Rover 820 Owners Workshop Manual

John S Mead

Models covered
Rover 820 Saloon and Fastback with 1994 cc 16-valve fuel injection engine

Does not cover Rover 825 or 827 models, base model 820 with 8-valve carburettor engine, or 820 Turbo 16V

(1380-4T1)

ABCDE
FGHIJ
KLMNO
P

Haynes Publishing Group
Sparkford Nr Yeovil
Somerset BA22 7JJ England

Haynes Publications, Inc
861 Lawrence Drive
Newbury Park
California 91320 USA

Acknowledgements

Thanks are due to the Champion Sparking Plug Company Limited who supplied the illustrations showing spark plug conditions, to Holt Lloyd Limited who supplied the illustrations showing bodywork repair, and to Duckhams Oils, who provided lubrication data. Certain illustrations are the copyright of the Austin Rover Group Limited, and are used with their permission. Thanks are also due to Sykes-Pickavant Limited, who provided a selection of workshop tools, and to all the staff at Sparkford who helped in the production of this manual.

© Haynes Publishing Group 1991

A book in the **Haynes Owners Workshop Manual Series**

Printed by J. H. Haynes & Co. Ltd., Sparkford, Nr Yeovil, Somerset BA22 7JJ, England

ISBN 1 85010 792 0

British Library Cataloguing in Publication Data
A catalogue record for this book is available from the British Library

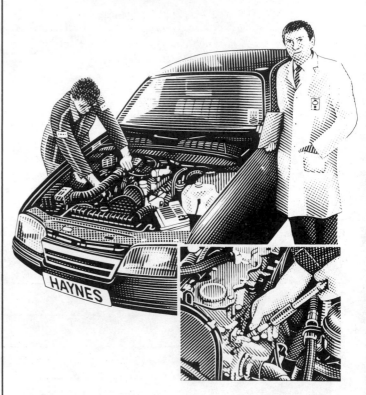

Contents

Rover 820i Saloon

Rover 820Se Fastback

About this manual

Its aim

The aim of this manual is to help you get the best value from your vehicle. It can do so in several ways. It can help you decide what work must be done (even should you choose to get it done by a garage), provide information on routine maintenance and servicing, and give a logical course of action and diagnosis when random faults occur. However, it is hoped that you will use the manual by tackling the work yourself. On simpler jobs it may even be quicker than booking the car into a garage and going there twice, to leave and collect it. Perhaps most important, a lot of money can be saved by avoiding the costs a garage must charge to cover its labour and overheads.

The manual has drawings and descriptions to show the function of the various components so that their layout can be understood. Then the tasks are described and photographed in a step-by-step sequence so that even a novice can do the work.

Its arrangement

The manual is divided into 13 Chapters, each covering a logical sub-division of the vehicle. The Chapters are each divided into Sections, numbered with single figures, eg 5; and the Sections into paragraphs (or sub-sections), with decimal numbers following on from the Section they are in, eg 5.1, 5.2, 5.3 etc.

It is freely illustrated, especially in those parts where there is a detailed sequence of operations to be carried out. There are two forms of illustration: figures and photographs. The figures are numbered in sequence with decimal numbers, according to their position in the Chapter – eg Fig. 6.4 is the fourth drawing/illustration in Chapter 6. Photographs carry the same number (either individually or in related groups) as the Section or sub-section to which they relate.

There is an alphabetical index at the back of the manual as well as a contents list at the front. Each Chapter is also preceded by its own individual contents list.

References to the 'left' or 'right' of the vehicle are in the sense of a person in the driver's seat facing forwards.

Unless otherwise stated, nuts and bolts are removed by turning anti-clockwise, and tightened by turning clockwise.

Vehicle manufacturers continually make changes to specifications and recommendations, and these, when notified, are incorporated into our manuals at the earliest opportunity.

Whilst every care is taken to ensure that the information in this manual is correct, no liability can be accepted by the authors or publishers for loss, damage or injury caused by any errors in, or omissions from, the information given.

Project vehicles

The main project vehicle used in the preparation of this manual, and appearing in the majority of the photographic sequences, was a 1986 Rover 820 Se Saloon. Additional work was carried out and photographed on a 1988 Rover 820 Si Fastback.

Introduction to the Rover 820 Series

Designed in conjunction with the Honda Motor Company of Japan, the Rover 820 series was launched in the UK in July 1986 as a replacement for the ageing Rover SD1. Initially available in four-door Saloon guise, a Fastback version was added to the range in mid-1988.

The cars covered by this manual are all powered by a 2.0 litre twin overhead camshaft, sixteen valve engine with single-point or multi-point fuel injection. The engines are based on the proven Austin Rover O-series engine used in the Montego and other Austin Rover vehicles, but with an all-new cylinder head and valve train. The engine is mounted transversely, and drives the front wheels through a five-speed manual gearbox or four-speed automatic transmission.

Suspension is independent at the front by double wishbones and coil springs, and at the rear by transverse trailing links and coil springs. Power-assisted steering is standard on all models.

A comprehensive range of electrical and interior features are offered as standard equipment, including electric front windows, central locking and stereo radio cassette player. Optional equipment is also extensive, including ABS braking system, air conditioning, headlamp wash, and electric rear windows available on most models.

General dimensions, weights and capacities

For information applicable to later models, see Supplement at end of manual

Dimensions

Overall length	4690.0 mm (184.6 in)
Overall width (including door mirrors)	1970.0 mm (77.6 in)
Overall height	1400.0 mm (55.0 in)
Wheelbase	2760.0 mm (108.7 in)
Front track	1490.0 mm (58.7 in)
Rear track	1450.0 mm (57.1 in)
Ground clearance	145.0 mm (5.7 in)
Turning circle..	11.9 m (39.0 ft)

Weights

Kerb weight:

820 e Saloon	1305 kg (2870 lb)
820 i Saloon	1300 kg (2860 lb)
820 Se Saloon	1325 kg (2915 lb)
820 Si Saloon	1320 kg (2905 lb)
820 e Fastback	1335 kg (2935 lb)
820 i Fastback	1330 kg (2925 lb)
820 Se Fastback	1355 kg (2980 lb)
820 Si Fastback	1350 kg (2970 lb)

Add 15 kg (33 lb) to the above weights for automatic transmission models

Maximum roof rack load	70 kg (154 lb)
Maximum towing weight:	
Braked trailer	1550 kg (3417 lb)
Unbraked trailer	500 kg (1102 lb)
Maximum towing hitch downward load	50 kg (110 lb)

Capacities

Engine oil (including filter)	4.5 litres (8.0 Imp pts)
Cooling system	10.0 litres (17.6 Imp pts)
Fuel tank	68.0 litres (15.0 Imp gals)
Manual gearbox	2.3 litres (4.0 Imp pts)
Automatic transmission:	
Total capacity	6.0 litres (10.5 Imp pts)
Service refill	2.0 litres (3.5 Imp pts)
Power steering reservoir	1.5 litres (3.0 Imp pts)
Windscreen/headlamps washer reservoir......................................	6.0 litres (10.5 Imp pints)

Jacking, towing and wheel changing

Jacking and wheel changing

To change a roadwheel, first remove the spare wheel and jack, which are located under the luggage compartment floor. Firmly apply the handbrake and engage first gear on manual gearbox models, or PARK on automatic transmission models. Place chocks at the front and rear of the wheel diagonally opposite the one to be changed.

Remove the wheel trim and slacken the wheel nuts with the tools provided in the tool kit. Position the jack head in the reinforced jacking point, at the base of the sill nearest to the wheel to be changed. Raise the jack to just take the weight of the car. If the tyre is flat, position the base of the jack so that it is flat on the ground. If the tyre is not flat, position the jack so that the base elbow is resting on the ground and the base is just clear. Raise the car until the wheel is clear of the ground, then remove the wheel nuts and the wheel. Fit the spare wheel, and screw on the wheel nuts. Lower the jack until the tyre is just touching the ground, and tighten the wheel nuts moderately tight. Now lower the jack fully and tighten the wheel nuts securely in a diagonal sequence. Refit the wheel trim, then remove the jack and stow it together with the wheel and tools in the luggage compartment.

When jacking up the car with a trolley jack, position the jack head under the front towing eye if the front is to be raised, or under the rear towing eye if the rear is to be raised. If the side of the car is to be raised, position the jack head under the reinforced areas at the front or rear of the side sills. Do not jack up the car by means of the sump, or any of the suspension or steering components. Supplement the jack using axle stands or sturdy blocks. The jacking points and axle stand positions are shown in the accompanying illustrations. **Never** *work under, around, or near a raised car, unless it is adequately supported in at least two places.*

Towing

Towing eyes are fitted to the front and rear of the vehicle for attachment of a tow rope. The front towing eye is situated under the centre of the front bumper, and the rear towing eye is located under the centre of the rear bumper behind a detachable trim plate. Always turn the ignition key to position one when the vehicle is being towed to prevent the steering lock operating. Note that if the engine is not running, greater effort will be required to apply the brakes and steer the car.

Before being towed, release the handbrake and place the gear lever in neutral. Do not tow at a speed greater than 30 mph (50 kph). On no account may the car be towed with the front wheels on the ground if the transmission is faulty, if the gearbox oil or transmission fluid is low, or if the towing distance is greater than 30 miles (50 km).

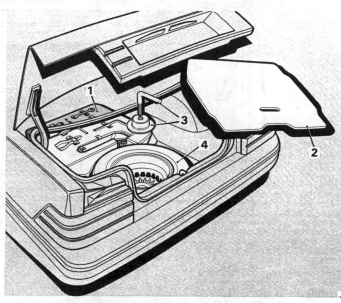

Spare wheel and tool locations

1 Tool kit	3 Spare wheel clamp
2 Floor panel	4 Spare wheel

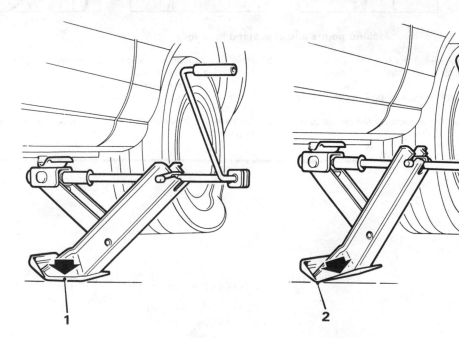

Using the vehicle tool kit jack

1   Jack base positioned flat on the ground (deflated tyre)
2   Jack positioned with base elbow on the ground, and base just clear (inflated tyre)

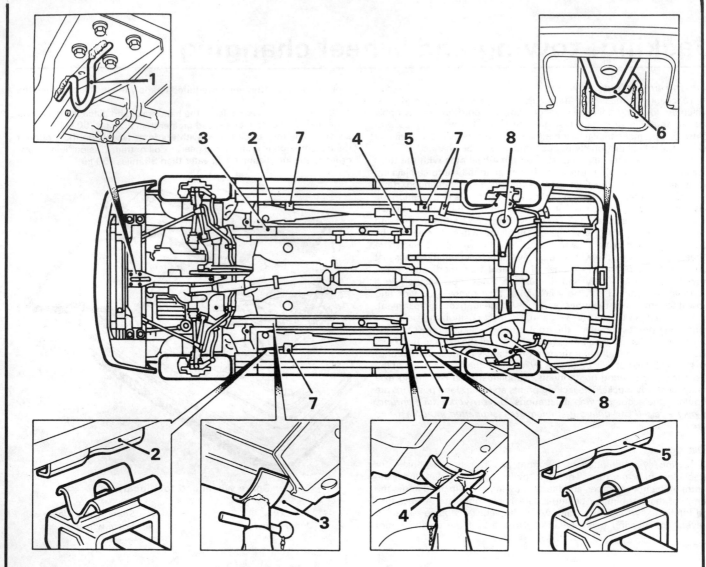

Jacking points and axle stand locations

1 Front towing eye – used for raising the front of the car
2 Reinforced sill area – used for raising the side of the car, or supporting on axle stands
3 Front chassis member – used for supporting the car on axle stands
4 Rear chassis member – used for supporting the car on axle stands

5 Reinforced sill area – used for raising the side of the car, or supporting on axle stands
6 Rear towing eye – used for raising the rear of the car
7 Square tubular chassis sections – **Not suitable for jacking or supporting**
8 Suspension components – **Not suitable for jacking or supporting**

Buying spare parts and vehicle identification numbers

Buying spare parts

Spare parts are available from many sources, for example: Rover garages, other garages and accessory shops, and motor factors. Our advice regarding spare part sources is as follows.

Officially appointed Rover garages – This is the best source for parts which are peculiar to your car, and are not generally available (eg complete cylinder heads, internal gearbox components, badges, interior trim etc). It is also the only place at which you should buy parts if the vehicle is still under warranty – non-Rover components may invalidate the warranty. To be sure of obtaining the correct parts, it will be necessary to give the storeman your car's vehicle identification number, and if possible, take the old part along for positive identification. Many parts are available under a factory exchange scheme – any parts returned should always be clean. It obviously makes good sense to go straight to the specialists on your car for this type of part, as they are best equipped to supply you.

Other garages and accessory shops – These are often very good places to buy materials and components needed for the maintenance of your car (eg oil filters, spark plugs, bulbs, drivebelts, oils and greases, touch-up paint, filler paste, etc). They also sell general accessories, usually have convenient opening hours, charge lower prices and can often be found not far from home.

Motor factors – Good factors will stock all the more important components which wear out comparatively quickly (eg exhaust systems, brake pads, seals and hydraulic parts, clutch components, bearing shells, pistons, valves etc). Motor factors will often provide new or reconditioned components on a part exchange basis – this can save a considerable amount of money.

Vehicle identification numbers

Modifications are a continuing and unpublicised process in vehicle manufacture, quite apart from major model changes. Spare parts manuals and lists are compiled upon a numerical basis, the individual vehicle identification numbers being essential to correct identification of the component concerned.

When ordering spare parts, always give as much information as possible. Quote the car model, year of manufacture, body and engine numbers as appropriate.

The vehicle identification number is stamped on a plate attached to the front body panel.

The body number is stamped on a plate attached to the front right-hand inner wing valance.

The engine number is stamped on the rear face of the cylinder block, below the cylinder head.

General repair procedures

Whenever servicing, repair or overhaul work is carried out on the car or its components, it is necessary to observe the following procedures and instructions. This will assist in carrying out the operation efficiently and to a professional standard of workmanship.

Joint mating faces and gaskets

Where a gasket is used between the mating faces of two components, ensure that it is renewed on reassembly, and fit it dry unless otherwise stated in the repair procedure. Make sure that the mating faces are clean and dry with all traces of old gasket removed. When cleaning a joint face, use a tool which is not likely to score or damage the face, and remove any burrs or nicks with an oilstone or fine file.

Make sure that tapped holes are cleaned with a pipe cleaner, and keep them free of jointing compound if this is being used unless specifically instructed otherwise.

Ensure that all orifices, channels or pipes are clear and blow through them, preferably using compressed air.

Oil seals

Whenever an oil seal is removed from its working location, either individually or as part of an assembly, it should be renewed.

The very fine sealing lip of the seal is easily damaged and will not seal if the surface it contacts is not completely clean and free from scratches, nicks or grooves. If the original sealing surface of the component cannot be restored, the component should be renewed.

Protect the lips of the seal from any surface which may damage them in the course of fitting. Use tape or a conical sleeve where possible. Lubricate the seal lips with oil before fitting and, on dual lipped seals, fill the space between the lips with grease.

Unless otherwise stated, oil seals must be fitted with their sealing lips toward the lubricant to be sealed.

Use a tubular drift or block of wood of the appropriate size to install the seal and, if the seal housing is shouldered, drive the seal down to the shoulder. If the seal housing is unshouldered, the seal should be fitted with its face flush with the housing top face.

Screw threads and fastenings

Always ensure that a blind tapped hole is completely free from oil, grease, water or other fluid before installing the bolt or stud. Failure to do this could cause the housing to crack due to the hydraulic action of the bolt or stud as it is screwed in.

When tightening a castellated nut to accept a split pin, tighten the nut to the specified torque, where applicable, and then tighten further to the next split pin hole. Never slacken the nut to align a split pin hole unless stated in the repair procedure.

When checking or retightening a nut or bolt to a specified torque setting, slacken the nut or bolt by a quarter of a turn, and then retighten to the specified setting.

Locknuts, locktabs and washers

Any fastening which will rotate against a component or housing in the course of tightening should always have a washer between it and the relevant component or housing.

Spring or split washers should always be renewed when they are used to lock a critical component such as a big-end bearing retaining nut or bolt.

Locktabs which are folded over to retain a nut or bolt should always be renewed.

Self-locking nuts can be reused in non-critical areas, providing resistance can be felt when the locking portion passes over the bolt or stud thread.

Split pins must always be replaced with new ones of the correct size for the hole.

Special tools

Some repair procedures in this manual entail the use of special tools such as a press, two or three-legged pullers, spring compressors etc. Wherever possible, suitable readily available alternatives to the manufacturer's special tools are described, and are shown in use. In some instances, where no alternative is possible, it has been necessary to resort to the use of a manufacturer's tool and this has been done for reasons of safety as well as the efficient completion of the repair operation. Unless you are highly skilled and have a thorough understanding of the procedure described, never attempt to bypass the use of any special tool when the procedure described specifies its use. Not only is there a very great risk of personal injury, but expensive damage could be caused to the components involved.

Tools and working facilities

Introduction

A selection of good tools is a fundamental requirement for anyone contemplating the maintenance and repair of a motor vehicle. For the owner who does not possess any, their purchase will prove a considerable expense, offsetting some of the savings made by doing-it-yourself. However, provided that the tools purchased meet the relevant national safety standards and are of good quality, they will last for many years and prove an extremely worthwhile investment.

To help the average owner to decide which tools are needed to carry out the various tasks detailed in this manual, we have compiled three lists of tools under the following headings: *Maintenance and minor repair, Repair and overhaul,* and *Special.* The newcomer to practical mechanics should start off with the *Maintenance and minor repair* tool kit and confine himself to the simpler jobs around the vehicle. Then, as his confidence and experience grow, he can undertake more difficult tasks, buying extra tools as, and when, they are needed. In this way, a *Maintenance and minor repair* tool kit can be built-up into a *Repair and overhaul* tool kit over a considerable period of time without any major cash outlays. The experienced do-it-yourselfer will have a tool kit good enough for most repair and overhaul procedures and will add tools from the *Special* category when he feels the expense is justified by the amount of use to which these tools will be put.

It is obviously not possible to cover the subject of tools fully here. For those who wish to learn more about tools and their use there is a book entitled *How to Choose and Use Car Tools* available from the publishers of this manual.

Maintenance and minor repair tool kit

The tools given in this list should be considered as a minimum requirement if routine maintenance, servicing and minor repair operations are to be undertaken. We recommend the purchase of combination spanners (ring one end, open-ended the other); although more expensive than open-ended ones, they do give the advantages of both types of spanner.

Combination spanners - 10, 11, 12, 13, 14 & 17 mm, and $7/16$, $1/2$, $9/16$, $5/8$, $11/16$, $3/4$, $13/16$, $7/8$, and $15/16$ in
Adjustable spanner - 9 inch
Gearbox drain plug key
Spark plug spanner (with rubber insert)
Spark plug gap adjustment tool
Set of feeler gauges
Brake adjuster spanner
Brake bleed nipple spanner
Screwdriver - 4 in long x $1/4$ in dia (flat blade)
Screwdriver - 4 in long x $1/4$ in dia (cross blade)
Combination pliers - 6 inch
Hacksaw (junior)
Tyre pump

Tyre pressure gauge
Oil can
Fine emery cloth (1 sheet)
Wire brush (small)
Funnel (medium size)

Repair and overhaul tool kit

These tools are virtually essential for anyone undertaking any major repairs to a motor vehicle, and are additional to those given in the *Maintenance and minor repair* list. Included in this list is a comprehensive set of sockets. Although these are expensive they will be found invaluable as they are so versatile - particularly if various drives are included in the set. We recommend the ½ in square-drive type, as this can be used with most proprietary torque wrenches. If you cannot afford a socket set, even bought piecemeal, then inexpensive tubular box spanners are a useful alternative.

The tools in this list will occasionally need to be supplemented by tools from the *Special* list.

Sockets (or box spanners) to cover range in previous list
Selection of Torx type socket bits
Reversible ratchet drive (for use with sockets)
Extension piece, 10 inch (for use with sockets)
Universal joint (for use with sockets)
Torque wrench (for use with sockets)
'Mole' wrench - 8 inch
Ball pein hammer
Soft-faced hammer, plastic or rubber
Screwdriver - 6 in long x $5/16$ in dia (flat blade)
Screwdriver - 2 in long x $5/16$ in square (flat blade)
Screwdriver - $11/2$ in long x $1/4$ in dia (cross blade)
Screwdriver - 3 in long x $1/8$ in dia (electricians)
Pliers - electricians side cutters
Pliers - needle nosed
Pliers - circlip (internal and external)
Cold chisel - $1/2$ inch
Scriber
Scraper
Centre punch
Pin punch
Hacksaw
Valve grinding tool
Steel rule/straight-edge
Allen keys (inc. splined/Torx type if necessary)
Selection of files
Wire brush (large)
Axle-stands
Jack (strong trolley or hydraulic type)

Special tools

The tools in this list are those which are not used regularly, are expensive to buy, or which need to be used in accordance with their manufacturers' instructions. Unless relatively difficult mechanical jobs are undertaken frequently, it will not be economic to buy many of these tools. Where this is the case, you could consider clubbing together with friends (or joining a motorists' club) to make a joint purchase, or borrowing the tools against a deposit from a local garage or tool hire specialist.

The following list contains only those tools and instruments freely available to the public, and not those special tools produced by the vehicle manufacturer specifically for its dealer network. You will find occasional references to these manufacturers' special tools in the text of this manual. Generally, an alternative method of doing the job without the vehicle manufacturers' special tool is given. However, sometimes, there is no alternative to using them. Where this is the case and the relevant tool cannot be bought or borrowed, you will have to entrust the work to a franchised garage.

> Valve spring compressor (where applicable)
> Piston ring compressor
> Balljoint separator
> Universal hub/bearing puller
> Impact screwdriver
> Micrometer and/or vernier gauge
> Dial gauge
> Stroboscopic timing light
> Dwell angle meter/tachometer
> Universal electrical multi-meter
> Cylinder compression gauge
> Lifting tackle
> Trolley jack
> Light with extension lead

Buying tools

For practically all tools, a tool factor is the best source since he will have a very comprehensive range compared with the average garage or accessory shop. Having said that, accessory shops often offer excellent quality tools at discount prices, so it pays to shop around.

There are plenty of good tools around at reasonable prices, but always aim to purchase items which meet the relevant national safety standards. If in doubt, ask the proprietor or manager of the shop for advice before making a purchase.

Care and maintenance of tools

Having purchased a reasonable tool kit, it is necessary to keep the tools in a clean serviceable condition. After use, always wipe off any dirt, grease and metal particles using a clean, dry cloth, before putting the tools away. Never leave them lying around after they have been used. A simple tool rack on the garage or workshop wall, for items such as screwdrivers and pliers is a good idea. Store all normal wrenches and sockets in a metal box. Any measuring instruments, gauges, meters, etc, must be carefully stored where they cannot be damaged or become rusty.

Take a little care when tools are used. Hammer heads inevitably become marked and screwdrivers lose the keen edge on their blades from time to time. A little timely attention with emery cloth or a file will soon restore items like this to a good serviceable finish.

Working facilities

Not to be forgotten when discussing tools, is the workshop itself. If anything more than routine maintenance is to be carried out, some form of suitable working area becomes essential.

It is appreciated that many an owner mechanic is forced by circumstances to remove an engine or similar item, without the benefit of a garage or workshop. Having done this, any repairs should always be done under the cover of a roof.

Wherever possible, any dismantling should be done on a clean, flat workbench or table at a suitable working height.

Any workbench needs a vice: one with a jaw opening of 4 in (100 mm) is suitable for most jobs. As mentioned previously, some clean dry storage space is also required for tools, as well as for lubricants, cleaning fluids, touch-up paints and so on, which become necessary.

Another item which may be required, and which has a much more general usage, is an electric drill with a chuck capacity of at least $5/16$ in (8 mm). This, together with a good range of twist drills, is virtually

essential for fitting accessories such as mirrors and reversing lights.

Last, but not least, always keep a supply of old newspapers and clean, lint-free rags available, and try to keep any working area as clean as possible.

Spanner jaw gap comparison table

Jaw gap (in)	Spanner size
0.250	$1/4$ in AF
0.276	7 mm
0.313	$5/16$ in AF
0.315	8 mm
0.344	$11/32$ in AF; $1/8$ in Whitworth
0.354	9 mm
0.375	$3/8$ in AF
0.394	10 mm
0.433	11 mm
0.438	$7/16$ in AF
0.445	$3/16$ in Whitworth; $1/4$ in BSF
0.472	12 mm
0.500	$1/2$ in AF
0.512	13 mm
0.525	$1/4$ in Whitworth; $5/16$ in BSF
0.551	14 mm
0.563	$9/16$ in AF
0.591	15 mm
0.600	$5/16$ in Whitworth; $3/8$ in BSF
0.625	$5/8$ in AF
0.630	16 mm
0.669	17 mm
0.686	$11/16$ in AF
0.709	18 mm
0.710	$3/8$ in Whitworth; $7/16$ in BSF
0.748	19 mm
0.750	$3/4$ in AF
0.813	$13/16$ in AF
0.820	$7/16$ in Whitworth; $1/2$ in BSF
0.866	22 mm
0.875	$7/8$ in AF
0.920	$1/2$ in Whitworth; $9/16$ in BSF
0.938	$15/16$ in AF
0.945	24 mm
1.000	1 in AF
1.010	$9/16$ in Whitworth; $5/8$ in BSF
1.024	26 mm
1.063	$11/16$ in AF; 27 mm
1.100	$5/8$ in Whitworth; $11/16$ in BSF
1.125	$11/8$ in AF
1.181	30 mm
1.200	$11/16$ in Whitworth; $3/4$ in BSF
1.250	$11/4$ in AF
1.260	32 mm
1.300	$3/4$ in Whitworth; $7/8$ in BSF
1.313	$15/16$ in AF
1.390	$13/16$ in Whitworth; $15/16$ in BSF
1.417	36 mm
1.438	$17/16$ in AF
1.480	$7/8$ in Whitworth; 1 in BSF
1.500	$11/2$ in AF
1.575	40 mm; $15/16$ in Whitworth
1.614	41 mm
1.625	$15/8$ in AF
1.670	1 in Whitworth; $11/8$ in BSF
1.688	$111/16$ in AF
1.811	46 mm
1.813	$113/16$ in AF
1.860	$11/8$ in Whitworth; $11/4$ in BSF
1.875	$17/8$ in AF
1.969	50 mm
2.000	2 in AF
2.050	$11/4$ in Whitworth; $13/8$ in BSF
2.165	55 mm
2.362	60 mm

Conversion factors

Length (distance)
Inches (in)	X	25.4	= Millimetres (mm)	X 0.0394	= Inches (in)
Feet (ft)	X	0.305	= Metres (m)	X 3.281	= Feet (ft)
Miles	X	1.609	= Kilometres (km)	X 0.621	= Miles

Volume (capacity)
Cubic inches (cu in; in³)	X	16.387	= Cubic centimetres (cc; cm³)	X 0.061	= Cubic inches (cu in; in³)
Imperial pints (Imp pt)	X	0.568	= Litres (l)	X 1.76	= Imperial pints (Imp pt)
Imperial quarts (Imp qt)	X	1.137	= Litres (l)	X 0.88	= Imperial quarts (Imp qt)
Imperial quarts (Imp qt)	X	1.201	= US quarts (US qt)	X 0.833	= Imperial quarts (Imp qt)
US quarts (US qt)	X	0.946	= Litres (l)	X 1.057	= US quarts (US qt)
Imperial gallons (Imp gal)	X	4.546	= Litres (l)	X 0.22	= Imperial gallons (Imp gal)
Imperial gallons (Imp gal)	X	1.201	= US gallons (US gal)	X 0.833	= Imperial gallons (Imp gal)
US gallons (US gal)	X	3.785	= Litres (l)	X 0.264	= US gallons (US gal)

Mass (weight)
Ounces (oz)	X	28.35	= Grams (g)	X 0.035	= Ounces (oz)
Pounds (lb)	X	0.454	= Kilograms (kg)	X 2.205	= Pounds (lb)

Force
Ounces-force (ozf; oz)	X	0.278	= Newtons (N)	X 3.6	= Ounces-force (ozf; oz)
Pounds-force (lbf; lb)	X	4.448	= Newtons (N)	X 0.225	= Pounds-force (lbf; lb)
Newtons (N)	X	0.1	= Kilograms-force (kgf; kg)	X 9.81	= Newtons (N)

Pressure
Pounds-force per square inch (psi; lbf/in²; lb/in²)	X	0.070	= Kilograms-force per square centimetre (kgf/cm²; kg/cm²)	X 14.223	= Pounds-force per square inch (psi; lbf/in²; lb/in²)
Pounds-force per square inch (psi; lbf/in²; lb/in²)	X	0.068	= Atmospheres (atm)	X 14.696	= Pounds-force per square inch (psi; lbf/in²; lb/in²)
Pounds-force per square inch (psi; lbf/in²; lb/in²)	X	0.069	= Bars	X 14.5	= Pounds-force per square inch (psi; lbf/in²; lb/in²)
Pounds-force per square inch (psi; lbf/in²; lb/in²)	X	6.895	= Kilopascals (kPa)	X 0.145	= Pounds-force per square inch (psi; lbf/in²; lb/in²)
Kilopascals (kPa)	X	0.01	= Kilograms-force per square centimetre (kgf/cm²; kg/cm²)	X 98.1	= Kilopascals (kPa)
Millibar (mbar)	X	100	= Pascals (Pa)	X 0.01	= Millibar (mbar)
Millibar (mbar)	X	0.0145	= Pounds-force per square inch (psi; lbf/in²; lb/in²)	X 68.947	= Millibar (mbar)
Millibar (mbar)	X	0.75	= Millimetres of mercury (mmHg)	X 1.333	= Millibar (mbar)
Millibar (mbar)	X	0.401	= Inches of water (inH₂O)	X 2.491	= Millibar (mbar)
Millimetres of mercury (mmHg)	X	0.535	= Inches of water (inH₂O)	X 1.868	= Millimetres of mercury (mmHg)
Inches of water (inH₂O)	X	0.036	= Pounds-force per square inch (psi; lbf/in²; lb/in²)	X 27.68	= Inches of water (inH₂O)

Torque (moment of force)
Pounds-force inches (lbf in; lb in)	X	1.152	= Kilograms-force centimetre (kgf cm; kg cm)	X 0.868	= Pounds-force inches (lbf in; lb in)
Pounds-force inches (lbf in; lb in)	X	0.113	= Newton metres (Nm)	X 8.85	= Pounds-force inches (lbf in; lb in)
Pounds-force inches (lbf in; lb in)	X	0.083	= Pounds-force feet (lbf ft; lb ft)	X 12	= Pounds-force inches (lbf in; lb in)
Pounds-force feet (lbf ft; lb ft)	X	0.138	= Kilograms-force metres (kgf m; kg m)	X 7.233	= Pounds-force feet (lbf ft; lb ft)
Pounds-force feet (lbf ft; lb ft)	X	1.356	= Newton metres (Nm)	X 0.738	= Pounds-force feet (lbf ft; lb ft)
Newton metres (Nm)	X	0.102	= Kilograms-force metres (kgf m; kg m)	X 9.804	= Newton metres (Nm)

Power
Horsepower (hp)	X	745.7	= Watts (W)	X 0.0013	= Horsepower (hp)

Velocity (speed)
Miles per hour (miles/hr; mph)	X	1.609	= Kilometres per hour (km/hr; kph)	X 0.621	= Miles per hour (miles/hr; mph)

Fuel consumption*
Miles per gallon, Imperial (mpg)	X	0.354	= Kilometres per litre (km/l)	X 2.825	= Miles per gallon, Imperial (mpg)
Miles per gallon, US (mpg)	X	0.425	= Kilometres per litre (km/l)	X 2.352	= Miles per gallon, US (mpg)

Temperature

Degrees Fahrenheit = (°C x 1.8) + 32

Degrees Celsius (Degrees Centigrade; °C) = (°F - 32) x 0.56

*It is common practice to convert from miles per gallon (mpg) to litres/100 kilometres (l/100km), where mpg (Imperial) x l/100 km = 282 and mpg (US) x l/100 km = 235

Safety first!

Professional motor mechanics are trained in safe working procedures. However enthusiastic you may be about getting on with the job in hand, do take the time to ensure that your safety is not put at risk. A moment's lack of attention can result in an accident, as can failure to observe certain elementary precautions.

There will always be new ways of having accidents, and the following points do not pretend to be a comprehensive list of all dangers; they are intended rather to make you aware of the risks and to encourage a safety-conscious approach to all work you carry out on your vehicle.

Essential DOs and DON'Ts

DON'T rely on a single jack when working underneath the vehicle. Always use reliable additional means of support, such as axle stands, securely placed under a part of the vehicle that you know will not give way.

DON'T attempt to loosen or tighten high-torque nuts (e.g. wheel hub nuts) while the vehicle is on a jack; it may be pulled off.

DON'T start the engine without first ascertaining that the transmission is in neutral (or 'Park' where applicable) and the parking brake applied.

DON'T suddenly remove the filler cap from a hot cooling system – cover it with a cloth and release the pressure gradually first, or you may get scalded by escaping coolant.

DON'T attempt to drain oil until you are sure it has cooled sufficiently to avoid scalding you.

DON'T grasp any part of the engine, exhaust or catalytic converter without first ascertaining that it is sufficiently cool to avoid burning you.

DON'T allow brake fluid or antifreeze to contact vehicle paintwork.

DON'T syphon toxic liquids such as fuel, brake fluid or antifreeze by mouth, or allow them to remain on your skin.

DON'T inhale dust – it may be injurious to health (see *Asbestos* below).

DON'T allow any spilt oil or grease to remain on the floor – wipe it up straight away, before someone slips on it.

DON'T use ill-fitting spanners or other tools which may slip and cause injury.

DON'T attempt to lift a heavy component which may be beyond your capability – get assistance.

DON'T rush to finish a job, or take unverified short cuts.

DON'T allow children or animals in or around an unattended vehicle.

DO wear eye protection when using power tools such as drill, sander, bench grinder etc, and when working under the vehicle.

DO use a barrier cream on your hands prior to undertaking dirty jobs – it will protect your skin from infection as well as making the dirt easier to remove afterwards; but make sure your hands aren't left slippery. Note that long-term contact with used engine oil can be a health hazard.

DO keep loose clothing (cuffs, tie etc) and long hair well out of the way of moving mechanical parts.

DO remove rings, wristwatch etc, before working on the vehicle – especially the electrical system.

DO ensure that any lifting tackle used has a safe working load rating adequate for the job.

DO keep your work area tidy – it is only too easy to fall over articles left lying around.

DO get someone to check periodically that all is well, when working alone on the vehicle.

DO carry out work in a logical sequence and check that everything is correctly assembled and tightened afterwards.

DO remember that your vehicle's safety affects that of yourself and others. If in doubt on any point, get specialist advice.

IF, in spite of following these precautions, you are unfortunate enough to injure yourself, seek medical attention as soon as possible.

Asbestos

Certain friction, insulating, sealing, and other products – such as brake linings, brake bands, clutch linings, torque converters, gaskets, etc – contain asbestos. *Extreme care must be taken to avoid inhalation of dust from such products since it is hazardous to health.* If in doubt, assume that they *do* contain asbestos.

Fire

Remember at all times that petrol (gasoline) is highly flammable. Never smoke, or have any kind of naked flame around, when working on the vehicle. But the risk does not end there – a spark caused by an electrical short-circuit, by two metal surfaces contacting each other, by careless use of tools, or even by static electricity built up in your body under certain conditions, can ignite petrol vapour, which in a confined space is highly explosive.

Always disconnect the battery earth (ground) terminal before working on any part of the fuel or electrical system, and never risk spilling fuel on to a hot engine or exhaust.

It is recommended that a fire extinguisher of a type suitable for fuel and electrical fires is kept handy in the garage or workplace at all times. Never try to extinguish a fuel or electrical fire with water.

Note: *Any reference to a 'torch' appearing in this manual should always be taken to mean a hand-held battery-operated electric lamp or flashlight. It does NOT mean a welding/gas torch or blowlamp.*

Fumes

Certain fumes are highly toxic and can quickly cause unconsciousness and even death if inhaled to any extent. Petrol (gasoline) vapour comes into this category, as do the vapours from certain solvents such as trichloroethylene. Any draining or pouring of such volatile fluids should be done in a well ventilated area.

When using cleaning fluids and solvents, read the instructions carefully. Never use materials from unmarked containers – they may give off poisonous vapours.

Never run the engine of a motor vehicle in an enclosed space such as a garage. Exhaust fumes contain carbon monoxide which is extremely poisonous; if you need to run the engine, always do so in the open air or at least have the rear of the vehicle outside the workplace.

If you are fortunate enough to have the use of an inspection pit, never drain or pour petrol, and never run the engine, while the vehicle is standing over it; the fumes, being heavier than air, will concentrate in the pit with possibly lethal results.

The battery

Never cause a spark, or allow a naked light, near the vehicle's battery. It will normally be giving off a certain amount of hydrogen gas, which is highly explosive.

Always disconnect the battery earth (ground) terminal before working on the fuel or electrical systems.

If possible, loosen the filler plugs or cover when charging the battery from an external source. Do not charge at an excessive rate or the battery may burst.

Take care when topping up and when carrying the battery. The acid electrolyte, even when diluted, is very corrosive and should not be allowed to contact the eyes or skin.

If you ever need to prepare electrolyte yourself, always add the acid slowly to the water, and never the other way round. Protect against splashes by wearing rubber gloves and goggles.

When jump starting a car using a booster battery, for negative earth (ground) vehicles, connect the jump leads in the following sequence: First connect one jump lead between the positive (+) terminals of the two batteries. Then connect the other jump lead first to the negative (–) terminal of the booster battery, and then to a good earthing (ground) point on the vehicle to be started, at least 18 in (45 cm) from the battery if possible. Ensure that hands and jump leads are clear of any moving parts, and that the two vehicles do not touch. Disconnect the leads in the reverse order.

Mains electricity and electrical equipment

When using an electric power tool, inspection light etc, always ensure that the appliance is correctly connected to its plug and that, where necessary, it is properly earthed (grounded). Do not use such appliances in damp conditions and, again, beware of creating a spark or applying excessive heat in the vicinity of fuel or fuel vapour. Also ensure that the appliances meet the relevant national safety standards.

Ignition HT voltage

A severe electric shock can result from touching certain parts of the ignition system, such as the HT leads, when the engine is running or being cranked, particularly if components are damp or the insulation is defective. Where an electronic ignition system is fitted, the HT voltage is much higher and could prove fatal.

Routine maintenance

For modifications, and information applicable to later models, see Supplement at end of manual

Maintenance is essential for ensuring safety, and desirable for the purpose of getting the best in terms of performance and economy from your car. Over the years, the need for periodic lubrication has been greatly reduced, if not totally eliminated. This has unfortunately tended to lead some owners to think that because no such action is required, the items either no longer exist, or will last forever. This is certainly not the case; it is essential to carry out regular visual examination as comprehensively as possible, in order to spot any potential defects at an early stage before they develop into major expensive repairs.

The following service schedules are a list of the maintenance requirements, and the intervals at which they should be carried out, as recommended by the manufacturers. Where applicable, these procedures are covered in greater detail throughout this manual, near the beginning of each Chapter.

Every 250 miles (400 km) or weekly – whichever occurs first

Engine, cooling system, steering and brakes
Check the oil level and top up if necessary
Check the coolant level and top up if necessary
Check the brake fluid level in the master cylinder, and top up if necessary
Check the fluid level in the power steering reservoir, and top up if necessary

Lights and wipers
Check the operation of all interior and exterior lamps, wipers and washers
Check and if necessary top up the washer reservoir

Tyres
Check the tyre pressures
Visually examine the tyres for wear or damage

Every 6000 miles (10 000 km) or 6 months – whichever occurs first

---

Engine (Chapter 1)
Renew the engine oil and filter
Visually check the engine for oil leaks

Every 12 000 miles (20 000 km) or 12 months – whichever occurs first

---

In addition to all the items in the previous services, carry out the following:

Cooling system (Chapter 2)
Check the hoses, hose clips and visible joint gaskets for leaks, and any signs of corrosion or deterioration
Check that the operation of the engine cooling fan is satisfactory
Check the specific gravity of the coolant, using a hydrometer

Fuel and exhaust systems (Chapter 3)
Check the operation of the accelerator cable and linkage
Visually check the fuel pipes and hoses for security, chafing, leaks and corrosion
Check the base idle speed and mixture settings, and adjust if required
Check the fuel tank for leaks and damage
Check the condition and security of the exhaust system

Ignition system (Chapter 4)
Renew the spark plugs
Clean the distributor cap, coil tower and HT leads. Check for signs of tracking

Clutch (Chapter 5)
Check the clutch hydraulic pipes and hoses for leaks, chafing and security

Manual gearbox (Chapter 6)
Visually check for oil leaks around the gearbox joint faces and oil seals
Check, and if necessary top up, the gearbox oil level

Automatic transmission (Chapter 7)
Visually check for fluid leaks around the transmission joint faces and seals
Check, and if necessary top up, the transmission fluid level

Driveshafts (Chapter 8)
Check the condition of the rubber gaiters, and of their securing clips
Check for excessive wear in the driveshaft CV joints

Braking system (Chapter 9)
Check the operation of the brake pad wear and low fluid level warning indicators
Check the front and rear brake pads for excessive wear, and renew if necessary
Check the condition of the front and rear brake discs
Visually check all brake pipes, hoses and unions for corrosion, chafing, leakage and security
Check the operation of the footbrake
Check the operation of the handbrake, and adjust if necessary

Suspension and steering (Chapter 10)
Check the condition and tension of the power steering pump drivebelt
Check the tightness of the roadwheel nuts, and the condition of the roadwheels
Check the front and rear shock absorbers for fluid leaks, damage or corrosion
Check the condition and security of the steering gear, and steering and suspension joints and rubber gaiters
Inspect the tyres for damage and abnormal wear, and if evident, check the front and rear wheel alignment

Bodywork (Chapter 11)
Lubricate all hinges and locks with a few drops of light oil (do not lubricate the steering lock)
Where applicable, check the condition and tension of the air conditioning compressor drivebelt
Carefully inspect the paintwork for damage, and the bodywork for corrosion
Check the condition of the underseal
Check the condition of the seat belts, the security of the seat belt mountings and the operation of the inertia reels

Electrical system (Chapter 12)
Check the operation of all electrical equipment and accessories (lights, indicators, horn, wipers, etc)
Check the condition and tension of the alternator drivebelt
Check the condition of the wiper blades
Check the condition and security of all accessible wiring connectors, harnesses and retaining clips
Check the screenwasher jets, and adjust their aim if necessary
Clean the battery terminals, and smear with petroleum jelly (also clean the battery tray, if necessary)
Check and if necessary adjust, the headlamp aim

Road test
Check the function of all instruments and warning lamps
Check the performance of the engine, transmission, brakes, clutch, steering and suspension, paying attention to any abnormalities or unusual noises

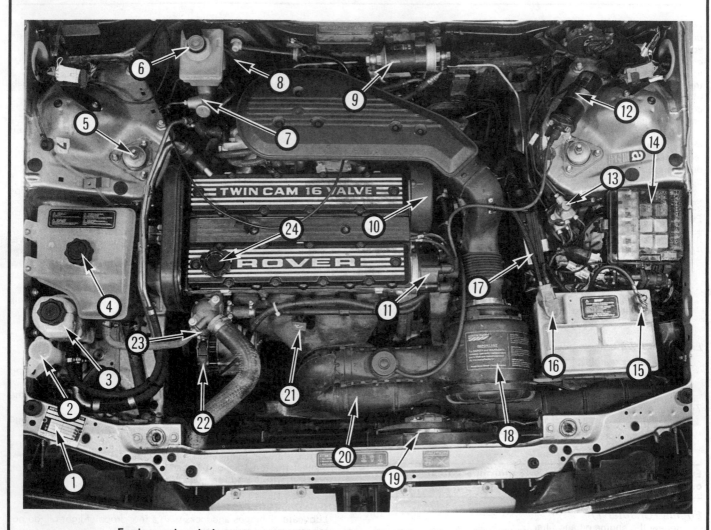

Engine and underbonnet component locations (models with single-point fuel injection)

1 Vehicle identification plate
2 Screen washer reservoir filler
3 Power steering fluid
   reservoir filler
4 Cooling system expansion
   tank filler
5 Front shock absorber top
   mounting

6 Brake and clutch fluid
   reservoir filler
7 Brake master cylinder
8 Brake vacuum servo unit
9 Fuel filter
10 Power steering pump
   drivebelt (models with
   rear-mounted pump)

11 Distributor cap
12 Ignition coil
13 Brake pressure reducing
   valve
14 Fuse and relay box
15 Battery negative terminal
16 Battery positive terminal
17 Ignition/fuel ECU

18 Air cleaner assembly
19 Radiator cooling fan
20 Air cleaner intake trunking
21 Engine oil dipstick
22 Alternator
23 Thermostat housing
24 Engine oil filler cap

Engine and underbonnet component locations (models with multi-point fuel injection)

1 Vehicle identification plate
2 Screen washer reservoir filler
3 Power steering fluid
   reservoir filler
4 Cooling system expansion
   tank filler
5 Front shock absorber top
   mounting
6 Brake and clutch fluid
   reservoir filler
7 Brake master cylinder
8 Brake vacuum servo unit
9 Fuel filter
10 Fuel system ECU
11 Ignition coil
12 Brake pressure reducing
   valve
13 Fuse and relay box
14 Battery negative terminal
15 Battery positive terminal
16 Air cleaner assembly
17 Radiator cooling fan
18 Air cleaner intake trunking
19 Engine oil dipstick
20 Airflow meter
21 Throttle housing
22 Plenum chamber
23 Engine oil filler cap
24 Alternator
25 Power steering pump
   (models with front-mounted
   pump)

Front underbody view

1	Engine undertray	6	Front tie-bar
2	Front towing eye	7	Gearbox drain plug
3	Longitudinal support member	8	Driveshaft inner constant velocity joint
4	Clutch slave cylinder	9	Gearbox filler plug
5	Reversing lamp switch	10	Front anti-roll bar

11	Gearchange rod
12	Gearbox steady rod
13	Fuel pipes
14	Exhaust section flange joint
15	Power steering gear
16	Steering tie-rod

17	Front lower suspension arm
18	Brake caliper
19	Oil filter
20	Driveshaft damper
21	Engine oil drain plug

Rear underbody view

1 Exhaust intermediate section	4 Handbrake cable	7 Fuel filler neck connection	10 Rear anti-roll bar
2 Fuel tank	5 Fuel pipes	8 Transverse link	11 Rear silencer
3 Exhaust rear heat shield	6 Trailing link	9 Fuel tank retaining straps	12 Brake caliper

Every 24 000 miles (40 000 km) or 24 months – whichever occurs first

In addition to all the items in the previous services, carry out the following:

Engine (Chapter 1)
Check the condition and tension of the timing belt
Check the condition of the crankcase ventilation system hoses, etc

Fuel and exhaust systems (Chapter 3)
Renew the fuel filter

Manual gearbox (Chapter 6)
Renew the gearbox oil

Automatic transmission (Chapter 7)
Renew the automatic transmission fluid

Braking system (Chapter 9)
Renew the brake fluid

Bodywork (Chapter 11)
Check the condition and security of the air conditioning system hoses (where applicable)

Every 48 000 miles (80 000 km) or 36 months – whichever occurs first

In addition to all the items in the previous services, carry out the following:

Engine (Chapter 1)
Renew the timing belt

Every 60 000 miles (96 000 km) or 36 months – whichever occurs first

In addition to all the items in the previous services, carry out the following:

Cooling system (Chapter 2)
Drain and flush the cooling system, and renew the coolant

Braking system (Chapter 9)
Renew the master cylinder and all wheel cylinder seals

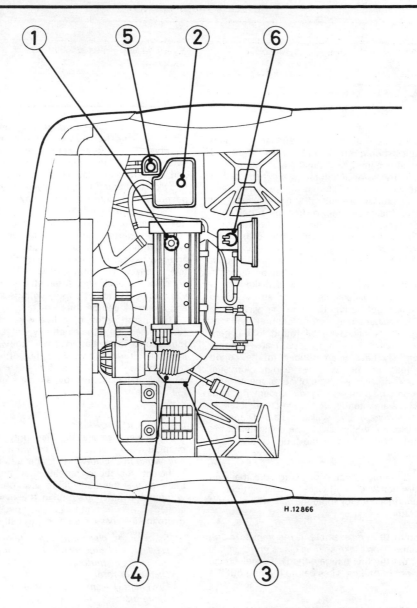

H.12866

Recommended lubricants and fluids

Component or system	Lubricant type/specification	Duckhams recommendation
Engine (1)*	Multigrade engine oil, viscosity SAE 10W/40 to API SF or SF/CD	Duckhams QXR, Hypergrade, or 10W/40 Motor Oil
Cooling system (2)	Ethylene glycol based antifreeze	Duckhams Universal Antifreeze and Summer Coolant
Manual gearbox (3)*	Multigrade engine oil, viscosity SAE 10W/40, to API SF or SF/CD	Duckhams QXR, Hypergrade, or 10W/40 Motor Oil
Automatic transmission (4)	Dexron IID type ATF	Duckhams D-Matic
Power steering reservoir (5)	Dexron IID type ATF	Duckhams D-Matic
Brake and clutch fluid reservoir (6)	Hydraulic fluid to FMVSS 116 DOT 4	Duckhams Universal Brake and Clutch Fluid
General greasing	Multipurpose lithium based grease	Duckhams LB 10

*Note: *Austin Rover specify a 10W/40 oil to meet warranty requirements. Duckhams QXR and 10W/40 Motor Oil are available to meet these requirements.*

Fault diagnosis

Introduction

The vehicle owner who does his or her own maintenance according to the recommended schedules should not have to use this section of the manual very often. Modern component reliability is such that, provided those items subject to wear or deterioration are inspected or renewed at the specified intervals, sudden failure is comparatively rare. Faults do not usually just happen as a result of sudden failure, but develop over a period of time. Major mechanical failures in particular are usually preceded by characteristic symptoms over hundreds or even thousands of miles. Those components which do occasionally fail without warning are often small and easily carried in the vehicle.

With any fault finding, the first step is to decide where to begin investigations. Sometimes this is obvious, but on other occasions a little detective work will be necessary. The owner who makes half a dozen haphazard adjustments or replacements may be successful in curing a fault (or its symptoms), but he will be none the wiser if the fault recurs and he may well have spent more time and money than was necessary. A calm and logical approach will be found to be more satisfactory in the long run. Always take into account any warning signs or abnormalities that may have been noticed in the period preceding the fault – power loss, high or low gauge readings, unusual noises or smells, etc – and remember that failure of components such as fuses or spark plugs may only be pointers to some underlying fault.

The pages which follow here are intended to help in cases of failure to start or breakdown on the road. There is also a Fault Diagnosis Section at the end of each Chapter which should be consulted if the preliminary checks prove unfruitful. Whatever the fault, certain basic principles apply. These are as follows:

Verify the fault. This is simply a matter of being sure that you know what the symptoms are before starting work. This is particularly important if you are investigating a fault for someone else who may not have described it very accurately.

Don't overlook the obvious. For example, if the vehicle won't start, is there petrol in the tank? (Don't take anyone else's word on this particular point, and don't trust the fuel gauge either!) If an electrical fault is indicated, look for loose or broken wires before digging out the test gear.

Cure the disease, not the symptom. Substituting a flat battery with a fully charged one will get you off the hard shoulder, but if the underlying cause is not attended to, the new battery will go the same way. Similarly, changing oil-fouled spark plugs for a new set will get you moving again, but remember that the reason for the fouling (if it wasn't simply an incorrect grade of plug) will have to be established and corrected.

Don't take anything for granted. Particularly, don't forget that a 'new' component may itself be defective (especially if it's been rattling round in the boot for months), and don't leave components out of a fault diagnosis sequence just because they are new or recently fitted. When you do finally diagnose a difficult fault, you'll probably realise that all the evidence was there from the start.

Electrical faults

Electrical faults can be more puzzling than straightforward mechanical failures, but they are no less susceptible to logical analysis if the basic principles of operation are understood. Vehicle electrical wiring exists in extremely unfavourable conditions – heat, vibration and chemical attack – and the first things to look for are loose or corroded connections and broken or chafed wires, especially where the wires pass through holes in the bodywork or are subject to vibration.

All metal-bodied vehicles in current production have one pole of the battery 'earthed', ie connected to the vehicle bodywork, and in nearly all modern vehicles it is the negative (–) terminal. The various electrical components – motors, bulb holders etc – are also connected to earth, either by means of a lead or directly by their mountings.

Electric current flows through the component and then back to the battery via the bodywork. If the component mounting is loose or corroded, or if a good path back to the battery is not available, the circuit will be incomplete and malfunction will result. The engine and/or gearbox are also earthed by means of flexible metal straps to the body or subframe; if these straps are loose or missing, starter motor, generator and ignition trouble may result.

Assuming the earth return to be satisfactory, electrical faults will be due either to component malfunction or to defects in the current supply. Individual components are dealt with in Chapter 12. If supply wires are broken or cracked internally this results in an open-circuit, and the easiest way to check for this is to bypass the suspect wire temporarily with a length of wire having a crocodile clip or suitable connector at each end. Alternatively, a 12V test lamp can be used to verify the presence of supply voltage at various points along the wire and the break can be thus isolated.

If a bare portion of a live wire touches the bodywork or other earthed metal part, the electricity will take the low-resistance path thus formed back to the battery: this is known as a short-circuit. Hopefully a short-circuit will blow a fuse, but otherwise it may cause burning of the insulation (and possibly further short-circuits) or even a fire. This is why it is inadvisable to bypass persistently blowing fuses with silver foil or wire.

Spares and tool kit

Most vehicles are supplied only with sufficient tools for wheel changing; the *Maintenance and minor repair* tool kit detailed in *Tools and working facilities,* with the addition of a hammer, is probably sufficient for those repairs that most motorists would consider attempting at the roadside. In addition a few items which can be fitted without too much trouble in the event of a breakdown should be carried. Experience and available space will modify the list below, but the following may save having to call on professional assistance:

Spark plugs, clean and correctly gapped
HT lead and plug cap – long enough to reach the plug furthest from the distributor
Distributor rotor
Drivebelt(s) – emergency type may suffice
Spare fuses
Set of principal light bulbs
Tin of radiator sealer and hose bandage
Exhaust bandage
Roll of insulating tape
Length of soft iron wire
Length of electrical flex
Torch or inspection lamp (can double as test lamp)
Battery jump leads
Tow-rope
Ignition water dispersant aerosol
Litre of engine oil
Sealed can of hydraulic fluid
Emergency windscreen
Worm drive clips

If spare fuel is carried, a can designed for the purpose should be used to minimise risks of leakage and collision damage. A first aid kit and a warning triangle, whilst not at present compulsory in the UK, are obviously sensible items to carry in addition to the above.

When touring abroad it may be advisable to carry additional spares which, even if you cannot fit them yourself, could save having to wait while parts are obtained. The items below may be worth considering:

Throttle cable
Cylinder head gasket
Alternator brushes
Tyre valve core

One of the motoring organisations will be able to advise on availability of fuel etc in foreign countries.

Carrying a few spares may save a long walk!

Engine will not start

Engine fails to turn when starter operated
    Flat battery (recharge, use jump leads, or push start)
    Battery terminals loose or corroded
    Battery earth to body defective
    Engine earth strap loose or broken
    Starter motor (or solenoid) wiring loose or broken
    Automatic transmission selector in wrong position, or inhibitor switch faulty
    Ignition/starter switch faulty
    Major mechanical failure (seizure)
    Starter or solenoid internal fault (see Chapter 12)

Starter motor turns engine slowly
    Partially discharged battery (recharge, use jump leads, or push start)
    Battery terminals loose or corroded
    Battery earth to body defective
    Engine earth strap loose
    Starter motor (or solenoid) wiring loose
    Starter motor internal fault (see Chapter 12)

Starter motor spins without turning engine
    Flat battery
    Starter motor pinion sticking on sleeve
    Flywheel gear teeth damaged or worn
    Starter motor mounting bolts loose

Engine turns normally but fails to start
    Damp or dirty HT leads and distributor cap (crank engine and check for spark)
    No fuel in tank
    Fouled or incorrectly gapped spark plugs (remove, clean and regap)
    Other ignition system fault (see Chapter 4)
    Other fuel system fault (see Chapter 3)
    Poor compression (see Chapter 1)
    Major mechanical failure (eg camshaft drive)

Engine fires but will not run
    Air leaks at inlet manifold
    Fuel starvation (see Chapter 3)
    Other ignition fault (see Chapter 4)

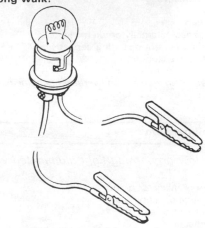

A simple test lamp is useful for tracing electrical faults

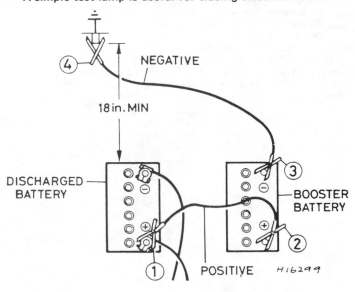

Jump start lead connections for negative earth vehicles - connect leads in order shown

Engine cuts out and will not restart

Engine cuts out suddenly – ignition fault
Loose or disconnected LT wires
Wet HT leads or distributor cap (after traversing water splash)
Coil failure (check for spark)
Other ignition fault (see Chapter 4)

Engine misfires before cutting out – fuel fault
Fuel tank empty
Fuel pump defective or filter blocked (check for delivery)
Fuel tank filler vent blocked (suction will be evident on releasing cap)
Other fuel system fault (see Chapter 3)

Engine cuts out – other causes
Serious overheating
Major mechanical failure (eg camshaft drive)

Engine overheats

Ignition (no-charge) warning light illuminated
Slack or broken drivebelt – retension or renew (Chapter 12)

Ignition warning light not illuminated
Coolant loss due to internal or external leakage (see Chapter 2)
Thermostat defective
Low oil level
Brakes binding
Radiator clogged externally or internally
Electric cooling fan not operating correctly
Engine waterways clogged

Note: *Do not add cold water to an overheated engine or damage may result*

Low engine oil pressure

Gauge reads low or warning light illuminated with engine running
Oil level low or incorrect grade
Defective gauge or sender unit
Wire to sender unit earthed
Engine overheating
Oil filter clogged or bypass valve defective
Oil pressure relief valve defective
Oil pick-up strainer clogged
Oil pump worn
Worn main or big-end bearings
Note: *Low oil pressure in a high-mileage engine at tickover is not necessarily a cause for concern. Sudden pressure loss at speed is far more significant. In any event, check the gauge or warning light sender before condemning the engine.*

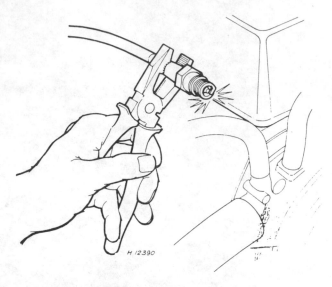

Crank engine and check for spark. Note use of insulated tool to hold plug lead

Engine noises

Pre-ignition (pinking) on acceleration
Incorrect grade of fuel
Ignition ECU fault
Excessive carbon build-up in engine

Whistling or wheezing noises
Leaking vacuum hose
Leaking manifold gasket
Blowing head gasket

Tapping or rattling
Worn valve gear
Worn timing belt
Broken piston ring (ticking noise)

Knocking or thumping
Unintentional mechanical contact (eg fan blades)
Worn drivebelt
Peripheral component fault (alternator, water pump etc)
Worn big-end bearings (regular heavy knocking, perhaps less under load)
Worn main bearings (rumbling and knocking, perhaps worsening under load)
Piston slap (most noticeable when cold)

Chapter 1 Engine

For modifications, and information applicable to later models, see Supplement at end of manual

Contents

Specifications

General

Type	M16 twin overhead camshaft
Designation	20 HD
Number of cylinders	4
Bore	84.45 mm (3.327 in)
Stroke	89.00 mm (3.506 in)
Capacity	1994 cc
Firing order	1-3-4-2 (No 1 at timing belt end)
Direction of crankshaft rotation	Clockwise
Valve operation	Overhead camshaft/ hydraulic tappets
Compression ratio	10.0:1

Cylinder block

Material	Cast iron
Block height	294.07 mm (11.192 in)
Bore diameter	84.456 to 84.469 mm (3.3275 to 3.3280 in)
Maximum cylinder bore taper	0.15 mm (0.006 in)
Maximum cylinder bore ovality	0.15 mm (0.006 in)
Maximum gasket face distortion	0.10 mm (0.004 in)

Crankshaft

Main bearing journal diameter	54.005 to 54.026 mm (2.1277 to 2.1286 in)
Crankpin journal diameter	47.635 to 47.647 mm (1.8768 to 1.8772 in)
Main bearing journal running clearance	0.03 to 0.38 mm (0.001 to 0.014 in)
Crankpin journal running clearance	0.04 to 0.08 mm (0.001 to 0.003 in)
Crankshaft endfloat	0.03 to 0.14 mm (0.001 to 0.005 in)

Pistons and piston rings

Piston-to-bore clearance:

Top of skirt	0.08 to 0.10 mm (0.003 to 0.004 in)
Bottom of skirt	0.04 to 0.05 mm (0.001 to 0.002 in)

Piston ring fitted gap:

Compression rings	0.30 to 0.50 mm (0.011 to 0.020 in)
Oil control rails	0.25 to 0.50 mm (0.010 to 0.020 in)

Gudgeon pin

Type	Fully floating
Diameter	23.810 to 23.815 mm (0.9381 to 0.9383 in)
Clearance in connecting rod	0.003 to 0.025 mm (0.0001 to 0.0010 in)
Clearance in piston	Hand push fit at 20°C (68°F)

Connecting rod

Small end bush reamed diameter	23.818 to 23.825 mm (0.9384 to 0.0387 in)

Camshafts

Drive	Toothed belt
Number of bearings	5 per shaft
Camshaft bearing clearance:	
New	0.043 to 0.094 mm (0.0016 to 0.0037 in)
Used	0.10 mm (0.039 in) maximum

Valves

Face angle	45° 30'
Head diameter:	
Inlet	31.70 to 32.00 mm (1.24 to 1.26 in)
Exhaust	29.20 to 29.40 mm (1.15 to 1.16 in)
Stem diameter:	
Inlet	7.09 to 7.10 mm (0.279 to 0.280 in)
Exhaust	7.07 to 7.09 mm (0.278 to 0.279 in)
Seat width	1.5 to 2.0 mm (0.060 to 0.078 in)
Installed height	44.00 mm (1.733 in) maximum
Valve spring free length	41.00 mm (1.615 in)

Cylinder head

Maximum gasket face distortion	0.20 mm (0.007 in)
Valve seat angle	45°
Valve seat width	1.50 to 2.00 mm (0.059 to 0.078 in)
Valve guide protrusion	12.00 mm (0.472 in) above head face

Lubrication system

System pressure:	
Idling	0.7 bar (10.15 lbf/ in) minimum
Running	3.8 bar (55.10 lbf/ in) minimum
Oil filter	Champion B101
Engine oil type/specification *	Multigrade engine oil, viscosity SAE 10W/40, to API SF or SF/CD (Duckhams QXR, Hypergrade, or 10W/40 Motor Oil)
Engine oil capacity (including filter)	4.5 litres (8.0 Imp pints)
Difference between MAX and MIN marks on dipstick	0.5 litre (0.9 Imp pint)

* **Note:** *Austin Rover specify a 10W/40 oil to meet warranty requirements. Duckhams QXR or 10W/40 Motor Oil is available to meet these requirements.*

Torque wrench settings

	Nm	lbf ft
Timing belt upper cover bolts	3	2
Timing belt lower cover bolts	6	4
Timing belt bottom cover bracket bolts	6	4
Timing belt tensioner retaining bolt	25	18
Timing belt idler pulley bolt	25	18
Camshaft sprocket retaining bolt	65	48
Cylinder head backplate	6	4
Crankshaft pulley retaining bolt	85	63
Camshaft cover bolts	10	7
Camshaft housing to cylinder head	25	18
Cylinder head bolts:		
Stage 1	45	33
Stage 2	80	59
Stage 3	Further 60°, or to 108 Nm (80 lbf ft) – whichever comes first	
Oil pump retaining bolts	6	4
Flywheel retaining bolts	85	63
Torque converter driveplate bolts	110	81
Starter ring gear to driveplate	32	23
Adaptor plate to engine:		
Bolts below crankshaft centre-line	25	18
Bolts above crankshaft centre-line	45	33
Sump drain plug	35	26
Sump pan bolts	8	6
Oil pick-up pipe bolts	6	4
Main bearing cap bolts	105	77
Big-end bearing cap nuts	55	40
Front and rear engine mounting-to-mounting bracket nuts	80	59
Front engine mounting bracket bolts	40	30
Rear engine mounting bracket to engine	90	66
Rear engine mounting bracket to body	25	18
Right-hand engine mounting through-bolt	45	33
Right-hand engine mounting to engine bracket	60	44
Right-hand engine mounting bracket to engine	25	18
Engine tie-bar through-bolts	45	33
Snubber to longitudinal support member	55	40
Snubber bracket to adaptor plate	80	59
Longitudinal support member bolts	45	33

1 General description

The M16 engine fitted to Rover 820 models is a water-cooled, four-cylinder, four-stroke petrol engine, of double overhead camshaft configuration, and 1994 cc capacity.

The combined crankcase and cylinder block is of cast iron construction, and houses the pistons, connecting rods and crankshaft. The solid skirt cast aluminium alloy pistons have two compression rings and an oil control ring, and are retained on the connecting rods by fully floating gudgeon pins. To reduce frictional drag and piston slap, the gudgeon pin is offset to the thrust side of the piston. The forged steel connecting rods are attached to the crankshaft by renewable shell type big-end bearings. The crankshaft is carried in five main bearings, also of the renewable shell type. Crankshaft endfloat is controlled by thrust washers which are located on either side of the centre main bearing.

The twin overhead camshafts are located in the cylinder head, and each is retained in position by a housing bolted to the cylinder head upper face. The camshafts are supported by five bearing journals machined directly into the head and housings. Drive to the camshafts is by an internally-toothed rubber timing belt, from a sprocket on the front end of the crankshaft. An idler pulley and adjustable tensioner pulley are fitted to eliminate backlash and prevent slackness of the belt. The distributor rotor arm is attached to the rear of the exhaust camshaft, and on early models, the power steering pump is belt-driven from a sprocket attached to the rear of the inlet camshaft. On later models, the power steering is located at the front of the engine, and is belt-driven from a sprocket on the crankshaft.

The M16 engine utilizes four valves per cylinder, mounted at an inclined angle, and running in guides which are pressed into the cylinder head. The valves are of small diameter, to improve breathing efficiency and reduce valve mass. Each valve is opened by a hydraulic tappet, acted upon directly by the lobe of the camshaft, and closed by a single valve spring.

Blow-by gases from the crankcase are vented by a positive crankcase ventilation system back into the intake air stream for combustion. The system incorporates an oil separator, to return oil droplets to the sump, and a diverter valve, which channels the vapour to inlets on either side of the throttle valve, depending on manifold depression.

Engine lubrication is by a conventional forced-feed system, and a detailed description of its operation will be found in Section 24.

2 Maintenance and inspection

1 At the intervals given in *Routine maintenance* at the beginning of this manual, carry out the following operations on the engine.

2 Visually inspect the engine joint faces, gaskets and seals for any signs of oil or water leaks. Pay particular attention to the areas around the camshaft covers, cylinder head, crankshaft front oil seal and sump joint faces. Rectify any leaks by referring to the appropriate Sections of this Chapter.

3 Place a suitable container beneath the oil drain plug, located on the rear-facing side of the sump (photo). Unscrew the plug using a spanner or socket, and allow the oil to drain. Inspect the condition of the drain plug sealing washer, and renew it if necessary. Refit and tighten the plug after draining.

4 Reposition the bowl to the side of the engine, under the oil filter.

5 Using a strap wrench or filter removal tool, slacken the filter initially, then unscrew it from the engine and discard (photo).

6 Wipe the filter housing mating face with a rag, then lubricate the seal of a new filter using clean engine oil.

7 Screw the filter into position, and tighten it by hand only – do not use any tools.

8 Unscrew the filler cap on the camshaft cover and fill the engine, using the correct grade of oil, until the level reaches the MAX mark on the dipstick (photo). Refit the filler cap, then start the engine and check for leaks around the filter seal. Switch off, wait for a few minutes for the oil to return to the sump, then check the level on the dipstick once more. Top up if necessary to bring the level back up to the MAX mark, and maintain the level between the MAX and MIN marks at all times. Approximately 0.5 litres (0.8 pts) will raise the level from MIN to MAX on the dipstick.

2.3 Engine oil drain plug location

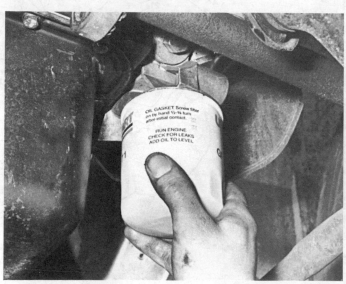

2.5 Removing the oil filter

2.8 Fill the engine with oil through the filler orifice on the camshaft cover

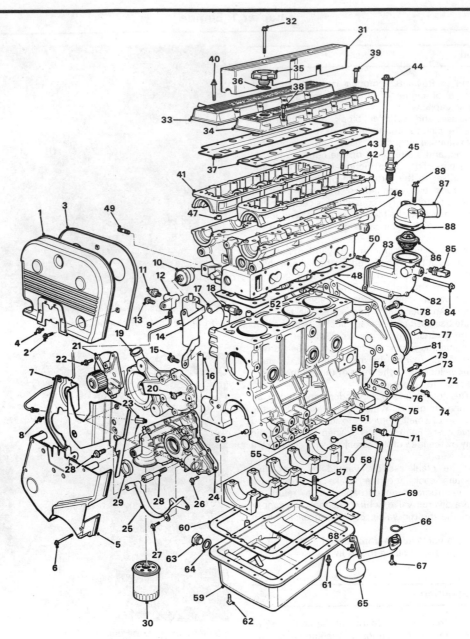

Fig. 1.1 Exploded view of the engine external components (Sec 1)

1 Timing belt upper cover
2 Upper cover bolt
3 Backplate
4 Backplate bolt
5 Timing belt lower cover
6 Lower cover bolt
7 Backplate
8 Backplate bolt
9 Oil pipe
10 Oil pressure transducer
11 Oil pressure switch
12 Adaptor
13 Adaptor bolt
14 Oil separator
15 Oil separator bolt
16 Breather hose
17 Breather hose
18 Knock sensor
19 Water pump housing
20 Water pump housing bolt
21 Water pump
22 Water pump bolt
23 Oil pipe adaptor

24 Oil pump housing
25 Timing belt bottom cover
26 Bottom cover bolt
27 Bottom cover bolt
28 Bolt adaptor
29 Crankshaft front oil seal
30 Oil filter cartridge
31 Spark plug cover
32 Spark plug cover bolt
33 Inlet camshaft cover
34 Exhaust camshaft cover
35 Oil filler cap
36 Filler cap seal
37 Baffle plates
38 Camshaft cover bolt
39 Camshaft cover bolt
40 Camshaft cover bolt
41 Inlet camshaft housing
42 Exhaust camshaft housing
43 Camshaft housing bolt
44 Cylinder head bolt
45 Spark plug
46 Cylinder head

47 Camshaft housing dowels
48 Cylinder head gasket
49 Inlet manifold stud
50 Exhaust manifold stud
51 Cylinder block
52 Cylinder head dowel
53 Oil pump housing dowel
54 Adaptor plate dowel
55 Main bearing caps
56 Bearing cap dowel
57 Main bearing cap bolt
58 Crankcase breather
   extension tube
59 Sump
60 Sump gasket
61 Sump bolt
62 Sump bolt
63 Drain plug
64 Drain plug washer
65 Oil pick-up pipe strainer
66 O-ring seal
67 Pick-up pipe bolt
68 Pick-up pipe bracket bolt

69 Oil dipstick
70 Dipstick tube
71 Dipstick tube bolt
72 Crankcase cover plate
73 Gasket
74 Cover plate bolt
75 Gearbox adaptor plate
76 Adaptor plate gasket
77 Gearbox locating dowel
78 Adaptor plate bolt
79 Adaptor plate bolt
80 Adaptor plate Torx bolt
81 Crankshaft rear oil seal
82 Thermostat housing
83 Gasket
84 Thermostat housing bolt
85 Coolant temperature
   thermistor
86 Thermostat
87 Water outlet elbow
88 Gasket
89 Outlet elbow bolt

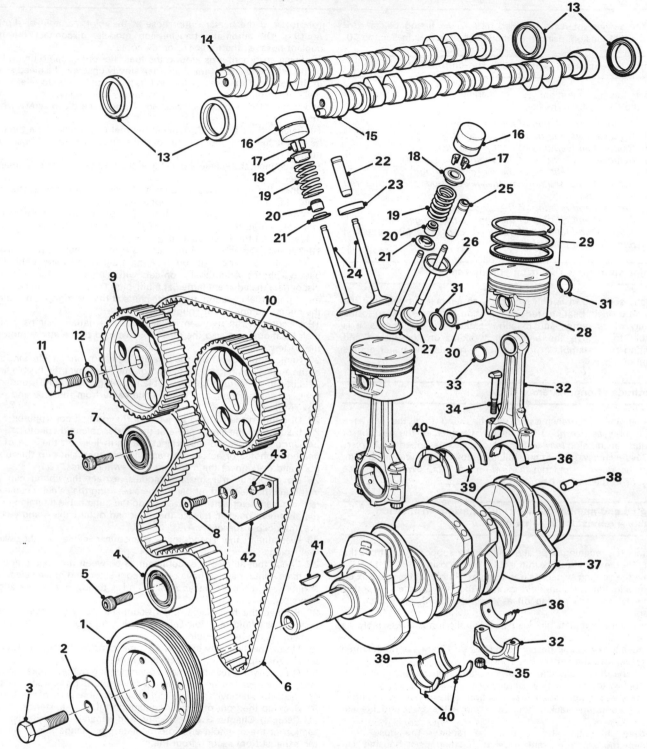

Fig. 1.2 Exploded view of the engine internal components (Sec 1)

1   Crankshaft pulley and sprocket
2   Flat washer
3   Crankshaft pulley bolt
4   Timing belt tensioner pulley
5   Pulley retaining bolt
6   Timing belt
7   Timing belt idler pulley
8   Mounting plate countersunk screw
9   Inlet camshaft sprocket
10 Exhaust camshaft sprocket

11 Sprocket retaining bolt
12 Washer
13 Camshaft front oil seals
14 Inlet camshaft
15 Exhaust camshaft
16 Hydraulic tappet
17 Valve collets
18 Valve spring top cup
19 Valve spring
20 Valve stem oil deal
21 Valve spring seat
22 Inlet valve guide

23 Inlet valve seat
24 Inlet valves
25 Exhaust valve guide
26 Exhaust valve seat
27 Exhaust valves
28 Piston
29 Piston rings
30 Gudgeon pin
31 Circlips
32 Connecting rod and cap
33 Connecting rod small end bush

34 Connecting rod bolt
35 Connecting rod cap nut
36 Big-end bearing shells
37 Crankshaft
38 Dowel
39 Main bearing shells
40 Crankshaft thrustwashers
41 Woodruff keys
42 Timing belt tensioner mounting plate
43 Mounting plate bolt

9 At the service intervals specified, renew the timing belt and/or adjust the belt tension, using the procedures described in Section 10.

3 Major operations possible with the engine in the car

The following operations can be carried out without having to remove the engine from the car:

(a) Removal and refitting of the timing belt
(b) Removal and refitting of the camshaft and tappets
(c) Removal and refitting of the cylinder head
(d) Removal and refitting of the sump
(e) Removal and refitting of the big-end bearings
(f) Removal and refitting of the piston and connecting rod assemblies
(g) Removal and refitting of the oil pump
(h) Removal and refitting of the engine mountings
(i) Removal and refitting of the flywheel or driveplate (after first removing the transmission)

4 Major operations requiring engine removal

Strictly speaking, it is only necessary to remove the engine if the crankshaft or main bearings require attention. However, owing to the possibility of dirt entry, and to allow greater working access, it is preferable to remove the engine if working on the piston and connecting rod assemblies, or when carrying out any major engine overhaul or repair.

5 Methods of engine removal

The engine and transmission can be lifted from the car as a complete unit, as described later in this Chapter, or the gearbox or automatic transmission may be first removed, as described in Chapters 6 and 7 respectively. It is not possible to remove the engine on its own, leaving the gearbox or transmission in the car, owing to space restrictions in the engine bay.

6 Engine and manual gearbox/automatic transmission assembly – removal and refitting

1 Extract the retaining clips and release the support struts from the bonnet. Tie the bonnet back in the fully-open position.
2 Drain the cooling system as described in Chapter 2, the gearbox oil or automatic transmission fluid as described in Chapters 6 and 7 respectively, and the engine oil as described in Section 2 of this Chapter.
3 Remove the complete air cleaner and intake trunking assembly, as described in Chapter 3.
4 Remove the battery as described in Chapter 12, then undo the three bolts and remove the battery tray (photo).
5 Undo the three bolts and remove the air cleaner support bracket, located below the battery tray (photo).
6 On cars with single-point fuel injection, undo the three ignition/fuel ECU mounting bracket bolts, and move the ECU and bracket aside.
7 Slacken the clips and remove the radiator top hose, then disconnect the expansion tank hose at the thermostat housing. On single-point injection models, disconnect the two heater outlet hoses at the inlet manifold.
8 Disconnect the remaining vacuum hose at the inlet manifold.
9 Undo the bolt securing the engine rear tie-bar support bracket to the inlet manifold (photo).
10 Undo the two through-bolts securing the engine rear tie-bar to the engine and body brackets, and recover the special forked nut (photo). Note that the forked end of the nut engages with a bracket projection to prevent the nut turning.
11 Withdraw the rear tie-bar from its brackets, noting that it is stamped with the word TOP on the upper face of the larger end, which must be refitted accordingly (photo).
12 Slacken the clips and disconnect the radiator bottom hose at the radiator and main coolant pipe (photo), the bottom hose take-off at the expansion tank pipe, the two heater hoses at the heater matrix

(photo), and the heater outlet hose at the inlet manifold or throttle housing. On automatic transmission models, disconnect the two coolant hoses at the transmission oil cooler.
13 Place absorbent rags around the fuel filter outlet banjo union bolt on the left-hand side of the filter, then slowly unscrew the bleed screw in the centre of the bolt, or the bolt itself as applicable, to release the fuel system pressure. When the pressure is released, remove the bolt and recover the two copper washers. Tighten the bleed screw where fitted.
14 Release the clip and disconnect the fuel return hose from the pipe below the fuel filter. Plug or tape over the disconnected fuel hoses and unions.
15 Disconnect the accelerator cable at the throttle end, as described in Chapter 3.
16 Undo the brake servo vacuum hose banjo union bolt at the inlet manifold, and recover the two copper washers.
17 On cars with single-point fuel injection, disconnect the wiring multi-plug from the ignition/fuel ECU, and remove the relay from its holder behind the ECU location (photo).
18 Separate the engine wiring harness from the main wiring harness by disconnecting the large round wiring multi-plug located behind the battery (photo). Additionally, on cars with single-point fuel injection, disconnect the adjacent large flat multi-plug (photo), and on cars with multi-point fuel injection, the multi-plugs at the rear right-hand side of the engine compartment (photo).
19 Disconnect the two sensing leads at the battery clamps, noting their locations, and also the main positive lead to the starter motor at the battery clamp.
20 Remove the cover from the fuse and relay box on the left-hand side of the engine compartment, then lift off the cover over the fusible links.
21 Lift out the engine harness cable retaining clip (photo), undo the cable retaining screw, and remove the cable from the fuse and relay box (photos).
22 Disconnect the HT and LT leads at the ignition coil (photos).
23 Disconnect the single cable at the starter solenoid (photo).
24 Undo the bolt and disconnect the earth lead on the side of the gearbox (photo) or automatic transmission, then slide up the rubber boot and disconnect the reversing light switch wires.
25 On automatic transmission models, extract the spring clip and withdraw the steel and rubber washers securing the selector cable end to the transmission selector lever. Undo the outer cable retaining nut at the abutment bracket, release the inner and outer cables, and recover the inner cable spacer.
26 Disconnect the speedometer transducer cable at the wiring multi-plug .
27 Check that all electrical connections between the engine and the car main wiring harness have been disconnected and moved clear. The engine wiring harness stays in situ, and is removed with the engine assembly.
28 Slacken the hose clips and disconnect the two power steering hoses at the fluid reservoir (photos). Plug the hoses and the outlets immediately to reduce fluid loss.
29 Undo the two power steering pipe support bracket bolts, and release the pipes from the brackets (photo).
30 On cars with a rear-mounted power steering pump, slacken the clip and disconnect the power steering fluid return hose from the pipe (photo), then remove the pipe and hose assembly clear of the engine.
31 Jack up the front of the car and support it on axle stands.
32 Refer to Chapter 3 if necessary, and separate the exhaust front section at the manifold and intermediate pipe flange joints. Remove the exhaust front section from the car.
33 On manual gearbox models, extract the spring clip and withdraw the clevis pin securing the clutch slave cylinder pushrod to the gearbox release arm. Undo the two slave cylinder retaining bolts and move the cylinder aside.
34 On manual gearbox models, undo the bolt in the centre of the gearbox steady rod. Remove the dished washer, slide off the steady rod and remove the inner flat washer. Remove the spring clip to expose the gearchange rod-to-gearchange shaft retaining roll pin. Using a parallel pin punch, tap out the roll pin and slide the gearchange rod rearwards off the shaft (photo).
35 Undo the eight bolts and remove the longitudinal support member from beneath the engine (photo).
36 On cars with a front-mounted power steering pump, undo the pipe union and remove the fluid pipe from the rear of the pump. Plug the unions to prevent fluid loss.

6.4 Undo the three bolts and remove the battery tray

6.5 Undo the three bolts and remove the air cleaner support bracket

6.9 Undo the engine tie-bar-to-inlet manifold bolt (arrowed)

6.10 Remove the tie-bar through-bolt (A), and recover the forked nut (B)

6.11 The tie-bar must be refitted with the word TOP (arrowed) uppermost

6.12A Disconnect the radiator hose (arrowed) at the main coolant pipe ...

6.12B ... and the heater hoses at the heater matrix (arrowed)

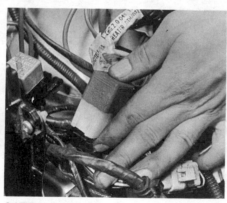

6.17 Remove the relay behind the ignition/fuel ECU

6.18A Disconnect the large round wiring multi-plug (arrowed) ...

6.18B ... and the adjacent flat multi-plug

6.18C Disconnect the appropriate multi-plugs at the rear of the engine compartment

6.21A Lift out the engine harness cable retaining clip ...

6.21B ... undo the cable retaining screw ...

6.21C ... and remove the cable from the fuse and relay box

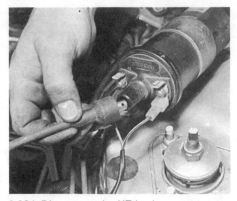

6.22A Disconnect the HT lead ...

6.22B .. and LT leads at the ignition coil

6.23 Disconnect the starter solenoid cable

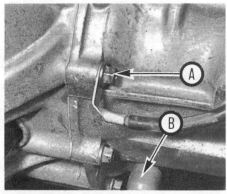

6.24 Disconnect the gearbox earth lead (A) and reversing light switch wires (B)

6.28A Slacken the power steering hose clips (arrowed) ...

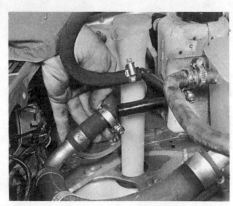

6.28B ... and disconnect the hoses

6.29 Undo the power steering pipe support bracket bolts (arrowed)

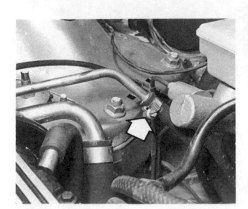

6.30 Disconnect the power steering fluid return hose (arrowed)

6.34 Separate the gearchange rod from the shaft after removing the roll pin

6.35 Undo the bolts and remove the longitudinal support member (arrowed)

37 Undo the nut securing the right-hand steering knuckle balljoint to the lower suspension arm (photo), then release the balljoint from the arm using a universal balljoint separator tool or two-legged puller.
38 Pull the steering knuckle outwards, then using a suitable flat bar or large screwdriver, lever between the driveshaft inner constant velocity joint and the differential housing to release the joint.
39 Move the driveshaft clear, then repeat these operations on the left-hand driveshaft.
40 Attach a suitable hoist to the engine using rope slings, or chains attached to brackets secured to the cylinder head. Adjust the ropes or chains so that the engine will hang at approximately 30° to the horizontal, with the timing cover end uppermost, when it is lifted out.
41 On automatic transmission models, undo the mounting bracket bolts and remove the engine lower tie-bar from under the front of the car, complete with mounting brackets.
42 Undo the right-hand engine mounting through-bolt, and recover the special nut. Note that the forked end of the nut plate locates over a stud on the body bracket.
43 Undo the two bolts securing the engine mounting to its mounting bracket, and remove the mounting (photo).
44 Undo the two bolts securing the air cleaner trunking support bracket to the front chassis member, and remove the bracket (photo).
45 Undo the nut securing the front engine mounting to its gearbox or transmission bracket (photo).
46 Undo the nut securing the rear engine mounting to its gearbox or transmission bracket.
47 Raise the engine slightly, then on cars with a rear-mounted power steering pump, undo the power steering pipe union nut at the rear of the pump, and remove the pipe. Plug the unions to prevent loss of fluid.
48 Make a final check that everything connecting the engine and gearbox or transmission to the car has been disconnected and moved well clear.
49 Carefully lift the power unit upwards, whilst moving and twisting it slightly to clear the various projections (photo). When the unit has been raised sufficiently, draw the hoist forwards to bring the engine

assembly over the front body panel, then lower the assembly to the floor.
50 Refitting is a straightforward reverse of the removal sequence, bearing in mind the following points:

(a) Refit all the engine mounting bolts loosely, then tighten them in the sequence shown in Fig. 1.3 or 1.4 as applicable
(b) Refill the cooling system as described in Chapter 2
(c) Refill the gearbox or automatic transmission as described in Chapters 6 or 7 respectively
(d) Fill the engine with oil as described in Section 2
(e) Refill and bleed the power steering system as described in Chapter 10
(f) Adjust the accelerator cable as described in Chapter 3, and where applicable, the automatic transmission kickdown cable as described in Chapter 7

7 Engine – separation from, and attachment to, manual gearbox/ automatic transmission

Separation – manual gearbox models
1 With the engine and gearbox removed from the car, undo the starter motor retaining bolts, and remove the unit from the gearbox bellhousing (photo).
2 Undo the three bolts and remove the engine snubber bracket from the gearbox adaptor plate beneath the engine sump.
3 Undo the two bolts securing the front engine mounting bracket to the gearbox, and remove the bracket (photo).
4 Undo the bolts securing the rear engine mounting bracket to the gearbox, noting the location of the crankshaft sensor bracket (photo). Move the sensor aside and remove the bracket.
5 Undo all the remaining bolts securing the gearbox to the engine.
6 With the gearbox well supported, release the locating dowels and draw the unit squarely away from the engine (photo).

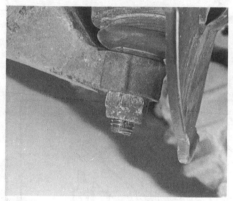
6.37 Undo the nut and separate the steering knuckle balljoint

6.43 Remove the right-hand engine mounting

6.44 Undo the bolts (arrowed) and remove the air cleaner trunking support bracket

6.45 Undo the nut securing the front engine mounting

6.49 Removing the engine and gearbox from the car

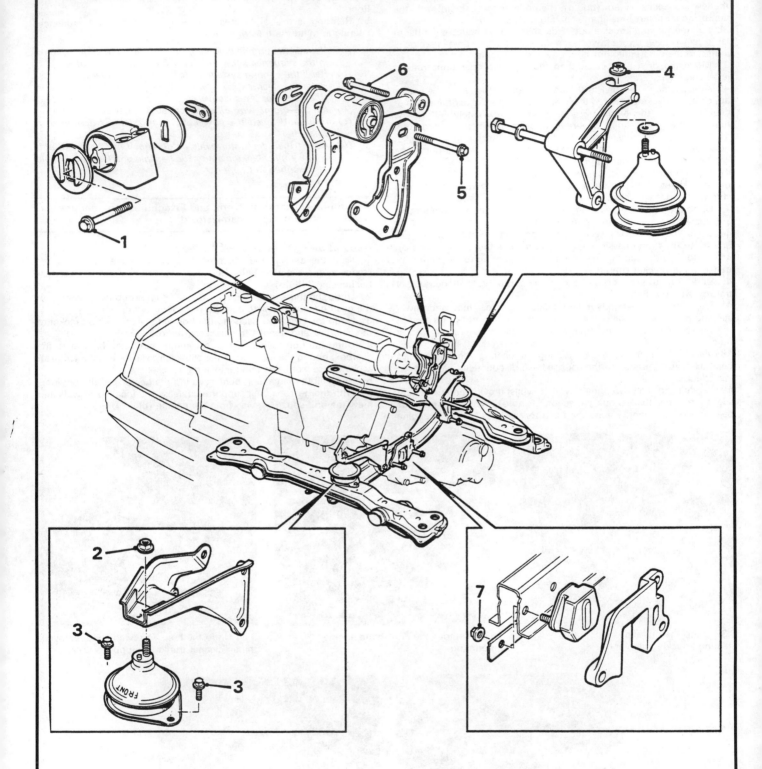

Fig. 1.3 Engine mounting tightening sequence – manual gearbox models (Sec 6)

Tighten the mountings in the numerical sequence shown

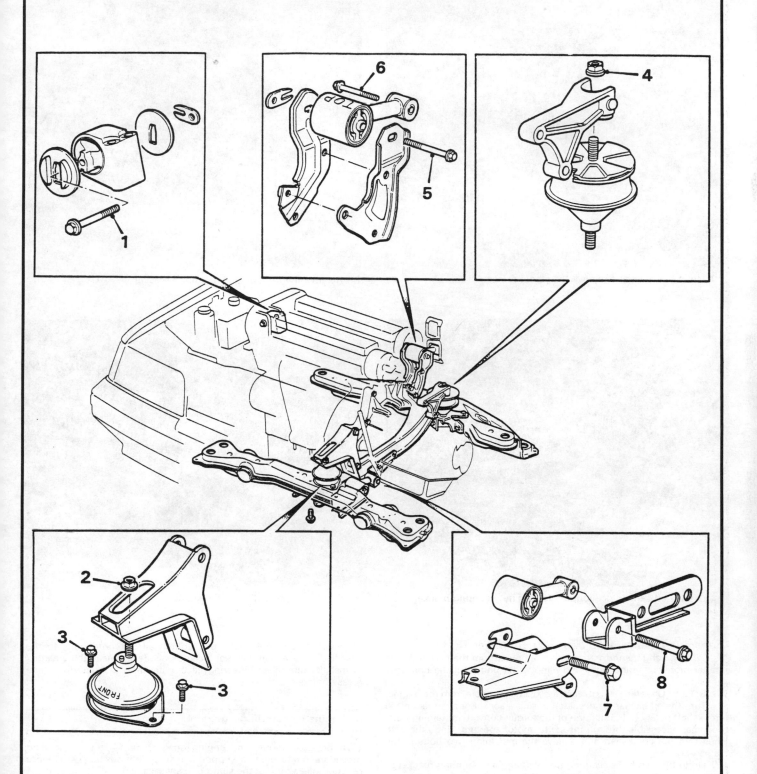

Fig. 1.4 Engine mounting tightening sequence – automatic transmission models (Sec 6)

Tighten the mountings in the numerical sequence shown

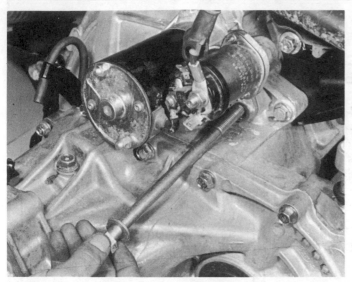

7.1 Undo the bolts and remove the starter motor

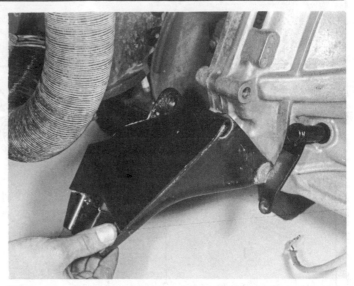

7.3 Remove the front engine mounting bracket

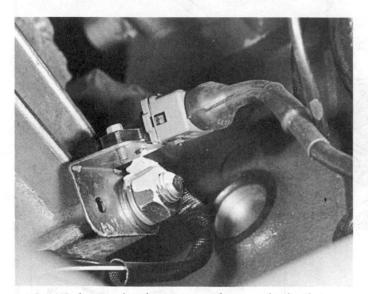

7.4 Crankshaft sensor location on rear engine mounting bracket

7.6 Gearbox separated from the engine

Separation – automatic transmission models

7   With the engine and transmission removed from the car, undo the starter motor retaining bolts and remove the unit from the converter housing.

8   Refer to Chapter 7 and release the kickdown cable from the engine.

9   Turn the crankshaft as necessary, using a socket or spanner on the crankshaft pulley bolt, until one of the torque converter retaining bolts becomes accessible through the starter motor aperture. Undo the bolt, then turn the crankshaft and remove the remaining two bolts in the same way

10   Undo the two bolts securing the front engine mounting bracket to the transmission, and remove the bracket.

11   Undo the bolts securing the rear engine mounting bracket to the gearbox, noting the location of the crankshaft sensor bracket. Move the sensor aside and remove the bracket.

12   Undo the remaining bolts securing the transmission to the engine.

13   With the transmission well supported, release the locating dowels and draw the unit squarely away from the engine. Ensure that the torque converter stays in place on the transmission.

Attachment – all models

14   Attachment is the straightforward reverse of the separation sequence, but where applicable, tighten all nuts and bolts to the specified torque. On manual gearbox models, smear the gearbox mainshaft and release bearing face with molybdenum disulphide grease before attachment.

---

8   Engine dismantling – general

1   If possible, mount the engine on a stand for the dismantling procedure, but failing this, support it in an upright position with blocks of wood placed under the sump or crankcase.

2   Drain the oil into a suitable container before cleaning the engine or commencing dismantling, if this has not already been done.

3   Cleanliness is most important, and if the engine is dirty, it should be cleaned with paraffin or a suitable solvent, while keeping it in an upright position.

4   Avoid working with the engine directly on a concrete floor, as grit presents a real source of trouble.

5   As parts are removed, clean them in a paraffin bath. However, do not immerse parts with internal oilways in paraffin, as it is difficult to remove, usually requiring a high pressure hose. Clean oilways with nylon pipe cleaners.

6 It is advisable to have suitable containers to hold small items, as this will help when reassembling the engine, and also prevent possible losses.

7 Always obtain complete sets of new gaskets, but retain the old ones with a view to using them as a pattern to make a replacement if a new one is not available.

8 When possible, refit nuts, bolts and washers in their location after being removed, as this helps to protect the threads, and will also be helpful when reassembling the engine.

9 Retain unserviceable components, in order to compare them with the new parts supplied.

9 Ancillary components – removal and refitting

1 If the engine has been removed from the car for major overhaul or repair, the following externally-mounted ancillary components can now be removed. The removal sequence need not necessarily follow the order given, nor will it always be necessary to remove all the components listed. This will depend on the extent of the work to be carried out, and the operations involved.

Thermostat housing and heater pipes (Chapter 2)
Water pump and housing (Chapter 2)
Inlet and exhaust manifolds (Chapter 3)
Distributor cap, spark plugs and HT leads (Chapter 4)
Knock sensor (Chapter 4)
Crankshaft sensor (Chapter 4)
Clutch assembly (Chapter 5)
Power steering pump (Chapter 10)
Alternator (Chapter 12)
Oil filter cartridge (Section 2 of this Chapter)
Engine mountings (Section 25 of this Chapter)
Dipstick tube (photo)
Alternator mounting bracket (photo)
Alternator adjustment arm or front mounted power steering pump bracket (photo)
Oil separator and oil pressure switch bracket (photo)

2 Refitting is essentially the reverse of the removal sequence, with reference to the Sections and Chapters indicated.

9.1A Remove the dipstick tube ...

9.1B ... the alternator mounting bracket ...

9.1C ... the alternator adjustment arm and bracket ...

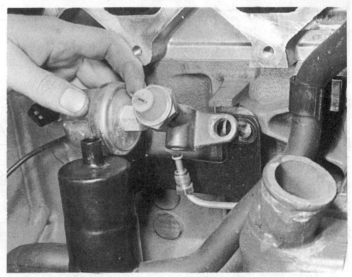

9.1D ... and oil pressure switch bracket

10 Timing belt – removal, refitting and adjustment

Note: *Accurate adjustment of the timing belt entails the use of a tension checking gauge, which is a Rover special tool. An approximate setting can be achieved using the method described in this Section, but the tension should be checked by a Rover dealer on completion.*

1 Disconnect the battery negative terminal. (Refer to Chapter 12, Section 1, before doing this).

2 Slacken the right-hand front wheel nuts, jack up the front of the car and support it on axle stands. Remove the roadwheel.

3 Undo the three bolts and remove the access panel under the wheel arch.

4 Position a jack and interposed block of wood under the sump, and just take the weight of the engine.

5 Undo the bolts securing the power steering pipe support brackets, and move the pipes slightly to gain access to the right-hand engine mounting (photo).

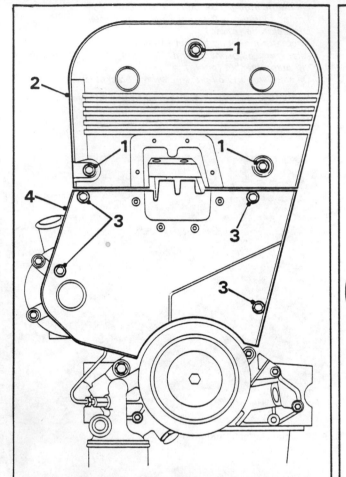
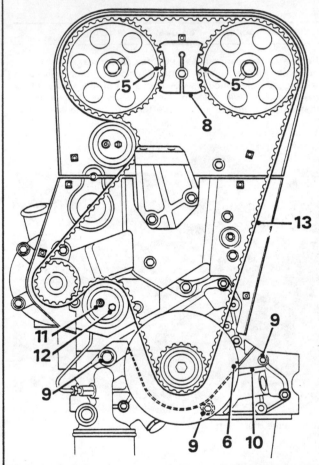

Fig. 1.5 Timing belt component details (Sec 10)

1 Upper cover retaining bolts	5 Camshaft sprocket timing marks	7 Locking the crankshaft through the hole in the adaptor plate	9 Bottom cover retaining bolts
2 Upper cover			10 Bottom cover
3 Lower cover retaining bolts	6 Crankshaft pulley timing mark	8 Special tool for locking camshaft sprockets	11 Tensioner retaining bolt
4 Lower cover			12 Tensioner adjusting hole
			13 Timing belt

6 Undo the engine mounting through-bolt (photo), and recover the special nut. Note that the forked end of the nut plate locates over a stud on the body bracket.

7 Undo the two bolts securing the engine mounting to its mounting bracket, and remove the mounting.

8 Raise the engine slightly, then undo the three bolts (photo) and lift off the timing belt upper cover.

9 Undo the four bolts (photo) and remove the timing belt lower cover.

10 Refer to Chapter 12 and remove the alternator drivebelt.

11 Using a socket or spanner on the crankshaft pulley, turn the crankshaft in an anti-clockwise direction until the timing notches on the camshaft sprockets are facing each other and aligned horizontally (photos). The notch on the crankshaft pulley should also be aligned with the edge of the metal bracket which forms the timing belt bottom cover (photo). In this position, the crankshaft is at 90° BTDC, with No 1 piston on its compression stroke.

12 If required, the crankshaft can be locked in this position, by inserting a dowel rod or drill of suitable diameter through the hole in the gearbox adaptor plate, near to the lower edge of the cylinder block on the front-facing side of the engine (Fig. 1.5). The dowel or drill will then engage with a corresponding hole in the flywheel.

13 Undo the three bolts and remove the timing belt bottom cover (photo).

14 Using a suitable Allen key, undo the timing belt tensioner retaining bolt, and remove the tensioner (photo).

15 Slip the belt off the sprockets, and remove it from the engine (photo).

16 If the timing belt is to be re-used, mark it in chalk with an arrow to indicate its running direction, and store it on its edge while it is off the engine.

17 Check the condition of the timing belt and the various sprockets, with reference to Section 23.

18 Before refitting the belt, check that the crankshaft is still at the 90° BTDC position, and that the timing marks on the two sprockets are still aligned.

19 Engage the timing belt with the teeth of the crankshaft sprocket, and then pull the belt vertically upright on its straight, right-hand run. Keep it taut, and engage it over the exhaust camshaft sprocket, then the inlet camshaft sprocket.

20 Check that none of the sprockets have moved, then feed the belt around the idler pulley and engage it with the teeth of the water pump sprocket.

21 Fit the timing belt tensioner and secure with the retaining bolt, tightened finger-tight only at this stage.

22 Engage an Allen key with the hexagonal adjusting hole in the tensioner (photo), and turn the tensioner body until there is moderate tension on the belt. Hold the tensioner in this position, and tighten the retaining bolt.

23 Remove the locking pin (if used) from the gearbox adaptor plate, and turn the crankshaft one complete turn clockwise, followed by one complete turn anti-clockwise, and re-align the timing marks.

24 Check that it is just possible to deflect the belt, using moderate hand pressure, by 19.0 mm (0.75 in) at a point midway between the crankshaft and exhaust camshaft sprockets. Re-adjust the tension if necessary by slackening the tensioner retaining bolt, and repositioning the tensioner body with the Allen key. Recheck the tension again after turning the crankshaft one turn clockwise, then one turn anti-clockwise. It must be emphasised that this is only an approximate setting, and the tension should be checked by a dealer, using the Rover tension gauge, at the earliest opportunity.

25 Refit the timing belt bottom cover, turn the crankshaft to align the pulley timing mark with the edge of the bottom cover, and make a final check that the camshaft sprocket timing marks are still aligned.

26 Refer to Chapter 12 and refit the alternator drivebelt.

27 Refit the timing belt upper and lower covers.

28 Refit the engine mounting to its mounting bracket, lower the engine and secure the mounting to the body with the through-bolt and special nut.

29 Refit the power steering pipe support brackets, the wheel arch access panel, and the roadwheel.

30 Lower the car to the ground, tighten the wheel nuts fully, and reconnect the battery.

10.5 Undo the power steering pipe support bracket bolts (arrowed) and move the pipes

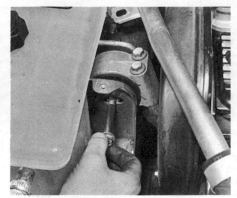

10.6 Undo the right-hand mounting through-bolt

10.8 Timing belt upper cover retaining bolt locations (arrowed)

10.9 Timing belt lower cover retaining bolt locations (arrowed)

10.11A Turn the crankshaft to align the sprocket timing marks (arrowed) ...

10.11B ... then check their horizontal alignment with a straight edge

10.11C Crankshaft pulley timing notch (arrowed) aligned with timing belt bottom cover edge

10.13 Removing the timing belt bottom cover

10.14 Removing the timing belt tensioner

10.15 Slip the timing belt off the sprockets

10.22 Tensioner hexagonal adjusting hole (arrowed)

11 Camshafts and tappets – removal and refitting

1 Remove the timing belt as described in the previous Section.

2 Using a suitable Allen key, undo the bolt securing the timing belt idler pulley to the cylinder head (photo). WIthdraw the pulley, noting that there is a spacing washer fitted between the pulley and cylinder head backplate (photo).

3 Undo the retaining bolt securing each sprocket to its respective camshaft (photo). To prevent the sprockets turning as the bolts are undone, either insert a large screwdriver through one of the sprocket holes and engage it with one of the backplate bolts behind, or make up a holding tool from scrap metal, as shown in photo 11.35, which is of a scissor shape, with a bolts at each end to engage with the holes in the sprocket.

4 Withdraw the two sprockets from the camshafts, noting that they are not identical, and are marked INLET and EXHAUST on their front faces to avoid confusion (photos).

5 Undo the four bolts and remove the cylinder head backplate (photos).

6 Undo the two retaining bolts, withdraw the distributor cap, and place it to one side.

7 Undo the retaining Allen screw, and remove the distributor rotor arm (photo).

8 Undo the two screws and remove the distributor adaptor plate from the cylinder head (photos).

9 On cars fitted with a rear-mounted power steering pump driven off the inlet camshaft, remove the power steering pump drivebelt as described in Chapter 10, then withdraw the spacer behind the camshaft pulley (photo). Undo the two nuts and two bolts, and remove the power steering pulley backplate (photos).

10 On cars fitted with a front-mounted power steering pump, undo the two bolts and remove the blanking plate from the cylinder head (photo).

11 Detach the breather hose from the rear of the inlet camshaft cover.

12 On cars with multi-point fuel injection, release the plastic covers

then undo the two bolts securing the plenum chamber support brackets to the plenum chamber.

13 Undo the two bolts and lift off the spark plug cover from the centre of the cylinder head. Note that the spark plug HT lead grommet engages with the end of the cover, and on certain models, an accelerator cable support bracket is also retained by the right-hand cover bolt.

14 Undo the ten bolts securing each camshaft cover to its respective camshaft housing, and lift off the two covers (photos).

15 Withdraw the baffle plates, taking care not to damage the sealing edges on both sides of the plates (photo).

16 Slacken the ten bolts securing each camshaft housing to the cylinder head, then remove all the bolts except two on each housing at diagonally opposite corners. Make sure that the heads of the bolts left in position are at least 5.0 mm (0.2 in) clear of the housing face. Note that two types of retaining bolts are used to secure the camshaft housings. The three bolts on the inner edge of each housing nearest to the spark plugs are plain bolts, while all the rest are patch bolts (photo). All the bolts are of the micro-encapsulated type, having their threads filled with a locking and sealing compound, and new bolts must be obtained prior to reassembly.

17 Using a plastic or hide mallet, carefully tap up each housing to release it from the locating dowels. When the housings are free, remove the remaining bolts and lift off the two housings (photo).

18 Carefully lift out the camshafts, and remove the oil seals at each end. Identify each camshaft, inlet or exhaust, with a label after removal.

19 Have a box ready with sixteen internal compartments, marked Inlet 1 to 8, and Exhaust 1 to 8, or alternatively mark a sheet of card in a similar way.

20 Lift out each tappet in turn (photo), and place it upside down in its respective position in the box or on the card. If the tappets are difficult to remove by hand, use the rubber sucker end of a valve grinding tool to lift them out.

21 Carry out a careful inspection of the components with reference to Section 23, and renew any parts as necessary. Prior to reassembly, obtain new camshaft oil seals, a complete set of camshaft housing

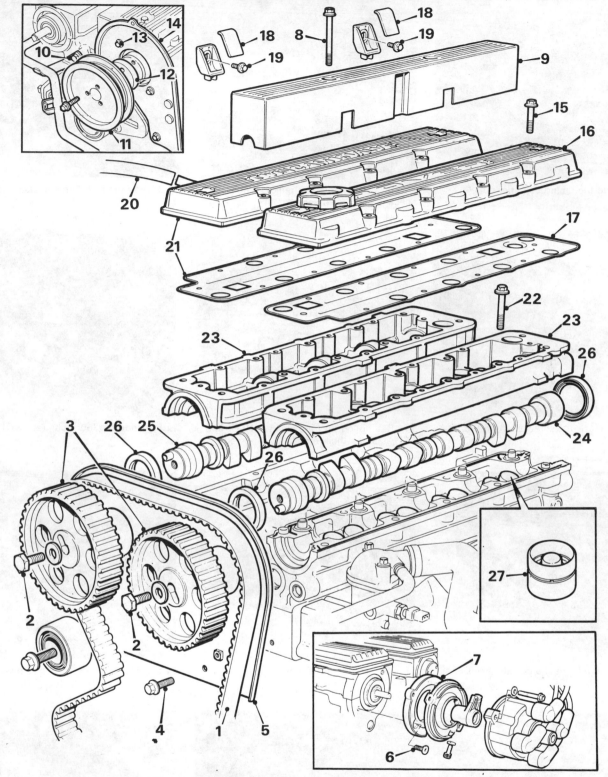

Fig. 1.6 Exploded view of the camshaft and tappet components (Sec 11)

1 Timing belt	8 Spark plug cover retaining bolt	15 Camshaft cover retaining bolt	20 Breather hose
2 Camshaft sprocket retaining bolts	9 Spark plug cover	16 Exhaust camshaft cover	21 Inlet camshaft cover and baffle plate
3 Camshaft sprockets	10 Heater bypass pipe bracket	17 Baffle plate	22 Camshaft housing retaining bolt
4 Backplate retaining bolt	11 Power steering pump pulley	18 Plastic covers (multi-point fuel injection models)	23 Camshaft housings
5 Backplate	12 Pulley spacer	19 Plenum chamber support bracket bolts (multi-point fuel injection models)	24 Exhaust camshaft
6 Distributor adaptor plate retaining screw	13 Pulley backplate retaining bolt		25 Inlet camshaft
7 Distributor adaptor plate	14 Pulley backplate		26 Oil seals
			27 Hydraulic tappets

11.2A Undo the timing belt idler pulley bolt ...

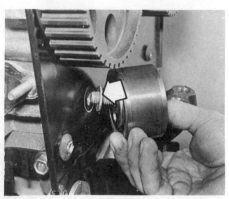
11.2B ... and remove the pulley, noting the spacer behind (arrowed)

11.3 Undo the camshaft sprocket retaining bolts

11.4A Withdraw the sprockets from the camshafts ...

11.4B ... noting they are marked INLET and EXHAUST on their front faces (arrowed)

11.5A Undo the four bolts (arrowed) ...

11.5B ... and remove the cylinder head backplate

11.7 Remove the rotor arm

11.8A Undo the two screws (arrowed) ...

11.8B ... and remove the distributor adaptor plate

11.9A Withdraw the spacer behind the power steering pulley ...

11.9B ... undo the two backplate nuts ...

11.9C ... and the two bolts, then remove the backplate

11.10 Undo the bolts (arrowed) and remove the blanking plate

11.14A Undo the camshaft cover retaining bolts ...

11.14B ... and remove the covers

11.15 Remove the baffle plates over the camshafts

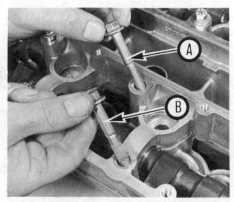

11.16 Camshaft housing plain bolts (A) and patch bolts (B)

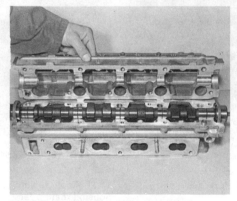

11.17 Removing the exhaust camshaft housing

11.20 Lift out the tappets and keep them in order

retaining bolts, and a tube of Loctite sealant 574.

22 Remove all traces of old sealant from the camshaft housing retaining bolt holes in the cylinder head, preferably using an M8 x 1.25 mm tap, but alternatively, using one of the old bolts with two file grooves cut into its threads. Also ensure that there is no oil remaining at the bottom of the bolt holes.

23 Thoroughly lubricate the tappet bores in the cylinder head, and refit the tappets in their original positions.

24 Lubricate the camshaft journals and lobes, then place the camshafts in position (photo). Set the camshafts so that when viewed head-on, the locating roll pin for the exhaust camshaft sprocket is in the 8 o'clock position, and the pin for the inlet camshaft sprocket is in the 2 o'clock position.

25 Lubricate the sealing lips of the new oil seals, carefully ease them over the camshaft journals, and position them against the shoulder in the cylinder head (photo),

26 Apply a thin bead of Loctite sealant 574 to the camshaft housing-to-cylinder head mating face (photo), then place both housings in position on the cylinder head.

27 Refit the housing retaining bolts, noting the location of the two different bolt types with reference to Fig. 1.7. Tighten the bolts progressively, and in a diagonal sequence, to the specified torque (photo).

28 Place the baffle plates in position over each housing.

29 Refit the camshaft covers, and tighten the bolts in a diagonal sequence to the specified torque. Refit the breather hose.

30 Refit the spark plug cover.

31 Where applicable, refit the two bolts securing the plenum chamber brackets to the plenum chamber, followed by the plastic covers.

32 On cars fitted with a rear-mounted power steering pump, refit the power steering pulley backplate, followed by the pulley spacer, then refit the pump drivebelt as described in Chapter 10.

33 On cars fitted with a front-mounted power steering pump, refit the blanking plate to the cylinder head.

34 Refit the distributor adaptor plate, followed by the rotor arm and distributor cap.

35 Refit the cylinder head backplate, then place the two sprockets in position on their respective camshafts. Fit the sprocket retaining bolts, then tighten the bolts to the specified torque while holding the sprockets to prevent them turning (photo).

36 Turn the sprockets as necessary to align the timing marks (photo).

37 Refit the timing belt idler pulley, noting that the hole in the pulley

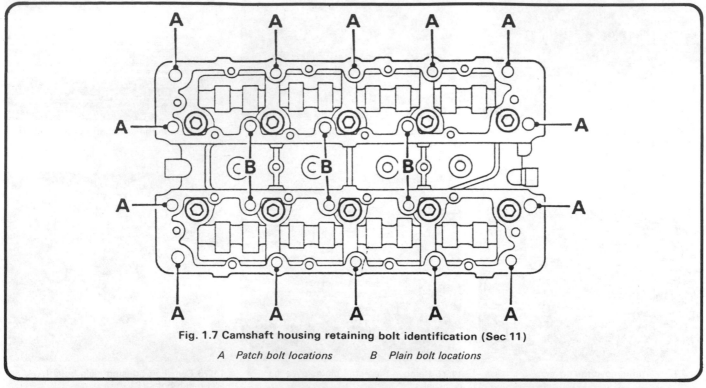

Fig. 1.7 Camshaft housing retaining bolt identification (Sec 11)

A   Patch bolt locations   B   Plain bolt locations

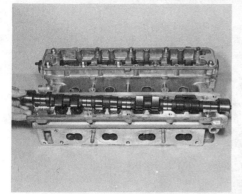
11.24 Placing the camshafts in position

11.25 Fitting the camshaft oil seals

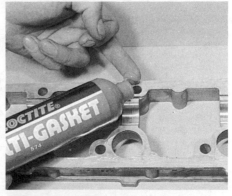
11.26 Apply sealant to the camshaft housing mating face

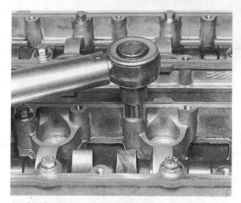
11.27 Tighten the housing retaining bolts to the specified torque

11.35 Home-made tool to prevent camshaft rotation

11.36 Align the sprocket timing marks (arrowed)

body engages over the peg in the backplate (photo).

38 Refer to Section 10 and refit the timing belt.

39 When the engine is started on completion of the work, be prepared for a considerable rattle from the tappets until they completely fill with oil. This may take a few minutes, and will be more pronounced if any of the tappets have been renewed.

12 Cylinder head (single-point fuel injection models) – removal and refitting

1 Drain the cooling system as described in Chapter 2.

2 Remove the air cleaner, air box and intake trunking as described in Chapter 3.

3 Remove the timing belt as described in Section 10 of this Chapter.

4 Undo the four nuts and separate the exhaust front pipe from the manifold flange. Recover the gasket.

5 Slacken the clips and disconnect the radiator top hose, and the expansion tank hose at the thermostat housing.

6 Disconnect the wiring multi-plug at the coolant temperature thermistor (photo).

7 Undo the brake servo vacuum hose banjo union bolt on the right-hand side of the inlet manifold, and recover the two copper washers.

8 Slacken the clip and disconnect the heater hose at the inlet manifold, behind the brake servo vacuum hose.

9 Undo the bolt securing the stay bar to the inlet manifold, below the heater hose.

10 Slacken the clips and disconnect the heater bypass hose at the thermostat housing (photo).

11 Slacken the clip and disconnect the heater hose at the other end of the bypass pipe.

12 Undo the bolts securing the bypass pipe to the exhaust manifold, cylinder head and main coolant pipe, release the clips securing the wiring harness (photo), and remove the bypass pipe from the engine.

13 Slacken the clip and disconnect the coolant hose at the left-hand end of the inlet manifold.

14 Disconnect the vacuum hoses from the inlet manifold, adjacent to the coolant hose. Mark the location of each vacuum hose as it is disconnected.

15 Undo the bolt securing the support bracket to the inlet manifold, below the vacuum hoses.

16 At the rear of the engine below the inlet manifold, release the wire clip and detach the breather hose from the top of the oil separator. Also detach the hose from the crankcase ventilation system diverter valve (photo).

17 Disconnect the two wires to the inlet manifold heater temperature sensor, on the underside of the manifold, and the single lead to the manifold heater at the wiring connector.

18 Slacken the accelerator cable locknuts, and unscrew the lower locknut off the outer cable end (photo). Open the throttle at the throttle cam, slip the cable end out of the cam slot, and remove the cable from the support bracket. Release the cable from the camshaft cover support bracket, and place it clear of the engine.

19 On automatic transmission models, disconnect the kickdown cable, using the same procedure as for the accelerator cable.

20 Disconnect the wiring multi-plugs at the idle speed stepper motor, the fuel injector, and the throttle potentiometer (photo). Move the wiring harness clear of the cylinder head.

21 Place absorbent rags around the fuel filter outlet union banjo bolt on the left-hand side of the filter, then slowly unscrew the bolt to release the fuel system pressure. Remove the bolt and recover the two copper washers after the pressure has been released. Tape over the filter orifice and banjo union to prevent fuel loss and dirt ingress.

22 Disconnect the fuel return hose at the pipe below the fuel filter.

23 Remove the dipstick from the dipstick tube.

24 Refer to Section 10, and carry out the operations described in paragraphs 6 to 15 inclusive, with the exception of paragraph 12.

25 On cars fitted with a rear-mounted power steering pump, extract the circlip from the end of the power steering pump drivebelt tension adjuster bolt (photo). Slide the adjuster rearwards, and undo all the accessible bolts securing the adjuster bracket to the cylinder head (photo). Now move the adjuster the other way, and undo the remaining bolts (photo), then remove the adjuster assembly complete.

26 Progressively slacken all the cylinder head retaining bolts, in the reverse sequence to that shown in Fig. 1.8. Remove the bolts when all

11.37 Timing belt idler pulley locating peg (arrowed)

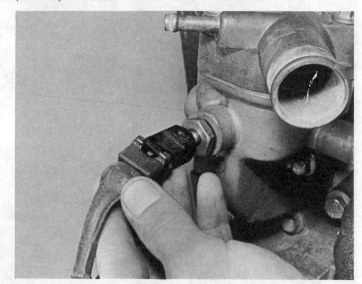

12.6 Disconnect the coolant temperature thermistor multi-plug

12.10 Disconnect the heater bypass hose at the thermostat housing

have been slackened.

27 With the help of an assistant, lift the cylinder head, complete with manifolds, off the engine. If the head is stuck, it can be carefully levered up using a large screwdriver between the cylinder block and the protruding cylinder head flanges. Do not insert the screwdriver under the head-to-block mating face. Place the head on blocks on the bench to protect the valves.

28 Remove the cylinder head gasket from the block.

29 If further dismantling is to be undertaken, refer to Section 14. Inspect the cylinder head and its related components, with reference to Section 23.

30 Prior to refitting, ensure that the cylinder block and head mating faces are thoroughly clean and dry, with all traces of old gasket removed. Clean the threads of the retaining bolts, and remove any oil, water and thread sealer from the bolt holes.

31 Locate a new gasket over the dowels on the cylinder block (photo). *Do not use any jointing compound on the cylinder head gasket.*

32 Check that the crankshaft is still positioned at 90° BTDC position, and that the timing marks on the camshaft sprockets are aligned (see Section 10).

33 Lower the cylinder head assembly onto the gasket, and refit the retaining bolts. Working in the sequence shown in Fig. 1.8, initially tighten the bolts to the Stage 1 torque setting given in the Specifications (photo), then to the Stage 2 setting. Finally tighten through a further 60° (one sixth of a turn), or to the Stage 3 setting – whichever comes first. If possible, use an angular torque gauge (photo) to determine accurately the 60° movement. These are readily available from motor factors at modest cost, or it may be possible to hire one from larger DIY outlets. Using the gauge in conjunction with a torque wrench, the bolt is tightened until either the pointer moves through 60°, or the torque wrench reaches the Stage 3 setting (photo).

12.12 Release the wiring harness clips from the bypass pipe

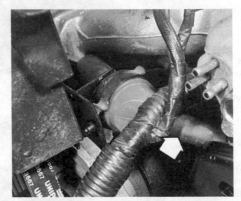

12.16 Detach the hose from the diverter valve (arrowed)

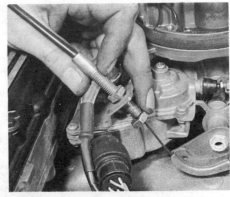

12.18 Disconnect the accelerator cable

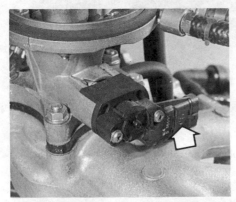

12.20 Disconnect the throttle potentiometer wiring multi-plug (arrowed)

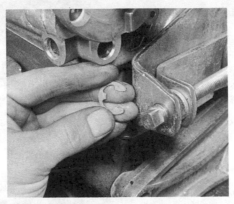

12.25A Extract the circlip from the adjuster bolt ...

12.25B ... move the adjuster one way and undo the accessible bolts ...

12.25C .. then move the adjuster the other way, and remove the remaining bolts

12.31 Locate a new cylinder head gasket over the dowels

12.33A Tighten the cylinder head bolts to the specified torque ...

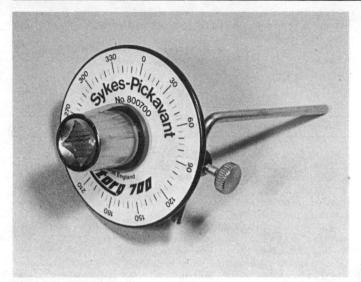

12.33B ... then using an angular torque gauge ...

12.33C ... tighten the bolts to the specified angular torque setting

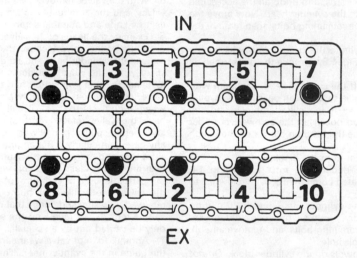

Fig. 1.8 Cylinder head bolt tightening sequence (Secs 12 and 13)

If an angular torque gauge is not available, an alternative is to draw two lines at 60° to each other on a piece of card, with a hole large enough to fit over the bolt head at the intersection of the two lines. Place the card over the bolt head, followed by the socket bit of the torque wrench, then align the torque wrench handle with the first line. Hold the card to prevent it moving, and torque the bolt until either the torque wrench handle is aligned with the other line on the card, or the Stage 3 setting is reached. Repeat this procedure for the other bolts in sequence.

34 Refit all the wiring, pipes, hoses and components to the cylinder head, using the reverse sequence to removal.

35 Refit the timing belt and adjust its tension, as described in Section 10.

36 Refit the power steering pump drivebelt and adjust its tension, as described in Chapter 10.

37 Refit the accelerator cable as described in Chapter 3, and the automatic transmission kickdown cable (where applicable) as described in Chapter 7.

38 Refit the air cleaner components as described in Chapter 3, and refill the cooling system as described in Chapter 2.

13 Cylinder head (multi-point fuel injection models) – removal and refitting

1   Drain the cooling system as described in Chapter 2.

2   Remove complete air cleaner assembly as described in Chapter 3.

3   Remove the timing belt as described in Section 10 of this Chapter.

4   Undo the four nuts and separate the exhaust front pipe from the manifold flange. Recover the gasket.

5   Slacken the clips and disconnect the radiator top hose, and the expansion tank hose at the thermostat housing.

6   Disconnect the wiring multi-plug at the coolant temperature thermistor on the side of the thermostat housing.

7   Undo the brake servo vacuum hose banjo union bolt on the right-hand side of the inlet manifold, and recover the two copper washers.

8   Slacken the clips and disconnect the heater bypass hose at the thermostat housing.

9   Slacken the clip and disconnect the heater hose at the other end of the bypass pipe.

10   Undo the bolts securing the bypass pipe to the exhaust manifold, cylinder head and main coolant pipe, and remove the bypass pipe from the engine.

11   Slacken the clips and disconnect the two coolant hoses from the underside of the throttle housing.

12   At the rear of the engine, disconnect the wiring multi-plugs and leads at the crankshaft sensor, knock sensor, oil pressure switch and oil pressure transducer.

13   Disconnect the main engine wiring loom multi-plug(s) on the right-hand side valance as necessary, to enable part of the loom to be removed with the cylinder head – see photo 6.18C.

14 Check that all the wiring likely to impede removal of the cylinder head and its ancillaries has been disconnected, and the harness moved clear. It may be necessary to disconnect additional wiring, depending on options or additional equipment fitted.

15 Disconnect the breather hoses from the oil separator.

16 Open the throttle fully by hand, and slip the accelerator inner cable end out of the slot on the throttle lever.

17 Slacken the outer cable locknuts, and unscrew the outer locknut, nearest to the cable end, fully. Remove the washer and rubber bush, then withdraw the cable from the support bracket.

18 On automatic transmission models, disconnect the kickdown cable, using the same procedure as for the accelerator cable.

19 Place absorbent rags around the fuel filter outlet union banjo bolt on the left-hand side of the filter, then slowly unscrew the bleed screw in the centre of the bolt to release the fuel system pressure. Tighten the bleed screw when the pressure has been released. Undo the outlet union banjo bolt, and recover the two copper washers. Tape over the filter orifice, and banjo union to prevent fuel loss and dirt entry.

20 Unscrew the union nut and disconnect the fuel return hose at the fuel pressure regulator, on the left-hand side of the inlet manifold.

21 Remove the dipstick from the dipstick tube.

22 Refer to Section 10, and carry out the operations described in paragraphs 6 to 15 inclusive.

23 On cars fitted with a rear-mounted power steering pump, extract the circlip from the end of the power steering pump drivebelt tension adjuster bolt. Slide the adjuster rearwards, and undo all the accessible bolts securing the adjuster bracket to the cylinder head. Now move the adjuster the other way, and undo the remaining bolts, then remove the adjuster assembly complete.

24 Progressively slacken all the cylinder head retaining bolts, in the reverse sequence to that shown in Fig. 1.8. Remove the bolts when all have been slackened.

25 With the help of an assistant, lift the cylinder head, complete with manifolds, off the engine. If the head is stuck, it can be carefully levered up using a large screwdriver between the cylinder block and the protruding cylinder head flanges. Do not insert the screwdriver under the head-to-block mating face. Place the head on blocks on the bench to protect the valves.

26 Remove the cylinder head gasket from the block.

27 If further dismantling is to be undertaken, refer to Section 14. Inspect the cylinder head and its related components, with reference to Section 23.

28 Prior to refitting, ensure that the cylinder block and head mating faces are thoroughly clean and dry, with all traces of old gasket removed. Clean the threads of the retaining bolts, and remove any oil, water and thread sealer from the bolt holes.

29 Locate a new gasket over the dowels on the cylinder block. *Do not use any jointing compound on the cylinder head gasket.*

30 Check that the crankshaft is still positioned at the 90° BTDC position, and that the timing marks on the camshaft sprockets are aligned (see Section 10).

31 Lower the cylinder head assembly onto the gasket, and refit the retaining bolts. Working in the sequence shown in Fig. 1.8, initially tighten the bolts to the Stage 1 torque setting given in the Specifications, then to the Stage 2 setting. Finally tighten through a further 60° (one sixth of a turn), or to the Stage 3 setting – whichever comes first. If possible, use an angular torque gauge (see photo 12.33B) to determine accurately the 60° movement. These are readily available from motor factors at modest cost, or it may be possible to hire one from larger DIY outlets. Using the gauge in conjunction with a torque wrench, the bolt is tightened until either the pointer moves through 60°, or the torque wrench reaches the Stage 3 setting. If an angular torque gauge is not available, an alternative is to draw two lines at 60° to each other on a piece of card, with a hole large enough to fit over the bolt head at the intersection of the two lines, Place the card over the bolt head, followed by the socket bit of the torque wrench, then align the torque wrench handle with the first line. Hold the card to prevent it moving, and torque the bolt until either the torque wrench handle is aligned with the other line on the card, or the Stage 3 setting is reached. Repeat this procedure for the other bolts in sequence.

32 Refit all the wiring, pipes, hoses and components to the cylinder head, using the reverse sequence to removal.

33 Refit the timing belt and adjust as described in Section 10.

34 Refit the power steering pump drivebelt and adjust its tension, as described in Chapter 10.

35 Refit the accelerator cable as described in Chapter 3, and the automatic transmission kickdown cable (where applicable) as described in Chapter 7.

36 Refit the air cleaner components as described in Chapter 3, and refill the cooling system as described in Chapter 2.

14 Cylinder head – overhaul

1 With the cylinder head on the bench, remove the camshafts and tappets (Section 11), thermostat housing (Chapter 2), inlet and exhaust manifolds (Chapter 3), and the spark plugs (Chapter 4).

2 To remove the valves, compress each spring in turn with a universal valve spring compressor, until the two retaining collets can be removed (photo).

3 Release the compressor, and lift off the spring top cup, valve spring, oil seal, valve spring seat and the valve (photos).

4 It is essential that the valves are kept in their correct order, unless they are so badly worn or burnt that they are to be renewed. If they are going to be refitted, place them in their correct sequence, along with the camshaft tappets removed previously. Also keep the valve springs, cups, seats and collets in the same order.

5 With the valves removed, scrape away all traces of carbon from the valves, and the combustion chambers and ports in the cylinder head, using a knife and suitable scraper, and with reference to Section 23.

6 Examine the heads of the valves for signs of cracking, burning away or pitting of the valve face, or the edge of the valve head. The valve seats in the cylinder head should also be examined for the same signs. Usually it is the valve that deteriorates first, but if a bad valve is not rectified, the seat will suffer, and this is more difficult to repair. If the valve face and seat are deeply pitted, or if the valve face is concave where it contacts the seat, it will be necessary to renew the valve, or have the valve refaced and the seat recut by a dealer or motor engineering specialist. It is worth considering having this work done in any case, particularly if the engine has covered a high mileage. A little extra time and money spent ensuring that the cylinder head and valve gear are in first-class condition will make a tremendous difference to the performance and economy of the engine after overhaul. If any of the valves are cracked or burnt away, it is essential that they are renewed. Any similar damage that may have occurred to the valve seats can be repaired by renewing the seat. However, this is a job that can only be carried out by a specialist.

7 Another form of valve wear can occur on the stem, where it runs in the guide in the cylinder head. This can be detected by trying to rock the valve from side to side. If there is anything but the slightest movement at all, it is an indication that the stem or guide is worn. Check the valve stem first, with a micrometer, at points along and around its length. If it is not within the specified size, a new valve will probably solve the problem. If the guide is worn, however, it will need renewing. This work should be carried out by a Rover dealer or motor engineering specialist.

8 Check the valve installed height by fitting each valve into its respective guide, and measuring the distance from the spring seat location in the cylinder head to the top of the valve stem. If the figure exceeds the installed height dimension given in the Specifications, the valve, or additionally the valve seat, must be renewed.

9 Assuming that the valve faces and seats are only lightly pitted, or that new valves are to be fitted, the valves should be lapped into their seats. This is done by placing a smear of fine carborundum on the valve seat, and using a suction-type valve holder, lapping the valve *in situ*. Using a semi-rotary action, rotate the handle of the valve holder between your hands, lifting it occasionally to redistribute the paste. As soon as a matt grey, unbroken line appears on both the valve face and cylinder head seat, the valve is 'ground in'.

10 When all work on the cylinder head and valves is complete, it is essential that all traces of carbon dust and grinding paste are removed. This should be done by thoroughly washing the components in paraffin or a suitable solvent, and blowing out with a jet of air.

11 With the valves and valve seats suitably prepared, and with the valves in their correct order, commence reassembly, starting with the first valve of No 1 cylinder as follows.

12 Place the valve spring seat in position, then fit a new oil seal over the valve guide, pushing it fully into position.

14.2 Compress the valve spring with a spring compressor, and remove the collets

14.3A Release the compressor, and remove the spring top cup ...

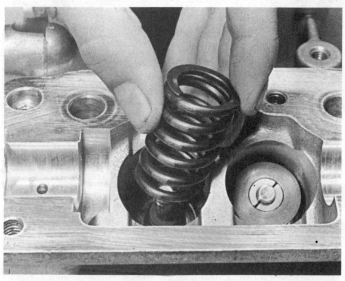

14.3B ... valve spring ...

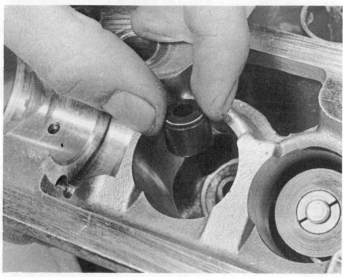

14.3C ... oil seal ...

14.3D .., spring seat ...

14.3E ... and the valve

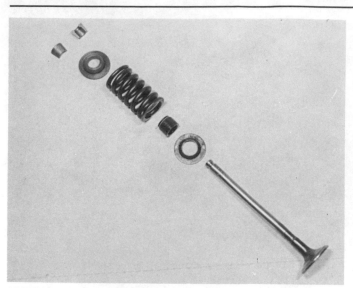

14.3F Valve components ready for inspection

15.7 Sump special retaining bolt location

13 Lubricate the valve stem with engine oil, then insert the valve into its guide.
14 Fit the valve spring, and place the top cup over the spring and valve.
15 Using the compressor tool, compress the valve spring until the two collets can be slid into position. Release the compressor carefully, in order not to displace the collets.
16 Refit the remaining valves in the same way. When they are all fitted, tap the end of each valve stem with a plastic mallet to settle the components.
17 Refit the components listed in paragraph 1, using the reverse sequence to removal, and with reference to the applicable Sections and Chapters of this manual.

15 Sump – removal and refitting

1 Disconnect the battery negative terminal. (Refer to Chapter 12, Section 1, before doing this).
2 Apply the handbrake, jack up the front of the car and support it on axle stands.
3 Drain the engine oil as described in Section 2.
4 Remove the exhaust front section as described in Chapter 3.
5 Undo the bolts securing the longitudinal support member to the underbody beneath the engine, and remove the member.
6 Disconnect the crankcase breather hose from the pipe stub on the side of the sump.
7 Slacken, then remove, the eighteen sump retaining bolts, noting that the corner bolt on the drain plug side at the flywheel end is longer than the rest, and has a flat washer and elongated washer in addition to the normal spring washer (photo).
8 Withdraw the sump from the crankcase, tapping it from side to side with a hide or plastic mallet if it is stuck. Recover the sump gasket.
9 If the oil pick-up tube and strainer are to be removed, undo the two bolts securing the tube flange to the crankcase, and the single bolt securing the support bracket to the main bearing cap (photos).
10 Slide the support bracket from under the crankcase breather oil return pipe, and remove the pick-up pipe and tube from the crankcase. Recover the O-ring from the pick-up pipe flange.
11 Clean the sump thoroughly, and remove all traces of old gasket and sealant from the mating faces of the sump and crankcase.
12 If removed, clean the pick-up pipe, and the filter gauze in the strainer.
13 Place a new O-ring seal on the pick-up pipe flange (photo), fit the pipe and strainer assembly, and secure with the retaining bolts, tightened to the specified torque.
14 Apply a bead of RTV sealant to the joint between Nos 1 and 5 main bearing caps and the edge of the crankcase (photo). Apply gasket sealant to the sump and crankcase mating faces, then place a new gasket in position (photos).

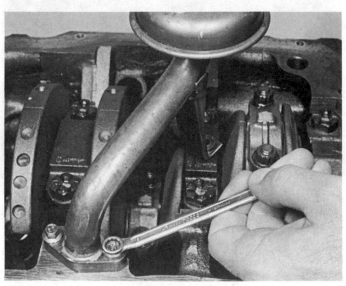

15.9A Undo the two pick-up pipe-to-crankcase bolts ...

15.9B ... and the support bracket bolt (arrowed)

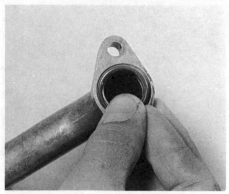

15.13 Fit a new O-ring to the pick-up pipe flange

15.14A Apply sealant to the main bearing cap joints ...

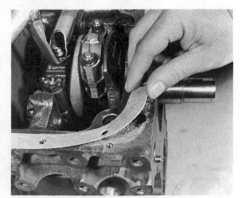

15.14B ... then place the sump gasket in position

15.15A Fit the sump ...

15.15B ... and tighten the bolts in sequence to the specified torque

15 Refit the sump, and tighten the retaining bolts progressively, and in the sequence shown in Fig. 1.9, to the specified torque (photos).
16 Refit the crankcase breather hose.
17 Refit the exhaust front section as described in Chapter 3.
18 Refit the longitudinal support member.
19 Lower the car to the ground, reconnect the battery and fill the engine with oil as described in Section 2.

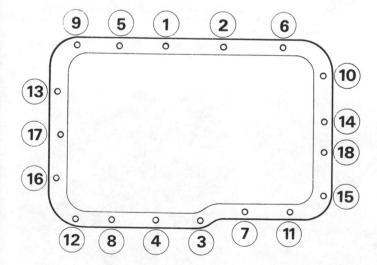

Fig. 1.9 Sump retaining bolt tightening sequence (Sec 15)

16 Oil pump and housing – removal and refitting

1 Using a socket and long handle, slacken the crankshaft pulley retaining bolt. To prevent the crankshaft turning, engage 1st gear and firmly apply the handbrake. On automatic transmission models, it will be necessary to remove the starter motor (Chapter 12) and lock the driveplate ring gear, through the starter motor aperture, using a large screwdriver or similar tool. If the engine is not in the car, engage a small strip of angle iron between the ring gear teeth and one of the adaptor plate dowels, to prevent rotation of the crankshaft.
2 Remove the timing belt as described in Section 10.
3 Drain the engine oil and remove oil filter as described in Section 2.
4 Unscrew the crankshaft pulley bolt and withdraw the pulley (photo). Carefully lever it off using two screwdrivers if it is tight.
5 Remove the Woodruff key from the slot in the crankshaft (photo).
6 Unscrew the oil pipe union on the side of the filter housing, then undo the bolt securing the oil pipe retaining clip and timing belt backplate to the crankcase (photo).
7 Undo the pump housing retaining bolts, and withdraw the assembly from the crankshaft and crankcase (photo). Recover the gasket.
8 Ensure that the pump housing and crankcase mating faces are thoroughly clean, with all traces of old gasket and sealer removed.
9 Apply a bead of RTV sealant to the vertical joint between the main bearing cap and the crankcase, and smear jointing compound to both faces of a new gasket. Place the gasket in position on the crankcase (photo).
10 Lubricate the lip of the oil seal, then locate the pump housing in place.
11 Fit the retaining bolts, and tighten them to the specified torque.
12 Refit the timing belt bottom cover.
13 Reconnect the oil pipe union, and refit the pipe support clip retaining bolt.

16.4 Removing the crankshaft pulley

16.5 Removing the Woodruff key

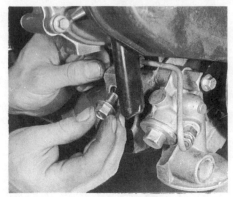

16.6 Undo the timing belt backplate and oil pipe clip retaining bolt

16.7 Undo the retaining bolts (arrowed) and remove the oil pump housing

16.9 Use a new gasket when refitting the housing

14 Place the Woodruff key in its crankshaft groove, then refit the crankshaft pulley, retaining bolt and washer.
15 Tighten the pulley retaining bolt to the specified torque.
16 Refit the timing belt as described in Section 10.
17 Fit a new oil filter, and fill the engine with oil as described in Section 2.

17 Oil pump and housing – dismantling and reassembly

1   With the pump housing removed from the engine, undo the four Torx retaining bolts on the housing rear face, and lift off the pump cover (photo). Inspect the condition of the inner and outer rotors for visual signs of scoring or wear ridges. Note that the pump internal parts

are not available separately, and if there is any sign of wear, a complete new oil pump and housing assembly must be obtained. Refit the pump cover.
2   To remove the pressure relief valve components, extract the split pin and withdraw the plug cap, spring and relief valve plunger (photo).
3   Check the plunger for scoring or wear ridges, and renew if necessary. Also renew the plug cap O-ring if it shows signs of deterioration.
4   Lubricate the relief valve components with engine oil, then refit the plunger, spring and plug cap. Secure the cap with a new split pin.
5   Using a screwdriver, prise out the crankshaft front oil seal from the oil pump housing (photo).
6   Place a new oil seal in position, and carefully tap it home with the aid of a mallet, block of wood and the old oil seal.

17.1 Oil pump cover retaining bolts (arrowed)

17.2 Oil pressure relief valve components

17.5 Using a screwdriver to remove the crankshaft front oil seal

18 Pistons and connecting rods – removal and refitting

1 Remove the cylinder head, the sump, and the oil pick-up pipe as described in earlier Sections of this Chapter.

2 Turn the crankshaft by means of the pulley bolt, until No 1 and No 4 pistons are at the bottom of their stroke.

3 Using a knife or scraper, clean the carbon ridge from the top of the cylinder bore, to facilitate removal of the piston.

4 Mark the No 1 cylinder connecting rod and cap on their sides, using a centre-punch and hammer, to indicate the cylinder the assembly is fitted to, and also the fitted relationship of the cap to the rod.

5 Undo the big-end cap nuts on No 1 connecting rod, then remove the cap, complete with the lower bearing shell (photo). If the cap is difficult to remove, tap it from side to side with a plastic mallet.

6 Push the piston/connecting rod upwards with the aid of the wooden handle of a hammer or similar tool, then withdraw the assembly from the top of the cylinder bore (photo).

7 Refit the bearing cap and shell to the connecting rod after removal.

8 Repeat paragraphs 3 to 7 for No 4 connecting rod.

9 Turn the crankshaft back through half a turn, until No 2 and No 3 pistons are at the bottom of their stroke.

10 Repeat paragraphs 3 to 6 for No 2 and No 3 connecting rods.

11 To remove the pistons from the connecting rods, extract the two gudgeon pin retaining circlips, using a small screwdriver (photo), then push out the gudgeon pin. If the pin is tight, warm the piston in hot water, which will expand the piston slightly, enabling the gudgeon pin to be pushed out. As each piston is removed, mark it on the inside with a punch, as before, indicating its cylinder number.

12 To remove the piston rings, slide them carefully over the top of the piston, taking care not to scratch the aluminium alloy of the piston. It is very easy to break piston rings if they are pulled off roughly, so this operation should be done with extreme caution. It is helpful to use an old feeler blade to facilitate their removal, as follows.

13 Turn the feeler blade slowly around the piston; as the ring comes out of its groove it rests on the land above. It can then be eased off the piston, with the feeler blade stopping it from slipping into empty grooves. If the old rings are to be re-used, identify each as it is removed using a label, marked No 1 top, No 1 second, etc.

14 Clean and examine the dismantled components, with reference to Section 23.

15 Check that the piston ring grooves and oilways are thoroughly clean and unblocked. Piston rings must always be fitted over the head of the piston, and never from the bottom.

16 The easiest method to use when fitting rings is to position two feeler blades on either side of the piston, and slide the rings down over the blades. This will stop the rings from dropping into a vacant ring groove. When the ring is adjacent to its correct groove, slide out the feeler blades, and the ring will drop in.

17 The procedure for fitting the rings is as follows. Start by sliding the bottom rail of the oil control ring down the piston, and position it below the bottom ring groove. Fit the oil control expander into the bottom ring groove, then slip the bottom rail into the bottom groove. Now fit the top rail of the oil control ring into the bottom groove. Make sure that the ends of the expander are butting together, and not overlapping. Position the gaps of the two rails and the expander at 90°

to each other.

·18 Fit the second compression ring to its groove, with the step towards the gudgeon pin, and the word TOP or the letter T facing the top of the piston.

19 Fit the top compression ring to its groove, with the word TOP or the letter T facing the top of the piston.

20 When all the piston rings are in place, set the ring gaps of the compression rings at 90° to each other, and away from the thrust side of the piston.

21 To refit the pistons to their connecting rods, start with No 1 and insert the connecting rod into the piston, so that the offset at the gudgeon pin end of the rod is towards the side of the piston marked FRONT on its top face (Fig. 1.10 and photo). Insert the gudgeon pin, and refit the retaining circlips. Ensure that the circlips fully enter their grooves.

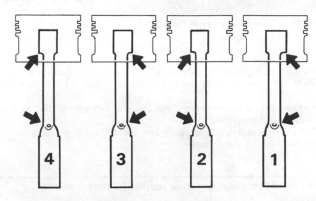

Fig. 1.10 Connecting rod offset and oil squirt hole relationship (Sec 18)

22 Assemble the No 3 piston and connecting rod in the same way.

23 Assemble the No 2 and No 4 pistons and connecting rods in the same way, but with the offset at the gudgeon pin end of the rod away from the side of the piston marked FRONT.

24 Wipe the cylinder bores clean with a cloth, then lubricate the bores and pistons with clean engine oil.

25 Starting with No 1 piston/connecting rod assembly, fit a universal piston ring compressor over the piston, and tighten it fully to compress the rings. Remove the bearing cap and shell from the connecting rod.

26 Insert the piston into its bore, making sure the word FRONT on the piston crown is towards the crankshaft pulley end of the engine.

27 Slide the assembly down the bore until the bottom of the piston ring compressor rests on the cylinder block face. Now gently, but firmly, tap the piston through the compressor, using the wooden handle of a hammer (photo).

28 As soon as the rings have entered the bore, remove the compressor, and continue pushing the piston down until the connecting rod approaches its crankshaft journal.

29 Wipe the connecting rod, crankshaft journal and bearing shell, then fit the shell to the rod, with its tag engaged with the notch in the rod.

30 Lubricate the crankshaft journal with engine oil, then draw the rod down onto the journal.

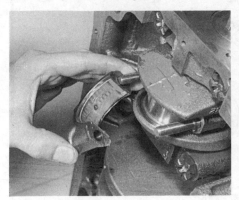

18.5 Removing the connecting rod big-end cap and bearing shell

18.6 Removing the piston and connecting rod assembly

18.11 Using a small screwdriver to extract the gudgeon pin circlip

18.21 The pistons are marked FRONT on their top face (arrowed)

18.27 Refitting the piston and connecting rod assemblies, with the aid of a ring compressor

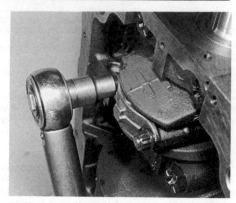

18.32 Tighten the bearing cap nuts to the specified torque

31 Fit the bearing shell to the big-end cap, then refit the cap to the rod.

32 Refit the cap retaining nuts, and tighten them to the specified torque (photo).

33 Repeat the refitting procedure for the remaining piston and connecting rod assemblies.

34 Refit the oil pick-up pipe, sump and cylinder head, as described in earlier Sections of this Chapter.

19 Flywheel (manual gearbox models) – removal and refitting

1 With the engine removed from the car and separated from the gearbox, or with the gearbox removed as described in Chapter 6,

remove the clutch assembly as described in Chapter 5.

2 Knock back the tabs of the locking plate, using a screwdriver or small chisel, and undo the six flywheel retaining bolts. To prevent the flywheel turning, lock the ring gear teeth using a small strip of angle iron engaged in the teeth and against the adaptor plate dowel. Note that the flywheel retaining bolts are of the encapsulated type, incorporating a locking compound in their threads, and new bolts must be obtained for reassembly.

3 Lift off the locking plate, then withdraw the flywheel from the crankshaft (photos).

4 Examine the flywheel and the ring gear teeth with reference to Section 23, and renew any components as required.

5 Refitting is the reverse sequence to removal. Tighten the bolts to the specified torque, then bend over the tabs of a new locking plate (photos).

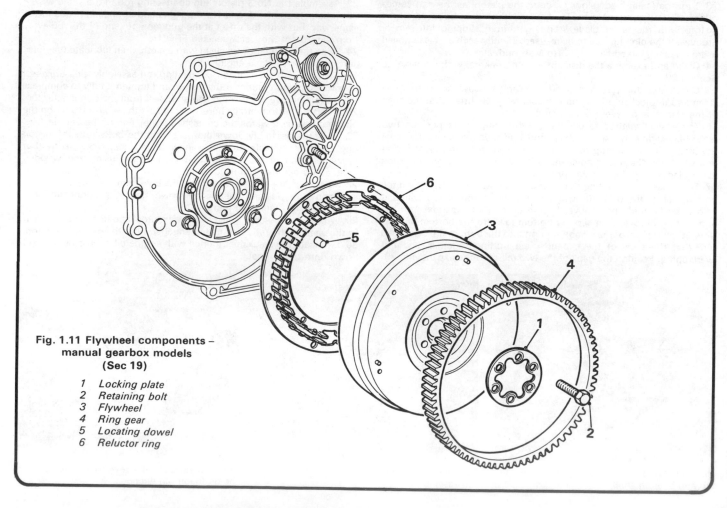

Fig. 1.11 Flywheel components – manual gearbox models (Sec 19)

1 Locking plate
2 Retaining bolt
3 Flywheel
4 Ring gear
5 Locating dowel
6 Reluctor ring

19.3A Lift off the locking plate ...

19.3B ... then withdraw the flywheel

19.5A Tighten the flywheel bolts to the specified torque ...

19.5B ... then bend over the locking plate tabs

20 Torque converter driveplate (automatic transmission models) – removal and refitting

1   With the engine removed from the car and separated from the transmission, or with the transmission removed as described in Chapter 7, undo the six bolts securing the driveplate to the crankshaft. To prevent the driveplate turning, lock the ring gear teeth using a small strip of angle iron engaged in the teeth and against the adaptor plate dowel. Note that the driveplate retaining bolts are of the encapsulated type, incorporating a locking compound in their threads, and new bolts must be obtained for reassembly.
2   Remove the reinforcing plate, then withdraw the driveplate from the crankshaft. Recover the spacer between the driveplate and crankshaft.
3   Examine the driveplate and the ring gear teeth with reference to Section 23, and renew any components as required.
4   Refitting is the reverse sequence to removal, but tighten the bolts to the specified torque.

21 Gearbox/transmission adaptor plate – removal and refitting

1   Remove the flywheel or torque converter driveplate as described in Sections 19 and 20 respectively.
2   On cars equipped with a rear-mounted power steering pump, refer to Chapter 10 and remove the power steering pump.
3   Undo the two bolts securing the crankshaft sensor to the adaptor plate, remove the sensor, and recover the spacer (photo).
4   Undo the bolts securing the adaptor plate to the cylinder block, noting the various bolt lengths and their locations. Note also that the four Torx type bolts are of the encapsulated type, incorporating a sealer in their threads, and new bolts must be obtained for reassembly (photo).
5   Remove the adaptor plate from the cylinder block, and recover the gasket.
6   The crankshaft rear oil seal should be renewed as a matter of course. Tap out the old seal, and fit a new one with its open side

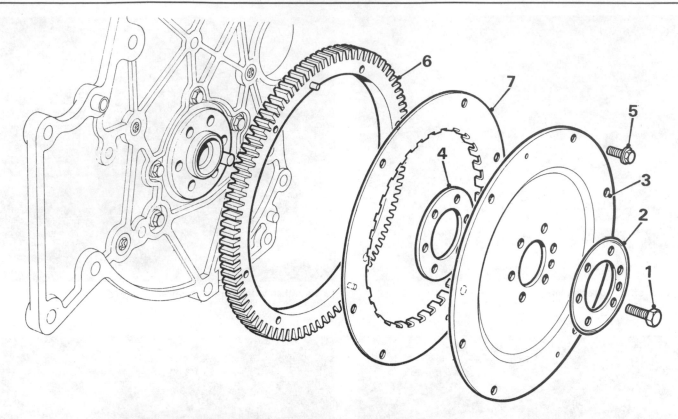

Fig. 1.12 Torque converter driveplate components – automatic transmission models (Sec 20)

1 Driveplate retaining bolt	3 Driveplate	5 Ring gear retaining bolt	7 Reluctor ring
2 Reinforcing plate	4 Spacer	6 Ring gear	

towards the engine. Tap the seal into place using a block of wood or the old seal.

7 Ensure that all traces of old gasket are removed from the adaptor plate and block mating faces.

8 Apply a bead of RTV jointing compound to the vertical joint of the rear main bearing cap, and lubricate the oil seal in the adaptor plate with engine oil.

9 Place a new gasket in position (photo), then fit the adaptor plate, taking care as the oil seal locates over the crankshaft.

10 Fit the retaining bolts, and tighten them progressively to the specified torque.

11 Refit the crankshaft sensor and spacer.

12 Refit the power steering pump as described in Chapter 10.

13 Refit the flywheel or torque converter driveplate.

22 Crankshaft and main bearings – removal and refitting

1 With the engine removed from the car, as described in Section 6, and with all the components removed from it, as described in earlier Sections, the crankshaft and main bearings can be removed as follows.

2 Withdraw the crankcase breather tube elbow from the outside of the cylinder block (photo).

3 From within the crankcase, remove the crankcase breather extension tube (photo). To do this, move the tube from side to side to release the sealing compound, then tap it out using a dowel rod inserted through the elbow aperture.

4 Note that the main bearing caps have their numbers cast on the face of each cap, and in addition, Nos 2, 3 and 4 have arrows

21.3 Crankshaft sensor location on gearbox adaptor plate

21.4 Adaptor plate Torx type retaining bolt locations (arrowed)

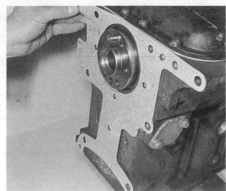

21.9 Place a new gasket in position, then refit the adaptor plate

indicating their fitted direction (photo).

5 Undo the main bearing cap retaining bolts, one turn at a time, then when all are slack, remove the bolts.

6 Lift away each main bearing cap and the bottom half of each bearing shell, taking care to keep the bearing shell with the right cap. If the caps are tight, tap them on their sides with a plastic mallet to release them from the locating dowels.

7 When removing the centre main bearing cap, note the bottom semi-circular halves of the thrustwashers, one located on each side of the cap. Lay them, with the centre bearing cap, along the correct side.

8 Lift out the crankshaft, followed by the bearing shell upper halves and the thrustwashers. Keep the bearing shells and thrustwashers with their correct caps.

9 Carry out a careful inspection of the crankshaft and main bearings, with reference to Section 23.

10 Prior to refitting, ensure that the crankshaft and crankcase are thoroughly clean, and that all oilways are clear. If possible, blow the drillings out with compressed air, then inject clean engine oil through them to ensure they are clear.

11 If new bearing shells are being fitted, carefully clean away all traces of the protective grease with which they are coated.

12 Fit the five upper halves of the main bearing shells to their location in the crankcase, after wiping the location clean (photo). Note that on the back of each bearing is a tab, which engages in locating grooves in either the crankcase or main bearing cap.

13 Wipe the bearing shell locations in the bearing caps, and fit the five lower bearing shells to their caps.

14 Wipe the recesses either side of the centre main bearing which locate the upper halves of the thrustwashers.

15 Place the upper halves of the thrustwashers (the halves without tabs) in position on either side of the centre main bearing, with their oil grooves facing outwards (photo). Use a little grease to retain them in place.

16 Generously lubricate the upper halves of the bearing shells, and carefully lower the crankshaft into position (photo).

17 Using a screwdriver between the crankcase and one crankshaft web, lever the crankshaft forwards, and check the endfloat using feeler gauges (photo). This should be as given in the Specifications. If excessive, new thrustwashers must be fitted.

18 Lubricate the crankshaft journals (photo), and fit Nos 2, 3 and 4 main bearing caps into their respective locations.

19 When fitting the centre main bearing cap, ensure that the thrustwashers, generously lubricated, are fitted with their oil grooves facing outwards, and the locating tab of each is engaged with the slot in the main bearing cap.

20 Apply RTV sealant into the vertical grooves on the edges of Nos 1 and 5 main bearing caps, then fit these caps to their locations.

21 Fit the main bearing cap retaining bolts, and tighten them moderately tightly at this stage, starting with the centre cap bolts, then working outwards to the others in turn. As each cap is tightened, test the crankshaft for freedom of rotation. Should it be very stiff to turn, or possess high spots, a most careful inspection must be made, preferably by a skilled mechanic with a micrometer, to trace the cause. It is very seldom that any trouble of this nature occurs, unless the bearing caps or shells have been fitted to the wrong locations.

22 Tighten the main bearing cap bolts to the specified torque (photo), and recheck the crankshaft for freedom of rotation.

23 Apply sealer to the crankcase breather tube extension, then fit the tube to its location. Apply sealant to the breather tube elbow, and fit the elbow, ensuring that it is tapped down until the shoulder contacts the crankcase.

23 Engine components – examination and renovation

Crankshaft

Inspect the main bearing journals and crankpins. If there are any scratches or score marks, then the shaft will need regrinding. Such

22.2 Withdraw the crankcase breather tube elbow

22.3 Remove the crankcase breather extension tube

22.4 Main bearing cap identification number and direction arrow

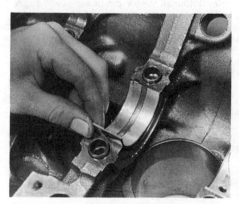
22.12 Fitting the main bearing shell upper halves

22.15 Fitting the crankshaft thrustwasher upper halves

22.16 Crankshaft installation

22.17 Checking crankshaft endfloat

22.18 Thoroughly lubricate the crankshaft journals

22.19 Fitting the crankshaft thrustwasher lower halves to the centre bearing cap

22.22 Tighten the bearing cap bolts to the specified torque

conditions will nearly always be accompanied by similar deterioration in the matching bearing shells.

Each bearing journal should also be round, and can be checked with a micrometer or caliper gauge around the periphery at several points. If there is more than 0.001 in (0.025 mm) of ovality, regrinding is necessary.

A Rover dealer or motor engineering specialist will be able to decide to what extent regrinding is necessary, and also supply the special undersize shell bearing to match whatever may need grinding off.

Before taking the crankshaft for grinding, also check the cylinder bores and pistons, as it may be advantageous to have the whole engine done at the same time.

Main and big-end bearings

With careful servicing and regular oil and filter changes, bearings will last for a very long time, but they can still fail for unforeseen reasons. With big-end bearings, the indication is a regular rhythmic loud knocking from the crankcase. The frequency depends on engine speed and is particularly noticeable when the engine is under load. This symptom is accompanied by a fall in oil pressure, although this is not normally noticeable unless an oil pressure gauge is fitted. Main bearing failure is usually indicated by serious vibration, particularly at

higher engine revolutions, accompanied by a more significant drop in oil pressure and a rumbling noise.

Bearing shells in good condition have bearing surfaces with a smooth, even matt silver/ grey colour all over. Worn bearings will show patches of a different colour, where the bearing metal has worn away and exposed the underlay. Damaged bearings will be pitted or scored. It is always well worthwhile fitting new shells, as their cost is relatively low. If the crankshaft is in good condition, it is merely a question of obtaining another set of standard size. A reground crankshaft will need new bearing shells as a matter of course.

Cylinder bores

A new cylinder is perfectly round, and the walls parallel throughout its length. The action of the piston tends to wear the walls at right-angles to the gudgeon pin, due to side thrust. This wear takes place principally on that section of the cylinder swept by the piston rings.

It is possible to get an indication of bore wear by removing the cylinder head with the engine still in the car. With the piston down in the bore, first signs of wear can be seen and felt just below the top of the bore where the top piston ring reaches, and there will be a noticeable lip. If there is no lip, it is fairly reasonable to assume that bore wear is not severe , and any lack of compression or excessive oil consumption is due to worn or broken piston rings or pistons.

If it is possible to obtain a bore-measuring micrometer, measure the bore in the thrust plane below the lip, and again at the bottom of the cylinder in the same plane. If the difference is more than 0.006 in (0.15 mm), a rebore is necessary. Similarly, a difference of 0.006 in (0.15 mm) or more between two measurements of the bore diameter taken at right-angles to each other is a sign of excessive ovality, calling for a rebore.

Any bore which is significantly scratched or scored will need reboring. This symptom usually indicates that the piston or rings are also damaged. Even in the event of only one cylinder in need of reboring, it will still be necessary for all four to be bored, and fitted with new oversize pistons and rings. A motor engineering specialist will be able to rebore the cylinders and supply the necessary matched pistons. If the crankshaft is also undergoing regrinding, it is a good idea to let the same firm renovate and reassemble the crankshaft and pistons to the block. A reputable firm normally gives a guarantee for such work.

Pistons and piston rings

If the old pistons are to be refitted, carefully remove the piston rings, and then thoroughly clean them. Take particular care to clean out the piston ring grooves. Do not scratch the aluminum in any way. If new rings are to be fitted to the old pistons, then the top ring should be of the stepped type, so as to clear the ridge left above the previous top ring. If a normal but oversize new ring is fitted, it will hit the ridge and break, because the new ring will not have worn in the same way as the old.

Before fitting the rings on the pistons, each should be inserted approximately 75 mm (3 in) down the cylinder bore, and the gap measured with a feeler gauge. This should be between the limits given in the Specifications at the beginning of this Chapter. It is essential that the gap is measured at the bottom of the ring travel, for if it is measured at the top of a worn bore and gives a perfect fit, it could easily seize at the bottom. If the ring gap is too small, rub down the ends of the ring with a very fine file until the gap is correct when fitted. To keep the rings square in the bore for measurement, line each one up in turn with an old piston inserted in the bore upside down, and use the piston to push the ring down about 75 mm (3 in). Remove the piston and measure the piston ring gap.

The groove clearance of the new rings in old pistons should be checked with the rings in place. If it is not enough, the rings could stick in the piston grooves, causing loss of compression. The ring grooves in the piston in this case will need machining out to accept the new rings.

Before fitting new rings onto an old piston, clean out the grooves with a piece of broken ring.

If new pistons are obtained, the rings will be included, so it must be emphasised that the top ring be stepped if fitted to a cylinder bore that has not been rebored, or has not had the top ridge removed.

Camshafts and tappets

Check the camshaft journals and lobes for scoring and wear. If there are very slight scoring marks, these can be removed with emery cloth or a fine oil stone. The greatest care must be taken to keep the cam profiles smooth.

Examine the camshaft bearing surfaces in the cylinder head and camshaft housings – if they are scored and worn it means a new cylinder head and camshaft housings will be required.

Check for scoring or pitting of the tappets, and check the fit of the tappets in their respective bores. Renew any that show signs of wear.

Timing belt and tensioner

Check the belt for any sign of cracks or splits in the belt, particularly around the roots of the teeth. Renew the belt if wear is obvious, if there are signs of oil contamination, or if the belt has exceeded its service life (see Routine maintenance). Also renew the sprockets if they show any signs of wear or chipping of the teeth.

Spin the tensioner, and ensure that there is no roughness or harshness in the bearing. Also check that the endfloat is not excessive. Renew the tensioner if worn.

Cylinder head and pistons – decarbonising

This can be carried out with the engine either in or out of the car. With the cylinder head removed, carefully use a wire brush and blunt scraper to clean all traces of carbon deposits from the combustion spaces and the ports. The valve head stems and valve guides should also be freed from any carbon deposits. Wash the combustion spaces and ports down with petrol, and scrape the cylinder head surface free of any foreign matter with the side of a steel rule or similar article.

If the engine is installed in the car, clean the pistons and the top of the cylinder bores. If the pistons are still in the block, then it is essential that great care is taken to ensure that no carbon gets into the cylinder bores, as this could scratch the cylinder walls or cause damage to the piston and rings. To ensure this does not happen, first turn the crankshaft so that two of the pistons are at the top of their bores. Stuff rag into the other two bores or seal them off with paper and masking tape. The waterways should also be covered with small pieces of masking tape, to prevent particles of carbon entering the cooling system and damaging the water pump.

Press a little grease into the gap between the cylinder walls and the two pistons which are to be worked on. With a blunt scraper carefully scrape away the carbon from the piston crown, taking great care not to scratch the aluminium. Also scrape away the carbon from the surrounding lip of the cylinder wall. When all carbon has been removed, scrape away the grease which will now be contaminated with carbon particles, taking care not to press any into the bores. To assist prevention of carbon build-up, the piston crown can be polished with a metal polish. Remove the rags or masking tape from the other two cylinders, and turn the crankshaft so that the two pistons which were at the bottom are now at the top. Place rag or masking tape in the cylinders which have now been decarbonised, and proceed as just described. Decarbonising is now complete.

Flywheel or torque converter driveplate

Inspect the starter ring gear on the flywheel or driveplate for wear or broken teeth. If evident, the ring gear should be renewed. On automatic transmission models, the ring gear is bolted to the driveplate, and renewal is straightforward. On manual gearbox models however, the ring gear is a shrink fit on the flywheel, and renewal entails drilling the old ring then splitting it with a chisel. The new ring must then be heated so that it expands slightly, and allowed to cool when in position on the flywheel. As it cools, it contracts to a smaller diameter than the flywheel so as to provide a tight interference fit. The temperatures involved in this operation are critical to avoid damaging the ring gear, and the work should be carried out by a Rover dealer or motor engineering works.

The clutch friction surface on the flywheel should be checked for grooving or cracks, the latter being caused by overheating. If these conditions are evident, renewal of the flywheel is necessary.

On manual and automatic models, check the condition of the reluctor ring teeth. If any are bent, broken. or in any way damaged, renew the ring, which is bolted to the flywheel or driveplate.

24 Lubrication system – description

The pressed-steel sump is attached to the underside of the crankcase, and acts as a reservoir for the engine oil. The oil pump draws oil through a strainer attached to the pick-up pipe and submerged in the oil. The pump passes the oil along a short passage and into the full-flow filter, which is screwed onto the pump housing. The freshly filtered oil flows from the filter and enters the main cylinder block oil gallery, which feeds the crankshaft main bearings. Oil passes from the main bearings, through drillings in the crankshaft to the big-end bearings.

As the crankshaft rotates, oil is squirted from the hole in each connecting rod, and splashes the thrust side of the pistons and cylinder bores.

A drilling from the main oil gallery feeds the cylinder head gallery, via a restrictor located just below the top face of the cylinder block. The cylinder head contains an oil gallery on each side, with drillings to lubricate each camshaft journal and hydraulic tappet bore. The oil then drains back into the sump via large drillings in the cylinder head and cylinder block.

A pressure relief valve is incorporated in the oil pump housing, to maintain the oil pressure within specified limits.

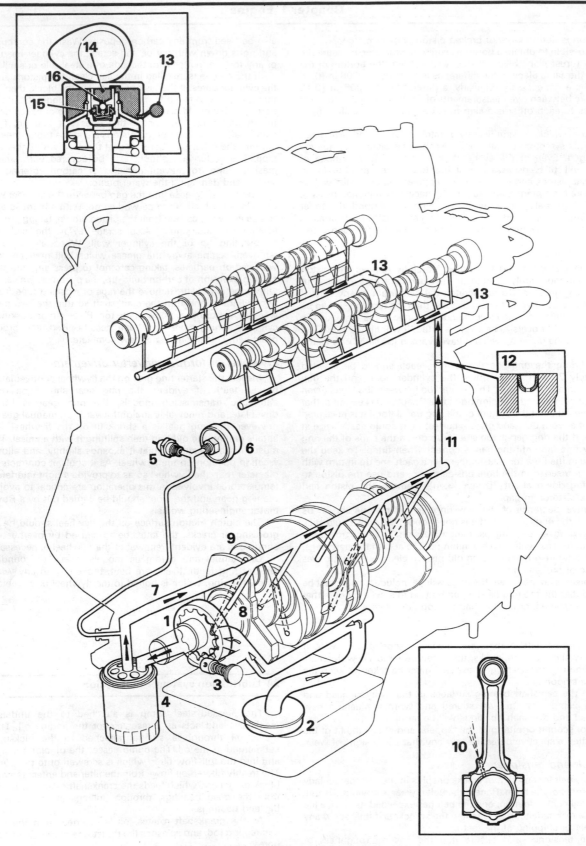

Fig. 1.13 Diagrammatic layout of the lubrication system (Sec 24)

1	Oil pump	6	Oil pressure transducer	10	Connecting rod oil squirt	14	Hydraulic tappet low
2	Pick-up pipe strainer	7	Main oil gallery		holes		pressure chamber
3	Pressure relief valve	8	Crankshaft main bearings	11	Feed to cylinder head	15	Tappet high pressure
4	Filter cartridge	9	Big-end bearing journals	12	Restrictor		chamber
5	Oil pressure switch			13	Cylinder head oil gallery	16	Ball valve

25 Engine mountings – removal and refitting

Front mounting

1 Remove the battery as described in Chapter 12, then undo the retaining bolts and remove the battery tray.

2 Remove the air intake trunking as described in Chapter 3.

3 Undo the nut securing the mounting to the engine mounting bracket, and the two bolts securing the mounting to the front chassis member.

4 Using a jack and interposed block of wood, raise the engine slightly until the mounting stud can be withdrawn from the bracket, then remove the mounting from the car.

5 Renew the mounting if it shows any sign of damage, contamination or separation of the rubber-to-metal bond.

6 Refitting is the reverse sequence to removal, but ensure that the small peg on the mounting top face engages with the hole in the bracket, and tighten the bolts and nut to the specified torque.

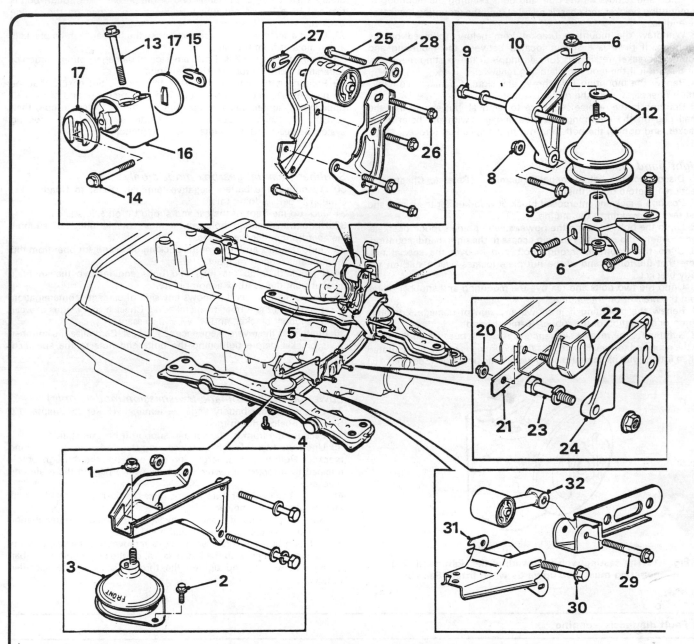

Fig. 1.14 Engine mounting components and attachments (Sec 25)

1 Front mounting-to-engine bracket retaining nut	6 Rear mounting-to-mounting bracket nuts
2 Front mounting-to-chassis member bolts	8 Engine bracket retaining nut
3 Front mounting	9 Engine bracket retaining bolt
4 Longitudinal support member retaining bolt	10 Engine bracket
5 Longitudinal support member	12 Rear mounting and spacer
	13 Right-hand mounting-to-engine bracket bolt
	14 Mounting through-bolt

15 Forked nut	26 Rear tie-bar-to-engine bracket through-bolt
16 Right-hand mounting	27 Forked nut
17 Snubber plates	28 Rear tie-bar
20 Snubber retaining nut	29 Lower tie-bar-to-engine bracket through-bolt
21 Backing plate	30 Lower tie-bar-to-chassis bracket through-bolt
22 Snubber	31 Forked nut
23 Snubber bracket bolt	32 Lower tie-bar
24 Snubber bracket	
25 Rear tie-bar-to-body bracket through-bolt	

Rear mounting

7 Disconnect the battery negative terminal. (Refer to Chapter 12, Section 1, before doing this).
8 Remove the air intake trunking as described in Chapter 3.
9 Jack up the front of the car and support it on axle stands.
10 Undo the bolts and remove the longitudinal support member from beneath the engine.
11 Support the engine and gearbox/transmission assembly on a jack with interposed block of wood.
12 Undo and remove all the nuts and bolts securing the mounting to its mounting bracket and chassis member, and the mounting bracket to the engine.
13 Withdraw the mounting bracket from below, followed by the mounting. If there is a spacer located between the mounting and mounting bracket, retain this for refitting with the existing mounting, but discard it if the mounting is being renewed.
14 Renew the mounting if it shows any sign of damage, contamination or separation of the rubber-to-metal bond.
15 Refitting is the reverse sequence to removal, but ensure that the small peg on the mounting top face engages with the hole in the bracket, and tighten the bolts and nut to the specified torque.

Right-hand mounting

16 Disconnect the battery negative terminal. (Refer to Chapter 12, Section 1, before doing this).
17 Position a jack and interposed block of wood under the sump, and just take the weight of the engine.
18 Undo the bolts securing the power steering pipe support brackets, and move the pipes slightly to gain access to the right-hand mounting.
19 Undo the mounting through-bolt, and recover the special nut. Note that the forked end of the nut plate locates over a stud on the body bracket.
20 Undo the two bolts and remove the mounting and snubber plates from the bracket on the engine.
21 Renew the mounting if it shows any sign of damage, contamination or separation of the rubber-to-metal bond.
22 Refitting is the reverse sequence to removal, but tighten the bolts to the specified torque. Ensure that the mounting is correctly orientated when fitting, with its central casting web facing upwards. (See Fig. 1.15.)

TB 0538

Fig. 1.15 The casting web (arrowed) of the right-hand engine mounting must face upwards when fitted (Sec 25)

Rear tie-bar

23 Disconnect the battery negative terminal. (Refer to Chapter 12, Section 1, before doing this).
24 On cars equipped with single-point fuel injection, remove the air cleaner assembly as described in Chapter 3.
25 Drain the cooling system as described in Chapter 2, then disconnect the heater hoses and coolant hoses in the vicinity of the tie-bar as necessary to provide access.
26 Undo the two through-bolts securing the tie-bar to its mounting brackets. Note that at the larger end of the tie-bar, the through-bolt is retained by a forked nut which engages over a peg on the engine bracket.
27 Using a screwdriver if necessary, prise the tie-bar from its brackets and remove it from the car.
28 Renew the tie-bar if it shows any sign of damage, contamination or separation from the rubber-to-metal bond.
29 Refitting is the reverse sequence to removal, but ensure that the tie-bar is positioned with the word TOP, on the larger end of the bar, uppermost. Tighten the through-bolts to the specified torque, then refit the air cleaner as described in Chapter 3, and refill the cooling system as described in Chapter 2 on completion.

Snubber (manual gearbox models only)

30 Disconnect the battery negative terminal. (Refer to Chapter 12, Section 1, before doing this).
31 Jack up the front of the car and support it on axle stands.
32 Undo the retaining bolts and remove the longitudinal support member from under the engine.
33 Undo the nuts and remove the backing plate and snubber from the longitudinal support member.
34 If required, undo the nuts and bolts and remove the snubber bracket from the gearbox adaptor plate.
35 Renew the snubber if it shows any sign of damage, contamination or separation of the rubber-to-metal bond. Check also for signs of wear on the snubber bracket, and renew if necessary.
36 Refitting is the reverse sequence to removal. Centralise the snubber in its bracket before tightening the bolts and nuts to the specified torque.

Lower tie-bar (automatic transmission models only)

37 Disconnect the battery negative terminal. (Refer to Chapter 12, Section 1, before doing this).
38 Jack up the front of the car and support it on axle stands.
39 Undo the two through-bolts securing the tie-bar to its mounting brackets. Note that at the larger end of the tie-bar, the through-bolt is retained by a forked nut which engages over a peg on the mounting bracket.
40 Using a screwdriver if necessary, prise the tie-bar from its brackets and remove it from the car.
41 Renew the tie-bar if it shows any signs of damage, contamination or separation of the rubber-to-metal bond.
42 Refitting is the reverse sequence to removal, but ensure that the tie-bar is positioned with the letters BTM, on the larger end of the bar, facing downwards, and tighten the through-bolts to the specified torque.

---

26 Fault diagnosis – engine

Symptom	Reason(s)
Engine fails to start	Discharged battery
	Loose battery connections
	Moisture on spark plugs, distributor cap or HT leads
	Incorrect spark plug gaps
	Cracked distributor cap or rotor arm
	Other ignition system fault (see Chapter 4)
	Empty fuel tank
	Other fuel system fault (see Chapter 3)
	Faulty starter motor
	Low cylinder compressions

Symptom	Reason(s)
Engine idles erratically	Idling adjustment incorrect Inlet manifold air leak Disconnected or damaged crankcase ventilation hoses Leaking cylinder head gasket Incorrect valve timing Worn camshaft lobes Faulty hydraulic tappet(s) Uneven cylinder compressions Other fuel system fault (see Chapter 3) Other ignition system fault (see Chapter 4)
Engine misfires	Spark plugs worn, or incorrectly gapped Burnt out valve Leaking cylinder head gasket Distributor cap cracked Incorrect valve timing Worn camshaft lobes Faulty hydraulic tappet(s) Disconnected or damaged crankcase ventilation hoses Uneven cylinder compressions Other fuel system fault (see Chapter 3) Other ignition system fault (see Chapter 4)
Engine stalls	Idling adjustments incorrect Disconnected or damaged crankcase ventilation hoses Inlet manifold air leak Other fuel system fault (see Chapter 3) Other ignition system fault (see Chapter 4)
Excessive oil consumption	Worn pistons, piston rings or cylinder bores Valve guides, valve stems or valve stem oil seals worn Oil seal or gasket leakage
Engine lacks power	Low cylinder compressions Excessive carbon build-up in engine Air cleaner choked Other fuel system fault (see Chapter 3) Other ignition system fault (see Chapter 4)

Chapter 2 Cooling system

Contents

Specifications

System type .... Pressurized, water pump-assisted thermo-syphon, with front-mounted radiator and electric cooling fan

Thermostat
Type .... Wax
Starts-to-open temperature .... 76° to 80°C (169° to 176°F)
Fully-open temperature .... 88°C (190°F)
Lift height .... 8.1 mm (0.32 in)

Expansion tank cap pressure .... 1.0 bar (14.5 lbf/in²)

Cooling fan operating temperature .... 90°C (194°F)

System capacity .... 10.0 litres (17.6 Imp pts)

Antifreeze
Type .... Ethylene glycol based antifreeze (Duckhams Universal Antifreeze and Summer Coolant)

33% antifreeze (by volume):
    Commences freezing .... −19°C (−2°F)
    Frozen solid .... −36°C (−33°F)

	Antifreeze	Water
Quantities (system refill)	3.3 litres (5.8 Imp pts)	6.7 litres (11.8 Imp pts)

50% antifreeze (by volume):
    Commences freezing .... −36°C (−33°F)
    Frozen solid .... −48°C (−54°F)

	Antifreeze	Water
Quantities (system refill)	5.0 litres (8.8 Imp pts)	5.0 litres (8.8 Imp pts)

Torque wrench settings

	Nm	lbf ft
Water outlet elbow to thermostat housing	25	18
Thermostat housing to cylinder head	25	18
Water pump bolts	6	4
Water pump housing bolts	6	4
Water pump support strut bolt	6	4
Engine mounting bracket bolts	25	18
Timing belt tensioner plate	See text – Section 12	
Lower backplate bolts	6	4
Coolant temperature thermistor	7	5
Radiator centre platform bolts	8	6
Cooling fan to radiator	6	4
Bonnet safety catch to centre platform	6	4

1 General description

The cooling system is of the pressurized, pump-assisted thermo-syphon type. The system consists of the radiator, water pump thermostat, electric cooling fan, expansion tank and associated hoses. The impeller type water pump is mounted on the right-hand end of the engine, and is driven by the timing belt.

The system functions as follows. Cold coolant in the bottom of the radiator left-hand tank passes, via hoses and pipes, to the water pump, where it is pumped around the cylinder block and head passages. After cooling the cylinder bores, combustion surfaces and valve seats, the coolant reaches the underside of the thermostat, which is initially closed, and is diverted through a bypass hose to the heater matrix. After passing through the heater, the coolant travels through the water jacket of the inlet manifold or throttle housing as applicable, before returning to the water pump inlet hose. When the engine is cold, the thermostat remains closed, and the coolant only circulates as described. When the coolant reaches a predetermined temperature,

however, the thermostat opens, and the coolant passes through the top hose to the radiator right-hand tank. As the coolant circulates around the radiator, it is cooled by the inrush of air when the car is in forward motion. Airflow is supplemented by the action of the electric cooling fan when necessary. Upon reaching the left-hand side of the radiator, the coolant is now cooled and the cycle is repeated.

When the engine is at normal operating temperature, the coolant expands, and some of it is displaced into the expansion tank. This coolant collects in the tank, and is returned to the radiator when the system cools.

The electric cooling fan mounted on the radiator is controlled by a thermostatic switch, located in the radiator right-hand side tank. At a predetermined coolant temperature, the switch contacts close, thus actuating the fan.

On models equipped with automatic transmission, a fluid cooler is mounted to the transmission casing by a hollow centre bolt. The fluid cooler is connected to the main cooling system, engine coolant being the transmission fluid cooling medium.

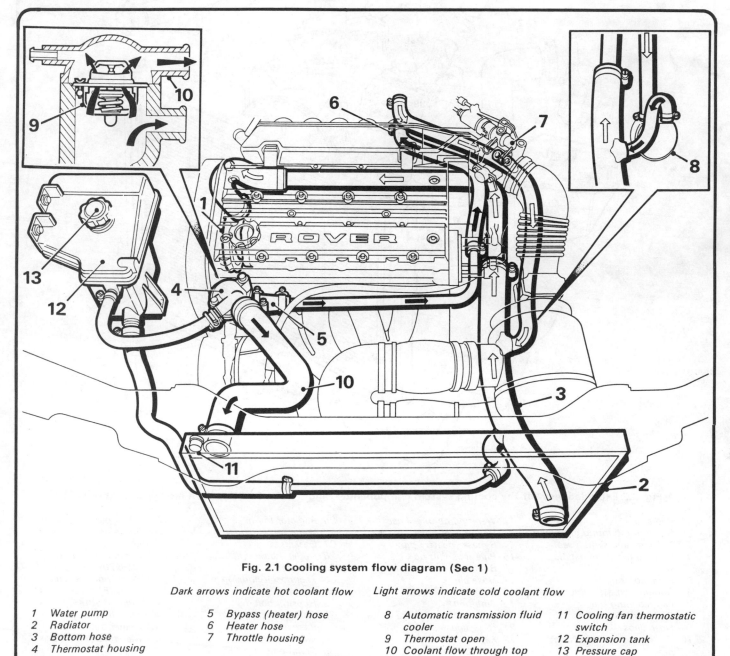

Fig. 2.1 Cooling system flow diagram (Sec 1)

Dark arrows indicate hot coolant flow   Light arrows indicate cold coolant flow

1	Water pump	5	Bypass (heater) hose
2	Radiator	6	Heater hose
3	Bottom hose	7	Throttle housing
4	Thermostat housing		

8	Automatic transmission fluid cooler	11	Cooling fan thermostatic switch
9	Thermostat open	12	Expansion tank
10	Coolant flow through top hose	13	Pressure cap

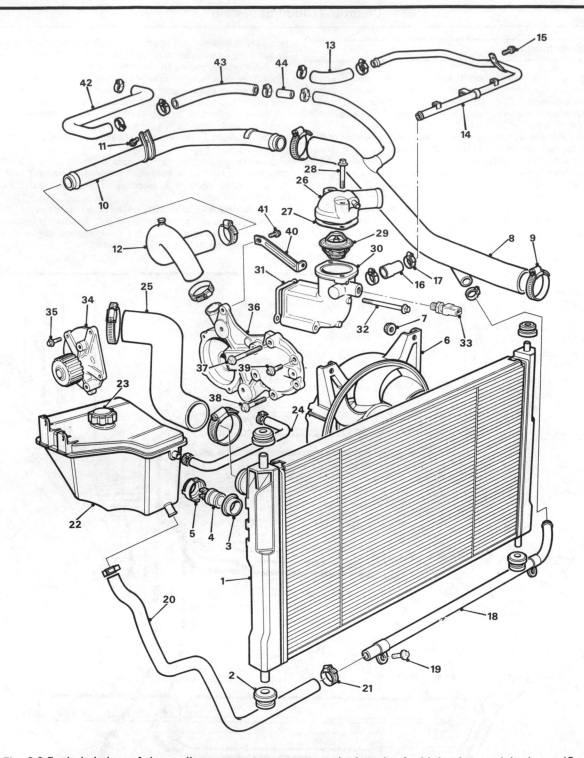

Fig. 2.2 Exploded view of the cooling system components – single-point fuel injection models shown (Sec 1)

1	Radiator	12	Water pump inlet hose	25	Radiator top hose	36	Water pump housing
2	Radiator mounting grommet	13	Heater inlet hose	26	Water outlet elbow	37	Pump housing bolt
3	Thermostatic switch seal	14	Bypass (heater) pipe	27	Gasket		(M8x60)
4	Cooling fan thermostatic	15	Pipe retaining bolt	28	Outlet elbow bolt	38	Pump housing bolt
	switch	16	Bypass (heater) hose	29	Thermostat		(M8x70)
5	Retaining ring	17	Hose clip	30	Thermostat housing	39	Pump housing bolt
6	Cooling fan assembly	18	Expansion tank pipe	31	Gasket		(M8x25)
7	Fan retaining nut	19	Pipe bolt	32	Housing bolt	40	Support strut
8	Radiator bottom hose	20	Expansion tank hose	33	Coolant temperature	41	Strut bolt
9	Hose clips	21	Hose clip		thermistor	42	Heater outlet hose
10	Bottom hose connecting	22	Expansion tank	34	Water pump	43	Manifold outlet hose
	pipe	23	Pressure cap	35	Pump bolt	44	Adaptor pipe
11	Pipe retaining bolts	24	Expansion tank vent hose				

2 Maintenance and inspection

1 Check the coolant level in the system weekly and, if necessary, top up when the engine is cold, using a water-and-antifreeze mixture (photo), until the level just covers the pipe outlet on the seam of the tank. With a sealed type cooling system, topping-up should only be necessary at very infrequent intervals. If this is not the case, and frequent topping-up is required, it is likely that there is a leak in the system, or that the engine is overheating. Check all hoses and joint faces for any staining or actual wetness, and rectify as necessary. If no leaks can be found, it is advisable to have the system pressure-tested, as the leak could possibly be internal. It is a good idea to keep a careful check on the engine oil level in these circumstances, as a serious internal coolant leak can often cause the level in the sump to rise, thus confirming suspicions.
2 At the service intervals given in *Routine maintenance* at the beginning of this manual, carefully inspect all the hoses, hose clips and visible joint gaskets for cracks, corrosion, deterioration or leakage. Renew any hoses and clips that are suspect, and also renew any gaskets or reseal any joint faces, if necessary.
3 At the less-frequent service intervals indicated drain, flush and refill the cooling system using fresh antifreeze, as described in Sections 3, 4, and 5 respectively.

2.1 Top up through the expansion tank with a water-and-antifreeze mixture

3 Cooling system – draining

1 It is preferable to drain the cooling system when the engine is cold. *If the engine is hot, the pressure in the cooling system must be released before attempting to drain the system.* Place a cloth over the pressure cap of the expansion tank to avoid scalding and turn the cap one complete turn anti-clockwise. Wait until all the pressure is released, then remove the cap slowly from the tank.
2 Undo the retaining bolts and remove the undertray from beneath the radiator (photo).
3 Place a suitable container beneath the left-hand side of the radiator. Slacken the hose clip and carefully ease the bottom hose off the radiator outlet (photo). Allow the coolant to drain into the container.
4 If the cooling system is to be flushed after draining, see the next Section, otherwise refit the bottom hose and undertray, then refill the system as described in Section 5.

3.2 Undo the five bolts and remove the undertray

4 Cooling system – flushing

1 With time, the cooling system may gradually lose its efficiency, as the radiator core becomes choked with rust, scale deposits from the water, and other sediment.
2 To flush the system, first drain the coolant as described in the previous Section.
3 Disconnect the top hose at the thermostat housing water outlet elbow, and leave the bottom hose disconnected at the radiator outlet.
4 Insert a garden hose into the top hose, and allow water to circulate through the radiator until it runs clear from the bottom outlet.
5 Disconnect the small hose that connects the heater pipe to the thermostat housing (photo). Connect the garden hose, and allow water to circulate through the heater and manifold and out through the bottom hose until clear. Refit the heater hose on completion.
6 To flush the engine, remove the thermostat as described in Section 10, and insert the garden hose into the thermostat housing. Allow water to flow through the engine until it runs clear from the bottom hose. Refit the thermostat on completion.
7 In severe cases of contamination, reverse-flushing of the radiator may be necessary. To do this, remove the radiator as described in Section 7, invert it and insert the garden hose into the bottom outlet. Continue flushing until clear water runs from the top hose outlet.
8 The use of chemical cleaners should only be necessary as a last resort. The regular renewal of antifreeze should prevent excessive contamination of the system.

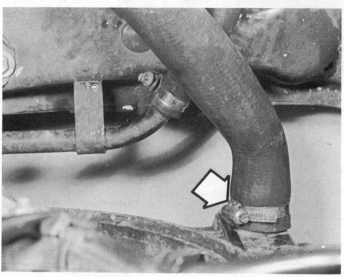

3.3 Slacken the hoseclip (arrowed) and remove the bottom hose

4.5 Disconnect the hose connecting the heater pipe to the thermostat housing

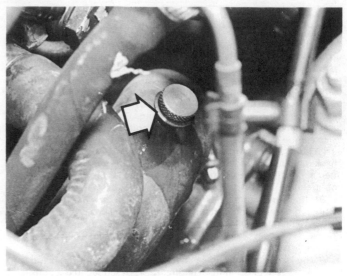

5.3 Tighten the bleed screw (arrowed) when coolant flows free from air bubbles

5 Cooling system – filling

1 If the system has been flushed, refit any hoses or components that were removed for this purpose.
2 Slacken the bleed screw, which is located on the hose connecting the main coolant pipe to the water pump at the rear of the engine.
3 Fill the system slowly through the expansion tank with the appropriate mixture of water and antifreeze (see Section 6), until the level is just below the filler neck. Tighten the bleed screw as soon as coolant flows out free of air bubbles (photo).
4 Recheck the coolant level in the expansion tank, then refit the pressure cap.
5 Start the engine, run it for approximately two minutes, then switch off.
6 Slowly unscrew the pressure cap one complete turn, wait until all the pressure escapes, then remove the cap. Check that the coolant just covers the pipe outlet on the seam of the tank, top up if necessary, then refit the cap.

6 Antifreeze mixture

1 The antifreeze should be renewed at regular intervals (see *Routine maintenance*). This is necessary not only to maintain the antifreeze properties, but also to prevent corrosion which would otherwise occur as the corrosion inhibitors become progressively less effective.
2 Always use an ethylene glycol based antifreeze with non-phosphate corrosion inhibitors, containing no methanol, and which is suitable for use in mixed metal cooling systems.
3 Before adding antifreeze, the cooling system should be completely drained and flushed, and all hoses checked for condition and security.
4 The ratio of antifreeze to water should be maintained at at least 33% all year round. The quantity of antifreeze and levels of protection are indicated in the Specifications.
5 After filling with antifreeze, a label should be attached to the radiator, stating the type and concentration of antifreeze used, and the date installed. Any subsequent topping-up should be made with the same type and concentration of antifreeze.
6 Do not use engine antifreeze in the screen washer system, as it will cause damage to the vehicle paintwork. Screen washer antifreeze is available from most motor accessory shops.

7 Radiator – removal, inspection, cleaning and refitting

1 Drain the cooling system as described in Section 3. Leave the bottom radiator hose disconnected.

2 Slacken the retaining clip and disconnect the radiator top hose (photo).
3 Disconnect the radiator cooling fan multi-plug at the wiring connector.
4 Disconnect the two wires at the thermostatic switch just below the top hose outlet.
5 Undo the radiator grille retaining screws, release the lower catches, and remove the grille from the front of the car.
6 Undo the two bolts each side securing the centre platform to the body side members (photo).
7 Undo the nut and retaining bolt securing the bonnet safety catch to the centre platform (photo).
8 Lift the centre platform upwards, turn it over, and cut off the cable ties securing the bonnet release cable to the platform underside (photo). Remove the platform from the car.
9 Lift the radiator upwards, and carefully remove it from the car.
10 Radiator repair is best left to a specialist, but minor leaks may be sealed using a proprietary coolant additive. Clear the radiator matrix of flies and small leaves with a soft brush, or by hosing.
11 Reverse-flush the radiator, as described in Section 4. Renew the top and bottom hoses and clips if they are damaged or have deteriorated.

7.2 Radiator top hose connection (arrowed)

12 Refitting the radiator is the reverse sequence to removal, but ensure that the lower mounting lugs engage in the rubber grommets (photo), and the centre platform grommets locate over the radiator upper lugs (photo). Re-secure the bonnet release cable to the centre platform, using new cable ties. On completion, fill the cooling system as described in Section 5.

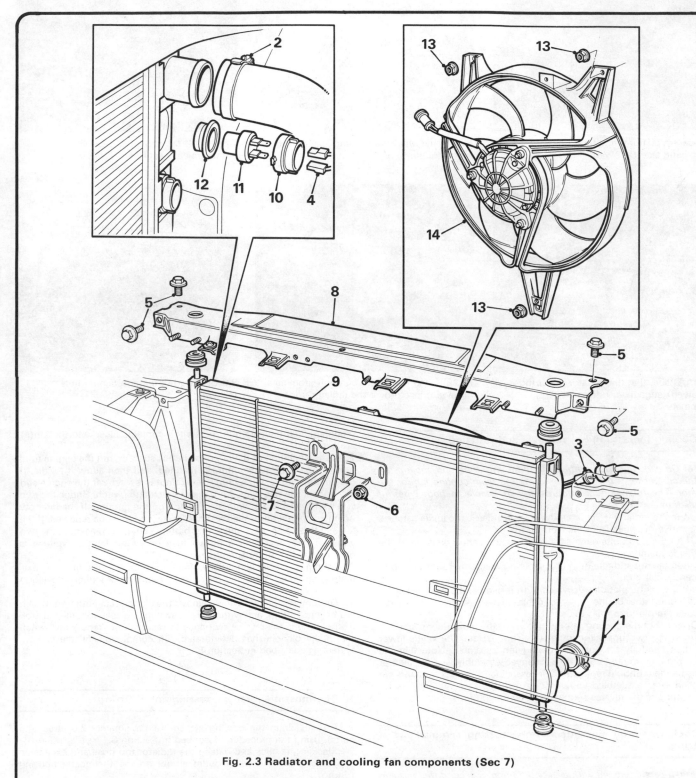

Fig. 2.3 Radiator and cooling fan components (Sec 7)

1 Bottom hose
2 Top hose
3 Cooling fan multi-plug
4 Thermostatic switch wires
5 Centre platform retaining bolts
6 Bonnet safety catch retaining nut
7 Bonnet safety catch retaining bolt
8 Centre platform
9 Radiator
10 Thermostatic switch retaining ring
11 Thermostatic switch
12 Seal
13 Fan shroud retaining nuts
14 Fan and shroud assembly

7.6 Centre platform retaining bolts – right-hand side (arrowed)

7.7 Remove the bonnet safety catch from the centre platform

7.8 Cut off the cable ties securing the bonnet release cable

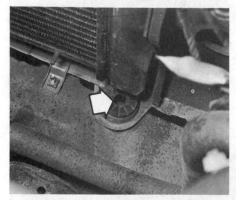

7.12A Ensure that the radiator lower lugs (arrowed) engage with the rubber grommets ...

7.12B ... and the centre platform grommets (arrowed) locate over the radiator upper lugs

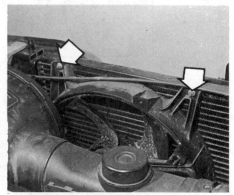

8.6 Cooling fan upper retaining nuts (arrowed)

8 Cooling fan assembly – removal and refitting

Note: *On cars equipped with air conditioning, a second cooling fan for the condensor is mounted alongside the main cooling fan for the radiator. The following procedures are applicable to both types of installation.*

1 Undo the radiator grille retaining screws, release the lower catches, and remove the grille from the front of the car.
2 Undo the two bolts each side securing the centre platform to the body side members.
3 Undo the nut and retaining bolt securing the bonnet safety catch to the centre platform.
4 Lift the centre platform upwards, turn it over, and cut off the cable ties securing the bonnet release cable to the platform underside. Remove the platform from the car.
5 Disconnect the cooling fan multi-plug at the wiring connector.
6 Undo the two upper retaining nuts (photo) and the single lower nut, then carefully lift out the cooling fan assembly. Note that the cooling fan, motor and cowl are a balanced assembly, and should not be dismantled. Should renewal be necessary, all three components are supplied as an assembled unit.
7 Refitting is the reverse sequence to removal.

9 Cooling fan thermostatic switch – testing, removal and refitting

Note: *On cars equipped with air conditioning, a second thermostatic switch for the condensor fan is mounted below the main thermostatic switch for the radiator cooling fan. The following procedures are applicable to both types of installation*

1 The radiator cooling fan (and condensor fan on cars equipped with air conditioning) are each operated by thermostatic switches, located on the right-hand side of the radiator. When the coolant exceeds a predetermined temperature, the switch contacts close and the fan(s) are activated.
2 If the operation of the fan or switch is suspect, run the engine until normal operating temperature is reached, and then allow it to idle. If the fan does not cut in within a few minutes, switch off the engine and disconnect the two wires from the thermostatic switch. Bridge the two wires with a length of wire, and switch on the ignition. If the fan now operates, the thermostatic switch is faulty, and must be renewed. If the fan still fails to operate, check that battery voltage is present at the two wires. If not, check for a blown fuse or wiring fault. If voltage is present, the fan motor is faulty.
3 To remove switch, partially drain the cooling system (approximately 2.5 litres/ 4.5 pints), using the procedure described in Section 3.
4 Disconnect the two wires, remove the switch retaining ring, which is a bayonet fitting, and withdraw the switch and seal from the radiator.
5 Refitting is the reverse sequence to removal, but renew the switch seal if the old one has deteriorated. On completion, fill the cooling system as described in Section 5.

10 Thermostat – removal, testing and refitting

1 Partially drain the cooling system (approximately 2.5 litres/ 4.5 pints), using the procedure described in Section 3.
2 Slacken the clips and detach the radiator top hose and expansion tank hose from the water outlet elbow on the thermostat housing (photo).
3 Undo the two bolts and remove the water outlet elbow (photos). Remove the gasket.
4 Withdraw the thermostat from its seat in the housing (photo).
5 To test the thermostat, suspend it on a string in a saucepan of cold water, together with a thermometer. Do not allow the thermostat or thermometer to touch the bottom of the pan. Heat the water, and note

10.2 Detach the radiator top hose and expansion tank hose at the water outlet elbow

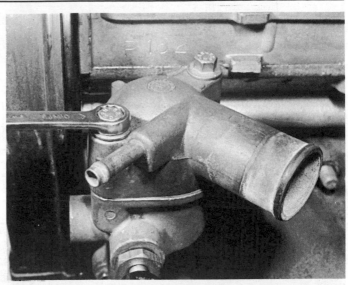

10.3A Undo the two retaining bolts ...

10.3B ... and remove the water outlet elbow

10.4 Withdraw the thermostat from the housing

the temperature at which the thermostat begins to open. Continue heating the water until the thermostat is fully open, note the temperature, then remove the unit from the water.

6   The temperatures at which the thermostat should start to open, and be fully open, are given in the Specifications. The fully-open temperature is also stamped on the wax capsule at the base of the thermostat. If the unit does not start to open, or is not fully open, at the specified temperatures, or if it does not close when removed from the water, then it must be discarded, and a new unit fitted. Under no circumstances should the car be used without a thermostat, as uneven cooling of the cylinder walls and head passages will occur, causing distortion and possible seizure of the engine internal components.

7   Refitting the thermostat is the reverse sequence to removal, bearing in mind the following points:

   (a) *Position the unit with its support legs across the heater outlet pipe, as shown in Fig. 2.4*
   (b) *Clean away all traces of old gasket from the mating faces, and use a new gasket, lightly smeared with jointing compound*

   (c) *Tighten the water outlet elbow retaining bolts to the specified torque*
   (d) *Top up the cooling system with reference to Section 5*

11 Thermostat housing – removal and refitting

1   Remove the thermostat as described in the previous Section.
2   Disconnect the coolant temperature thermistor wiring multi-plug.
3   Slacken the retaining clips, and disconnect the heater pipe connecting hose from the side of the housing.
4   Undo the two bolts, and remove the thermostat housing and gasket from the cylinder head (photos).
5   Refitting is the reverse sequence to removal, bearing in mind the following points:

   (a) *Clean away all traces of old gasket from the mating faces, and use a new gasket, lightly smeared with jointing compound*
   (b) *Tighten the retaining bolts to the specified torque*

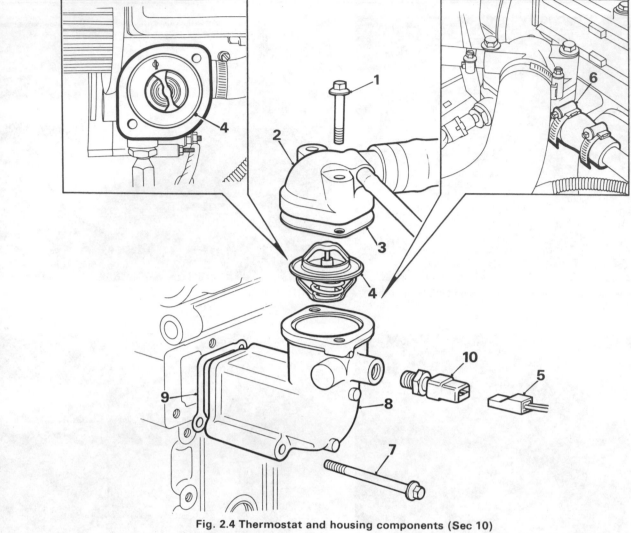

Fig. 2.4 Thermostat and housing components (Sec 10)

1	Outlet elbow bolt	4	Thermostat (inset shows	6	Connecting hose clip	9	Gasket
2	Water outlet elbow		correct fitted position)	7	Housing bolt	10	Coolant temperature
3	Gasket	5	Wiring plug	8	Thermostat housing		thermistor

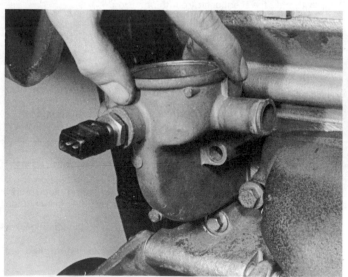

11.4A Remove the thermostat housing ...

11.4B ... followed by the gasket

12 Water pump – removal and refitting

Note: *Water pump failure is indicated by water leaking from the gland at the front of the pump, or by rough and noisy operation, usually accompanied by excessive play of the pump spindle. Repair or overhaul of a faulty pump is not possible, as internal parts are not available separately. In the event of failure, a replacement pump must be obtained.*

1 Drain the cooling system as described in Section 3.
2 Remove the alternator drivebelt as described in Chapter 12.
3 Refer to Chapter 1 and remove the timing belt.
4 Undo the three remaining bolts securing the lower backplate to the engine, noting that one bolt also retains a breather hose clip, and one retains an oil pipe clip. Remove the lower backplate (photo).
5 Undo the three bolts or Torx type / socket-headed screws, as applicable, and remove the timing belt tensioner mounting plate (photo).
6 Undo the five bolts securing the water pump to its housing (photo).
7 Have a container handy to catch any remaining coolant, then withdraw the pump from the housing. If necessary, carefully tap the pump body with a soft-faced mallet to free it.
8 With the pump removed, scrape away all traces of RTV sealant from the pump and housing mating faces, ensuring that both are competely clean and dry.
9 Before refitting the pump, it will be necessary to obtain three new bolts or socket-headed screws, as applicable, that retain the timing belt tensioner mounting plate. These are all of the micro-encapsulated type that incorporate a locking compound in their threads, and consequently, they can only be used once. Note also that considerable modification has taken place in this area during the course of

production, and there are currently three versions of mounting plate and fastenings available. These are shown in Figs. 2.5 to 2.7. To identify the type fitted to the engine being worked on, compare the part number stamped on the mounting plate face with those shown in the illustrations, and obtain new screws or bolts from a Rover dealer accordingly.
10 Apply a thin, continuous bead of RTV sealant to the pump mating face, and place the pump in position on the housing.
11 Refit the pump retaining bolts and tighten them progressively, and in a diagonal sequence, to the specified torque.
12 Locate the timing belt tensioner mounting plate in position, and fit the three bolts or screws finger-tight. These must now be tightened in the correct sequence, according to type as follows:

First version (Fig. 2.5)
Tighten screws 'A' progressively to 9 to 12 Nm (6.6 to 8.8 lbf ft) then tighten bolt 'B' to 7 to 10 Nm (5.1 to 7.3 lbf ft)

Second version (Fig. 2.6)
Tighten in numerical order shown, to 11 to 14 Nm (8.1 to 10.3 lbf ft) for screws 1 and 2, and 7 to 10 Nm (5.1 to 7.3 lbf ft) for bolt 3

Third version (Fig. 2.7)
Tighten all, in the numerical order shown, to 11 to 14 Nm (8.1 to 10.3 lbf ft)

Do not attempt to retighten any of the screws or bolts after the locking compound has set (approximately two minutes), otherwise the locking properties will be destroyed, and the screws may loosen in service.
13 Refit the lower backplate to the engine, and secure with the three bolts.
14 Refer to Chapter 1 and refit the timing belt.
15 Refit the alternator drivebelt as described in Chapter 12, then refill the cooling system as described in Section 5.

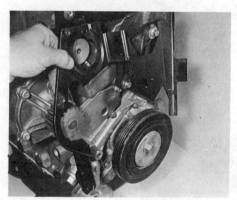

12.4 Remove the lower backplate from the engine

12.5 Timing belt tensioner mounting plate bolts/screws (arrowed)

12.6 Undo the five bolts (arrowed) and remove the water pump

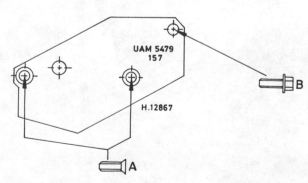

Fig. 2.5 Timing belt tensioner mounting plate – first version (Sec 12)

A Hexagon drive countersunk screws
B Flange head bolt

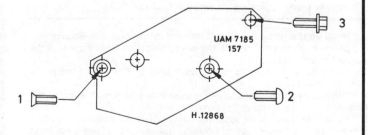

Fig. 2.6 Timing belt tensioner mounting plate – second version (Sec 12)

1 Torx type countersunk screw
2 Torx type pan head screw
3 Flange head bolt

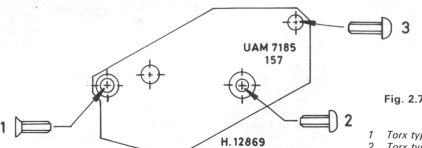

Fig. 2.7 Timing belt tensioner mounting plate – third
version (Sec 12)

1   Torx type countersunk screw   3   Torx type pan head screw
2   Torx type pan head screw

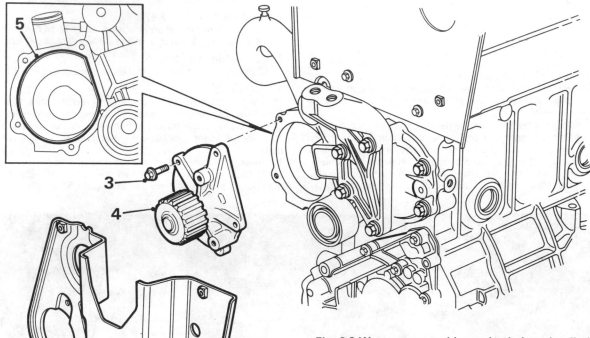

Fig. 2.8 Water pump and lower backplate details (Sec 12)

1   Lower backplate bolts   4   Water pump assembly
2   Lower backplate   5   Bead of RTV sealant applied
3   Water pump bolts   to pump housing face

13 Water pump housing – removal and refitting

1   Remove the water pump as described in the previous Section.
2   Slacken the clip and detach the water inlet hose from the rear of the
pump housing (photo).
3   Undo the bolt securing the support strut to the rear of the pump
housing (photo).
4   Using a suitable jack and interposed block of wood, support the
engine under the sump at the timing belt end.
5   Undo the four bolts securing the right-hand engine mounting
bracket to the water pump housing (photo), and the two bolts
securing the bracket to the engine mounting, then remove the bracket.
6   Undo the remaining two retaining bolts (photo), and remove the
water pump housing from the cylinder block.
7   Clean away all traces of RTV sealant from the housing and cylinder
block mating faces, ensuring that both surfaces are clean and dry.
8   Apply a thin, continuous bead of RTV sealant to the cylinder block
mating face (photo), and locate the housing in position.

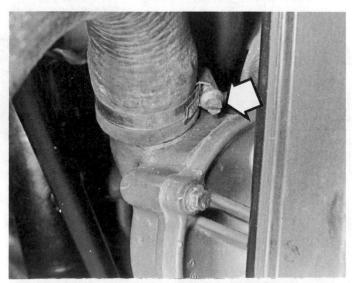

13.2 Water inlet hose connection (arrowed) at rear of water pump
housing

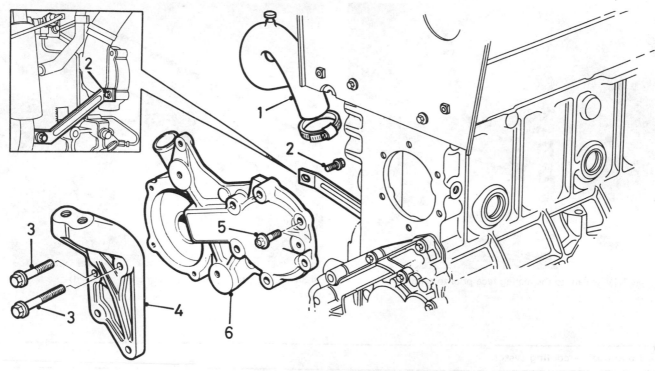

Fig. 2.9 Water pump housing details (Sec 13)

1 Water inlet hose
2 Support strut bolt

3 Engine mounting bracket
   bolts

4 Engine mounting bracket
5 Pump housing bolts

6 Water pump housing

9 Apply thread sealer to the two housing retaining bolts, and fit them finger-tight at this stage.
10 Apply thread sealer to the four engine mounting bracket-to-pump housing bolts, fit the bracket and tighten the bolts to the specified torque. Now tighten the two pump bolts fitted previously.
11 Secure the engine mounting bracket to the mounting, and remove the support jack.
12 Refit the bolt securing the support strut to the rear of the pump housing.
13 Reconnect the inlet water hose to the housing.
14 Refit the water pump as described in the previous Section.

14 Expansion tank – removal and refitting

1 Drain the cooling system as described in Section 3.
2 Slacken the clips and detach the two hoses on the side of the tank.

3 Undo the two upper (photo) and one lower retaining screw(s), and remove the tank.
4 Refitting is the reverse sequence to removal.

15 Coolant temperature thermistor – removal and refitting

1 The thermistor contains an element, the resistance of which alters according to coolant temperature. The unit controls the operation of the temperature gauge, and is also used by the fuel and ignition system control units to determine engine temperature.
2 Partially drain the cooling system (approximately 2.5 litres/ 4.5 pints), using the procedure described in Section 3.
3 Disconnect the wiring multi-plug, then unscrew the thermistor from its location in the thermostat housing.
4 Refitting is the reverse sequence to removal, but refill the cooling system with reference to Section 5.

13.3 Undo the bolt (arrowed) securing the support strut to the housing

13.5 Engine mounting bracket bolt locations (arrowed)

13.6 Water pump housing retaining bolts (arrowed)

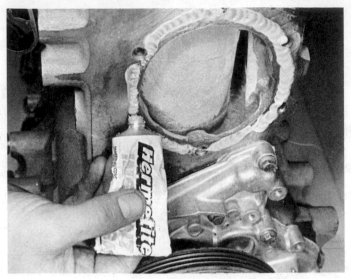

13.8 Apply RTV sealant to the mating face prior to refitting

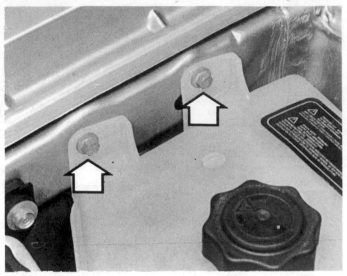

14.3 Expansion tank upper retaining bolts (arrowed)

16 Fault diagnosis – cooling system

Symptom	Reason(s)
Overheating	Low coolant level (this may be the result of overheating for other reasons) Radiator blockage (internal or external), or grille restricted Thermostat defective Ignition system fault Faulty cooling fan thermostatic switch Faulty cooling fan Blown cylinder head gasket Water pump defective Expansion tank pressure cap faulty Brakes binding
Overcooling	Thermostat missing, defective or wrong heat range Incorrect reading on gauge (faulty gauge or temperature thermistor)
Water loss – external	Loose hose clips Perished or cracked hoses Radiator core leaking Heater matrix leaking Expansion tank pressure cap leaking Boiling due to overheating Water pump or thermostat housing leaking Core plug leaking Other joint face leak
Water loss – internal	Cylinder head gasket blown Cylinder head cracked or warped Cylinder head cracked
Corrosion	Infrequent draining and flushing Incorrect antifreeze mixture, or inappropriate type Combustion gases contaminating coolant

Chapter 3 Fuel and exhaust systems

For modifications, and information applicable to later models, see Supplement at end of manual

Contents

Specifications

Part A : Single-point fuel injection system

System type .... Indirect single-point injection, with microprocessor control

Fuel pump

Type .... Electric, self-priming centrifugal
Make .... Nippon Denso FP3
Output pressure .... 4.1 bar (59.4 lbf/in²)
Regulated pressure .... 1.0 bar (14.5 lbf/in²)
Delivery rate (at 1.0 bar/14.5 lbf/in², and 12 volts) .... 85 litres/hr (150 pints/hr)
Voltage at pump .... 9.0 to 10.0 volts

General

ECU-controlled idle speed:
  Manual gearbox models .... 700 to 800 rpm
  Automatic transmission models .... 650 to 750 rpm
Base idle speed:
  Manual gearbox models .... 625 to 675 rpm
  Automatic transmission models .... 575 to 625 rpm
Idle mixture CO content .... 2.0 to 3.0%
Throttle potentiometer voltage .... 315 to 335 mV
Throttle lever lost motion gap .... 0.5 to 0.9 mm (0.020 to 0.035 in)
Fuel octane rating .... 4 star (97 RON – leaded) or Premium (95 RON – unleaded)
Fuel filter .... Champion L208
Air cleaner element .... Champion W114

Torque wrench settings

	Nm	lbf ft
Inlet air temperature sensor	7	5
Fuel filter banjo union bolts	50	37
Throttle body-to-manifold nuts	25	18
Fuel pump banjo union bolt	22	16
Fuel pump retaining nuts	6	4
Fuel tank drain plug	50	37
Fuel tank strap locknuts	18	13
Inlet manifold support stay bolts	25	18
Inlet manifold to cylinder head	25	18
Inlet manifold heater bolts	10	7
Exhaust manifold to cylinder head	45	33
Exhaust front pipe to manifold	30	22
Exhaust section flange nuts	30	22
Exhaust heat shield retaining bolts	25	18

Part B : Multi-point fuel injection system

System type

System type .... Indirect multi-point injection, with microprocessor control

Fuel pump

Type	Electric, self-priming centrifugal
Make	Nippon Denso FP3
Output pressure	4.1 bar (59.4 lbf/in²)
Regulated pressure range	3.0 to 2.3 bar (43.5 to 33.4 lbf/in²)
Delivery rate (at 3.0 bar/43.5 lbf/in², and 12 volts)	70 litres/hr (123.2 pints/hr)

General

ECU-controlled idle speed:	
Manual gearbox models	850 to 950 rpm
Automatic transmission models	800 to 900 rpm
Base idle speed:	
Manual gearbox models	725 to 775 rpm
Automatic transmission models	675 to 725 rpm
Idle mixture CO content	0.5 to 1.5%
Throttle potentiometer voltage	315 to 335 mV
Fuel octane rating	4 star (97 RON – leaded) or Premium (95 RON – unleaded)
Fuel filter	Champion L208
Air cleaner element	Champion W114

Torque wrench settings

	Nm	lbf ft
Airflow meter retaining bolts	6	4
Throttle housing retaining nuts	8	6
Fuel filter banjo union bolts	50	37
Fuel pressure regulator retaining bolts	6	4
Brake servo hose banjo union bolt	50	37
Plenum chamber to camshaft cover	6	4
Plenum chamber to inlet manifold	8	6
Fuel rail to inlet manifold	8	6
Fuel pump banjo union bolt	22	16
Fuel pump retaining nuts	6	4
Fuel tank drain plug	50	37
Fuel tank strap locknuts	18	13
Inlet manifold to cylinder head	25	18
Exhaust manifold to cylinder head	45	33
Exhaust front pipe to manifold	30	22
Exhaust section flange nuts	30	22
Exhaust heat shield retaining bolts	25	18

PART A : SINGLE-POINT FUEL INJECTION SYSTEM

1 General description

The fuel system used on Rover 820e and Se models consists of a centrally-mounted fuel tank, electric fuel pump and single-point fuel injection (SPi) system, together with its related electrical and mechanical components. A more detailed description of the SPi system is contained in Section 10.

The exhaust system consists of a front, intermediate and rear section, suspended from the underbody on rubber mountings, and bolted to a cast iron manifold at the front. A ball-and-socket universal joint is incorporated in the front section, to allow for engine and exhaust system movement.

Warning: *Many of the procedures in this Chapter entail the removal of fuel pipes and connections, which may result in some fuel spillage. Before carrying out any operations on the fuel system, refer to the precautions given in* Safety first! *at the beginning of this manual, and follow them implicitly. Petrol is a highly dangerous and volatile liquid, and the precautions necessary when handling it cannot be overstressed.*

2 Maintenance and inspection

1 At the intervals given in *Routine maintenance* at the beginning of this manual, carry out the following service operations on the fuel and exhaust system components.

2 With the car raised on a vehicle lift or securely supported on axle stands, carefully inspect the fuel pipes, hoses and unions for chafing, leaks, and corrosion. Renew any pipes that are severely pitted with corrosion, or in any way damaged. Renew any hoses that show signs of cracking or other deterioration.

3 Check the security of the fuel tank mountings, and check the tank

for signs of corrosion or damage. Refer to Section 7 if the tank condition is suspect.

4 Check condition of the exhaust system as described in Section 26.

5 From within the engine compartment, check the security of all fuel hose attachments, and inspect the fuel hoses and vacuum hoses for kinks, chafing or deterioration.

6 Renew the air cleaner element, and clean the air cleaner body and cover, as described in Section 3.

7 Check the operation of the accelerator linkage, and lubricate the linkage, cable and pedal pivot with a few drops of oil.

8 Renew the fuel filter as described in Section 4.

9 Check the fuel injection system base idle speed and mixture settings as described in Section 12.

3 Air cleaner and element – removal and refitting

1 To renew the air cleaner element, remove the cover from the air cleaner body by carefully prising it off using a screwdriver around the periphery (photo).

2 Withdraw the element from the body, and bend it upwards to clear the front body panel (photo).

3 Using a clean rag, wipe out the inside of the body and cover.

4 Carefully fit the new element, ensuring that its centre is located over the lip at the base of the air cleaner body.

5 Refit the cover, and push it firmly into place.

6 To remove the complete air cleaner assembly, slacken the hose clip securing the intake trunking to the air cleaner body, and release the HT cable from the support clip.

7 Undo the five upper bolts securing the air box to the injector housing and support bracket.

8 Lift up the air box, and disconnect the wiring multi-plug at the air temperature sensor, and the vacuum hose at the fuel trap (photos).

9 Disconnect the vacuum hose from the inlet manifold connection, and from the vacuum motor on the air cleaner (photos). Remove the air box and intake trunking assembly.

10 Undo the bolts securing the air cleaner body and the forward air trunking assembly to their support brackets (photos). Lift the body and trunking, disconnect the hot air intake tube, and release the trunking

3.1 Remove the air cleaner cover ...

3.2 ... and withdraw the element

3.8A Lift up the air box ...

3.8B ... and disconnect the air temperature sensor multi-plug

3.9A Disconnect the vacuum hose at the inlet manifold ...

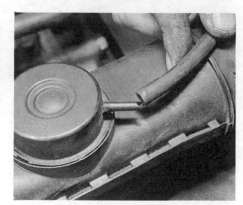

3.9B ... and at the vacuum motor

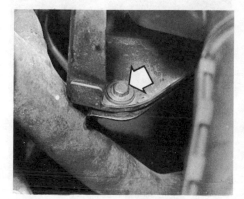

3.10A Undo the air cleaner body left-hand retaining bolt (arrowed) ...

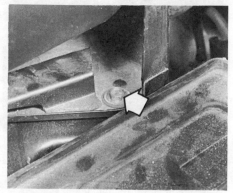

3.10B ... and right-hand retaining bolt (arrowed) ...

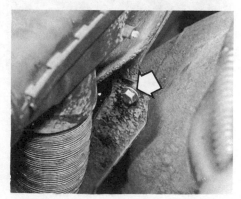

3.10C ... and the air cleaner trunking-to-support bracket bolt (arrowed)

from the connecting duct at the front of the car. Remove the air cleaner body and trunking.

11 If the cold air side intake is to be removed, refer to Chapter 12 and remove the battery.

12 Undo the bolt securing the side intake to the body, and remove the intake and duct (photo).

13 Refitting is the reverse sequence to removal, but ensure that all the ducts and trunking are fully engaged before tightening the various retaining bolts.

4 Fuel filter – removal and refitting

Note: Refer to the warning note in Section 1 before proceeding.

1 Disconnect the battery negative terminal. (Refer to Chapter 12, Section 1, before doing this.)

2 Place absorbent rags around the fuel filter outlet union banjo bolt (photo), then slowly unscrew the bolt to release the fuel system pressure.

3 Unscrew the filter inlet and outlet union banjo bolts, and recover the copper washers (photo).

4 Undo the filter bracket retaining nuts, and remove the filter.

5 Refitting is the reverse sequence to removal, but use new copper washers on the banjo unions.

5 Fuel pump – removal and refitting

Note: Refer to the warning note in Section 1 before proceeding.

1 Disconnect the battery negative terminal. (Refer to Chapter 12, Section 1, before doing this).

2 Release the fuel system pressure as described in Section 4,

paragraph 2. Tighten the fuel filter banjo bolt after the pressure has been released.

3 Remove the floor carpet from the luggage compartment.

4 Refer to Chapter 11 and remove the rear seats.

5 Release the eight studs and remove the seat squab backing from the body.

6 Release the two studs and remove the luggage compartment backboard from the body.

7 Remove the cover board over the spare wheel, and remove the tool kit.

8 Undo the four screws and lift off the pump access panel (photos). Move the panel to one side.

9 Disconnect the pump wiring multi-plug, then unscrew the fuel hose banjo union bolt and recover the copper washers (photo).

10 Slacken the clip and disconnect the fuel return hose.

11 Undo the pump retaining nuts, and withdraw the pump from the tank. Remove the seal from the pump flange.

12 Refitting is the reverse sequence to removal, but renew the flange seal if it shows any sign of deterioration.

6 Fuel gauge sender unit – removal and refitting

Note: Refer to the warning note in Section 1 before proceeding.

1 Follow the procedure given in Section 5, paragraphs 1 to 8 inclusive, with the exception of paragraph 2.

2 Disconnect the two leads at the sender unit.

3 Engage a screwdriver, flat bar or other suitable tool with the lugs of the locking ring, and turn the ring anti-clockwise to release it.

4 Withdraw the locking ring, seal and sender unit.

5 Refitting is the reverse sequence to removal, but renew the seal if it shows any sign of deterioration.

3.12 Side intake-to-body retaining bolt (arrowed)

4.2 Fuel filter outlet union banjo bolt (arrowed)

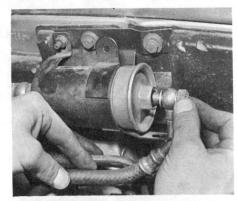

4.3 Undo the banjo unions and recover the copper washers

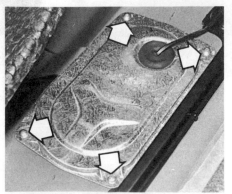

5.8A Undo the four retaining screws (arrowed) ...

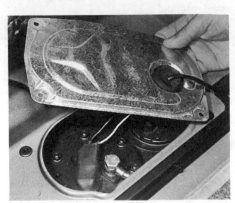

5.8B ... and lift off the fuel pump access panel

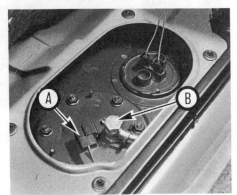

5.9 Fuel pump wiring multi-plug connection (A) and fuel hose banjo union (B)

7 Fuel tank – removal and refitting

Note: *Refer to the warning note in Section 1 before proceeding.*

1 Follow the procedure given in Section 5, paragraphs 1 to 8 inclusive.

2 Disconnect the fuel pump wiring multi-plug, and the two leads at the fuel gauge sender unit.

3 Remove the fuel tank filler cap.

4 With suitable sealed containers handy, undo the drain plug at the base of the tank, and drain the fuel into the containers. Recover the drain plug sealing washer. When all the fuel has drained, refit the plug, using a new sealing washer if necessary.

5 Chock the front wheels, prise off the rear wheel trim and slacken the wheel nuts. Jack up the rear of the car and support it on axle stands. Remove the left-hand rear roadwheel.

6 Slacken the retaining clip and disconnect the filler hose from the filler neck. Move the hose aside.

7 Slacken the retaining clips and disconnect the five breather hoses from the breather pipes.

8 Refer to Section 26 and remove the exhaust system rear and intermediate sections, together with the rear heat shield.

9 Slacken the retaining clip and disconnect the fuel return hose from the pipe on the side of the tank. Plug the disconnected pipe and hose.

10 Undo the union connector and disconnect the fuel feed hose from the pipe. Plug the disconnected pipe and hose.

11 Support the tank on a jack with interposed block of wood.

12 Slacken the two tank retaining strap locknuts (photo), release the hook bolts from the body slots, and move the straps clear.

13 Lower the tank and remove it from under the car.

14 If the tank is contaminated with sediment or water, remove the sender unit as described in Section 6, and swill the tank out with clean fuel. If the tank is damaged, or leaks, it should be repaired by a specialist, or alternatively renewed. **Do not** *under any circumstances solder or weld the tank.*

15 Refitting is the reverse sequence to removal.

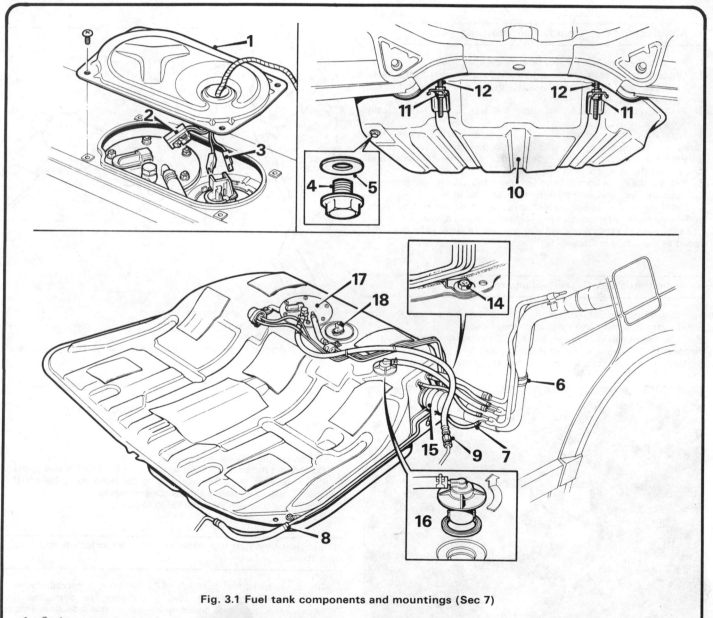

Fig. 3.1 Fuel tank components and mountings (Sec 7)

1 Fuel pump access panel	6 Filler hose-to-filler neck connection	10 Fuel tank	15 Filler hose-to-tank connection
2 Pump wiring multi-plug	7 Breather hose	11 Retaining strap locknuts	16 Cut-off valve
3 Sender unit wiring	8 Fuel return hose	12 Hook bolts	17 Fuel pump
4 Drain plug	9 Fuel feed hose union	14 Breather pipe support bracket	18 Fuel gauge sender unit
5 Sealing washer			

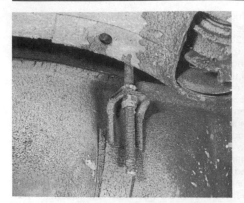

7.12 Fuel tank retaining strap and locknut

8.2 Undo the accelerator cable locknut ...

8.3 ... and release the cable end (arrowed) from the throttle cam

8 Accelerator cable – removal and refitting

1   Refer to Section 3 and remove the air cleaner air box.
2   Unscrew the accelerator outer cable locknut nearest to the cable end, pull the outer cable upwards, and slide the inner cable out of the slot in the support bracket (photo).
3   Release the inner cable end from the slot in the throttle cam (photo).
4   From inside the car, release the turnbuckles and lift out the trim panel over the clutch, brake and accelerator pedals.
5   Prise the retaining clip from the top of the accelerator pedal, and disconnect the inner cable.
6   Release the cable from the engine compartment bulkhead and from the support clips, and withdraw the complete cable from the car.
7   Refitting is the reverse sequence to removal. Adjust the cable initially by means of the outer cable locknuts, to give a small amount of free play with the throttle closed. On completion, check the base idle speed as described in Section 12.

9 Accelerator pedal – removal and refitting

1   From inside the car, release the turnbuckles and lift out the trim panel over the clutch, brake and accelerator pedals.
2   Prise the retaining clip from the top of the accelerator pedal, and disconnect the inner cable from the pedal arm.
3   Undo the bolts securing the pedal bracket to the bulkhead (photo),

9.3 Accelerator pedal bracket retaining bolts (arrowed)

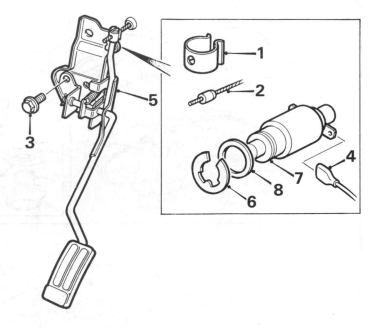

Fig. 3.2 Accelerator pedal and pedal switch components (Sec 9)

1 Cable retaining clip	5 Pedal and bracket assembly
2 Accelerator cable	6 C-clip
3 Pedal bracket retaining bolts	7 Pedal switch
4 Pedal switch wiring	8 Washer

and withdraw the bracket and pedal assembly.
4   Disconnect the switch wiring and remove the bracket and pedal.
5   If the accelerator pedal switch is to be removed, prise off the retaining C-clip and remove the switch and washer.
6   Refitting is the reverse sequence to removal.

10 Single-point fuel injection system – description and operation

The single-point fuel injection (SPi) system is a microprocessor-controlled fuel management system, designed to overcome the limitations associated with conventional carburettor induction. This is achieved by continuously monitoring the engine using various sensors, whose data is input to the fuel system electronic control unit (ECU). Based on this information, the ECU program and memory then determine the exact amount of fuel necessary, which is injected into the throttle body by a single injector, for all actual and anticipated driving conditions.

The main components of the system are shown in Figs. 3.3 and 3.4, and their individual operation is as follows.

Fuel ECU: The fuel ECU is a microprocessor which controls the injector opening time, and therefore the amount of fuel supplied. Contained in the ECU memory is a program from which a pulse is derived, the length of which determines the fuel injector opening duration. Information received from the various engine sensors will cause the ECU to alter the fuel requirements, by changing the pulse length. Airflow measurement is based on the speed/density method, in which the inlet air temperature and inlet manifold pressure are measured under the assumption that the engine is a calibrated vacuum pump, with its characteristics stored in the ECU memory. The air/fuel ratio requirements for all engine speeds and loads are also stored in the ECU. This information on the engine's basic fuel requirements is constantly amended, according to the information received from the various sensors. In addition to this, the engine idle speed is also controlled by the ECU, which uses a stepper motor to open or close the throttle as required. Two separate programs control the ECU functions.

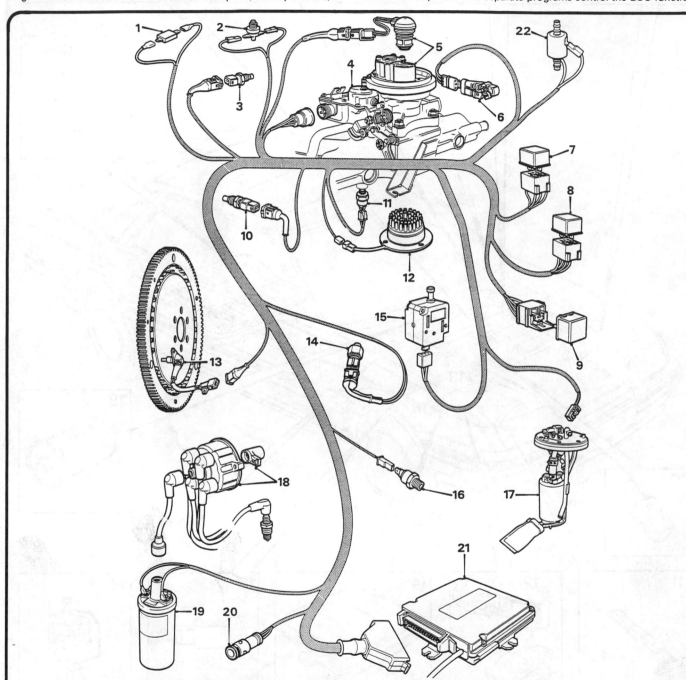

Fig. 3.3 Main components of the single-point fuel injection system (Sec 10)

1	Ambient air temperature sensor	6 Throttle potentiometer	12 Manifold heater	18 Distributor cap and rotor arm
2	Accelerator pedal switch	7 Main fuel system relay	13 Crankshaft sensor	19 Ignition coil
3	Inlet air temperature sensor	8 Fuel pump relay	14 Knock sensor	20 Diagnostic plug connector
4	Throttle body and idle speed stepper motor	9 Oil pressure relay	15 Inertia switch	21 Fuel/ignition ECU
5	Fuel injector and fuel pressure regulator	10 Coolant temperature thermistor	16 Oil pressure switch	22 Idle solenoid (models with air conditioning)
		11 Manifold heater temperature sensor	17 Fuel pump	

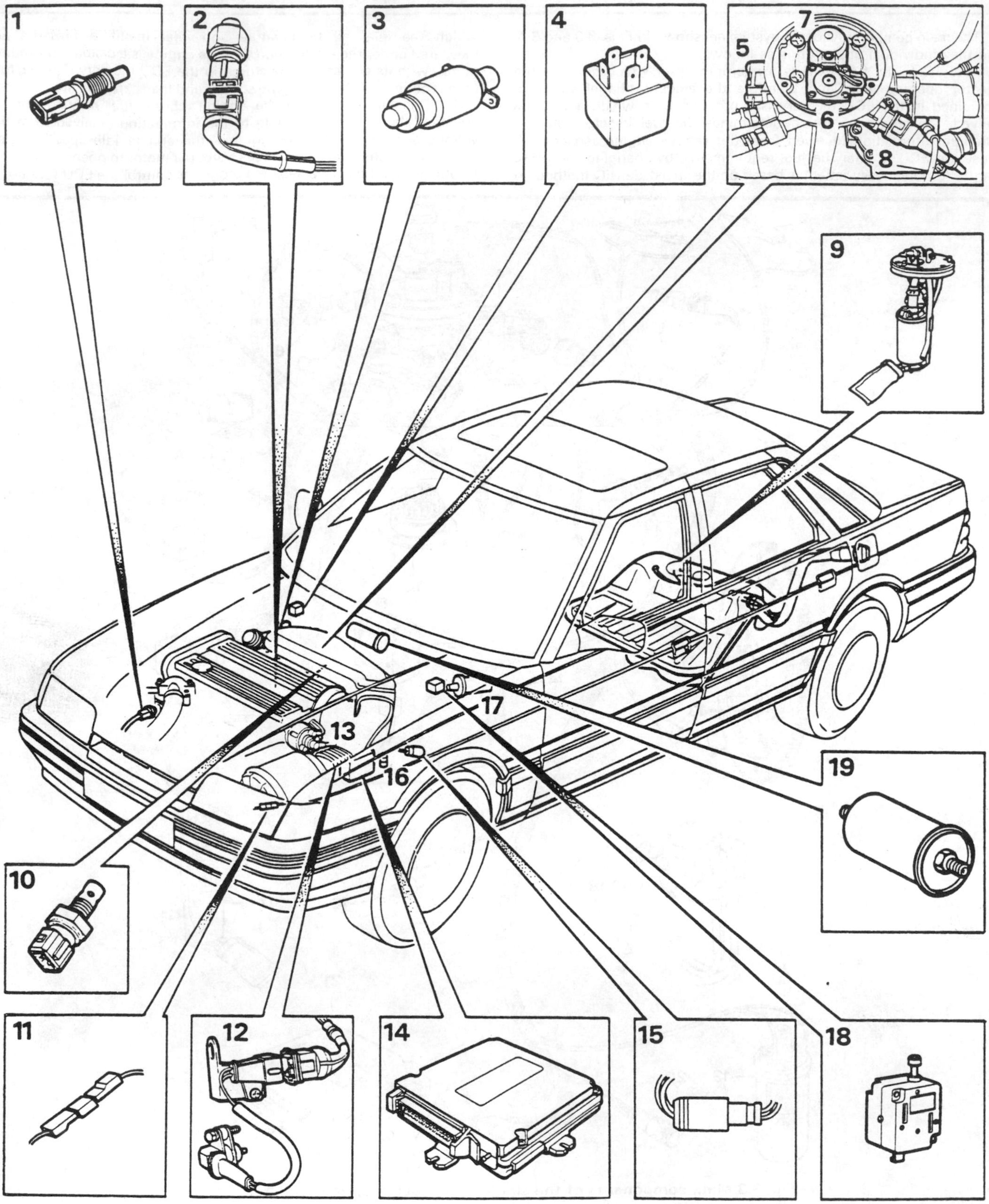

Fig. 3.4 Single-point injection system component location (Sec 10)

1	Coolant temperature thermistor	6	Fuel pressure regulator
2	Knock sensor	7	Fuel injector
3	Accelerator pedal switch	8	Idle speed stepper motor
4	Fuel pump relay	9	Fuel pump
5	Throttle potentiometer	10	Inlet air temperature sensor

11	Ambient air temperature sensor	15	Diagnostic plug connector
12	Crankshaft sensor	16	Main fuel system relay
13	Distributor cap and rotor arm	17	Ignition coil
14	Fuel/ignition ECU	18	Inertia switch
		19	Fuel filter

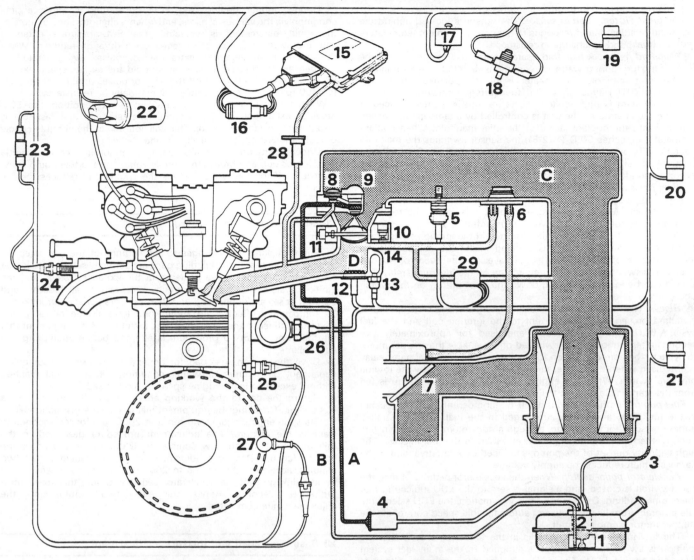

Fig. 3.5 Schematic layout of the single-point fuel injection system (Sec 10)

1 Fuel return swirl pot	11 Throttle potentiometer
2 Fuel pump	12 Manifold heater
3 Fuel pump resistive wire	13 Manifold heater temperature sensor
4 Fuel filter	14 Inlet manifold vacuum port
5 Inlet air temperature senose	15 Fuel/ignition ECU
6 Thermac switch	16 Diagnostic plug
7 Vacuum motor and air flap	17 Inertia switch
8 Fuel pressure regulator	18 Accelerator pedal switch
9 Fuel injector	
10 Idle speed stepper motor	
19 Main fuel system relay	26 Oil pressure switch
20 Oil pressure relay	27 Crankshaft sensor
21 Fuel pump relay	28 Fuel trap
22 Ignition coil	29 Idle solenoid (models with air conditioning)
23 Ambient air temperature sensor	A Regulated fuel pressure
24 Coolant temperature thermistor	B Return fuel
25 Knock sensor	C Inlet airflow
	D Manifold vacuum

One program operates under cruise conditions, and the other at idle. The idle program can be altered completely using electronic test equipment, or partially by using the procedures described in Section 13. Any changes to this program do not affect the cruise program, which cannot be accessed. Whenever the battery is disconnected, the idle program is lost, and the ECU reverts back to a set of nominal parameters until the information is reintroduced into the memory. This can only be done using the manufacturer's test equipment, but the performance of the engine at idle is only marginally affected in this condition. As well as control of the fuel injection system, the ECU is also used to control the ignition timing.

Fuel injector: The single fuel injector is a solenoid-operated ball valve, containing a fine gauze filter and a nozzle wirh six spray holes for complete fuel atomization. When a pulse is received from the ECU, the injector sprays fuel into the air stream through the throttle body.

Throttle potentiometer: The potentiometer is a variable resistor, attached to the throttle shaft on the throttle body. The unit is supplied with a constant input voltage, and as the resistance of the potentiometer varies with throttle shaft movement, the output voltage is proportionally affected. This allows the ECU to determine throttle valve position, and rate of change.

Idle speed stepper motor: This is a small electric motor, having four control windings to enable it to rotate in either direction. Under a signal from the ECU, the stepper motor will rotate in whichever direction is necessary, to open or close the throttle by means of pushrod acting directly against the base idle speed adjusting screw.

Inlet air temperature sensor: Located in the airflow through the air cleaner air box, the sensor is a thermistor (resistive device whose resistance quickly decreases with temperature increase).

Coolant temperature thermistor: This resistive device is screwed into the thermostat housing, where its element is in direct contact with the engine coolant. Changes in coolant temperature are detected by the ECU as a change in the thermistor resistance.

Ambient air temperature sensor: The sensor is located behind the left-hand headlamp, and responds to changes in ambient temperature with a corresponding change in resistance.

Manifold heater: A manifold heater, to improve atomization of the fuel/air mixture during warm-up conditions, is fitted to the underside of the inlet manifold. The heater is of the positive temperature coefficient (PTC) type, in which the current consumption of the heating element is high while it heats up, but is greatly reduced at operating temperature. The unit is controlled by a temperature sensor, screwed into the coolant jacket of the inlet manifold. When coolant temperature reaches 50°C (122°F), the sensor switches the manifold heater off. To avoid a heavy drain on the battery, current for the heater is supplied via the oil pressure switch relay, and consequently only switches on after the engine has started.

Fuel pressure regulator: The fuel pressure regulator is attached to the throttle body, and maintains fuel pressure at a constant 1.0 bar (14.5 lbf/in²). When the pressure exceeds this value, the regulator returns excess fuel to the tank via the fuel return line.

Inertia switch: An inertia switch is fitted in the ignition switch feed to the fuel pump relay, and is situated inside the car behind the left-hand side of the radio cassette player. In the event of sudden impact, the switch trips out, thus switching off the fuel pump relay. The switch can be reset by pressing down the reset button on the switch body.

Relays: The main fuel system relay is energised when the ignition is switched on, and supplies current to the ignition coil and the fuel system ECU. The relay remains energised for approximately five seconds after the ignition is switched off, to enable the stepper motor to cycle to the correct position for engine starting. The fuel pump relay is energised when the oil pressure relay is de-energised by the low oil pressure switch. When the engine is cranking, the fuel pump is fed from the starter solenoid via the de-energised fuel pump relay.

Fuel pump: The fuel pump is a self-priming centrifugal unit, located in the fuel tank, and totally submerged in the fuel. Fuel is supplied under pressure from the pump, through a non-return valve and in-line filter, to the fuel pressure regulator, and then to the fuel injector. The high capacity output of the pump is reduced by a resistive wire in the harness which reduces the supply voltage.

Accelerator pedal switch: When the accelerator pedal is at rest, the pedal switch is closed, and a signal is sent to the ECU indicating that the engine is idling. On receipt of this information, the ECU selects the idle program from its memory, and automatic idle speed control via the stepper motor is implemented.

The fuel injection system works in the following way. When the ignition is switched on, voltage is supplied to the main fuel system relay and to the ECU. The ECU relay is energised and voltage is supplied to the fuel injector, the ignition coil and to the stepper motor. This causes the stepper motor to cycle to the fast idle position (providing that the engine has cooled since last being run), and the throttle is opened by the stepper motor pushrod.

When the starter is operated, voltage is supplied to the fuel pump via the starter solenoid, and the various sensors send data on engine cranking speed, coolant temperarure, inlet air temperature and manifold pressure. From this data, the ECU calculates the amount of fuel required and the injector opening time. To provide fuel enrichment for starting, the injector-open time is extended above the normal rate for idling, but the number of pulses in which the injector opens are limited, to prevent flooding.

Once the engine starts and the solenoid is released, the ECU senses from the crankshaft sensor that the engine speed is in excess of 400 rpm. As the oil pressure builds up, the oil pressure switch opens, and the fuel pump relay is activated. The pump is now supplied with a lower voltage through the resistive wire in the harness. The open oil pressure switch also activates the manifold heater, which will operate until the coolant temperature reaches 50°C (122°F). Until the ambient air temperature sensor senses that air temperature has reached 14°C (57°F) the ECU will continue to extend the injector-open time to improve cold drivability.

During the warm-up period, the engine fast idle speed is controlled by the stepper motor. As the ECU senses engine temperature rise via the coolant thermistor, the stepper motor is allowed to progressively return to the idle speed setting. Should engine speed drop by more than 15 rpm from the idle setting, due for example to an additional electrical load on the alternator, the stepper motor will be operated to maintain a stabilised setting.

During normal driving, the ECU constantly monitors engine condition via the various sensors, and when a change in one or more of the input parameters is detected, the ECU program enters a sub-routine to determine the injector-open duration required. When the engine is accelerating, extra injector pulses are generated to compensate for throttle movement. Should the engine speed exceed 6700 rpm, the ECU will cut off the injector pulses until the speed falls to 6400 rpm, at which time they will gradually be re-instated.

When the engine is being restarted in a hot condition, the ECU provides extra fuel for two seconds after starting, and fast idle is instated via the stepper motor. This will counteract the possible effects of fuel vaporisation, and prevent engine stalling.

Under conditions of abrupt deceleration or impact, the inertia switch trips out, and breaks the supply voltage to the fuel pump relay. This cuts off the fuel supply, stops the engine and reduces the fire hazard.

11 Engine tuning – procedure

1   Before making any changes to the settings of the fuel injection system, ensure that the spark plug gaps are correctly set, the air cleaner element is clean, there are no leaks in the exhaust system, and the ignition system is operating correctly. Ensure that all breather and vacuum hoses are connected, and that none are perished or kinked.
2   Temperature effects, and engine and transmission oil drag, can adversely influence the base idle speed setting, and it is important that the following warm-up procedure is adopted before attempting any adjustments.
3   Drive the car on the road for approximately two to four miles, dependent on summer or winter conditions, in a normal manner, without excessive load, engine speed or road speed.
4   Return the car to the working area, switch off and connect a tachometer, following the equipment manufacturer's instructions.
5   Start the engine again, and run it at 2000 rpm for ten seconds to stabilise the mixture. The adjustment procedure described in the following Section can now commence. If during the procedure the cooling fan operates, or if adjustment is not completed within two minutes, accelerate the engine to 2000 rpm again, by means of the throttle linkage (not the accelerator pedal) and hold this speed for a further ten seconds. Repeat this every two minutes until the adjustments are completed.

12 Base idle speed and mixture – adjustment

Note: *The function of the fuel injection system is such that the base idle speed and idle mixture settings are controlled by the electronic control unit, and of these two, only the base idle speed can be adjusted without the use of the manufacturer's test equipment. The idle mixture setting will not normally require attention unless the battery is disconnected, in which case the settings in the ECU memory will be lost. If the battery is disconnected for any reason, the ECU can be recalibrated using the procedure described in Section 13 as a temporary measure. Should poor idle quality be experienced, the base idle speed should be checked, and if necessary adjusted, using the following procedure. If the idle quality is still poor after adjustment, the idle mixture should be checked by a dealer.*
1   Refer to the information contained in Section 11 before starting.
2   Switch off the engine, and ensure also that all electrical circuits are switched off throughout the procedure.
3   Undo the five bolts and lift off the air cleaner air box. Place the air box alongside the engine, without disconnecting any of the hoses or ducts.
4   Operate the throttle by hand, and check that it opens fully and returns to rest against the stepper motor pushrod.
5   Start the engine and using the throttle linkage, not the accelerator pedal, increase the engine speed to 1200 rpm, and hold it at this speed. Check that the stepper motor pushrod has retracted fully, then disconnect the stepper motor multi-plug (the round plug on the side of the throttle body below the accelerator cable).
6   Release the throttle and allow the engine to stabilise at idle speed.
7   Check the engine base idle speed on the tachometer, and compare the reading with the figure given in the Specifications. If adjustment is required, slacken the adjusting screw locknut and turn the adjusting

screw as necessary to obtain the correct setting (photos). Tighten the locknut when the speed is correct.

8 Check the lost motion gap by inserting a feeler gauge of the specified size between the forked end of the throttle lever and the peg on the linkage (photo). If the gap requires adjustment, slacken the accelerator cable locknuts and reposition the outer cable until the correct setting is achieved (photo). Tighten the locknuts when the gap is correct.

9 Reconnect the stepper motor multi-plug.

10 Switch off the ignition, wait three seconds and switch the ignition on once more. After a further three seconds, switch off the ignition again. The stepper motor will now be in the correct position for the next engine start.

11 On cars equipped with automatic transmission, refer to Chapter 7 and check the kickdown cable adjustment.

12 Refit the air cleaner air box on completion.

13 Electronic control unit – calibration

Note: *Whenever the battery is disconnected, the idle mixture setting stored in the ECU memory will be lost. On reconnection of the battery,*

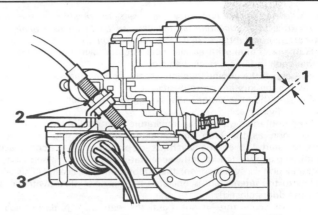

Fig. 3.6 Base idle speed adjustment (Sec 12)

1 Lost motion gap
2 Accelerator cable locknuts for lost motion gap adjustment
3 Stepper motor multi-plug
4 Base idle speed adjusting screw

12.7A Slacken the base idle speed adjusting screw locknut ...

12.7B ... and turn the adjusting screw (arrowed) to obtain the correct setting

12.8A Insert a feeler gauge between the throttle lever and peg ...

12.8B ... then adjust the lost motion gap at the accelerator cable

the following procedure may be used to recalibrate the unit temporarily, until such time as the car can be taken to a dealer for accurate setting on Rover dedicated test equipment.

1   Run the engine with all electrical circuits switched off, until the engine cooling fan operates then stops.
2   Switch off the engine immediately the cooling fan stops.
3   Switch the ignition on to position two of the key.
4   Depress the accelerator pedal through at least half its travel, then release it, five times.
5   Wait until the high engine temperature warning light starts to flash.
6   As soon as the high engine temperature warning light stops flashing, start the engine **without depressing the accelerator pedal,** and allow it to idle. If the accelerator pedal is depressed, or if an electrical unit is switched on, the calibration will cease. (This also applies to the interior lights operated by the door pillar switches, so keep the doors closed).
7   Wait for two to three minutes until the warning light flashes again, indicating that calibration is complete.

14 Thermac switch – removal and refitting

1   Refer to Section 3 and remove the air cleaner air box.
2   Disconnect the two vacuum hoses at the thermac switch on the base of the air box (photo).
3   Remove the air box intake trunking for access to the switch.
4   Carefully prise off the switch retaining clip, and remove the switch from inside the air box.
5   Refitting is the reverse sequence to removal, but position the unit so that the large diameter pipe is towards the air temperature sensor. Connect the vacuum hose from the manifold to the pipe with the small diameter hole, and the vacuum hose from the air cleaner vacuum motor to the pipe with the large diameter hole.

15 Inlet air temperature sensor – removal and refitting

1   Refer to Section 3 and remove the air cleaner air box.
2   Unscrew the sensor from the adaptor on the base of the air box. If

the adaptor unscrews with the sensor, unscrew the adaptor and refit it to the air box.
3   Refit the sensor to the adaptor, and refit the air box.

16 Throttle potentiometer – removal and refitting

1   Refer to Section 3 and remove the air cleaner air box.
2   Disconnect the multi-plug from the side of the potentiometer body.
3   Using a dab of paint, mark the position of the throttle potentiometer in relation to the mounting adaptor.
4   Undo the two screws, remove the potentiometer, and lift off the adaptor (photo).
5   Refitting is the reverse sequence to removal. Ensure that the potentiometer lever engages to the right of the throttle lever, and align the previously-made mark before tightening the retaining screws.
6   Have the potentiometer position adjusted accurately by a Rover dealer on completion.

17 Injector housing – removal and refitting

1   Refer to Section 4, paragraphs 1 to 3 inclusive, and carry out the operations described to release the fuel system pressure. Tighten the fuel filter banjo union bolt after the pressure has been released.
2   Refer to Section 3 and remove the air cleaner air box.
3   Using pliers, release the two fuel hose retaining clips at the injector housing, and disconnect the two hoses (photos). Plug the hoses after removal.
4   Disconnect the injector wiring multi-plug.
5   Undo the four screws securing the injector housing to the throttle body, and lift off the housing (photos). The housing may be initially tight, due to the two locating dowels. Recover the gasket from the throttle body.
6   This is the limit of dismantling that can be undertaken on the injector housing assembly. Should it be necessary to renew the fuel injector or fuel pressure regulator, a complete injector housing assembly must be obtained.
7   Clean the mating faces of the injector housing and throttle body,

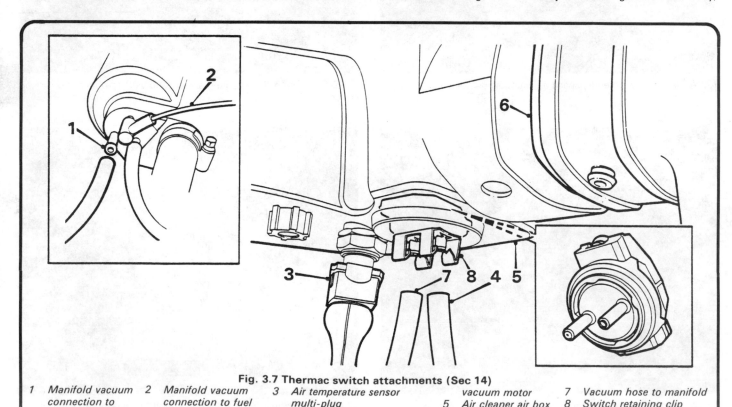

Fig. 3.7 Thermac switch attachments (Sec 14)

1 *Manifold vacuum connection to thermac switch*	2 *Manifold vacuum connection to fuel trap and ECU*	3 *Air temperature sensor multi-plug*	*vacuum motor*	7 *Vacuum hose to manifold*
		4 *Vacuum hose-to-air cleaner*	5 *Air cleaner air box*	8 *Switch retaining clip*
			6 *Intake trunking*	

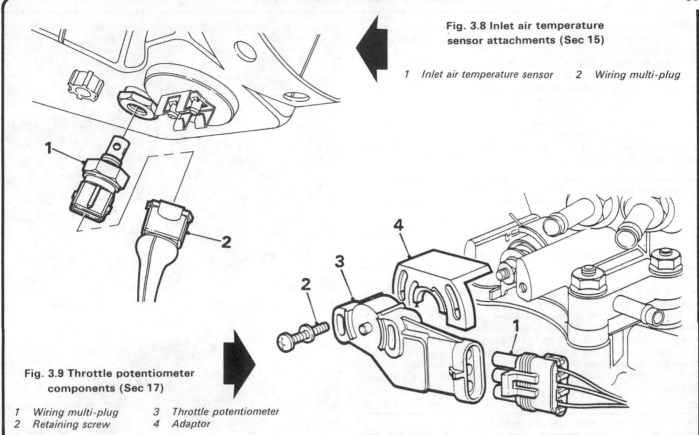

Fig. 3.8 Inlet air temperature
sensor attachments (Sec 15)

1   Inlet air temperature sensor   2   Wiring multi-plug

Fig. 3.9 Throttle potentiometer
components (Sec 17)

1   Wiring multi-plug   3   Throttle potentiometer
2   Retaining screw   4   Adaptor

14.2 Thermac switch vacuum hoses
(arrowed)

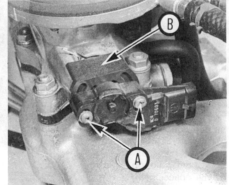

16.4 Throttle potentiometer retaining
screws (A) and adaptor (B)

17.3A Release the fuel hose retaining clips
(arrowed) ...

17.3B ... and disconnect the two hoses

17.5A Undo the four injector housing
retaining screws (arrowed) ...

17.5B ... and lift off the housing

and remove all the old locking compound from the threads of the retaining screws. Obtain a new gasket if the original shows any signs of deterioration.

8 Place the gasket in position on the throttle body, and locate the injector housing over the gasket.

9 Apply a thread-locking compound to the four retaining screws, then fit and tighten the screws securely.

10 Reconnect the injector wiring multi-plug.

11 Reconnect the two fuel hoses, then locate the retaining clips 3.0 mm (0.12 in) from the hose ends.

12 Refit the air cleaner air box, then adjust the base idle speed as described in Section 12.

18 Stepper motor unit – removal and refitting

1 Refer to Section 17 and remove the injector housing.

2 Disconnect the wiring multi-plug from the side of the stepper motor.

3 Undo the four outermost screws that secure the stepper motor to the throttle body (photo). Do not remove the two screws near the centre of the unit.

4 Lift off the accelerator cable support bracket, with cable still attached, and place it to one side.

5 Carefully lift off the stepper motor unit (photo), and where fitted. recover the gasket. Note that the gasket was only fitted to early models, and if present, discard it, and do not fit another on reassembly.

6 Clean the components with a clean cloth, and remove all the old locking compound from the threads of the retaining screws.

7 Refitting is the reverse sequence to removal, but use a thread-locking compound on the retaining screw threads.

19 Throttle body – removal and refitting

1 Refer to Section 17 and remove the injector housing.

2 Disconnect the wiring multi-plugs to the stepper motor and throttle potentiometer.

3 Disconnect the two breather hoses on the side of the throttle body (photo).

4 Slacken the accelerator cable locknuts, open the throttle fully and slip the cable end out of the throttle cam. Unscrew the lower cable locknut fully, and remove the accelerator cable from the support bracket.

5 On automatic transmission models, disconnect the kickdown cable, using the same procedure as for the accelerator cable.

6 Undo the four nuts securing the throttle body to the manifold.

7 Lift off the throttle body, and recover the manifold spacer, with gaskets.

8 Clean the mating faces on the manifold and throttle body, and renew the gaskets on the spacer if they show any sign of deterioration. If the gaskets are being renewed, attach them to the spacer using non-drying jointing compound.

9 Place the spacer with gaskets over the manifold studs, then place the throttle body in position. Secure the throttle body with the four nuts tightened securely.

10 Reconnect the breather hoses and the wiring multi-plugs.

11 Refit the accelerator cable and adjust it, by means of the locknuts, to give a small amount of free play in the throttle-closed position.

12 On automatic transmission models, refit and adjust the kickdown cable as described in Chapter 7.

13 Refer to Section 17 and refit the injector housing.

20 Electronic control unit – removal and refitting

1 Disconnect the battery negative terminal. (Refer to Chapter 12, Section 1, before doing this).

2 Disconnect the wiring multi-plug from the ECU, which is located on the left-hand side of the engine compartment behind the battery. To do this, press the retaining tab upwards, release the bottom of the multi-plug, then disengage the top lug (photo).

3 Disconnect the vacuum supply hose.

4 Undo the two retaining screws, disengage the locating lug and remove the unit from its mounting bracket.

18.3 Undo the four stepper motor retaining screws (arrowed) ...

18.5 ... and lift off the stepper motor unit

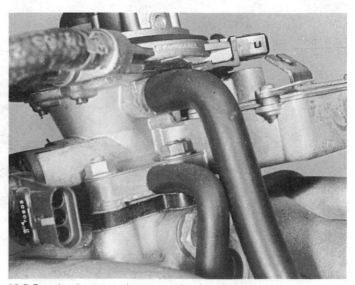

19.3 Breather hose attachments at the throttle body

5   Refitting is the reverse sequence to removal.

21 Resonator unit – removal and refitting

1   Apply the handbrake, jack up the front of the car and support it on axle stands.
2   Undo the two screws and one bolt securing the access panel to the underside of the front wheel arch on the left-hand side.
3   Disengage the access panel from the front spoiler, and remove it from under the car.
4   Undo the two bolts and withdraw the resonator from under the front wheel arch.
5   Remove the spacers and rubber mountings from the resonator.
6   Refitting is the reverse sequence to removal.

22 Inertia switch – removal and refitting

1   From inside the car, remove the stud from the centre console side cover on the left-hand side, and remove the cover.
2   Undo the two screws securing the inertia switch to the mounting plate, disconnect the wiring multi-plug and remove the switch.
3   Check the operation of the switch by striking the forward-facing side hard against the palm of your hand. The setting button should trip out when this is done. If not, renew the switch.
4   Refitting is the reverse sequence to removal. Press the button down to reset the switch after installation.

23 Manifold heater – removal and refitting

1   Disconnect the battery negative terminal. (Refer to Chapter 12, Section 1, before doing this).
2   Refer to Section 3 and remove the air cleaner air box.

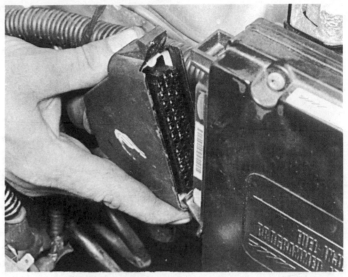

20.2 Disconnect the ECU wiring multi-plug

3   Refer to Section 4, paragraphs 1 to 3 inclusive, and carry out the operations described to release the fuel system pressure. Tighten the fuel filter banjo union bolt after the pressure has been released.
4   Release the clips and disconnect the two fuel hoses at the injector housing.
5   Disconnect the manifold heater wiring connector.
6   Undo the two bolts securing the fuel pipe clips and the heater to the manifold, and move the pipes aside (photo).
7   Undo the remaining heater retaining bolt.
8   Open the throttle fully, and remove the heater by pushing down with a long screwdriver through the throttle aperture.

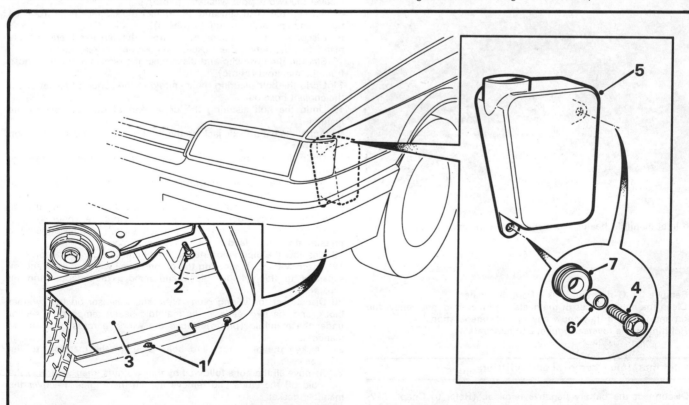

Fig. 3.10 Resonator unit location and mountings (Sec 21)

1	Access panel retaining screws	2	Access panel retaining bolt	4	Resonator unit retaining bolt	6	Spacer
		3	Access panel	5	Resonator unit	7	Rubber mounting

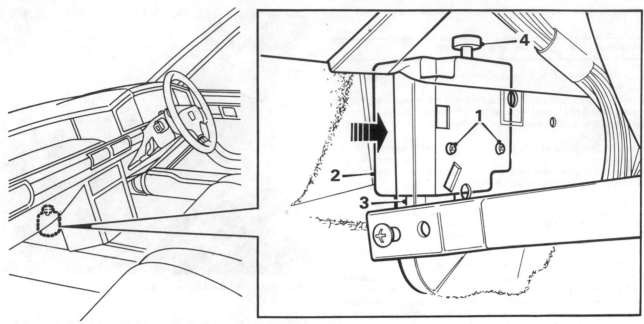

Fig. 3.11 Inertia switch location and mountings (Sec 22)

1 *Switch retaining screws*   2 *Inertia switch*   3 *Wiring multi-plug*   4 *Setting button*

23.6 Inlet manifold heater and fuel pipe clip retaining bolts

9 Remove the O-ring and gasket from the heater.
10 Clean the mating faces of the heater and manifold, and renew the gasket and O-ring if they show any sign of deterioration.
11 Refitting is the reverse sequence to removal.

24 Inlet manifold – removal and refitting

1 Disconnect the battery negative terminal. (Refer to Chapter 12, Section 1, before doing this).
2 Refer to Section 3 and remove the air cleaner air box.
3 Refer to Section 4, paragraphs 1 to 3 inclusive, and carry out the operations described to release the fuel system pressure. Tighten the filter banjo union bolt after the pressure has been released.

4 Release the hose clips and disconnect the two fuel hoses from the fuel pipes (photo).
5 Refer to Section 19 and remove the throttle body.
6 Refer to Chapter 2 and drain the cooling system.
7 Undo the brake servo banjo hose union at the manifold, and recover the two copper washers (photo).
8 Slacken the hose clip and disconnect the coolant hose from the right-hand end of the manifold (photo).
9 Disconnect the vacuum hoses from the left-hand end of the manifold, after noting their respective positions for reassembly.
10 Slacken the hose clip and disconnect the remaining coolant hose from the manifold (photo).
11 Undo the bolt securing the manifold to the support bracket under the coolant hose outlet.
12 Undo the bolt securing the upper end of the stay bar to the manifold.
13 Apply the handbrake, jack up the front of the car and support it on axle stands.
14 Undo the manifold stay bar lower retaining bolt and remove the stay (photo).
15 Release the clip and disconnect the breather hose from the oil separator (photo).
16 Disconnect the breather hose from the lower end of the oil separator at the cylinder block, and at the sump outlet (photos).
17 Disconnect the lead at the oil pressure switch and disconnect the pressure transducer lead at the wiring connector.
18 Unscrew the pipe union nut at the oil pressure switch adaptor.
19 Unscrew the bolt securing the oil pressure switch adaptor and oil separator to the cylinder block and remove the adaptor and oil separator.
20 Disconnect the wiring plug at the knock sensor on the cylinder block, and the two leads at the manifold heater temperature sensor under the manifold (photo). Move the wiring harness clear of the manifold.
21 Slacken the nine nuts and bolts securing the manifold to the cylinder head.
22 Remove all the bolts followed by the two nuts, then withdraw the manifold off the studs and remove it from the engine. Recover the manifold gasket.
23 Clean the manifold and cylinder head mating faces, and obtain a new gasket if the sealing lips of the original are in any way damaged.
24 Refitting is the reverse sequence to removal, but tighten the manifold retaining nuts and bolts in the sequence shown in Fig. 3.13, to the specified torque.

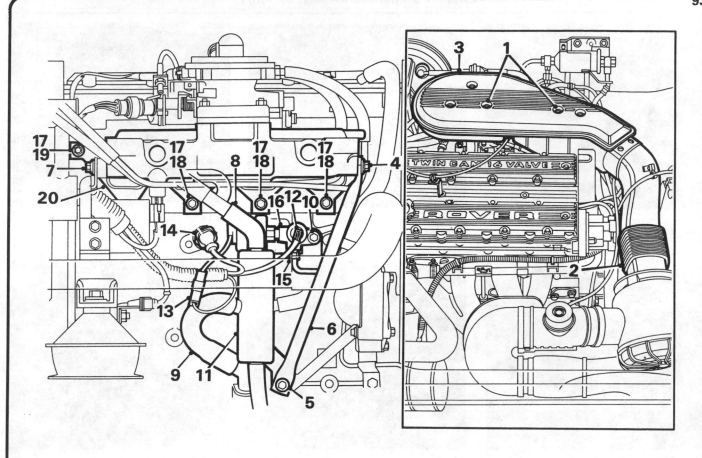

Fig. 3.12 Inlet manifold and related component attachments (Sec 24)

1 Air box retaining bolts
2 Intake trunking
3 Air box
4 Stay bar upper retaining bolt
5 Stay bar lower retaining bolt
6 Manifold stay bar
7 Manifold-to-support bracket bolt
8 Breather hose
9 Breather hose
10 Oil pressure switch adaptor, and oil separator retaining bolt
11 Oil separator
12 Oil pressure switch lead
13 Oil pressure transducer lead
14 Knock sensor wiring plug
15 Oil pipe union nut
16 Oil pressure switch adaptor
17 Manifold retaining nuts and bolts
18 Manifold bolt locations
19 Manifold nut locations
20 Manifold gasket

24.4 Release the clips and disconnect the fuel hoses

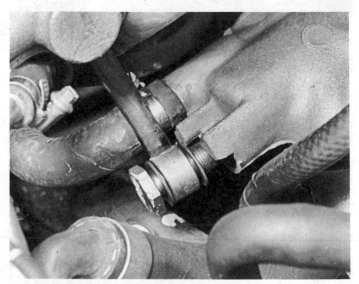

24.7 Undo the brake servo vacuum hose union

24.8 Disconnect the manifold right-hand coolant hose

24.10 Disconnect the remaining coolant hose from the manifold

24.14 Manifold stay bar lower retaining bolt location (arrowed)

24.15 Disconnect the breather hose (A) from the oil separator (B)

24.16A Disconnect the breather hose at the cylinder block ...

24.16B ... and at the sump

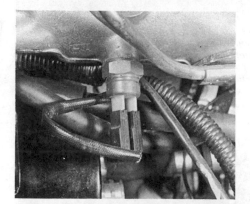

24.20 Disconnect the leads at the manifold heater temperature sensor

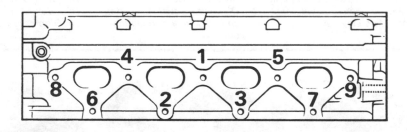

Fig. 3.13 Inlet manifold nut and bolt tightening sequence
(Sec 24)

25 Exhaust manifold – removal and refitting

1 Disconnect the battery negative terminal. (Refer to Chapter 12, Section 1, before doing this).
2 Refer to Section 3 and remove the air cleaner components as necessary to provide total access to the front and side of the engine.
3 Drain the cooling system as described in Chapter 2.
4 Remove the dipstick from the dipstick tube.
5 Remove the distributor cap and place it to one side.
6 Apply the handbrake, jack up the front of the car and support it on axle stands.
7 Undo the four bolts securing the exhaust front pipe flange to the manifold (photo). Separate the flange and recover the gasket (photo).
8 Undo the bolts on both sides securing the two halves of the manifold stove together, and remove the outer half (photos).
9 Undo the bolt securing the heater bypass pipe to the cylinder head

and to the main coolant pipe support bracket (photos).
10 Slacken the clip securing the bypass pipe connecting hose to the thermostat housing.
11 Undo the five nuts and bolts securing the manifold to the cylinder head, noting that the upper nut also secures the bypass pipe bracket (photo).
12 Release the connecting hose from the thermostat housing, and withdraw the bypass pipe from the manifold stud.
13 Remove the manifold from the cylinder head, followed by the inner half of the stove and the manifold gasket (photos).
14 Clean the manifold and cylinder head mating faces, and obtain a new gasket if the original is in any way damaged.
15 Refitting is the reverse sequence to removal, but tighten the manifold retaining nuts and bolts in the sequence shown in Fig. 3.15, to the specified torque. Make sure that the inner half of the stove is in position before fitting the manifold.

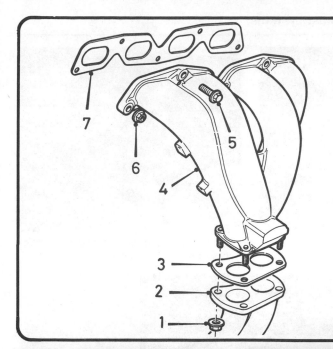

Fig. 3.14 Exhaust manifold attachments (Sec 25)

1 Front pipe flange retaining nuts
2 Front pipe
3 Flange gasket
4 Exhaust manifold
5 Retaining bolts
6 Retaining nuts
7 Manifold gasket

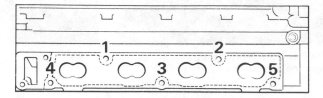

Fig. 3.15 Exhaust manifold nut and bolt tightening sequence (Sec 25)

25.7A Undo the front pipe-to-manifold flange retaining bolts ...

25.7B ... and recover the gasket

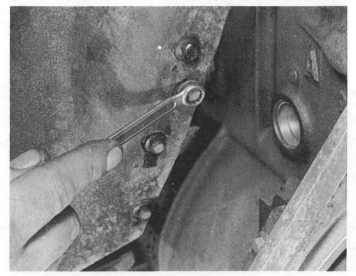

25.8A Undo the bolts on both sides of the manifold stove ...

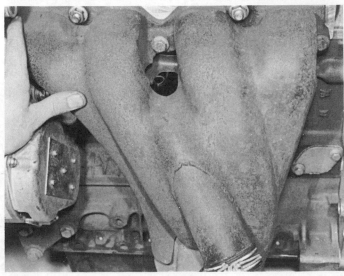

25.8B ... and remove the stove outer half

25.9A Undo the bolt securing the bypass pipe to the cylinder head (arrowed) ...

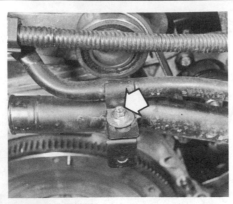

25.9B ... and to the main coolant pipe bracket (arrowed)

25.11 Undo the nut securing the front of the bypass pipe to the manifold

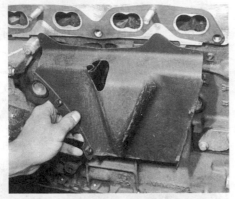

25.13A Remove the inner half of the manifold stove ...

25.13B ... and the exhaust manifold gasket

26 Exhaust system – checking, removal and refitting

1   The exhaust system should be examined for leaks, damage and security at regular intervals (see *Routine maintenance*). To do this, apply the handbrake, and allow the engine to idle in a well-ventilated area. Lie down on each side of the car in turn, and check the full length of the system for leaks, while an assistant temporarily places a wad of cloth over the end of the tailpipe. If a leak is evident, stop the engine and use a proprietary repair kit to seal it. If the leak is excessive, or damage is evident, renew the section. Check the rubber mountings for deterioration, and renew them if necessary.
2   To remove the system, raise the vehicle by means of axle stands or ramps to provide adequate working clearance underneath.
3   To remove the rear section, undo the three nuts securing the rear section to the intermediate section at the flange joint, and separate the joint (photo). Recover the flange gasket. Disengage the rubber

mountings at the side and rear (photos), and remove the section from under the car.
4   To remove the intermediate section, undo the nuts securing the intermediate section to the front and rear sections at the flange joints (photo), and separate the joints. Recover the flange gaskets. Disengage the side rubber mountings and remove the section from under the car (photo).
5   To remove the front section, undo the nuts securing the front section to the manifold and intermediate section, separate the flange joints and remove the section from under the car. Recover the flange gaskets.
6   If necessary, the front and rear heat shields can be removed after removing the relevant exhaust section, then undoing the heat shield retaining bolts.
7   Refitting is the reverse sequence to removal, but use new gaskets if the originals show any sign of deterioration. Tighten the flange retaining nuts to the specified torque.

26.3A Exhaust rear section flange joint ...

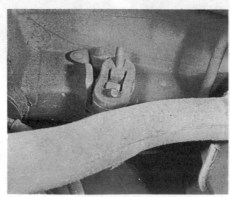

26.3B ... side rubber mounting ...

26.3C ... and rear rubber mounting

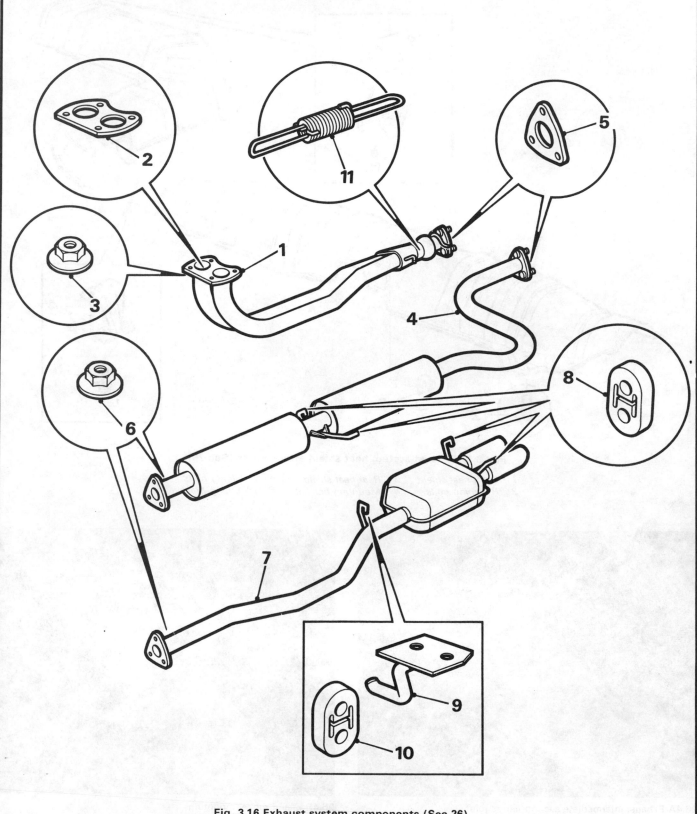

Fig. 3.16 Exhaust system components (Sec 26)

1	Front pipe	5	Flange gasket	9	Mounting bracket
2	Flange gasket	6	Locknut	10	Rubber mounting
3	Locknut	7	Rear section	11	Tensioning spring
4	Intermediate section	8	Rubber mountings		

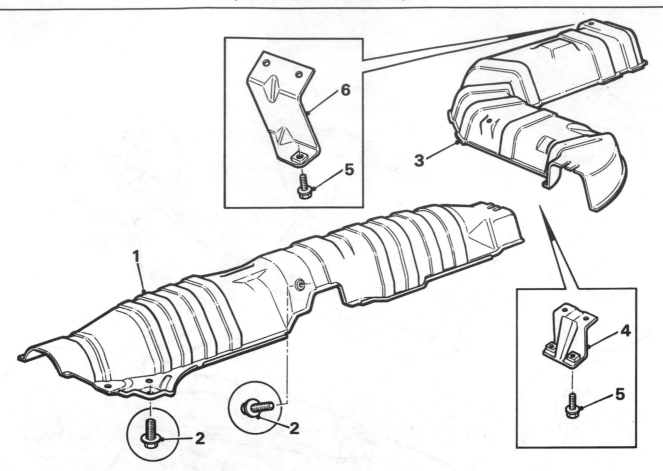

Fig. 3.17 Exhaust system heat shield attachments (Sec 26)

1 Front heat shield	3 Rear heat shield	5 Retaining bolts
2 Retaining bolts	4 Mounting bracket	6 Mounting bracket

26.4A Exhaust intermediate section flange joint ...

26.4B ... and rubber mountings

27 Fault diagnosis – fuel and exhaust systems (single-point fuel injection system)

Owing to the complexity of the electronic circuitry, and the nature of the computer-controlled operation, special test equipment has been developed for fault diagnosis on the fuel injection system. Therefore, any suspected faults on the system or its related components should be referred to a suitably-equipped Rover dealer.

PART B:
MULTI-POINT FUEL INJECTION SYSTEM

28 General description

The fuel system used on Rover 820i and Si models consists of a centrally-mounted fuel tank, electric fuel pump and indirect multi-point fuel injection (MPi) system, together with its related electrical and mechanical components. A more detailed description of the MPi system is contained in Section 37.

The exhaust system consists of a front, intermediate and rear section, suspended from the underbody on rubber mountings, and bolted to a cast iron manifold at the front. A ball-and-socket universal joint is incorporated in the front section, to allow for engine and exhaust system movement.

Warning: *Many of the procedures in this Chapter entail the removal of fuel pipes and connections, which may result in some fuel spillage. Before carrying out any operations on the fuel system, refer to the precautions given in* Safety first! *at the beginning of this manual and follow them implicitly. Petrol is a highly dangerous and volatile liquid, and the precautions necessary when handling it cannot be overstressed.*

29 Maintenance and inspection

1 At the intervals given in *Routine maintenance* at the beginning of this manual, carry out the following service operations on the fuel and exhaust system components.
2 With the car raised on a vehicle lift, or securely supported on axle stands, carefully inspect the fuel pipes, hoses and unions for chafing, leaks, and corrosion. Renew any pipes that are severely pitted with corrosion, or in any way damaged. Renew any hoses that show signs of cracking or other deterioration.
3 Check the security of the fuel tank mountings, and check the tank for signs of corrosion or damage. Refer to Section 34 if the tank condition is suspect.
4 Check the condition of exhaust system as described in Section 53.
5 From within the engine compartment, check the security of all fuel hose attachments, and inspect the fuel hoses and vacuum hoses for kinks, chafing or deterioration.
6 Renew the air cleaner element, and clean the air cleaner body and cover, as described in Section 30.
7 Check the operation of the accelerator linkage, and lubricate the linkage, cable and pedal pivot with a few drops of oil.
8 Renew the fuel filter as described in Section 31.
9 Check the fuel injection system base idle speed and mixture settings as described in Section 39.

30 Air cleaner and element – removal and refitting

1 To renew the air cleaner element, disconnect the vacuum hose from the air cleaner body cover (photo), release the retaining spring clips and lift off the cover.
2 Withdraw the element from the body, and bend it upwards to clear the front body panel.
3 Using a clean rag, wipe out the inside of the body and cover.
4 Carefully fit the new element, ensuring that its centre is located over the lip at the base of the air cleaner body.
5 Refit the cover and clip it into place.
6 To remove the complete air cleaner assembly, slacken the hose clip and disconnect the air trunking at the throttle housing (photo).
7 Disconnect the airflow meter wiring connector, and release the cable from the support clip.
8 Undo the two air cleaner body and airflow meter support bracket bolts, and the two bolts securing the forward air trunking to its support bracket (photo).
9 Withdraw the air cleaner body, complete with airflow meter and forward air trunking, release the trunking from the connecting duct at the front of the car, and remove the assembly from the engine compartment.
10 If the cold air side intake is to be removed, refer to Chapter 12 and remove the battery.
11 Undo the bolt securing the side intake to the body, and remove the intake and duct.
12 Refitting is the reverse sequence to removal, but ensure that all the ducts and trunking are fully engaged before tightening the various retaining bolts.

31 Fuel filter – removal and refitting

Note: *Refer to the warning note in Section 28 before proceeding.*
1 Disconnect the battery negative terminal.
2 Place absorbent rags around the fuel filter outlet union banjo bolt, then slowly unscrew the bleed screw in the centre of the bolt to release the fuel system pressure. Tighten the bleed screw when the pressure is released.
3 Unscrew the filter inlet and outlet union banjo bolts, and recover the copper washers.
4 Undo the filter bracket retaining nuts and remove the filter.
5 Refitting is the reverse sequence to removal, but use new copper washers on the banjo unions.

32 Fuel pump – removal and refitting

Note: *Refer to the warning note in Section 28 before proceeding.*
1 Disconnect the battery negative terminal.
2 Release the fuel system pressure as described in Section 31, paragraph 2.
3 Remove the floor carpet from the luggage compartment.
4 Refer to Chapter 11 and remove the rear seats.
5 Release the eight studs and remove the seat squab backing from the body.
6 Release the two studs and remove the luggage compartment backboard from the body.

30.1 Disconnect the vacuum hose at the air cleaner body cover

30.6 Disconnect the air trunking at the throttle housing

30.8 Forward air trunking-to-support bracket bolt

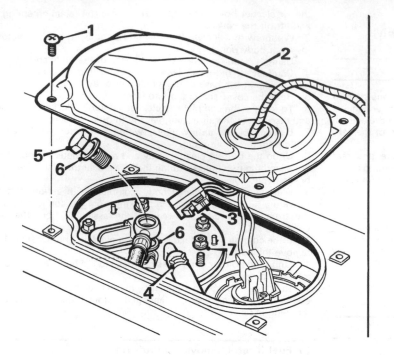
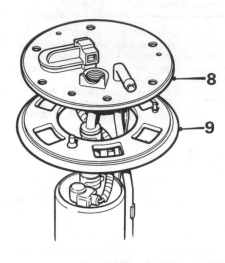

Fig. 3.18 Fuel pump and related component attachments (Sec 32)

1 Access panel retaining screws	4 Fuel return hose	7 Pump retaining nuts
2 Access panel	5 Fuel feed hose banjo union bolt	8 Fuel pump
3 Pump wiring multi-plug	6 Copper washers	9 Pump seal

7 Remove the cover board over the spare wheel, and remove the tool kit.

8 Undo the four screws and lift off the pump access panel. Move the panel to one side.

9 Disconnect the pump wiring multi-plug, then unscrew the fuel hose banjo union bolt and recover the copper washers.

10 Slacken the clip and disconnect the fuel return hose.

11 Undo the pump retaining nuts, and withdraw the pump from the tank. Remove the seal from the pump flange.

12 Refitting is the reverse sequence to removal, but renew the flange seal if it shows any sign of deterioration.

33 Fuel gauge sender unit – removal and refitting

Note: *Refer to the warning note in Section 28 before proceeding.*

1 Follow the procedure given in Section 32, paragraphs 1 to 8 inclusive, with the exception of paragraph 2.

2 Disconnect the two leads at the sender unit.

3 Engage a screwdriver, flat bar or other suitable tool with the lugs of the locking ring, and turn the ring anti-clockwise to release it.

4 Withdraw the locking ring, seal and sender unit.

5 Refitting is the reverse sequence to removal, but renew the seal if it shows any sign of deterioration.

34 Fuel tank – removal and refitting

Note: *Refer to the warning note in Section 28 before proceeding.*

1 Follow the procedure given in Section 32, paragraphs 1 to 8 inclusive.

2 Disconnect the fuel pump wiring multi-plug, and the two leads at the fuel gauge sender unit.

3 Remove the fuel tank filler cap.

4 With suitable sealed containers handy, undo the drain plug at the base of the tank, and drain the fuel into the containers. Recover the drain plug sealing washer. When all the fuel has drained, refit the plug, using a new sealing washer if necessary.

5 Chock the front wheel, prise off the rear wheel trim and slacken the

wheel nuts. Jack up the rear of the car and support it on axle stands. Remove the left-hand rear roadwheel.

6 Slacken the retaining clip and disconnect the filler hose from the filler neck. Move the hose aside.

7 Slacken the retaining clips and disconnect the five breather hoses from the breather pipes.

8 Refer to Section 53 and remove the exhaust system rear and intermediate sections, together with the rear heat shield.

9 Slacken the retaining clip and disconnect the fuel return hose from the pipe on the side of the tank. Plug the disconnected pipe and hose.

10 Undo the union connector and disconnect the fuel feed hose from the pipe. Plug the disconnected pipe and hose.

11 Support the tank on a jack with interposed block of wood.

12 Slacken the two tank retaining strap locknuts (photo), release the hook bolts from the body slots, and move the straps clear.

13 Lower the tank and remove it from under the car.

14 If the tank is contaminated with sediment or water, remove the sender unit as described in Section 34, and swill the tank out with clean fuel. If the tank is damaged, or leaks, it should be repaired by a specialist, or alternatively renewed. **Do not** *under any circumstances solder or weld the tank.*

15 Refitting is the reverse sequence to removal.

35 Accelerator cable – removal and refitting

1 Open the throttle fully by hand, and slip the inner cable end out of the slot on the throttle lever (photo).

2 Slacken the outer cable locknuts, and unscrew the outer locknut, nearest to the cable end, fully.

3 Remove the washer and rubber bush, then withdraw the cable from the support bracket.

4 From inside the car, release the turnbuckles and lift out the trim panel over the clutch, brake and accelerator pedals.

5 Prise the retaining clip from the top of the accelerator pedal, and disconnect the inner cable.

6 Release the cable from the engine compartment bulkhead, and from the support clips, and withdraw the complete cable from the car.

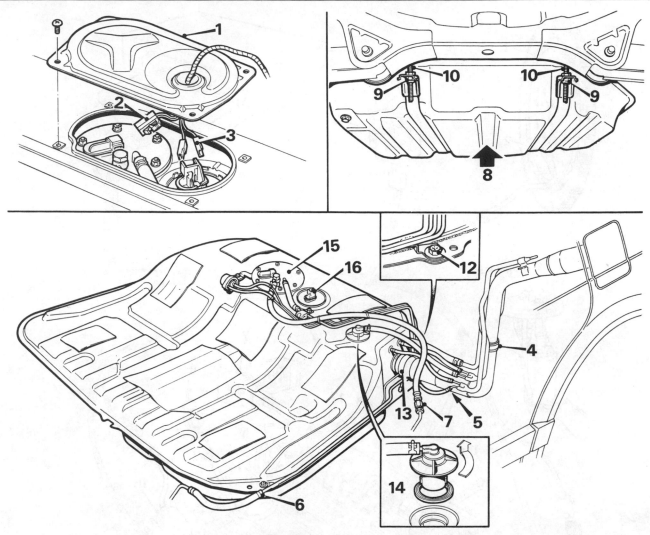

Fig. 3.19 Fuel tank components and mountings (Sec 34)

1	Fuel pump access panel	5	Breather hose
2	Pump wiring multi-plug	6	Fuel return hose
3	Sender unit wiring	7	Fuel feed hose union
4	Filler hose-to-filler neck connection	8	Fuel tank
		9	Retaining strap locknuts

10	Hook bolts	14	Cut-off valve
12	Breather pipe support bracket	15	Fuel pump
13	Filler hose-to-tank connection	16	Fuel gauge sender unit

35.1 Accelerator cable end fitting attachment at the throttle lever (A) and outer cable locknuts (B)

7   Refitting is the reverse sequence to removal. Adjust the cable initially by means of the outer cable locknuts, to give a small amount of free play with the throttle closed. On completion, check the base idle speed as described in Section 39.

36 Accelerator pedal – removal and refitting

Refer to Part A, Section 9.

37 Multi-point fuel injection system – description and operation

The multi-point fuel injection (MPi) system is a microprocessor-controlled fuel management system, designed to overcome the limitations associated with conventional carburettor induction. This is achieved by continuously monitoring the engine using various sensors, whose data is input to the fuel system electronic control unit (ECU). Based on this information, the ECU program and memory then determine the exact amount of fuel necessary, which is then injected directly into the inlet manifold, for all actual and anticipated driving conditions.

The main components of the system are shown in Figs. 3.20 and 3.21, and their individual operation is as follows.

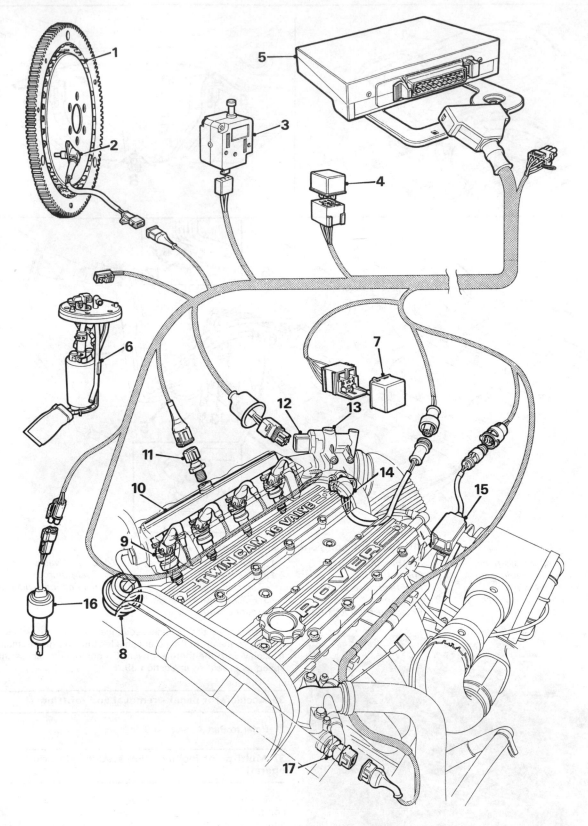

Fig. 3.20 Main components of the multi-point fuel injection system (Sec 37)

1	Flywheel reluctor ring	6	Fuel pump
2	Crankshaft sensor	7	Fuel system main relay
3	Inertia switch	8	Fuel pressure regulator
4	Fuel pump relay	9	Fuel injector
5	Fuel ECU	10	Fuel rail

11	Fuel temperature switch	15	Airflow meter
12	Idle speed stepper motor	16	Speedometer transducer
13	Throttle housing	17	Coolant temperature
14	Throttle potentiometer		thermistor

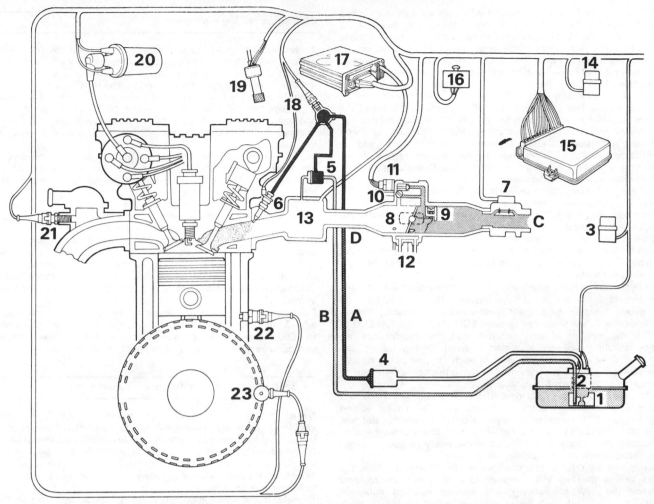

Fig. 3.21 Schematic layout of the multi-point fuel injection system (Sec 37)

1 Fuel return swirl pot	9 Base idle speed adjusting screw	14 Fuel system main relay	21 Coolant temperature thermistor
2 Fuel pump		15 Fuel ECU	
3 Fuel pump relay	10 Idle mixture adjustment screw	16 Inertia switch	22 Knock sensor
4 Fuel filter		17 Ignition ECU	23 Crankshaft sensor
5 Fuel pressure regulator	11 Idle speed stepper motor	18 Fuel temperature switch	A Regulated fuel pressure
6 Fuel injectors	12 Coolant and crankcase breather ports	19 Speedometer transducer	B Return fuel
7 Airflow meter		20 Ignition coil	C Inlet airflow
8 Throttle potentiometer	13 Inlet manifold and plenum chamber		D Manifold vacuum

Fuel ECU: The fuel ECU is a microprocessor, which controls the entire operation of the fuel system. Contained in the ECU memory is a program which controls the fuel supply to the injectors, and their opening duration. The program enters sub-routines to alter these parameters, according to inputs from the other components of the system. In addition to this, the engine idle speed is also controlled by the ECU, which uses a stepper motor to open or close an air valve as required.

Fuel injectors: Each fuel injector consists of a solenoid-operated needle valve, which opens under commands from the fuel ECU. Fuel from the fuel rail is then delivered through the injector nozzle into the inlet manifold.

Coolant temperature thermistor: This resistive device is screwed into the thermostat housing, where its element is in direct contact with the engine coolant. Changes in coolant temperature are detected by the ECU as a change in thermistor resistance.

Airflow meter: The airflow meter contains two resistive elements mounted in the intake air stream, one of which is heated by a current passing through it. Air passing over the heated wire alters its resistance by cooling it, while the temperature of the air is sensed by the other wire. An electronic module within the airflow meter monitors the reaction of the elements to the airflow, and provides a proportional signal to the fuel ECU.

Throttle potentiometer: The potentiometer is a variable resistor, attached to the throttle shaft in the throttle housing. The unit is supplied with a constant input voltage, and as the resistance of the potentiometer varies with throttle shaft movement, the output voltage is proportionally affected. This allows the fuel ECU to determine throttle valve position, and rate of change.

Idle speed stepper motor: This is a small electric motor, having two control windings to enable it to rotate in either direction. Under a signal from the fuel ECU, the stepper motor will rotate in whichever direction is necessary, to open or close the air valve in the throttle housing. This allows air to bypass the throttle valve and maintain a stabilised idling speed.

Fuel pump: The fuel pump is a self-priming centrifugal unit, located in the fuel tank, and totally submerged in the fuel. Fuel is supplied under pressure from the pump, through an in-line filter, to the fuel rail and fuel pressure regulator.

Fuel pressure regulator: The regulator is a vacuum-operated mechanical device, which ensures that the pressure differential between fuel in the fuel rail and fuel in the inlet manifold is maintained at a constant value. As manifold depression increases, the regulated fuel pressure is reduced in direct proportion. When fuel pressure in the fuel rail exceeds the regulator setting, the regulator opens to allow fuel to return via the return line to the tank.

Relays: The main relay is energised when the ignition is switched on, and provides the fuel ECU supply voltage. The fuel relay is energised by the fuel ECU for a short period after the ignition is initially switched on, and then continuously when the engine is running.

Fuel temperature switch: The fuel temperature switch contacts remain open during normal engine operation, and only close when the temperature of the fuel in the fuel rail exceeds a preset value. When the contacts close, a signal is sent to the fuel ECU, overriding the coolant thermistor signal. The ECU then alters the opening duration of the injectors accordingly, to minimise the effects of fuel vaporisation.

Inertia switch: The switch is a mechanically-controlled accelerator, connected in the electrical circuit between the ignition switch and the fuel ECU and fuel relay. Under violent deceleration or impact, the switch trips out, and cuts off the supply voltage. Depressing a button on the switch body resets the switch.

The fuel injection system works in the following way. When the ignition is switched on, a voltage is supplied via the inertia switch to the main relay and fuel ECU. The ECU energises the fuel pump relay, and voltage is supplied to the pump. The pump is allowed to run for a short period of time to pressurise the system. Excess fuel is returned to the tank by the action of the fuel pressure regulator. At the same time, the stepper motor cycles to close off the air valve, thus maintaining a richer mixture for starting.

When the starter is operated, voltage is supplied directly to the fuel pump, bypassing the fuel pump relay. Inputs to the fuel ECU from the road speed transducer, coolant temperature thermistor, throttle potentiometer, airflow meter and ignition ECU enables the fuel ECU to establish the amount of fuel required, and the injector opening duration, to allow the engine to start and run. During starting, the injectors operate simultaneously, and at each ignition pulse, so that fuel is sprayed into the inlet manifold at twice the normal rate, giving the necessary enrichment for starting.

When the engine fires and runs, the supply voltage for the fuel pump is diverted back through the fuel pump relay. During engine idling, the fuel ECU modifies the injector opening duration and fuel supply rate, according to data received from the various sensors. Additionally, the stepper motor cycles as necessary to open or close the air valve, to maintain a stabilised idling speed.

During normal driving, any changes in the information from the sensors causes the fuel ECU program to enter a sub-routine, and determine the new fuel supply and injector opening durations accordingly.

During full throttle acceleration, the injectors are held open for a longer duration, thus providing the necessary enrichment to avoid hesitation. Under overrun conditions, the fuel supply is cut off by the fuel ECU, providing the engine has reached a predetermined temperature, and the accelerator pedal is released. When the engine speed decreases, or the accelerator pedal is depressed, the fuel supply is gradually re-instated to eliminate hesitation.

During hot start conditions, inputs to the fuel ECU from the coolant temperature thermistor and fuel temperature switch cause the fuel ECU to alter the injector opening duration accordingly, to counteract vaporisation.

Under conditions of abrupt deceleration or impact, the inertia switch opens, and breaks the system supply voltage. This shuts down the fuel system, stops the engine, and reduces the fire hazard.

38 Engine tuning – procedure

1   Before making any changes to the settings of the fuel injection system, ensure that the spark plug gaps are correctly set, the air cleaner element is clean, there are no leaks in the exhaust system, and the ignition system is operating correctly. Ensure that all breather and vacuum hoses are connected, and that none are perished or kinked.
2   Check that there is at least 5.0 mm (0.20 in) of free play in the accelerator cable, and that the throttle lever rests against its stop in the released condition. Adjust the cable as described in Section 35 if necessary.
3   Temperature effects, and engine and transmission oil drag, can adversely influence the idle speed and mixture settings, and it is important that the following warm-up procedure is adopted before attempting any adjustments.
4   Drive the car on the road for approximately two to four miles, dependent on summer or winter conditions, in a normal manner, without excessive load, engine speed or road speed.
5   Return the car to the working area, and without switching off the engine, connect an exhaust gas analyser (CO meter) in accordance with the equipment manufacturer's instructions. The analyser should be warmed up, correctly calibrated and ready for immediate use. Commence the adjustment procedure described in Section 39 immediately.
6   If, during the adjustment procedure, the cooling fan operates, or if adjustment is not completed within two minutes, accelerate the engine to 2000 rpm, and hold this speed for ten seconds. Repeat this every two minutes until the adjustments are completed.

39 Base idle speed and mixture – adjustment

Note: *The fuel injection system is such that the engine idle speed and mixture settings are controlled by the fuel ECU. Unless a new component has been fitted, the idle speed or mixture screws have been tampered with, or the idle quality is unsatisfactory, no adjustment should normally be necessary. If, however, the settings are to be altered, an accurate exhaust gas analyser (CO meter), tachometer, and voltmeter will be required.*

1   Refer to the information contained in Section 38 before starting.
2   Switch off all electrical accessories, and ensure that they remain switched off throughout the adjustment procedure.
3   With the engine idling and the exhaust gas analyser connected, take a reading of the exhaust gas CO content. If this is not as given in the Specifications, hook out the tamperproof plug over the idle mixture adjustment screw (photo), and turn the screw clockwise to enrich the mixture, or anti-clockwise to weaken it as necessary.
4   With the CO content correctly adjusted, switch off the engine and connect a tachometer according to the equipment manufacturer's instructions.
5   Before adjusting the base idle speed, the stepper motor must be cycled to its fully-extended position, using the following procedure.

   (a)   Switch on the ignition

39.3 Idle mixture adjustment screw tamperproof plug (arrowed)

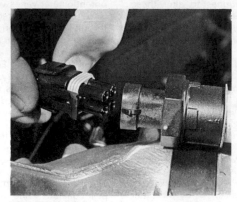
39.5 Disconnect the stepper motor wiring multi-plug

39.8 Base idle speed adjusting screw tamperproof plug (arrowed)

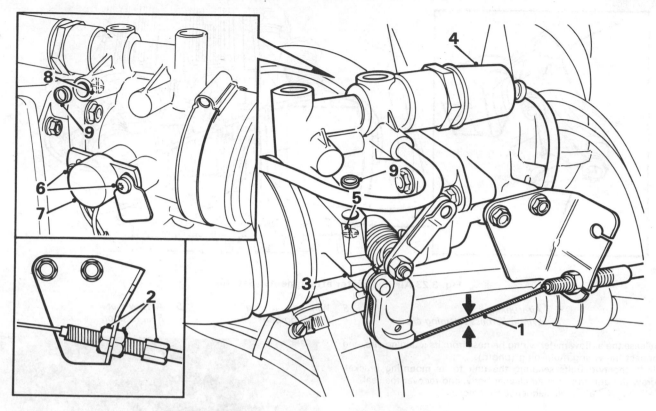

Fig. 3.22 Base idle speed and mixture adjustment (Sec 39)

1	Accelerator cable free play
2	Cable locknuts for free play adjustment
3	Throttle lever stop

4	Stepper motor multi-plug
5	Base idle speed adjusting screw

6	Throttle potentiometer retaining screws
7	Throttle potentiometer

8	Idle mixture adjustment screw
9	Tamperproof plug

(b) Disconnect the stepper motor wiring multi-plug on the top of the throttle housing (photo)

(c) Switch off the ignition, wait five seconds, and reconnect the stepper motor multi-plug

(d) Switch on the ignition, wait five seconds, and disconnect the stepper motor multi-plug again

(e) Switch off the ignition, wait five seconds, and reconnect the stepper motor multi-plug

(f) Switch on the ignition, wait five seconds, and disconnect the stepper motor multi-plug once more. The stepper motor is now fully extended

6 Start the engine, and allow it to idle until normal operating temperature is again reached.

7 Check the reading on the tachometer, and compare this with the base idle speed figure given in the Specifications.

8 If adjustment is necessary, hook out the tamperproof plug over the idle speed adjusting screw (photo), and turn the adjusting screw as necessary to achieve the correct setting.

9 Increase the engine speed to 2000 rpm for ten seconds, then return it to idle.

10 Recheck the exhaust CO content, as described earlier in this Section.

11 Switch off the ignition, and pull back the dust cover over the throttle potentiometer wiring multi-plug.

12 Insert the probes from the voltmeter into the back of the multi-plug so that the voltmeter black lead is connected to the pink/black wire, and the red lead is connected to the light green/pink wire.

13 Select millivolts on the voltmeter, then switch on the ignition.

14 Check that the reading on the voltmeter scale is now equal to the throttle potentiometer voltage, as given in the Specifications. If this is not the case, slacken the two retaining screws (photo), and slowly move the potentiometer body until the correct reading is obtained. Tighten the screws securely.

15 Open and close the throttle several times, then with it closed, check the voltmeter reading once more. Repeat the adjustment if the reading

is now outside the specified tolerance.

16 With the adjustments complete, switch off the engine and disconnect the test instruments.

39.14 Throttle potentiometer retaining screws (arrowed)

40 Airflow meter – removal and refitting

1 Slacken the hose clip and detach the air trunking from the airflow meter.

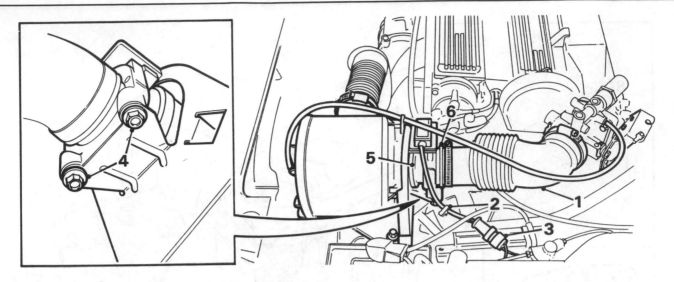

Fig. 3.23 Airflow meter attachments (Sec 40)

1 Air trunking   3 Wiring multi-plug   5 Airflow meter
2 Wiring harness retaining clip   4 Retaining bolts   6 Seal location

2   Release the airflow meter wiring harness from its retaining clip, and disconnect the wiring multi-plug (photo).
3   Undo the two bolts securing the unit to its mounting bracket, withdraw the unit from the air cleaner body, and recover the seal.
4   Refitting is the reverse sequence to removal.

41 Idle speed stepper motor – removal and refitting

1   Slide back the rubber dust cover (where fitted), and disconnect the stepper motor wiring multi-plug.
2   Using a 32 mm spanner, unscrew the stepper motor from the throttle housing.
3   Refitting is the reverse sequence to removal.

42 Throttle potentiometer – removal and refitting

1   Disconnect the throttle potentiometer wiring harness multi-plug.
2   Using a dab of paint, mark the position of the potentiometer in relation to the throttle housing, so that if the original unit is refitted, its position can be restored.
3   Undo the two screws, remove the unit from the throttle housing, and recover the gasket.
4   Refit the potentiometer and gasket, align the previously-made mark, then tighten the two retaining screws. If a new unit is being fitted, position it centrally within its adjustment range.
5   Adjust the base idle speed and mixture settings as described in Section 39.

43 Throttle housing – removal and refitting

1   Drain the cooling system as described in Chapter 2.
2   Slacken the hose clip and detach the air intake trunking from the throttle housing.
3   Disconnect the throttle potentiometer and stepper motor wiring multi-plugs.
4   Disconnect the air valve hose from the top of the housing (photo), and the breather hose from below.
5   Slacken the clips and disconnect the two coolant hoses from the housing.
6   Open the throttle fully by hand, and slip the accelerator inner cable end out of the slot on the throttle lever.
7   Slacken the outer cable locknuts, and unscrew the outer locknut, nearest to the cable end, fully.

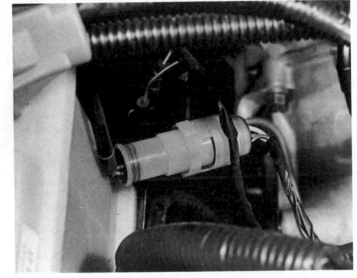

40.2 Airflow meter wiring multi-plug

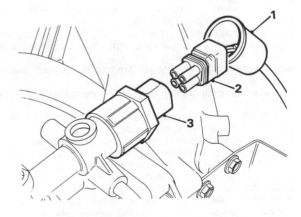

Fig. 3.24 Idle speed stepper motor details (Sec 41)

1 Multi-plug dust cover   3 Stepper motor
2 Wiring multi-plug

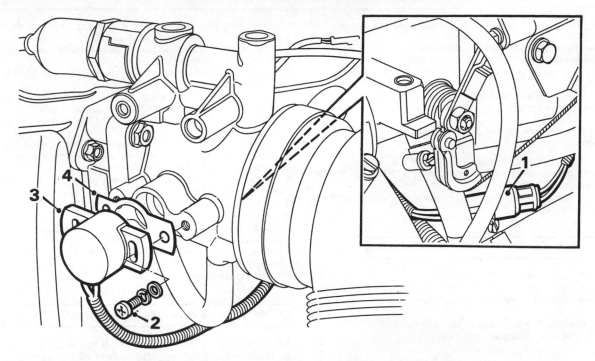

Fig. 3.25 Throttle potentiometer components (Sec 42)

1 Wiring multi-plug   2 Retaining screws   3 Throttle potentiometer   4 Gasket

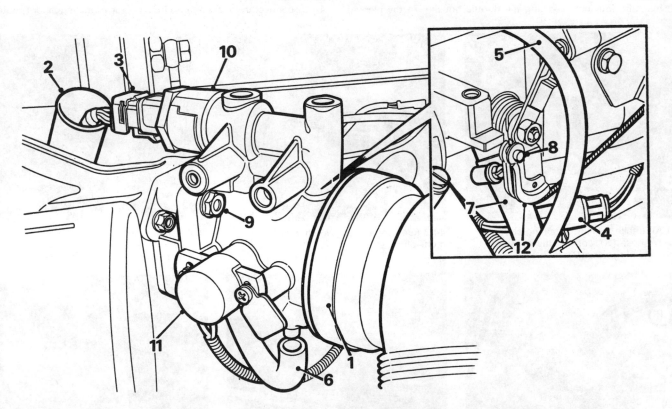

Fig. 3.26 Throttle housing components and attachments (Sec 43)

1 Air intake trunking	4 Throttle potentiometer multi-plug	7 Coolant hoses	10 Stepper motor
2 Stepper motor multi-plug cover	5 Air valve hose	8 Accelerator cable end fitting	11 Throttle potentiometer
3 Stepper motor multi-plug	6 Breather hose	9 Throttle housing retaining nuts	12 Throttle lever

8 Remove the washer and rubber bush, then withdraw the accelerator cable from the support bracket.
9 On automatic transmission models, disconnect the kickdown cable using the same procedure as for the accelerator cable.
10 Undo the four retaining nuts and remove the throttle housing from its mounting.
11 If further dismantling is required, the stepper motor and throttle potentiometer can be removed, with reference to Sections 41 and 42 respectively.
12 Refitting is the reverse sequence to removal, bearing in mind the following points:

(a) Refill the cooling system as described in Chapter 2
(b) On automatic transmission models, adjust the kickdown cable as described in Chapter 7
(c) Adjust the base idle speed and mixture settings as described in Section 39

44 Fuel temperature switch – removal and refitting

1 Disconnect the battery negative terminal.
2 Disconnect the wiring multi-plug from the temperature switch, located in the centre of the fuel rail behind the plenum chamber (photo).
3 Unscrew the switch and remove it from the fuel rail.
4 Refitting is the reverse sequence to removal.

45 Plenum chamber – removal and refitting

1 Disconnect the battery negative terminal.
2 Slacken the hose clip and detach the air intake trunking from the throttle housing.
3 Undo the four nuts securing the throttle housing to the plenum chamber, ease the housing off the studs, and move it slightly to one side.
4 Disconnect the two vacuum hoses at the throttle housing end of the plenum chamber (photo).
5 At the other end of the plenum chamber, unscrew the brake servo vacuum hose banjo union bolt, disconnect the vacuum hose adjacent to the banjo union, and undo the fuel pressure regulator mounting bracket bolt (photo). Recover the two copper washers from the banjo union, and note that the hose locates between two locating pegs in its fitted position.
6 Remove the fuel temperature switch as described in Section 44.
7 Undo the two bolts securing the plenum chamber mounting brackets to the camshaft cover (photo).
8 Undo the six bolts securing the rear of the plenum chamber to the inlet manifold (photo).
9 Lift the plenum chamber off the manifold, and recover the four locating sleeves and O-ring seals.
10 Clean the manifold and plenum chamber mating faces, and renew the O-ring seals if they show any sign of deterioration.
11 Refitting is the reverse sequence to removal. Fit the locating sleeves to the manifold before the O-ring seals, and tighten all nuts and bolts to the specified torque.

46 Fuel pressure regulator – removal and refitting

Note: *Refer to the warning note in Section 28 before proceeding.*
1 Disconnect the battery negative terminal.
2 Place absorbent rags around the fuel filter outlet union banjo bolt, then slowly unscrew the bleed screw in the centre of the bolt to release the fuel system pressure. Tighten the bleed screw when the pressure is released.
3 Detach the breather hose from the camshaft cover, and move the hose aside (photo).
4 Disconnect the vacuum hose from the top of the regulator (photo).

43.4 Air intake trunking retaining clip (A), air valve hose (B), and throttle housing upper retaining nuts (C)

44.2 Fuel temperature switch wiring multi-plug

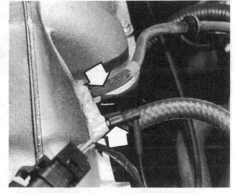
45.4 Vacuum hose connections at the throttle housing end of the plenum chamber (arrowed)

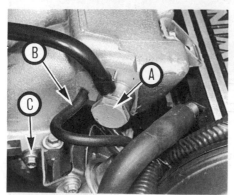
45.5 Brake servo vacuum hose banjo union (A), additional vacuum hose (B), and fuel pressure regulator mounting bracket bolt (C)

45.7 Plenum chamber mounting bracket-to-camshaft cover bolt (arrowed)

45.8 Plenum chamber-to-inlet manifold retaining bolts

46.3 Detach the breather hose from the camshaft cover

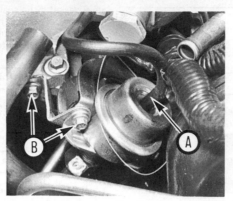

46.4 Fuel pressure regulator vacuum hose (A) and mounting bracket bolts (B)

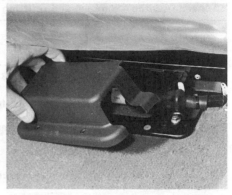

48.3 Remove the ECU cover from under the driver's seat

5 Unscrew the fuel return hose union from the base of the regulator.
6 Undo the regulator bracket retaining bolts, and withdraw the regulator from the fuel rail.
7 Refitting is the reverse sequence to removal.

47 Fuel injectors – removal and refitting

Note: *Refer to the warning note in Section 28 before proceeding.*
1 Disconnect the battery negative terminal.
2 Place absorbent rags around the fuel filter outlet union banjo bolt, then slowly unscrew the bleed screw in the centre of the bolt to release the fuel system pressure. Tighten the bleed screw when the pressure is released.
3 Remove the plenum chamber as described in Section 45.
4 Remove the fuel temperature switch as described in Section 44.
5 Detach the breather hose from the camshaft cover, and move the hose aside.
6 Disconnect the fuel pressure regulator vacuum hose.
7 Undo the fuel pressure regulator mounting bracket bolts.
8 Undo the union nut, and disconnect the fuel supply hose from the fuel rail.
9 Undo the union nut, and disconnect the fuel return hose from the fuel pressure regulator.
10 Disconnect the multi-plugs from each of the four injectors.
11 Undo the two bolts securing the fuel rail to the inlet manifold.
12 Ease the four injectors out of their inlet manifold locations, and lift up the injector and fuel rail assembly. Recover the O-ring seal from each injector outlet.
13 Extract the retaining clips, and remove the injectors from the fuel rail. Recover the O-ring seal from each injector inlet.
14 Refitting is the reverse sequence to removal, but renew the injector inlet and outlet O-rings.

48 Electronic control unit – removal and refitting

1 Disconnect the battery negative terminal.
2 Slide the driver's seat fully forwards.
3 From under the driver's seat, undo the two screws and lift off the ECU cover (photo).
4 Undo the bolt securing the rear of the mounting bracket to the floor (photo).
5 Slide the driver's seat fully rearwards, and undo the two bolts securing the front of the mounting bracket to the floor.
6 Withdraw the ECU and mounting bracket assembly from under the seat.
7 Depress the multi-plug retaining tab, and pull the plug straight from the socket.
8 Remove the ECU from the car.
9 Refitting is the reverse sequence to removal.

49 Resonator unit – removal and refitting

Refer to Part A, Section 21.

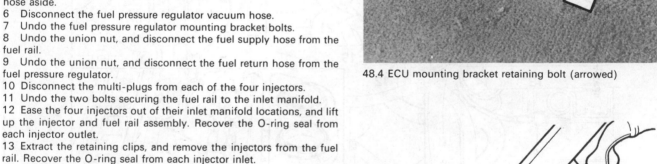

48.4 ECU mounting bracket retaining bolt (arrowed)

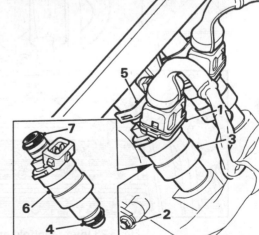

Fig. 3.27 Fuel injector and fuel rail details (Sec 47)

1 Injector multi-plug
2 Fuel rail retaining bolt
3 Fuel injector location on inlet manifold
4 Injector outlet O-ring seal
5 Injector-to-fuel rail retaining clip
6 Injector body
7 Injector inlet O-ring seal

50 Inertia switch – removal and refitting

Refer to Part A, Section 22.

51 Inlet manifold – removal and refitting

1   Remove the fuel injectors, complete with fuel rail, as described in Section 47.
2   Release the clip and disconnect the breather hose from the oil separator.
3   Disconnect the breather hose from the lower end of the oil separator and the sump outlet.
4   Disconnect the wires at the oil pressure switch, oil pressure transducer and knock sensor.
5   Slacken the nine nuts and bolts securing the manifold to the cylinder head.
6   Remove all the bolts, followed by the two nuts, then withdraw the manifold off the studs and remove it from the engine. Recover the manifold gasket.
7   Clean the manifold and cylinder head mating faces, and obtain a new gasket if the sealing lips of the original are in any way damaged.
8   Refitting is the reverse sequence to removal, but tighten the manifold retaining nuts and bolts in the sequence shown in Fig. 3.13 and to the specified torque.

52 Exhaust manifold – removal and refitting

Refer to Part A, Section 25, but ignore the instructions to remove the manifold stove, which is not fitted to models with multi-point fuel injection.

53 Exhaust system – checking, removal and refitting

Refer to Part A, Section 26.

54 Fault diagnosis – fuel and exhaust systems (multi-point fuel injection system)

Refer to Part A, Section 27.

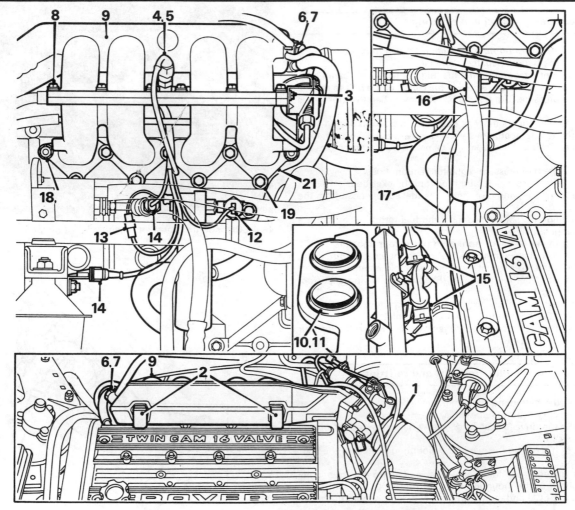

Fig. 3.28 Inlet manifold and related component attachments (Sec 15)

1 Air intake trunking	11 O-ring seals
2 Plenum chamber mounting brackets	12 Oil pressure switch wire
3 Fuel pressure regulator mounting bracket bolt	13 Oil pressure transducer wire
4 Fuel temperature switch multi-plug	14 Knock sensor and crankshaft sensor wiring multi-plugs
5 Fuel temperature switch	15 Fuel injector wiring multi-plugs
6 Brake servo vacuum hose banjo union bolt	16 Oil separator upper breather hose
7 Banjo union copper washers	17 Oil separator lower breather hose
8 Plenum chamber-to-inlet manifold retaining bolts	18 Manifold retaining nuts
9 Plenum chamber	19 Manifold retaining bolts
10 Locating sleeves	21 Inlet manifold

Chapter 4 Ignition system

For modifications, and information applicable to later models, see Supplement at end of manual

Contents

Specifications

System type .... Programmed electronic ignition

Firing order .... 1-3-4-2 (No 1 at timing belt end)

Direction of rotor arm rotation .... Anti-clockwise

Ignition coil
Type .... Unipart GCL 141
Current consumption – engine idling .... 0.25 to 0.75 amps (average)
Primary resistance at 20°C (68°F) .... 0.71 to 0.81 ohms

Ignition timing*
Engines with single-point fuel injection:
· Vacuum connected .... 16° BTDC at ECU-controlled idle speed
Engines with multi-point fuel injection:
Vacuum connected .... 22° to 28° BTDC at 1500 rpm
Vacuum disconnected .... 12° BTDC at 1500 rpm
* Non-adjustable, for information only

Spark plugs
Type.. Champion RC9YCC or RC9YC
Electrode gap .... 0.8 mm (0.032 in)

Torque wrench settings

	Nm	lbf ft
Spark plugs	18	13
Spark plug cover bolts	6	4
Crankshaft sensor bolts	6	4
Knock sensor	12	9
Ignition coil mounting bracket	24	18

1 General description

All models covered by this manual are equipped with a programmed electronic ignition system, which utilizes computer technology and electro-magnetic circuitry to simulate the main functions of a conventional ignition distributor.

A reluctor ring on the periphery of the engine flywheel, and a crankshaft sensor whose inductive head runs between the reluctor ring teeth, replace the operation of the contact breaker points in a conventional system. The reluctor ring utilizes 34 teeth spaced at 10° intervals, with two spaces, 180° apart, corresponding to TDC for Nos 1 and 4 pistons, and Nos 2 and 3 pistons respectively. As the crankshaft rotates, the reluctor ring teeth pass over the crankshaft sensor, which transmits a pulse to the ignition electronic control unit (ECU) every time a tooth passes over it. The ECU recognises the absence of a pulse every 180°, and consequently establishes the TDC position. Each subsequent pulse then represents 10° of crankshaft rotation. This, and the time interval between pulses, allows the ECU to determine accurately crankshaft position and speed.

A small bore pipe connecting the inlet manifold to a pressure transducer within the ECU supplies the unit with information on engine load. From this constantly-changing data, the ECU selects a particular advance from a range of ignition characteristics stored in its memory. The basic setting can be further advanced or retarded, according to information sent to the ECU from the coolant temperature thermistor and knock sensor.

With the firing point established, the ECU triggers the ignition coil, which delivers HT voltage to the spark plugs in the conventional manner. The cycle is then repeated many times a second for each cylinder in turn.

In addition to the above operations, many of the ignition system components have a second function in the control and operation of the fuel injection system. Further details will be found in Chapter 3.

Warning: *The voltages produced by the electronic ignition system are considerably higher than those produced by a conventional system. Extreme care must be used when working on the system with the ignition switched on, particularly by persons fitted with a cardiac pacemaker.*

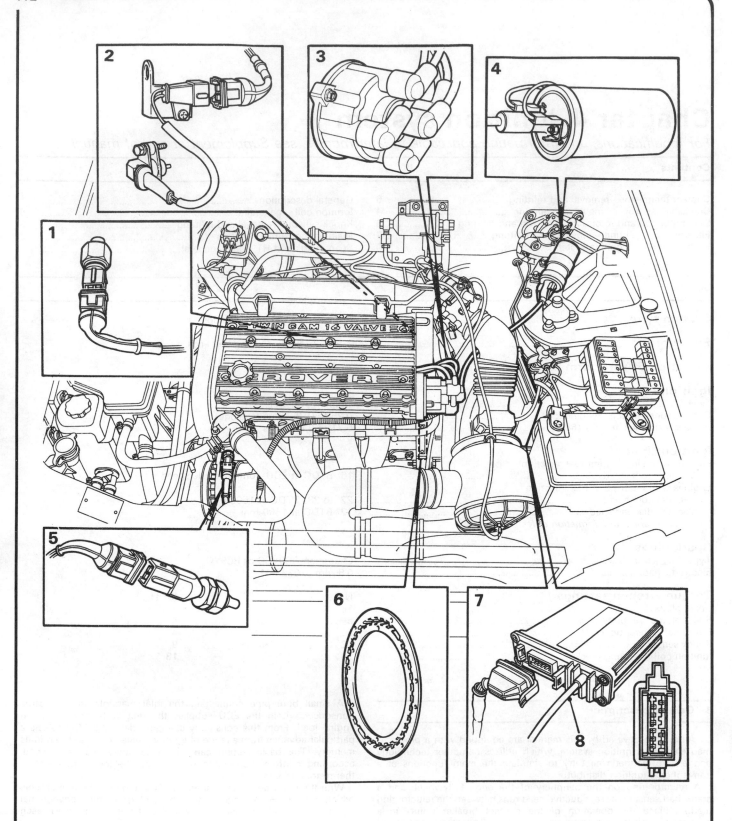

Fig. 4.1 Layout of the programmed electronic ignition system components (Sec 1)

1 Knock sensor	3 Distributor cap	5 Coolant thermistor	7 Electronic control unit
2 Crankshaft sensor	4 Ignition coil	6 Reluctor ring	8 Vacuum hose

2   Maintenance and inspection

1   At the intervals given in *Routine maintenance* at the beginning of this manual, remove the distributor cap and thoroughly clean it inside and out with a dry lint-free cloth. Examine the four HT lead segments inside the cap. If the segments appear badly burnt or pitted, renew the cap. Check the carbon brush in the centre of the cap, ensuring that it is free to move and that it stands proud of its holder.
2   Check all ignition wiring, cables and HT leads for security and cleanliness, and wipe them over with a clean rag if necessary. Pay particular attention to the wiring and HT lead connection at the coil tower. Dirt or moisture in this area can increase the likelihood of HT leakage due to arcing.
3   Remove, clean and reset, or renew, the spark plugs, using the procedure described in Section 9. It is recommended by the manufacturers that the spark plugs should be renewed every 24 000 miles (40 000 km) or two years, whichever occurs first. Practical experience has shown that this, in some circumstances, is considerably in excess of the practical working life of some makes of spark plug. In terms of performance and reliability, it may be considered beneficial to renew the plugs at the 12 000 mile (20 000 km), or 12 month, service interval.
4   This is the limit of routine maintenance necessary on the ignition system, as adjustment of the ignition timing, for example, is not necessary – nor is it possible.

3   Distributor cap and rotor arm – removal and refitting

1   Using an open-ended spanner, undo the two retaining screws and lift off the distributor cap from the cylinder head (photo). Clean and check the cap as described in Section 2.
2   If the cap is to be renewed, record the position of the HT leads in relation to the cap, then pull them off. Transfer the leads to a new cap, refitting them in the same position.
3   To renew the rotor arm, withdraw the plastic shield (photo), then undo the grub retaining screw using a suitable Allen key (photo). Withdraw the rotor arm from the end of the camshaft.
4   Refitting the rotor arm, shield and distributor cap is the reverse sequence to removal.

4   Crankshaft sensor – removal and refitting

1   Jack up the front of the car and support it on stands.
2   Disconnect the multi-plug from the crankshaft sensor wiring socket, attached to the gearbox/transmission adaptor plate on the rear-facing side of the engine.
3   Undo the retaining screw and remove the wiring socket from its mounting bracket.
4   Undo the two bolts securing the crankshaft sensor to the adaptor plate, and withdraw the sensor, complete with spacer and wiring socket.
5   Refitting is the reverse sequence to removal.

5   Knock sensor – removal and refitting

1   The knock sensor is located in the centre of the rear-facing side of the cylinder block, beneath the inlet manifold.
2   Jack up the front of the car and support it on stands.
3   Disconnect the wiring multi-plug, then unscrew the sensor from its location (photos).
4   Refitting is the reverse sequence to removal, but ensure that the sensor and cylinder block mating faces are clean.

6   Coolant thermistor – removal and refitting

Removal and refitting procedures for this component are contained in Chapter 2.

3.1 Undo the distributor cap screws using an open-ended spanner

3.3A Withdraw the plastic shield ...

3.3B ... then undo the rotor arm grub screw with an Allen key

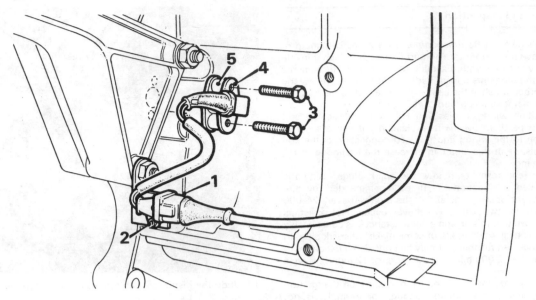

Fig. 4.2 Crankshaft sensor attachments (Sec 4)

1 *Wiring multi-plug*

2 *Wiring socket retaining
  screw*

3 *Sensor retaining bolts*
4 *Crankshaft sensor*

5 *Spacer*

5.3A Disconnect the knock sensor wiring multi-plug (arrowed) ...

5.3B ... then unscrew the sensor

7 Electronic control unit – removal and refitting

Note: *The following procedure is applicable to engines with
multi-point fuel injection. For engines equipped with single-point fuel
injection, reference should be made to the procedures contained in
Chapter 3.*

1   Disconnect the battery negative terminal.
2   Disconnect the wiring multi-plug from the electronic control unit
(ECU), which is located on the left-hand side of the engine
compartment, behind the battery. To do this, press the retaining tab
upwards, release the bottom of the multi-plug, then disengage the top
lug.
3   Disconnect the vacuum supply hose.
4   Undo the retaining screw, slide the unit out of its mounting bracket
to disengage the retaining lug, and remove the ECU from the engine
compartment.
5   Refitting is the reverse sequence to removal.

8 Ignition coil – general

1   The ignition coil is mounted on the left-hand side of the engine
compartment, on the suspension strut tower.
2   To remove the coil, disconnect the LT leads at the coil positive and
negative terminals, and the HT lead at the centre terminal.
3   Undo the mounting bracket retaining bolt and remove the coil.
4   Note the position of the positive and negative terminals in relation
to the mounting bracket, then slacken the mounting bracket screw and
slide out the coil.
5   Refitting is the reverse sequence to removal.
6   Accurate checking of the coil output requires the use of special test
equipment, and should be left to a Rover dealer or suitably-equipped
automotive electrician. It is however possible to check the primary
winding resistance, using an ohmmeter as follows.
7   To check the primary winding resistance, disconnect the LT and HT
wiring at the coil, and connect an ohmmeter across the positive and

negative LT terminals. The resistance should be as given in the Specifications at the beginning of this Chapter. If the resistance is not as specified, the coil should be renewed.

8 If the coil is to be renewed, ensure that the new coil is of the manufacturer's specified type for use in programmed electronic ignition systems. Failure to do so could cause irreparable damage to the electronic control unit.

9 Spark plugs and HT leads – general

1 The correct functioning of the spark plugs is vital for the correct running and efficiency of the engine. It is essential that the plugs fitted are appropriate for the engine (the correct type is specified at the beginning of this Chapter). If this type is used, and the engine is in good

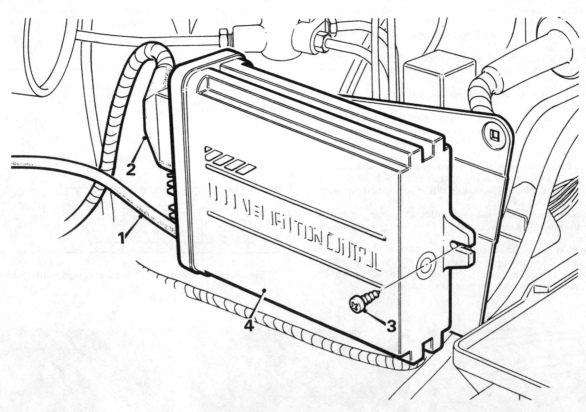

Fig. 4.3 Electronic control unit attachments (Sec 7)

1 Vacuum hose
2 Wiring multi-plug
3 Retaining screw
4 Electronic control unit

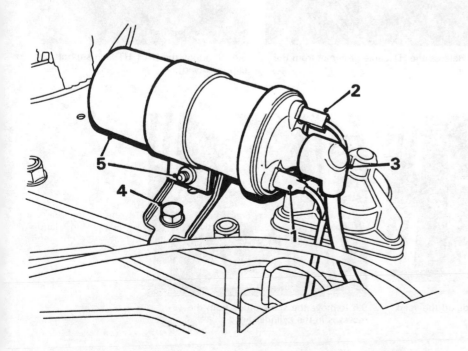

Fig. 4.4 Ignition coil details (Sec 8)

1 LT negative lead
2 LT positive lead
3 HT lead
4 Mounting bracket retaining bolt
5 Coil-to-bracket retaining screw

condition, the spark plugs should not need attention between scheduled service renewal intervals. Spark plug cleaning is rarely necessary, and should not be attempted unless specialised equipment is available, as damage can easily be caused to the firing ends.

2   To remove the spark plugs, undo the two bolts securing the plastic spark plug cover to the centre of the cylinder head. Note the location of the accelerator cable support bracket on the right-hand bolt (photo).

3   Lift off the cover and release the HT cable support grommet from the distributor cap end (photo).

4   With the cover removed, withdraw the No 1 HT lead support clip from the lead and the retaining bolt stud (photo).

5   Mark the HT leads to ensure correct refitment, and carefully pull them off the plugs (photo).

6   Using a spark plug spanner or suitable deep socket and extension bar, unscrew each spark plug in turn and remove it from the engine (photo).

7   The condition of the spark plugs will also tell much about the condition of the engine.

8   If the insulator nose of the spark plug is clean and white, with no deposits, this is indicative of a weak mixture, or too hot a plug (a hot plug transfers heat away from the electrode slowly – a cold plug transfers it away quickly).

9   If the tip and insulator nose are covered with hard, black-looking deposits then this is indicative that the mixture is too rich. Should the plug be black and oily, then it is likely that the engine is fairly worn, as well as the mixture being too rich.

10 If the insulator nose is covered with light tan to greyish-brown deposits, then the mixture is correct, and it is likely that the engine is in good condition.

11 The spark plug gap is of considerable importance, as if it is too large or too small, the size of the spark and its efficiency will be seriously impaired. The spark plug gap should be set to the figure given in the Specifications at the beginning of this Chapter.

12 To set it, measure the gap with a feeler gauge, and then bend open, or close, the *outer* earth electrode until the correct gap is obtained. The centre electrode should *never* be bent, as this may crack the insulation and cause plug failure, if nothing worse.

13 To refit the plugs, first clean the seat area in the cylinder head, then screw the plugs in by hand initially, finally tightening to the specified torque. If a torque wrench is not available, tighten the plugs until initial resistance is felt as the sealing washer contacts its seat, and then tighten by a further quarter of a turn. Refit the HT leads in the correct order, ensuring that they are a tight fit over the plug ends. Refit the spark plug cover using the reverse of the removal sequence.

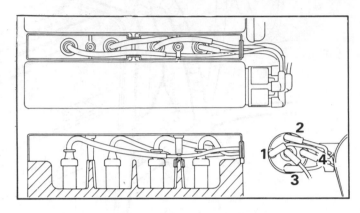

Fig. 4.5 Spark plug (HT) lead arrangement (Sec 9)

9.2 Accelerator cable support bracket location on spark plug cover

9.3 Release the HT cable grommet from the cover

9.4 Withdraw the No 1 HT lead support clip (arrowed)

9.5 Carefully pull the HT leads off the spark plugs

9.6 Remove the spark plugs from the recesses in the cylinder head

Are your plugs trying to tell you something?

Normal.
Grey-brown deposits, lightly coated core nose. Plugs ideally suited to engine, and engine in good condition.

Heavy Deposits.
A build up of crusty deposits, light-grey sandy colour in appearance.
Fault: Often caused by worn valve guides, excessive use of upper cylinder lubricant, or idling for long periods.

Lead Glazing.
Plug insulator firing tip appears yellow or green/yellow and shiny in appearance.
Fault: Often caused by incorrect carburation, excessive idling followed by sharp acceleration. Also check ignition timing.

Carbon fouling.
Dry, black, sooty deposits.
Fault: over-rich fuel mixture.
Check: carburettor mixture settings, float level, choke operation, air filter.

Oil fouling.
Wet, oily deposits. Fault: worn bores/piston rings or valve guides; sometimes occurs (temporarily) during running-in period.

Overheating.
Electrodes have glazed appearance, core nose very white – few deposits. Fault: plug overheating. Check: plug value, ignition timing, fuel octane rating (too low) and fuel mixture (too weak).

Electrode damage.
Electrodes burned away; core nose has burned, glazed appearance. Fault: pre-ignition. Check: for correct heat range and as for 'overheating'.

Split core nose.
(May appear initially as a crack). Fault: detonation or wrong gap-setting technique. Check: ignition timing, cooling system, fuel mixture (too weak).

WHY DOUBLE COPPER IS BETTER FOR YOUR ENGINE.

Unique Trapezoidal Copper Cored Earth Electrode — 50% Larger Spark Area — Copper Cored Centre Electrode

Champion Double Copper plugs are the first in the world to have copper core in both centre <u>and</u> earth electrode. This innovative design means that they run cooler by up to 100°C – giving greater efficiency and longer life. These double copper cores transfer heat away from the tip of the plug faster and more efficiently. Therefore, Double Copper runs at cooler temperatures than conventional plugs giving improved acceleration response and high speed performance with no fear of pre-ignition.

TRAPEZOIDAL COPPER CORED EARTH ELECTRODE
NEW TRAPEZOIDAL COPPER CORED EARTH ELECTRODE   CONVENTIONAL SOLID NICKEL ALLOY EARTH ELECTRODE
50% INCREASE IN SPARK AREA

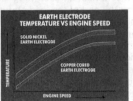

EARTH ELECTRODE TEMPERATURE VS ENGINE SPEED
SOLID NICKEL EARTH ELECTRODE
COPPER CORED EARTH ELECTRODE
TEMPERATURE
ENGINE SPEED

Champion Double Copper plugs also feature a unique trapezoidal earth electrode giving a 50% increase in spark area. This, together with the double copper cores, offers greatly reduced electrode wear, so the spark stays stronger for longer.

 FASTER COLD STARTING

 FOR UNLEADED OR LEADED FUEL

 ELECTRODES UP TO 100°C COOLER

 BETTER ACCELERATION RESPONSE

 LOWER EMISSIONS

 50% BIGGER SPARK AREA

 THE LONGER LIFE PLUG

Plug Tips/Hot and Cold.
Spark plugs must operate within well-defined temperature limits to avoid cold fouling at one extreme and overheating at the other.
Champion and the car manufacturers work out the best plugs for an engine to give optimum performance under all conditions, from freezing cold starts to sustained high speed motorway cruising.
Plugs are often referred to as hot or cold. With Champion, the higher the number on its body, the hotter the plug, and the lower the number the cooler the plug. For the correct plug for your car refer to the specifications at the beginning of this chapter.

Plug Cleaning
Modern plug design and materials mean that Champion no longer recommends periodic plug cleaning. Certainly don't clean your plugs with a wire brush as this can cause metal conductive paths across the nose of the insulator so impairing its performance and resulting in loss of acceleration and reduced m.p.g.
However, if plugs are removed, always carefully clean the area where the plug seats in the cylinder head as grit and dirt can sometimes cause gas leakage.
Also wipe any traces of oil or grease from plug leads as this may lead to arcing.

10 Fault diagnosis – ignition system

Problems associated with the programmed electronic ignition system can usually be grouped into one of two areas, those caused by the more conventional HT side of the system such as spark plugs, HT leads, rotor arm and distributor cap, and those caused by the LT circuitry, including the electronic control unit and its related components.

The following checks are concerned with the HT side of the system, where the majority of ignition system problems occur. If, after carrying out these checks the fault still exists, then it will be necessary to seek the help of a Rover dealer, who will have the necessary dedicated test equipment to check accurately the remainder of the system.

Before carrying out any of the following tests, ensure that the battery terminals are clean and secure, and that the battery is fully charged and capable of cranking the engine on the starter motor. If this is not the case, refer to Chapter 12.

Engine fails to start

1   One of the most common reasons for bad starting is wet or damp spark plug leads and distributor cap. Remove the distributor cap. If condensation is visible internally, dry the cap with a rag and wipe over the leads. Refit the cap.

2   If the engine still fails to start, check that current is reaching the plugs, by disconnecting each plug lead in turn at the spark plug end, and holding the end of the lead about $3/16$ inch (5 mm) away from the cylinder block. Spin the engine on the starter motor.

3   Sparking between the end of the lead and the block should be fairly strong, with a regular blue spark. (Hold the lead with rubber to avoid electric shocks). If current is reaching the plugs, then remove and regap them. The engine should now start.

4   If there is no spark at the plug leads, disconnect the HT lead from the centre of the distributor cap, and hold it to the block as before. Spin the engine on the starter once more. A rapid succession of blue sparks between the end of the lead and the block indicates that the coil is in good order, and that the distributor cap is cracked, the rotor arm faulty, or the carbon brush in the top of the distributor cap is not making good contact with the rotor arm.

5   If there are no sparks from the end of the coil lead, check the connections at the coil for security. If these are in order, check the coil primary resistance (see Section 8), which will give some idea of the condition of the coil, or preferably test by substitution of a new coil.

6   If all these checks have failed to highlight the problem, then the fault is likely to lie with the electronic control unit or its related components. It will therefore be necessary to refer the problem to a Rover dealer, as further checks can only be carried out using the manufacturer's test equipment and systematic checking procedure.

Engine misfires

7   If the misfire is regular and even, run the engine at a fast idle and pull off each of the plug HT leads in turn while listening to the note of the engine. Hold the lead with a dry cloth or rubber glove as additional protection against shock from the HT supply.

8   No difference in engine running will be noticed when the lead from the defective cylinder is removed. Removing the lead from one of the good cylinders will accentuate the misfire.

9   Stop the engine, remove the plug lead from the end of the defective plug and hold it about $3/16$ inch (5 mm) away from the block. Restart the engine. If the sparking is fairly strong and regular, the fault must lie in the spark plug.

10 The plug may be loose, the insulation may be cracked, or the electrodes may have burnt away, giving too wide a gap for the spark to jump. Either renew the plug, or reset the gap, and then test it

11 If there is no spark at the end of the plug lead, or if it is weak and intermittent, check the HT lead from the distributor cap to the plug. If the insulation is cracked or perished, renew the lead. Even if the lead appears to be sound externally, there may be an internal break which will not be visually apparent. Substitute a known good lead for the suspect one, and repeat the checks.

12 If there is still no spark, examine the distributor cap carefully for tracking. This can be recognised by a very thin black line running between two or more electrodes, or between an electrode and some other part of the cap. These lines are paths which now conduct electricity across the cap, thus letting it run to earth. The only answer in this case is a new distributor cap.

13 Other causes of misfiring have already been described under the section dealing with failure of the engine to start. To recap, these are:

(a) The coil may be faulty giving an intermittent misfire
(b) There may be a damaged wire or loose connection in the low tension circuit
(c) There may be a fault in the electronic control unit

14 If all these areas appear satisfactory, then the fault may lie with the fuel system, or there may be an internal engine fault. Further information will be found in Chapters 3 and 1 respectively.

Chapter 5 Clutch

Contents

Specifications

Type .... Single dry plate, diaphragm spring, hydraulically operated

Clutch disc diameter .... 215 mm (8.47 in)

Clutch fluid type .... Hydraulic fluid to FMVSS 116 DOT 4 (Duckhams Universal Brake and Clutch Fluid)

Clutch pedal height .... 179.0 mm (7.0 in)

Torque wrench settings

	Nm	lbf ft
Clutch cover to flywheel	26	19
Master cylinder retaining nuts	12	9
Fluid damper retaining nuts	12	9
Slave cylinder retaining bolts	22	16
Pedal bracket retaining nuts	12	9
Pedal bracket retaining bolt	25	18

1 General description

All manual transmission models are equipped with a single dry plate diaphragm spring clutch, operated hydraulically by a master and slave cylinder.

The clutch components comprise a steel cover assembly, clutch disc, release bearing and release mechanism. The cover assembly, which is bolted and dowelled to the rear face of the flywheel, contains the pressure plate and diaphragm spring.

The clutch disc is free to slide along the gearbox mainshaft splines, and is held in position between the flywheel and pressure plate by the pressure of the diaphragm spring.

Friction material is riveted to the clutch disc, which has a spring-cushioned hub to absorb transmission shocks, and to help ensure a smooth take-up of the drive.

The hydraulic components of the clutch mechanism consist of a master cylinder, mounted on the engine compartment side of the bulkhead in front of the driver, and a slave cylinder, mounted on the front of the gearbox. The two are connected by a hydraulic fluid pipe, incorporating a hydraulic damper for smooth operation. Hydraulic fluid is supplied by a combined brake and clutch fluid reservoir, mounted on the brake master cylinder. A short pushrod connects the clutch master cylinder to the pendant clutch pedal.

Depressing the clutch pedal moves the piston in the master cylinder forwards, so forcing hydraulic fluid through the hydraulic pipe to the slave cylinder, via the damper. The piston in the slave cylinder moves forward under the action of the fluid, and actuates the clutch release arm by means of a short pushrod. The opposite end of the release arm is forked, and is located behind the release bearing. As the release arm moves backwards, the release bearing moves forward to bear against the fingers of the diaphragm spring, so moving the centre of the diaphragm spring inwards. The spring is sandwiched between two annular rings, which act as fulcrum points. As the release bearing pushes the spring fingers in, the outer circumference pivots out, so moving the pressure plate away from the flywheel and releasing its grip on the clutch disc.

When the pedal is released, the diaphragm spring forces the pressure plate into contact with the friction linings of the clutch disc. The disc is now firmly sandwiched between the pressure plate and the flywheel, thus transmitting drive to the gearbox.

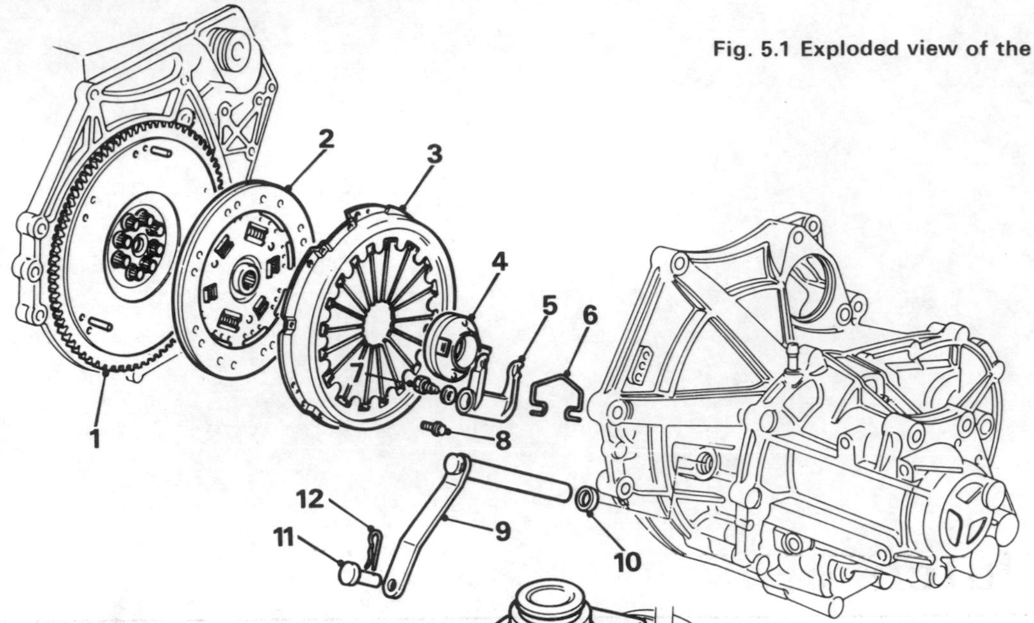

Fig. 5.1 Exploded view of the clutch components (Sec 1)

1 Flywheel
2 Clutch disc
3 Cover assembly
4 Release bearing
5 Release fork
6 Bearing spring clip
7 Release fork retaining bolt
8 Cover assembly retaining bolts
9 Release arm
10 Seal
11 Clevis pin
12 Spring clip

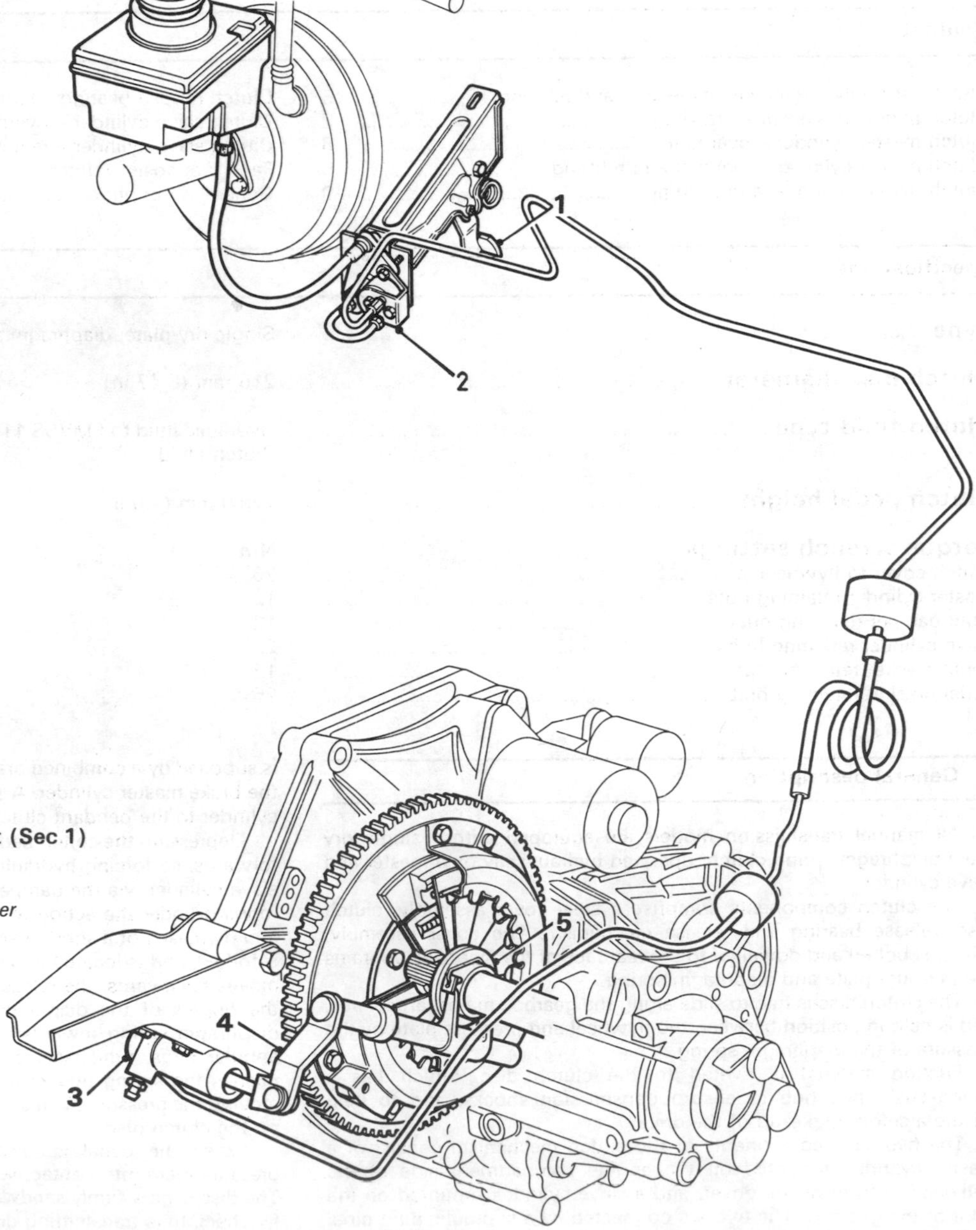

Fig. 5.2 Clutch component layout (Sec 1)

1 Clutch pedal
2 Master cylinder and damper
3 Slave cylinder
4 Release arm
5 Release bearing

2 Clutch hydraulic system – bleeding

1   Obtain a clean glass jar, a length of plastic or rubber tubing which will fit tightly over the bleed screw on the slave cylinder, a tin of the specified brake and clutch hydraulic fluid, and the help of an assistant. Alternatively, if a one-man brake bleeding kit is available, this can be used equally well for the clutch hydraulic system (see Chapter 9 for further information on these kits).

2   Check that the hydraulic fluid reservoir on top of the brake master cylinder is full, and top up if necessary. Also pour some fluid into the glass jar.

3   Remove the dust cap from the slave cylinder bleed screw, located on the lower front facing side of the gearbox (photo), and place one end of the rubber tube securely over the screw. Insert the other end of the tube into the glass jar, so that the end of the tube is below the level of the fluid.

4   Using a suitable spanner, slacken the bleed screw approximately one turn.

5   Have your assistant depress the clutch pedal, and hold it down at the end of its stroke. Close the bleed screw, then allow the pedal to return to its normal position.

6   Continue this series of operations (paragraphs 4 and 5) until clean fluid, without any trace of air bubbles, emerges from the end of the tubing. Make sure that the fluid reservoir is checked frequently to ensure that the level does not drop too far, thus letting further air into the system.

7   When no more air bubbles appear, tighten the bleed screw at the end of a downstroke and remove the tubing. Discard the expelled fluid, as it is unsuitable for further use in the hydraulic system.

8   Finally, check the level of fluid in the reservoir once more, top up if necessary, and refit the filler cap.

3 Clutch assembly – removal, inspection and refitting

1   Remove the gearbox as described in Chapter 6.

2   In a diagonal sequence, half a turn at a time, slacken the bolts securing the clutch cover assembly to the flywheel (photo).

3   When all the bolts are slack, remove them, and then ease the cover assembly off the locating dowels. Collect the clutch disc, which will drop out when the clutch cover is removed (photo).

4   With the clutch assembly removed, clean off all traces of asbestos dust using a dry cloth. This is best done outside or in a well-ventilated area; *asbestos dust is harmful and must not be inhaled.*

5   Examine the linings of the clutch disc for wear and loose rivets, and the disc for rim distortion, cracks, broken torsion springs, and worn splines. The surface of the friction linings may be highly glazed, but as long as the friction material pattern can be clearly seen, this is satisfactory. If there is any sign of oil contamination, indicated by a continuous, or patchy, shiny black discolouration, the disc must be renewed, and the source of the contamination traced and rectified. This will be either a leaking crankshaft oil seal or gearbox mainshaft oil seal – or both. Renewal procedures are given in Chapters 1 and 6 respectively. The disc must also be renewed if the lining thickness has worn down to, or just above, the level of the rivet heads.

6   Check the machined faces of the flywheel and pressure plate. If either is grooved, or heavily scored, renewal is necessary. The pressure plate must also be renewed if any cracks are apparent, or if the diaphragm spring is damaged, or its pressure suspect.

7   With the gearbox removed, it is advisable to check the condition of the release bearing, as described in the following Section.

8   To refit the clutch assembly, place the clutch disc in position with the raised portion of the spring housing facing away from the flywheel. The words FLYWHEEL SIDE will also usually be found on the other side of the disc that faces the flywheel (photo).

9   Hold the disc in place, and refit the cover assembly loosely on the dowels. Refit the retaining bolts, and tighten them finger-tight, so that the clutch disc is gripped, but can still be moved.

10 The disc must now be centralised, so that when the engine and gearbox are mated, the gearbox mainshaft splines will pass through the splines in the centre of the disc hub.

11 Centralisation can be carried out quite easily by inserting a round bar, or long screwdriver through the centre of the hub, so that the end of the bar rests in the hole in the centre of the crankshaft. Moving the

2.3 Clutch slave cylinder bleed screw and dust cap (arrowed)

3.2 Slacken the cover plate bolts in a diagonal sequence

3.3 Collect the clutch disc

3.8 Clutch disc marking

3.11 Using a clutch aligning tool to centralise the disc

bar sideways, or up-and-down, will move the disc in whichever direction is necessary to achieve centralisation. With the bar removed, view the clutch disc hub in relation to the hole in the centre of the crankshaft. When the hub appears exactly in the centre, all is correct. Alternatively, if a clutch aligning tool can be obtained, this will eliminate all the guesswork, obviating the need for visual alignment (photo).

12 Tighten the cover retaining bolts gradually, in a diagonal sequence, to the specified torque.

13 The gearbox can now be refitted, as described in Chapter 6.

4 Clutch release bearing – removal, inspection and refitting

1 Remove the gearbox as described in Chapter 6.

2 Disengage the ends of the retaining spring clip from the release fork, and slide the bearing off the gearbox mainshaft sleeve (photo).

3 Check the bearing for smoothness of operation, and renew it if there is any roughness or harshness as the bearing is spun.

4 If required, the release shaft and fork can be removed after undoing the bolt securing the fork to the shaft (photo). Slide the shaft out of the gearbox and recover the fork. Check the condition of the shaft and the oil seal, and renew any components as necessary.

5 Refitting is the reverse sequence to removal, but lubricate the shaft and mainshaft sleeve with molybdenum disulphide grease, and ensure that the retaining spring clip ends locate behind the release fork.

5 Clutch master cylinder – removal and refitting

1 From within the engine compartment, clamp the fluid supply hose from the fluid reservoir to the master cylinder, using a brake hose clamp, a G-clamp, or other similar tool. This will minimise fluid loss during subsequent operations.

2 Release the hose clip and disconnect the fluid supply hose at the master cylinder (photo).

3 Undo the union nut and disconnect the rigid fluid pipe at the upper connection on the damper. Release the retaining clip and carefully move the pipe aside for access.

4 From inside the car, release the turnbuckles and lift out the trim panel over the clutch, brake and accelerator pedals (photo).

5 Extract the retaining clip and withdraw the clevis pin securing the master cylinder pushrod to the clutch pedal (photo).

6 Undo the two nuts securing the master cylinder to the bulkhead, then remove the cylinder and damper assembly from the engine compartment. Recover the master cylinder-to-bulkhead gasket.

7 With the assembly on the bench, undo the two union nuts and remove the connecting fluid pipe between the cylinder and damper.

8 Undo the two nuts and separate the master cylinder from the damper.

9 Refit the master cylinder and damper using the reverse sequence to removal, then bleed the hydraulic system as described in Section 2.

10 After installation, it is advisable to check the clutch pedal height with reference to Fig. 5.4. To do this, measure the distance from the centre of the pedal pad to the floor (carpets removed), and if necessary alter the pedal position by slackening the locknut and turning the master cylinder pushrod. Tighten the locknut when the height is as specified.

6 Clutch master cylinder – overhaul

1 Remove the master cylinder as described in Section 5.

2 Ease back the rubber dust cover from the pushrod end, and then, using circlip pliers, release the circlip that retains the pushrod assembly. Lift out the pushrod complete with disc cover, circlip and washers.

3 Tap the end of the master cylinder on a block of wood to release the piston assembly complete with seals. Also withdraw the return spring

4.2 Removing the release bearing from the mainshaft sleeve

4.4 Clutch release fork-to-shaft retaining bolt (arrowed)

5.2 Fluid supply hose (A) and rigid fluid pipe connection (B) at the master cylinder

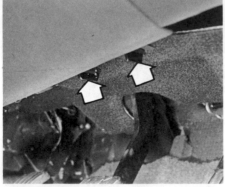

5.4 Interior trim panel retaining turnbuckles (arrowed)

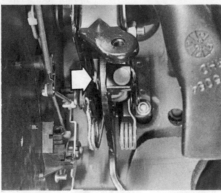

5.5 Extract the clevis pin retaining spring clip (arrowed)

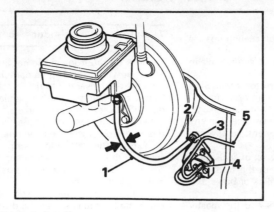

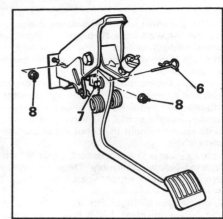

Fig. 5.3 Master cylinder attachment details (Sec 5)

1   Fluid supply hose (arrows indicate clamping
    point)
2   Supply hose clip
3   Supply hose-to-master cylinder connection
4   Rigid pipe connection at fluid damper
5   Rigid pipe retaining clip
6   Clevis pin retaining clip
7   Clevis pin
8   Master cylinder retaining nuts
9   Master cylinder
10 Flange gasket
11 Connecting fluid pipe master cylinder union
12 Connecting fluid pipe damper union
13 Connecting fluid pipe
14 Damper retaining nut
15 Damper

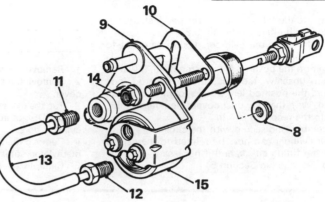

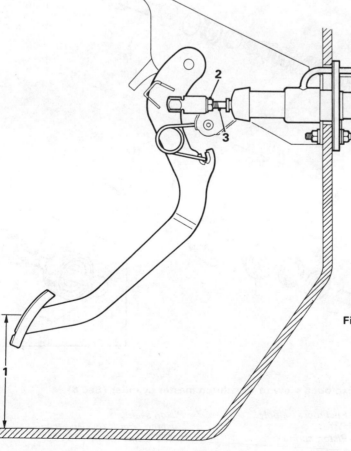

**Fig. 5.4 Clutch pedal height adjustment
details (Sec 5)**

1   Pedal height dimension =
    179 mm (7.0 in)
2   Locknut
3   Pushrod

noting that the small end is towards the piston.

4   Remove the seals from the piston, noting that their sealing lips are towards the return spring.

5   Thoroughly clean all the components in methylated spirit or clean brake fluid.

6   Carefully examine the internal cylinder bore and piston for scoring or wear, and all components for damage or distortion. In order for the seals to maintain hydraulic fluid pressure adequately without leakage, the condition of the cylinder bore and piston must be perfect. If in any doubt whatsoever about the condition of the components, renew the complete master cylinder.

7   If the cylinder is in a satisfactory condition, a new set of seals must be obtained before reassembly. These are available in the form of a master cylinder repair kit, obtainable from Rover dealers or brake and clutch factors.

8   Before reassembly, lubricate all the internal parts and the master cylinder bore with clean brake fluid, and make sure that they are assembled wet.

9   Insert the return spring into the cylinder bore, large end first, then fit the new seals to the piston with reference to Fig. 5.5.

10   Carefully insert the piston into the cylinder, taking care not to damage the seal edges.

11   If the rubber dust cover on the pushrod is to be renewed, it will be necessary to slacken, then unscrew, the locknut and pushrod fork. Before doing this, measure the pushrod length as shown in Fig. 5.5, and record this dimension. With the new dust cover fitted, reassemble the pushrod and reset it to the recorded length.

12   Refit the pushrod assembly, and secure with the circlip.

13   The assembled master cylinder can now be refitted to the car, as described in Section 5. After fitting check, and if necessary reset, the clutch pedal height (also described in Section 5).

7   Clutch slave cylinder – removal and refitting

1   Jack up the front of the car and support it on stands.

2   From within the engine compartment, clamp the fluid supply hose from the fluid reservoir to the clutch master cylinder, using a brake hose clamp, a G-clamp, or other similar tool. This will minimise fluid loss during subsequent operations.

3   From under the front of the car, unscrew the union nut and remove the fluid pipe at the slave cylinder (photo).

4   Extract the retaining spring clip, and withdraw the clevis pin securing the slave cylinder pushrod to the clutch release arm (photo).

5   Undo the two slave cylinder retaining bolts, and remove the cylinder from the car.

6   Refitting is the reverse sequence to removal, but on completion bleed the hydraulic system as described in Section 2.

8   Clutch slave cylinder – overhaul

1   Remove the slave cylinder from the car as described in Section 7.

2   Remove the pushrod from the cylinder, then release the rubber dust cover.

3   Tap the cylinder on a block of wood to release the piston and return spring. Do not attempt to remove the plastic filter from the base of the cylinder bore.

4   Remove the seal from the piston, then clean all the components in methylated spirit or clean brake fluid.

5   Carefully examine the internal cylinder bore and piston for signs of

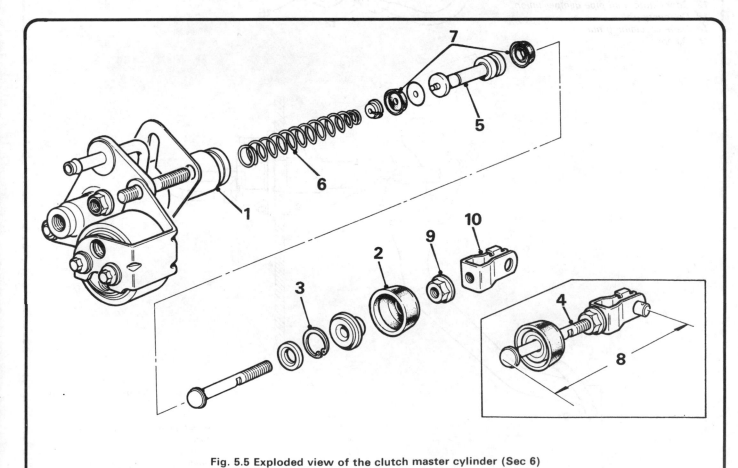

Fig. 5.5 Exploded view of the clutch master cylinder (Sec 6)

1 Master cylinder	4 Pushrod assembly	7 Piston seals	9 Locknut
2 Dust cover	5 Piston	8 Pushrod length (measured	10 Pushrod fork
3 Circlip	6 Piston spring	before dismantling)	

7.3 Fluid pipe union nut (A) and slave cylinder retaining bolts (B)

7.4 Removing the pushrod clevis pin retaining spring clip

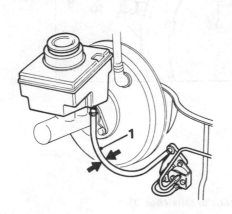

Fig. 5.6 Slave cylinder attachment details (Sec 7)

1	Fluid supply hose (arrows indicate clamping point)	2	Fluid pipe	4	Clevis pin	6	Slave cylinder
		3	Clevis pin retaining clip	5	Slave cylinder retaining bolts	

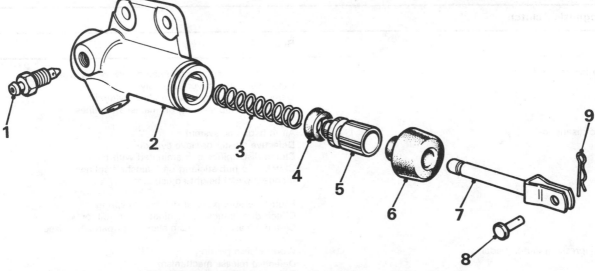

Fig. 5.7 Exploded view of the clutch slave cylinder (Sec 8)

1	Bleed screw	4	Piston seal	6	Dust cover	8	Clevis pin
2	Slave cylinder	5	Piston	7	Pushrod	9	Clevis pin retaining clip
3	Return spring						

scoring or wear, and if evident, renew the complete slave cylinder. If the components are in a satisfactory condition, a new set of rubber seals must be obtained before reassembly. These are available in the form of a repair kit, obtainable from Rover dealers or brake and clutch factors.

6   Lubricate the piston, seal, and cylinder bore with clean brake fluid, and assemble the components wet.

7   Fit the new seal to the piston, with the sealing lip towards the return spring.

8   Fit the return spring to the cylinder bore, followed by the piston, dust cover and pushrod.

9   The assembled slave cylinder can now be fitted to the car as described in Section 7.

9   Clutch pedal – removal and refitting

1   From inside the car, release the turnbuckles and lift out the trim panel over the clutch, brake and accelerator pedals.

2   Depress the clutch pedal fully, release the pedal return spring from the pedal, then remove the spring from the pedal bracket.

3   Extract the retaining spring clip, and withdraw the clevis pin securing the master cylinder pushrod to the pedal.

4   Undo the two nuts and one bolt securing the pedal bracket to the bulkhead, and remove the bracket and pedal assembly from the car.

5   Undo the pedal pivot bolt and remove the pedal from the bracket.

6   Prise out the two pedal bushes and withdraw the centre spacer tube.

7   Check the condition of the components and renew as necessary.

8   Refitting is the reverse sequence to removal.

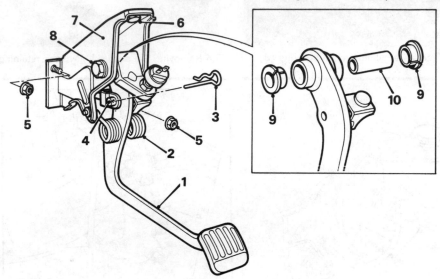

Fig. 5.8 Clutch pedal attachment details (Sec 9)

1 Clutch pedal	4 Clevis pin	7 Pedal bracket	9 Pedal bushes
2 Pedal return spring	5 Pedal bracket retaining nuts	8 Pedal pivot bolt	10 Centre spacer tube
3 Clevis pin retaining clip	6 Pedal bracket retaining bolt		

10   Fault diagnosis – clutch

Symptom	Reason(s)
Judder when taking up drive	Clutch disc linings contaminated with oil, or worn Defective clutch cover assembly Defective master cylinder or slave cylinder Clutch disc hub sticking on mainshaft splines
Clutch fails to disengage	Air in hydraulic system Defective master or slave cylinder Clutch disc linings contaminated with oil Clutch disc hub sticking on mainshaft splines Incorrect pedal height adjustment
Clutch slips	Faulty pressure plate or diaphragm spring Clutch disc linings contaminated with oil, or worn Clutch release mechanism sticking or partially seized
Noise when depressing clutch pedal	Worn release bearing Defective release mechanism Defective clutch cover assembly
Noise when releasing clutch pedal	Broken clutch disc torsion springs Defective clutch cover assembly Dry or worn pedal pivot bushes Gearbox internal wear

Chapter 6 Manual gearbox

For modifications, and information applicable to later models, see Supplement at end of manual

Contents

Specifications

Type .... Five forward speeds (all synchromesh) and reverse. Final drive integral with main gearbox

Identification number .... G6 DT

Gear ratios

Up to approximately June 1988:

1st	3.25:1
2nd	1.89:1
3rd	1.31:1
4th	1.00:1
5th	0.85:1
Reverse	3.00:1
Final drive	3.94:1

From approximately June 1988 onwards:

1st	3.25:1
2nd	1.89:1
3rd	1.22:1
4th	0.93:1
5th	0.76:1
Reverse	3.00:1
Final drive	4.20:1

Lubrication

Lubricant type/specification* .... Multigrade engine oil, viscosity SAE 10W/40, to API SF or SF/CD (Duckhams QXR, Hypergrade, or 10W/40 Motor Oil)

Lubricant capacity .... 2.3 litres (4.0 Imp pts)

* Note: *Austin Rover specify a 10W/40 oil to meet warranty requirements. Duckhams QXR and 10W/40 Motor Oil are available to meet these requirements.*

Gearbox overhaul data

Mainshaft endfloat	0.14 to 0.21 mm (0.005 to 0.008 in)
Endfloat adjustment	Selective circlips
Mainshaft bearing clearances:	
2nd to 3rd gear clearance:	
Standard	0.06 to 0.21 mm (0.002 to 0.008 in)
Wear limit	0.30 mm (0.012 in)
3rd gear thickness:	
Standard	35.42 to 35.47 mm (1.395 to 1.397 in)
Wear limit	35.30 mm (1.390 in)
4th gear to distance collar:	
Standard	0.06 to 0.21 mm (0.002 to 0.008 in)
Wear limit	0.30 mm (0.012 in)

Distance collar dimension 'A':
    Standard .... 26.03 to 26.08 mm (1.025 to 1.027 in)
    Wear limit .... 26.01 mm (1.024 in)
4th gear thickness:
    Standard .... 33.45 to 33.47 mm (1.317 to 1.318 in)
    Wear limit .... 33.33 mm (1.313 in)
5th gear to distance collar:
    Standard .... 0.06 to 0.21 mm (0.002 to 0.008 in)
    Wear limit .... 0.3 mm (0.012 in)
Distance collar dimension 'B':
    Standard .... 26.03 to 26.08 mm (1.025 to 1.027 in)
    Wear limit .... 26.01 mm (1.024 in)
5th gear thickness:
    Standard .... 31.92 to 31.97 mm (1.257 to 1.259 in)
    Wear limit .... 31.80 mm (1.252 in)
Countershaft endfloat:
    Standard .... 0.03 to 0.08 mm (0.0012 to 0.003 in)
    Wear limit .... 0.18 mm (0.007 in)
Endfloat adjustment .... Selective distance collars and thrustwashers
Synchro baulk ring to gear clearance:
    Standard .... 0.85 to 1.10 mm (0.033 to 0.043 in)
    Wear limit .... 0.40 mm (0.016 in)
Selector fork to synchro sleeve clearance:
    Standard .... 0.45 to 0.65 mm (0.017 to 0.025 in)
    Wear limit .... 1.00 mm (0.039 in)
Selector fork thicknesses:
    1st/2nd .... 8.90 to 9.00 mm (0.350 to 0.354 in)
    3rd/4th .... 8.40 to 8.50 mm (0.330 to 0.334 in)
    5th .... 5.40 to 5.50 mm (0.212 to 0.216 in)
Reverse gear fork to gear clearance:
    Standard .... 0.50 to 1.10 mm (0.019 to 0.043 in)
    Wear limit .... 1.80 mm (0.070 in)
Shift arm guide to 3rd/4th selector fork clearance:
    Standard .... 0.20 to 0.50 mm (0.007 to 0.019 in)
    Wear limit .... 0.80 mm (0.031 in)
Gearchange arm to shift arm clearance:
    Standard .... 0.05 to 0.35 mm (0.002 to 0.013 in)
    Wear limit .... 0.60 mm (0.023 in)
Gearchange arm to interlock clearance:
    Standard .... 0.05 to 0.25 mm (0.002 to 0.009 in)
    Wear limit .... 0.50 mm (0.020 in)
Shift arm to guide clearance:
    Standard .... 0.20 to 0.30 mm (0.007 to 0.012 in)
    Wear limit .... 0.55 mm (0.021 in)
Differential endfloat .... 0.15 mm (0.006 in)
Endfloat adjustment .... Selective circlips

Torque wrench settings

	Nm	lbf ft
Oil filler plug	45	33
Oil drain plug	40	30
Speedometer pinion retainer plate bolt	11	8
Gearbox steady rod bolt	25	18
Gear lever to gearchange rod	22	16
Remote control housing to underbody	22	16
Clutch slave cylinder bolts	22	16
Front engine mounting to gearbox bracket	80	59
Front engine mounting bracket to gearbox	40	30
Rear engine mounting bracket to gearbox	40	30
Engine rear tie-bar to mounting bracket	45	33
Longitudinal support member to underbody	45	33
Engine snubber bracket to gearbox	45	33
Reversing light switch	25	18
Gearcase to bellhousing bolts	45	33
Reverse idler shaft retaining bolt	55	41
Countershaft access plug	70	52
Reverse gear fork bracket bolts	15	11
Gearchange holder and interlock assembly:		
Long bolt	28	21
Intermediate bolt	15	11
Short bolt	12	9
Gearchange shaft detent plug	22	16
Gearchange arm to shaft bolt	30	22
Countershaft bearing retaining plate bolts	12	9
Countershaft nut	110	81
Roadwheel nuts	70	52

1 General description

The manual gearbox fitted to all 820 series models is of Honda design, incorporating five forward gears and one reverse. Synchromesh gear engagement is used on all forward gears.

The mainshaft and countershaft carry the constant mesh gear cluster assemblies, and are supported on ball and roller bearings. The short input end of the mainshaft eliminates the need for additional support from a crankshaft spigot bearing. The synchromesh gear engagement is by spring rings which act against baulk rings under the movement of the synchroniser sleeves. Gear selection is by means of a floor-mounted lever, connected by a remote control housing and gear change rod to the gearchange shaft in the gearbox. Gearchange shaft movement is transmitted to the selector forks via the gearchange holder and interlock assembly.

The final drive differential unit is integral with the main gearbox, and is located between the bellhousing and gearcase. The gearbox and final drive components both share the same lubricating oil.

2 Maintenance and inspection

1 At the intervals given in *Routine maintenance* at the beginning of this manual, carry out the following service operations on the gearbox.
2 Carefully inspect the gearbox joint faces and oil seals for signs of damage, deterioration or oil leakage.
3 At the same service intervals, check and if necessary top up the gearbox oil. The filler plug is located on the left-hand side of the gearcase, and can be reached from above the engine compartment. Wipe the area around the filler plug with a rag before unscrewing the plug. Top up if necessary, using the specified grade of oil, to bring the level up to the filler plug orifice (photo).
4 At the specified intervals, the gearbox oil should be renewed. To do this, jack up the front of the car and support it on axle stands. Place a suitable container beneath the drain plug, which is located below the driveshaft inner constant velocity joint on the same side as the filler plug (photo). Undo the plug using a square key, and allow the oil to drain. If a suitable key is not available, the $3/8$ in square drive end of a socket bar will suffice. Refit the plug after draining, then refill with fresh oil through the filler orifice.
5 At less-frequent intervals, check for excess free play or wear in the gear linkage and gear lever joints and pivots.

3 Gearbox – removal and refitting

1 Disconnect the battery negative terminal. (Refer to Chapter 12, Section 1, before doing this).
2 Remove the air cleaner assembly as described in Chapter 3.
3 Remove the starter motor as described in Chapter 12.
4 Extract the retaining clips and release the support struts from the bonnet. Tie the bonnet back in the fully open position.
5 Apply the handbrake, prise off the front wheel trim and slacken the wheel nuts. Jack up the front of the car and support it on axle stands. Remove the front roadwheels.

6 Drain the gearbox oil as described in Section 2.
7 Remove the engine undershield and the access panel from the left-hand inner wing.
8 Remove the front suspension tie-rod on the left-hand side, as described in Chapter 10.
9 Undo the bolt and disconnect the earth lead from the gearbox (photo).
10 Slide up the rubber boot and disconnect the leads at the reversing light switch.
11 Disconnect the speedometer transducer wiring multi-plug.
12 Undo the bolts securing the longitudinal support member to the underbody, and remove the member.
13 Undo the three bolts and remove the engine snubber bracket from the gearbox (photo).
14 Extract the spring clip and withdraw the clevis pin securing the clutch slave cylinder pushrod to the release arm (photo).
15 Undo the two slave cylinder retaining bolts, and move the cylinder aside.
16 Undo the bolt in the centre of the gearbox steady rod. Remove the dished washer, slide off the steady rod and remove the inner flat washer (photos).
17 Remove the spring clip to expose the gearchange rod-to-gearchange shaft retaining roll pin (photo).
18 Using a parallel pin punch, tap out the roll pin, and slide the gearchange rod rearwards, off the shaft (photo).
19 Undo the nut securing the right-hand steering knuckle balljoint to the lower suspension arm, then release the balljoint from the arm using a universal balljoint separator tool or two-legged puller – refer to Chapter 10 if necessary.
20 Pull the steering knuckle outwards, then using a suitable flat bar or large screwdriver, lever between the driveshaft inner constant velocity joint and the differential housing to release the joint from the gearbox (photo).
21 Move the driveshaft clear of the gearbox, then repeat these procedures on the left-hand driveshaft.
22 Attach a suitable hoist to the engine using rope slings, or chains attached to brackets secured to the cylinder head. Raise the hoist to just take the weight of the engine.
23 Support the gearbox using a jack and interposed block of wood.
24 Undo the nut securing the front engine mounting to its gearbox bracket.
25 Undo the two bolts securing the front mounting bracket to the gearbox, and remove the bracket.
26 Undo the bolts securing the rear engine mounting bracket to the gearbox, noting the location of the crankshaft sensor bracket. Remove the bolts and move the sensor aside (photo).
27 Undo the bolt securing the larger end of the engine rear tie-bar to its mounting bracket. Remove the through-bolt, and recover the special nut.
28 Undo all the remaining bolts securing the gearbox to the engine.
29 Ease the gearbox away from the engine after releasing it from the locating dowels, then lower the jack and engine hoist until clearance exists to enable the gearbox to be withdrawn fully from the side of the engine. Withdraw the unit from under the car.
30 Refitting the gearbox is the reverse sequence to removal. Tighten all nuts and bolts to the specified torque, and fill the gearbox with oil as described in Section 2 on completion.

2.3 Topping-up the gearbox oil

2.4 Gearbox drain plug location (arrowed)

3.9 Gearbox earth lead retaining bolt (arrowed)

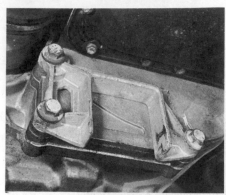

3.13 Undo the three bolts and remove the snubber bracket

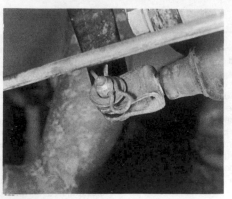

3.14 Clutch slave cylinder pushrod clevis pin and spring clip

3.16A Undo the bolt in the centre of the steady rod (arrowed) ...

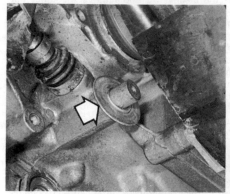

3.16B ... slide off the steady rod and remove the inner flat washer (arrowed)

3.17 Remove the gearchange rod spring clip ...

3.18 ... tap out the roll pin, and withdraw the gearchange rod off the shaft

3.20 Removing the driveshaft inner constant velocity joint

3.26 Crankshaft sensor bracket location

4 Gearbox overhaul – general

1   Dismantling, overhaul and reassembly of the gearbox is reasonably straightforward, and can be carried out without recourse to the manufacturer's special tools, although a reasonably comprehensive standard tool kit will be required. It should be noted, however, that any repair or overhaul work on the final drive differential must be limited to the renewal of the carrier support bearings. Owing to the complicated nature of this unit and the costs involved, the advice of a Rover dealer should be sought if further repair is necessary.

2   Read through all the applicable Sections of this Chapter, and familiarise yourself with the procedures involved before contemplating any repair or overhaul task. Make sure that you have all the necessary tools required (or have access to any you don't have), and enquire about the availability of any parts thay may be needed for repair.

3   Before starting any work on the gearbox, clean the exterior of the casings using paraffin or a suitable solvent. Dry the unit with a lint-free rag. Make sure that an uncluttered working area is available, with some small containers and trays handy to store the various parts. Label everything as it is removed.

4   Before starting reassembly, all the components must be spotlessly clean, and should be lubricated with the specified grade of oil during reassembly.

5 Gearbox – dismantling

1 Stand the gearbox on its bellhousing face on the bench, and begin dismantling by removing the reversing light switch.
2 Undo the bolt, remove the retaining plate, and lift out the speedometer transducer and pinion assembly.
3 Undo all the gearcase-to-bellhousing retaining bolts, noting the location of the breather hose and bracket, which are also retained by one of the case bolts. Remove the breather hose and bracket (photo).
4 Undo the reverse idler shaft retaining bolt, located on the side of the gearcase (photo).
5 Using a large Allen key, hexagonal bar, or suitable bolt with two nuts locked together, undo the countershaft access plug on the end of the gearcase (photo).
6 Using circlip pliers inserted through the access plug aperture, spread the countershaft retaining circlip, while at the same time lifting

upwards on the gearcase. Tap the case with a soft mallet if necessary. When the circlip is clear of its groove, lift the case up and off the bellhousing and gear clusters (photos).
7 Undo the two retaining bolts and remove the reverse gear fork and bracket.
8 Lift out the reverse gear idler shaft, then remove the gear and thrustwasher from the shaft.
9 Undo the three bolts and remove the gearchange holder and interlock assembly. Note that the holder locates in a slot in the 1st/2nd selector shaft.
10 With the help of an assistant, lift the mainshaft and countershaft as an assembly upwards slightly, then withdraw the selector shafts and forks from the bellhousing and gear clusters (photo).
11 Lift the mainshaft and countershaft out of their respective bearings in the bellhousing (photo).
12 Finally, remove the differential from the bellhousing (photo).

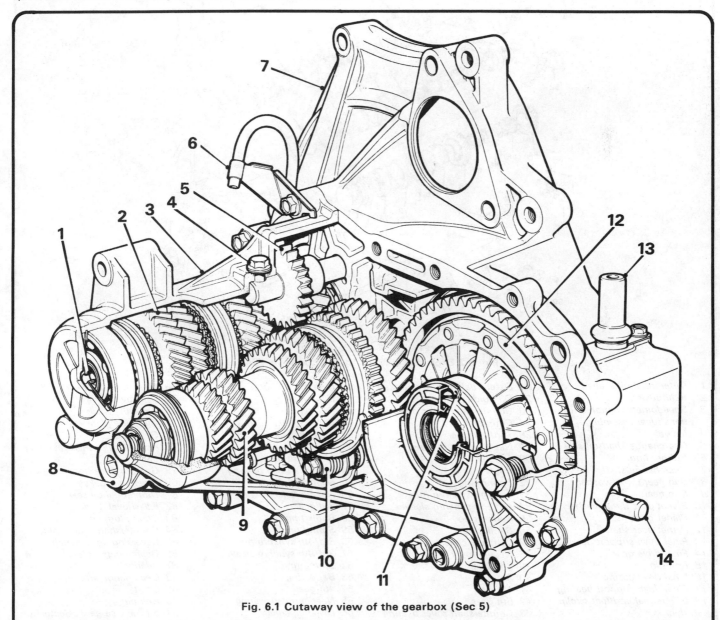

Fig. 6.1 Cutaway view of the gearbox (Sec 5)

1 Oil guide plate
2 Mainshaft assembly
3 Gearcase
4 Reverse idler shaft retaining bolt
5 Reverse idler gear
6 Gearbox breather and bracket
7 Bellhousing
8 Countershaft access plug
9 Countershaft assembly
10 Gearchange holder and interlock assembly
11 Differential endfloat circlip shim
12 Final drive differential
13 Speedometer pinion and transducer assembly
14 Gearchange shaft

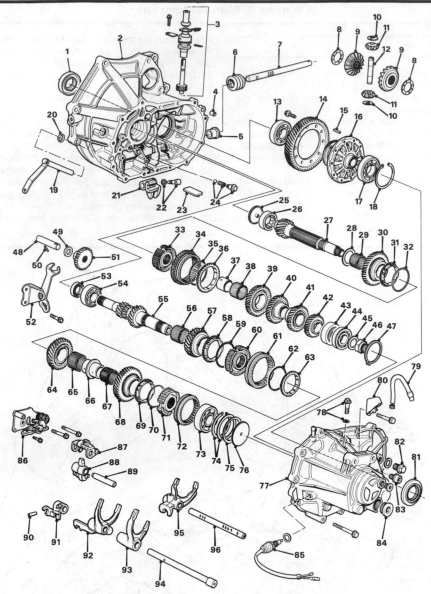

Fig. 6.2 Exploded view of the components (Sec 5)

1	Differential oil seal
2	Bellhousing
3	Speedometer pinion and transducer assembly
4	Dowel
5	Gearchange shaft oil seal
6	Rubber boot
7	Gearchange shaft
8	Sun gear thrustwasher
9	Sun gear
10	Planet gear thrustwasher
11	Planet gear
12	Planet gear shaft
13	Final drive support bearing
14	Final drive gear
15	Roll pin
16	Final drive casing
17	Final drive support bearing
18	Differential endfloat circlip shim
19	Clutch operating lever
20	Clutch operating lever oil seal
21	Gearchange arm
22	Dowel bolt and washer
23	Magnet
24	Detent ball, spring and plug
25	Oil guide plate
26	Countershaft roller bearing
27	Countershaft
28	Thrustwasher
29	Needle roller bearing
30	1st gear
31	Baulk ring
32	Spring ring
33	1st/2nd synchro hub
34	1st/2nd synchro sleeve
35	Spring ring
36	Baulk ring
37	Distance collar
38	Needle roller bearing
39	2nd gear
40	3rd gear
41	4th gear
42	5th gear
43	Countershaft roller bearing
44	Countershaft ball bearing
45	Washer
46	Retaining nut
47	Circlip
48	Reverse idler shaft
49	Reverse idler gear thrustwasher
50	Roll pin
51	Reverse idler gear
52	Reverse gear fork and bracket
53	Mainshaft oil seal
54	Mainshaft ball bearing
55	Mainshaft
56	Needle roller bearing
57	3rd gear
58	Baulk ring
59	Spring ring
60	3rd/4th synchro hub
61	3rd/4th synchro sleeve
62	Spring ring
63	Baulk ring
64	4th gear
65	Needle roller bearing
66	Distance collar
67	Needle roller bearing
68	5th gear
69	Baulk ring
70	Spring ring
71	5th gear synchro hub
72	5th gear synchro sleeve
73	Mainshaft ball bearing
74	Selective circlips
75	Belleville washer
76	Oil guide plate
77	Gearcase
78	Reverse idler shaft retaining bolt
79	Gearbox breather
80	Breather bracket
81	Differential oil seal
82	Filler/level plug
83	Drain plug
84	Countershaft access plug
85	Reversing light switch
86	Gearchange holder
87	Interlock
88	Gearchange arm
89	Shaft
90	Roll pin
91	5th/reverse gear selector
92	3rd/4th gear selector fork
93	5th gear selector fork
94	5th/reverse selector shaft
95	1st/2nd gear selector shaft
96	1st/2nd gear selector shaft

5.3 Gearbox breather bracket and case retaining bolt

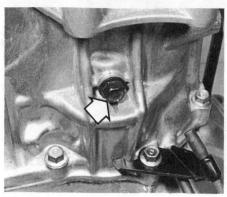

5.4 Reverse idler shaft retaining bolt (arrowed)

5.5 Countershaft access plug (arrowed)

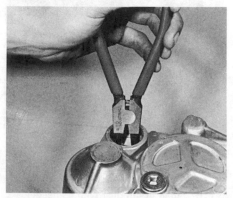

5.6A Release the countershaft bearing retaining circlip ...

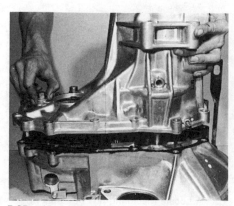

5.6B ... then withdraw the gearcase

5.10 Lift the mainshaft and countershaft, then remove the selector shafts and forks

5.11 Remove the mainshaft and countershaft together from the bellhousing

5.12 Remove the differential from the bellhousing

6 Mainshaft – dismantling and reassembly

1   Remove the mainshaft bearing using a two-or three-legged puller if necessary, unless the bearing remained in the gearcase during removal.
2   Withdraw the 5th gear synchroniser hub and sleeve assembly from the mainshaft, using a puller if it is tight. Recover the 5th gear baulk ring from the cone face of 5th gear and place it, together with the spring ring, on the synchroniser unit.
3   Slide off 5th gear, followed by the 5th gear needle roller bearing.
4   Withdraw the distance collar, followed by 4th gear and the needle roller bearing.
5   Remove the 3rd/4th synchro hub and sleeve assembly, complete with baulk rings and spring rings.
6   Remove 3rd gear and its needle roller bearing.
7   Carry out a careful inspection of the mainshaft components as

described in Section 10, and obtain any new parts as necessary.
8   During reassembly, lightly lubricate all the parts with the specified grade of oil as the work proceeds.
9   Slide the 3rd gear needle roller bearing onto the mainshaft, followed by the 3rd gear, with its flat face towards the other gears on the shaft (photos).
10 Place the 3rd gear baulk ring and spring ring on the cone face of 3rd gear, then fit the 3rd/4th synchro hub and sleeve assembly. Ensure that the lugs on the baulk ring engage with the slots in the synchro hub (photos).
11 Locate the 4th gear spring ring and baulk ring in the synchro unit, then slide on 4th gear with its needle roller bearing (photos).
12 Fit the distance collar (photo).
13 Place the 5th gear needle roller bearing over the collar, then slide 5th gear onto the bearing (photos).
14 Locate the 5th gear baulk ring and spring ring in the 5th gear

6.9A Fit the 3rd gear needle roller bearing to the mainshaft ...

6.9B ... followed by 3rd gear

6.10A Place the baulk ring and spring ring on 3rd gear ...

6.10B ... then fit the 3rd/4th synchro hub and sleeve assembly

6.11A Locate the spring rig and baulk ring on the synchro unit ...

6.11B ... then fit 4th gear with its needle roller bearing

6.12 Fit the distance collar

6.13A Place the 5th gear needle roller bearing over the collar ...

6.13B ... then slide on 5th gear

synchro unit, then fit this assembly to the mainshaft (photo).

15 Fit the mainshaft bearing, and drive it fully home using a hammer and tube of suitable diameter in contact with the bearing inner race.

16 The mainshaft bearing clearances should now be checked, using feeler gauges as follows. If any of the clearances are found to be outside the tolerances given in the Specifications, it will be necessary to dismantle the mainshaft again so that the adjacent gear or distance collar can be measured, and then renewed if necessary. To avoid having to dismantle the mainshaft repeatedly, measure *all* the clearances first, then dismantle and renew the components as required.

17 Measure the clearance between 2nd gear and 3rd gear, and compare the figure obtained with that given in the Specifications. If the clearance is excessive, dismantle the mainshaft and measure the thickness of 3rd gear. If this is outside the specified tolerance, renew the gear. If the thickness is satisfactory, renew the 3rd/4th synchro hub.

18 Measure the clearance between 4th gear and the distance collar flange. If the clearance is excessive, dismantle the mainshaft and measure the distance from the 4th gear side of the distance collar

shoulder to the end of the collar (dimension 'A' in Fig. 6.3). If this dimension is outside the specified tolerance, renew the distance collar. If the measured distance is satisfactory, measure the 4th gear thickness. If this is outside the specified tolerance, renew the gear. If the thickness is satisfactory, renew the 3rd/4th synchro hub.

19 Measure the clearance between 5th gear and the distance collar flange. If the clearance is excessive, dismantle the mainshaft and measure the distance from the 5th gear side of the distance collar shoulder to the end of the collar (dimension 'B' in Fig. 6.3). If this dimension is outside the specified tolerance, renew the distance collar. If the measured distance is satisfactory, measure the 5th gear thickness. If this is outside the specified tolerance, renew the gear. If the thickness is satisfactory, renew the 5th gear synchro hub.

20 If the mainshaft, mainshaft components, the gearcase or bellhousing have been renewed, then the mainshaft endfloat must be checked and if necessary adjusted. To do this, it will be necessary to remove the mainshaft ball-bearing in the gearcase, remove the selective circlips, Belleville washer and oil guide, then refit the bearing.

21 Position the assembled mainshaft in the bellhousing, fit the

gearcase, and temporarily secure it with several evenly-spaced bolts. Tighten the bolts securely.

22 Support the bellhousing face of the gearbox on blocks, so as to provide access to the protruding mainshaft.

23 Place a straight edge across the bellhousing face, in line with the mainshaft, then accurately measure and record the distance from straight edge to mainshaft (Fig. 6.4).

24 Turn the gearbox over so that the bellhousing is uppermost, and gently tap the mainshaft back into the gearcase using a soft-faced mallet. Take a second measurement of the mainshaft-to-straight edge distance.

25 Subtract the first measurement from the second measurement, and identify this as dimension A.

26 Measure the thickness of the Belleville washer, and add an allowance of 0.17 mm (0.006 in), which is the nominal mainshaft endfloat. Identify this as dimension B.

27 Subtract dimension B from dimension A, and the value obtained is the thickness of selective circlip(s) required to give the specified mainshaft endfloat.

28 Remove the gearcase and mainshaft. Remove the bearing from the gearcase, refit the oil guide, Belleville washer, and circlips of the required thickness, then refit the bearing.

6.14 Fit the 5th gear synchro unit, complete with spring ring and baulk ring

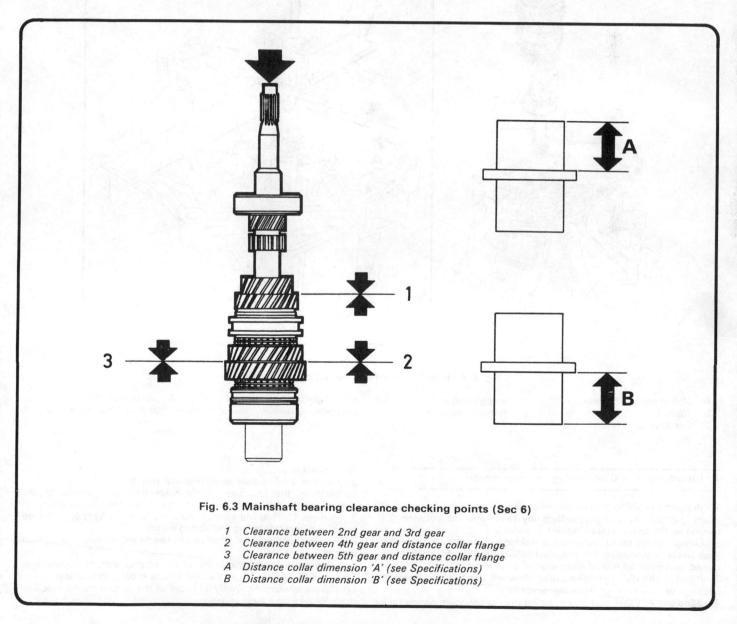

Fig. 6.3 Mainshaft bearing clearance checking points (Sec 6)

1 Clearance between 2nd gear and 3rd gear
2 Clearance between 4th gear and distance collar flange
3 Clearance between 5th gear and distance collar flange
A Distance collar dimension 'A' (see Specifications)
B Distance collar dimension 'B' (see Specifications)

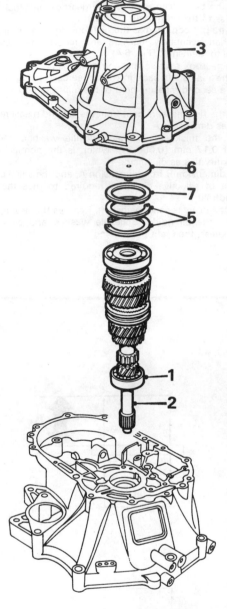
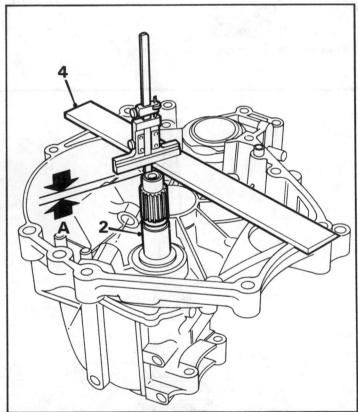

Fig. 6.4 Mainshaft endfloat adjustment (Sec 6)

1 Mainshaft ball-bearing   4 Straight edge   6 Oil guide plate   A Measured clearance –
2 Mainshaft   5 Selective circlips   7 Belleville washer   straight edge-to-mainshaft
3 Gearcase

7 Countershaft – dismantling and reassembly

1 Support the pinion gear on the countershaft between two blocks of wood. Tighten the vice just sufficiently to prevent the countershaft turning as the bearing retaining nut is undone.
2 Using a small punch, release the staking on the countershaft nut, then undo and remove the nut. Note that the nut has a left-hand thread, and must be turned clockwise to unscrew it.
3 Remove the dished washer, then draw off the two countershaft bearings using a two- or three-legged puller.
4 Slide 5th, 4th, 3rd, and 2nd gears off the countershaft, noting their

fitted directions.
5 Remove the 2nd gear baulk ring and spring ring.
6 Slide off the 2nd gear needle roller bearing, followed by the distance collar. Use two screwdrivers to lever off the collar if it is tight.
7 Remove the 1st/2nd synchro hub and sleeve assembly, followed by the 1st gear baulk ring and spring ring.
8 Slide off first gear, followed by the needle roller bearing and thrust washer.
9 Carry out a careful inspection of the countershaft components as described in Section 10, and obtain any new parts as necessary.
10 During reassembly, lightly lubricate all the parts with the specified grade of oil as the work proceeds.

11 Fit the thrustwasher to the countershaft, followed by the needle roller bearing and 1st gear (photos).

12 Fit the baulk ring and spring ring to the cone face of 1st gear, then slide on the 1st/2nd synchro unit. The synchro unit must be fitted with the selector fork groove in the synchro sleeve away from 1st gear. As the unit is fitted, ensure that the lugs on the baulk ring engage with the slots in the synchro hub (photos).

13 Warm the distance collar in boiling water, then slide it onto the countershaft with the oil hole offset towards 1st gear (photo).

14 Fit the 2nd gear needle roller bearing to the distance collar (photo).

15 Locate the 2nd gear baulk ring and spring ring on the synchro unit, then slide 2nd gear into place over the needle roller bearing (photos).

16 Fit 3rd gear to the countershaft with its longer boss away from 2nd gear (photo).

17 Fit 4th gear with its boss towards the 3rd gear boss (photo).

18 Fit 5th gear with its flat face towards 4th gear (photo), then tap the countershaft bearings into position using a hammer and suitable tube.

19 Fit the dished washer with its dished side towards the bearings, followed by a new countershaft nut. Hold the pinion between blocks of wood in the vice as before, and tighten the nut to the specified torque.

20 Using feeler gauges, measure the clearance between the thrustwasher and 1st gear, and between the 2nd and 3rd gear faces (photos). Compare the measurements with the endfloat dimension given in the Specifications. If the recorded clearances are outside the tolerance range, dismantle the countershaft again, and fit an alternative thickness thrustwasher or distance collar from the range available.

21 With the countershaft assembled and the endfloat correctly set, recheck the torque of the countershaft nut, then peen its edge into the countershaft groove using a small punch.

7.11A Fit the thrustwasher to the countershaft ...

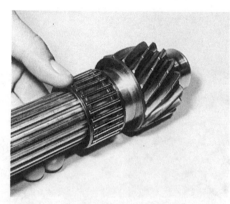

7.11B ... followed by the needle roller bearing ...

7.11C ... and 1st gear

7.12A Fit the baulk ring and spring ring to 1st gear ...

7.12B ... then slide on the 1st/2nd synchro unit

7.13 Fit the distance collar with its oil hole (arrowed) offset towards 1st gear

7.14 Locate the 2nd gear needle roller bearing over the collar

7.15A Fit the baulk ring and spring ring ...

7.15B ... followed by 2nd gear

7.16 Fit 3rd gear with its boss away from 2nd gear

7.17 Fit 4th gear with its boss towards 3rd gear

7.18 Fit 5th gear with its flat face towards 4th gear

7.20A Check the clearance between the thrustwasher and 1st gear ...

7.20B ... and between 2nd and 3rd gears

8 Gearcase – inspection and overhaul

1   Check the gearcase for cracks, or any damage to its bellhousing mating face. Renew the case if damaged.
2   Check the condition of the mainshaft bearing in the gearcase, and ensure that it spins smoothly, with no trace of roughness or harshness. The bearing must be removed if it is worn, if the gearcase is to be renewed, or if it is necessary to gain access to the mainshaft endfloat selective circlips located behind it.
3   Removal of the bearing entails the use of a slide hammer, with adaptor consisting of externally-expanding flange or legs, to locate behind the inner race. A Rover special tool is available for this purpose, but it should be possible to make up a suitable alternative with readily-available tools. Whichever option is chosen, it is quite likely that the oil guide plate will be damaged or broken in the process. If so a new one must be obtained.
4   If any of the mainshaft components are being renewed during the course of overhaul, do not refit the bearing, the circlips, the Belleville washer or the oil guide plate until after the mainshaft endfloat has been checked and adjusted.
5   When the bearing is fitted, this can be done by tapping it squarely into place, using a hammer and tube of suitable diameter in contact with the bearing outer race.
6   If there is any sign of leakage, the differential oil seal in the gearcase should be renewed. Drive or hook out the old seal, and install the new one with its open side facing inwards, ie towards the bearing. Tap the seal squarely into place, using a suitable tube or the old seal. Smear a little grease around the sealing to aid refitting of the driveshaft. **Note:** *If the differential or differential bearings have been renewed or disturbed from their original positions, do not fit the oil seal until the gearbox has been completely reassembled.* The differential bearing clearances are checked through the oil seal aperture, and cannot be done with the seal in place.

9 Bellhousing – inspection and overhaul

1   With the mainshaft and countershaft removed, lift out the magnet from its location in the bellhousing edge (photo).
2   Remove the clutch release bearing, release fork and arm as described in Chapter 5.
3   Undo the gearchange shaft detent plug bolt, and lift out the detent spring and ball (photos).
4   Undo the bolt securing the gearchange arm to the shaft, and slide the arm off the shaft (photo).
5   Withdraw the gearchange shaft from the bellhousing, and recover the rubber boot.
6   Check the condition of the ball and roller bearings in the bellhousing, ensuring that they spin smoothly, with no trace of roughness or harshness.
7   Removal of the bearing entails the use of a slide hammer, with adaptor consisting of externally-expanding flange or legs, to locate behind the inner race. A Rover special tool is available for this purpose, but it should be possible to make up a suitable alternative with readily-available tools. Another alternative would be to take the bellhousing along to your dealer, and have him renew the bearings for you. Whichever option is chosen, it is quite likely that the oil guide plate behind the countershaft roller bearing will be damaged or broken in the process (assuming this bearing is to be renewed), and if so a new one must be obtained (photo).
8   Refit the bearings by tapping them squarely into place, using a hammer and tube of suitable diameter. Ensure that the oil hole in the countershaft bearing faces the gearbox interior.
9   Carefully inspect all the oil seals in the bellhousing, and renew any that show signs of leakage or deterioration. The old seals can be driven out with a tube or punch, and the new seals tapped squarely into place using a block of wood or the old seal. Ensure that in all cases the open side of the seal faces inwards. In the case of the mainshaft oil seal, it

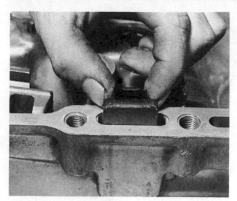

9.1 Remove the magnet from the bellhousing

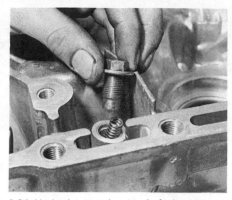

9.3A Undo the gearchange shaft detent plug bolt ...

9.3B ... then lift out the spring ...

9.3C ... and detent ball

9.4 Gearchange arm retaining bolt (arrowed)

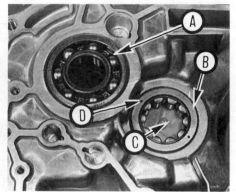

9.7 Mainshaft ballbearing (A) countershaft roller bearing(B), oil guide plate (C), and bearing oil holes (D)

will be necessary to remove the mainshaft bearing to enable a new seal to be fitted.

10 Inspect the gearchange shaft for distortion or wear across the detent grooves, and check the gearchange arm for wear of the forks. Renew these components if wear is evident.

11 With the new bearings and seals in position, and any other new parts obtained as necessary, refit the gearchange shaft and rubber boot with the detent grooves facing outwards, ie towards the gear clusters.

12 Slide on the gearchange arm so that its forked side is facing away from the bellhousing starter motor aperture. Refit the retaining bolt and washer, and tighten to the specified torque.

13 Refit the detent ball, followed by the spring and plug bolt. Tighten the bolt to the specified torque.

14 Refit the clutch release mechanism as described in Chapter 5.

15 Refit the magnet to its location in the bellhousing edge.

10 Mainshaft and countershaft components and synchro units – inspection and overhaul

1 With the mainshaft and countershaft dismantled, examine the shafts and gears for signs of pitting, scoring, wear ridges or chipped teeth. Check the fit of the gears on the mainshaft and countershaft splines, and ensure that there is no lateral free play.

2 Check the smoothness of the bearings, and check for any signs of scoring on the needle roller bearing tracks and distance collars.

3 Check the mainshaft and countershaft for straightness, check for damaged threads or splines, and ensure that the lubrication holes are clear (photos).

4 Mark one side of each synchro hub and sleeve before separating the two parts, so that they may be refitted in the same position.

5 Withdraw the hub from the sleeve, and examine the internal gear teeth for wear ridges. Ensure that the hub and sleeve are a snug sliding

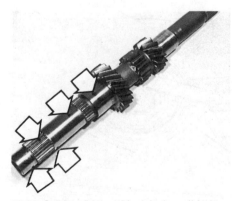

10.3A Gearbox mainshaft showing oil holes (arrowed) ...

10.3B ... and gearbox countershaft

10.8 Oversized teeth in synchro sleeve (arrowed) engaged with corresponding grooves in hub

fit, with the minimum of lateral movement.

6   Check the fit of the selector forks in their respective synchro sleeve grooves. If the clearance exceeds the figure given in the Specifications, measure the selector fork thicknesses, and renew any that are outside the specified tolerance range.

7   Place each baulk ring on the cone face of its respective gear, and measure the distance between the baulk ring and the gear face. If the clearance is less than specified, renew the baulk ring. Renew them also if there is excessive wear or rounding-off of the dog teeth around the periphery, if they are cracked, or if they are in any way damaged. If the gearbox is in reasonable condition and is to be rebuilt, it is advisable to renew all the baulk rings as a matter of course. The improvement in the synchromesh action when changing gear will justify the expense.

8   When reassembling the synchro units, make sure that the two oversize teeth in the synchro sleeve engage with the two oversize grooves in the hub (photo).

9   If any of the gears on the mainshaft are to be renewed, then the corresponding gear on the countershaft must also be renewed, and *vice-versa*. This applies to the countershaft and differential final drive gear as well.

11 Selector forks, shafts and gearchange mechanism – inspection and overhaul

1   Visually inspect the selector forks for obvious signs of wear ridges, cracks or deformation.

2   Slide the selector forks off the shafts, noting their fitted positions, and check the detent action as the fork is removed. Note that the detent balls and springs are located in the selector forks themselves, and cannot be removed. If the detent action is weak, or if there is evidence of a broken spring or damaged ball, the fork must be renewed.

3   Check the fit of the selector forks in their respective synchro sleeve grooves. If the clearance exceeds the figure given in the Specifications, measure the selector fork thicknesses, and renew any that are outside the specified tolerance range.

4   Examine the selector shafts for wear ridges around the detent grooves, and for any obvious signs of distortion. Renew any suspect shafts.

5   Examine the gearchange and interlock assembly for any visible signs of wear or damage, then measure the clearances as shown in the accompanying illustrations. It is advisable not to dismantle the mechanism unless it is obviously worn and in need of renewal. If this is the case, it can be separated into three main units, and the worn parts can be renewed.

6   Having obtained any new parts as required, reassemble the selector forks back onto the shafts, and reassemble the gearchange holder and interlock components if these were dismantled for renewal.

12 Final drive differential – inspection and renewal

1   As mentioned earlier, the only parts that can be renewed as a practical proposition are the two main support bearings on the final drive casing. The differential unit should be examined for any signs of wear or damage, but if any is found, it is recommended that you seek the advice of your dealer. Differential parts are supplied in sets, ie final drive gear and matching countershaft; sun gears and matching planet gears etc, and consequently are extremely expensive. The cost of individual parts may even equal, or exceed, the price of a complete exchange reconditioned gearbox.

2   Check that the bearings spin freely, with no sign of harshness or roughness. If renewal is necessary, remove the bearings by levering them off the differential using two screwdrivers or a small puller.

3   Fit the new bearings by tapping them into place, using a hammer and tube in contact with the bearing inner race.

13 Gearbox – reassembly

1   Position the differential in its location in the bellhousing, and tap it down gently, using a soft-faced mallet, to ensure that the bearing is fully seated.

2   Fit the gearcase to the bellhousing, and secure it temporarily with several bolts tightened to the specified torque.

3   Using feeler gauges inserted through the oil seal aperture in the

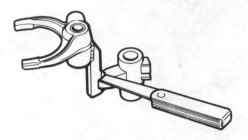

Fig. 6.5 Checking shift arm guide-to-3rd/4th selector fork clearance (Sec 11)

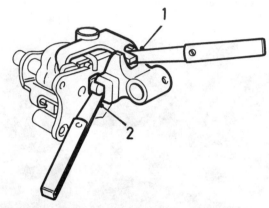

Fig. 6.6 Checking gearchange arm-to-shift arm clearance (1), and gearchange arm-to-interlock clearance (2) (Sec 11)

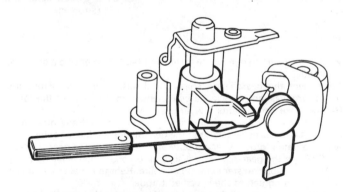

Fig. 6.7 Checking shift arm-to-guide clearance (Sec 11)

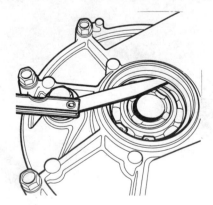

Fig. 6.8 Checking differential endfloat (Sec 13)

Feeler gauges inserted through oil seal aperture

gearcase, measure the clearance between the bearing and the circlip in the bearing recess. If the clearance is not equal to the differential endfloat dimension given in the Specifications, slacken the gearcase retaining bolts, extract the circlip through the oil seal aperture, and substitute a thicker or thinner circlip as required from the range available. Repeat this procedure until the correct endfloat is obtained, then remove the gearcase. Gearbox reassembly can now proceed as follows.

4   Insert the magnet into its location in the edge of the bellhousing.
5   Refit the gearchange shaft and arm as described in Section 9, if this has not already been done.
6   With the bearings in place in the bellhousing, hold the assembled mainshaft and countershaft together, and insert them into their locations.
7   With the help of an assistant, lift up the mainshaft and countershaft assemblies together, approximately 12.0 mm (0.5 in). Engage the selector forks with their respective synchro sleeves, and locate the selector shafts in the bellhousing (photo). Return the mainshaft and countershaft to their original positions, ensuring that the selector shafts engage fully with their holes in the bellhousing.
8   Refit the gearchange holder and interlock assembly, noting that the holder locates in a slot in the 1st/2nd selector shaft (photo).
9   Refit the three gearchange holder and interlock retaining bolts, and tighten them to the specified torque (photo).
10 Refit the reverse gear idler shaft, thrustwasher and reverse gear, and engage the roll pin on the shaft with the slot in the bellhousing (photo).
11 Engage the reverse gear fork over the reverse gear teeth, and over the peg on the 5th/reverse selector. Secure the reverse gear fork bracket with the two retaining bolts, tightened to the specified torque (photo).
12 Apply a thin, continuous bead of RTV sealant to the gearcase mating face. Lower the gearcase over the gear clusters, and engage the shafts and bearings in their locations. Using circlip pliers inserted through the countershaft access plug aperture, spread the circlip, and tap the gearcase fully into position using a soft-faced mallet. Release the circlip, ensuring that it enters the groove on the countershaft bearing.
13 Refit the gearcase retaining bolts and breather bracket, then tighten the bolts progressively and in a diagonal sequence to the specified torque.
14 Refit the reverse idler shaft retaining bolt, and tighten it to the specified torque.
15 Apply thread sealant to the countershaft access plug, refit the plug and tighten it to the specified torque.
16 Refit the speedometer transducer and pinion assembly, and the reversing light switch.
17 Refit the final drive differential oil seal to the gearcase, if not already done.
18 Check the operation of the gearchange mechanism, ensuring that all gears can be engaged, then refit the gearbox to the car as described in Section 3.

14 Gear lever and remote control housing – removal and refitting

Gear lever
1   Jack up the front of the car and support it on axle stands.
2   Undo the bolts securing the front heat shield to the underbody.
3   Release the exhaust system front rubber mounting, then remove the heat shield by twisting it around the exhaust front pipe.
4   Undo the nut and remove the bolt securing the gear lever to the gearchange remote control rod (photo).
5   Remove the centre console as described in Chapter 11.
6   Remove the rubber boot and dust cover over the gear lever (photos).
7   Extract the retaining circlip, and withdraw the gear lever from the remote control housing (photo).
8   Release the sealing washers, extract the bushes, and slide out the spacer, complete with O-ring seals, located at the base of the gear lever. Examine the components for wear.
9   Inspect the O-rings and gear lever seat in the remote control housing for signs of wear or damage.
10 Renew any worn or damaged parts, then reassemble and refit the gear lever, using the reverse sequence to removal.

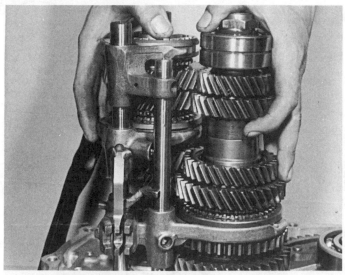

13.7 Lift up the mainshaft and countershaft to allow fitment of the selector forks and shafts

13.8 Fit the gearchange holder and interlock assembly ...

13.9 ... and secure with the three retaining bolts (arrowed)

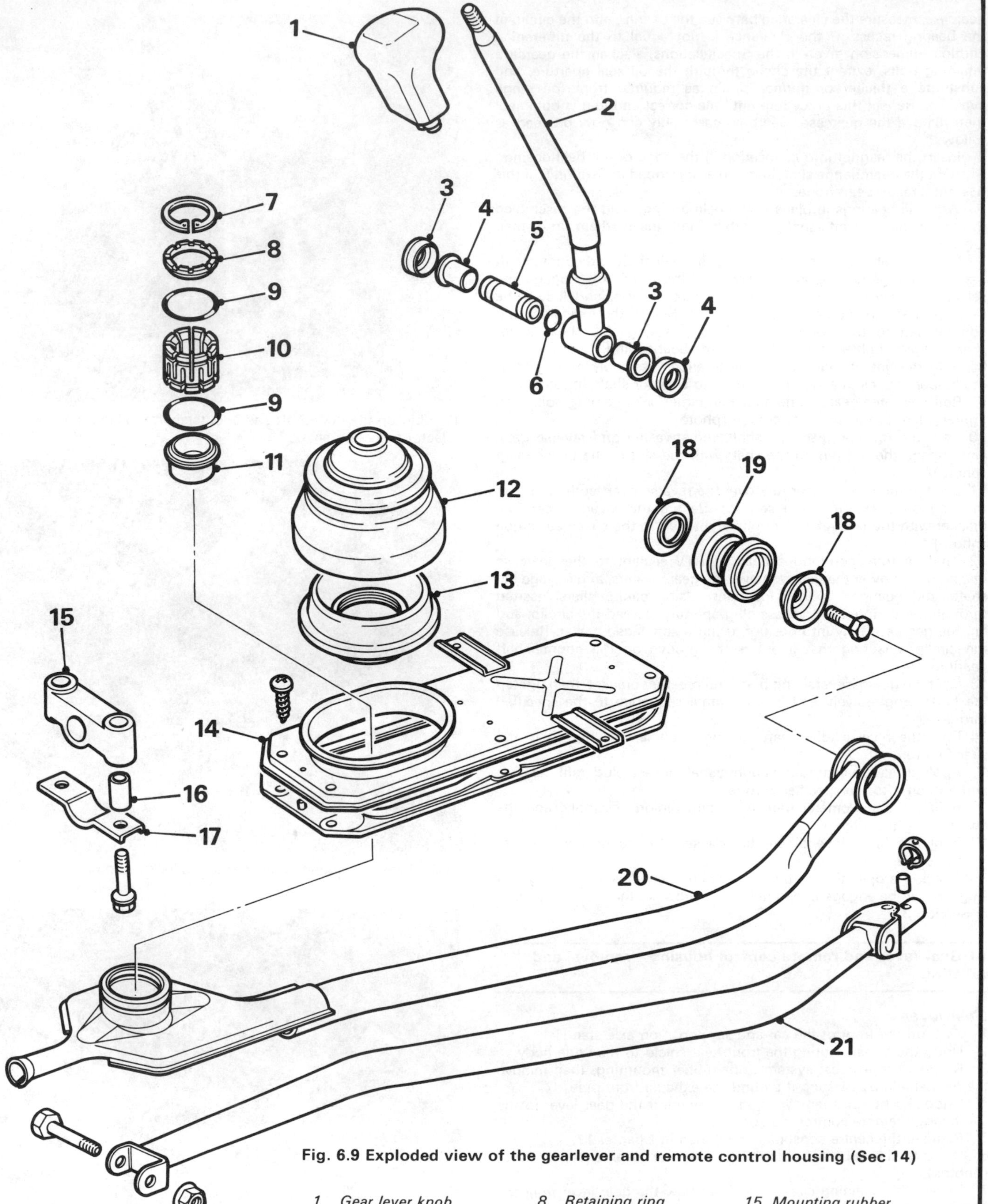

Fig. 6.9 Exploded view of the gearlever and remote control housing (Sec 14)

1 Gear lever knob	8 Retaining ring	15 Mounting rubber
2 Gear lever	9 O-ring	16 Spacer
3 Sealing washers	10 Gear lever seat	17 Bracket
4 Bushes	11 Dust cover	18 Washers
5 Spacer	12 Rubber boot	19 Bush
6 O-ring	13 Dust cover	20 Steady rod
7 Circlip	14 Retainer plate	21 Gearchange rod

13.10 Fit the reverse idler shaft, thrustwasher and gear

13.11 Engage the reverse gear fork with reverse gear, and with the 5th/reverse selector peg (arrowed)

14.4 Gear lever-to-gearchange remote control rod retaining bolt (arrowed)

14.6A Remove the gear lever rubber boot ...

14.6B ... and dust cover

14.7 Gear lever retaining circlip location (arrowed)

Remote control housing

11 Carry out the operations described previously in paragraphs 1 to 5 inclusive.

12 Undo the bolt in the centre of the gearbox steady rod. Remove the dished washer, slide off the steady rod and remove the inner flat washer.

13 Remove the spring clip to expose the gearchange rod-to-gearchange shaft retaining roll pin.

14 Using a parallel pin punch, tap out the roll pin and slide the gearchange rod rearwards, off the shaft.

15 At the remote control housing end, undo the two bolts securing the mounting bracket to the underbody (photo), and withdraw the remote control assembly from under the car.

16 Refitting is the reverse sequence to removal.

14.14 Remote control housing mounting bracket retaining bolts (arrowed)

19 Fault diagnosis – manual gearbox

Symptom	Reason(s)
Gearbox noisy in neutral	Mainshaft bearings worn
Gearbox noisy only when moving (in all gears)	Countershaft bearings worn Differential bearings worn Differential final drive gear or countershaft pinion chipped or worn
Gearbox noisy in only one gear	Worn, damaged or chipped gear teeth Worn needle roller bearings
Gearbox jumps out of gear	Worn synchro hubs or synchro sleeves Weak or broken selector shaft detent spring Weak or broken gearchange shaft detent spring Worn shaft detent grooves Worn selector forks Excessive mainshaft or countershaft endfloat
Ineffective synchromesh	Worn baulk rings or synchro hubs
Difficulty in engaging gears	Clutch fault Ineffective synchromesh Worn gear lever bushes and/or linkage

Chapter 7 Automatic transmission

Contents

Specifications

General

Transmission type	ZF Type 4 HP 14
Transmission ratios:	
1st	2.412 : 1
2nd	1.369 : 1
3rd	1.000 : 1
4th	0.739 : 1
Reverse	2.828 : 1

Automatic transmission fluid

Fluid type	Dexron IID type ATF (Duckhams D-Matic)
Fluid capacity:	
From dry	6.0 litres (10.5 Imp pts)
At service fluid change	2.0 litres (3.5 Imp pts)

Torque wrench settings

	Nm	lbf ft
Drain plugs	15	11
Selector cable clamp nut	8	6
Selector cable-to-selector housing nut	15	11
Oil cooler retaining bolt	50	37
Starter inhibitor/reversing light switch	40	30
Sump pan screws	10	7
Dipstick/filler tube bracket bolt	9	6
Fluid filter housing screws	10	7
Front engine mounting bracket-to-transmission bolts	40	30
Longitudinal support member bolts	45	33
Engine tie-bars-to-mounting bracket through-bolts	45	33
Engine mountings-to-transmission bracket nuts	80	59
Roadwheel nuts	70	52

1 General description

The ZF four-speed automatic transmission fitted to Rover 820 series models comprises a hydrodynamic torque converter, a planetary gear set controlled by hydraulically operated clutches and brakes, and an integral final drive differential.

The torque converter operates on the split-torque principle, whereby engine torque is transmitted to the geartrain by hydraulic or mechanical means, in accordance with the gear selected. In first, second and reverse gears, the torque converter provides a totally hydraulic coupling between engine and geartrain. In third gear, approximately 40% of engine torque is transmitted hydraulically, the remaining 60% being transmitted mechanically by the torque converter's integrated torsion damper. In fourth gear, 100% of engine torque is transmitted mechanically, thus eliminating the hydraulic slip within the torque converter at high engine speeds, and resulting in greater efficiency and improved fuel economy.

The planetary geartrain provides one of the four forward or single reverse gear ratios, according to which of its component parts are held

stationary or allowed to turn. In addition to two mechanical one-way clutches, the geartrain components are held or released by three clutches and three brake bands, which are activated by hydraulic valves. An oil pump within the transmission provides the necessary hydraulic pressure to operate the clutches and brakes.

Driver control of the transmission is by a seven-position selector lever, which provides fully-automatic operation with a hold facility on the first, second and third gear ratios. A kickdown (downshift) facility is provided for overtaking, actuated by flooring the accelerator pedal.

Fluid used in the transmission is common to the geartrain and final drive, but separate drain plugs are provided in the casing to ensure complete draining. An oil cooler is located on the side of the transmission, and uses engine coolant flow as the fluid cooling medium.

Due to the complexity of the automatic transmission, any repair or overhaul work must be entrusted to a Rover dealer or automatic transmission specialist with the necessary equipment for fault diagnosis and repair. The contents of this Chapter are therefore confined to supplying general information and any service information and instructions that can be used by the owner.

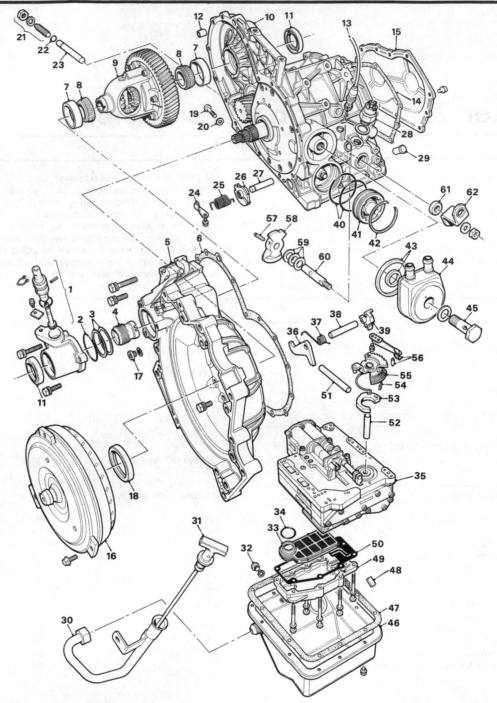

Fig. 7.1 Exploded view of the ZF HP14 automatic transmission (Sec 1)

1 Speedometer pinion assembly	16 Torque converter	31 Dipstick	47 Gasket
2 O-ring	17 Drain plug	32 Drain plug	48 Magnet
3 Selective shims	18 Oil seal	33 Fluid filter	49 Filter housing
4 Speedometer drivegear	19 Countershaft bearing locating bolt	34 O-ring	50 Gasket
5 Torque converter housing	20 Washer	35 Valve block	51 Parking pawl pushrod
6 Gasket	21 Brake band adjuster	36 Parking pawl	52 Park lock cam shaft
7 Bearing outer track	22 O-ring	37 Spring	53 Locking cam
8 Differential taper roller bearing	23 Adjuster plate	38 Parking pawl shaft	54 Spring
9 Final drive differential	24 Retaining plate	39 Oil diverter	55 Selector stop-plate
10 Transmission casing	25 Spring	40 O-rings	56 Detent spring and roller
11 Oil seal	26 Kickdown cam	41 Servo cover	57 Roll pin
12 Dowel	27 Kickdown cam shaft	42 Snap-ring	58 Selector cam
13 Kickdown cable	28 Starter/inhibitor switch	43 Oil cooler seals	59 Shims
14 Gasket	29 Transmission breather	44 Oil cooler	60 Selector shaft
15 End cover	30 Dipstick/filler tube	45 Oil cooler retaining bolt	61 Oil seal
		46 Sump pan	62 Selector lever

2 Maintenance and inspection

1   At the intervals given in *Routine maintenance* at the beginning of this manual, carefully inspect the transmission joint faces and oil seals for any signs of damage, deterioration or oil leakage.
2   Check the transmission fluid level as described in the following Section, and at the less-frequent intervals specified, renew the fluid as described in Section 4.
3   Carry out a thorough road test, ensuring that all gear changes occur smoothly without snatching and without an increase in engine speed between changes. Check that all gear positions can be engaged with the appropriate movement of the gear selector and, with the vehicle at rest, check the operation of the parking pawl when 'P' is selected.

3 Automatic transmission fluid – level checking

1   Check the fluid level at the intervals specified in *Routine maintenance*, with the car standing on a level surface. The check may be carried out with the engine/transmission hot or cold, but hot is preferable.

Engine/transmission cold

2   Apply the handbrake and select 'P'. Start the engine, and as soon as it idles evenly, withdraw the dipstick and wipe it clean on paper or a non-fluffy cloth.
3   Insert the dipstick fully, and immediately withdraw it. The fluid level should be between the MIN and MAX marks on the COLD side of the dipstick.
4   If more fluid is required, top up via the dipstick/filler tube, using the specified fluid, to the mid-point between the marks. Do not overfill. The difference between the MAX and MIN marks is 0.3 litres (0.5 Imp pts). Note that checking the fluid level cold is only approximate – ideally it should be checked hot.

Engine/transmission hot

5   The engine/transmission should be at normal operating temperature, preferably after a short journey.
6   Level checking and topping-up are as described in paragraphs 2 to 4, but check the level against the HOT side of the dipstick.

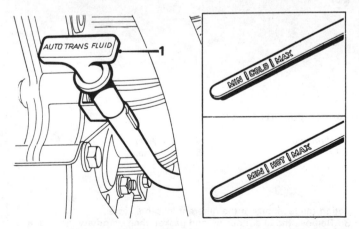

Fig. 7.2 Transmission fluid dipstick (1) and level markings (Sec 3)

4 Automatic transmission fluid – draining and refilling

1   Prior to draining, the engine/transmission should be at normal operating temperature, preferably after a short journey.
2   Apply the handbrake, select 'P', jack up the front of the car and support it on axle stands.
3   Position a large container beneath the transmission, and undo the two socket-headed drain plugs – one on the side of the sump pan, and one on the transmission casing (Fig. 7.3). Allow the fluid to drain into

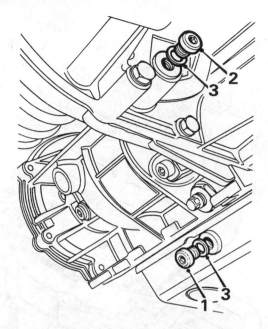

Fig. 7.3 Drain plug locations (Sec 4)

1   Sump pan drain plug   *3   Sealing washers*
2   Transmission casing drain plug

the container. **Warning:** *Take care to avoid scalding – the transmission fluid will be very hot.*
4   Clean and refit the drain plugs, using new sealing washers if the old ones are damaged.
5   Lower the car to the ground.
6   Refill through the dipstick/filler tube, using the specified fluid, until the fluid level is at MAX on the cold side of the dipstick.
7   Start the engine, and as soon as it idles evenly, move the selector lever slowly through all gear positions to circulate fluid through the transmission, then return it to 'P'.
8   Check the fluid level against the COLD side of the dipstick, as described in the previous Section, and top up if necessary.
9   Recheck the fluid level with the engine/transmission hot after taking the car for a short journey.

5 Transmission sump pan – removal and refitting

1   Remove the front suspension tie-rod on the left-hand side, as described in Chapter 10.
2   Drain the automatic transmission fluid as described in the previous Section.
3   Undo the bolt securing the dipstick/filler tube to the engine.
4   Undo the retaining screws and withdraw the sump pan and gasket.
5   Clean the interior of the sump pan, and remove and clean the swarf-collecting magnet.
6   Refit the sump pan using a new gasket, and tighten the retaining screws progressively and in a diagonal sequence to the specified torque.
7   Refit the dipstick/filler tube retaining bolt.
8   Refit the tie-rod as described in Chapter 10.
9   Lower the car to the ground, and refill the transmission with fresh fluid as described in Section 4.

6 Transmission fluid filter – removal, cleaning and refitting

1   This is not a routine maintenance operation, and will normally only be required after very high mileage, or if contaminants are evident in the fluid at the time of regular fluid renewal.
2   Remove the transmission sump pan as described in the previous Section.
3   Undo the nine screws securing the filter housing to the valve block,

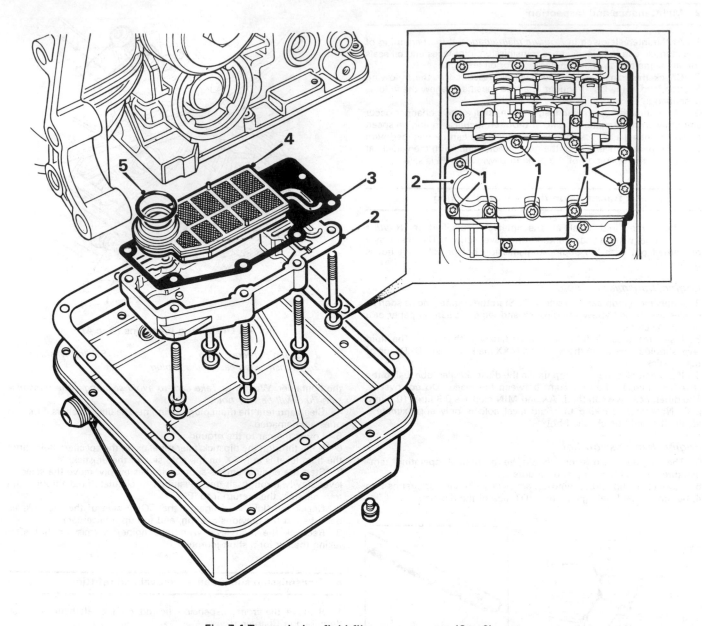

Fig. 7.4 Transmission fluid filter components (Sec 6)

1 *Filter housing retaining screws*	2 *Filter housing*	4 *Fluid filter*
	3 *Gasket*	5 *O-ring seal*

noting the locations of the different length screws.

4   Remove the filter housing and gasket, then withdraw the filter and O-ring seal.

5   Clean the filter and filter housing in clean transmission fluid. If the filter is badly contaminated, it should be renewed. Also renew the filter housing gasket and the O-ring seal as a matter of course.

6   Refit the components using the reverse sequence to removal, tightening the housing retaining screws to the specified torque. Refit the sump pan as described in the previous Section.

7   Valve block – removal and refitting

1   Remove the transmission sump pan as described in Section 5.

2   Undo the nine screws securing the filter housing to the valve block,

noting the locations of the different length screws.

3   Remove the filter housing and gasket, then withdraw the filter and O-ring seal.

4   Undo the remaining screws securing the valve block, and withdraw the valve block from the transmission.

5   Clean the valve block, filter and filter housing in clean transmission fluid. If the filter is badly contaminated, it should be renewed. Also renew the filter housing gasket and the O-ring seal as a matter of course.

6   Move the selector lever in the car to position '1'.

7   Fit the valve block to the transmission, ensuring that the manual shift valve engages with the kickdown cable cam.

8   With the O-ring in position, fit the filter to the valve block followed by the filter housing and gasket. Secure the housing and valve block with the retaining screws, tightened to the specified torque.

9   Refit the sump pan as described in Section 5.

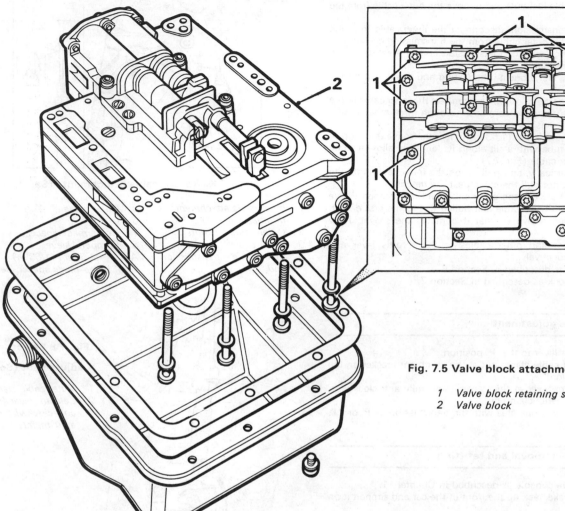

Fig. 7.5 Valve block attachments (Sec 7)

1 Valve block retaining screws
2 Valve block

8 Kickdown cable – adjustment

1 Refer to Chapter 3 and remove the air cleaner components as necessary to gain access to the kickdown cable and linkage.
2 Slacken the kickdown cable locknuts at the abutment bracket on the side of the throttle housing to release the tension in the cable.
3 Open the throttle and hold it in the fully-open position.
4 Pull the kickdown inner cable upwards until the detent is felt, then adjust the outer cable locknuts to eliminate the slack in the inner cable.
5 Release the throttle, and check that the gap between the crimped sleeve on the inner cable, and the end of the outer cable, is between 0.5 and 1.0 mm (0.02 and 0.04 in) (Fig. 7.6). Reposition the crimped sleeve if the gap is incorrect.
6 Tighten the cable locknuts securely, and refit the air cleaner components.

9 Kickdown cable – removal and refitting

1 Refer to Chapter 3 and remove the air cleaner components as necessary to gain access to the kickdown cable and linkage.
2 Remove the valve block as described in Section 7.
3 Record the routing of the cable so that the cable can be refitted in the same way.

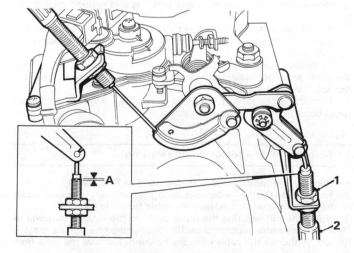

Fig. 7.6 Kickdown cable adjustment (Sec 8)

1 Kickdown cable locknuts
2 Outer cable
A = 0.5 to 1.0 mm (0.02 to 0.04 in) – see text

4 Release the kickdown inner cable from the throttle lever, then unscrew the outer cable locknuts and remove the outer cable from the abutment bracket.

5 Working at the transmission, disconnect the inner cable from the kickdown cam, and the outer cable from the transmission casing.

6 Remove the O-ring from the transmission end of the cable, then remove the cable from the car.

7 To refit the cable, first lubricate the O-ring and position it on the outer cable.

8 Fit the cable to the transmission, and connect the inner cable to the kickdown cam after turning the cam back through three-quarters of a turn against its spring tension.

9 Make up a spacer, 41.5 mm (1.63 in) in length, from a thin strip of metal, or from metal tube with a slit along its length to allow it to be slipped over the inner cable (Fig. 7.7).

10 Hold the cable vertically, and pull up on the inner cable until the first detent is felt. Do not pull the cable past the detent.

11 Insert the spacer between the outer cable and the crimped sleeve on the inner cable. With the cable still pulled out to the first detent, reposition the crimped sleeve so that it contacts the spacer. Now remove the spacer.

12 Connect the inner and outer cables to the throttle lever and abutment bracket respectively.

13 Adjust the cable as described in Section 8.

14 Refit the valve block as described in Section 7.

10 Selector cable – adjustment

1 Move the selector lever to the 'P' position.

2 Slacken the outer cable clamp nut at the abutment bracket on the side of the transmission.

3 Rotate the selector lever at the transmission fully anti-clockwise, and then tighten the cable clamp nut.

4 Check the starter only operates with the transmission in 'P' or 'N'.

11 Selector cable – removal and refitting

1 Remove the centre console as described in Chapter 11.

2 Apply the handbrake, jack up the front of the car and support it on axle stands.

3 From inside the car, extract the spring clip securing the inner cable to the selector lever, and release the cable from the lever.

4 Undo the nut securing the outer cable to the selector housing. A $^{15}/_{16}$ inch crowfoot spanner is useful for undoing this nut, as space is limited. Withdraw the cable from the housing.

5 Release the cable from the body brackets and support clips under the car.

6 At the transmission end, extract the spring clip and withdraw the steel and rubber washers securing the inner cable to the transmission selector lever.

7 Undo the outer cable retaining nut at the abutment bracket, release the inner and outer cables, and recover the inner cable spacer. Remove the selector cable from the car.

8 Refitting is the reverse sequence to removal. Adjust the cable as described in Section 10 on completion.

12 Selector lever – removal and refitting

1 Remove the centre console as described in Chapter 11.

2 From inside the car, extract the spring clip securing the inner cable to the selector lever, and release the cable from the lever.

3 Undo the nut securing the outer cable to the selector housing. A $^{15}/_{16}$ inch crowfoot spanner is useful for undoing this nut, as space is limited. Withdraw the cable from the housing. Remove the olive from the cable.

4 Apply the handbrake, jack up the front of the car and support it on axle stands.

5 Undo the five bolts and remove the engine undertray.

6 Undo the nuts securing the exhaust front pipe to the manifold.

7 Release the exhaust system front rubber mounting, and lower the

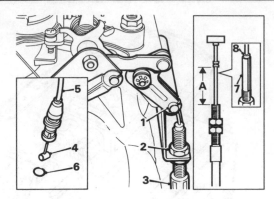

Fig. 7.7 Kickdown cable attachments (Sec 9)

1 Inner cable attachments at throttle cam	5 Outer cable
2 Outer cable locknuts	6 O-ring
3 Outer cable	7 Home made spacer
4 Inner cable – transmission end	8 Crimped sleeve
	A = 41.5 mm (1.63 in) – length of home-made spacer (see text)

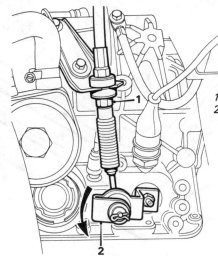

Fig. 7.8 Selector cable adjustment (Sec 10)

1 Outer cable clamp nut
2 Selector lever (rotate anti-clockwise during adjustment)

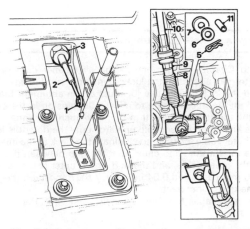

Fig. 7.9 Selector cable attachments (Sec 11)

1 Selector cable-to-lever spring clip	6 Steel washer
2 Inner cable	7 Rubber washer
3 Outer cable-to-housing retaining nut	8 Rubber gaiter
4 Underbody bracket	9 Outer cable-to-abutment bracket retaining nut
5 Spring clip	10 Outer cable
	11 Inner cable spacer

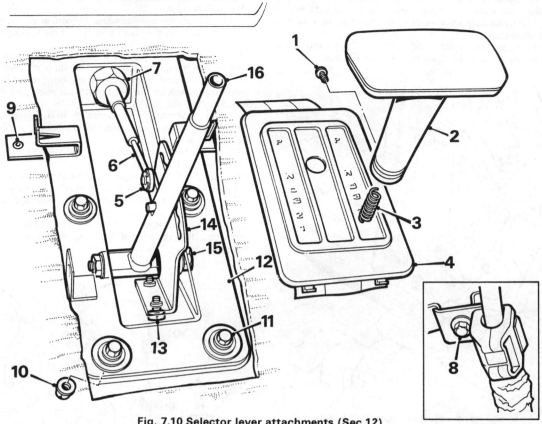

Fig. 7.10 Selector lever attachments (Sec 12)

1	Grub screw	5	Selector cable-to-lever
2	Selector lever knob		spring clip
3	Spring	6	Inner cable
4	Top panel	7	Outer cable-to-housing
			retaining nut

8	Underbody bracket	13	Detent bracket retaining
9	Housing rivets		bolts
10	Housing retaining nut	14	Detent bracket
11	Housing retaining bolt	15	Selector lever pivot bolt
12	Selector housing	16	Selector lever

exhaust slightly at the front. Recover the front pipe-to-manifold gasket.

8 Undo the retaining bolts and remove the exhaust front heat shield.

9 Undo the bolt and release the cable support bracket from the underbody.

10 Withdraw the selector cable from the selector housing.

11 From inside the car, move the carpets aside and drill out the four rivets on the sides of the housing.

12 Undo the nuts and bolts securing the housing and console mounting bracket, then remove the selector housing from the car.

13 With the assembly on the bench, undo the two bolts and remove the detent bracket from the housing.

14 Undo the nut, remove the selector lever pivot bolt and withdraw the lever from the housing.

15 Refitting is the reverse sequence to removal, but adjust the selector cable as described in Section 10 on completion.

13 Starter inhibitor/reversing light switch – removal and refitting

1 From within the engine compartment, release the ignition/fuel electronic control unit from its mounting bracket below the battery, and move the unit to one side.

2 Slide up the rubber grommet over the starter inhibitor/reversing light switch wiring terminals, and disconnect the four wires. Note that the two white/red wires are connected to the two larger terminals on the switch.

3 Unscrew the switch from the transmission and recover the sealing washer.

4 Refitting is the reverse sequence to removal, but use a new sealing

washer if necessary. On completion, check the operation of the reversing lights, and check that the starter only operates with the selector lever in 'P' or 'N'.

14 Brake band – adjustment

1 This is not a routine operation but is worth checking, along with the other adjustments contained in this Chapter, in the event of an elementary malfunction, or suspected fault in the transmission.

2 Apply the handbrake, jack up the front of the car and support it on axle stands.

3 Move the selector lever to 'N'.

4 Slacken the brake band adjuster locknut located above the sump pan drain plug.

5 Tighten the adjuster screw to 10 Nm (7.0 lbf ft), then unscrew the adjuster exactly two turns.

6 Hold the adjuster screw in this position, and tighten the locknut.

7 Lower the car to the ground.

15 Oil cooler – removal and refitting

1 Drain the cooling system as described in Chapter 2.

2 Undo the air cleaner bracket retaining bolts, and release the bracket for access.

3 Slacken the retaining clips and disconnect the two coolant hoses at the oil cooler.

4 Undo the centre retaining bolt and recover the seal.

5 Withdraw the oil cooler from the transmission, and recover the two seals.

6 Check the condition of the seals, and renew if necessary. Clean the oil cooler and the cooler-to-transmission mating faces.
7 Lubricate the new seals with transmission fluid, and refit the oil cooler using the reverse sequence to removal. Tighten the retaining bolt to the specified torque.
8 Refill the cooling system as described in Chapter 2, and top up the transmission fluid as described in Section 3 of this Chapter.

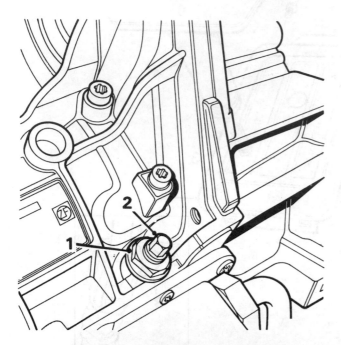

Fig. 7.11 Brake band adjuster locknut (1) and adjuster screw (2) (Sec 14)

16 Speedometer pinion – removal and refitting

1 Disconnect the speedometer transducer wiring multi-plug.
2 Slide up the rubber boot and extract the transducer retaining spring clip.
3 Withdraw the transducer from the pinion housing.
4 Undo the screw and remove the pinion housing retaining plate.
5 Withdraw the pinion housing from the transmission, and recover the O-ring seals.
6 Tap out the retaining pin in the housing and withdraw the pinion. Recover the small O-ring seal.
7 Check the condition of the components, and renew as necessary.
8 Lubricate the pinion shaft and O-rings with transmission fluid, then refit using the reverse sequence to removal.

17 Automatic transmission – removal and refitting

1 Disconnect the battery negative terminal. (Refer to Chapter 12, Section 1, before doing this).
2 Remove the air cleaner assembly as described in Chapter 3.
3 Drain the cooling system as described in Chapter 2.
4 Extract the retaining clips and release the support struts from the bonnet. Tie the bonnet back in the fully-open position.
5 Disconnect the earth lead at the transmission.
6 Slacken the clips and disconnect the two coolant hoses at the transmission oil cooler.
7 Slide up the rubber boot and disconnect the four wires at the reversing light/starter inhibitor switch. Note that the two white/red wires are connected to the two larger switch terminals.
8 Extract the spring clip and withdraw the steel and rubber washers securing the selector cable end to the transmission selector lever.
9 Undo the outer cable retaining nut at the abutment bracket, release the inner and outer cables, and recover the inner cable spacer.

10 Release the kickdown inner cable from the throttle lever, then unscrew the outer cable locknuts and remove the outer cable from the abutment bracket.
11 Disconnect the speedometer transducer wiring multi-plug.
12 Slide up the rubber boot and extract the transducer retaining spring clip.
13 Withdraw the transducer from the pinion housing.
14 Remove the starter motor as described in Chapter 12.
15 Apply the handbrake, prise off the front wheel trim and slacken the wheel nuts. Jack up the front of the car and support it on axle stands. Remove the front roadwheels.
16 Drain the automatic transmission fluid as described in Section 4.
17 Remove the engine undershield and the access panel from the left-hand inner wing.
18 Remove the front suspension tie-rod on the left-hand side, as described in Chapter 10.
19 Undo the nut securing the right-hand steering knuckle balljoint to the lower suspension arm, then release the balljoint from the arm using a universal balljoint separator tool or two-legged puller.
20 Pull the steering knuckle outwards, then using a suitable flat bar or large screwdriver, lever between the driveshaft inner constant velocity joint and the differential housing to release the joint from the transmission.

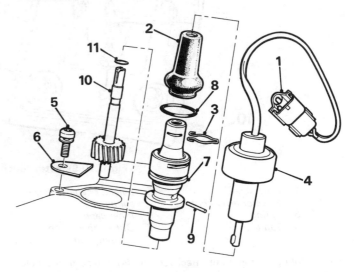

Fig. 7.12 Exploded view of the speedometer pinion components (Sec 16)

1 Transducer wiring multi-plug
2 Rubber boot
3 Spring clip
4 Transducer
5 Retaining screw
6 Pinion housing retaining plate
7 Pinion housing
8 O-ring
9 Pinion retaining pin
10 Speedometer pinion
11 O-ring

21 Move the driveshaft clear of the transmission, then repeat these procedures on the left-hand driveshaft.
22 Attach a suitable hoist to the engine using rope slings, or chains attached to brackets secured to the cylinder head. Raise the hoist to just take the weight of the engine.
23 From under the front of the car, undo the bolt securing the larger end of the engine lower tie-bar to its mounting bracket. Remove the through-bolt and recover the special nut.
24 Undo the bolts securing the longitudinal support member to the underbody, and remove the member.
25 Undo the two bolts securing the bracket at the smaller end of the engine lower tie-bar to the transmission. Undo the mounting bracket bolts and remove the lower tie-bar assembly.
26 Turn the crankshaft as necessary, using a socket or spanner on the crankshaft pulley bolt, until one of the torque converter retaining bolts becomes accessible through the starter motor aperture. Undo the bolt, then turn the crankshaft and remove the remaining two bolts in the same way.
27 Support the transmission using a jack and interposed block of wood positioned under the sump pan.

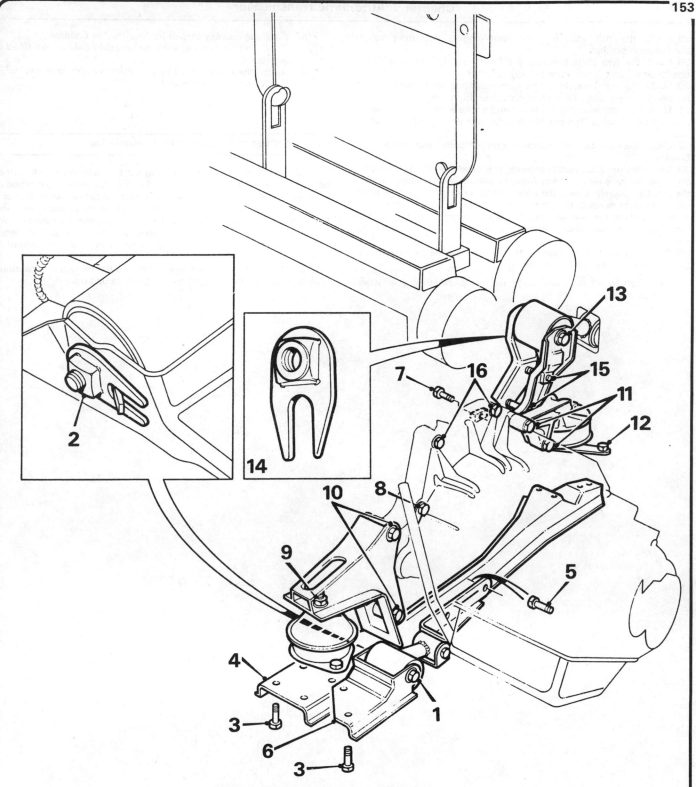

Fig. 7.13 Automatic transmission mounting details (Sec 17)

1 Engine lower
  tie-bar-to-mounting bracket
  bolt
2 Special nut
3 Longitudinal support
  member and tie-bar bracket
  bolts
4 Longitudinal support
  member

5 Engine lower
  tie-bar-to-transmission
  bracket bolts
6 Engine lower tie-bar
  assembly
7 Torque converter retaining
  bolts
8 Transmission-to-engine bolt

9 Front engine
  mounting-to-transmission
  bracket nut
10 Front engine mounting
  bracket retaining bolts
11 Rear engine mounting
  bracket retaining bolts
12 Rear engine mounting bolts

13 Engine rear
  tie-bar-to-mounting bracket
  bolt
14 Special nut
15 Rear tie-bar mounting
  bracket bolts
16 Transmission-to-engine
  bolts

28 Undo the nut securing the front engine mounting to its transmission bracket.

29 Undo the two bolts securing the front mounting bracket to the transmission, and remove the bracket.

30 Undo the bolts securing the rear mounting and bracket, then remove the mounting and bracket complete, from the car.

31 Undo the bolt securing the larger end of the engine rear tie-bar to its mounting bracket. Remove the through-bolt and recover the special nut.

32 Undo the rear tie-bar mounting bracket bolts, and remove the bracket.

33 Undo the remaining bolts securing the transmission to the engine.

34 Ease the transmission away from the engine, after releasing it from the locating dowels. Lower the transmission jack and the engine hoist, until clearance exists to enable the transmission to be withdrawn fully from the side of the engine. Ensure that the torque converter stays in place on the transmission, and remove the assembly from under the car.

35 Refitting the transmission is the reverse sequence to removal, bearing in mind the following points:

(a) *Tighten all nuts and bolts to the specified torque, where applicable*

(b) *Refill the cooling system as described in Chapter 2*

(c) *Refill the transmission with the specified fluid as described in Section 4*

(d) *Adjust the kickdown cable and selector cable as described in Sections 8 and 10 respectively*

18 Fault diagnosis – automatic transmission

In the event of a fault occurring on the transmission which cannot be cured by attention to the fluid level or the adjustments described in this Chapter, it is first necessary to determine whether the fault is of a mechanical or hydraulic nature. For this to be done accurately, the transmission must be in the car. Special test equipment is necessary for this purpose, together with a systematic test procedure, and the work should be entrusted to a suitably-equipped Rover dealer, or automatic transmission specialist.

Do not remove the transmission from the car for repair or overhaul until professional fault diagnosis has been carried out.

Chapter 8 Driveshafts

Contents

Specifications

Type .... Unequal-length solid steel, splined to inner and outer constant velocity joints

Lubrication
Overhaul only – see text
Lubricant type:
    Outer constant velocity joint .... Mobil 171A-M3 grease or equivalent
    Inner constant velocity joint .... Mobil 525 grease or equivalent
Quantity:
    Outer constant velocity joint .... 80 to 100 ml
    Inner constant velocity joint .... 175 to 185 ml

Torque wrench settings

	Nm	lbf ft
Driveshaft retaining nut	290	214
Strut forked member clamp bolt	50	37
Strut forked member to lower arm	90	66
Steering knuckle balljoint nut	100	74
Steering tie-rod balljoint nut	44	32
Roadwheel nuts	70	52

---

1 General description

Drive is transmitted from the differential to the front wheels by means of two unequal-length, solid steel driveshafts.

Both driveshafts are fitted with constant velocity joints at each end. The outer joints are of the ball-and-cage type, and are splined to accept the driveshaft and wheel hub drive flange. The inner joints are of the sliding tripod type, allowing lateral movement of the driveshaft to cater for suspension travel. The inner joints are splined to accept the driveshaft and differential sun gears.

To eliminate driveshaft-induced harmonic vibrations and resonance, a rubber-mounted steel damper is attached to the longer, right-hand, driveshaft.

Driveshaft repair procedures are limited, as only the inner and outer rubber boots, and outer constant velocity joints, are available separately. The driveshafts and inner joints are supplied as complete assemblies.

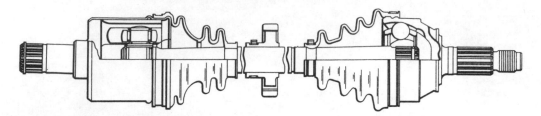

Fig. 8.1 Sectional view of the right-hand driveshaft assembly (Sec 1)

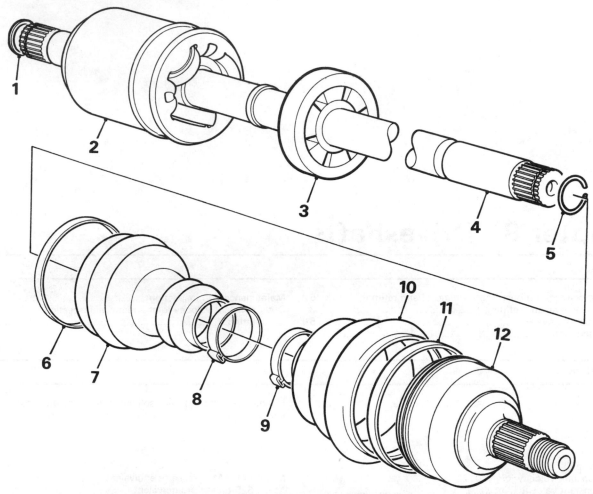

Fig. 8.2 Exploded view of the right-hand driveshaft components (Sec 1)

1 Circlip	4 Driveshaft	7 Inner joint rubber boot	10 Outer joint rubber boot
2 Inner constant velocity joint	5 Circlip	8 Rubber boot retaining clip	11 Rubber boot retaining clip
3 Damper	6 Rubber boot retaining clip	9 Rubber boot retaining clip	12 Outer constant velocity joint

2 Maintenance and inspection

1   At the intervals given in *Routine maintenance* at the beginning of this manual carry out a thorough inspection of the driveshafts and joints as follows.

2   Jack up the front of the car and securely support it on stands.

3   Slowly rotate the roadwheel, and inspect the condition of the outer joint rubber boots. Check for signs of cracking, splits or deterioration of the rubber, which may allow the grease to escape and lead to water and grit entry into the joint. Also check the condition and security of the retaining clips. Repeat these checks on the inner constant velocity joints. If any damage or deterioration is found, the boots should be renewed as described in Section 5.

4   Continue rotating the roadwheel, and check for any distortion or damage to the driveshaft itself. Check for any free play in the joints by first holding the driveshaft and attempting to rotate the wheel. Repeat this check by holding the inner joint and attempting to rotate the driveshaft. Any appreciable movement indicates wear in the joints, wear in the driveshaft splines, or a loose driveshaft retaining nut. Further investigation will be necessary if any wear is detected.

5   Road test the car and listen for a metallic clicking from the front as the car is driven slowly in a circle with the steering on full lock. If a clicking noise is heard, this indicates wear in the outer constant velocity joint(s), caused by excessive clearance between the balls in the joint and the tracks in which they run. Remove and inspect the joint as described in Section 4.

6   If vibration consistent with roadspeed is felt through the car when accelerating, there is a possibility of wear in the inner constant velocity joint(s). If so, renewal of the relevant driveshaft complete with inner joint will be necessary.

3 Driveshaft – removal and refitting

1 While the car is standing on its wheels, firmly apply the handbrake and put the transmission in gear (PARK on automatic transmission models).

2 Remove the wheel trim and, using a small punch, knock up the staking that secures the driveshaft retaining nut to the groove in the constant velocity joint stub shaft. Note that a new retaining nut will be needed for reassembly.

3 Using a socket, sturdy T-bar and long extension tube for leverage, slacken the retaining nut half a turn. Note that the retaining nut is tightened to a very high torque setting, and considerable effort will be required to slacken it.

4 Slacken the wheel nuts, jack up the front of the car and support it on stands. Remove the roadwheel and return the transmission to neutral.

5 Drain the gearbox oil as described in Chapter 6, or the automatic transmission fluid as described in Chapter 7.

6 Unscrew the nut and remove the clamp bolt securing the front suspension strut forked member to the strut – refer to Chapter 10 if necessary (photo).

7 Unscrew the nut and remove the bolt securing the forked member to the suspension lower arm (photo).

8 Remove the forked member from the strut and lower arm. If the member is tight on the strut, tap a screwdriver into the slot below the clamp bolt hole to spread the member slightly.

9 Undo the nut securing the steering knuckle balljoint to the lower arm, then release the balljoint from the arm using a universal balljoint separator tool or two-legged puller.

10 Extract the split pin and undo the nut securing the steering tie-rod balljoint to the steering knuckle arm. Release the balljoint using a universal balljoint separator tool or two-legged puller.

11 Remove the previously-slackened retaining nut.

12 Twist the steering knuckle onto full lock, then push the constant velocity joint out of the hub flange. It may be necessary to tap the end

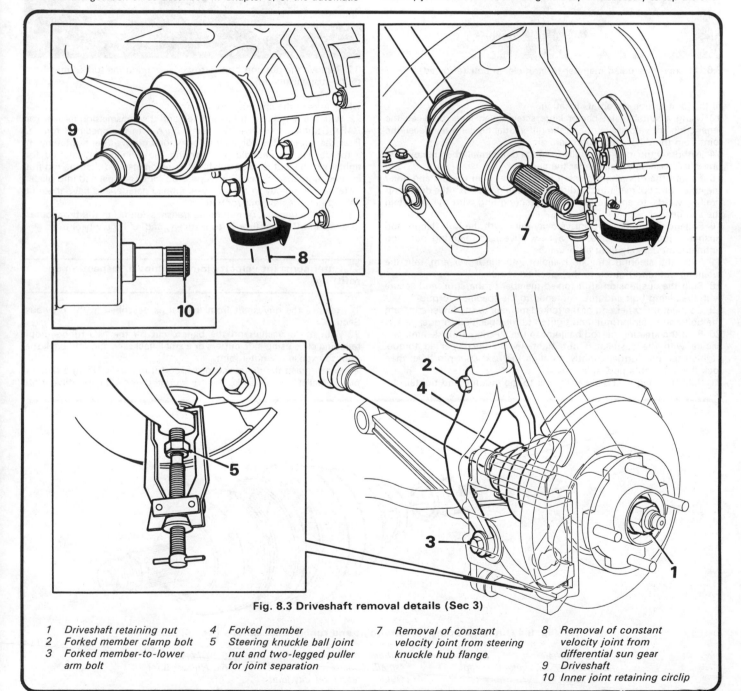

Fig. 8.3 Driveshaft removal details (Sec 3)

1	Driveshaft retaining nut	4	Forked member
2	Forked member clamp bolt	5	Steering knuckle ball joint
3	Forked member-to-lower		nut and two-legged puller
	arm bolt		for joint separation

7	Removal of constant velocity joint from steering knuckle hub flange

8	Removal of constant velocity joint from differential sun gear
9	Driveshaft
10	Inner joint retaining circlip

3.6 Unscrew the forked member-to-strut clamp bolt (arrowed)

3.7 Remove the nut and bolt (arrowed) securing the forked member to the suspension arm

of the joint to free it from its location.

13 Using a suitable flat bar or large screwdriver, lever between the inner constant velocity joint and the differential housing to release the joint from the differential sun gear.

14 Withdraw the inner joint fully from the differential, then remove the driveshaft assembly from under the car.

15 To refit the driveshaft, place it in position under the car and enter the inner joint splines into the differential sun gear. Push the driveshaft firmly inwards, to engage the retaining spring ring with the groove in the sun gear.

16 Engage the outer constant velocity joint with the hub flange, and push the joint fully home. Fit a new driveshaft retaining nut, and tighten it moderately tight at this stage.

17 Enter the steering knuckle balljoint into the lower arm, refit the retaining nut, and tighten to the specified torque.

18 Refit the suspension strut forked member to the strut, and secure with the clamp bolt and nut, tightened to the specified torque.

19 Connect the other end of the forked memebr to the lower arm, refit the bolt and retaining nut, and tighten to the specified torque.

20 Refit the steering tie-rod balljoint to the steering knuckle arm, and secure with the castellated nut, tightened to the specified torque. Tighten the nut further slightly, to align the next split pin hole, then lock the nut with a new split pin.

21 Refit the roadwheel, lower the car to the ground, and tighten the

wheel nuts to the specified torque.

22 With the handbrake firmly applied and the transmission in gear (or PARK), tighten the driveshaft retaining nut to the specified torque. Peen the nut into the constant velocity joint groove after tightening. If a torque wrench capable of recording the high figure required for tightening this nut is not available, it is recommended that the old nut is fitted, tightened as securely as possible, and then peened into place. Take the car directly to a suitably-equipped garage, and have them fit and tighten the new nut for you.

23 Refill the gearbox or automatic transmission using the procedures described in Chapter 6 or 7 respectively, and refit the wheel trim.

4 Outer constant velocity joint – removal, inspection and refitting

1 Remove the driveshaft from the car as described in the previous Section.

2 With the driveshaft on the bench, cut off the two rubber boot retaining clips using side cutters or a small hacksaw, and fold back the boot to expose the outer joint.

3 Firmly grasp the driveshaft or support it in a vice. Using a hide or plastic mallet, sharply strike the outer edge of the joint and drive it off

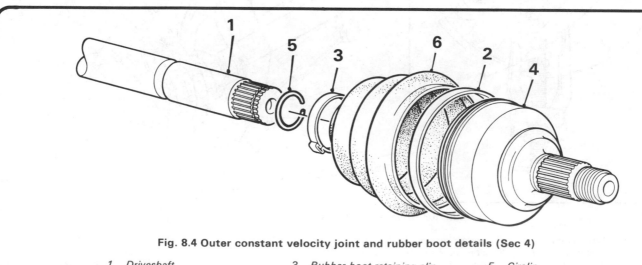

Fig. 8.4 Outer constant velocity joint and rubber boot details (Sec 4)

1 Driveshaft
2 Rubber boot retaining clip (large)
3 Rubber boot retaining clip (small)
4 Outer constant velocity joint
5 Circlip
6 Rubber boot

the shaft. The outer joint is retained on the driveshaft by an internal circular section circlip, and striking the joint in the manner described forces the circlip to contract into a groove, so allowing the joint to slide off.

4   Remove the rubber boot from the driveshaft.

5   Thoroughly clean the constant velocity joint using paraffin or a suitable solvent, and dry it, preferably using compressed air. Ensure that the joint is completely dry inside, with all traces of paraffin or the solvent removed.

6   Move the inner splined driving member from side to side, to expose each ball in turn at the top of its track. Examine the balls for cracks, flat spots, surface pitting or severe scuff marks,

7   Inspect the ball tracks on the inner and outer members. If the tracks have worn, the balls will no longer be a tight fit. At the same time, check the ball cage windows for wear or for cracking between the balls.

8   If any of the above checks indicate wear in the joint, it will be necessary to renew it complete, as the internal parts are not available separately. If the joint is in a satisfactory condition, obtain a repair kit consisting of a new rubber boot and retaining clips. Also obtain a suitable quantity of the special lubricating grease (see Specifications).

9   Slide the small retaining clip and the new rubber boot over the end of the driveshaft, and locate the boot end in the driveshaft groove.

10   Place the retaining clip over the rubber boot, and fully tighten it by gently squeezing the raised portion with pliers.

11   The help of an assistant will be necessary while fitting the constant velocity joint to the driveshaft. Ensure that the circlip is undamaged and correctly located in its driveshaft groove.

12   Fold back the rubber boot and position the constant velocity joint over the splines on the driveshaft until it abuts the circlip.

13   Using two small screwdrivers placed either side of the circlip, compress the clip, and at the same time have your assistant firmly strike the end of the joint with a hide or plastic mallet.

14   The joint should slide over the compressed circlip and into position on the shaft. It will probably take several attempts until you achieve

success. If the joint does not spring into place the moment it is struck, remove it, reposition the circlip and try again. Do not force the joint, otherwise the circlip will be damaged.

15   With the joint tapped fully home, pack it thoroughly with the specified quantity of the special grease. Work the grease well into the ball tracks while twisting the joint, and fill the rubber boot with any excess.

16   Fold the rubber boot back over the joint, fit the large retaining clip, and secure the clip by squeezing the raised portion with pliers.

17   The driveshaft can now be refitted to the car as described in Section 3.

5   Constant velocity joint rubber boots – removal and refitting

1   Remove the driveshaft from the car as described in Section 3.

Outer joint rubber boot

2   Remove the outer constant velocity joint from the driveshaft as described in Section 4. Renewal of the rubber boot is also covered in Section 4, as it is an integral part of the outer joint removal and refitting procedure.

Inner joint rubber boot

3   Remove the outer constant velocity joint and rubber boot as described in Section 4.

4   If working on the right-hand driveshaft, cut off the damper retaining clips using side cutters or a small hacksaw, and slide the damper off the driveshaft.

5   Cut off the inner joint rubber boot retaining clips, and slide the boot off the driveshaft.

6   Clean out as much of the grease in the inner constant velocity joint as possible, using a wooden spatula and old rags. It is advisable not to

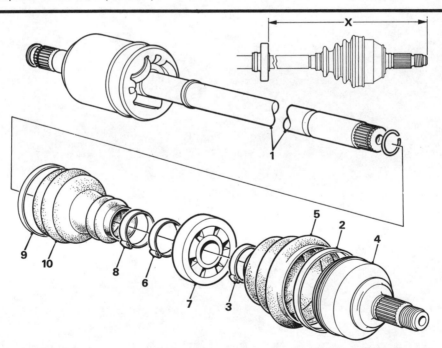

Fig. 8.5 Inner constant velocity joint, damper and rubber boot details (Sec 5)

1 Driveshaft	4 Outer constant velocity joint	8 Rubber boot retaining clip (small)
2 Rubber boot retaining clip (large)	5 Outer joint rubber boot	9 Rubber boot retaining clip (large)
3 Rubber boot retaining clip (small)	6 Damper retaining clip	10 Inner joint rubber boot
	7 Damper (right-hand driveshaft only)	

X = Damper setting dimension:
Manual gearbox models .... 538.25 to 546.25 mm (21.20 to 21.52 in)

Automatic transmission
models .... 522.25 to 527.25 mm (20.57 to 20.77 in)

clean this type of joint using paraffin or solvents, as it is impossible to remove all the solvent and dry the joint thoroughly after cleaning.

7 Examine the bearing tracks in the joint outer member for signs of scoring, wear ridges or evidence of lack of lubrication. Also examine the three bearing caps in the same way, and check for evidence of excessive play between the roller bearing caps and their tracks in the outer member.

8 If any of the above checks indicate wear in the joint, it will be necessary to renew the driveshaft and inner joint as an assembly; they are not available separately. If the joint is in a satisfactory condition, obtain a repair kit consisting of a new rubber boot and retaining clips. Also obtain a suitable quantity of the special lubricating grease (see Specifications).

9 Pack the constant velocity joint with the specified quantity of the special grease. Work the grease well into the joint while moving it from side to side. Fill the rubber boot with any excess.

10 Fit the new rubber boot and large retaining clip to the driveshaft, and locate the boot and clip over the joint. Secure the boot by squeezing the raised portion of the clip using side cutters.

11 Secure the other end of the boot in the same way with the small retaining clip.

12 Refit the damper and retaining clip to the driveshaft (where applicable), position the damper as shown in Fig. 8.5, and secure with the clip.

13 Refit the outer constant velocity joint and rubber boot as described in Section 4, then refit the driveshaft as described in Section 3.

6 Fault diagnosis – driveshafts

Symptom	Reason(s)
Vibration and/or noise on turns	Worn outer constant velocity joint(s)
Vibration when accelerating	Worn inner constant velocity joint(s) Bent or distorted driveshaft
Vibration or resonance at a particular roadspeed	Loose, incorrectly positioned or damaged vibration damper
Noise on taking up drive	Worn driveshaft or constant velocity joint splines Worn constant velocity joints Loose driveshaft retaining nut

See also Fault diagnosis – suspension and steering (Chapter 10)

Chapter 9 Braking system

For modifications, and information applicable to later models, see Supplement at end of manual

Contents

Specifications

System type ....

Diagonally-split, dual-circuit hydraulic with pressure-reducing valve in rear hydraulic circuit, and cable-operated handbrake. Anti-lock braking system available on later models.

Front brakes

Type	Ventilated disc with single-piston sliding calipers
Make	Girling
Disc diameter	262.0 mm (10.32 in)
Disc thickness:	
New	21.0 mm (0.827 in)
Minimum	19.0 mm (0.748 in)
Maximum thickness variation	0.015 mm (0.0006 in)
Maximum disc run-out	0.075 mm (0.003 in)
Caliper piston diameter	57.0 mm (2.24 in)
Brake pad thickness (including backing, but excluding shims):	
New	17.4 mm (0.68 in)
Minimum	8.2 mm (0.32 in)

Rear brakes

Type	Solid disc with single-piston sliding calipers
Make	Girling
Disc diameter	260.0 mm (10.24 in)
Disc thickness:	
New	10.0 mm (0.394 in)
Minimum	8.0 mm (0.315 in)
Maximum thickness variation	0.015 mm (0.0006 in)
Maximum disc run-out	0.075 mm (0.003 in)
Caliper piston diameter	38.0 mm (1.49 in)
Brake pad thickness (including backing):	
New	14.5 mm (0.57 in)
Minimum	7.2 mm (0.28 in)

Handbrake
Handbrake linkage lever-to-stop pin clearance .... 0.5 to 2.0 mm (0.019 to 0.078 in)

General
Brake fluid type .... Hydraulic fluid to FMVSS 116 DOT 4 (Duckhams Universal Brake and Clutch Fluid)

Master cylinder bore diameter .... 23.81 mm (0.938 in)
Servo unit boost ratio 4.6:1
Wheel speed sensor-to-reluctor ring clearance (ABS):
    Front .... 0.30 to 1.02 mm (0.011 to 0.04 in)
    Rear .... 0.16 to 1.03 mm (0.006 to 0.04 in)

Torque wrench settings

	Nm	lbf ft
Caliper guide pin bolts	33	24
Front caliper carrier bracket to steering knuckle	75	55
Rear caliper carrier bracket to hub carrier	45	33
Caliper bleed screws	10	7
Brake hose banjo union bolts	35	26
Brake pipe union nuts:		
Without ABS	14	10
With ABS	22	16
Brake disc retaining screws	12	9
Handbrake linkage cover to rear caliper	10	7
Handbrake lever to floor	25	18
Handbrake front cable guide plate bolts	25	18
Handbrake rear cable support clip bolts	10	7
Master cylinder-to-servo unit nuts	25	18
Servo unit-to-bulkhead nuts	25	18
Brake pedal pivot bolt	25	18
Pressure reducing valve mounting bracket bolts	10	7
Hydraulic modulator mounting nuts (ABS)	10	7
Wheel speed sensor-to-sensor bracket bolt (ABS)	10	7
Wheel speed sensor bracket bolts (ABS)	25	18
Wheel speed sensor wiring clips and bracket bolts (ABS)	10	7
Roadwheel nuts	70	52

1 General description

The braking system is of the servo-assisted, dual-circuit hydraulic type, incorporating disc brakes at the front and rear. A diagonally-split dual circuit hydraulic system is employed, in which each circuit operates one front and one diagonally opposite rear brake from a tandem master cylinder. Under normal conditions, both circuits operate in unison; however, in the event of hydraulic failure in one circuit, full braking force will still be available at two wheels. A pressure-reducing valve is incorporated in the rear brake hydraulic circuit. This valve regulates the hydraulic pressure applied to each rear brake, and reduces the possibility of the rear wheels locking under heavy braking.

Self-adjusting single-piston sliding type calipers are used in conjunction with ventilated and solid discs at the front and rear respectively. A cable-operated handbrake provides an independent mechanical means of rear brake application.

An anti-lock braking system (ABS) is available as an optional extra on models produced from approximately June 1988 onwards. Further information on this system will be found in the relevant Sections of this Chapter.

2 Maintenance and inspection

1 At the intervals given in *Routine maintenance* at the beginning of this manual, the following service operations should be carried out on the braking system components.
2 Check the brake fluid level, and if necessary top up with the specified fluid to the MAX mark on the reservoir (photos). Any need for frequent topping-up indicates a fluid leak somewhere in the system, which must be investigated and rectified immediately.
3 Check the front and rear brake pads for wear, and inspect the condition of the discs using the procedures described in Sections 3 and 7 respectively.
4 Check the condition of the hydraulic pipes and hoses as described in Section 15. At the same time, check the condition of the handbrake cables, lubricate the exposed cables and linkages, and if necessary adjust the handbrake as described in Section 18.

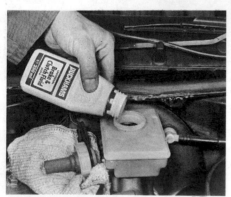
2.2A Top up with the specified fluid ...

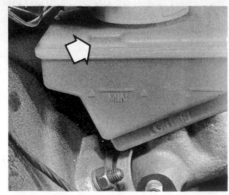
2.2B ... to the MAX mark on the reservoir (arrowed)

2.5 Brake pad wear warning light wiring plug (arrowed)

5   The operation of the three-function braking system warning light should be tested as follows. Apply the handbrake with the ignition switched on, and check that the light illuminates as the handbrake is applied. To test the low brake fluid warning function, place the car in gear (or in PARK on automatic transmission models), release the handbrake and switch on the ignition. The light should illuminate when the flexible contact cover in the centre of the brake fluid reservoir filler cap is depressed. To check the brake pad wear warning function, disconnect the warning lamp wiring plug attached to the left-hand front brake caliper (photo) and connect a bridging wire across the two terminals in the harness plug. With the ignition switched on, the warning light should illuminate when the bridging wire is earthed. Repeat this check at the left-hand rear caliper as a test for wiring continuity. If the warning light fails to illuminate under any of the test conditions, then either the bulb is blown, a fuse is at fault, or there is a wiring fault in the circuit concerned.

6   Renew the brake hydraulic fluid at the specified intervals by draining the system and refilling with fresh fluid, using the bleeding procedure described in Section 16.

7   The flexible brake hoses and rubber seals in the brake calipers and master cylinder should also be renewed at the intervals given. Details of these operations will be found in the relevant Sections of this Chapter.

3 Front brake pads – inspection and renewal

1   Apply the handbrake, prise off the front wheel trim and slacken the wheel nuts. Jack up the front of the car and support it on axle stands. Remove the front roadwheels.

2   The thickness of the brake pads can now be checked by viewing through the slot in the front of the caliper body. If any of the pads has worn down to, or below, the minimum specified thickness, all four pads must be renewed as a complete set. The pads must also be renewed if there is any sign of oil or fluid contamination caused by leaking seals. If so, the cause of the contamination must be traced and rectified before new pads are fitted.

3   Disconnect the pad wear warning light wiring plug (left-hand caliper only) and using a suitable spanner, unscrew the lower guide pin bolt (photo) while holding the guide pin with a second spanner.

4   Pivot the caliper body upwards (photo) and tie it up using a length of string to a suitable place under the wheelarch.

5   Lift out the two brake pads together with their shims (photo), then, where fitted, remove the upper and lower anti-rattle shims from the caliper carrier bracket (photos). If the pads are to be re-used, suitably identify them so that they can be refitted in their original positions.

6   Remove the heat shield from the caliper piston (photo).

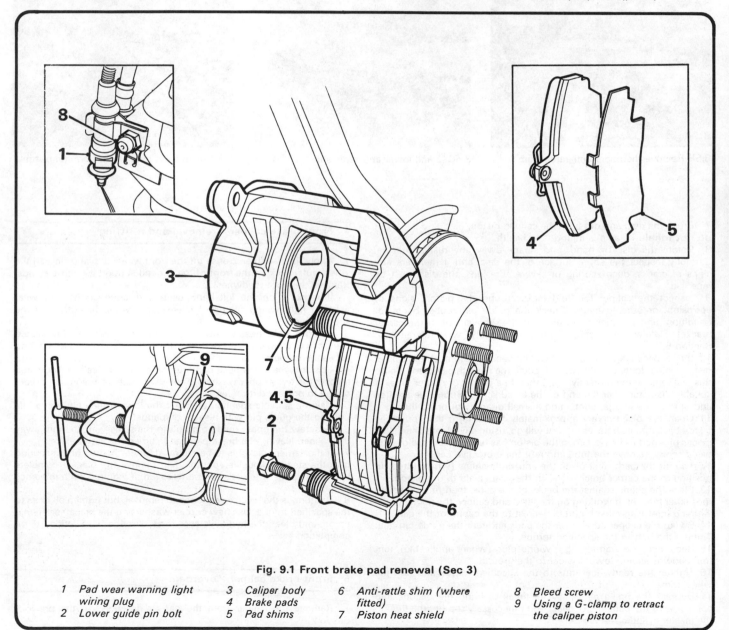

Fig. 9.1 Front brake pad renewal (Sec 3)

1	Pad wear warning light wiring plug	3	Caliper body	6	Anti-rattle shim (where fitted)	8	Bleed screw
2	Lower guide pin bolt	4	Brake pads	7	Piston heat shield	9	Using a G-clamp to retract the caliper piston
		5	Pad shims				

3.3 Unscrew the caliper lower guide pin bolt

3.4 Pivot the caliper body upwards

3.5A Lift out the brake pads together with their shims

3.5B Remove the upper anti-rattle shim ...

3.5C ... and lower anti-rattle shim

3.6 Remove the heat shield from the piston

7   Brush the dust and dirt from the caliper, piston, disc, and pads, but **do not inhale it,** as it is injurious to health.

8   Rotate the disc by hand, and scrape away any rust and scale. Carefully inspect the entire surface of the disc, and if there are any signs of cracks, deep scoring or severe abrasions, the disc must be renewed.

9   Inspect the caliper for fluid leaks around the piston, signs of corrosion, or other damage. Check the guide pin rubber boots for condition, and the pins themselves for free movement in the carrier bracket. Renew any suspect parts as necessary, with reference to Section 5.

10   If new pads are to be fitted, it will be necessary to push the caliper piston back into its bore to accommodate the new, thicker pads. To do this first remove the protective cap, then fit a plastic or rubber tube, of suitable diameter, over the end of the bleed screw. Submerge the free end of the tube in a jar containing a small quantity of brake fluid.

11   Open the bleed screw approximately half a turn, then push the piston back into its bore, as far as it will go, using a G-clamp or suitable pieces of wood as levers. When the piston has fully retracted, close the bleed screw, remove the tube and refit the protective cap.

12   To refit the pads, first place the anti-rattle shims (where fitted) in position in the carrier bracket and fit the heat shield to the piston.

13   Place the shims against the backs of the pads, then fit the pads to the carrier bracket. If working on the left-hand caliper, the pad with the warning light lead must be fitted nearest to the centre of the car.

14   Swing the caliper down over the pads and refit the guide pin bolt. Tighten the bolt to the specified torque.

15   Reconnect the warning light wiring plug (where applicable), refit the roadwheels and lower the car to the ground.

16   Tighten the roadwheel nuts to the specified torque and refit the wheel trims.

17   Depress the brake pedal several times to bring the pistons into contact with the pads then check, and if necessary top up, the fluid in the master cylinder reservoir.

4   Front brake caliper – removal and refitting

1   Apply the handbrake, prise off the front wheel trim and slacken the wheel nuts. Jack up the front of the car and support it on axle stands. Remove the front roadwheel.

2   If working on the left-hand caliper, disconnect the pad wear warning light wiring plug and release the wiring harness from the support clip.

3   Using a brake hose clamp, or self-locking wrench with protected jaws, clamp the flexible brake hose. This will minimise fluid loss during subsequent operations.

4   Unscrew the brake hose banjo union bolt at the caliper body, and recover the two copper washers. Tape over the hose union and caliper orifice to prevent dirt ingress.

5   Using a suitable spanner, unscrew the lower guide pin bolt while holding the guide pin with a second spanner.

6   Unscrew the upper guide pin bolt in the same way, then lift away the caliper, leaving the brake pads and carrier bracket in place.

7   If the carrier bracket is to be removed, undo the two bolts securing it to the steering knuckle (photo), and remove the bracket complete with brake pads. The pads can be removed, if required, with reference to Section 3.

8   Refitting is the reverse sequence to removal, but tighten all bolts to the specified torque. Use new copper washers on the brake hose banjo union, and bleed the hydraulic system as described in Section 16, on completion.

5   Front brake caliper – overhaul

1   Remove the caliper from the car as described in the previous Section.

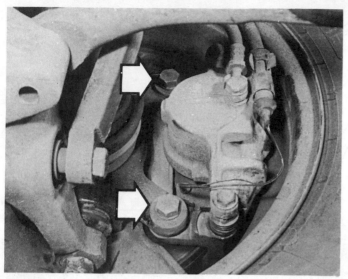

4.7 Carrier bracket-to-steering knuckle retaining bolts (arrowed)

7 Clean all the parts in methylated spirit, or clean brake fluid, and dry with a lint-free cloth. Inspect the piston and caliper bore for signs of damage, scuffing or corrosion, and if these conditions are evident, renew the caliper assembly complete. Also renew the guide pins in the carrier bracket if they are bent or damaged, or if their rubber boots are split or perished.
8 If the components are in a satisfactory condition, a repair kit consisting of new seals and dust cover should be obtained.
9 Thoroughly lubricate the caliper bore, piston, piston seal and dust cover with clean brake fluid, and carefully fit the seal to the caliper bore.
10 Position the dust cover over the innermost end of the piston, so that the caliper bore sealing lip protrudes beyond the base of the piston. Using a blunt instrument, if necessary, engage the sealing lip of the dust cover with the groove in the caliper. Now push the piston into the caliper bore until the other sealing lip of the dust cover can be engaged with the groove in the piston. Having done this, push the piston fully into its bore. Ease the piston out again slightly, and make sure that the dust cover lip is correctly seating in the piston groove.
11 Remove the guide pins from the carrier bracket, if not already done, and smear them with high-melting-point brake grease. Fit new rubber boots to the guide pins if necessary, and refit them to the carrier bracket.
12 The caliper can now be refitted as described in the previous Section.

2 With the caliper on the bench wipe away all traces of dust and dirt, but **avoid inhaling the dust,** as it is injurious to health.
3 Remove the shim from the caliper piston.
4 Using low air pressure, such as that generated by a tyre foot pump, eject the piston by holding the pump hose against the caliper fluid inlet port.
5 Remove the dust cover from the piston.
6 Using a blunt instrument such as a knitting needle, carefully extract the piston seal from the caliper bore.

6 Front brake disc – inspection, removal and refitting

1 Apply the handbrake, prise off the front wheel trim and slacken the wheel nuts. Jack up the front of the car and support it on axle stands. Remove the front roadwheel.
2 Undo the two bolts securing the brake caliper carrier bracket to the steering knuckle.
3 Withdraw the carrier bracket, complete with caliper and brake pads, from the disc and steering knuckle. Tie the caliper assembly from a

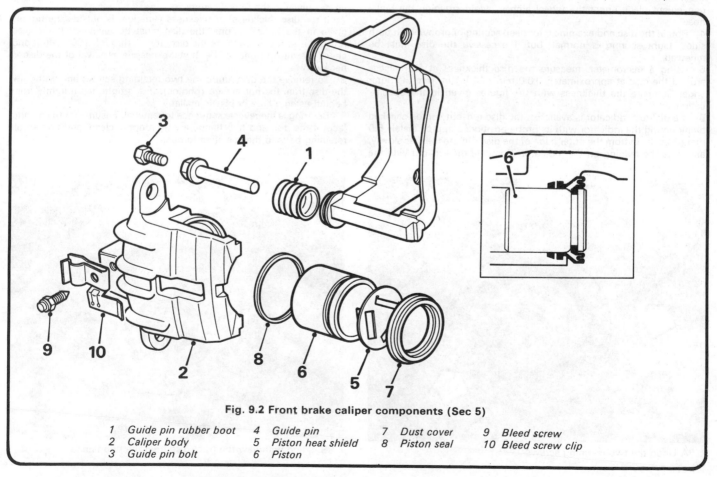

Fig. 9.2 Front brake caliper components (Sec 5)

1 Guide pin rubber boot   4 Guide pin   7 Dust cover   9 Bleed screw
2 Caliper body   5 Piston heat shield   8 Piston seal   10 Bleed screw clip
3 Guide pin bolt   6 Piston

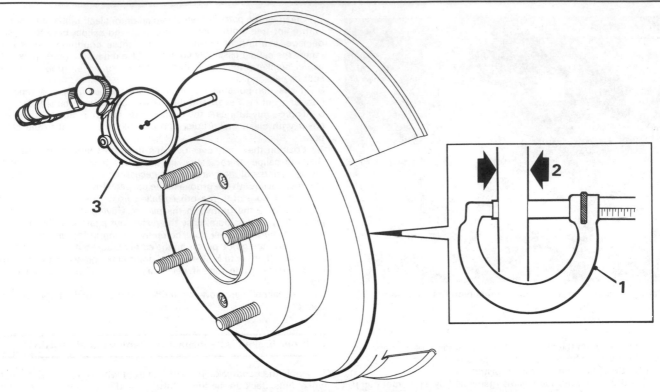

Fig. 9.3 Checking front brake disc thickness and run-out (Sec 6)

1   *Micrometer*   2   *Specified disc thickness*   3   *Dial test indicator*

convenient place under the wheel arch to avoid straining the brake hose.

4   Rotate the disc and examine it for deep scoring or grooving on both sides. Light scoring is normal, but if excessive the disc must be renewed.

5   Using a micrometer, measure the disc thickness at four places around the disc at approximately 10.0 mm (0.4 in) in from the outer edge. Compare the thickness with the figures given in the Specifications.

6   If a dial test indicator is available, the disc run-out can be checked by mounting the indicator with its probe positioned approximately 6.0 mm (0.25 in) in from the outer edge of the disc. Rotate the disc slowly, and note the reading on the indicator. Compare the run-out with the

figures given in the Specifications.

7   If the disc thickness, or thickness variation, is outside the figures given in the Specifications, the disc must be renewed. If the disc run-out is excessive, remove the disc, turn it through 180°, refit it and check the run-out once more. If still excessive, renewal of the disc is necessary.

8   To remove the disc, undo the two retaining screws and withdraw the disc from the hub flange (photos). If it is tight, tap it lightly from behind using a hide or plastic mallet.

9   Refitting is the reverse sequence to removal. Ensure that the mating face of the disc and hub flange are thoroughly clean, and tighten all retaining bolts to the specified torque.

6.8A Undo the two retaining screws ...

6.8B ... and withdraw the front disc from the hub flange

7   Rear brake pads – inspection and renewal

1   Chock the front wheels, remove the rear wheel trim and slacken the rear wheel nuts. Jack up the rear of the car and support it on axle stands. Remove the rear roadwheels and ensure that the handbrake is released.

2   The thickness of the brake pads can now be checked by viewing through the slot in the front of the caliper. If any of the pads has worn down to, or below, the minimum specified thickness, all four pads must be renewed as a complete set. The pads must also be renewed if there is any sign of oil or fluid contamination caused by leaking seals. If so, the cause of the contamination must be traced and rectified before new pads are fitted.

3   Undo the three bolts securing the handbrake linkage cover (photo), and remove the cover from the side of the caliper.

4   Disconnect the pad wear warning light wiring plug (left-hand caliper only).

5   Using a suitable spanner, unscrew the upper and lower guide pin bolts (photo).

6   Withdraw the caliper and handbrake linkage assembly off the brake pads and carrier bracket.

7   Lift out the two brake pads, then, where fitted, remove the upper and lower anti-rattle shims from the caliper carrier bracket (photos). If the pads are to be re-used, suitably identify them so that they can be refitted in their original positions.

8   Brush the dust and dirt from the caliper, piston, disc, and pads, but **do not inhale it,** as it is injurious to health.

9   Rotate the disc by hand, and scrape away any rust and scale. Carefully inspect the entire surface of the disc, and if there are any signs of cracks, deep scoring or severe abrasions, the disc must be renewed.

10   Inspect the caliper for fluid leaks around the piston, signs of corrosion, or other damage. Check the guide pin rubber boots for condition, and the pins themselves for free movement in the carrier bracket. Renew any suspect parts as necessary, with reference to Section 9.

11   If new pads are to be fitted, it will be necessary to retract the caliper piston back into its bore to accommodate the new, thicker pads. To do this first remove the protective cap, then fit a plastic or rubber tube, of suitable diameter, over the end of the bleed screw. Submerge the free end of the tube in a jar containing a small quantity of brake fluid.

12   Open the bleed screw approximately half a turn, then screw the piston back fully into its bore by turning it clockwise with a pair of angled circlip pliers (photo) or other similar tool. With the piston fully retracted, close the bleed screw, remove the tube and refit the protective cap.

13   To refit the pads, first place the anti-rattle shims (where fitted) in position in the carrier bracket.

14   Fit the pads to the carrier bracket, noting that the pad with the warning light lead (left-hand caliper only) must be fitted nearest to the centre of the car.

15   Place the caliper over the pads, and secure with the guide pin bolts, tightened to the specified torque.

16   Refit the warning light wiring plug (where applicable) and the handbrake linkage cover.

17   Refit the roadwheels and lower the car to the ground. Tighten the roadwheel nuts to the specified torque and refit the wheel trim.

18   Depress the brake pedal several times to bring the pistons into contact with the pads then check, and if necessary top up, the fluid in the master cylinder reservoir. There may be excessive free travel of the handbrake initially after completing these operations, but this will self-adjust automatically after the car has been driven a few miles.

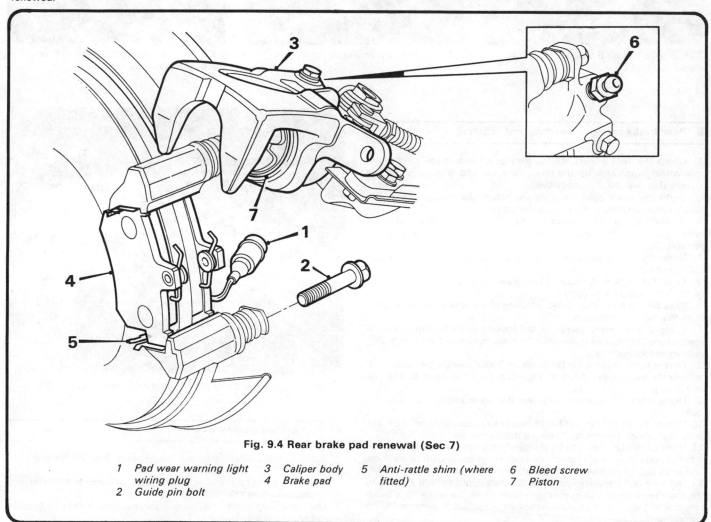

Fig. 9.4 Rear brake pad renewal (Sec 7)

1	Pad wear warning light wiring plug	3	Caliper body	5	Anti-rattle shim (where fitted)
2	Guide pin bolt	4	Brake pad	6	Bleed screw
				7	Piston

7.3 Undo the three handbrake linkage cover retaining bolts (arrowed)

7.5 Rear caliper upper and lower guide pin bolt locations (arrowed)

7.7A Lift out the two brake pads ...

7.7B ... followed by the upper anti-rattle shim ...

7.7C ... and lower anti-rattle shim

7.12 Using angled circlip pliers to screw the piston back into the caliper

8 Rear brake caliper – removal and refitting

1   Chock the front wheels, remove the rear wheel trim and slacken the rear wheel nuts. Jack up the rear of the car and support it on axle stands. Remove the rear roadwheel.
2   Undo the three bolts securing the handbrake linkage cover, and remove the cover from the side of the caliper.
3   If working on the left-hand caliper, disconnect the pad wear warning light wiring plug and release the wiring harness from the support clip.
4   Undo the two bolts and remove the front half of the handbrake linkage cover.
5   Extract the retaining clip and withdraw the clevis pin from the end of the handbrake cable (photo).
6   Prise off the handbrake cable retaining clip and withdraw the cable from the mounting bracket.
7   Using a brake hose clamp, or self-locking wrench with protected jaws, clamp the flexible brake hose. This will minimise fluid loss during subsequent operations.
8   Unscrew the brake hose banjo union bolt at the caliper body, and recover the two copper washers. Tape over the hose union and caliper orifice to prevent dirt ingress.
9   Using a suitable spanner, unscrew the upper and lower guide pin bolts.
10 Withdraw the caliper and handbrake linkage assembly off the brake pads and carrier bracket, and remove it from the car.
11 If the carrier bracket is to be removed, undo the two bolts securing it to the hub carrier, and remove the bracket complete with brake pads. The pads can be removed, if required, with reference to Section 7.
12 Refitting is the reverse sequence to removal, but tighten all bolts to the specified torque. Use new copper washers on the brake hose banjo union, and bleed the hydraulic system as described in Section 16, on completion.

8.5 Handbrake cable clevis pin (A) and cable retaining clip (B)

9 Rear brake caliper – overhaul

1   Remove the caliper from the car as described in the previous Section.
2   With the caliper on the bench, wipe away all traces of dust and dirt, but **avoid inhaling the dust,** as it is injurious to health.
3   Undo the two bolts and remove the handbrake linkage bracket assembly from the caliper.

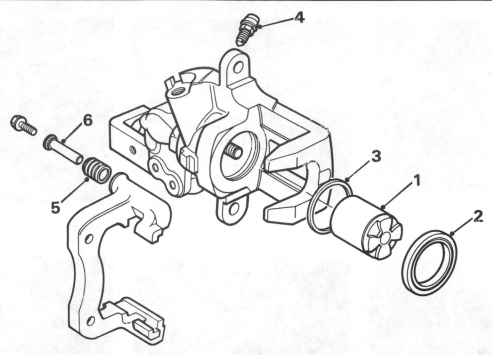

Fig. 9.5 Rear brake caliper components (Sec 9)

1 Piston	3 Piston seal	5 Guide pin rubber boot
2 Dust cover	4 Bleed screw	6 Guide pin

4   Using a pair of angled circlip pliers or other similar tool, turn the piston anti-clockwise to unscrew it from the caliper.

5   Remove the dust cover from the piston.

6   Using a blunt instrument such as a knitting needle, carefully extract the piston seal from the caliper bore.

7   Clean all the parts in methylated spirit, or clean brake fluid, and dry with a lint-free cloth. Inspect the piston and caliper bore for signs of damage, scuffing or corrosion, and if these conditions are evident, renew the caliper assembly complete. Also renew the guide pins in the carrier bracket if they are bent or damaged, or if their rubber boots are split or perished.

8   If the components are in a satisfactory condition, a repair kit consisting of new seals and dust cover should be obtained.

9   Thoroughly lubricate the caliper bore, piston, piston seal and dust cover with clean brake fluid, and carefully fit the seal to the caliper bore.

10 Position the dust cover over the innermost end of the piston, so that the caliper bore sealing lip protrudes beyond the base of the piston. Using a blunt instrument, if necessary, engage the sealing lip of the dust cover with the groove in the caliper. Screw the piston into the caliper bore until the other sealing lip of the dust cover can be engaged with the groove in the piston. With the piston screwed in all the way, make sure that the dust cover is correctly located in the piston and caliper grooves.

11 Remove the guide pins from the carrier bracket, if not already done, and smear them with high-melting-point brake grease. Fit new rubber boots to the guide pins if necessary, and refit them to the carrier bracket. Ensure that the guide pin with the rubber insert is fitted in the rearmost position.

12 Attach the handbrake linkage bracket assembly to the caliper and secure with the two bolts.

13 The caliper can now be refitted to the car as described in the previous Section.

10 Rear brake disc – inspection, removal and refitting

1   Chock the front wheels, remove the rear wheel trim and slacken the rear wheel nuts. Jack up the rear of the car and support it on axle stands. Remove the rear roadwheel.

2   Undo the two bolts securing the brake caliper carrier bracket to the rear hub carrier (photo).

3   Undo the retaining bolt and release the flexible brake hose support clip from the suspension strut (photo).

4   Withdraw the carrier bracket, complete with caliper and brake pads, from the disc and hub carrier. Tie the caliper assembly from a convenient place under the wheel arch to avoid straining the brake hose (photo).

5   The inspection procedures are the same as for the front brake disc, and reference should be made to Section 6, paragraphs 4 to 7 inclusive.

6   To remove the disc, undo the two retaining screws and withdraw the disc from the hub flange (photos). If it is tight, tap it lightly from behind using a hide or plastic mallet.

7   Refitting is the reverse sequence to removal. Ensure that the mating face of the disc and hub flange are thoroughly clean, and tighten all retaining bolts to the specified torque.

11 Master cylinder – removal and refitting

1   Working under the front of the car, remove the dust cover from the bleed screw on each front brake caliper. Obtain two plastic or rubber tubes of suitable diameter to fit snugly over the bleed screws, and place the other ends in suitable receptacles.

2   Open both bleed screws approximately half a turn, then operate the brake pedal until the master cylinder reservoir is empty. Tighten the bleed screws and remove the tubes. Discard the expelled brake fluid.

3   Disconnect the warning light wiring plug from the reservoir filler cap.

4   Place rags beneath the master cylinder to absorb any remaining brake fluid when the pipe unions are undone. If any brake fluid is spilled on the car paintwork, wash it off immediately with copious amounts of cold water.

5   On manual gearbox models, detach the clutch fluid supply hose from the side of the reservoir.

6   Unscrew the two brake pipe union nuts, and carefully withdraw the pipes from the master cylinder (photo). Tape over the pipe ends to prevent dirt ingress.

7   Undo the two nuts, remove the washers, and withdraw the master

10.2 Carrier bracket-to-rear hub carrier retaining bolts (arrowed)

10.3 Release the rear flexible brake hose support clip from the suspension strut

10.4 Tie up the caliper assembly to avoid straining the brake hose

10.6A Undo the two retaining screws ...

10.6B ... and withdraw the rear disc from the hub flange

11.6 Unscrew the two brake pipe unions (arrowed) at the master cylinder

cylinder from the servo unit. Recover the O-ring seal between master cylinder and servo.

8   Refitting is the reverse sequence to removal. Renew the master cylinder-to-servo O-ring seal, and tighten all retaining nuts to the specified torque. Bleed the hydraulic system as described in Section 16 on completion. On manual gearbox models, bleed the clutch hydraulic system as described in Chapter 5.

12 Master cylinder (non-ABS models) – overhaul

Note: *The following procedure is applicable to cars which are not fitted with an anti-lock braking system (ABS). For cars with ABS, refer to Section 13.*

1   Remove the master cylinder from the car as described in the previous Section. Drain any fluid remaining in the reservoir, and prepare a clean, uncluttered working surface ready for dismantling.
2   Hold the cylinder body firmly, and push the reservoir sideways to release it from its seals. Lift the reservoir off, and remove the two seals from the fluid inlet ports.
3   Push the primary piston down the cylinder bore slightly, and hold it there. Locate the stop-pin in the secondary inlet port, and withdraw the pin using pointed-nose pliers.
4   With the piston still held down, extract the circlip, using circlip pliers, from the end of the cylinder bore, and remove the washer behind the circlip.
5   Using a small blunt screwdriver, hook out the O-ring seal from the groove in the cylinder bore.
6   Remove the primary piston.
7   Lubricate the cylinder bore with clean brake fluid to aid removal of the secondary piston.
8   Tap the cylinder body on a block of wood to release the secondary piston, then withdraw the piston from the cylinder bore.
9   Refer to Fig. 9.6 and remove the secondary piston spring, seal retainer, rear seal, washer and front seal.

10   Remove the seal housing, seal and washer from the primary piston. Do not dismantle the primary piston further, as seals are not available separately. If the master cylinder is in a serviceable condition, and is to be re-used, a complete new primary piston assembly is included in the repair kit.
11   With the master cylinder dismantled, clean all the components in methylated spirit, or clean brake fluid, and dry with a lint-free cloth.
12   Carefully examine the cylinder bore and secondary piston for signs of wear, scoring or corrosion, and if evident, renew the complete master cylinder assembly.
13   If the components are in a satisfactory condition, obtain a repair kit consisting of new seals, springs and primary piston assembly.
14   Lubricate the cylinder bore, pistons and seals thoroughly in clean brake fluid, and assemble them wet.
15   Using your fingers only, fit the front seal to the secondary piston, followed by the washer, rear seal, seal retainer and spring.
16   Fit the washer, seal housing and seal to the primary piston.
17   Insert the secondary piston into the cylinder bore, using a circular rocking motion to avoid turning over the lips of the seals.
18   Fit the primary piston in the same way.
19   Fit a new O-ring seal to the groove in the cylinder bore, then refit the washer and circlip.
20   Push the primary piston down the bore, and refit the stop-pin to the secondary inlet port.
21   Fit two new seals to the reservoir fluid inlet ports, then push the reservoir firmly into place.
22   Fit a new seal to the reservoir filler cap, then refit the master cylinder to the car as described in Section 11.

13 Master cylinder (ABS models) – overhaul

Note: *The following procedure is applicable to cars which are fitted with an anti-lock braking system (ABS). For cars without ABS, refer to Section 12.*

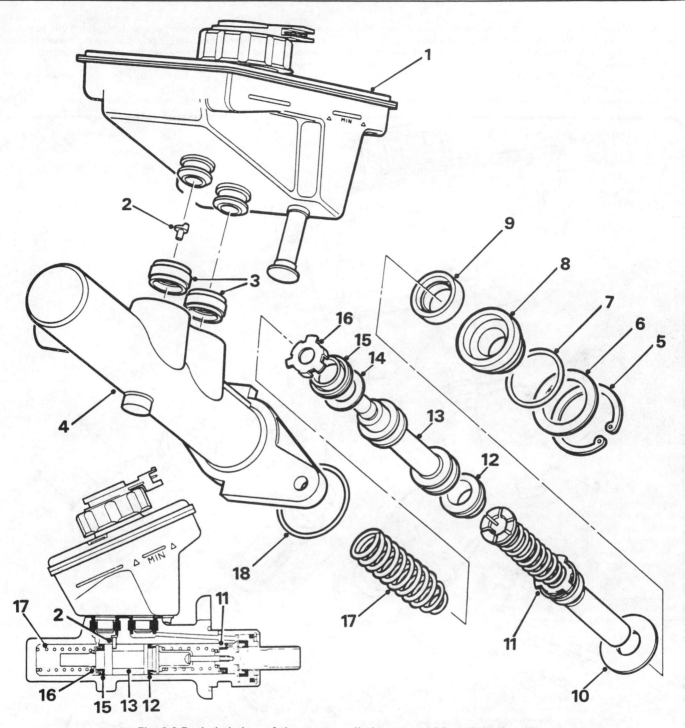

Fig. 9.6 Exploded view of the master cylinder – non-ABS models (Sec 12)

1 Reservoir	6 Washer	11 Primary piston assembly	15 Secondary piston rear seal
2 Stop-pin	7 O-ring seal	12 Secondary piston front seal	16 Secondary piston seal
3 Reservoir seals	8 Primary piston seal housing	13 Secondary piston	retainer
4 Cylinder body	9 Primary piston seal	14 Secondary piston washer	17 Secondary piston spring
5 Piston retaining circlip	10 Primary piston washer		18 O-ring

1   Remove the master cylinder from the car as described in Section 11. Drain any fluid remaining in the reservoir, and prepare a clean, uncluttered working surface ready for dismantling.

2   Hold the cylinder body firmly, and push the reservoir sideways to release it from its seals. Lift the reservoir off, and remove the two seals from the fluid inlet ports.

3   Push the primary piston down the cylinder bore slightly, and hold it there. Locate the stop-pin in the secondary inlet port, and withdraw

the pin using pointed-nose pliers.

4   With the piston still held down, extract the circlip, using circlip pliers, from the end of the cylinder bore, and remove the washer behind the circlip.

5   Using a small blunt screwdriver, hook out the O-ring seal from the groove in the cylinder bore.

6   Remove the primary piston.

7   Lubricate the cylinder bore with clean brake fluid to aid removal of

the secondary piston.

8 Tap the cylinder body on a block of wood to release the secondary piston, then withdraw the piston from the cylinder bore.

9 Refer to Fig. 9.7 and remove the seal housing, seal and washer from the primary piston. Do not dismantle either of the pistons further as seals are not available separately. If the master cylinder is in a serviceable condition, and is to be re-used, a repair kit including new primary and secondary piston assemblies will be required.

10 With the master cylinder dismantled, clean all the components in methylated spirit, or clean brake fluid, and dry with a lint-free cloth.

11 Carefully examine the cylinder bore for signs of wear, scoring or corrosion, and if evident, renew the complete master cylinder assembly.

12 If the components are in a satisfactory condition, obtain a repair kit and two new piston assemblies.

13 Lubricate the cylinder bore, pistons and seals thoroughly in clean

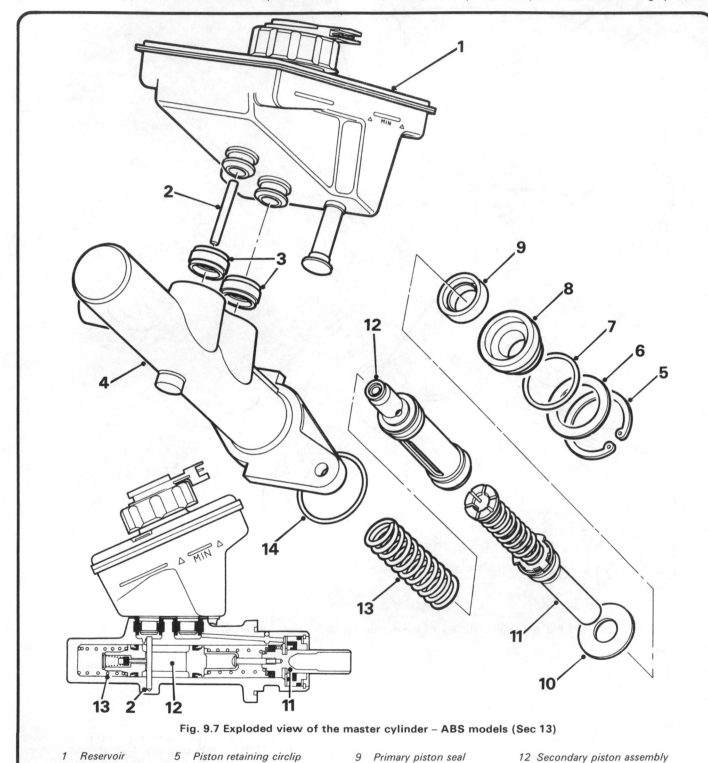

Fig. 9.7 Exploded view of the master cylinder – ABS models (Sec 13)

1 Reservoir	5 Piston retaining circlip	9 Primary piston seal	12 Secondary piston assembly
2 Stop-pin	6 Washer	10 Primary piston washer	13 Secondary piston spring
3 Reservoir seals	7 O-ring seal	11 Primary piston assembly	14 O-ring
4 Cylinder body	8 Primary piston seal housing		

brake fluid, and assemble them wet.

14 Fit the washer, seal housing and seal to the primary piston.

15 Insert the secondary piston into the cylinder bore, using a circular rocking motion to avoid turning over the lips of the seals. Align the slot in the piston with the stop-pin hole in the cylinder secondary inlet port.

16 Fit the primary piston in the same way.

17 Fit a new O-ring seal to the groove in the cylinder bore, then refit the washer and circlip.

18 Push the primary piston down the bore, and refit the stop-pin to the secondary inlet port.

19 Fit two new seals to the reservoir fluid inlet ports, then push the reservoir firmly into place.

20 Fit a new seal to the reservoir filler cap, then refit the master cylinder to the car as described in Section 11.

14 Pressure-reducing valve – description, removal and refitting

1 The pressure-reducing valve is mounted on the left-hand side of the engine compartment behind the battery.

2 The purposes of the valve is to distribute brake fluid to the front and rear brakes (rear brakes only on cars fitted with ABS), and to limit the fluid pressure supplied to the rear brakes under heavy braking.

3 The operation of the valve may be suspect if one or both rear wheels continually lock under heavy braking. It is essential, however, before condemning the valve to ensure that the brake assemblies themselves, or adverse road conditions, are not causing this condition. In the event of a valve internal failure, brake fluid will be seen seeping from the vent plug on the front of the valve which is covered by a plastic strap. Repair or overhaul of the valve is not possible, and the unit must be renewed as a complete assembly if faulty.

4 Remove the master cylinder reservoir filler cap, place a piece of polythene over the filler neck, and seal it tightly with an elastic band. This will minimise brake fluid loss during subsequent operations.

5 Place rags beneath the valve to collect any brake fluid that may escape when the pipe unions are undone. If any brake fluid is spilled on the car paintwork, wash it off immediately with copious amounts of cold water.

6 Identify the locations of each of the brake pipe unions, unscrew the union nuts and carefully withdraw the pipes clear of the valve (photo). Tape over the pipe ends and valve orifices to prevent dirt ingress.

7 Undo the two bolts securing the valve mounting bracket to the inner wing, and remove the valve assembly.

8 Refitting is the reverse sequence to removal. Bleed the hydraulic system as described in Section 16 on completion.

15 Hydraulic pipes and hoses – inspection, removal and refitting

1 At the intervals given in *Routine maintenance*, carefully examine all brake pipes, hoses, hose connections and pipe unions.

2 First check for signs of leakage at the pipe unions. Then examine the flexible hoses for signs of cracking, chafing or deterioration of the rubber.

3 The brake pipes must be examined carefully and methodically. They must be cleaned off and checked for signs of dents, corrosion or other damage. Corrosion should be scraped off and, if the depth of pitting is significant, the pipes renewed. The pipes are however protected by a plastic sleeve, and any corrosion that does occur is likely to be near the pipe unions where the sleeve protection ends.

4 If any section of pipe or hose is to be removed, first unscrew the master cylinder reservoir filler cap and place a piece of polythene over the filler neck. Secure the polythene with an elastic band, ensuring that an airtight seal is obtained. This will minimise brake fluid loss when the pipe or hose is removed.

5 As the front-to-rear brake pipes run inside the car, it will be necessary to determine the route of the pipe, then remove any interior trim panels as necessary for access (see Chapter 11). Once this is done, the union nuts at each end can be unscrewed, the pipe and union pulled out, and the pipe removed from the car or underbody clips as applicable. Where the union nuts are exposed, unprotected from the full force of the weather, they can sometimes be quite tight. As only an open-ended spanner can be used, burring of the flats on the nuts is not uncommon when attempting to undo them. For this reason, a self-locking wrench is often the only way to separate a stubborn union.

6 To remove a flexible hose, wipe the unions and brackets free of dirt and undo the union nut at the brake pipe end.

7 Next extract the hose retaining clip, and lift the end of the hose out of its bracket (photo).

8 If a front hose is being removed, undo the two bolts securing the hose support bracket to the steering knuckle (photo). At the rear, a single bolt secures the support bracket to the shock absorber strut.

9 Undo the banjo bolt securing the hose to the brake caliper (photo), recover the two copper washers, one on each side of the union, and remove the hose. Use new copper washers when refitting.

10 Brake pipes can be obtained individually, or in sets, from Rover dealers or larger accessory shops, cut to length and with the end flares and union nuts in place. The pipe is then bent to shape, using the old pipe as a guide, and is ready for fitting to the car.

11 Refitting the pipes and hoses is a reverse of the removal sequence. Make sure that the hoses are not kinked when in position, and will not chafe any suspension or steering component with suspension movement. Ensure also that the brake pipes are securely supported in their clips. After refitting, remove the polythene from the reservoir and bleed the hydraulic system as described in Section 16.

16 Hydraulic system – bleeding

1 The correct functioning of the brake hydraulic system is only possible after removing all air from the components and circuit; this is achieved by bleeding the system. Note that only clean, unused brake fluid of the specified type may be used.

2 If there is any possibility of incorrect fluid being used in the system, the brake lines and components must be completely flushed with uncontaminated fluid and new seals fitted to the components.

3 **Never** re-use brake fluid which has been bled from the system.

14.6 Pressure-reducing valve mountings and pipe attachments

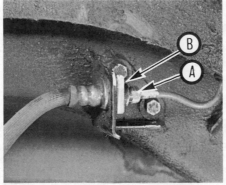
15.7 Flexible brake hose rigid pipe union nut (A) and hose retaining clip (B)

15.8 Front brake hose support bracket on the steering knuckle

15.9 Front brake hose-to-caliper banjo union bolt (arrowed)

4   During the procedure, do not allow the level of brake fluid to drop below the MIN mark on the reservoir.
5   Before starting work, check that all pipes and hoses are secure, unions tight, and bleed screws closed. Take great care not to allow brake fluid to come into contact with the car paintwork, otherwise the finish will be seriously damaged. Wash off any spilled fluid immediately with cold water.
6   If brake fluid has been lost from the master cylinder due to a leak in the system, ensure that the cause is traced and rectified before proceeding further.
7   There are a number of one-man, do-it-yourself, brake bleeding kits currently available from motor accessory shops. It is recommended that one of these kits is used wherever possible, as they greatly simplify the bleeding operation, and also reduce the risk of expelled air and fluid being drawn back into the system. If one of these kits is not available, it will be necessary to gather together a clean jar and a suitable length of plastic or rubber tubing, which is a tight fit over the bleed screw, and also to engage the help of an assistant.
8   If the hydraulic system has only been partially disconnected and suitable precautions were taken to minimise fluid loss, it should only be necessary to bleed that part of the system (ie primary or secondary circuit).
9   If the complete system is to be bled, then it should be done in the following sequence:

   Secondary circuit: Left-hand front, then right-hand rear
   Primary circuit: Right-hand front, then left-hand rear

Bleeding – two-man method

10   Check the fluid level in the master cylinder reservoir, and top up if necessary.
11   Clean the area around the bleed screw on the appropriate brake caliper, and remove the dust cap.
12   Push one end of the bleed tube onto the bleed screw and immerse the other end in the jar, which should contain enough fluid to cover the end of the tube.
13   Open the bleed screw approximately half a turn, and have your assistant depress the brake pedal with a smooth steady stroke, then release it. Tighten the bleed screw at the end of each pedal downstroke to obviate any chance of air or fluid being drawn back into the system.
14   Repeat this operation (paragraph 13) until clean brake fluid, free from air bubbles, can be seen flowing from the end of the tube.
15   Tighten the bleed screw at the end of a pedal downstroke, remove the bleed tube and refit the dust cap. Repeat these procedures on the remaining bleed screws as necessary.

Bleeding – using a one-way valve kit

16   Follow the instructions supplied with the kit, as the procedure may

vary slightly according to the type being used, but generally they are as follows.
17   Clean the area around the bleed screw on the appropriate brake caliper, and remove the dust cap.
18   Attach the tube to the bleed screw, and open the screw approximately half a turn.
19   Depress the brake pedal with a smooth steady stroke, then release it. The one-way valve in the kit will prevent expelled air and fluid from returning at the end of each pedal downstroke. Repeat this operation several times to be sure of ejecting all air from the system. Some kits incorporate a translucent container, which can be positioned so that the air bubbles can be seen flowing from the end of the tube.
20   Tighten the bleed screw, remove the tube and refit the dust cap. Repeat these procedures on the remaining bleed screws as necessary.

Bleeding – using a pressure-bleeding kit

21   These kits are also available from accessory shops, and are usually operated by air pressure from the spare tyre.
22   By connecting a pressurised, fluid-filled container to the master cylinder reservoir, bleeding is then carried out by simply opening each bleed screw in turn and allowing the fluid to run out, rather like turning on a tap, until no air is visible in the expelled fluid.
23   By using this method, the large reservoir of brake fluid provides a safeguard against air being drawn into the master cylinder during bleeding, which often occurs if the fluid level in the reservoir is not maintained.
24   Pressure bleeding is particularly effective when bleeding 'difficult' systems, or when bleeding the complete system at the time of routine fluid renewal. It is also advisable to use this method if the car is equipped with an anti-lock braking system.

All methods

25   When bleeding is completed, check and top up the fluid level in the master cylinder reservoir.
26   Check the feel of the brake pedal. If it feels at all spongy, air must still be present in the system, and further bleeding is indicated. Failure to bleed satisfactorily after a reasonable repetition of the bleeding operations may be due to worn master cylinder seals.
27   Discard brake fluid which has been bled from the system. It is almost certain to be contaminated with moisture and air, making it unsuitable for further use. Clean fluid should always be stored in an airtight container, as it is hygroscopic (absorbs moisture readily). This lowers its boiling point, and could affect braking performance under severe conditions.

17 Brake pedal – removal and refitting

1   From inside the car, release the turnbuckles and lift out the trim panel over the clutch, brake and accelerator pedals.
2   Disconnect the return spring from the brake pedal and pedal bracket.
3   Extract the retaining spring clip and withdraw the clevis pin securing the brake servo pushrod to the pedal.
4   Undo the nut, remove the washer and withdraw the brake pedal pivot bolt from the pedal bracket. Remove the pedal from the car.
5   Prise out the two pedal bushes and withdraw the spacer tube.
6   Check the condition of the components, and renew as necessary.
7   Refitting is the reverse sequence to removal.

18 Handbrake – adjustment

1   Due to the self-adjusting action of the rear brakes, adjustment of the handbrake should normally only be necessary after removal and refitting of any of the handbrake components.
2   To check the adjustment, chock the front wheels, remove the rear wheel trim and slacken the roadwheel nuts. Jack up the rear of the car and support it on axle stands. Remove both rear roadwheels and release the handbrake.
3   Undo the three bolts each side securing the handbrake linkage covers to the rear brake calipers, and remove the covers.
4   Check the clearance between the handbrake linkage lever and the stop-pin on both calipers (Fig. 9.9). If the clearance on either side is outside the tolerance given in the Specifications, adjust the handbrake

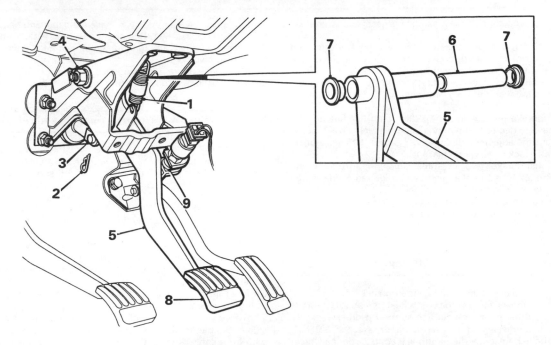

Fig. 9.8 Brake pedal mounting details (Sec 17)

1 Return spring	4 Pedal pivot bolt	6 Spacer tube	8 Pedal pad
2 Clevis pin spring clip	5 Brake pedal	7 Pedal bushes	9 Stop-light switch
3 Clevis pin			

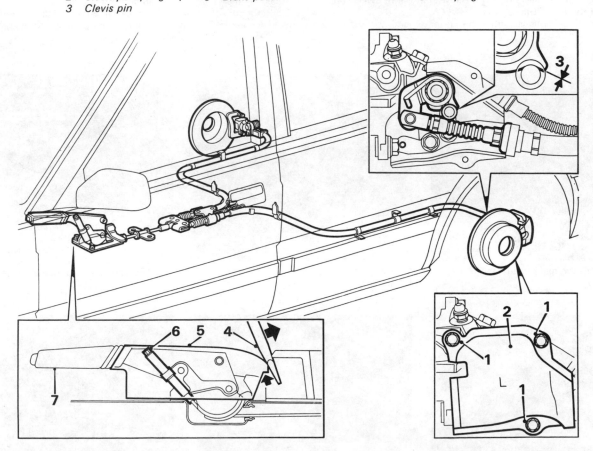

Fig. 9.9 Handbrake adjustment details (Sec 18)

1 Handbrake linkage cover retaining bolts	3 Handbrake linkage lever-to-stop-pin clearance measuring point	4 Using a lever to prise up the handbrake lever trim cover	6 Handbrake adjuster
2 Handbrake linkage cover		5 Handbrake lever trim cover	7 Handbrake lever

using the following procedure. If the clearance is satisfactory, proceed to paragraph 9.

5   From inside the car, carefully prise out the coin holders or switch panels on each side of the centre console, then raise the lid on the cassette holder at the rear of the console.

6   Using a screwdriver as a lever, carefully prise up the rear of the handbrake lever trim cover (photos), and remove the cover from the lever.

7   Turn the handbrake adjuster on the side of the handbrake lever (photo) to increase or decrease the previously-measured clearance, as necessary. Turning the adjuster clockwise will decrease the clearance, and turning it anti-clockwise will increase it.

8   Operate the handbrake two or three times, and recheck the clearance once more. Make a final adjustment if required, then refit the trim cover to the lever.

9   Refit the linkage covers to the brake calipers, refit the roadwheels and lower the car to the ground. Tighten the wheel nuts and refit the wheel trim.

19 Handbrake lever – removal and refitting

1   Refer to Chapter 11 and remove the centre console.

2   Chock the front wheels, remove the rear wheel trim and slacken the wheel nuts. Jack up the rear of the car and support it on axle stands. Remove the rear roadwheels and release the handbrake.

3   From inside the car, unscrew the handbrake adjuster on the side of the lever, and remove the adjuster and spacing washer from the front cable (photo).

4   Detach the front cable from the handbrake lever.

5   Disconnect the wiring plug from the warning light switch on the other side of the lever (photo).

6   Undo the four bolts securing the lever assembly to the floor (photo).

7   Lift up the lever assembly, release the cable and gaiter, and recover the lever to floor gasket. Remove the lever assembly from the car.

8   If required, the warning light switch can be removed after undoing the two screws.

9   Refitting is the reverse sequence to removal. Adjust the handbrake as described in Section 18 before lowering the car to the ground.

20 Handbrake cable (front) – removal and refitting

1   Refer to Chapter 11 and remove the centre console.

2   Chock the front wheels, remove the rear wheel trim and slacken the wheel nuts. Jack up the rear of the car and support it on axle stands. Remove the rear roadwheels and release the handbrake.

3   Undo the bolts securing the exhaust system front heat shield to the underbody. Release the exhaust system front rubber mountings, and remove the heat shield by twisting it around the exhaust system (photo).

4   Extract the spring clip and withdraw the clevis pin securing the front handbrake cable to the compensator (photo).

5   Undo the two bolts securing the front cable guide plate to the underbody (photo).

6   From inside the car, undo the four bolts securing the handbrake lever assembly to the floor.

7   Disconnect the wiring plug from the warning light switch on the side of the handbrake lever, then remove the lever assembly, complete with front cable, from the car. Recover the lever-to-floor gasket.

8   Unscrew the handbrake adjuster on the side of the lever, and remove the adjuster and spacing washer from the front cable.

9   Release the front cable and gaiter from the handbrake lever assembly, then remove the cable from the gaiter.

10   Refitting is the reverse sequence to removal. Adjust the handbrake as described in Section 18 before lowering the car to the ground.

18.6A Prise up the rear of the handbrake lever trim cover ...

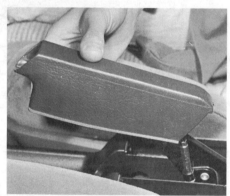

18.6B ... and remove the cover from the lever

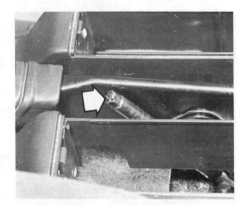

18.7 Handbrake adjuster location (arrowed)

19.3 Undcrew the handbrake adjuster on the side of the lever

19.5 Disconnect the warning light switch wiring plug (arrowed)

19.6 Undo the four handbrake lever retaining bolts (arrowed)

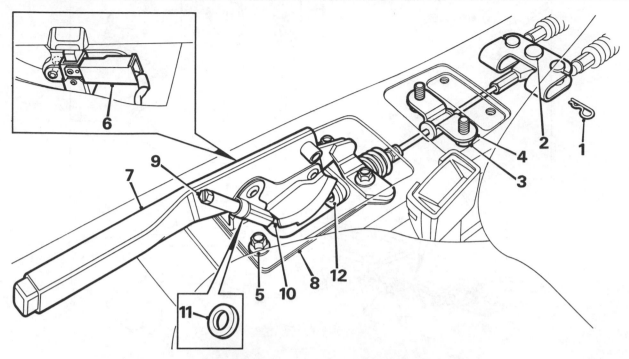

Fig. 9.10 Front handbrake cable attachments (Sec 20)

1	Clevis pin spring clip		10 Front cable-to-lever
2	Clevis pin	wiring plug	attachment
3	Cable guide plate retaining	7 Handbrake lever	11 Spacing washer
	bolts	8 Lever-to-floor gasket	12 Gaiter
4	Cable guide plate	9 Handbrake adjuster	
5	Handbrake lever retaining		
	bolts		
6	Warning light switch		

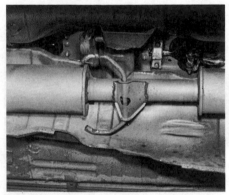

20.3 Removing the front heat shield from the exhaust system

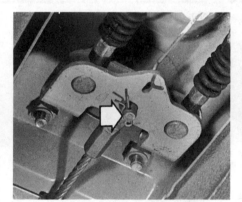

20.4 Extract the cable retaining spring clip and clevis pin (arrowed)

20.5 Undo the front cable guide plate retaining bolts (arrowed)

21 Handbrake cable (rear) – removal and refitting

1   Chock the front wheels, remove the rear wheel trim and slacken the wheel nuts. Jack up the rear of the car and support it on axle stands. Remove the rear roadwheels and release the handbrake.
2   Release the exhaust system rubber mountings, lower the system at the rear, and support it on blocks to avoid straining the front flexible joint.
3   Undo the retaining bolts and remove the front and rear exhaust system heat shields (photo).
4   Undo the three bolts and remove the handbrake linkage cover from the brake caliper.
5   Extract the spring clip and withdraw the clevis pin securing the handbrake cable to the linkage lever on the caliper (see Section 8, photo 8.5).
6   Withdraw the spring clip securing the cable to the abutment bracket, and remove the cable from the caliper.

7   Undo the bolts and release the cable support clips on the suspension arm, chassis member and underbody (photos).
8   Disconnect the return spring, extract the spring clip and withdraw the clevis pin securing the front handbrake cable to the compensator (photo).
9   Turn the rear cable end through 90°, and release it from the slot in the compensator.
10 Withdraw the cable from the abutment bracket, and remove it from under the car. Remove the support clips from the cable.
11 Refitting is the reverse sequence to removal. Adjust the handbrake as described in Section 18 before lowering the car to the ground.

22 Stop-light switch – removal, refitting and adjustment

1   From inside the car, release the turnbuckles and lift out the trim panel over the clutch, brake and accelerator pedals.

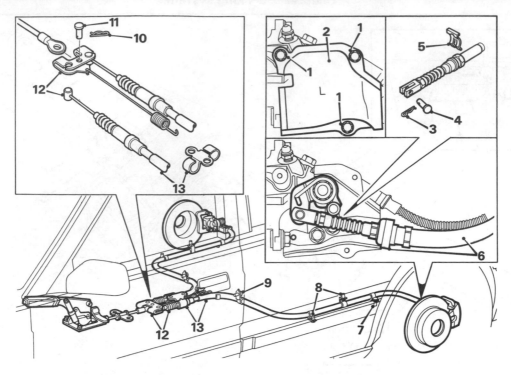

Fig. 9.11 Rear handbrake cable attachments (Sec 21)

1	Handbrake linkage cover retaining bolts	4	Clevis pin
2	Handbrake linkage cover	5	Cable retaining spring clip
3	Clevis pin spring clip	6	Handbrake cable
		7	Suspension arm support clip
8	Chassis member support clips	11	Clevis pin
9	Underbody support clip	12	Cable attachment at compensator
10	Clevis pin spring clip	13	Abutment bracket

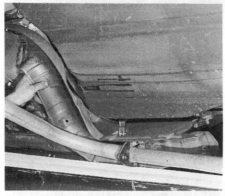

21.3 Removing the rear heat shield from the exhaust system

21.7A Cable support on the chassis member ...

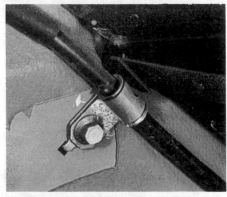

21.7B ... and rear underbody

21.7C Front cable support retaining bolts (arrowed)

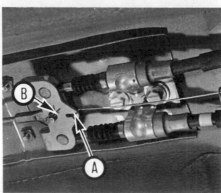

21.8 Handbrake cable return spring (A) and retaining clevis pin (B)

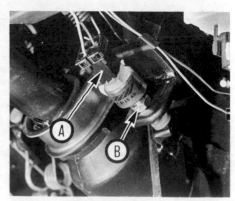

22.2 Stop-light switch wiring multi-plug (A) and locknut (B)

2 Disconnect the switch wiring multi-plug, then slacken the locknut and unscrew the switch from the brake pedal bracket (photo).
3 Refit the switch using the reverse of the removal procedure, and adjust its position so that the stop-lights illuminate after 6.0 mm (0.25 in) of brake pedal travel. When turning the switch during adjustment, disconnect the wiring multi-plug to avoid twisting the harness.
4 When adjustment is correct, tighten the locknut, then refit the trim panel.

23 Vacuum servo unit – description and testing

1 A vacuum servo unit is located between the brake pedal and master cylinder, to provide assistance to the driver when the brake pedal is depressed. This reduces the effort required by the driver to operate the brakes under all braking conditions.
2 The unit operates by vacuum obtained from the inlet manifold, and consists basically of a diaphragm, control valve and non-return valve.
3 With the brake pedal released, vacuum is channelled to both sides of the diaphragm, but when the pedal is depressed, one side is opened to atmosphere. The resultant unequal pressures are harnessed to assist in depressing the master cylinder pistons.
4 Normally, the servo unit is very reliable, but if the unit becomes faulty it must be renewed complete, as repair is not possible. In the event of failure, the hydraulic system is in no way affected, except that higher pedal pressures will be necessary.
5 To test the servo unit, depress the brake pedal several times with the engine switched off, to destroy the vacuum.
6 Apply moderate pressure to the brake pedal, then start the engine. The pedal should move down slightly as the vacuum is restored, if the servo is operating correctly.
7 Now switch off the engine and wait five minutes. Vacuum should still be available for at least one assisted operation of the pedal.

24 Vacuum servo unit – removal and refitting

1 Remove the master cylinder as described in Section 12 or 13 as applicable.
2 From inside the car, release the turnbuckles and lift out the trim panel over the clutch, brake and accelerator pedals.
3 Extract the retaining clip and withdraw the clevis pin securing the servo pushrod to the brake pedal.
4 From within the engine compartment, remove the vacuum hose elbow from the front face of the servo by prising it out of its grommet.
5 Unscrew the four retaining nuts inside the car, and withdraw the servo unit from the engine compartment bulkhead.
6 With the servo removed, the air filter can be renewed if necessary. Withdraw the dust cover over the air filter and pushrod. Hook out the washer and old filter, and cut the filter to allow removal over the pushrod fork. Similarly cut the new filter, place it in position in the housing, and refit the washer and dust cover.
7 Refitting is the reverse sequence to removal. Use a new gasket on the servo-to-bulkhead mating face, and tighten the retaining nuts to the specified torque. Refit the master cylinder as described in Sections 12 or 13 as applicable.

25 Anti-lock braking system – description and operation

Later Rover 820 models are available with an anti-lock braking system (ABS) as an optional extra. The system is used in conjunction with the normal braking system to provide greater stability, improved steering control and shorter stopping distances under all braking conditions. A brief description of the system operation is as follows. Each wheel is provided with a wheel speed sensor, which monitors the wheel rotational speed. The sensor consists of a magnetic core and coil, and is mounted at a predetermined distance from a toothed reluctor ring. The reluctor rings for the front wheels are pressed onto the driveshaft outer constant velocity joints, and those for the rear wheels are pressed onto the rear hubs. When each hub turns, the magnetic field of the sensor is altered as the reluctor ring teeth pass the sensor head, thus inducing an alternating voltage, the frequency of which varies according to wheel speed.

Signals from the wheel speed sensors are sent to an electronic control unit, which can accurately determine whether a wheel is accelerating or decelerating in relation to a reference speed. Information from the electronic control unit is sent to the hydraulic modulator, which contains four solenoids, each operating one inlet and one exhaust valve for one brake, and all working independently of each other in three distinct phases:
Pressure build-up phase: The solenoid inlet valves are open, and hydraulic pressure from the master cylinder is applied directly to the brake calipers.
Constant pressure phase: The solenoid inlet and exhaust valves are closed, and hydraulic pressure at the calipers is maintained at a constant level, even though master cylinder pressure may increase.
Pressure reduction phase: The solenoid inlet valve is closed to prevent further hydraulic pressure reaching the caliper and, in addition, the exhaust valve is open, to reduce existing pressure and release the brake. Fluid is returned to the master cylinder in this phase via the return pump in the hydraulic modulator.
The braking cycle for one wheel is therefore as follows, and will be the same for all four wheels, although independently.
Wheel rotational speed is measured by the wheel speed sensors, the information is processed by the electronic control unit. By comparing the signals received from each wheel, the control unit can determine a reference speed, and detect any variation from this speed, which would indicate a locking brake. Should a lock-up condition be detected, the control unit initiates the constant pressure phase, and no further increase in hydraulic pressure is applied to the affected brake. If the lock-up condition is still detected, the pressure reduction phase is initiated to allow the wheel to turn. The control unit returns to the constant pressure phase until the wheel rotational speed exceeds a predetermined value, then the cycle repeats with the control unit re-initiating the pressure build-up phase. This control cycle is continuously and rapidly repeated, until the brake pedal is released or the car comes to a stop.
Additional circuitry within the electronic control unit monitors the functioning of the system, and informs the driver of any fault condition by means of a warning light. Should a fault occur, the system switches off allowing normal braking, without ABS, to continue.

26 Anti-lock braking system components – removal and refitting

Hydraulic modulator
1 Refer to Chapter 12 and remove the battery.
2 To remove the modulator control relays, undo the screw and lift off the plastic cover. Remove the relays by pulling them out of their location. The large relay controls the return pump operation, and the small relay controls the solenoid valve operation. Refitting is the reversal of removal.
3 To remove the complete modulator unit, remove the relay cover, unscrew the cable clamp and disconnect the modulator wiring multi-plug. Undo the earth terminal nut and disconnect the earth lead from the modulator.
4 Remove the master cylinder reservoir filler cap, and place a piece of polythene over the filler neck. Seal the polythene with an elastic band, ensuring that an airtight seal is obtained. This will minimise brake fluid loss during subsequent operations. Place rags beneath the modulator as an added precaution against fluid spillage.
5 If no identification labels are present on the modulator brake pipe unions, identify each pipe and its location as an aid to refitting. The modulator ports should be stamped on the modulator body with a two-letter code as follows:

VR = Right-hand front
VL = Left-hand front
HR = Right-hand rear
HL = Left-hand rear

6 Unscrew each brake pipe union at the modulator, withdraw the pipe, and immediately plug the pipe end and orifice. Release the pipe support bracket from the side of the modulator, and carefully ease the pipes clear.
7 Slacken the modulator mounting nuts and remove the unit from its location. Do not attempt to dismantle the modulator, as it is a sealed

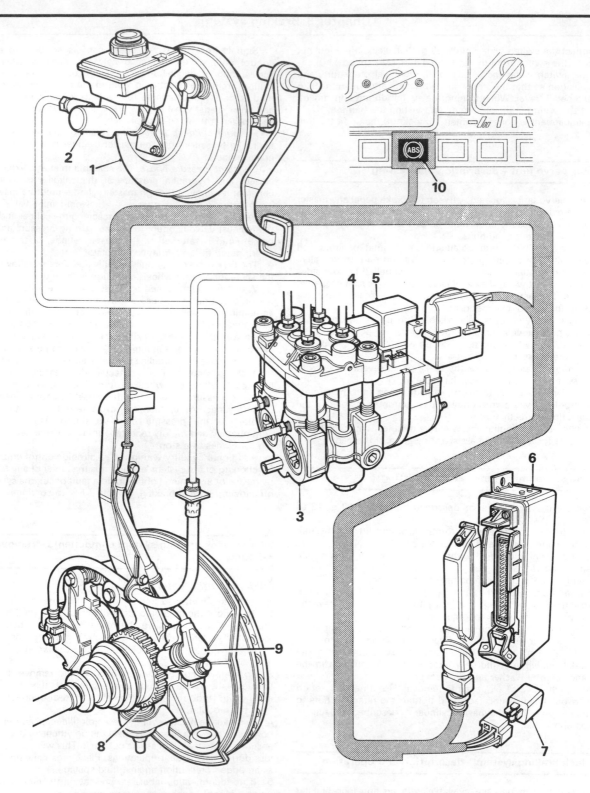

Fig. 9.12 Anti-lock braking system main components (Sec 25)

1 Vacuum servo unit
2 Master cylinder
3 Hydraulic modulator
4 Modulator control relay – solenoid valve operation
5 Modulator control relay – return pump operation
6 Electronic control unit
7 Over-voltage protection relay
8 Front wheel speed sensor reluctor ring
9 Front wheel speed sensor
10 ABS warning light

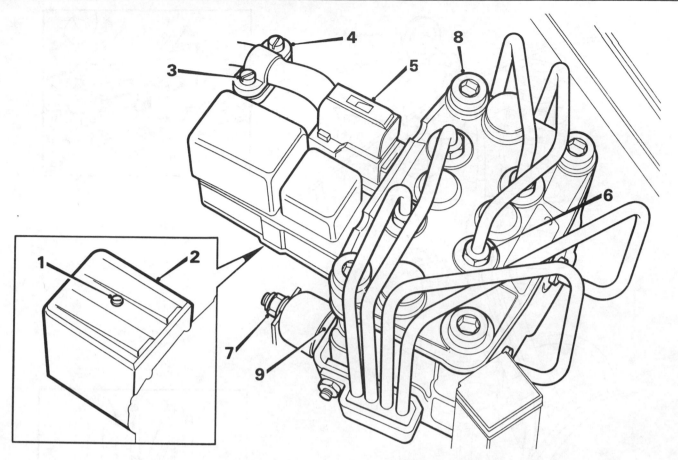

Fig. 9.13 Hydraulic modulator attachments (Sec 26)

1 Cover retaining screw	4 Cable clamp	6 Brake pipe unions	8 Modulator
2 Modulator relay cover	5 Multi-plug	7 Mounting nuts	9 Mounting rubbers
3 Cable clamp screws		

unit, and no repairs are possible.

8   Refitting is the reverse sequence to removal. Bleed the hydraulic system as described in Section 16 on completion.

Electronic control unit

9   Disconnect the battery negative terminal. (Refer to Chapter 12, Section 1, before doing this).

10   Working in the luggage compartment on the left-hand side, release the turnbuckle and lift off the control unit cover.

11   Disconnect the wiring multi-plug by depressing the spring tab at the cable end, lift the plug up at the cable end, then disengage the tab at the other end.

12   Undo the retaining bolts and remove the unit from its location.

13   Refitting is the reverse sequence to removal, but ensure that the wiring multi-plug engages securely with an audible click from the spring tab.

Over-voltage protection relay

14   Working in the luggage compartment, release the turnbuckle and lift off the cover over the electronic control unit.

15   Withdraw the relay from its socket located below the control unit.

16   Refitting is the reverse sequence to removal.

Front wheel speed sensor

17   Apply the handbrake, prise off the front wheel trim and slacken the wheel nuts. Jack up the front of the car and support it on axle stands. Remove the front roadwheel.

18   Undo the bolts securing the cable harness support brackets to the steering knuckle and inner wheel arch panel.

19   From within the engine compartment, release the wiring connector from its holder, and separate the connector. Release the wheel arch

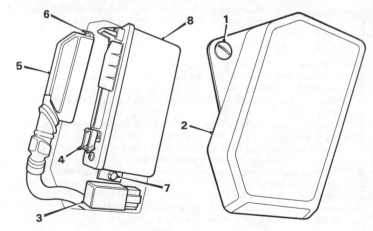

Fig. 9.14 Electronic control unit and over-voltage protection relay details (Sec 26)

1 Turnbuckle	5 Wiring multi-plug
2 Control unit cover	6 Multi-plug tab
3 Over-voltage protection relay	7 Retaining bolt
4 Spring tab	8 Electronic control unit

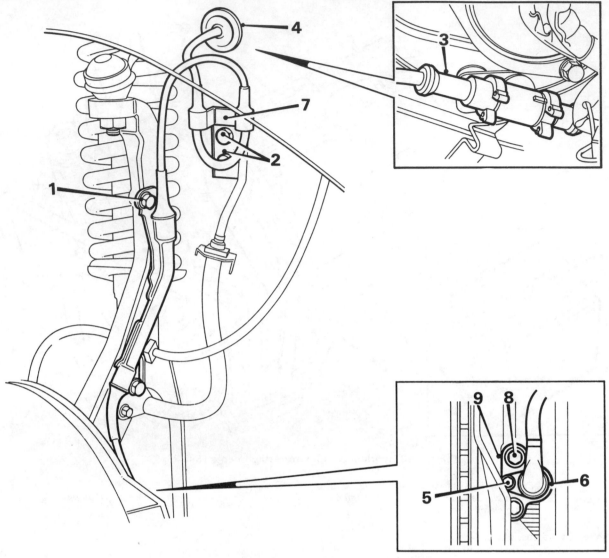

Fig. 9.15 Front wheel speed sensor attachments (Sec 26)

1	Cable harness support bracket bolt on steering knuckle	5	Sensor-to-sensor bracket retaining bolt
2	Cable harness support	6	Sensor
3	Wiring connector	7	Harness support bracket
4	Wheel arch grommet	8	Sensor bracket-to-steering knuckle retaining bolt
	bracket and bolt on inner wheel arch panel	9	Sensor bracket

grommet and pull the wiring through to the wheel arch.

20 Undo the bolt securing the sensor to the sensor bracket on the steering knuckle, and carefully prise the sensor out of the bracket.

21 Release the sensor wiring from the support bracket, and remove the unit from the car.

22 Undo the two bolts and remove the sensor bracket from the steering knuckle.

23 Prior to refitting, clean the sensor, sensor bracket and the mounting area on the steering knuckle, removing all traces of dirt and grit.

24 Refitting is the reverse sequence to removal. Lubricate the sensor and sensor bracket with Rocol J166 or Molykote FB180, and ensure that the bracket bosses face the hub when fitting. Tighten all bolts to the specified torque, and check the sensor-to-reluctor ring clearance, which should be as given in the Specifications.

Rear wheel speed sensor

25 Chock the front wheels, prise off the rear wheel trim and slacken the wheel nuts. Jack up the rear of the car and support it on axle stands. Remove the rear roadwheel.

26 Working in the luggage compartment on the left-hand side, release the turnbuckle and lift off the cover over the electronic control unit.

27 Remove the left-hand side trim panel for access to the wiring around the control unit.

28 Disconnect the wheel speed sensor wiring at the cable connector.

29 Undo the two screws and remove the plastic liner on the front face of the rear wheel arch.

30 Release the grommets in the luggage compartment floor and inner wheel arch, then pull the wiring through to the wheel arch.

31 Undo the two bolts and remove the cable cover and guide from the chassis member.

32 Release the cable ties and retaining clips securing the sensor wiring to the chassis member.

33 Undo the three bolts securing the cable harness support bracket to the rear suspension arm.

34 Undo the three bolts and remove the handbrake linkage cover from the brake caliper.

35 Undo the bolt securing the sensor to the sensor bracket on the hub carrier, and carefully prise the sensor out of the bracket.

36 Manipulate the sensor and wiring out from under the wheel arch, and remove it from car.

37 Prior to refitting, clean the sensor, sensor bracket and the mounting area on the hub carrier, removing all traces of dirt and grit.

38 Refitting is the reverse sequence to removal. Lubricate the sensor and sensor bracket with Rocol J166 or Molykote FB180, and tighten all bolts to the specified torque. Check the sensor-to-reluctor ring clearance, which should be as given in the Specifications.

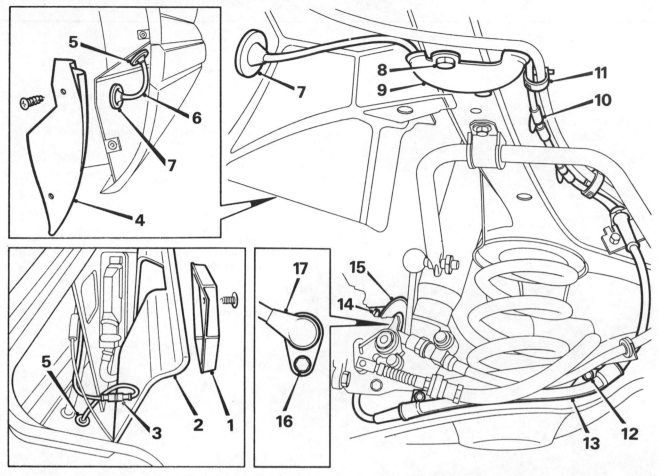

Fig. 9.16 Rear wheel speed sensor attachments (Sec 26)

1 Electronic control unit cover	6 Sensor wiring
2 Left-hand side trim panel	7 Inner wheel arch grommet
3 Cable connector	8 Cover bolts
4 Rear wheel arch plastic liner	9 Cable cover and guide
5 Luggage compartment floor grommet	10 Cable retaining clip

11 Cable tie
12 Support bracket bolt
13 Cable harness support bracket on suspension arm
14 Handbrake linkage cover bolts
15 Handbrake linkage cover
16 Sensor-to-sensor bracket retaining bolt
17 Wheel speed sensor

Wheel speed sensor reluctor rings

39 The reluctor rings for the front and rear wheel speed sensors are an integral part of the driveshaft outer constant velocity joints (front) and rear wheel hub flanges (rear), and cannot be renewed separately.

40 If a reluctor ring is damaged, or in any way unserviceable, a new driveshaft outer constant velocity joint or rear hub flange must be obtained as applicable. Removal and refitting procedures are covered in Chapters 8 and 10 respectively.

27 Fault diagnosis – braking system

Note: *Fault diagnosis on the anti-lock braking system (where fitted) should be entrusted to a suitably-equipped Rover dealer, due to the need for special gauges and test equipment.*

Symptom	Reason(s)
Excessive pedal travel	Rear brake self-adjust mechanism inoperative Air in hydraulic system Faulty master cylinder Worn or incorrectly adjusted hub bearings
Brake pedal feels spongy	Air in hydraulic system Faulty master cylinder

Symptom	Reason(s)
Judder felt through brake pedal or steering wheel when braking	Excessive run-out or thickness variation of discs Brake pads worn Brake caliper guide pins worn Brake caliper mounting bolts loose Wear in suspension or steering components – see Chapter 10
Excessive pedal pressure required to stop car	Faulty vacuum servo unit Leaking or disconnected servo vacuum supply hose Vacuum servo air filter choked Brake caliper piston seized Brake pads worn or contaminated Incorrect grade of brake pads fitted Primary or secondary hydraulic circuit failure
Brakes pull to one side	Brake pads worn or contaminated Brake caliper piston seized Seized rear brake self-adjust mechanism Brake pads renewed on one side only Tyre, steering or suspension defect – see Chapter 10
Brakes binding	Brake caliper piston seized Handbrake incorrectly adjusted Faulty master cylinder

Chapter 10 Suspension and steering

For modifications, and information applicable to later models, see Supplement at end of manual

Contents

Specifications

Front suspension

Type .... Independent, by unequal length upper and lower suspension arms, with coil springs, telescopic shock absorbers and anti-roll bar

Trim height (measured from the centre of the front hub to the edge of the wheel arch) .... 397 to 417 mm (15.6 to 16.4 in)
Hub bearing endfloat .... 0.05 mm (0.02 in)

Rear suspension

Type .... Independent, by transverse and trailing links, with coil springs, telescopic shock absorbers and anti-roll bar. Self-levelling suspension optional on certain models

Trim height (measured from the centre of the rear hub to the edge of the wheel arch):
    Standard suspension .... 379 to 399 mm (14.9 to 15.7 in)
    Self-levelling suspension (after being driven for 0.6 mile/ 1.0 km) .... 348 to 368 mm (13.7 to 14.5 in)
Hub bearing endfloat .... 0.10 mm (0.004 in)

Steering

Type .... Power-assisted rack and pinion
Turns lock-to-lock 3.2
Fluid type .... Dexron II D type ATF (Duckhams D-Matic)

Front wheel alignment

Toe setting .... Parallel ± 0° 8′
Camber .... 0° 11′ ± 0° 30′ positive
Castor .... 1° 54′ ± 0° 15′ positive
Steering axis inclination .... 8°

Rear wheel alignment

Toe setting .... 0° 10′ ± 0° 4′ toe-in
Camber .... 0° ± 30′

Roadwheels

Wheel size:
    Standard .... 6J x 14 or 6J x 15 pressed-steel
    Optional .... 6J x 15 light alloy

Tyres

Tyre size.. 195/70 HR x 14 or 195/65 VR x 15
Tyre pressures – cold, bar (lbf/ in²): **Front** **Rear**
    195/70 HR x 14 and 195/65 VR x 15................................... 1.9 (28) 1.9 (28)
For speeds in excess of 100 mph (160 kph), increase pressure by 0.4 bar (6.0 lbf/in²) for 195/70 HR x 14 tyres, and by 0.7 bar (10.0 lbf/in²) for 195/65 VR x 15 tyres

Torque wrench settings

	Nm	lbf ft
Front suspension		
Anti-roll bar connecting link bolts	50	37
Anti-roll mounting bracket bolts	22	16
Driveshaft retaining nut	290	214
Steering knuckle balljoint nut	100	74
Upper suspension arm balljoint nut	50	37
Strut forked member to lower arm	90	66
Strut forked member clamp bolt	50	37
Shock absorber top mounting nuts	25	18
Shock absorber spindle nut	50	37
Upper suspension arm mounting nuts	80	59
Upper suspension arm pivot bolt	90	66
Lower suspension arm inner mounting bolt	50	37
Tie-bar front mounting nut	90	66
Tie-bar-to-lower suspension arm bolts	170	125
Rear suspension		
Anti-roll bar connecting link nuts	45	33
Anti-roll bar mounting bracket bolts	22	16
Hub carrier-to-trailing link bolt	70	52
Hub carrier-to-transverse link bolt	70	52
Shock absorber-to-hub carrier clamp bolt	70	52
Shock absorber upper mounting nuts	25	18
Shock absorber spindle nut	52	38
Hub flange retaining nut	245	181
Transverse link inner mounting bolt	50	37
Trailing link front mounting nut	45	33
Trailing link adjustment plate retaining bolt	70	52
Trailing link adjustment plate eccentric bolt	70	52
Steering		
Steering wheel nut	50	37
Steering column upper mounting nuts	14	10
Steering column lower mounting bolts	22	16
Column universal joint clamp bolts	22	16
Steering tie-rod balljoint nut	44	32
Tie-rod setting locknuts	45	33
Steering rack hydraulic unions	20	15
Steering gear fluid pipe unions	18	13
Steering gear mounting bolts	45	33
Drivebelt tensioner wheel retaining nut (rear-mounted pump)	45	33
Drivebelt idler pulley retaining nut (front-mounted pump)	45	33
Camshaft pulley retaining bolts	10	7
Longitudinal support member bolts	45	33
Power steering pump retaining bolts:		
Rear-mounted pump	25	18
Front-mounted pump	10	7
Power steering pump pulley nut (rear-mounted pump)	82	61
Power steering pump pulley bolts (front-mounted pump)	25	18
Roadwheels		
Roadwheel nuts	70	52

1 General description

The independent front suspension is by unequal length upper and lower suspension arms, and utilizes coil springs and telescopic shock absorbers. Each spring and shock absorber assembly is attached to the body turret at its upper end by a rubber-cushioned mounting, and to the lower suspension arm by a forged, forked-shaped member. Fore and aft location of each suspension assembly is by a tie-bar, and an anti-roll bar is used to minimise body roll. The front steering knuckles, which carry the hub bearings, brake calipers and the hub/ disc assemblies, pivot on balljoints – one incorporated in the upper suspension arm, and one secured to the lower part of the steering knuckle itself.

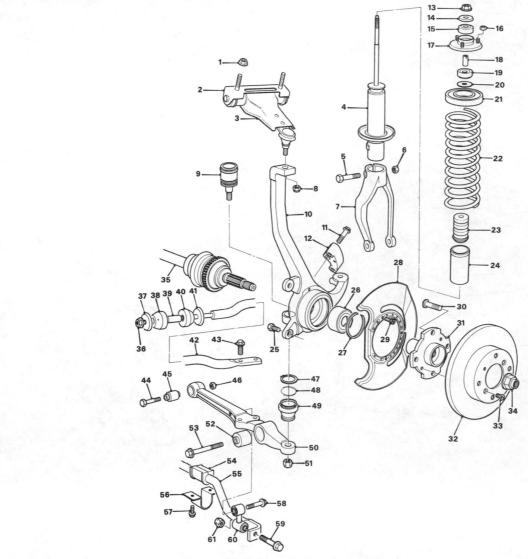

Fig. 10.1 Exploded view of the front suspension components (Sec 1)

1 Mounting bracket nut
2 Upper suspension arm mounting bracket
3 Upper suspension arm
4 Shock absorber
5 Forked member clamp bolt
6 Clamp bolt nut
7 Forked member
8 Balljoint nut
9 Steering knuckle balljoint
10 Steering knuckle
11 Wheel speed sensor bolt (where applicable)
12 Wheel speed sensor bracket (where applicable)
13 Shock absorber spindle nut
14 Washer
15 Upper bush

16 Upper mounting nut
17 Shock absorber upper mounting plate
18 Threaded collar
19 Lower bush (where fitted)
20 Washer
21 Spring seat
22 Coil spring
23 Bump-stop
24 Dust cover
25 Brake caliper carrier bracket bolt
26 Hub bearing
27 Bearing retaining circlip
28 Disc shield
29 Disc shield bolt
30 Wheel stud
31 Hub flange

32 Brake disc
33 Disc retaining screw
34 Driveshaft retaining nut
35 Driveshaft
36 Tie-bar front mounting nut
37 Washer
38 Outer mounting bush
39 Spacer
40 Inner mounting bush
41 Washer
42 Tie-bar
43 Tie-bar-to-lower suspension arm bolt
44 Lower suspension arm inner mounting bolt
45 Inner mounting bush
46 Mounting bolt nut
47 Balljoint retaining circlip

48 Dust cover locking ring
49 Balljoint dust cover
50 Lower suspension arm
51 Balljoint retaining nut
52 Forked member mounting bush
53 Forked member through bolt
54 Anti-roll bar mounting bush
55 Anti-roll bar
56 Anti-roll bar mounting bracket
57 Mounting bracket bolt
58 Connecting link bolt
59 Connecting link bolt
60 Connecting link
61 Connecting link nut

The independent rear suspension is by transverse and trailing links with coil springs, telescopic shock absorbers, and an anti-roll bar. The shock absorbers are attached to the body at their upper ends by rubber-cushioned mountings, and clamped to the hub carriers at their lower ends. Lateral location of each suspension assembly is provided by the transverse link, which also provides the lower location of the coil spring. Fore and aft location of each suspension assembly is controlled by the trailing link, which is attached to the hub carrier by means of a bracket incorporating an eccentric mounting bolt for rear wheel toe adjustment.

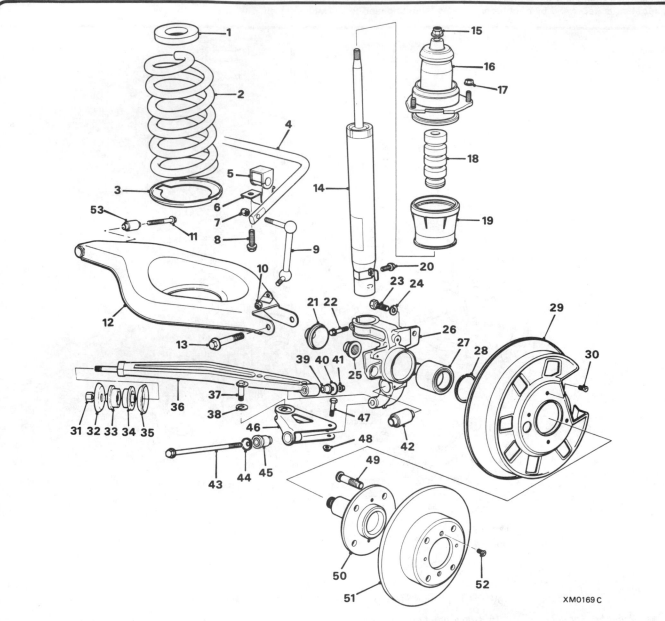

XM0169C

Fig. 10.2 Exploded view of the rear suspension components (Sec 1)

1 Upper spring seat	14 Shock absorber	27 Hub bearing	41 Through-bolt nut
2 Coil spring	15 Shock absorber spindle nut	28 Bearing retaining circlip	42 Transverse link-to-hub
3 Lower spring seat	16 Shock absorber upper	29 Disc shield	carrier mounting bush
4 Anti-roll bar	mounting	30 Disc shield screw	43 Trailing link-to-hub carrier
5 Anti-roll bar mounting bush	17 Upper mounting nut	31 Trailing link front mounting	through-bolt
6 Anti-roll bar mounting	18 Bump-stop	nut	44 Washer
bracket	19 Dust cover	32 Outer washer	45 Rear mounting bush
7 Connecting link nut	20 Brake hose bracket bolt	33 Outer bush	46 Adjustment plate
8 Mounting bracket bolt	21 Nut cover	34 Inner bush	47 Adjustment plate bolt
9 Connecting link	22 Shock absorber clamp bolt	35 Inner washer	48 Adjustment plate nut
10 Connecting link nut	23 Brake caliper carrier bracket	36 Trailing link	49 Wheel stud
11 Transverse link inner	bolt	37 Eccentric bolt	50 Hub flange
mounting bolt	24 Washer	38 Eccentric washer	51 Brake disc
12 Transverse link	25 Hub flange retaining nut	39 Rear mounting bush	52 Brake disc screw
13 Transverse link-to-hub	26 Hub carrier	40 Washer	53 Transverse link bush
carrier bolt			

Self-levelling rear suspension, which reacts to vehicle loading and automatically maintains the normal trim heights, is available as an option on all later models.The self-levelling units are sealed dampers fitted in place of the normal rear shock absorbers. A pump in the damper operates under the action of the suspension to raise the rear of the car until normal trim height is regained. On an undulating road, this process will be carried out within one mile. When the additional load is removed, the suspension remains at the correct level.

Power-assisted rack and pinion steering gear is standard equipment on all models. Movement of the steering wheel is transmitted to the steering gear by a steering column shaft containing two universal joints. These allow for provision of a rake-adjustable column assembly, and also allow the necessary upward deflection of the column, for driver safety, in the event of front end impact. The front wheels are connected to the steering gear by tie-rods, each having an inner and outer balljoint. On early models, hydraulic fluid pressure for the power assistance is provided by a pump, mounted on the left-hand end of the engine and belt-driven from a pulley on the inlet camshaft. On later models, the pump is mounted on the forward-facing side of the engine, for improved access, and is belt-driven from the crankshaft pulley.

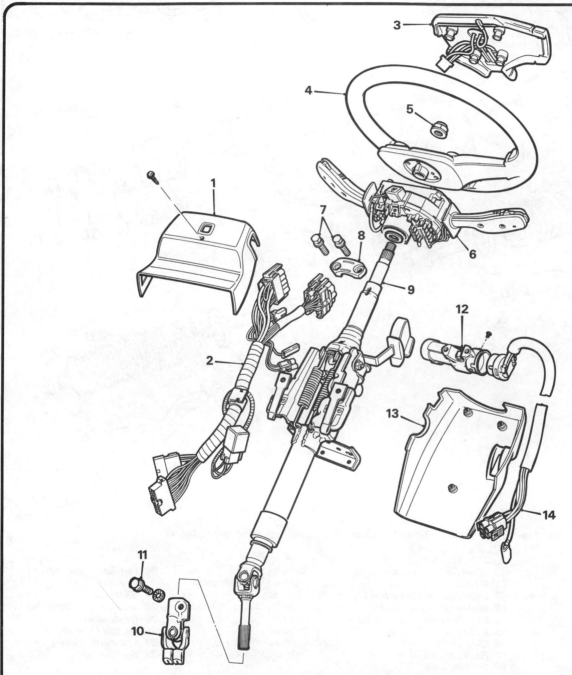

Fig. 10.3 Exploded view of the steering column components (Sec 1)

1	Steering column upper shroud	5 Steering wheel nut	10 Universal joint
2	Wiring harness	6 Steering column switches	11 Clamp bolt
3	Steering wheel pad	7 Steering lock shear-bolts	12 Steering column lock/ignition switch
4	Steering wheel	8 Lock saddle	13 Steering column lower shroud
		9 Steering column shaft	14 Ignition switch wiring harness

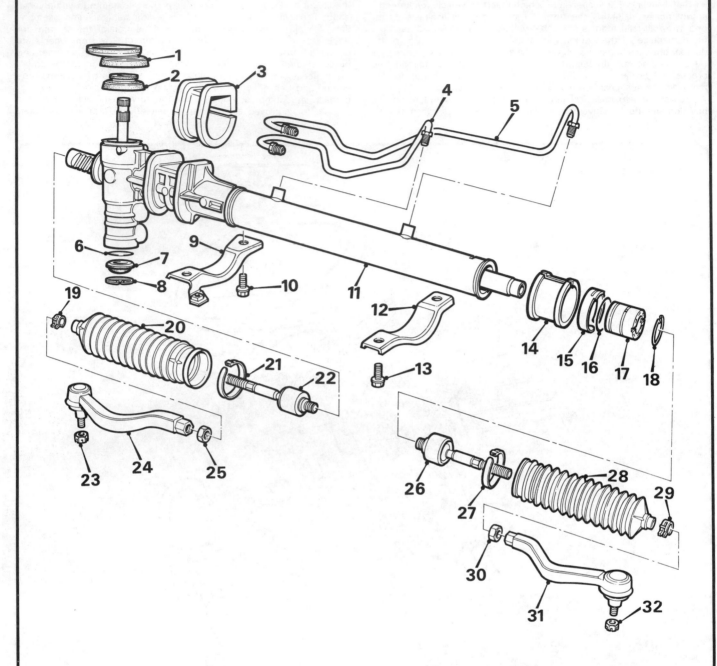

Fig. 10.4 Exploded view of the rack and pinion steering gear (Sec 1)

1	Pinion shield	10	Mounting bracket bolt	19	Gaiter clip	26	Left-hand inner tie-rod
2	Pinon dust cover	11	Rack housing	20	Right-hand rubber gaiter		balljoint
3	Right-hand rubber mounting	12	Left-hand mounting bracket	21	Gaiter clip	27	Gaiter clip
4	Fluid pipe	13	Mounting bracket bolt	22	Right-hand inner tie-rod	28	Left-hand rubber gaiter
5	Fluid pipe	14	Left-hand rubber mounting		balljoint	29	Gaiter clip
6	O-ring	15	Bush retainer	23	Balljoint	30	Tie-rod locknut
7	Pinion cover	16	O-ring	24	Right-hand steering tie-rod	31	Left-hand steering tie-rod
8	Circlip	17	Rack support bush	25	Tie-rod locknut	32	Balljoint nut
9	Right-hand mounting bracket	18	Locking wire				

2 Maintenance and inspection

1 At the intervals given in *Routine maintenance* at the beginning of this manual, a thorough inspection of all suspension and steering components should be carried out, using the following procedures as a guide.

Front suspension and steering

2 With the engine switched off, check the fluid level in the power steering reservoir as follows.
3 Wipe the area around the black filler cap on the reservoir (photo),turn the cap anti-clockwise and remove it.
4 Wipe the dipstick on a clean cloth, refit the cap fully, then remove it once more. Check the fluid level, which must be between the MIN mark on one side of the dipstick, and the MAX mark on the other. If necessary, top up using the specified fluid to bring the level up to the MAX mark (photo). Refit the cap and tighten it securely.
5 Apply the handbrake, jack up the front of the car and support it securely on axle stands.
6 Visually inspect the upper and lower balljoint dust covers and the steering gear rubber gaiters for splits, chafing or deterioration. Renew any components showing signs of wear or damage as described in the appropriate Section of this Chapter.
7 Check the power steering fluid hoses for chafing or deterioration, and the pipe and hose unions for fluid leaks. Also check for any signs of fluid leakage from the rubber gaiters, which would indicate failed fluid seals within the steering gear itself. Rectify any faults found using the procedures described later in this Chapter.
8 Grasp the roadwheel at the 12 o'clock and 6 o'clock positions, and try to rock it. Very slight free play may be felt, but if the movement is appreciable, further investigation is necessary to determine the source. Continue rocking the wheel while an assistant depresses the footbrake. If the movement is now eliminated or significantly reduced, it is likely that the hub bearings are at fault. If the free play is still evident with the footbrake depressed, then there is wear in the suspension joints or mountings. Pay close attention to the upper and lower balljoints and the suspension arm mounting bushes. Renew any worn components as described in the appropriate Sections of this Chapter.
9 Now grasp the wheel at the 9 o'clock and 3 o'clock positions, and try to rock it as before. Any excessive movement felt now may again be caused by wear in the hub bearings or the steering tie-rod inner or outer balljoints. If the outer balljoint is worn, the visual movement will be obvious. If the inner joint is suspect, it can be felt by placing a hand over the rack and pinion rubber gaiter and grasping the tie-rod. If the wheel is now rocked, movement will be felt at the inner joint if wear has taken place. Repair procedures are described in Section 25.
10 Using a large screwdriver or flat bar, check for wear in the anti-roll bar mountings by carefully levering against these components. Some movement is to be expected as the mounting bushes are made of rubber, but excessive wear should be obvious. Renew any bushes that are worn.
11 With the car standing on its wheels, have an assistant turn the steering wheel back and forth about one-eighth of a turn each way. There should be minimal lost movement between the steering wheel and roadwheels (some free play within the rack and pinion steering gear itself is normal, due to design tolerances). If the free play is excessive, closely observe the joints and mountings previously described, but in addition check the steering column shaft and universal joints for wear, and also the rack and pinion steering gear itself. Any wear should be visually apparent and must be rectified, as described in the appropriate Sections of this Chapter.
12 Have the front wheel alignment checked, and if necessary adjusted, (see Section 30) if there is any sign of abnormal wear of the front tyres.

Rear suspension

13 Chock the front wheels, jack up the rear of the car and support it securely on axle stands.
14 Visually check the rear suspension components, attachments and linkages for any visible signs of wear or damage.
15 Grasp the roadwheel at the 12 o'clock and 6 o'clock positions, and try to rock it. Any excess movement here indicates wear in the hub bearings, which may also be accompanied by a rumbling sound when the wheel is spun, or wear in the hub carrier lower mounting bush. Repair procedures are described in later Sections of this Chapter.

2.3 Power steering reservoir and filler cap

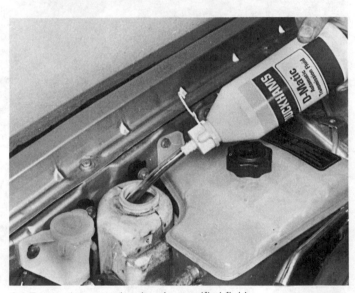

2.4 Top up the reservoir using the specified fluid

16 Have the rear wheel alignment checked, and if necessary adjusted, (see Section 30) if there is any sign of abnormal wear of the rear tyres.

Wheels and tyres

17 Carefully inspect each tyre, including the spare, for signs of uneven wear, lumps, bulges or damage to the sidewalls or tread face. Refer to Section 31 for further details.
18 Check the condition of the wheel rims for distortion, damage or excessive run-out. Also make sure that the balance weights are secure, with no obvious signs that any are missing. Check the torque of the roadwheel nuts, and check the tyre pressures.

Shock absorbers

19 Check for signs of fluid leakage around the shock absorber body, or from the rubber boot around the piston rod (where fitted). Should any fluid be noticed, the shock absorber is defective internally, and renewal is necessary.
20 The efficiency of the shock absorber may be checked by bouncing the car at each corner. Generally speaking, the body will return to its normal position and stop after being depressed. If it rises and returns on a rebound, the shock absorber is probably suspect. Examine also the shock absorber upper and lower mountings for any signs of wear. Renewal procedures are contained in Section 6, 7 and 14.

3 Front steering knuckle assembly – removal and refitting

1   While the car is standing on its wheels, firmly apply the handbrake and put the transmission in gear (PARK on automatic transmission models),

2   Remove the wheel trim, and using a small punch, knock up the staking that secures the driveshaft retaining nut to the groove in the constant velocity joint stub shaft (photo). Note that a new retaining nut will be needed for reassembly.

3   Using a socket, sturdy T-bar and long extension tube for leverage, slacken the retaining nut half a turn. Note that the retaining nut is tightened to a very high torque setting, and considerable effort will be required to slacken it.

4   Slacken the wheel nuts, jack up the front of the car and support it on stands. Remove the roadwheel and return the transmission to neutral.

5   Remove the driveshaft retaining nut.

6   Undo the two bolts securing the brake caliper carrier bracket to the steering knuckle (photo), and the two bolts securing the brake hose bracket to the knuckle.

7   Withdraw the caliper and carrier bracket assembly, complete with brake pads, off the disc, and tie it up using string or wire from a convenient place under the wheel arch. Take care to avoid straining the brake hose.

8   Undo the two retaining screws (photo) and remove the disc from the hub flange.

9   On cars equipped with ABS brakes, remove the front wheel speed sensor and wiring harness from the steering knuckle, as described in Chapter 9.

10   Extract the split pin and unscrew the nut securing the steering tie-rod balljoint to the steering knuckle arm (photo). Release the balljoint from the arm using a universal balljoint separator tool.

11   Undo the nut securing the steering knuckle balljoint to the lower suspension arm. Release the balljoint from the arm using a separator tool or two-legged puller (photo).

12   Undo the nut securing the upper suspension arm balljoint to the steering knuckle (photo), and release the balljoint using the same

3.2 Knock up the staking (arrowed) securing the driveshaft retaining nut

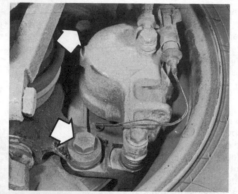

3.6 Brake caliper carrier bracket retaining bolts (arrowed)

3.8 Brake disc retaining screws (arrowed)

3.10 Extract the tie-rod balljoint nut split pin (arrowed)

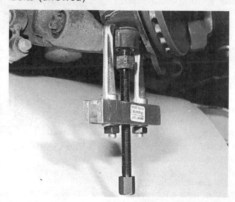

3.11 Using a two-legged puller to release the steering knuckle balljoint

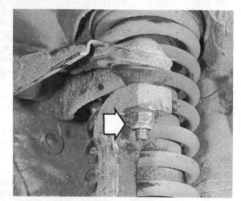

3.12 Undo the upper suspension arm balljoint nut (arrowed)

3.13 Removing the steering knuckle from the driveshaft

3.14 Tighten the new driveshaft retaining nut fully **only** when the weight of the car is on the roadwheels

procedure as for the lower balljoint.

13 Disengage the balljoint shanks, then withdraw the steering knuckle from the driveshaft (photo). If necessary, tap the end of the driveshaft with a copper or plastic mallet to release it from the hub splines. Remove the steering knuckle assembly from the car.

14 Refitting the steering knuckle is the reverse sequence to removal, bearing in mind the following points:

(a) Tighten all retaining nuts and bolts to the specified torque and use a new split pin to secure the steering tie-rod balljoint nut

(b) Use a new driveshaft retaining nut but **do not attempt to tighten this nut fully until the weight of the car is on the roadwheels** (photo). Peen the nut into the driveshaft groove using a small punch after tightening. If a torque wrench capable of recording the high figure required for tightening is not available, it is recommended that the old nut is fitted, tightened as securely as possible, then peened into place. Take the car directly to a suitably-equipped garage, and have them fit and tighten the new nut for you.

(c) On cars equipped with ABS brakes, refit the wheel speed sensor as described in Chapter 9

4 Front hub bearing – renewal

1 Remove the steering knuckle from the car as described in the previous Section.

2 Support the steering knuckle on blocks with the hub flange facing downwards. Using a hammer and socket or tube of suitable diameter in contact with the inner edge of the hub flange (photo), drive the flange

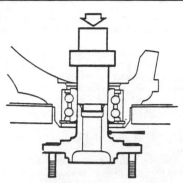

Fig. 10.5 Removing the hub flange from the steering knuckle and bearing (Sec 4)

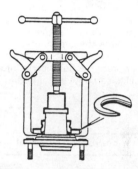

Fig. 10.6 Using a puller and horseshoe-shaped strip of metal to draw off the bearing inner race from the hub flange (Sec 4)

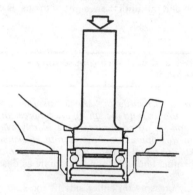

Fig. 10.7 Removing the hub bearing from the steering knuckle (Sec 4)

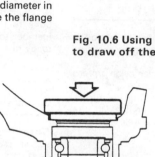

Fig. 10.8 Fitting the new hub bearing to the steering knuckle (Sec 4)

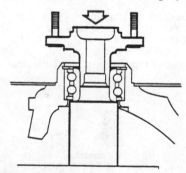

Fig. 10.9 Fitting the hub flange to the new bearing (Sec 4)

4.2A Remove the hub flange using a socket or tube in contact with its outer edge (arrowed) ...

4.2B ... or preferably, use a hydraulic press

out of the hub bearing. Alternatively, if a press is available, support the steering knuckle on the press bed and press the hub flange out (photo).

3 As the hub flange is withdrawn, one of the bearing inner races will come away with it, and must now be removed. To do this, engage the legs of a two-legged puller under the inner race and draw it off. It may be easier to do this if a horseshoe-shaped strip of metal is placed under the inner race, to give the puller legs greater purchase (Fig. 10.6).

4 With the hub flange removed, undo the four screws and remove the disc shield.

5 Using circlip pliers, extract the bearing retaining circlip from the steering knuckle.

6 Support the steering knuckle face-down on blocks, or on the press bed as before, and with the tube or mandrel in contact with the edge of the outer bearing, drive or press the bearing out.

7 Fit the new bearing in the same way, ensuring that it is pressed fully home to the shoulder in the steering knuckle. Keep the bearing square as it is fitted, otherwise it will jam and continued pressure could cause the outer race to crack. If the bearing does jam, tap or press it out, remove any burrs in the bore of the steering knuckle and try again.

8 Secure the bearing with the circlip, then refit the disc shield.

9 Support the bearing inner race on a socket or tube of suitable diameter, and drive or press the hub flange into place.

10 The steering knuckle can now be refitted to the car as described in the previous Section.

5 Steering knuckle balljoint – removal and refitting

1 Remove the steering knuckle from the car as described in Section 3.

2 Extract the balljoint retaining circlip (photo) and remove the dust cover.

3 Support the steering knuckle in a wide-opening vice or on a press bed, and using suitable tubes as mandrels and distance pieces, press the balljoint out of the knuckle. Fig. 10.10 shows the manufacturer's special tools being used for this purpose, to give an idea of the arrangement, but lengths of tubular steel work equally well.

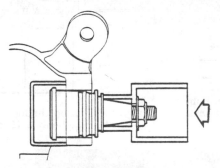

Fig. 10.10 Rover special tool for steering knuckle balljoint removal (Sec 5)

4 Using the same basic procedure, fit the new balljoint until its shoulder contacts the steering knuckle flange.

5 Fit the new dust cover and secure the assembly with the circlip.

6 Refit the steering knuckle to the car as described in Section 3.

6 Front shock absorber and coil spring assembly – removal and refitting

1 Apply the handbrake, prise off the front wheel trim and slacken the wheel nuts. Jack up the front of the car and support it on axle stands. Remove the front roadwheel.

2 Place a jack beneath the lower suspension arm and raise the arm slightly.

3 Undo the nut and remove the through-bolt securing the forked member to the lower suspension arm.

4 Undo the nut and remove the clamp bolt securing the forked member to the shock absorber.

5 Slowly lower the jack, and remove the forked member from the shock absorber and lower suspension arm (photo). It may be necessary to tap the member down using a copper or plastic mallet to release it from the shock absorber.

6 Have an assistant hold the assembly, from below, then undo the three nuts securing the shock absorber top mounting to the body turret in the engine compartment (photo).

7 Remove the shock absorber and spring assembly from under the wheel arch.

8 Refitting is the reverse sequence to removal. Tighten all nuts and bolts to the specified torque, but do not fully tighten the forked member-to-lower arm bolt and nut until the weight of the car is on the roadwheels.

7 Front shock absorber and coil spring assembly – dismantling and reassembly

Note: *Before attempting to dismantle the shock absorber and coil spring assembly, a suitable tool to hold the spring in compression must be obtained. Adjustable coil spring compressors are readily available, and are recommended for this operation. Any attempt at dismantling without such a tool is likely to result in damage or personal injury.*

1 Remove the shock absorber and coil spring assembly as described in the previous Section.

2 Position the spring compressors on either side of the spring, and compress the spring evenly until there is no tension on the spring seat or upper mounting.

5.2 Balljoint retaining circlip (arrowed)

6.5 Removing the front suspension forked member

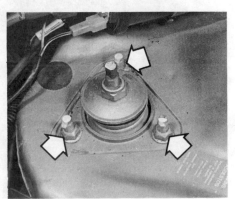

6.6 Shock absorber top mounting retaining nuts (arrowed)

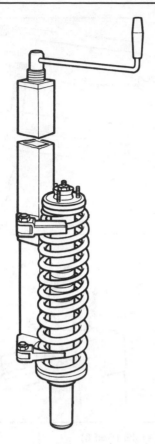

Fig. 10.11 Coil spring and shock absorber assembly,
showing spring compressor tool in position (Sec 7)

3   Hold the unthreaded end of the shock absorber spindle with a
self-locking wrench or similar tool, and unscrew the upper mounting
retaining nut (photo).
4   Withdraw the washer under the nut, followed by the upper bush,
the upper mounting plate and the spring seat.
5   To remove the threaded collar on the shock absorber spindle, it will
be necessary to make up a suitable tool which will engage in the slots
on the collar, enabling it to be unscrewed. A tool can be made out of a

7.3 Remove the retaining nut (arrowed) from the shock absorber
spindle

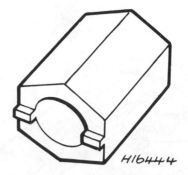

Fig. 10.12 Shock absorber threaded collar home-made
removal tool (Sec 7)

large nut, with one end suitably shaped by cutting or filing so that two
projections are left, which will engage with the collar slots (Fig.
10.12).
6   Engage the home-made tool with the threaded collar slots, then
screw two 10 mm nuts onto the threaded end of the spindle, and lock
them together. Hold these locknuts to prevent the spindle turning, and
unscrew the threaded collar.
7   Remove the locknuts, home-made tool and collar, then withdraw
the lower bush and washer.
8   Lift off the spring, then remove the bump-stop and shock absorber
dust cover.
9   Examine the shock absorber for signs of fluid leakage. Check the
spindle for signs of wear or pitting along its entire length, and check
the shock absorber body for signs of damage or corrosion. Test the
operation of the shock absorber, while holding it in an upright position,
by moving the spindle through a full stroke, and then through short
strokes of 50 to 100 mm (2 to 4 in). In both cases, the resistance felt
should be smooth and continuous. If the resistance is jerky or uneven,
or if there is any visible sign of wear, damage or fluid leakage, renewal
is necessary.
10 If any doubt exists about the condition of the coil spring, remove
the spring compressors and check the spring for distortion or damage.
The spring free length can only be assessed by comparing it with a new
item, and this should be done if the spring is suspect or if the vehicle
ride height has been measured and found to be less than the specified
figure. Renew the spring if necessary, ideally in pairs (both sides).
11 Check the condition of the spring seat and upper mounting
components, and renew any parts which are suspect.
12 Begin reassembly by refitting the shock absorber dust cover and
bump-stop.
13 Refit the spring compressors, if previously removed, and place the
spring in position on the shock absorber.
14 Refit the washer, lower bush and threaded collar. Tighten the collar
using the same procedure as for removal.
15 Refit the spring seat, upper mounting plate, upper bush and
washer. Secure the upper mounting assembly with the retaining nut,
tightened to the specified torque.
16 Remove the spring compressors, and refit the spring and shock
absorber to the car as described in Section 6.

8   Front upper suspension arm – removal and refitting

Note: *The upper suspension arm incorporates the steering knuckle
upper support balljoint as a riveted integral assembly. If wear of the
balljoint necessitates renewal, a complete upper suspension arm must
be obtained*

1   Apply the handbrake, prise off the front wheel trim and slacken the
wheel nuts. Jack up the front of the car and support it on axle stands.
Remove the front roadwheel.
2   Undo the nut securing the upper suspension arm balljoint to the
steering knuckle (photo). Release the balljoint using a separator tool or
two-legged puller.
3   From within the engine compartment, undo the two nuts securing
the suspension arm mounting bracket to the inner wing valance. For
access to the rearmost nut, it may be necessary to move the wiring
harness connectors aside, or if working on the left-hand suspension

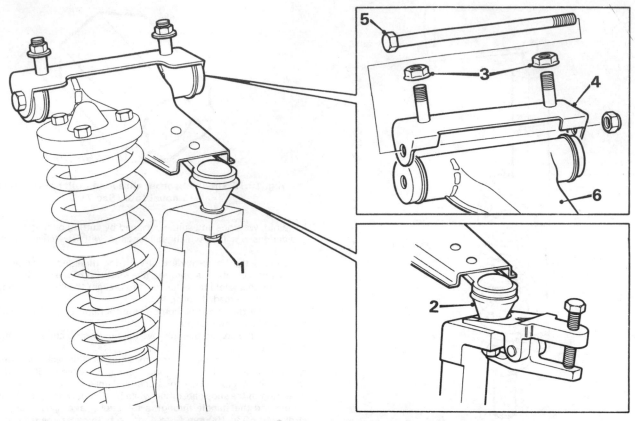

Fig. 10.13 Upper suspension arm attachment details (Sec 8)

1	Balljoint-to-steering knuckle retaining nut	2	Releasing the balljoint with a separator tool	3	Mounting bracket retaining nuts	4	Mounting bracket
						5 Pivot bolt
						6 Upper suspension arm

arm, to undo the bolts and move the wiper motor bracket slightly.

4   Withdraw the upper suspension arm assembly from under the wheel arch.

5   With the arm on the bench, undo the nut and withdraw the pivot bolt then remove the arm from its mounting bracket.

6   Check the condition of the balljoint dust cover, and check the joint itself for excess free play. Also check the condition of the pivot bushes and the arm itself. The bushes can be renewed by drifting them out then pressing in new ones. If the balljoint, balljoint dust cover or the suspension arm show signs of damage or wear, a complete new assembly must be obtained. Examine the pivot bolt for signs of wear ridges, and check the mounting bracket for elongation of the pivot bolt holes. Renew any components as necessary.

7   Refitting is the reverse sequence to removal, but tighten all nuts and bolts to the specified torque.

9   Front lower suspension arm – removal and refitting

1   Apply the handbrake, prise of the front wheel trim and slacken the wheel nuts. Jack up the front of the car and support it on axle stands. Remove the front roadwheel.

2   Undo the nut securing the steering knuckle balljoint to the lower suspension arm (photo). Release the balljoint using a separator tool or two-legged puller.

3   Undo the nut and remove the through-bolt securing the shock absorber forked member to the arm.

4   Undo the bolt securing the anti-roll bar connecting link to the arm.

5   Undo the two bolts securing the tie-bar to the arm.

6   Undo the nut and remove the suspension arm inner mounting bolt (photo).

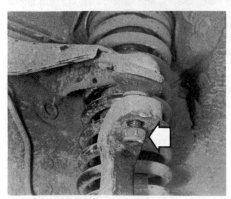

8.2 Undo the nut securing the balljoint to the steering knuckle (arrowed)

9.2 Undo the nut securing the steering knuckle balljoint to the lower suspension arm

9.6 Lower suspension arm inner mounting bolt (arrowed)

7 Withdraw the suspension arm from its inner mounting location, and remove it from under the wheel arch.
8 Check the condition of the two suspension arm bushes, and renew these if worn or damaged. To do this, a press will be required, together with suitable mandrels and distance tubes. If this equipment is not available, have this work done by a Rover dealer or suitably-equipped garage.
9 Refitting is the reverse sequence to removal, but tighten all nuts and bolts to the specified torque. Do not fully tighten the inner mounting bolt or the forked member retaining bolt until the weight of the car is on its roadwheels.

10 Front anti-roll bar – removal and refitting

1 Apply the handbrake, prise off the front wheel trim and slacken the

wheel nuts. Jack up the front of the car and support it on axle stands. Remove the front roadwheels.
2 Undo the single bolt each side securing the anti-roll bar connecting links to the lower suspension arms (photo).
3 Undo the two bolts each side securing the anti-roll bar mounting brackets to the chassis members (photo), and remove the bar from under the car.
4 If required, the connecting links can be removed after undoing the retaining nut and bolt on each side.
5 Check the condition of the connecting link bushes and the anti-roll bar mounting bushes, and renew any that show signs of deterioration. The connecting link bushes come complete with new connecting links, and the mounting bushes are slit along their length to allow removal and refitting over the bar.
6 Refitting is the reverse sequence to removal. Tighten the mounting and connecting link bushes to the specified torque only with the weight of the car on its roadwheels.

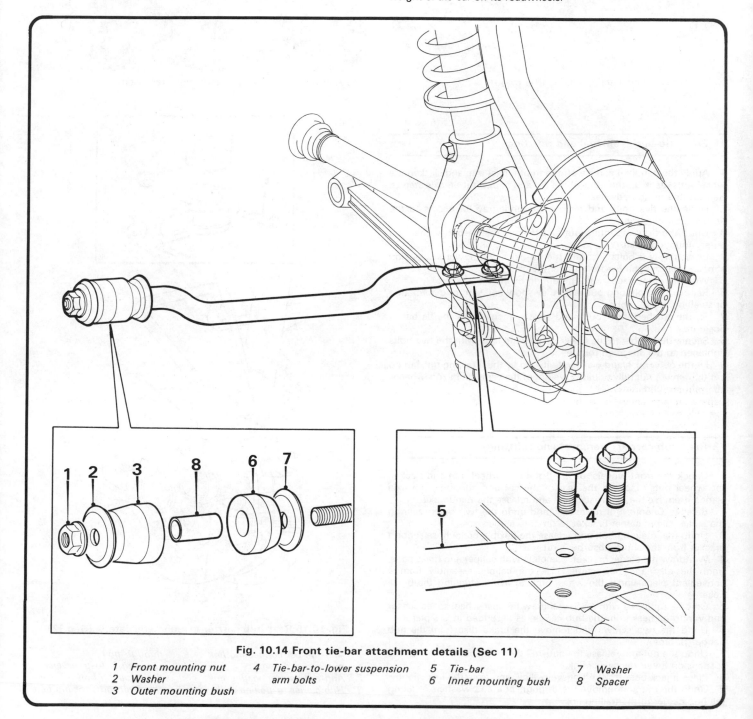

Fig. 10.14 Front tie-bar attachment details (Sec 11)

1	Front mounting nut	4	Tie-bar-to-lower suspension arm bolts	5	Tie-bar	7	Washer
2	Washer			6	Inner mounting bush	8	Spacer
3	Outer mounting bush						

10.2 Anti-roll bar connecting link bolt (arrowed)

10.3 Anti-roll bar mounting bracket bolts (arrowed)

11 Front tie-bar – removal and refitting

1   Apply the handbrake, prise off the front wheel trim and slacken the wheel nuts. Jack up the front of the car and support it on axle stands. Remove the front roadwheel.
2   Undo the five bolts and remove the undertray for access to the tie-bar front mounting.
3   Undo the front mounting nut and remove the tie-bar washer and outer mounting bush.
4   Undo the two bolts securing the tie-bar to the lower suspension arm, and remove the bar from under the car.
5   Withdraw the spacer, inner mounting bush and washer.
6   Renew the mounting bushes if they show any sign of deformation or swelling of the rubber.
7   Fit the washer, inner bush and spacer, then locate the tie-bar in position.
8   Secure the tie-bar to the lower suspension arm, with the two bolts tightened to the specified torque.
9   Fit the outer bush and washer, followed by the retaining nut, but do not tighten the nut fully until the weight of the car is on its roadwheels.
10 Refit the undertray.

12 Rear hub carrier – removal and refitting

1   Chock the front wheels, prise off the rear wheel trim and slacken the wheel nuts. Jack up the rear of the car and support it on axle stands. Remove the rear roadwheel and release the handbrake.
2   Refer to Chapter 9 if necessary, and undo the two bolts securing the brake caliper carrier bracket to the hub carrier.
3   Undo the retaining bolt and release the flexible brake hose support bracket from the shock absorber strut.
4   Withdraw the carrier bracket, complete with caliper and brake pads, from the disc and hub carrier. Tie the caliper assembly from a convenient place under the wheel arch to avoid straining the brake hose.
5   On cars equipped with ABS, withdraw the rear wheel speed sensor and wiring harness from the hub carrier, as described in Chapter 9.
6   Undo the two screws and remove the brake disc from the hub flange (photos).
7   Undo the nut and release the anti-roll bar connecting link from the suspension lower transverse link.
8   Place a jack beneath the transverse link, and raise the link slightly.
9   Undo the nut and remove the through-bolt and washers securing the hub carrier to the trailing link.

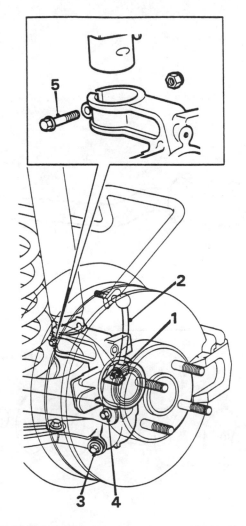

Fig. 10.15 Rear hub carrier attachment details (Sec 12)

1   Anti-roll bar connecting link nut
2   Anti-roll bar connecting link
3   Hub carrier-to-trailing link

        through-bolt
4   Hub carrier-to-transverse link retaining bolt
5   Shock absorber clamp bolt

12.6A Undo the two screws (arrowed) ...

12.6B ... and remove the brake disc

10 Undo the nut and remove the bolt securing the hub carrier to the transverse link.
11 Undo the nut and clamp bolt securing the shock absorber strut to the hub carrier.
12 Lower the jack slightly, and release the hub carrier from the shock absorber strut. If the strut is tight, spread the slot in the hub carrier with a screwdriver, and tap the carrier down with a copper or plastic mallet.
13 Withdraw the hub carrier from the transverse and trailing links, and remove it from the car.
14 Refitting is the reverse sequence to removal. Tighten all nuts and bolts to the specified torque, but do not fully tighten the transverse and trailing link retaining nuts until the weight of the car is on the roadwheels.

13 Rear hub bearing – renewal

1 Remove the rear hub from the car as described in the previous Section.
2 Prise off the cover over the hub flange retaining nut at the rear of the hub carrier, then secure the hub flange in a vice.

3 Using a small punch or screwdriver, tap up the staking, then unscrew the hub flange retaining nut. Note that a new nut will be required for reassembly.
4 Support the hub carrier in a vice, and tap the hub flange out of the bearing.
5 Undo the four screws and remove the disc shield.
6 Extract the bearing retaining circlip, then support the hub carrier face-down on blocks or on a press bed. Using a tube or mandrel in contact with the edge of the outer bearing, drive or press the bearing out.
7 Fit the new bearing in the same way, ensuring that it is pressed fully home to the shoulder in the hub carrier. Keep the bearing square as it is fitted, otherwise it will jam, and continued pressure could cause the outer race to crack. If the bearing does jam, tap or press it out, remove any burrs in the bore of the carrier and try again.
8 Secure the bearing with the circlip, then refit the disc shield.
9 Tap the hub flange into the bearing and fit a new retaining nut. Tighten the nut to the specified torque, and secure by staking the nut flange into the groove in the hub. Tap on the nut cover.
10 Refit the hub carrier to the car as described in the previous Section.

Fig. 10.16 Cover (1) and hub flange retaining nut (2) at the rear of the hub carrier (Sec 13)

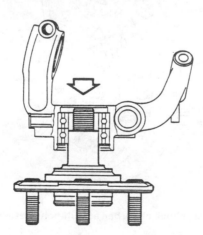

Fig. 10.17 Removing the hub flange from the bearing (Sec 13)

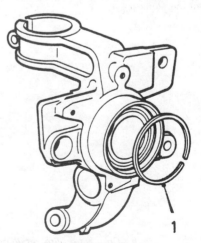

Fig. 10.18 Rear hub bearing retaining circlip (1) (Sec 13)

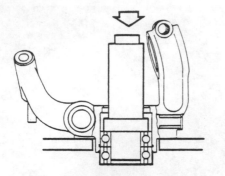

Fig. 10.19 Using a suitable mandrel for removal of the hub bearing (Sec 13)

14 Rear shock absorber – removal and refitting

Note: *The following procedures are applicable equally to cars with standard suspension or self-levelling damper units*

1   Chock the front wheels, prise of the rear wheel trim and slacken the wheel nuts. Jack up the rear of the car and support it on axle stands. Remove the rear roadwheel.
2   Undo the retaining bolt and release the flexible brake hose support bracket from the shock absorber strut.
3   Undo the nut and release the anti-roll bar connecting link from the suspension lower transverse link.
4   Place a jack below the transverse link, and raise the link slightly.
5   Undo the nut and remove the through-bolt and washers securing the hub carrier to the trailing link.
6   Undo the nut and remove the bolt securing the hub carrier to the transverse link.
7   Undo the nut and clamp bolt securing the shock absorber strut to the hub carrier.
8   Lower the jack slightly, and release the hub carrier from the shock

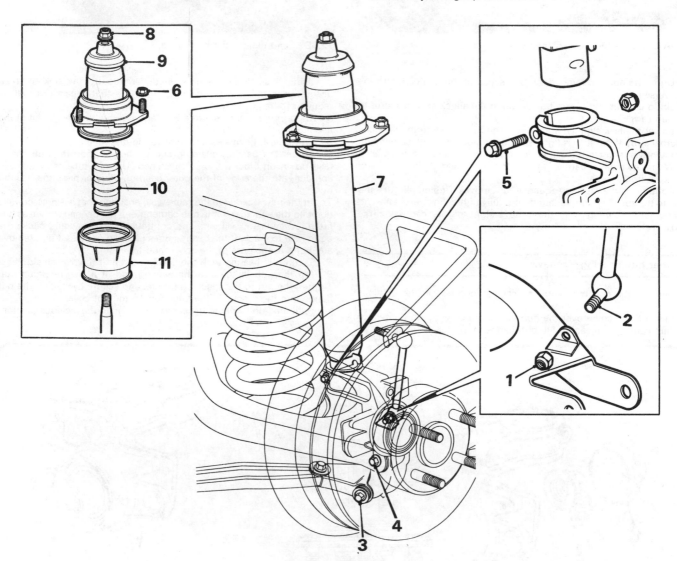

Fig. 10.20 Rear shock absorber attachment details (Sec 14)

1 Connecting link retaining nut	4 Transverse link retaining bolt	8 Shock absorber spindle nut
2 Anti-roll bar connecting link	5 Shock absorber clamp bolt	9 Upper mounting
3 Trailing link retaining through-bolt	6 Upper mounting retaining nut	10 Bump-stop
	7 Shock absorber	11 Dust cover

absorber strut. If the strut is tight, spread the slot in the hub carrier with a screwdriver, and tap the carrier down with a copper or plastic mallet.
9 From inside the luggage compartment, remove the trim as necessary to gain access to the shock absorber upper mounting.
10 Undo the three nuts securing the upper mounting to the body, and remove the shock absorber from under the wheel arch.
11 If the upper mounting is to be removed, undo the shock absorber spindle nut and withdraw the upper mounting, followed by the bump-stop and dust cover.
12 Examine the shock absorber for signs of fluid leakage. Check the spindle for signs of wear or pitting along its entire length, and check the shock absorber body for signs of damage or corrosion. Test the operation of the shock absorber, while holding it in an upright position, by moving the spindle through a full stroke, and then through short strokes of 50 to 100 mm (2 to 4 in). In both cases, the resistance felt should be smooth and continuous. If the resistance is jerky or uneven, or if there is any visible sign of wear, damage or fluid leakage, renewal is necessary. Also check the condition of the upper mounting, bump-stop and dust cover, and renew any components as necessary.
13 Refitting is the reverse sequence to removal. Tighten all nuts and bolts to the specified torque, but do not fully tighten the transverse and trailing link retaining nuts until the weight of the car is on the roadwheels.

15 Rear coil spring – removal and refitting

1 Refer to Section 14 and carry out the operations described in paragraphs 1 to 6 inclusive, with the exception of paragraph 2.
2 Ease the hub carrier away from the trailing link, and move the trailing link end clear as much as possible.
3 Lower the jack slowly and carefully to release the tension on the coil spring.
4 When all the tension is released, withdraw the spring from its location, and recover the upper and lower spring seats. Note the fitted position of the lower seat in the transverse link as it is removed.
5 Examine the spring carefully for signs of distortion or damage. The spring free length can only be assessed by comparing it with a new item, and this should be done if the spring is suspect or if the vehicle ride height has been measured and found to be less than the specified figure. Renew the spring if necessary, ideally in pairs (both sides). Also check the condition of the upper and lower spring seats, and renew any components as necessary.
6 Refitting is the reverse sequence to removal, but ensure that the tang on the lower spring seat engages with the slot in the transverse link. Tighten all nuts and bolts to the specified torque, but do not fully tighten the transverse and trailing link retaining nuts until the weight of the car is on the roadwheels.

16 Transverse link – removal and refitting

1 Remove the rear coil spring as described in the previous Section.
2 Undo the nut and remove the transverse link inner mounting bolt (photo).
3 Ease the link away from its inner location, and remove it from under the car.
4 If the transverse link inner mounting bush requires renewal, a hydraulic press and suitable mandrels will be needed to press out the old bush and press in a new one. If this equipment is not available, have the work carried out by a Rover dealer or suitably-equipped garage. A similar procedure must be used for renewal of the outer bush, which is located in the hub carrier, after removal of this component from the car (see Section 12).
5 Refitting is the reverse sequence to removal, but do not fully tighten the inner mounting nut until the weight of the car is on the roadwheels.

17 Trailing link – removal and refitting

1 Chock the front wheels, prise off the rear wheel trim and slacken the wheel nuts. Jack up the rear of the car and support it on axle stands. Remove the rear roadwheel.

16.2 Transverse link inner mounting bolt (arrowed)

17.2 Trailing link front mounting

17.3 Trailing link-to-hub carrier through-bolt (arrowed)

2   Undo the trailing link front mounting nut (photo) and remove the outer washer and bush.
3   Undo the nut and remove the through-bolt and washers securing the trailing link to the hub carrier (photo).
4   Ease the link away from the hub carrier, withdraw the front mounting from its location and remove the link from under the car.
5   Withdraw the front mounting inner bush and washer, and the two rear mounting bushes.
6   If the adjustment plate is to be removed, first mark the position of the forward eccentric bolt in relation to the plate, so that an approximate rear wheel toe setting can be obtained on reassembly. Undo the nuts, remove the retaining bolt and eccentric bolt, then withdraw the adjustment plate from the trailing link.
7   Examine all the mounting bushes for damage, deformation or swellling of the rubber, and check the remaining components for damage or distortion. Renew any parts as necessary.
8   Refit the adjustment plate to the link, and secure with the retaining

and adjustment bolts and nuts. Before fully tightening the nuts, set the eccentric adjustment bolt in the position marked before removal.
9   The remainder of the refitting procedure is the reverse sequence to removal. Do not fully tighten the trailing link-to-hub carrier through-bolt until the weight of the car is on the roadwheels.
10 On completion, have the rear wheel alignment checked and if necessary adjusted (see Section 30).

18 Rear anti-roll bar – removal and refitting

1   Apply the handbrake, prise off the rear wheel trim and slacken the wheel nuts. Jack up the rear of the car and support it on axle stands. Remove the rear roadwheels.
2   Undo the single nut each side securing the anti-roll bar connecting links to the rear suspension transverse links.
3   Undo the two bolts each side securing the anti-roll bar mounting

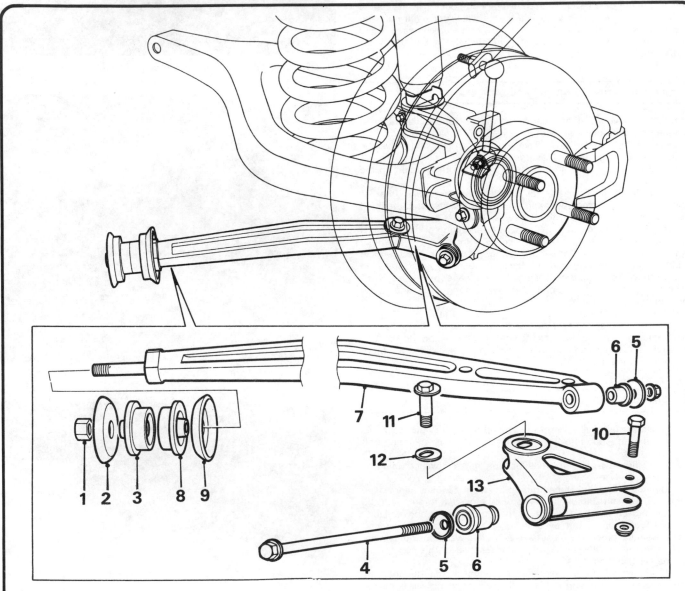

Fig. 10.21 Exploded view of the trailing link components and attachments (Sec 17)

1 Front mounting nut	5 Washer	9 Inner washer	11 Eccentric bolt
2 Outer washer	6 Bush	10 Adjustment plate retaining	12 Eccentric washer
3 Outer bush	7 Trailing link	bolt	13 Adjustment plate
4 Trailing link through-bolt	8 Inner bush		

brackets to the chassis members (photo), and remove the bar from under the car.
4 If required, the connecting links can be removed after undoing the retaining nut on each side.
5 Check the condition of the connecting link bushes and the anti-roll bar mounting bushes, and renew any that show signs of deterioration. The mounting bushes are slit along their length to allow removal and refitting over the bar.
6 Refitting is the reverse sequence to removal. Tighten the mounting and connecting link bushes to the specified torque only with the weight of the car on its roadwheels.

19 Steering wheel – removal and refitting

1 Disconnect the battery negative terminal. (Refer to Chapter 12, Section 1, before doing this).

2 Set the front wheels in the straight-ahead position.
3 Carefully prise off the steering wheel pad, disconnect the two horn switch leads and remove the pad (photos).
4 With an assistant holding the wheel, undo and remove the centre retaining nut using a socket and bar (photo).
5 Mark the steering wheel and column shaft in relation to each other, and withdraw the wheel from the shaft splines.
6 Before refitting, check that the wheels are still in the straight-ahead position, and turn the direction indicator cancelling bush so that the slot is pointing upwards (photo).
7 Engage the steering wheel over the shaft splines, ensuring that the previously-made marks are aligned, and make sure that the lug on the wheel boss engages with the slot in the direction indicator cancelling bush (photo).
8 Refit the retaining nut and tighten it to the specified torque while your assistant holds the wheel.
9 Reconnect the horn switch wires and refit the steering wheel pad.
10 Reconnect the battery.

18.3 Anti-roll bar right-hand side mounting bracket

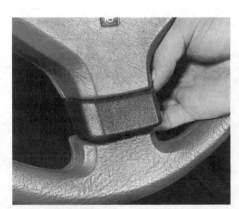
19.3A Prise off the steering wheel pad ...

19.3B ... and disconnect the two horn switch leads

19.4 Undo the steering wheel retaining nut

19.6 Position the direction indicator cancelling bush with the slot pointing upwards

19.7 Ensure that the lug on the steering wheel boss (A) engages the cancelling bush slot (B)

20 Steering column lock – removal and refitting

1 Disconnect the battery negative terminal. (Refer to Chapter 12, Section 1, before doing this).
2 From inside the car, release the turnbuckles and lift out the trim panels over the clutch, brake and accelerator pedals.
3 Release the rake lock on the side of the steering column, and move the column to its lowest position.
4 Undo the single upper screw and the three lower screws, and remove the upper and lower steering column shrouds.
5 Undo the two nuts and remove the washers from the steering column upper mounting.

6 Undo the two bolts and remove the mounting strap from the column lower mounting. Lower the column slightly, and support it in this position.
7 Disconnect the ignition switch wiring multi-plug and the additional switch lead.
8 Centre-punch the steering column lock shear-bolts, then drill off the bolt heads.
9 Remove the lock saddle, then withdraw the lock from the column.
10 With the lock removed, unscrew the shear-bolt studs with a self-locking wrench or a pair of grips on the protruding bolt ends.
11 Refitting is the reverse sequence to removal, but tighten all the mounting bolts and nuts to the specified torque. Use new shear-bolts to secure the lock, and tighten them until the heads shear off, but check the operation of the lock before doing this.

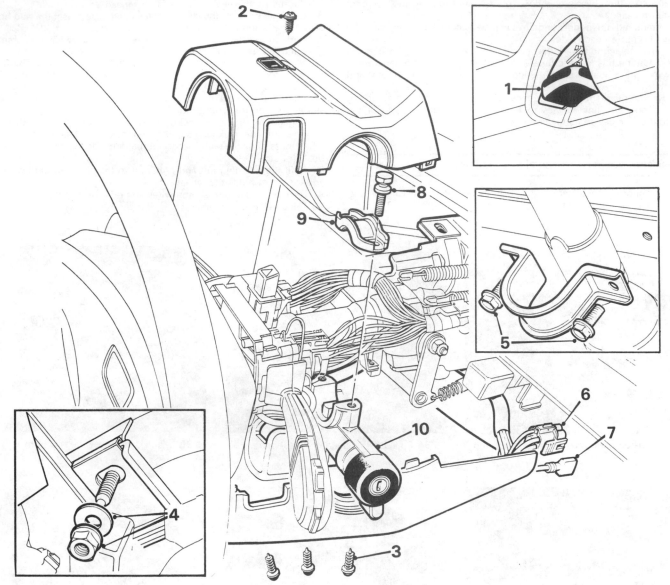

Fig. 10.22 Steering column lock attachments (Sec 20)

1 Steering column rake lock	4 Column upper mounting nut	6 Ignition switch wiring	8 Shear-bolt
2 Upper shroud retaining	and washer	multi-plug	9 Lock saddle
screw	5 Column lower mounting	7 Additional switch lead	10 Steering column lock
3 Lower shroud retaining	bolts		
screws			

21 Steering column – removal and refitting

1   Disconnect the battery negative terminal. (Refer to Chapter 12, Section 1, before doing this).

2   Remove the steering wheel as described in Section 19.

3   From inside the car, release the turnbuckles and lift out the trim panels over the clutch, brake and accelerator pedals (photos).

4   Release the rake lock on the side of the steering column, and move the column to its lowest position.

5   Undo the single upper screw and the three lower screws, and remove the upper and lower steering column shrouds.

6   At the base of the steering column, release the two retaining clips and slide up the cover over the column shaft universal joint.

7   Move the carpets aside to gain access to the floor-mounted cover plate.

8   Prise out the retaining studs to release the cover plate and gasket from the floor.

9   Undo the clamp bolt securing the universal joint to the steering gear pinion.

10   Undo the two nuts and remove the washers from the steering column upper mounting (photo).

11   Undo the two bolts and remove the mounting strap from the column lower mounting (photo). Lower the column slightly, and support it in this position.

12   Release the flasher unit from its bracket above the fusebox.

13   Disconnect the two main wiring harness multi-plugs adjacent to the fusebox.

14   Lift the steering column assembly upwards to disengage the universal joint from the steering gear pinion, then remove the column from the car.

15   If the universal joint is to be removed, first mark the joint in relation to the column shaft. Undo the clamp bolt and slide the joint off the shaft.

16   Before refitting the column, set the roadwheels to the straight-ahead position.

17   Refit the universal joint to the column shaft (if previously removed), ensuring that the marks made during removal are aligned.

18   Engage the universal joint with the steering gear pinion, and push it fully home.

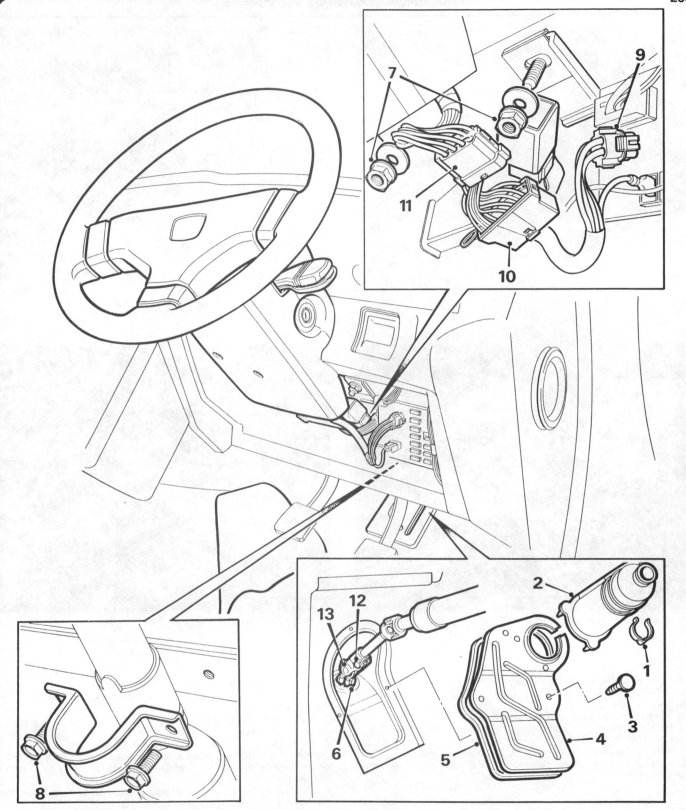

Fig. 10.23 Steering column attachments and components (Sec 21)

1 Universal joint cover
   retaining clip
2 Universal joint cover
3 Cover plate retaining studs
4 Cover plate

5 Gasket
6 Universal joint clamp bolt
7 Column upper mounting
   nuts

8 Column lower mounting
   bolts
9 Flasher unit
10 Main wiring multi-plug

11 Main relay harness
   multi-plug
12 Universal joint clamp bolt
13 Universal joint

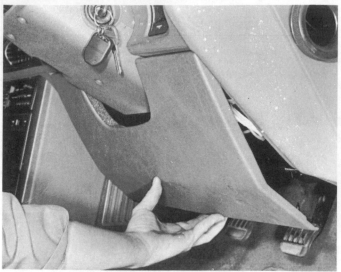

21.3A Remove the upper trim panel ...

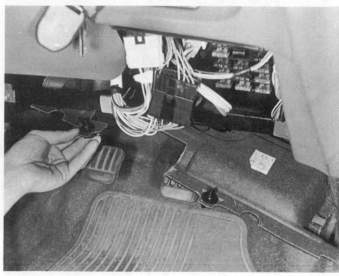

21.3B ... and lower trim panel over the pedals

21.10 Steering column upper mounting nut (arrowed)

21.11 Steering column lower mounting bolt (arrowed)

19 Reconnect the wiring multi-plugs and refit the flasher unit.
20 Refit the column mountings, and tighten the nuts and bolts to the specified torque.
21 Tighten the universal joint clamp bolt.
22 Refit the cover plate and gasket, followed by the universal joint cover.
23 Refit the steering column shrouds and the trim panels.
24 Refit the steering wheel as described in Section 19, then reconnect the battery.

22 Steering tie-rod – removal and refitting

1 Apply the handbrake, prise off the front wheel trim and slacken the wheel nuts. Jack up the front of the car and support it on axle stands. Remove the front roadwheel.
2 Slacken the tie-rod retaining locknut by a quarter of a turn (photo).
3 Extract the split pin, then unscrew the nut securing the tie-rod balljoint to the steering knuckle arm (photo).
4 Using a universal balljoint separator tool, release the tapered ball-pin from the arm (photo).

5 Engage a spanner over the flats on the inner tie-rod that protrudes from the rubber gaiter, then unscrew the steering tie-rod and outer balljoint assembly.
6 Fit the new tie-rod by screwing it on to the inner tie-rod until it contacts the locknut.
7 Insert the balljoint into the steering knuckle arm and refit the retaining nut. Tighten the nut to the specified torque, then tighten it further, slightly, to align the next split pin hole. Secure the nut with a new split pin.
8 Tighten the tie-rod retaining locknut securely, refit the roadwheel and lower the car to the ground.
9 Check the front wheel alignment as described in Section 30.

23 Steering gear rubber gaiter – renewal

1 Remove the steering tie-rod as described in the previous Section.
2 Count and record the number of exposed threads from the end of the inner tie-rod to the locknut, then unscrew and remove the locknut.
3 Release the rubber gaiter retaining clips, and withdraw the gaiter from the steering gear and inner tie-rod.

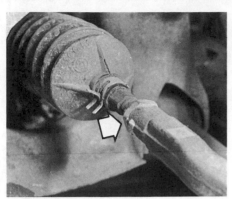

22.2 Tie-rod retaining locknut (arrowed)

22.3 Extract the split pin and remove the tie-rod retaining nut (arrowed)

22.4 Using a universal balljoint separator tool to release the tie-rod balljoint

4   Slide the new gaiter into position and secure it with new retaining clips.
5   Refit the locknut to the inner tie-rod, and position it so that the same number of threads are exposed as counted on removal.
6   Refit the steering tie-rod as described in the previous Section.

24 Steering gear – removal and refitting

1   From inside the car, release the two retaining clips and slide up the cover over the universal joint at the base of the steering column.
2   Move the carpets aside to gain access to the floor-mounted cover plate.
3   Prise out the retaining studs to release the cover plate and gasket from the floor.
4   Undo the clamp bolt securing the universal joint to the steering gear pinion.
5   Apply the handbrake, prise off the front wheel trim and slacken the wheel nuts. Jack up the front of the car and support it on axle stands. Remove the front roadwheels.
6   Remove the exhaust front pipes as described in Chapter 3.
7   Extract the split pins, then unscrew the nuts securing each tie-rod balljoint to the steering knuckle arm.
8   Using a universal balljoint separator tool, release the balljoint tapered ball-pins from the arms.
9   Position a suitable container beneath the pinion end of the steering gear.
10 Wipe clean the area around the fluid pipe unions, then unscrew the two rearward-facing union nuts on the pinion housing (photo). Allow the power steering fluid to drain into the container.
11 Remove the two O-ring seals from the disconnected pipes, then plug or tape over the pipe ends and orifices.
12 Undo the two bolts each side securing the steering gear to the chassis members, and remove the mounting brackets (photos).

13 Lower the steering gear to release the pinion from the column universal joint, then manipulate the assembly sideways and out through the wheel arch.
14 Check the condition of the rubber mountings, and renew them if there is any sign of deterioration or swelling of the rubber.
15 Refitting the steering gear is the reverse sequence to removal, bearing in mind the following points:

   (a) Tighten all nuts, bolts and unions to the specified torque
   (b) Use new O-ring seals on the pipe unions, and new split pins on the balljoint retaining nuts
   (c) Fill the system with fresh fluid, and bleed the steering gear as described in Section 26
   (d) If necessary, reposition the steering wheel so that the spokes are horizontal when the steering gear is in the straight-ahead position (see Section 19)

25 Steering gear – overhaul

1   Remove the steering gear from the car as described in the previous Section.
2   Clean the assembly externally with a rag, paying particular attention to the area around the pipe unions.
3   Remove both steering tie-rods and rubber gaiters, with reference to the procedures contained in Sections 22 and 23 respectively.
4   To remove the inner tie-rods and balljoints, ideally Rover tool 18G 1440 should be used. This tool consists of two clamps, one for the balljoint housing and one for the rack itself. The clamps are tightened securely, allowing the balljoint housing complete with inner tie-rod to be unscrewed using one clamp, while the rack is held with the other clamp. Fig. 10.25 shows the arrangement. In practice however, it is possible to do this using self-locking wrenches, pipe-grips, or similar tools, provided that the jaws are protected and care is taken not to

24.10 Unscrew the two fluid pipe union nuts (arrowed)

24.12A Steering gear right-hand mounting bracket bolts (arrowed) ...

24.12B ... and left-hand mounting bracket bolts (arrowed)

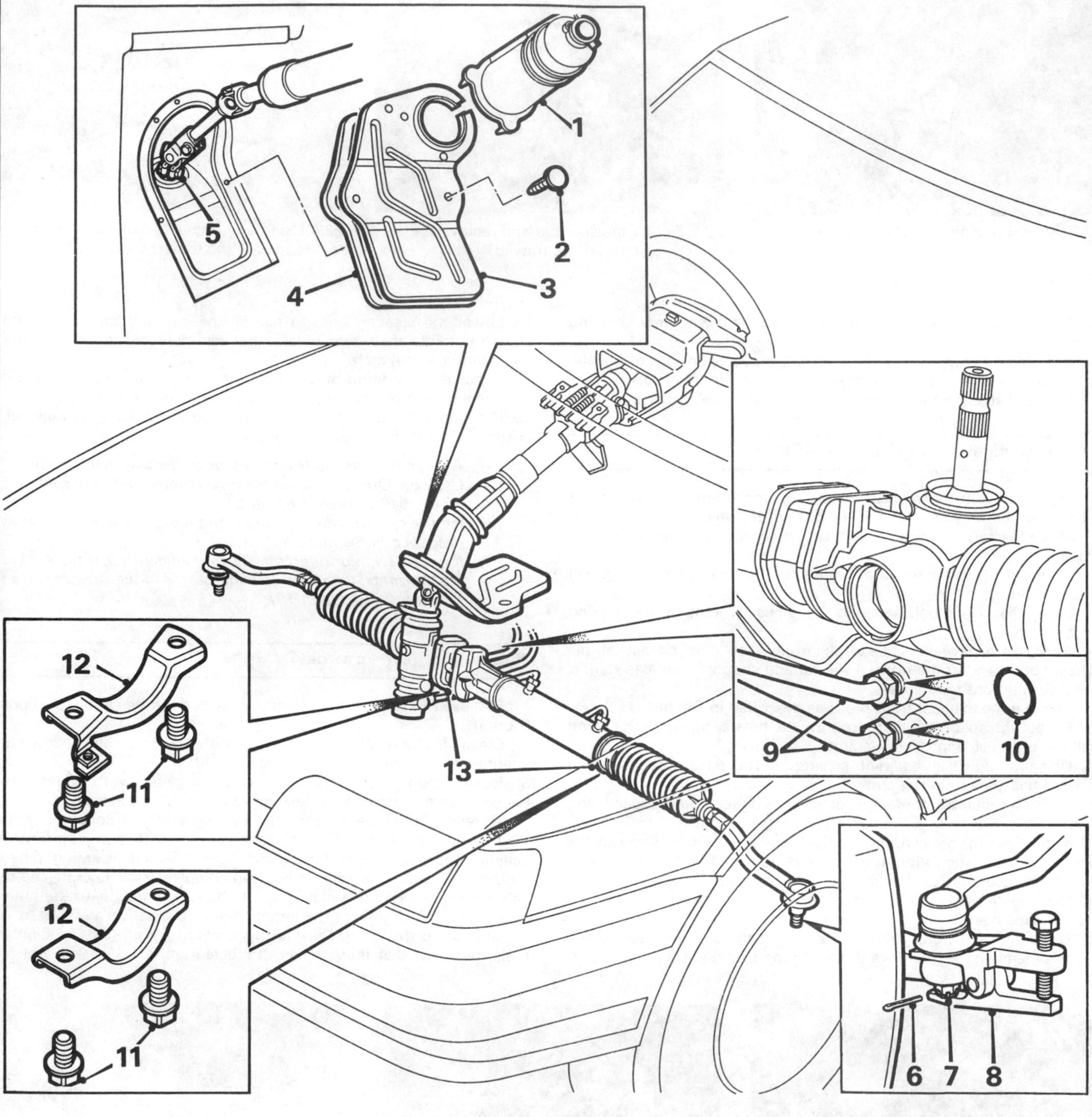

Fig. 10.24 Steering gear removal details (Sec 24)

1	Universal joint cover	5	Universal joint clamp bolt
2	Cover plate retaining studs	6	Split pin
3	Cover plate	7	Tie-rod balljoint retaining nut
4	Gasket		

8	Balljoint separator tool
9	Fluid pipe unions
10	O-ring

11	Mounting bracket bolts
12	Mounting brackets
13	Mounting points

score the parts being gripped, particularly the rack. Note that the balljoint housing is peened into place on the rack, so it will be tight to unscrew initially.

5   With the inner tie-rod and balljoint assemblies removed, prise out the rack support bush retainer, followed by the O-ring seal, support bush and bush locking wire.

6   Unscrew the remaining four pipe unions, and remove the two fluid pipes.

7   Extract the circlip at the base of the pinion housing, remove the pinion cover and withdraw the O-ring seal.

8   This is the limit of dismantling that can be undertaken on the steering gear, as no other parts are available separately.

9   Examine all the dismantled components, and renew any that are worn. The O-ring seals and rubber gaiters should be renewed as a matter of course.

10   Reassembly of the steering gear is the reverse sequence to removal, bearing in mind the following points:

(a) Clean all the old sealant from the bush retainer sealant hole in the rack housing, and apply fresh RTV sealant on reassembly

(b) Lubricate all the seals with the specified power steering fluid

(c) Tighten the inner tie-rod balljoint housing using the same procedure as used for removal, then peen the rack, using a small punch, to secure the assembly

(d) Refit the steering tie-rods and rubber gaiters, with reference to Sections 22 and 23

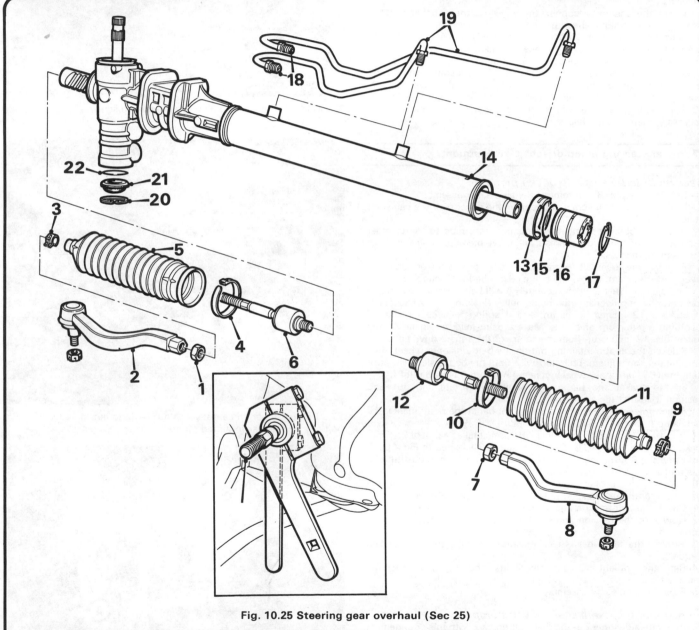

Fig. 10.25 Steering gear overhaul (Sec 25)

1 Right-hand steering tie-rod locknut	7 Left-hand steering tie-rod locknut	12 Left-hand inner tie-rod balljoint	17 Locking wire
2 Right-hand steering tie-rod	8 Left-hand steering tie-rod	13 Bush retainer	18 Fluid pipe unions
3 Gaiter clip	9 Gaiter clip	14 Bush retainer sealant hole	19 Fluid pipes
4 Gaiter clip	10 Gaiter clip	15 O-ring	20 Circlip
5 Right-hand rubber gaiter	11 Left-hand rubber gaiter	16 Rack support bush	21 Pinion cover
6 Right-hand inner tie-rod balljoint			22 O-ring

Inset shows Rover special tool for removal of the inner tie-rod balljoints

26 Power steering gear – bleeding

1   Remove the filler cap on the power steering fluid reservoir, and fill the reservoir with the specified fluid until the level is up to the MAX mark on the cap dipstick.
2   Disconnect the HT lead from the centre of the ignition coil.
3   Crank the engine on the starter motor for five seconds to prime the power steering pump.
4   Top up the reservoir, then crank the engine again for a further five seconds.
5   Turn the steering onto full right-hand lock, and crank the engine for five seconds.
6   Turn the steering onto full left-hand lock, and crank the engine for five seconds.
7   Top up the reservoir, reconnect the HT lead to the coil, then turn the steering to the straight-ahead position.
8   Start the engine and run it for approximately two minutes. During this time, turn the steering wheel one turn each way.
9   With the engine stopped, check the condition of the power steering fluid. If it is aerated, leave it until clear. If it is not aerated, top up the reservoir, start the engine again and run it for a further two minutes. During this time, turn the steering wheel one turn each way as before.
10   Stop the engine, make a final check of the fluid level and top up if necessary, then refit the filler cap.

27 Power steering pump drivebelt – adjustment

Rear-mounted, camshaft-driven pump
1   Refer to Chapter 3 and remove the air cleaner assembly.
2   Undo the retaining screw and remove the cover over the camshaft pulley (photo).
3   Undo the bolts securing the coolant bypass pipe to the cylinder head and to the main coolant pipe, and move the bypass pipe aside as necessary for access.
4   Examine the drivebelt for signs of cracking, fraying or excessive wear, and if evident, renew the belt as described in Section 28.
5   To adjust the belt tension accurately it will be necessary to obtain a socket to fit the power steering pump pulley retaining nut, a socket bar of at least 12 inches in length, and a spring balance capable of recording a minimum of 25 lbs. Make a paint mark or similar on the socket bar, 12 inches up from the centre of the square drive end.
6   Slacken the centre retaining nut on the belt tensioner wheel, then turn the tension adjuster bolt clockwise until the belt is slack (photo). Retighten the tensioner wheel retaining nut to 5.0 Nm (3.6 lbf ft).
7   Fit the socket and bar to the pump pulley retaining nut, and position it so that the socket bar is vertical.
8   Attach the spring balance to the socket bar at the point marked 12 inches up from the square drive end.
9   Turn the adjuster bolt anti-clockwise until it takes a pull of 25 lbs to make the pump pulley slip. This procedure is illustrated in Fig. 10.26, but using the Rover special tool. The socket and bar are a substitute for this tool.
10   Remove the socket, bar and spring balance, then turn the crankshaft until the camshaft pulley has turned through 180°.
11   Check the belt tension again, and re-adjust if necessary.
12   Now turn the tension adjuster bolt anti-clockwise two complete turns.
13   Tighten the tensioner wheel retaining nut fully to the specified torque.
14   Refit the coolant pipe retaining bolts, and the cover over the camshaft pulley.
15   Refit the air cleaner assembly.

Front-mounted, crankshaft-driven pump
16   Accurate adjustment of the drivebelt on cars with this arrangement can only be achieved with the Rover belt tensioning tool, and ideally this operation should be carried out by a Rover dealer. However, if a new belt has been fitted, or if the existing tension is extremely slack, a rough approximation as a temporary measure can be achieved using the following procedure.
17   Jack up the front of the car and securely support it on axle stands.
18   From under the front of the car, examine the drivebelt for signs of cracking, fraying or excessive wear, and if evident, renew the belt as described in Section 28.

27.2 Undo the camshaft pulley cover retaining screw

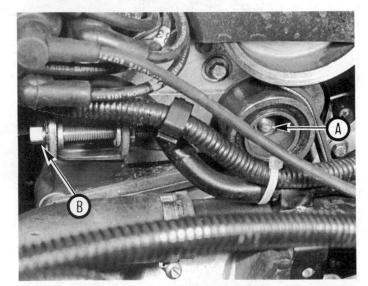
27.6 Belt tensioner wheel retaining nut (A) and tension adjuster bolt (B) on the rear-mounted pump

27.19 Idler pulley retaining nut (A) and adjuster bolt (B) on the front-mounted pump

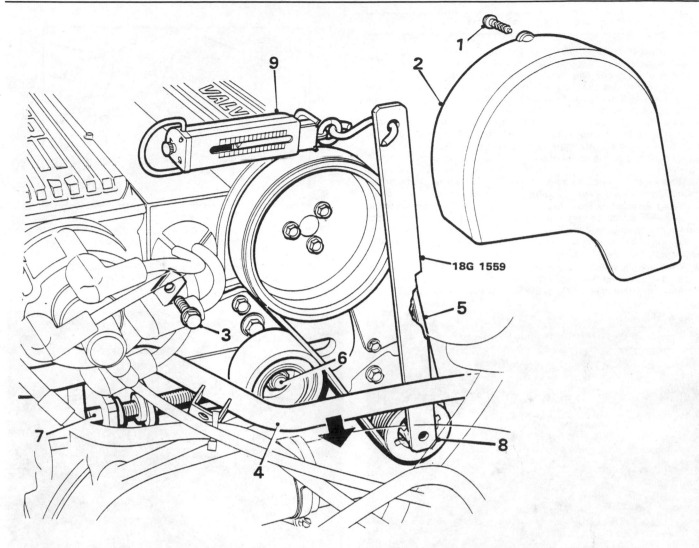

Fig. 10.26 Power steering pump drivebelt adjustment – rear-mounted pump (Sec 27)

1 Camshaft pulley cover retaining screw	4 Coolant bypass pipe	6 Belt tensioner wheel centre retaining nut
2 Camshaft pulley cover	5 Drivebelt	7 Tension adjuster bolt
3 Coolant pulley pipe		8 Rover special tool for checking tension
		9 Spring balance

19 To adjust the belt tension, refer to Fig. 12.1 (Chapter 12) and slacken the idler pulley retaining nut (photo), then turn the adjuster bolt clockwise to increase the tension or anti-clockwise to decrease it, until it is just possible to twist the belt by hand through 90° at a point midway between the crankshaft and power steering pump pulleys.

20 When the tension is correct, tighten the idler pulley retaining nut to the specified torque and lower the car to the ground.

21 Refit the air cleaner assembly.

28 Power steering pump drivebelt – removal and refitting

Rear-mounted, camshaft-driven pump

1 Refer to Chapter 3 and remove the air cleaner assembly.

2 Undo the retaining screw and remove the cover over the camshaft pulley.

3 Undo the bolts securing the coolant bypass pipe to the cylinder head and to the main coolant pipe, and move the bypass pipe aside as necessary for access.

4 Slacken the centre retaining nut on the belt tensioner wheel, then

turn the tensioner adjuster bolt clockwise until the belt is slack.

5 Undo the three camshaft pulley retaining bolts, withdraw the pulley and recover the spacer behind the pulley.

6 Remove the belt from the camshaft and power steering pump pulleys.

7 Place the new belt in position, then fit the spacer and camshaft pulley. Tighten the pulley retaining bolts to the specified torque.

8 Tension the belt using the procedure described in Section 27, but on completion, do not refit the camshaft cover or coolant pipe retaining bolts.

9 Start the engine, and run it for approximately 10 minutes at 1500 rpm to settle the new belt.

10 Switch off the engine, then refer to Section 27 again, and carry out the complete adjustment procedure once more.

Front-mounted, crankshaft-driven pump

11 Jack up the front of the car and securely support it on axle stands.

12 Slacken the idler pulley retaining nut, then turn the adjuster bolt anti-clockwise until all the tension is removed from the drivebelt.

13 Slip the drivebelt off the pulleys, then place a new belt in position.

14 Adjust the belt tension using procedure contained in Section 27.

29 Power steering pump – removal and refitting

Rear-mounted, camshaft-driven pump

1   Drain the cooling system as described in Chapter 2.
2   Refer to Chapter 3 and remove the air cleaner assembly.
3   Slacken the hose clips and disconnect the heater bypass hose from the thermostat housing, and the radiator bottom hose from the main coolant pipe below the distributor.
4   Undo the bolts securing the heater pipe and coolant pipe to their support brackets, and move the pipe and hose assembly away from the vicinity of the power steering pump as far as possible.
5   Undo the retaining screw and remove the cover over the camshaft pulley.
6   Slacken the centre retaining nut on the drivebelt tensioner wheel (photo), then turn the tension adjuster clockwise until the bolt is slack.
7   Using a socket and bar, unscrew and remove the power steering pump pulley retaining nut (photo). To prevent the pulley turning as the nut is undone, engage a large screwdriver with one of the slots on the pulley, rest the screwdriver over the socket, and apply clockwise leverage to the screwdriver.
8   Withdraw the pulley and drivebelt from the pump (photo). Use two screwdrivers to lever off the pulley if it is tight.
9   Apply the handbrake, jack up the front of the car and support it on

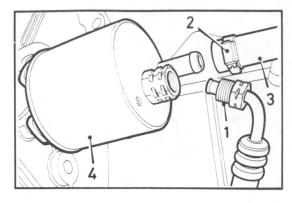

Fig. 10.27 Fluid pipe connections at the rear-mounted power steering pump (Sec 29)

1   *High pressure pipe union*   3   *Return hose*
2   *Return hose clip*   4   *Power steering pump*

29.6 Slacken the tensioner wheel retaining nut

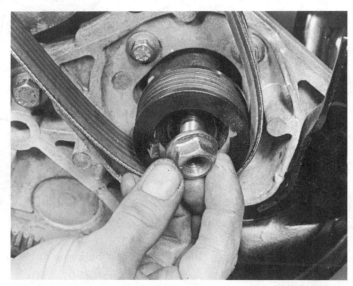

29.7 Unscrew the pump pulley retaining nut

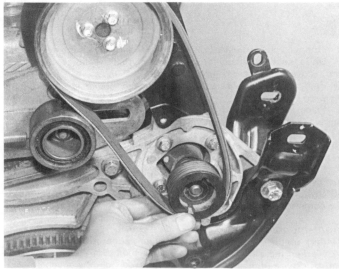

29.8 Remove the pulley and drivebelt

29.14 Undo the four pump retaining bolts

axle stands.
10 Undo the bolts securing the longitudinal support member to the underbody beneath the engine and remove the member.
11 Position a suitable container beneath the engine, below the power steering pump.
12 Wipe clean the area around the pipe and hose unions at the rear of the pump.
13 Unscrew the union nut and slacken the hose clip, then disconnect the high pressure pipe and return hose from the pump. Allow the power steering fluid to drain into the container. Plug or tape over the disconnected unions when the fluid has drained.
14 Undo the four power steering pump retaining bolts (photo), and remove the pump from under the car.
15 Refitting is the reverse sequence to removal, bearing in mind the following points:

    (a) *Tighten all nuts, bolts and unions to the specified torque*
    (b) *Adjust the drivebelt tension as described in Section 27*
    (c) *Bleed the power steering gear as described in Section 26*
    (d) *Refill the cooling system and refit the air cleaner as described in Chapters 2 and 3 respectively*

Front-mounted, crankshaft-driven pump

16 Position a suitable container beneath the engine, below the power steering pump.
17 Wipe clean the area around the pipe and hose unions at the rear of the pump.
18 Unscrew the union nut and slacken the hose clip, then disconnect the high pressure pipe and return hose from the pump. Allow the power steering fluid to drain into the container. Plug or tape over the disconnected unions when the fluid has drained.
19 Jack up the front of the car and securely support it on axle stands.
20 Slacken the idler pulley retaining nut, then turn the adjuster bolt anti-clockwise until all the tension is removed from the drivebelt.
21 Remove the belt from the pulleys.
22 Undo the three bolts and remove the power steering pump pulley.
23 Undo the four bolts securing the pump to its mounting bracket. Slide the pump out of the bracket, and remove it from under the car.
24 Refitting is the reverse sequence to removal, bearing in mind the following points:

    (a) *Tighten all nuts, bolts and unions to the specified torque*
    (b) *Adjust the drivebelt tension as described in Section 27*
    (c) *Bleed the power steering gear as described in Section 26*

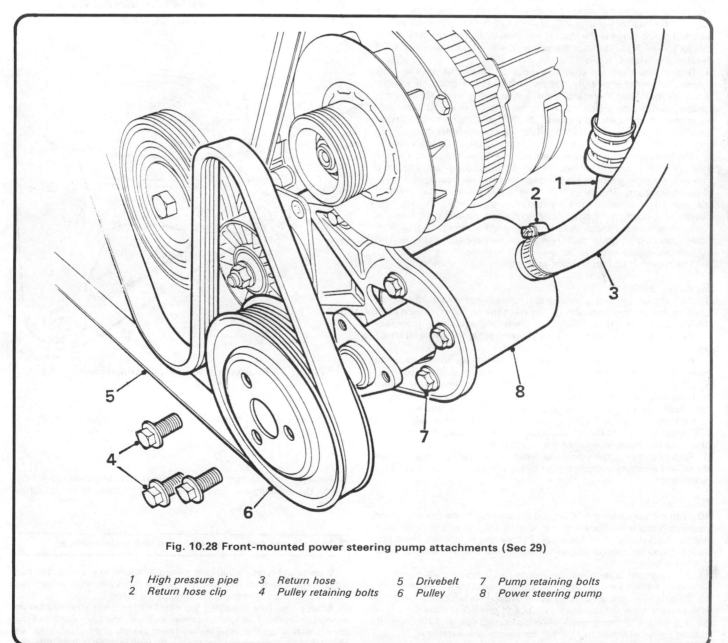

Fig. 10.28 Front-mounted power steering pump attachments (Sec 29)

1 *High pressure pipe*	3 *Return hose*	5 *Drivebelt*	7 *Pump retaining bolts*
2 *Return hose clip*	4 *Pulley retaining bolts*	6 *Pulley*	8 *Power steering pump*

30 Wheel alignment and steering angles

1   Accurate wheel alignment is essential to provide positive steering and handling characteristics, and to prevent excessive tyre wear. Before considering the steering/ suspension geometry, check that the tyres are correctly inflated, the front wheels are not buckled, and the steering linkage and suspension joints are in good order, without slackness or wear.

2   Wheel alignment consists of four factors:
Camber is the angle at which the roadwheels are set from the vertical when viewed from the front or rear of the vehicle. Positive camber is the angle (in degrees) that the wheels are tilted outwards at the top from the vertical.
Castor is the angle between the steering axis and a vertical line when viewed from each side of the vehicle. Positive castor is indicated when the steering axis is inclined towards the rear of the vehicle at its upper end.
Steering axis inclination, also known as kingpin inclination or KPI, is the angle, when viewed from the front or rear of the vehicle, between the vertical and an imaginary line drawn between the steering knuckle upper and lower balljoints.
Toe is the amount by which the distance between the front inside edges of the roadwheel rims differs from that between the rear inside edges. If the distance at the front is less than at the rear, the wheels are said to 'toe-in'. If the distance at the front inside edges is greater than at the rear, the wheels 'toe-out'.

3   Due to the need for special gauges to check the steering and suspension angles accurately, it is preferable to leave this work to your Rover dealer. Apart from the front and rear toe settings, all other steering and suspension angles are set in production, and are not adjustable. If these angles are ever checked and found to be outside specification, then either the suspension components are damaged or distorted, or wear has occurred in the bushes at the attachment points.

4   The front and rear toe settings are adjustable, and two methods are available to the home mechanic for doing this. One method is to use a gauge to measure the distance between the front and rear inside edges of the roadwheels. The other method is to use a scuff plate, in which the roadwheel is rolled across a movable plate which records any deviation, or scuff, of the tyre relative to the straight-ahead position, as it moves across the plate. Relatively inexpensive equipment of both types is available from accessory outlets to enable these checks, and subsequent adjustments, to be carried out at home.

5   The checking and adjustment procedures are as follows.

Front toe setting

6   With the car on level ground and the steering in the straight-ahead position, bounce the front and rear to settle the suspension, then push the car backwards then forwards. Follow the equipment manufacturer's instructions according to the equipment being used, and check the toe setting.

7   If adjustment is required, slacken the steering tie-rod locknuts on both sides (photo), and release the rubber gaiter retaining clips.

8   Using a spanner engaged with the flat on the inner tie-rod, turn both tie-rods, by equal amounts clockwise to increase the toe-in, or anti-clockwise to increase the toe-out. Push the car forwards, then recheck the setting. If a gauge is being used, take three readings, at 120° intervals around the wheel, pushing the car forward a little each time. Use the mean average of the three readings as the setting.

9   Repeat this procedure until the setting is as specified, then tighten the tie-rod locknuts and refit the gaiter clips. Ensure that the gaiters are not twisted.

Rear toe setting

10   With the car on level ground and the steering in the straight-ahead position, bounce the front and rear to settle the suspension, then push the car backwards then forwards. Follow the equipment manufacturer's instructions according to the equipment being used, and check the toe setting.

11   If adjustment is required, slacken the adjustment plate-to-trailing link retaining bolt locknut, and the eccentric bolt locknut on each side.

12   Turn both eccentric bolts, by equal amounts in whichever direction is necessary, then tighten the locknuts and recheck the toe setting.

13   If a gauge is being used, take three readings, at 120° intervals around the wheel, pushing the car forward a little each time. Use the mean average of the three readings as the setting.

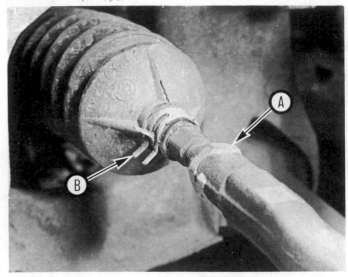

30.7 Steering tie-rod locknut (A) and gaiter clip (B)

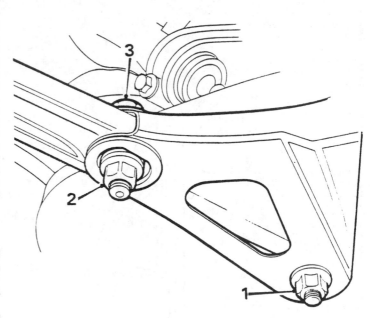

**Fig. 10.29 Rear wheel toe setting adjustment points
(Sec 30)**

1   Adjustment plate retaining   2   Eccentric bolt locknut
     bolt locknut   3   Eccentric bolt

14   Repeat this procedure until the setting is as specified, then fully tighten the retaining bolt and eccentric bolt locknuts to the specified torque.

31 Wheels and tyres – general care and maintenance

Wheels and tyres should give no real problems in use provided that a close eye is kept on them with regard to excessive wear or damage. To this end, the following points should be noted.

Ensure that tyre pressures are checked regularly and maintained correctly. Checking should be carried out with the tyres cold and not immediately after the vehicle has been in use. If the pre___ res are checked with the tyres hot, an apparently high reading will be obtained owing to heat expansion. Under no circumstances should an attempt be made to reduce the pressures to the quoted cold reading in this instance, or effective underinflation will result.

Underinflation will cause overheating of the tyre owing to excessive flexing of the casing, and the tread will not sit correctly on the road surface. This will cause a consequent loss of adhesion and excessive wear, not to mention the danger of sudden tyre failure due to heat build-up.

Overinflation will cause rapid wear of the centre part of the tyre tread coupled with reduced adhesion, harsher ride, and the danger of shock damage occurring in the tyre casing.

Regularly check the tyres for damage in the form of cuts or bulges, especially in the sidewalls. Remove any nails or stones embedded in the tread before they penetrate the tyre to cause deflation. If removal of a nail *does* reveal that the tyre has been punctured, refit the nail so that its point of penetration is marked. Then immediately change the wheel and have the tyre repaired by a tyre dealer. Do *not* drive on a tyre in such a condition. In many cases a puncture can be simply repaired by the use of an inner tube of the correct size and type. If in any doubt as to the possible consequences of any damage found, consult your local tyre dealer for advice.

Periodically remove the wheels and clean any dirt or mud from the inside and outside surfaces. Examine the wheel rims for signs of rusting, corrosion or other damage. Light alloy wheels are easily damaged by 'kerbing' whilst parking, and similarly steel wheels may become dented or buckled. Renewal of the wheel is very often the only course of remedial action possible.

The balance of each wheel and tyre assembly should be maintained to avoid excessive wear, not only to the tyres but also to the steering and suspension components. Wheel imbalance is normally signified by vibration through the vehicle's bodyshell, although in many cases it is particularly noticeable through the steering wheel. Conversely, it should be noted that wear or damage in suspension or steering components may cause excessive tyre wear. Out-of-round or out-of-true tyres, damaged wheels and wheel bearing wear/maladjustment also fall into this category. Balancing will not usually cure vibration caused by such wear.

Wheel balancing may be carried out with the wheel either on or off the vehicle. If balanced on the vehicle, ensure that the wheel-to-hub relationship is marked in some way prior to subsequent wheel removal so that it may be refitted in its original position.

General tyre wear is influenced to a large degree by driving style – harsh braking and acceleration or fast cornering will all produce more rapid tyre wear. Interchanging of tyres may result in more even wear, but this should only be carried out where there is no mix of tyre types on the vehicle. However, it is worth bearing in mind that if this is completely effective, the added expense of replacing a complete set of tyres simultaneously is incurred, which may prove financially restrictive for many owners.

Front tyres may wear unevenly as a result of wheel misalignment. The front wheels should always be correctly aligned according to the settings specified by the vehicle manufacturer.

Legal restrictions apply to the mixing of tyre types on a vehicle. Basically this means that a vehicle must not have tyres of differing construction on the same axle. Although it is not recommended to mix tyre types between front axle and rear axle, the only legally permissible combination is crossply at the front and radial at the rear. When mixing radial ply tyres, textile braced radials must always go on the front axle, with steel braced radials at the rear. An obvious disadvantage of such mixing is the necessity to carry two spare tyres to avoid contravening the law in the event of a puncture.

In the UK, the Motor Vehicles Construction and Use Regulations apply to many aspects of tyre fitting and usage. It is suggested that a copy of these regulations is obtained from your local police if in doubt as to the current legal requirements with regard to tyre condition, minimum tread depth, etc.

32 Fault diagnosis – suspension and steering

Note: *Before diagnosing suspension or steering faults, be sure that the trouble is not due to incorrect tyre pressures, mixture of tyre types, or binding brakes. More detailed fault diagnosis on the power-assisted steering gear entails the use of special test equipment. Apart from the general references listed below, faults on this system should be referred to a dealer*

Symptom	Reason(s)
Vehicle wanders or pulls to one side	Incorrect wheel alignment Wear in front suspension or steering components Wear in rear suspension components Weak shock absorbers Faulty tyre
Steering stiff and heavy	Power steering pump drivebelt slipping or broken Power steering system fault Seized steering or suspension balljoint Incorrect wheel alignment Steering rack or column bent or damaged
Excessive play in steering	Worn steering or suspension joints Worn steering column universal joint Worn rack and pinion steering gear
Wheel wobble and vibration	Roadwheels out-of-balance Roadwheels buckled or distorted Faulty or damaged tyre Worn steering or suspension joints Weak shock absorbers Worn hub bearings
Excessive tyre wear	Wheel alignment incorrect Worn steering or suspension components Roadwheels out-of-balance Accident damage

Chapter 11 Bodywork

For modifications, and information applicable to later models, see Supplement at end of manual

Contents

Specifications

Torque wrench settings

	Nm	lbf ft
Bonnet hinge bolts	10	7
Boot lid hinge bolts	10	7
Door hinge-to-body bolts	30	22
Door hinge-to-pillar bolts	22	16
Front seat retaining bolts	32	23
Seat belt retaining bolts	32	23
Bumper retaining bolts	22	16

1 General description

The bodyshell and underframe is of all-steel welded construction, and is of computer-originated design. The assembly and welding of the main body unit is completed entirely by computer-controlled robots, and the finished unit is checked for dimensional accuracy using modern computer and laser technology. In accordance with current practice, the bodyshell incorporates computer-calculated impact crumple zones at the front and rear, with a centre safety cell passenger compartment. During manufacture the body is dip-primed, fully sealed and undercoated, then painted with multi-layered base and top coats.

2 Maintenance – bodywork and underframe

The general condition of a vehicle's bodywork is the one thing that significantly affects its value. Maintenance is easy but needs to be regular. Neglect, particularly after minor damage, can lead quickly to further deterioration and costly repair bills. It is important also to keep watch on those parts of the vehicle not immediately visible, for instance the underside, inside all the wheel arches and the lower part of the engine compartment.

The basic maintenance routine for the bodywork is washing – preferably with a lot of water, from a hose. This will remove all the loose solids which may have stuck to the vehicle. It is important to flush these off in such a way as to prevent grit from scratching the finish. The wheel arches and underframe need washing in the same way to remove any accumulated mud which will retain moisture and tend to encourage rust. Paradoxically enough, the best time to clean the underframe and wheel arches is in wet weather when the mud is thoroughly wet and soft. In very wet weather the underframe is usually cleaned of large accumulations automatically and this is a good time for inspection.

Periodically, except on vehicles with a wax-based underbody protective coating, it is a good idea to have the whole of the underframe of the vehicle steam cleaned, engine compartment included, so that a thorough inspection can be carried out to see what minor repairs and renovations are necessary. Steam cleaning is available at many garages and is necessary for removal of the accumulation of oily grime which sometimes is allowed to become thick in certain areas. If steam cleaning facilities are not available, there are one or two excellent grease solvents available, such as Holts Engine Cleaner or Holts Foambrite, which can be brush applied. The dirt can then be simply hosed off. Note that these methods should not be used on vehicles with wax-based underbody protective coating or the coating will be removed. Such vehicles should be inspected annually, preferably just prior to winter, when the underbody should be washed down and any damage to the wax coating repaired using Holts Undershield. Ideally, a completely fresh coat should be applied. It would also be worth considering the use of such wax-based protection for injection into door panels, sills, box sections, etc, as an additional safeguard against rust damage where such protection is not provided by the vehicle manufacturer.

After washing paintwork, wipe off with a chamois leather to give an unspotted clear finish. A coat of clear protective wax polish, like the many excellent Turtle Wax polishes, will give added protection against chemical pollutants in the air. If the paintwork sheen has dulled or oxidised, use a cleaner/polisher combination such as Turtle Extra to restore the brilliance of the shine. This requires a little effort, but such dulling is usually caused because regular washing has been neglected. Care needs to be taken with metallic paintwork, as special non-abrasive cleaner/polisher is required to avoid damage to the finish. Always check that the door and ventilator opening drain holes and pipes are completely clear so that water can be drained out. Bright work should be treated in the same way as paint work. Windscreens and windows can be kept clear of the smeary film which often appears by the use of a proprietary glass cleaner like Holts Mixra. Never use any form of wax or other body or chromium polish on glass.

3 Maintenance – upholstery and carpets

Mats and carpets should be brushed or vacuum cleaned regularly to keep them free of grit. If they are badly stained remove them from the vehicle for scrubbing or sponging and make quite sure they are dry before refitting. Seats and interior trim panels can be kept clean by wiping with a damp cloth and Turtle Wax Carisma. If they do become stained (which can be more apparent on light coloured upholstery) use a little liquid detergent and a soft nail brush to scour the grime out of the grain of the material. Do not forget to keep the headlining clean in the same way as the upholstery. When using liquid cleaners inside the vehicle do not over-wet the surfaces being cleaned. Excessive damp could get into the seams and padded interior causing stains, offensive odours or even rot. If the inside of the vehicle gets wet accidentally it is worthwhile taking some trouble to dry it out properly, particularly where carpets are involved. *Do not leave oil or electric heaters inside the vehicle for this purpose.*

4 Minor body damage – repair

The photographic sequences on pages 218 and 219 illustrate the operations detailed in the following sub-sections.
Note: *For more detailed information about bodywork repair, the Haynes Publishing Group publish a book by Lindsay Porter called The Car Bodywork Repair Manual. This incorporates information on such aspects as rust treatment, painting and glass fibre repairs, as well as details on more ambitious repairs involving welding and panel beating.*

Repair of minor scratches in bodywork

If the scratch is very superficial, and does not penetrate to the metal of the bodywork, repair is very simple. Lightly rub the area of the scratch with a paintwork renovator like Turtle Wax New Color Back, or a very fine cutting paste like Holts Body + Plus Rubbing Compound to remove loose paint from the scratch and to clear the surrounding bodywork of wax polish. Rinse the area with clean water.

Apply touch-up paint, such as Holts Dupli-Color Color Touch or a paint film like Holts Autofilm, to the scratch using a fine paint brush; continue to apply fine layers of paint until the surface of the paint in the scratch is level with the surrounding paintwork. Allow the new paint at least two weeks to harden: then blend it into the surrounding paintwork by rubbing the scratch area with a paintwork renovator or a very fine cutting paste, such as Holts Body + Plus Rubbing Compound or Turtle Wax New Color Back. Finally, apply wax polish from one of the Turtle Wax range of wax polishes.

Where the scratch has penetrated right through to the metal of the bodywork, causing the metal to rust, a different repair technique is required. Remove any loose rust from the bottom of the scratch with a penknife, then apply rust inhibiting paint, such as Turtle Wax Rust Master, to prevent the formation of rust in the future. Using a rubber or nylon applicator fill the scratch with bodystopper paste like Holts Body + Plus Knifing Putty. If required, this paste can be mixed with cellulose thinners, such as Holts Body + Plus Cellulose Thinners, to provide a very thin paste which is ideal for filling narrow scratches. Before the stopper-paste in the scratch hardens, wrap a piece of smooth cotton rag around the top of a finger. Dip the finger in cellulose thinners, such as Holts Body + Plus Cellulose Thinners, and then quickly sweep it across the surface of the stopper-paste in the scratch; this will ensure that the surface of the stopper-paste is slightly hollowed. The scratch can now be painted over as described earlier in this Section.

Repair of dents in bodywork

When deep denting of the vehicle's bodywork has taken place, the first task is to pull the dent out, until the affected bodywork almost attains its original shape. There is little point in trying to restore the original shape completely, as the metal in the damaged area will have stretched on impact and cannot be reshaped fully to its original contour. It is better to bring the level of the dent up to a point which is about $\frac{1}{8}$ in (3 mm) below the level of the surrounding bodywork. In cases where the dent is very shallow anyway, it is not worth trying to pull it out at all. If the underside of the dent is accessible, it can be hammered out gently from behind, using a mallet with a wooden or plastic head. Whilst doing this, hold a suitable block of wood firmly against the outside of the panel to absorb the impact from the hammer blows and thus prevent a large area of the bodywork from being 'belled-out'.

Should the dent be in a section of the bodywork which has a double skin or some other factor making it inaccessible from behind, a different technique is called for. Drill several small holes through the metal inside the area – particulary in the deeper section. Then screw long self-tapping screws into the holes just sufficiently for them to gain a good purchase in the metal. Now the dent can be pulled out by pulling on the protruding heads of the screws with a pair of pliers.

The next stage of the repair is the removal of the paint from the damaged area, and from an inch or so of the surrounding 'sound' bodywork. This is accomplished most easily by using a wire brush or abrasive pad on a power drill, although it can be done just as effectively by hand using sheets of abrasive paper. To complete the preparation for filling, score the surface of the bare metal with a screwdriver or the tang of a file, or alternatively, drill small holes in the affected area. This will provide a really good 'key' for the filler paste.

To complete the repair see the Section on filling and re-spraying.

1 This photographic sequence shows the steps taken to repair the dent and paintwork damage shown above. In general, the procedure for repairing a hole will be similar; where there are substantial differences, the procedure is clearly described and shown in a separate photograph.

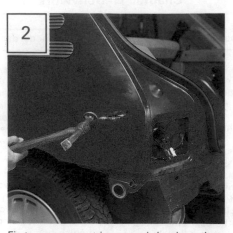

2 First remove any trim around the dent, then hammer out the dent where access is possible. This will minimise filling. Here, after the large dent has been hammered out, the damaged area is being made slightly concave.

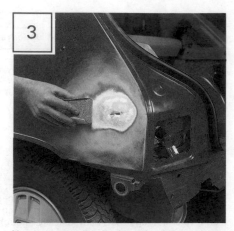

3 Next, remove all paint from the damaged area by rubbing with coarse abrasive paper or using a power drill fitted with a wire brush or abrasive pad. 'Feather' the edge of the boundary with good paintwork using a finer grade of abrasive paper.

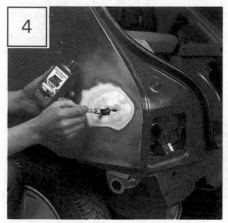

4 Where there are holes or other damage, the sheet metal should be cut away before proceeding further. The damaged area and any signs of rust should be treated with Turtle Wax Hi-Tech Rust Eater, which will also inhibit further rust formation.

5 *For a large dent or hole* mix Holts Body Plus Resin and Hardener according to the manufacturer's instructions and apply around the edge of the repair. Press Glass Fibre Matting over the repair area and leave for 20-30 minutes to harden. Then ...

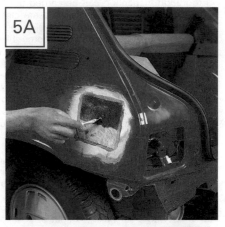

5A ... brush more Holts Body Plus Resin and Hardener onto the matting and leave to harden. Repeat the sequence with two or three layers of matting, checking that the final layer is lower than the surrounding area. Apply Holts Body Plus Filler Paste as shown in Step 5B.

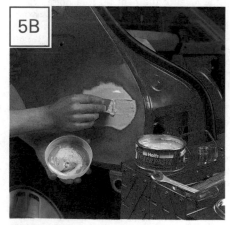

5B *For a medium dent,* mix Holts Body Plus Filler Paste and Hardener according to the manufacturer's instructions and apply it with a flexible applicator. Apply thin layers of filler at 20-minute intervals, until the filler surface is slightly proud of the surrounding bodywork.

5C *For small dents and scratches* use Holts No Mix Filler Paste straight from the tube. Apply it according to the instructions in thin layers, using the spatula provided. It will harden in minutes if applied outdoors and may then be used as its own knifing putty.

6 Use a plane or file for initial shaping. Then, using progressively finer grades of wet-and-dry paper, wrapped round a sanding block, and copious amounts of clean water, rub down the filler until glass smooth. 'Feather' the edges of adjoining paintwork.

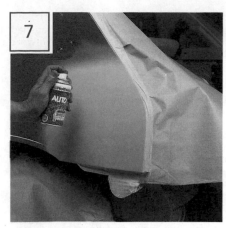

Protect adjoining areas before spraying the whole repair area and at least one inch of the surrounding sound paintwork with Holts Dupli-Color primer.

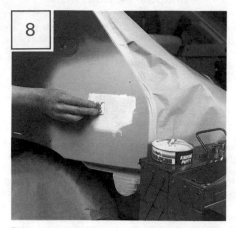

Fill any imperfections in the filler surface with a small amount of Holts Body Plus Knifing Putty. Using plenty of clean water, rub down the surface with a fine grade wet-and-dry paper – 400 grade is recommended – until it is really smooth.

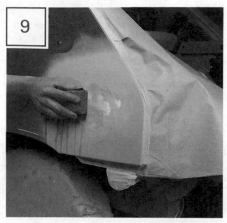

Carefully fill any remaining imperfections with knifing putty before applying the last coat of primer. Then rub down the surface with Holts Body Plus Rubbing Compound to ensure a really smooth surface.

Protect surrounding areas from overspray before applying the topcoat in several thin layers. Agitate Holts Dupli-Color aerosol thoroughly. Start at the repair centre, spraying outwards with a side-to-side motion.

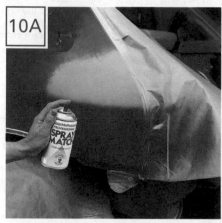

If the exact colour is not available off the shelf, local Holts Professional Spraymatch Centres will custom fill an aerosol to match perfectly.

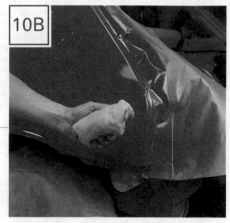

To identify whether a lacquer finish is required, rub a painted unrepaired part of the body with wax and a clean cloth.

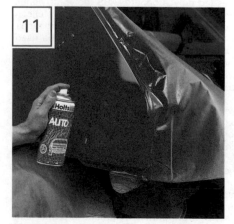

If *no* traces of paint appear on the cloth, spray Holts Dupli-Color clear lacquer over the repaired area to achieve the correct gloss level.

The paint will take about two weeks to harden fully. After this time it can be 'cut' with a mild cutting compound such as Turtle Wax Minute Cut prior to polishing with a final coating of Turtle Wax Extra.

When carrying out bodywork repairs, remember that the quality of the finished job is proportional to the time and effort expended.

Repair of rust holes or gashes in bodywork

Remove all paint from the affected area and from an inch or so of the surrounding 'sound' bodywork, using an abrasive pad or a wire brush on a power drill. If these are not available a few sheets of abrasive paper will do the job just as effectively. With the paint removed you will be able to gauge the severity of the corrosion and therefore decide whether to renew the whole panel (if this is possible) or to repair the affected area. New body panels are not as expensive as most people think and it is often quicker and more satisfactory to fit a new panel than to attempt to repair large areas of corrosion.

Remove all fittings from the affected area except those which will act as a guide to the original shape of the damaged bodywork (eg headlamp shells etc). Then, using tin snips or a hacksaw blade, remove all loose metal and any other metal badly affected by corrosion. Hammer the edges of the hole inwards in order to create a slight depression for the filler paste.

Wire brush the affected area to remove the powdery rust from the surface of the remaining metal. Paint the affected area with rust inhibiting paint like Turtle Rust Master; if the back of the rusted area is accessible treat this also.

Before filling can take place it will be necessary to block the hole in some way. This can be achieved by the use of aluminium or plastic mesh, or aluminium tape.

Aluminium or plastic mesh or glass fibre matting, such as the Holts Body + Plus Glass Fibre Matting, is probably the best material to use for a large hole. Cut a piece to the approximate size and shape of the hole to be filled, then position it in the hole so that its edges are below the level of the surrounding bodywork. It can be retained in position by several blobs of filler paste around its periphery.

Aluminium tape should be used for small or very narrow holes. Pull a piece off the roll and trim it to the approximate size and shape required, then pull off the backing paper (if used) and stick the tape over the hole; it can be overlapped if the thickness of one piece is insufficient. Burnish down the edges of the tape with the handle of a screwdriver or similar, to ensure that the tape is securely attached to the metal underneath.

Bodywork repairs – filling and re-spraying

Before using this Section, see the Sections on dent, deep scratch, rust holes and gash repairs.

Many types of bodyfiller are available, but generally speaking those proprietary kits which contain a tin of filler paste and a tube of resin hardener are best for this type of repair, like Holts Body + Plus or Holts No Mix which can be used directly from the tube. A wide, flexible plastic or nylon applicator will be found invaluable for imparting a smooth and well contoured finish to the surface of the filler.

Mix up a little filler on a clean piece of card or board – measure the hardener carefully (follow the maker's instructions on the pack) otherwise the filler will set too rapidly or too slowly. Alternatively, Holts No Mix can be used straight from the tube without mixing, but daylight is required to cure it. Using the applicator apply the filler paste to the prepared area; draw the applicator across the surface of the filler to achieve the correct contour and to level the filler surface. As soon as a contour that approximates to the correct one is achieved, stop working the paste – if you carry on too long the paste will become sticky and begin to 'pick up' on the applicator. Continue to add thin layers of filler paste at twenty-minute intervals until the level of the filler is just proud of the surrounding bodywork.

Once the filler has hardened, excess can be removed using a metal plane or file. From then on, progressively finer grades of abrasive paper should be used, starting with a 40 grade production paper and finishing with 400 grade wet-and-dry paper. Always wrap the abrasive paper around a flat rubber, cork, or wooden block – otherwise the surface of the filler will not be completely flat. During the smoothing of the filler surface the wet-and-dry paper should be periodically rinsed in water. This will ensure that a very smooth finish is imparted to the filler at the final stage.

At this stage the 'dent' should be surrounded by a ring of bare metal, which in turn should be encircled by the finely 'feathered' edge of the good paintwork. Rinse the repair area with clean water, until all of the dust produced by the rubbing-down operation has gone.

Spray the whole repair area with a light coat of primer, either Holts Body + Plus Grey or Red Oxide Primer – this will show up any imperfections in the surface of the filler. Repair these imperfections with fresh filler paste or bodystopper, and once more smooth the surface with abrasive paper. If bodystopper is used, it can be mixed with cellulose thinners to form a really thin paste which is ideal for filling small

holes. Repeat this spray and repair procedure until you are satisfied that the surface of the filler, and the feathered edge of the paintwork are perfect. Clean the repair area with clean water and allow to dry fully.

The repair area is now ready for final spraying. Paint spraying must be carried out in a warm, dry, windless and dust free atmosphere. This condition can be created artificially if you have access to a large indoor working area, but if you are forced to work in the open, you will have to pick your day very carefully. If you are working indoors, dousing the floor in the work area with water will help to settle the dust which would otherwise be in the atmosphere. If the repair area is confined to one body panel, mask off the surrounding panels; this will help to minimise the effects of a slight mis-match in paint colours. Bodywork fittings (eg chrome strips, door handles etc) will also need to be masked off. Use genuine masking tape and several thicknesses of newspaper for the masking operations.

Before commencing to spray, agitate the aerosol can thoroughly, then spray a test area (an old tin, or similar) until the technique is mastered. Cover the repair area with a thick coat of primer; the thickness should be built up using several thin layers of paint rather than one thick one. Using 400 grade wet-and-dry paper, rub down the surface of the primer until it is really smooth. While doing this, the work area should be thoroughly doused with water, and the wet-and-dry paper periodically rinsed in water. Allow to dry before spraying on more paint.

Spray on the top coat using Holts Dupli-Color Autospray, again building up the thickness by using several thin layers of paint. Start spraying in the centre of the repair area and then, with a single side-to-side motion, work outwards until the whole repair area and about 2 inches of the surrounding original paintwork is covered. Remove all masking material 10 to 15 minutes after spraying on the final coat of paint.

Allow the new paint at least two weeks to harden, then, using a paintwork renovator or a very fine cutting paste such as Turtle Wax New Color Back or Holts Body + Plus Rubbing Compound, blend the edges of the paint into the existing paintwork. Finally, apply wax polish.

Plastic components

With the use of more and more plastic body components by the vehicle manufacturers (eg bumpers, spoilers, and in some cases major body panels), rectification of more serious damage to such items has become a matter of either entrusting repair work to a specialist in this field, or renewing complete components. Repair of such damage by the DIY owner is not really feasible owing to the cost of the equipment and materials required for effecting such repairs. The basic technique involves making a groove along the line of the crack in the plastic using a rotary burr in a power drill. The damaged part is then welded back together by using a hot air gun to heat up and fuse a plastic filler rod into the groove. Any excess plastic is then removed and the area rubbed down to a smooth finish. It is important that a filler rod of the correct plastic is used, as body components can be made of a variety of different types (eg polycarbonate, ABS, polypropylene).

Damage of a less serious nature (abrasions, minor cracks etc) can be repaired by the DIY owner using a two-part epoxy filler repair material like Holts Body + Plus or Holts No Mix which can be used directly from the tube. Once mixed in equal proportions (or applied direct from the tube in the case of Holts No Mix), this is used in similar fashion to the bodywork filler used on metal panels. The filler is usually cured in twenty to thirty minutes, ready for sanding and painting.

If the owner is renewing a complete component himself, or if he has repaired it with epoxy filler, he will be left with the problem of finding a suitable paint for finishing which is compatible with the type of plastic used. At one time the use of a universal paint was not possible owing to the complex range of plastics encountered in body component applications. Standard paints, generally speaking, will not bond to plastic or rubber satisfactorily, but Holts Professional Spraymatch paints to match any plastic or rubber finish can be obtained from dealers. However, it is now possible to obtain a plastic body parts finishing kit which consists of a pre-primer treatment, a primer and coloured top coat. Full instructions are normally supplied with a kit, but basically the method of use is to first apply the pre-primer to the component concerned and allow it to dry for up to 30 minutes. Then the primer is applied and left to dry for about an hour before finally applying the special coloured top coat. The result is a correctly coloured component where the paint will flex with the plastic or rubber, a property that standard paint does not normally possess.

5 Major body damage – repair

Where serious damage has occurred, or large areas need renewal due to neglect, it means that complete new sections or panels will need welding in, and this is best left to professionals. If the damage is due to impact, it will also be necessary to check completely the alignment of the bodyshell, and this can only be carried out successfully using special jigs. If the body is left misaligned, it is primarily dangerous as the car will not handle properly, and secondly, uneven stresses will be imposed on the steering, suspension, and possibly transmission, causing abnormal wear, or complete failure, particularly to such items as the tyres.

6 Maintenance – hinges and locks

1   Oil the hinges of the bonnet, boot lid or tailgate, and doors with a few drops of light oil at regular intervals (photo).
2   At the same time lightly lubricate the bonnet release mechanism and the door locks (photo).
3   **Do not** attempt to lubricate the steering lock.

7 Bonnet – removal, refitting and adjustment

1   Open the bonnet and remove the sound-deadening material on the left-hand side by releasing the clip retainers (photo).
2   Undo the two screws securing the illumination lamp to the bonnet (photo), feed the lamp and wiring down behind the sound-deadening material and retrieve it from the bottom of the bonnet. Place the lamp and wiring to one side.

3   Disconnect the windscreen washer fluid feed hose at the two-way connector (photo).
4   Place some rags beneath the bonnet corners, by the hinges.
5   Mark the position of the hinges by drawing around them with a soft pencil, then loosen the retaining bolts (photo).
6   Engage the help of an assistant to support the bonnet.
7   Using a small screwdriver, prise out the clips securing the support struts to the pegs on the bonnet (photo). Release both struts from their pegs.
8   Undo the retaining bolts and carefully lift away the bonnet.
9   Refitting is the reverse sequence to removal, but adjust the bonnet position on the hinges to its original position initially, then check the alignment as follows.
10 Close the bonnet and check the alignment with the adjacent body panels. The bonnet can be moved forward and backward by adjusting its position at each hinge. If the bonnet is too low with respect to the adjacent wing, fit small shims between the hinge and bonnet.
11 Check the bonnet closure and ease of opening. If the striker pins do not engage smoothly with the lock plates, slacken the striker plate retaining bolts and reposition the plates. If necessary, slacken the locknut and adjust the striker pin height by turning the slotted end with a screwdriver.

8 Bonnet support strut – removal and refitting

1   Open the bonnet, and support it in the open position with the aid of an assistant or with a suitable prop.
2   Using a small screwdriver, prise out the retaining clips securing the strut ends to the mounting pegs.
3   Release the strut from the pegs and remove it from the bonnet.
4   Refitting is the reverse sequence to removal.

6.1 Lubricate the hinges with a few drops of light oil

6.2 Lubricate the bonnet release mechanism and the door locks

7.1 Release the sound-deadening material retaining clips

7.2 Remove the bonnet illumination lamp

7.3 Disconnect the windscreen washer fluid feed hose (arrowed)

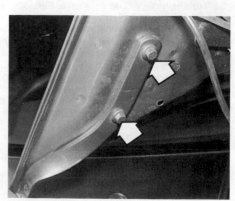

7.5 Loosen the bonnet hinge retaining bolts (arrowed)

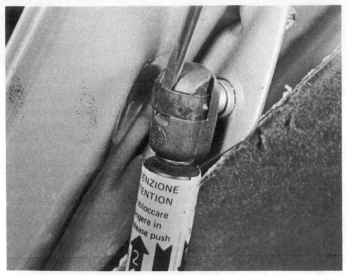

7.7 Prise out the support strut retaining clips

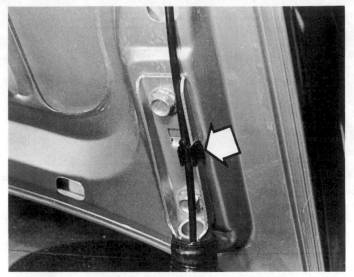

10.6 Release the cable from the retaining clip (arrowed)

10.10 Boot lid striker plate retaining bolts (arrowed)

9 Bonnet lock and release cable – removal and refitting

1   From inside the car, undo the bolts and withdraw the release lever from the right-hand side of the footwell.
2   Disengage the cables from the lever.
3   Working in the engine compartment, undo the bolts securing the relevant bonnet lock to the front body panel.
4   Withdraw the lock from under the body panel and disengage the release cable.
5   Release the cable from the retaining clips and ties in the engine compartment, and from the bulkhead grommet.
6   Feed the cable through into the engine compartment and remove it from the car.
7   Refitting is the reverse sequence to removal. Adjust the bonnet lock as described in Section 7, if necessary.

10 Boot lid (Saloon models) – removal, refitting and adjustment

1   Open the boot lid and remove the plastic cover over the lock.
2   Release the retaining clip and disconnect the link rod from the lock lever.
3   Disconnect the wiring at the connector adjacent to the lock.
4   Undo the two bolts and withdraw the lock from the boot lid.
5   Withdraw the lock release cable outer sheath from the lock bracket, and disconnect the inner cable from the lock lever.
6   Withdraw the grommet from the cable entry point above the boot lid hinge, and release the cable from the hinge cable clips and ties (photo). Withdraw the release cable and wiring from the bonnet.
7   With an assistant supporting the boot lid, undo the four hinge bolts and lift the boot lid away.
8   Refitting is the reverse sequence to removal. Engage the centre groove of the lock release cable sheath into the lock bracket slot initially, but use an alternative groove if the release lever action is unsatisfactory.
9   With the boot lid closed, check the relationship of the lid with the adjacent panels. If necessary, the boot can be repositioned by altering the position of the hinges at their body attachment. To do this, remove the rear seats as described in Section 42, and remove the parcel shelf. Slacken the hinge nuts and reposition the hinges as required. Tighten the nuts, then close the boot lid and check the operation of the lock. If necessary, slacken the striker plate bolts, reposition the striker plate and tighten the bolts (photo).
10   Refit the parcel shelf and rear seats on completion.

11 Boot lock (Saloon models) – removal and refitting

1   Open the boot lid and remove the plastic cover over the lock.
2   Release the retaining clip and disconnect the link rod from the lock lever.
3   Disconnect the wiring at the connector adjacent to the lock.
4   Undo the two bolts and withdraw the lock from the boot lid.
5   Withdraw the lock release cable outer sheath from the lock bracket, disconnect the inner cable from the lock lever, and remove the lock.
6   Refitting is the reverse sequence to removal. Engage the centre groove of the lock release cable sheath into the lock bracket slot initially, but use an alternative groove if the release lever action is unsatisfactory.

12 Boot lid private lock (Saloon models) – removal and refitting

1   Remove the number plate from the boot lid.
2   From inside the boot lid, undo the screws and remove the centre lens and reflector assembly (photo).
3   Extract the retaining circlip from the private lock lever, and withdraw the link rod.

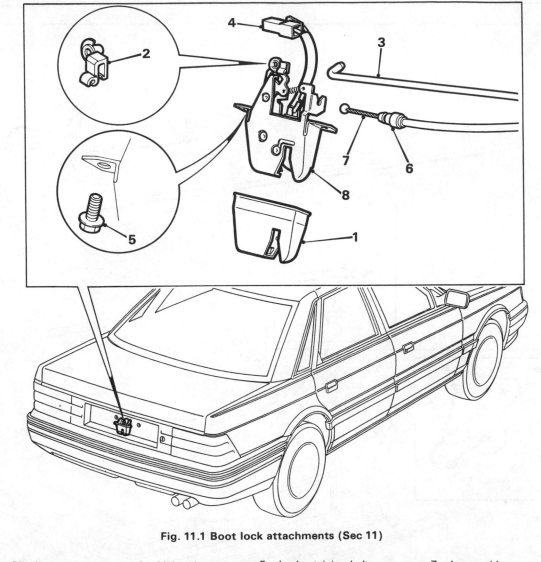

Fig. 11.1 Boot lock attachments (Sec 11)

1 Plastic cover	3 Link rod	5 Lock retaining bolts	7 Inner cable
2 Link rod retaining clip	4 Wiring connector	6 Release cable outer sheath	8 Boot lock

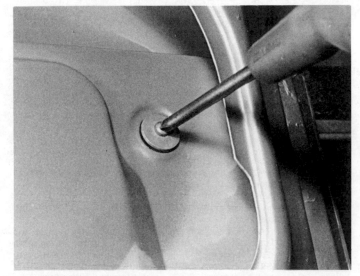

12.2 Undo the centre lens and reflector retaining screw

12.4 Boot lid private lock retaining rivets

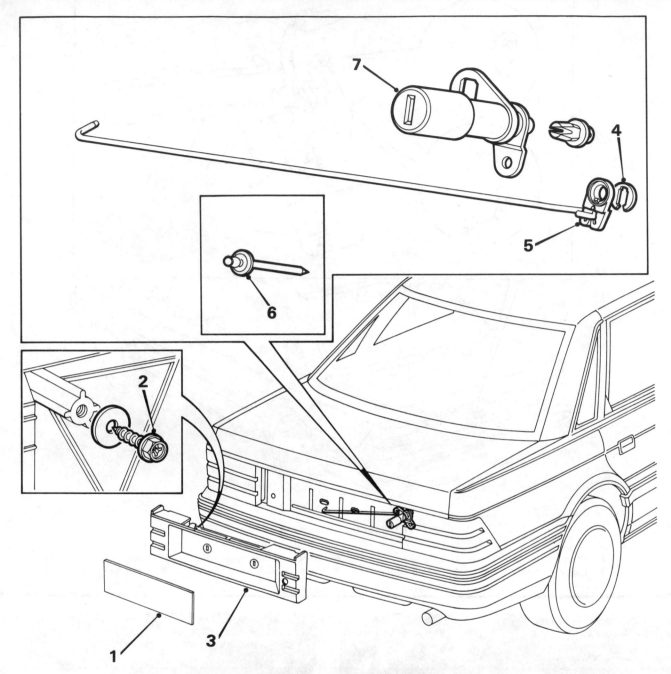

Fig. 11.2 Boot private lock attachments (Sec 12)

1 Number plate	3 Centre lens and reflector	4 Lever retaining circlip	6 Retaining rivets
2 Centre lens and reflector	assembly	5 Lever	7 Private lock
assembly screws			

4   Drill out the three retaining rivets (photo), and remove the private lock from the boot lid.
5   Refitting is the reverse sequence to removal.

13 Boot lid/tailgate and fuel filler flap release control – removal and refitting

1   Withdraw the knobs from the release levers inside the car (photo).
2   Undo the two screws securing the release control cover – one on the side face (photo), and one under a flap at the rear.
3   Withdraw the cover retaining stud on the inner face, then lift the cover off the release control (photo).
4   Undo the screws securing the front sill tread plate, lift off the tread plate, and pull back the carpet around the release control.
5   Undo the three screws and withdraw the release control (photo).
6   Disconnect the inner cable ends and outer cable sheaths, and remove the control from the car.
7   Refitting is the reverse sequence to removal. Note that the boot/tailgate release cable with the single groove in the outer cable sheath is fitted to the upper location, and the fuel filler flap release with the three grooves in the outer cable sheath is fitted to the lower location. Engage the centre groove with the bracket when fitting the filler flap cable, and check the release operation. If unsatisfactory, use an alternate groove.

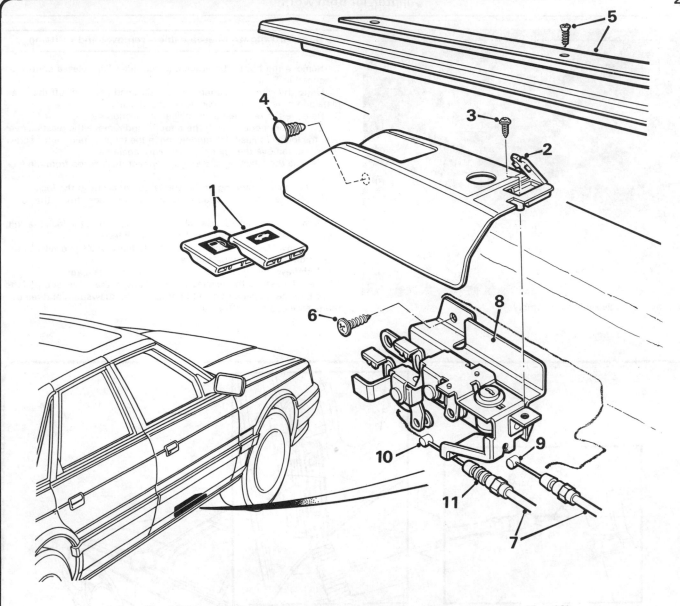

Fig. 11.3 Boot lid/tailgate fuel filler flap release control attachments (Sec 13)

1	Release lever knobs	5	Front sill tread plate screws
2	Access flap	6	Release control retaining
3	Cover retaining screws		screws
4	Cover retaining stud	7	Control cables

8	Release control	11	Three grooves on fuel filler
9	Boot release inner cable		flap release outer cable
10	Fuel filler flap release inner		sheath
	cable		

13.1 Withdraw the boot lid/tailgate and fuel filler flap release lever knobs

13.2 Undo the release lever control cover retaining screws

13.3 Withdraw the cover ...

13.5 ... over the release lever assembly

14 Boot lid/tailgate release cable – removal and refitting

1   Remove the boot lid/tailgate and fuel filler flap release control as described in Section 13.
2   Undo the screws securing the rear sill tread plate, lift off the tread plate and move aside the carpet around the sill.
3   Remove the rear seat as described in Section 42.
4   On Saloon models, open the boot lid and remove the plastic cover over the lock. On Fastback models, open the tailgate, release the screw studs and remove the tailgate inner trim panel.
5   Release the retaining clip and disconnect the link rod from the lock lever.
6   Disconnect the wiring at the connector adjacent to the lock.
7   Undo the two bolts and withdraw the lock from the boot lid/tailgate.
8   Withdraw the lock release cable outer sheath from the lock bracket, and disconnect the inner cable from the lock lever.
9   Withdraw the grommet from the cable entry point and release the cable from the cable clips and ties.
10   Withdraw the release cable from the boot lid/tailgate.
11   Tie a drawstring to the release control end of the cable, and pull the cable into the luggage compartment. Untie the drawstring and remove the release cable from the car.

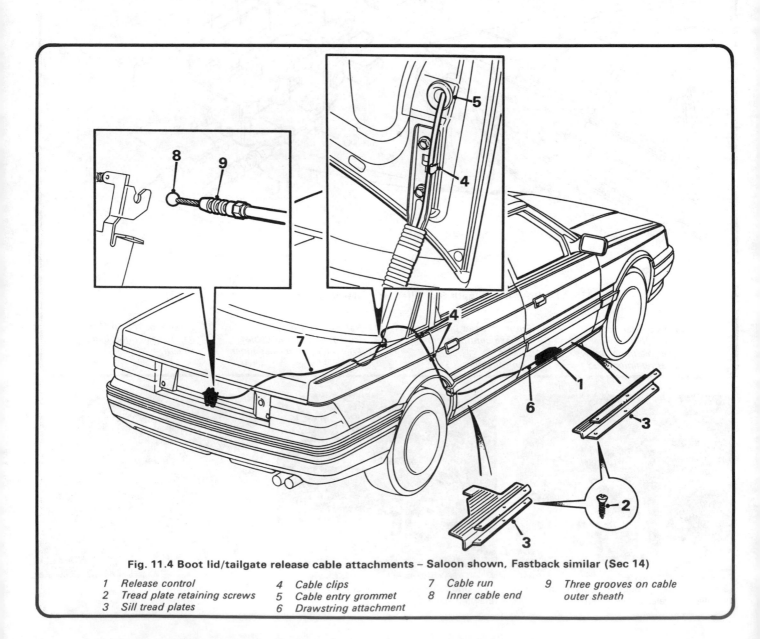

Fig. 11.4 Boot lid/tailgate release cable attachments – Saloon shown, Fastback similar (Sec 14)

1 Release control	4 Cable clips	7 Cable run	9 Three grooves on cable
2 Tread plate retaining screws	5 Cable entry grommet	8 Inner cable end	outer sheath
3 Sill tread plates	6 Drawstring attachment		

12 Tie the drawstring to the new cable, and pull it through into the car interior.

13 Refit the cable to the release lever and lock, then reassemble the components using the reverse sequence to removal. When refitting the cable to the lock, engage the centre groove of the cable sheath into the lock bracket slot initially, but use an alternative groove if the release lever action is unsatisfactory.

15 Fuel filler flap release cable – removal and refitting

1 Open the fuel filler flap, then remove the boot lid/tailgate and fuel filler flap release control, as described in Section 13.

2 Undo the screws securing the rear sill tread plate, lift off the tread plate and move aside the carpet around the sill.

3 Remove the rear seat as described in Section 42.

4 Extract the retaining clip securing the cable end at the filler flap end, and push the cable through into the luggage compartment (photo).

5 Release the cable from the retaining clips, and pull it into the car interior.

6 Where fitted, undo the screws and remove the cover strip over the cable beneath the rear seat location.

7 Release the cable from any further clips and ties, and remove it from the car.

8 Refitting is the reverse sequence to removal, with reference to Section 13 when refitting the cable to the release control.

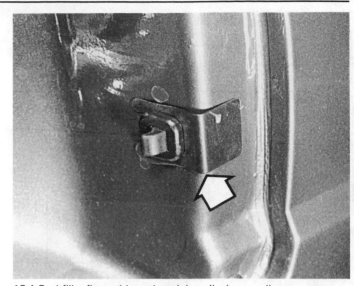

15.4 Fuel filler flap cable end retaining clip (arrowed)

16 Tailgate (Fastback models) – removal and refitting

1 Open the tailgate and release the parcel shelf support strings.

2 From inside the car, remove the headliner rear finisher for access to the tailgate hinge retaining nuts.

3 Disconnect the screen washer hose, and the tailgate wiring harness connectors.

4 Support the tailgate with the help of an assistant, or using a prop.

5 Extract the wire spring retainer securing each support strut to its tailgate ball-stud, and release the struts.

6 Undo the tailgate hinge retaining nuts and remove the tailgate from the car.

7 Refitting is the reverse sequence to removal, in conjunction with the following adjustment procedure.

8 With the tailgate closed, check the relationship of the tailgate with the adjacent panels. If necessary, it can be repositioned by altering the position of the hinges at their body attachment. Slacken the hinge nuts, and reposition the hinges are required. Tighten the nuts, then close the tailgate and check the operation of the lock. If necessary, slacken the striker plate bolts, reposition the striker plate and tighten the bolts.

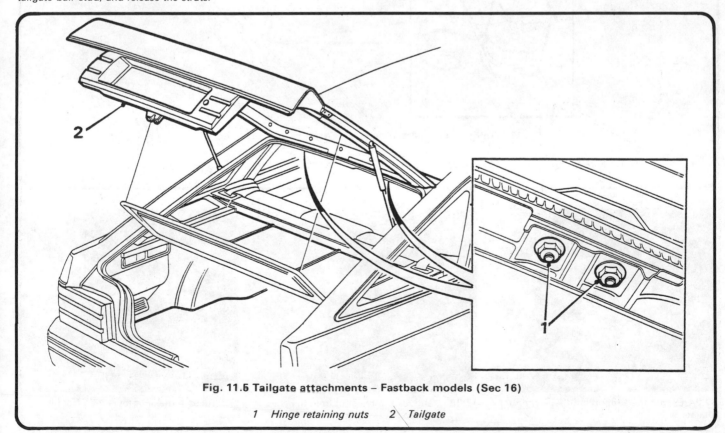

Fig. 11.5 Tailgate attachments – Fastback models (Sec 16)

1 Hinge retaining nuts   2 Tailgate

17 Tailgate support strut (Fastback models) – removal and refitting

1 Open the tailgate and support it with the help of an assistant, or using a prop.

2 Extract the wire spring retainer securing the upper end of the support strut to its tailgate ball-stud, and release the strut (photos).
3 Release the strut lower end clip, ease the strut from its stud (photo) and remove it from the car.
4 Refitting is the reverse sequence to removal.

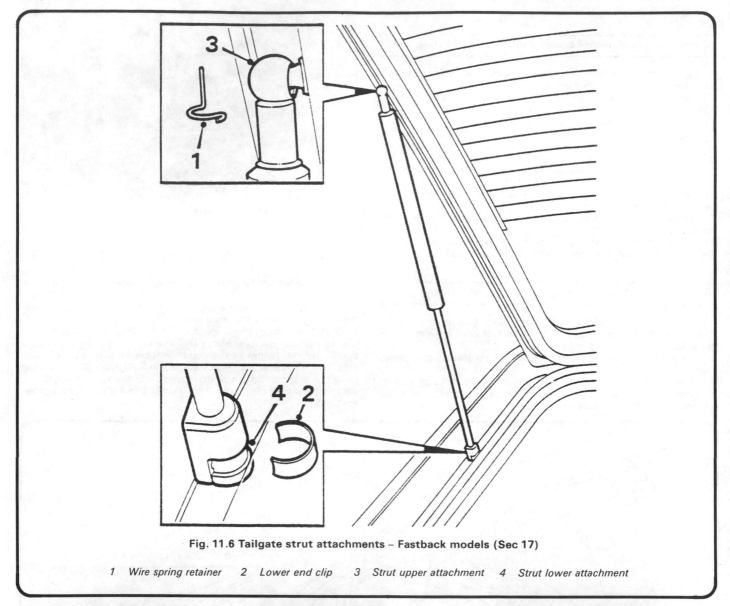

Fig. 11.6 Tailgate strut attachments – Fastback models (Sec 17)

1   Wire spring retainer   2   Lower end clip   3   Strut upper attachment   4   Strut lower attachment

17.2A Extract the support strut wire spring retainer ...

17.2B ... and release the strut from the stud

17.3 Release the strut lower end from its stud

18 Tailgate lock (Fastback models) – removal and refitting

1 Open the tailgate, release the screw studs (photo) and remove the tailgate inner trim panel.
2 Remove the plastic cover from the lock (photo).

3 Release the retaining clip from the link rod, and remove the link rod from the lock lever.
4 Disconnect the wiring multi-plugs, undo the two lock retaining bolts (photo) and remove the lock from the door.
5 Refitting is the reverse sequence to removal.

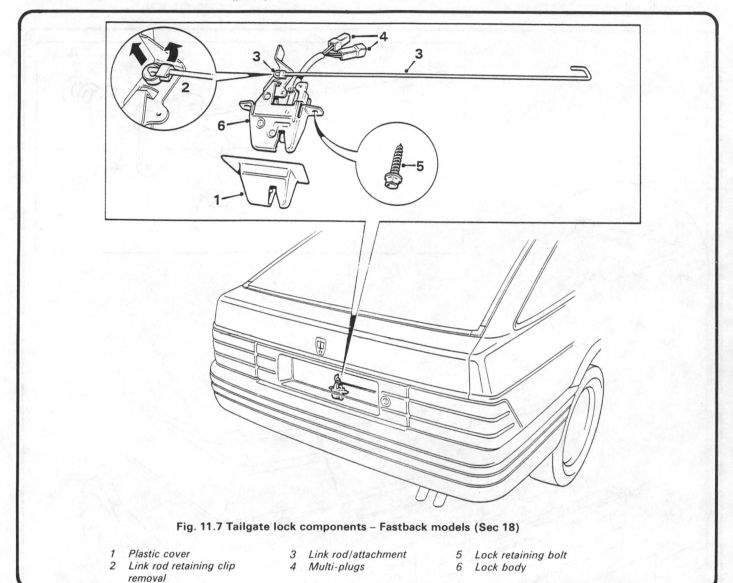

Fig. 11.7 Tailgate lock components – Fastback models (Sec 18)

1 Plastic cover	3 Link rod/attachment	5 Lock retaining bolt
2 Link rod retaining clip removal	4 Multi-plugs	6 Lock body

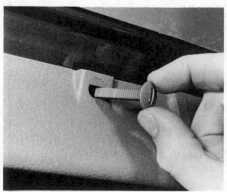

18.1 Release the screw studs and remove the tailgate inner trim panel

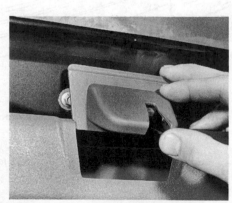

18.2 Remove the plastic cover from the lock

18.4 Undo the two lock retaining bolts (arrowed)

19 Tailgate private lock (Fastback models) – removal and refitting

1   Open the tailgate, release the screw studs and remove the tailgate inner trim panel.
2   Remove the number plate from the tailgate.

3   From inside the tailgate, undo the screws and remove the centre lens and reflector assembly.
4   Extract the retaining circlip from the private lock lever, and withdraw the lever from the lock (photo).
5   Drill out the three retaining rivets and remove the private lock from the tailgate.
6   Refitting is the reverse sequence to removal.

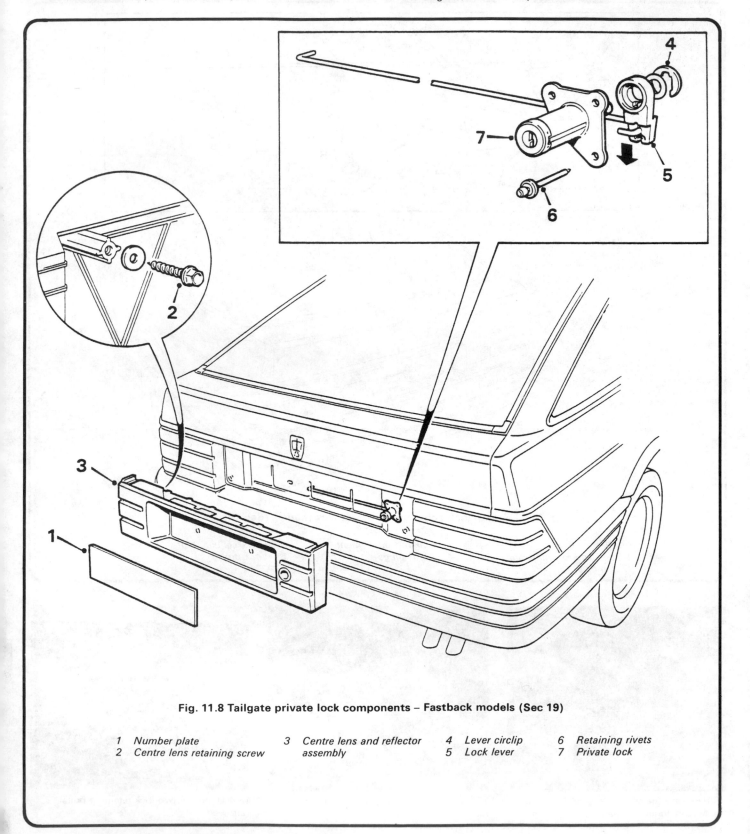

Fig. 11.8 Tailgate private lock components – Fastback models (Sec 19)

1 Number plate	3 Centre lens and reflector	4 Lever circlip	6 Retaining rivets
2 Centre lens retaining screw	assembly	5 Lock lever	7 Private lock

19.4 Private lock lever retaining circlip (arrowed)

21.1 Radiator grille upper retaining screws (arrowed)

21.2 Radiator grille lower retaining clip

20 Tailgate lock solenoid (Fastback models) – removal and refitting

1   Open the tailgate, release the screw studs and remove the tailgate inner trim panel.
2   Remove the number plate from the tailgate.
3   From inside the tailgate, undo the screws and remove the centre lens and reflector assembly.
4   Disconnect the solenoid wiring multi-plug.
5   Undo the two screws and remove the solenoid from the tailgate.
6   Refitting is the reverse sequence to removal.

21 Radiator grille – removal and refitting

1   Undo the four grille upper retaining screws (photo).
2   Release the two lower retaining clips (photo) and withdraw the grille from the car.
3   Refitting is the reverse sequence to removal.

22 Windscreen, rear window and tailgate window glass – removal and refitting

The primary window glass on Rover 820 models is flush-glazed, and secured to the body shell by direct bonding. Due to this method of retention, special tools and equipment are required for removal and refitting, and this task is definitely beyond the scope of the home mechanic. If it is necessary to have windscreen, rear window or tailgate window glass removed, this job should be left to a suitably-equipped specialist.

23 Front door inner trim panel – removal and refitting

Saloon models
1   Insert a small screwdriver into the slot at the rear of the interior locking button, and prise apart the outer moulded half of the locking button. Lift off the outer half, then remove the inner half from the locking rod (photos).
2   Carefully prise out the finisher trim from the inner handle, disconnect the tweeter speaker leads and remove the finisher (photos).

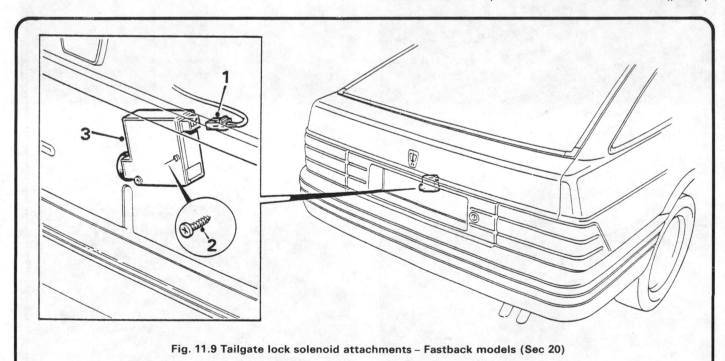

Fig. 11.9 Tailgate lock solenoid attachments – Fastback models (Sec 20)

1   *Wiring multi-plug*   2   *Retaining screws*   3   *Solenoid*

3   Carefully prise out the blanking plate from the bottom of the panel (photo).

4   Ease back the padded trim at the bottom of the panel to expose the retaining screw, then undo the screw (photo).

5   Pull out the blanking plug on the rear side of the panel, and undo the recessed screw behind (photos).

6   Undo the screw at the upper front corner of the panel (photo).

7   Undo the screw at each end of the storage bin (photos).

8   Working through the blanking plate aperture, undo the screw in the recess (photo).

9   Undo the screw at the top of the door pull below the interior handle (photo).

10 Using a suitable flat tool or your fingers, release the eight studs securing the panel to the door by prising the panel out, or sharply pulling it out, in the vicinity of each stud. Lift the panel upwards and withdraw it from the door (photo).

11 Disconnect the switch panel wiring multi-plug from the rear of the panel and remove the panel (photo).

12 Refitting is the reverse sequence to removal.

Fastback models

13 Insert a small screwdriver into the slot at the rear of the interior locking button, and prise apart the outer moulded half of the locking button. Lift off the outer half, then remove the inner half from the locking rod (photo).

14 Prise out the door inner handle centre finisher trim, and undo the two screws securing the trim surround to the door (photos).

15 Pull the door handle outwards, and manipulate the trim surround off the handle and door panel (photo).

16 Disconnect the tweeter speaker leads from the rear of the trim surround, and remove the surround (photo).

17 Where fitted, undo the screw from the bottom of the door pull finger grip, and remove the finger grip from the panel.

18 If the panel incorporates a moulded door pull, prise out the blanking plug and undo the recessed screw behind (photos).

19 Lift up the cap over the screw at the bottom rear corner of the panel, and undo the screw (photo).

20 Pull out the blanking plug on the rear side of the panel, and undo the recessed screw behind (photos).

21 Undo the screw at the upper front corner of the panel (photo).

22 Undo the screw at each end of the storage bin (photos).

23 Undo the screw at the top of the door pull below the interior handle (photo).

24 Release the rubber boot over the door mirror adjustment stalk, release the stalk retaining clips and push the stalk through to the inside of the panel (photos).

25 Using a suitable flat tool or your fingers, release the eight studs securing the panel to the door by prising the panel out, or sharply pulling it out, in the vicinity of each stud. Lift the panel upwards and withdraw it from the door.

26 Refitting is the reverse sequence to removal but push the door mirror stalk into position from the rear before refitting the panel (photo).

23.1A Prise apart the interior lock button ...

23.1B ... and lift out the outer half ...

23.1C ... followed by the inner half

23.2A Prise out the inner handle finisher trim ...

23.2B ... and disconnect the tweeter speaker leads

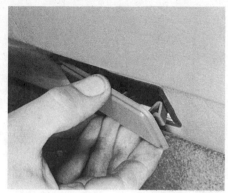

23.3 Prise out the blanking plate

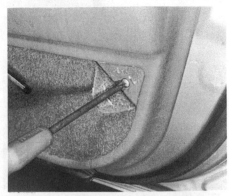

23.4 Undo the screw behind the padded trim

25.5A Pull out the blanking plug ...

23.5B ... and undo the recessed screw behind

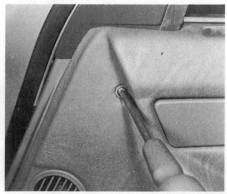

23.6 Undo the screw at the upper front corner

23.7A Undo the screw at the front ...

23.7B ... and rear of the storage bin

23.8 Undo the screw in the blanking plate recess

23.9 Undo the screw at the top of the door pull

23.10 Withdraw the panel from the door

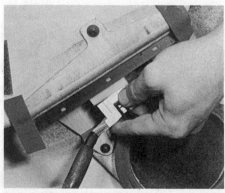

23.11 Disconnect the switch panel wiring multi-plug

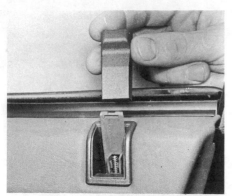

23.13 Remove the two halves of the locking button

23.14A Prise out the inner handle centre finisher trim ...

23.14B ... and undo the two trim surround screws

23.15 Manipulate the surround off the handle

23.16 Disconnect the tweeter speaker leads

23.18A Prise out the blanking plug ...

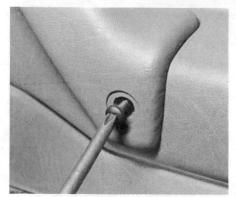

23.18B ... and undo the screw behind

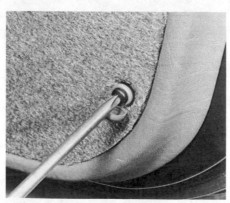

23.19 Lift off the cap and undo the panel bottom rear corner screw

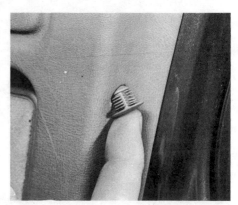

23.20A Pull out the blanking plug ...

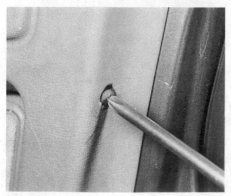

23.20B ... and undo the recessed rear side screw

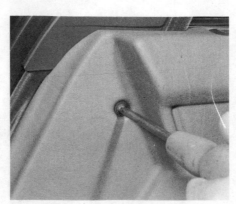

23.21 Undo the screw at the upper front corner

23.22A Undo the screw at the front ...

23.22B ... and rear of the storage bin

23.23 Undo the screw at the top of the door pull

23.24A Withdraw the rubber boot ...

23.24B ... and release the mirror adjustment stalk

23.26 Refit the mirror adjustment stalk before fitting the panel

24 Front door – removal, refitting and adjustment

1   Remove the front door inner trim panel as described in Section 23.
2   Release the masking tape and carefully peel back the polythene condensation barrier as necessary for access to the internal wiring multi-plugs.
3   Identify the multi-plugs for refitting, then disconnect them from the door components. Withdraw the wiring harness from the door.
4   Using a suitable drift, tap out the door check strap retaining roll pin (photo).

5   With the help of an assistant, support the door on a padded jack, undo the four hinge retaining bolts and withdraw the door from the car.
6   Refitting is the reverse sequence to removal.
7   Check the fit of the door against the surrounding panels, and if necessary slacken the hinge bolts and reposition the door.
8   When the door fit is correct, check the operation of the lock, and if necessary slacken the striker plate screws and reposition the striker plate (photo). Tighten all the bolts and screws securely on completion.

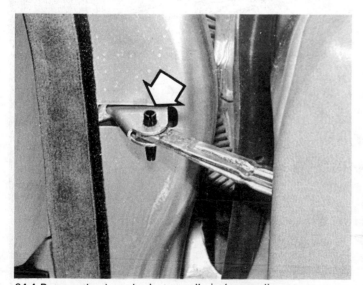

24.4 Remove the door check strap roll pin (arrowed)

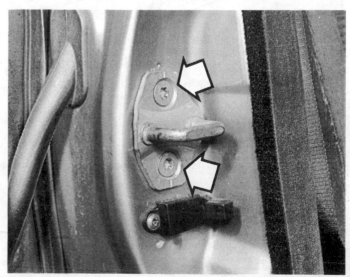

24.8 Door striker plate retaining screws (arrowed)

25 Front door lock – removal and refitting

1   Remove the front door inner trim panel as described in Section 23.
2   Release the masking tape and carefully peel back the polythene condensation barrier as necessary for access to the door lock area.
3   Carefully prise out the door lock link rod and control rod from their attachments at the private lock lever and exterior handle lever respectively.
4   Undo the three screws securing the lock assembly to the door (photo).
5   Lower the lock assembly, and release the interior handle control rod and locking button rod from the lock levers.
6   Disconnect the central locking motor wiring multi-plug, and manipulate the lock assembly from the door.
7   Refitting is the reverse sequence to removal.

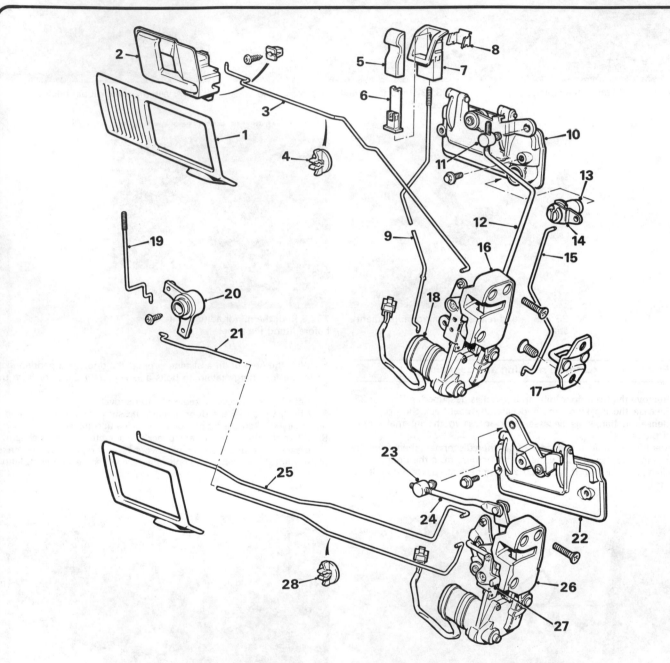

Fig. 11.10 Exploded view of the front and rear door locks and related components (Sec 25)

Front door
1   Finisher trim
2   Inner handle
3   Control rod
4   Rod guide
5   Locking button outer half
6   Locking button inner half
7   Sleeve

8   Clip
9   Link rod
10 Exterior handle
11 Trunnion
12 Control rod
13 Private lock
14 Private lock lever
15 Link rod

16 Door lock
17 Striker plate
18 Central locking motor

Rear door
19 Link rod
20 Bellcrank
21 Control rod

22 Exterior handle
23 Trunnion
24 Link rod
25 Link rod
26 Door lock
27 Childproof lock lever
28 Rod guide

25.4 Door lock retaining screws

26 Front door private lock – removal and refitting

1 Remove the front door inner trim panel as described in Section 23.
2 Release the masking tape and carefully peel back the polythene condensation barrier as necessary for access to the door lock area.
3 Extract the circlip from the end of the lock barrel, and remove the washer, plate and operating lever (photo).
4 Extract the private lock retaining wire clip, and withdraw the lock from the outside of the door.
5 Refitting is the reverse sequence to removal.

27 Front door exterior handle – removal and refitting

1 Remove the front door private lock as described in Section 26.
2 Carefully prise out the door lock control rod from the exterior handle lever.
3 Undo the two retaining bolts and remove the handle from the outside of the door (photo).

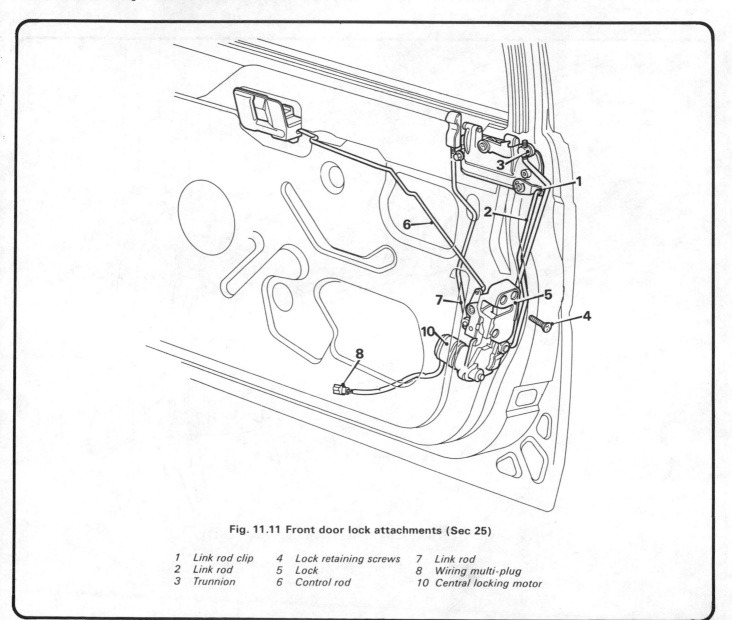

Fig. 11.11 Front door lock attachments (Sec 25)

1 Link rod clip	4 Lock retaining screws	7 Link rod
2 Link rod	5 Lock	8 Wiring multi-plug
3 Trunnion	6 Control rod	10 Central locking motor

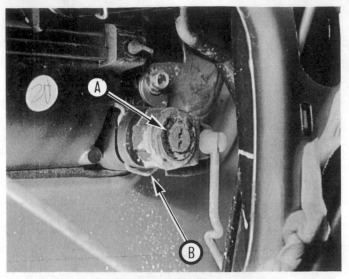

26.3 Lock barrel operating lever retaining circlip (A) and private lock retaining wire clip (B)

27.3 Front door exterior handle retaining bolts (arrowed)

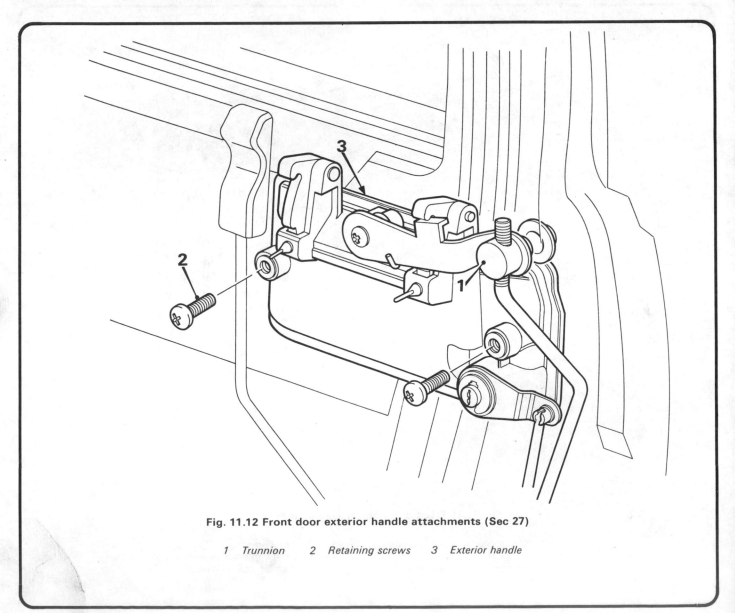

Fig. 11.12 Front door exterior handle attachments (Sec 27)

1 Trunnion   2 Retaining screws   3 Exterior handle

28 Front door interior handle – removal and refitting

1 Remove the front door inner trim panel as described in Section 23.
2 Remove the foam pad from the handle (photo).
3 Where applicable, undo the screws securing the handle to the door panel.
4 Lift the locking tab at the front of the handle body, slide the handle rearwards and withdraw it from the door (photo).
5 Disconnect the operating rod and remove the handle.
6 Refitting is the reverse sequence to removal.

28.2 Remove the foam pad

28.4 Withdraw the handle from the door

29 Front door window glass – removal and refitting

1 Remove the front door inner trim panel as described in Section 23.
2 Using a screwdriver and protective rag, carefully prise up the waist seal from the upper edge of the door panel to release the retaining clips (photos).
3 Remove the front door main speaker, referring to Chapter 12 if necessary.
4 Where fitted, undo the three screws and remove the trim panel support bracket (photo).
5 Release the masking tape securing the wiring loom and loom connectors to the door panel (photo).
6 Release the wiring loom retaining clips and ease the loom away from the door (photos).
7 Undo the three screws securing the relay mounting plate, then move the plate and relays aside (photos).
8 Carefully peel back the condensation barrier, and pull it downwards to provide access inside the door (photo).
9 Lower the window until the two glass-to-lifting member retaining bolts are accessible through one of the door apertures.
10 Undo the two bolts securing the door glass to the lifting member, and lift the glass up and out of the door (photo).
11 Refitting is the reverse sequence to removal. Ensure that the condensation barrier is refitted securely over the entire door panel face, and position the waist seal retaining clips in the waist seal before refitting the seal to the door (photo).

30 Front door window lift motor – removal and refitting

1 Remove the front door window glass as described in Section 29.
2 Disconnect the motor wiring multi-plug (photo).
3 Undo the two lower bolts and one upper bolt securing the lifting channel to the door.
4 Undo the three nuts securing the motor to the door, then manipulate the motor and lifting channel out through the lower door aperture (photos).
5 Refitting is the reverse sequence to removal.

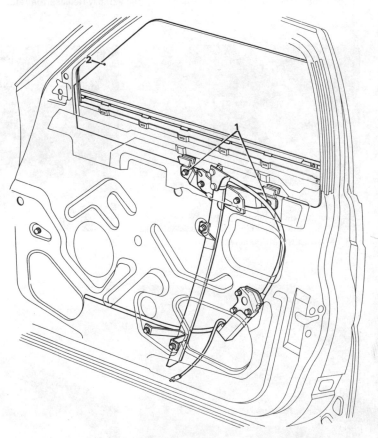

Fig. 11.13 Front door window glass attachments (Sec 29)

1   Glass-to-lifting member
    retaining bolts
2   Window glass

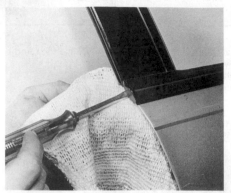

29.2A Prise up the waist seal ...

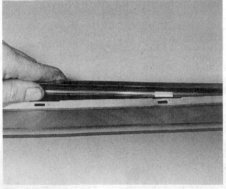

29.2B ... and release the retaining clips

29.4 Remove the trim panel support bracket

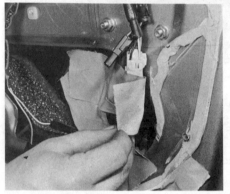

29.5 Release the masking tape

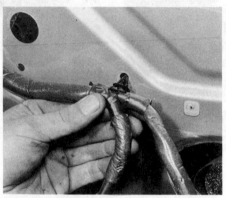

29.6A Release the retaining clips ...

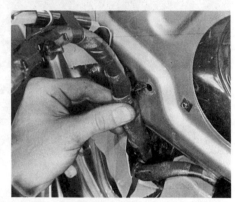

29.6B ... and ease the wiring loom from the door

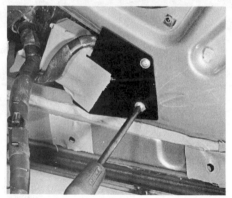

29.7A Undo the three screws ...

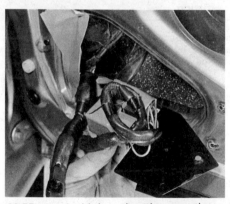

29.7B ... and withdraw the relay mounting plate

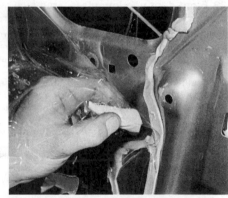

29.8 Peel back the condensation barrier

29.10 Lift the glass up and out of the door

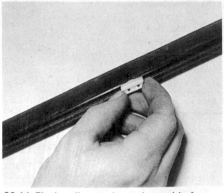

29.11 Fit the clips to the waist seal before refitting the seal

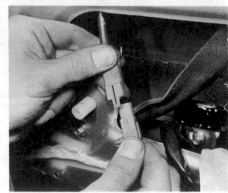

30.2 Disconnect the motor wiring multi-plug

30.4A Undo the three motor retaining nuts (arrowed) ...

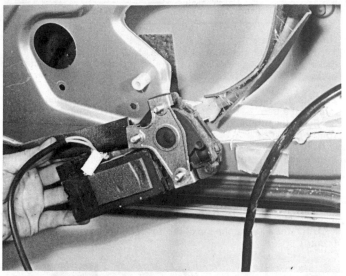

30.4B ... and remove the motor from the door

31 Front door mirror – removal and refitting

Manually controlled mirror

1   Remove the front door inner trim panel as described in Section 23.
2   Carefully prise off the triangular trim panel from the upper corner of the door (photo).
3   Undo the three mirror retaining screws (photo), release the cables from their retaining strap inside the door, and remove the mirror and cables from the door (photo).
4   Refitting is the reverse sequence to removal.

Electrically controlled mirror

5   Remove the front door inner trim panel as described in Section 23.
6   Carefully prise off the triangular trim panel from the upper corner of the door.
7   Peel back the condensation barrier as necessary to gain access to the mirror wiring multi-plugs, then disconnect them.
8   Undo the three mirror retaining screws and withdraw the mirror from the door.
9   Refitting is the reverse sequence to removal.

Fig. 11.14 Front door mirror details (Sec 31)

1   Trim panel   3   Mirror
2   Retaining screws   4   Wiring multi-plugs

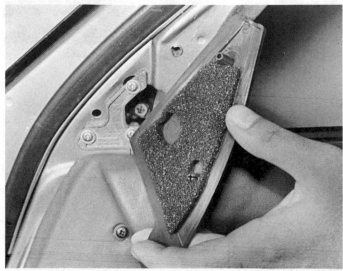

31.2 Prise out the trim panel

31.3 Undo the mirror retaining screws

32 Rear door inner trim panel – removal and refitting

Saloon models

1   Insert a small screwdriver into the slot at the rear of the interior locking button, and prise apart the outer moulded half of the locking button. Lift off the outer half, then remove the inner half from the locking rod (photos).
2   Carefully prise out the finisher trim from the inner handle, and remove the trim.
3   Carefully prise out the blanking plate from the bottom of the panel (photo).
4   If the window is manually operated, push in the escutcheon behind the regulator handle, extract the handle retaining clip and withdraw the handle from the regulator spindle.
5   Ease back the padded trim at the bottom of the panel to expose the retaining screw then undo the screw.
6   Working through the blanking plate aperture, undo the screw in the recess (photo).
7   Undo the screw at the top of the door pull below the interior handle (photo).

8   Pull out the blanking plug near the bottom of the panel, and undo the recessed screw behind (photos).
9   Using a suitable flat tool or your fingers, release the eight studs securing the panel to the door by prising the panel out, or sharply pulling it out, in the vicinity of each stud. Lift the panel upwards and withdraw it from the door.
10 Disconnect the wiring multi-plug at the rear of the window lift switches (where fitted) and remove the panel (photo).
11 Refitting is the reverse sequence to removal. Where fitted, locate the window regulator handle retaining clip in the handle groove before fitting the handle to the door.

Fastback models

12 Insert a small screwdriver into the slot at the rear of the interior locking button, and prise apart the outer moulded half of the locking button. Lift off the outer half, then remove the inner half from the locking rod.
13 Prise out the door inner handle centre finisher trim, and undo the two screws securing the trim surround to the door.
14 Pull the door handle outwards, and manipulate the trim surround off the handle and door panel.

32.1A Prise apart the locking button ...

32.1B ... and remove the inner and outer half

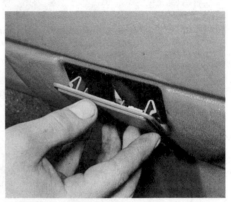

32.3 Prise out the blanking plate

32.6 Undo the screw in the blanking plate aperture

32.7 Undo the screw at the top of the door pull

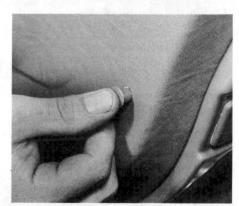

32.8A Pull out the blanking plug ...

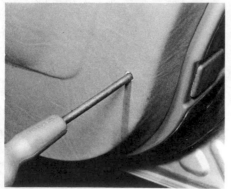

32.8B ... and remove the screw behind

32.10 Disconnect the wiring multi-plug

15 Undo the screw from the bottom of the door pull finger grip, and remove the finger grip from the panel.

16 Using a suitable flat tool or your fingers, release the eight studs securing the panel to the door by prising the panel out, or sharply pulling it out, in the vicinity of each stud. Lift the panel upwards and withdraw it from the door.

17 Refitting is the reverse sequence to removal. Where fitted, locate the window regulator handle retaining clip in the handle groove before fitting the handle to the door.

33 Rear door – removal, refitting and adjustment

The procedure for the rear door is virtually identical to that for the front door, and reference should be made to Section 24.

34 Rear door exterior handle – removal and refitting

1 Remove the rear door inner trim panel as described in Section 32.
2 Release the masking tape and carefully peel back the polythene condensation barrier as necessary for access to the door lock area.
3 Remove the access plug from the rear of the door.
4 Undo the screw securing the interior lock button control rod bellcrank.
5 Withdraw the bellcrank from the door, and disconnect the door lock control rod.
6 Undo the bolt securing the rear glass channel to the door, and remove the glass channel.
7 Undo the three screws securing the door lock to the rear face of the door.
8 Release the door lock control rod from the plastic guide on the inner face of the door.
9 Move the door lock aside, and undo the bolts securing the exterior handle to the door.
10 Withdraw the exterior handle, release the collar and remove the control rod from the exterior handle lever.
11 Remove the exterior handle from the door.
12 Refitting is the reverse sequence to removal.

35 Rear door lock – removal and refitting

1 Remove the rear door exterior handle as described in Section 34.
2 Release the door inner handle control rod from its plastic guide on the outer face of the door.
3 Carefully prise out the two control rods from their respective levers on the door lock.
4 Disconnect the central locking motor wiring multi-plug, and manipulate the lock assembly from the door.
5 Refitting is the reverse sequence to removal.

36 Rear door interior handle – removal and refitting

The procedure for the rear door is virtually identical to that for the front door, and reference should be made to Section 28.

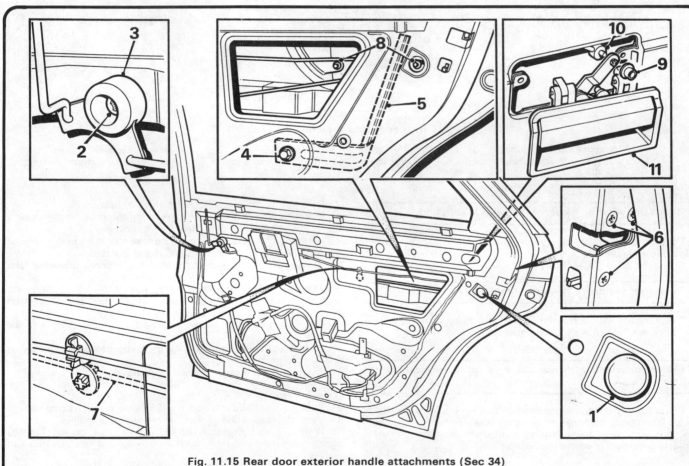

Fig. 11.15 Rear door exterior handle attachments (Sec 34)

1 Access plug	4 Rear glass channel retaining bolt	7 Control rod and guide
2 Bellcrank retaining screw	5 Rear glass channel	8 Exterior handle retaining bolts
3 Bellcrank	6 Lock retaining screws	9 Collar
		10 Trunnion
		11 Exterior handle

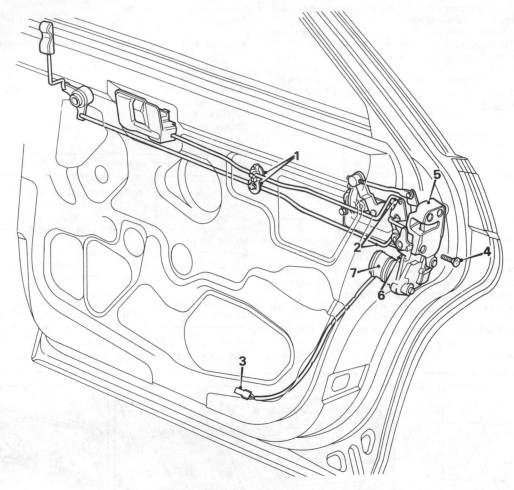

Fig. 11.16 Rear door lock attachments (Sec 35)

1 Control rod and guide	3 Wiring multi-plug	5 Door lock retaining screws
2 Control rod attachments	4 Lock retaining screws	6 Central locking motor 7 Central locking motor

37 Rear door window glass – removal and refitting

The procedure for the rear door is virtually identical to that for the front door, and reference should be made to Section 29.

38 Rear door window lift motor – removal and refitting

The procedure for the rear door is virtually identical to that for the front door, and reference should be made to Section 30.

39 Rear door window lift manual regulator – removal and refitting

The procedure is virtually identical to that for the front door with electric lift motor, except that the regulator is secured to the door with two bolts, and there are no wiring multi-plugs to disconnect. The complete procedure is covered in Section 30.

40 Bumpers – removal and refitting

Front bumper

1 Refer to Chapter 12 and remove the headlamp lens units, and where fitted, the headlamp washer jets.

2 Remove the radiator grille as described in Section 21.
3 Undo the bolt and two screws securing the access panels below the front of each wheel arch. Remove both panels.
4 Undo the two nuts securing the bumper moulding to the frame at the front. Withdraw the washers and clamp plates.
5 Release the wheel arch liner from the bumper moulding, and release the moulding from the side retaining clips.
6 Withdraw the moulding from the bumper.
7 Where fitted, release the washer pipe clips and studs, and disconnect the wiring multi-plug.
8 Undo the two bolts securing the centre support member to the bumper.
9 Undo the two end bolts securing the bumper to the frame (photo) and remove the bumper.
10 Refitting is the reverse sequence to removal.

Rear bumper

11 Remove the plastic trim from the rear of the luggage compartment.
12 Undo the screws and remove the two wheel arch liners.
13 Withdraw the grommets from the rear face of the luggage compartment, and undo the two bumper moulding retaining nuts and washers.
14 Release the moulding from the side retaining clips, and withdraw the moulding from the bumper.
15 Remove the plastic cover over the rear towing eye.
16 Withdraw the grommets, and undo the two bolts each side securing the bumper to the frame (photo).
17 Remove the bumper from the car.
18 Refitting is the reverse sequence to removal.

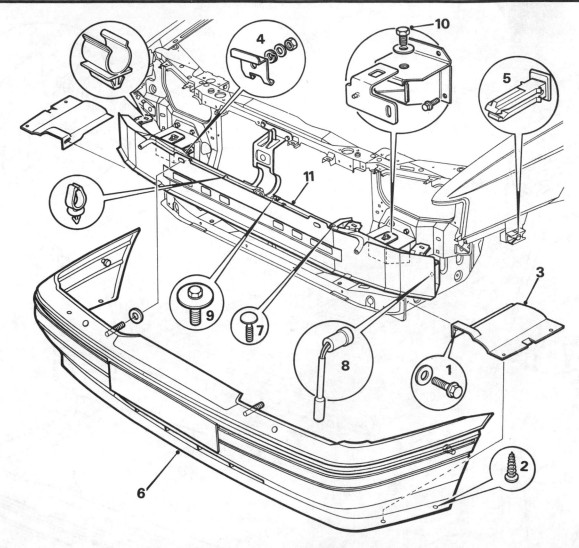

Fig. 11.17 Front bumper components (Sec 40)

1	Access panel retaining bolt	4 Bumper moulding clamp	7 Stud	10 Bumper retaining bolts
2	Access panel retaining screws	5 Bumper moulding side clips	8 Wiring multi-plug	11 Bumper mounting
3	Access panel	6 Bumper moulding	9 Centre support member bolts	

40.9 Front bumper retaining bolt

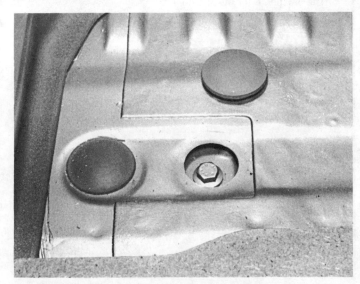

40.16 Rear bumper retaining bolt and cover grommet

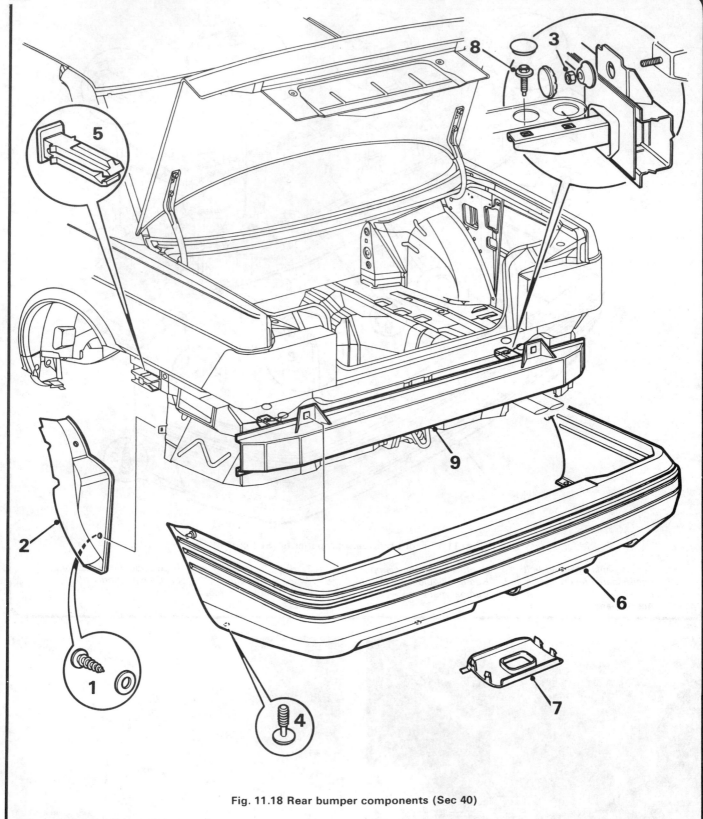

Fig. 11.18 Rear bumper components (Sec 40)

1 Wheel arch liner screws	4 Bumper moulding retaining bolts	6 Bumper moulding	8 Bumper mounting bolts and grommets
2 Wheel arch liner		7 Towing eye cover	
3 Bumper moulding nuts and grommets	5 Bumper moulding retaining clips		9 Bumper mounting

41 Front seats – removal and refitting

1   Carefully prise off the trim caps, and undo the two screws securing the trim panel below the seat base. Remove the trim panel.
2   Undo the bolt securing the seat belt at the base of the seat.
3   Undo the four bolts securing the seat runners.
4   Undo the bolt securing the seat belt stalk, and remove the stalk.
5   Withdraw the seat from the car.
6   Refitting is the reverse sequence to removal.

42 Rear seats – removal and refitting

Saloon models
1   Push the seat base rearwards, and at the same time lift it up at the front to release the two retainers. Remove the seat base from the car.
2   Undo the four bolts at the base of the seat squab.
3   Release the two seat belts from the retainers.
4   Slide the squab downwards and forwards to release the rear locating pegs, then remove the squab from the car.
5   Refitting is the reverse sequence to removal.

Fastback models
6   Push the seat base rearwards, and at the same time lift it up at the front to release the two retainers. Remove the seat base from the car.
7   Undo the bolt at the base of each side cushion extension, lift the cushion extensions upwards to release the rear wire retainers, and remove the side cushions (photo).
8   Operate the release levers and tip the two seat squabs forward.
9   Undo the two bolts securing the hinge brackets at the ends of each squab (photo).
10 Release the seat belt stalks and remove the squabs from the car.
11 Refitting is the reverse sequence to removal.

43 Rear seat squab release lever and cable (Fastback models) – removal and refitting

1   Remove the luggage compartment lamp from the release lever surround.
2   Undo the screw in the lamp aperture, move the release lever surround forwards and outwards, then disengage the two rear locating lugs (photos).
3   Extract the outer cable retaining clip at the rear of the lever surround (photo).
4   Disengage the inner cable from the release lever, and remove the lever and surround assembly.
5   Extract the outer cable retaining clip at the squab locking mechanism (photo).
6   Disengage the inner cable from the lever, and remove the cable from the car.
7   Refitting is the reverse sequence to removal.

44 Seat belts – removal and refitting

Front seat belts
1   Move the front seat rearwards as far as it will go.
2   Carefully prise off the lower trim from the centre door pillar.
3   Undo the bolt at the seat belt anchorage.
4   Remove the trim cap over the top anchorage, undo the retaining bolt and recover the spacer and fibre washer.
5   Undo the retaining screw and remove the belt guide.
6   Undo the bolt at the base of the inertia reel, and remove the seat belt components.
7   Undo the bolt securing the seat belt stalk to the seat, and remove the stalk.
8   Refitting is the reverse sequence to removal.

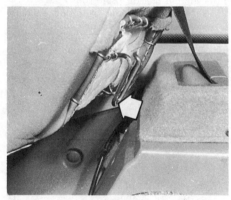

42.7 Release the side cushion wire retainer (arrowed)

42.9 Undo the hinge bracket bolts

43.2A Undo the release lever surround retaining screw ...

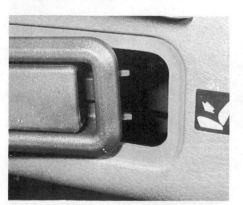

43.2B ... and disengage the locating lugs

43.3 Extract the outer cable retaining clip (arrowed) at the lever surround ...

43.5 ... and the clip at the locking mechanism (arrowed)

Rear seat belts

9   Remove the rear seat base and squab as described in Section 42.
10 Undo the bolt at the seat belt anchorage.
11 Remove the belt guide from the rear parcel shelf.
12 Remove the trim cap over the top anchorage, undo the retaining bolt and recover the spacer and fibre washer.
13 From within the luggage compartment, undo the bolt at the base of the inertia reel, and remove the seat belt assembly from the luggage compartment.
14 Undo the retaining bolts and remove the individual static belts as required.
15 Refitting is the reverse sequence to removal.

45 Sunroof – general

A mechanically operated steel sunroof is available as standard or optional equipment according to model.

The sunroof is maintenance-free, but any adjustment or removal and refitting of the component parts should be entrusted to a dealer, due to the complexity of the unit and the need to remove much of the interior trim and headlining to gain access. The latter operation is involved, and requires care and specialist knowledge to avoid damage.

46 Centre console – removal and refitting

1   On manual gearbox models, unscrew the gear lever knob and remove the gear lever boot (photo).
2   On automatic transmission models, undo the retaining screw and lift off the selector lever. Carefully prise up the selector lever quadrant, disconnect the wiring multi-plugs and remove the quadrant.
3   Prise up the coin trays (photo) or switch panels on each side of the handbrake lever. Remove the coin trays, or disconnect the multi-plugs and remove the switch panels.
4   Insert a screwdriver under the rear end of the cover trim over the handbrake lever. Prise up the cover rear end, then withdraw the cover

from the handbrake lever (photo).
5   Lift back the edges of the carpet under the coin holder or switch panel locations, and undo the two console retaining bolts under the carpet (photo).
6   Remove the rear ashtray, followed by the ashtray insert, then undo the two screws securing the rear of the console (photos).
7   Open the cassette holder lid, and undo the two screws at the base of the cassette racks (photo).
8   Apply the handbrake as hard as possible, then lift the rear of the console over the handbrake lever (photos). Slide the forward end of the console out from under the facia and remove the console from the car. There is barely sufficient clearance to allow the console to clear the handbrake under normal conditions, and if it proves impossible to do this, refer to Chapter 9 and slacken the handbrake adjuster to allow the lever to be pulled up further.
9   Refitting is the reverse sequence to removal. Adjust the handbrake as described in Chapter 9 if the adjuster position was disturbed.

47 Facia – removal and refitting

1   Remove the instrument panel and the radio cassette player as described in Chapter 12.
2   Release the turnbuckles and remove the trim panel under the facia on the driver's side. Remove the additional panel over the clutch, brake and accelerator pedals (photo).
3   Release the heater outer cable retaining clips on the lower right-hand side of the heater, and slip the inner cable ends off the lever studs (photo).
4   Pull off the control knobs on the heater control switches (photo).
5   Undo the two nuts and two bolts securing the steering column clamp and mounting bracket under the facia. Remove the clamp and lower the column.
6   Release the retaining button and withdraw the triangular-shaped trim panels at the base of the lower facia (photo).
7   Undo the retaining screw on each side now exposed, securing the lower facia side braces to the support bracket (photo).
8   Using a screwdriver, release the radio mounting plate side retainers

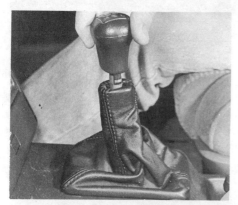

46.1 Unscrew the gear lever knob

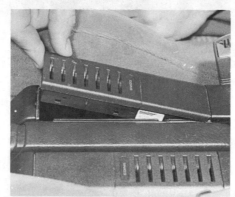

46.3 Prise up the coin trays

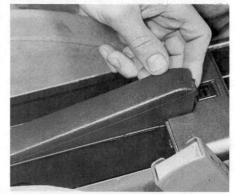

46.4 Lift up the handbrake lever cover trim at the rear

46.5 Console left-hand retaining bolt (arrowed)

46.6A Remove the rear ashtray ...

46.6B ... and undo the two rear screws

and remove the mounting plate (photos).

9 Undo the two screws at the base of the oddments tray below the digital clock (photo).

10 Withdraw the clock and oddments tray housing from the lower facia, and disconnect the clock wiring multi-plug (photo).

11 Undo the two upper screws securing the lower facia, and withdraw the lower facia from its location (photos).

12 Disconnect the wiring multi-plug at the rear (photo), and remove the lower facia from the car.

13 Undo the screw at each end of the cross-brace under the facia on the driver's side (photo).

14 Undo the bolt at each lower end of the facia (photo).

15 Undo the two bolts on the front support plate at the base of the console (photo).

16 Lift up the cover plate on the console top, at the centre below the windscreen (photo), and undo the bolt below the plate (photo).

17 Prise out the trim caps at each side of the console, adjacent to the door apertures, and undo the bolt behind (photos).

18 With the help of an assistant, lift the console from its location and withdraw it into the passenger compartment.

19 Disconnect the wiring multi-plug at the inertia switch, and at the fusebox, and disconnect the two main loom multi-plugs (photos).

20 With all the wiring disconnected, remove the facia from the car (photo).

21 Refitting is the reverse sequence to removal. When connecting the heater cables, adjust the position of the outer cables in their retaining clips so as to give full travel of the heater levers, consistent with full travel of the control levers.

46.7 Undo the two screws at the base of the cassette rack

46.8A Apply the handbrake fully

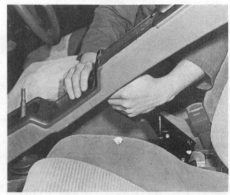
46.8B ... and lift the console over the handbrake

47.2 Remove the trim panel under the facia

47.3 Release the heater cables at the heater (arrowed)

47.4 Pull off the heater knobs

47.6 Withdraw the trim panel at the base of the lower facia

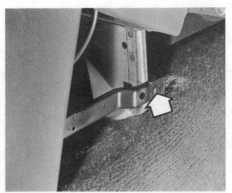
47.7 Undo the side brace retaining screws (arrowed)

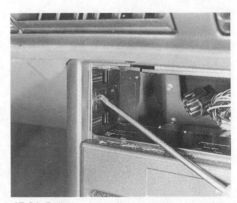
47.8A Release the radio mounting plate retainers ...

47.8B ... and remove the mounting plate

47.9 Undo the screws in the oddments tray

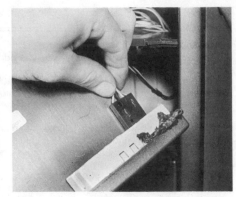

47.10 Disconnect the clock wiring multi-plug

47.11A Undo the lower facia upper screws ...

47.11B ... and remove the lower facia

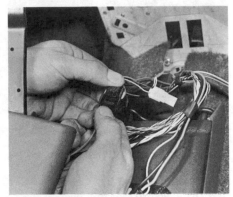

47.12 Disconnect the lower facia multi-plug

47.13 Undo the cross-brace screws

47.14 Undo the bolt at the facia lower end

47.15 Undo the front support plate bolts (arrowed)

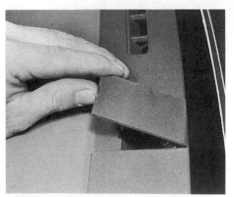

47.16A Lift up the centre cover plate ...

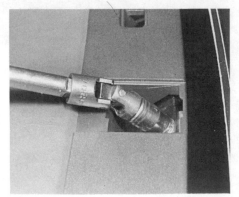

47.16B ... and undo the retaining bolt

47.17A Prise out the trim caps ...

47.17B ... and undo the bolts in the door apertures

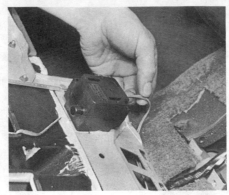

47.19A Disconnect the inertia switch wiring ...

47.17B ... the fusebox multi-plug ...

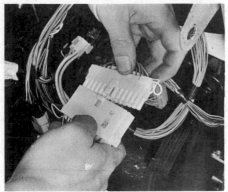

47.19C ... the large main wiring multi-plug

47.19D ... and the smaller main wiring multi-plug

47.20 Withdraw the facia with the help of an assistant

48 Heater blower motor and housing assembly – removal and refitting

1   Disconnect the battery negative terminal. (Refer to Chapter 12, Section 1, before doing this).
2   Remove the trim panel under the facia on the passenger's side.
3   Open the glovebox, undo the two screws securing the glovebox bar, and remove the glovebox.
4   Disconnect the air duct from the side of the unit, and recover the seals.
5   Release the screw cap and undo the facia retaining bolt at the extreme end, adjacent to the door aperture.
6   Disconnect the blower motor wiring multi-plug (photo).
7   Disconnect the vacuum hose at the solenoid (photo).
8   Undo the two upper bolts and one lower nut securing the heater housing assembly in position, and remove the unit from under the facia (photos).

9   Refitting is the reverse sequence to removal.

49 Heater blower motor – removal and refitting

1   Remove the assembly from the car as described in Section 48.
2   Extract the clips securing the two halves of the housing assembly, and lift off the upper half.
3   Remove the separator plate.
4   Undo the nut and remove the fan from the motor.
5   Disconnect the cooling hose and wiring multi-plug from the side of the motor.
6   Undo the motor retaining nuts, withdraw the motor and collect the gasket.
7   Refitting is the reverse sequence to removal.

48.6 Blower motor wiring multi-plug

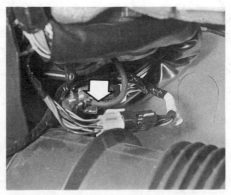

48.7 Solenoid vacuum hose (arrowed)

48.8A Undo the two upper bolts (arrowed) ...

48.8B ... and lower nut (arrowed)

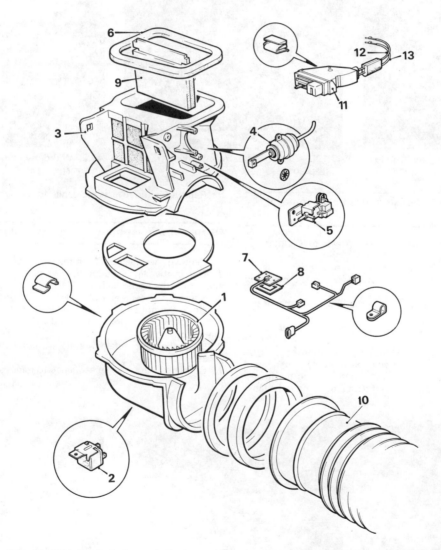

Fig. 11.19 Exploded view of the heater blower motor housing assembly (Sec 48)

1 Fan	5 Vacuum solenoid	8 Gasket	11 Control assembly
2 Relay	6 Seal	9 Air flap	12 Distribution cable
3 Air box	7 Harness	10 Air duct	13 Temperature cable
4 Vacuum actuator			

50 Heater vacuum servo unit – removal and refitting

1 Disconnect the battery negative terminal. (Refer to Chapter 12, Section 1, before doing this).
2 Remove the trim panel under the facia on the passenger's side.
3 Open the glovebox, undo the two screws securing the glovebox bar, and remove the glovebox.
4 Disconnect the air duct from the side of the heater blower assembly, and recover the two seals.
5 Disconnect the vacuum hose at the servo unit.
6 Extract the retaining spire clip, and release the servo arm from the heater lever.
7 Undo the two screws and remove the servo from the heater assembly.
8 Refitting is the reverse sequence to removal.

51 Heater solenoid valve – removal and refitting

1 Disconnect the battery negative terminal. (Refer to Chapter 12, Section 1, before doing this).
2 Remove the trim panel under the facia on the passenger's side.
3 Open the glovebox, undo the two screws securing the glovebox bar, and remove the glovebox.
4 Disconnect the air duct from the side of the heater blower assembly, and recover the two seals.
5 Disconnect the vacuum hose at the solenoid valve.
6 Disconnect the solenoid wiring multi-plug.
7 Undo the retaining screw and remove the solenoid from the car.
8 Refitting is the reverse sequence to removal.

52 Heater control unit and cables – removal and refitting

1 Remove the instrument cowl as described in Chapter 12.
2 Remove the trim panel under the facia on the driver's side.
3 Extract the outer cable retaining clips, and slip the cable ends off the heater levers.
4 Withdraw the control unit and cables from the facia.
5 Release the two inner and outer cables from the control unit.
6 Refitting is the reverse sequence to removal. When connecting the heater cables, adjust the position of the outer cables in their retaining clips so as to give full travel of the heater levers, consistent with full travel of the control levers.

53 Heater matrix – removal and refitting

1 Remove the facia as described in Section 47.
2 Drain the cooling system as described in Chapter 2.
3 From within the engine compartment, disconnect the heater hoses at the matrix pipe stubs.

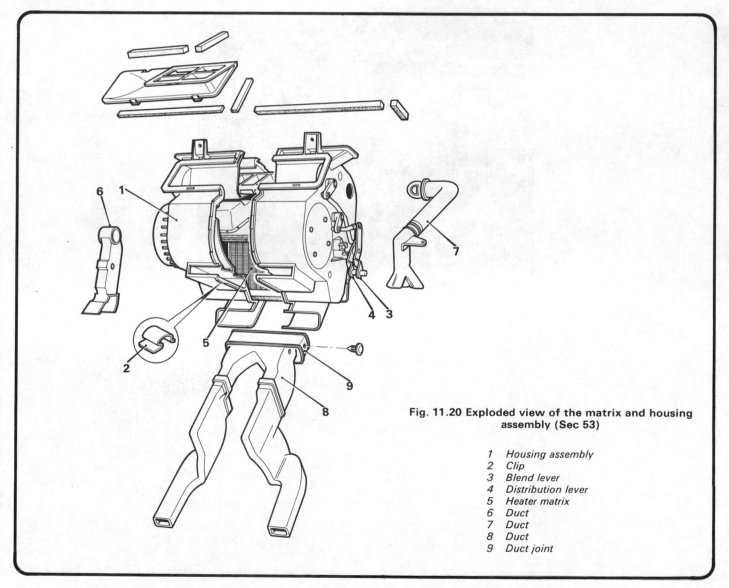

Fig. 11.20 Exploded view of the matrix and housing assembly (Sec 53)

1 Housing assembly
2 Clip
3 Blend lever
4 Distribution lever
5 Heater matrix
6 Duct
7 Duct
8 Duct
9 Duct joint

4   Remove the duct between the heater blower motor assembly and the matrix housing. Collect the two seals.
5   Extract the retaining stud from the driver's side footwell duct and remove the duct.
6   Extract the two studs securing the rear compartment duct to the matrix casing, and slide the duct rearwards.
7   Remove the two retaining clips at the base of the matrix housing.
8   Undo the two upper retaining bolts (photo) and remove the matrix housing from the car.
9   Remove the seal from the top of the housing.
10 Undo the screw and remove the left-hand duct.
11 Release the clips around the upper face aperture, and remove the face panel.
12 Release the clips securing the two halves of the matrix housing, and separate the housing.
13 Remove the matrix
14 Refitting is the reverse sequence to removal.

54 Air conditioning system – precautions and maintenance

1   Air conditioning is available as optional equipment on certain models covered by this manual. Due to the complexity of the system, the need for special equipment to carry out virtually all operations, and the dangers involved in any service or repair procedure, work on the air conditioning system components is considered beyond the scope of this manual. If, however, it is necessary to remove or disconnect a component as part of some other maintenance or repair procedure, observe the following.
2   Never disconnect any part of the air conditioner refrigerant circuit unless the system has been discharged by a dealer or qualified refrigerant engineer.
3   Where the compressor or condenser obstructs other mechanical operations, such as engine removal, it is permissible to unbolt their mountings and move them to the limit of their flexible hose deflection, but **not** to disconnect the hoses. If there is still insufficient room to carry out the required work, then the system must be discharged before disconnecting and removing the assemblies.
4   The system will, of course, have to be recharged on completion.
5   Regularly check the condenser for clogging with flies or dirt. Hose clean with water or compressed air.
6   Check the drivebelt condition, and if necessary adjust, or have it adjusted by a Rover dealer. The belt adjustment procedure requires a special tool to check the deflection, but the procedure is similar to that described in Chapter 12 for the alternator drivebelt.

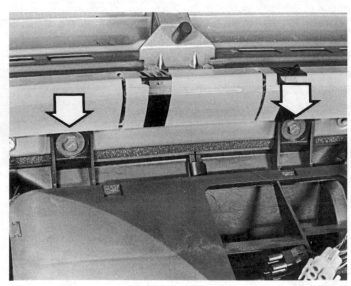

53.8 Matrix housing upper retaining bolts (arrowed)

Chapter 12 Electrical system

For modifications, and information applicable to later models, see Supplement at end of manual

Contents

Specifications

System type	12 volt, negative earth
Battery	
Type	Unipart 'sealed for life'
Capacity	54 amp-hour
Performance – cold start current (amps)/reserve capacity (minutes) ..	480/90
Alternator	
Type	Lucas A127/65
Maximum output	65 amps
Brush length:	
New	20.0 mm (0.8 in)
Minimum	10.0 mm (0.4 in)
Starter motor	
Type	Lucas M78R
Power	1.0 or 1.4 kW
Wiper blades	Champion X-5103

Bulbs

	Wattage
Headlamp dipped beam	60/55
Headlamp main beam	55
Sidelamps	5
Direction indicators	21
Side repeater lamps	5
Stop/tail lamps	21/5
Reversing lamps	21
Rear foglamp	21
Number plate lamps	5
Engine compartment lamp	5
Interior courtesy lamps	10
Map reading and courtesy lamps	4
Footwell and glovebox illumination lamps	5
Luggage compartment lamp	10
Instrument panel illumination and warning lamps	1.2
Ignition warning lamp	2
Switch illumination bulbs	0.36
Heater control illumination bulbs	0.36 and 1.2

Torque wrench settings

	Nm	lbf ft
Alternator pivot bolt	25	18
Alternator adjustment bracket bolts	12	9
Alternator drivebelt idler pulley nut	45	33
Alternator pulley nut	47	35
Starter motor retaining bolts:		
Manual gearbox	85	63
Automatic transmission	45	33

1 General description

The electrical system is of the 12 volt negative earth type, and consists of a 12 volt battery, alternator, starter motor and related electrical accessories, components and wiring. The battery is of the maintenance-free 'sealed for life' type, and is charged by an alternator which is belt-driven from the crankshaft pulley. The starter motor is of the pre-engaged type, incorporating an integral solenoid. On starting, the solenoid moves the drive pinion into engagement with the flywheel or driveplate ring gear before the starter motor is energised. Once the engine has started, a one-way clutch prevents the motor armature being driven by the engine until the pinion disengages from the ring gear.

Note: *On cars equipped with single-point fuel injection, the idle mixture settings stored in the memory of the fuel system electronic control unit will be lost whenever the battery is disconnected. When the battery is reconnected, the control unit will adopt a set of nominal parameters which will allow the engine to run, but the mixture setting will be outside the manufacturer's specification. Should the engine performance be unsatisfactory, the control unit can be calibrated as a temporary measure using the procedure described in Chapter 3, Section 13, until such time as the setting can be accurately adjusted by a dealer.*

2 Electrical system – precautions

1 It is necessary to take extra care when working on the electrical system to avoid damage to semi-conductor devices (diodes and transistors), and to avoid the risk of personal injury. In addition to the precautions given in *Safety first!* at the beginning of this manual, observe the following when working on the system.

2 *Always remove rings, watches, etc before working on the electrical system.* Even with the battery disconnected, capacitive discharge could occur if a component live terminal is earthed through a metal object. This could cause a shock or nasty burn.

3 *Do not reverse the battery connections.* Components such as the alternator, fuel and ignition control units, or any other having semi-conductor circuitry could be irreparably damaged.

4 If the engine is being started using jump leads and a slave battery, connect the batteries *positive to positive* and *negative to negative*. This also applies when connecting a battery charger.

5 Never disconnect the battery terminals, any electrical wiring or any test instruments, when the engine is running.

6 Never use an ohmmeter of the type incorporating a hand-cranked generator for circuit or continuity testing.

3 Maintenance and inspection

1 At regular intervals, (see *Routine maintenance*) carry out the following maintenance and inspection operations on the electrical system components.

2 Check the operation of all the electrical equipment, ie wipers, washers, lights, direction indicators, horn etc. Refer to the appropriate Sections of this Chapter if any of the components are found to be inoperative.

3 Visually check all accessible wiring connectors, harnesses and retaining clips for security, or signs of chafing or damage. Rectify any problems encountered.

4 Check the alternator drivebelt for cracks, fraying or damage. Renew the belt if worn, or if satisfactory, check and adjust the belt tension as described in Section 6.

5 Check the condition of the wiper blades, and if they show signs of deterioration or fail to clean the screen effectively, renew them as described in Section 37.

6 Check the operation of the windscreen, tailgate and headlamp washers, as applicable and adjust the windscreen or tailgate washers using a pin if necessary. Top up the screen washer reservoir (photo) and check the condition and security of the pump wires and water pipes.

7 Check the battery terminals and if there is any sign of corrosion, disconnect and clean them thoroughly. Smear the terminals and battery posts with petroleum jelly before refitting the plastic covers. If there is any corrosion on the battery tray, remove the battery, clean the deposits away and treat the affected metal with an anti-rust preparation. Repaint the tray in the original colour after treatment.

8 It is advisable to have the headlamp aim adjusted using optical beam setting equipment.

9 When carrying out a road test, check the operation of all the instruments and warning lights, and the various electrical accessories as applicable.

4 Battery – removal and refitting

Note: *Refer to Section 1 before proceeding.*

1 The 'sealed for life' battery is located on the left-hand side of the engine compartment.

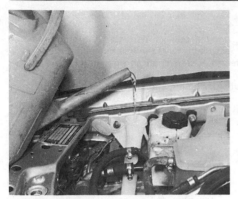
3.6 Topping-up the washer reservoir

4.3 Lift off the plastic cover and disconnect the battery positive terminal

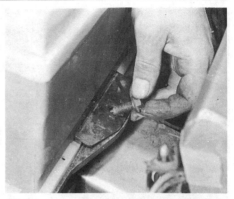
4.4 Removing the battery clamp retaining bolt

2 Slacken the negative (–) terminal clamp bolt and lift the terminal off the battery post.
3 Lift the plastic cover from the positive (+) terminal, slacken the clamp bolt and lift the terminal off the battery post (photo).
4 Undo the retaining bolt and remove the battery clamp plate (photo).
5 Lift the battery out of its tray and remove it from the car.
6 If required, the battery tray can be removed after undoing the three retaining bolts.
7 Refitting is the reverse sequence to removal, but make sure that the positive lead is connected first and the negative lead last. Do not overtighten the clamp bolts.

5 Battery charging

1 In winter, when a heavy demand is placed on the battery, such as when starting from cold and using more electrical equipment, it may be necessary to have the battery fully charged from an external source.
2 Charging should be done overnight, with the battery removed from the car, and at a 'trickle' rate of 1 to 1.5 amps. Owing to the design of certain maintenance-free batteries, rapid or boost charging is not recommended. If in any doubt about the suitability of certain types of charging equipment, consult a dealer or automotive electrical specialist.
3 The terminals of the battery and the leads of the charger must be connected positive to positive and negative to negative.
4 Battery charging must be carried out in a well-ventilated area. Explosive gases are given off as the battery is charged, and every precaution must be taken to avoid naked flames and sparks.

6 Alternator drivebelt – removal, refitting and adjustment

Note: *Accurate adjustment of the drivebelt can only be achieved with a Rover belt tensioning tool, and ideally this operation should be carried out by a dealer. However, if a new belt is to be fitted, or if the existing tension is extremely slack, a rough approximation as a temporary measure can be achieved using the following procedure.*

Cars with a rear-mounted power steering pump

1 Disconnect the battery negative terminal. (Refer to Section 1 before doing this).
2 Slacken the two alternator adjustment bracket bolts and the alternator pivot bolt and nut (photos).
3 Undo the timing belt lower cover retaining bolt below the drivebelt run.
4 Push the alternator in towards the engine and slip the drivebelt off the alternator pulley (photo).
5 Lift the lower edge of the timing belt cover and remove the belt from the crankshaft pulley.
6 Check the drivebelt for signs of fraying, splitting of the internal ribs, a build-up of rubber within the rib grooves, oil contamination, or general deterioration. Renew the belt if any of these conditions are evident.
7 Fit the new drivebelt over the pulleys, then lever the alternator away from the engine until the drivebelt is moderately tight. The alternator must only be levered with care at the drive end bracket. Hold the alternator in this position and tighten the adjustment bracket bolts.
8 Refit the timing belt lower cover bolt.
9 Check that it is just possible to twist the belt by hand through 90° at a point midway between the two pulleys. If necessary, slacken the adjustment bracket bolts and re-adjust the belt tension. When the tension is correct, tighten the pivot bolt and nut.
10 Reconnect the battery, then run the engine at a fast idle for five minutes. Switch off, recheck the tension and re-adjust if necessary.

Cars with a front-mounted power steering pump

11 Disconnect the battery negative terminal. (Refer to Section 1 before doing this).
12 Jack up the front of the car and support it on axle stands.
13 Slacken the nut in the centre of the idler pulley, then turn the adjuster bolt anti-clockwise until all tension is removed from the belt (photo).
14 Slip the belt off the crankshaft, alternator, power steering pump and idler pulleys, and remove it from under the car.
15 Check the drivebelt for signs of fraying, splitting of the internal ribs, a build-up of rubber within the rib grooves, oil contamination, or

6.2A Alternator adjustment bracket bolts (arrowed) ...

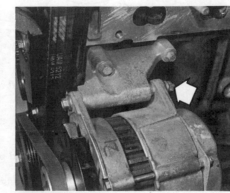
6.2B ... and pivot bolt retaining nut (arrowed)

6.4 Slip the drivebelt off the alternator pulley

6.13 Drivebelt adjuster bolt (arrowed) on cars with a front-mounted power steering pump

general deterioration. Renew the belt if any of these conditions are evident.
16 Fit a new drivebelt over the pulleys, then turn the adjuster bolt clockwise until it is just possible to twist the belt by hand through 90° at a point midway between the crankshaft and power steering pump pulleys.
17 Tighten the idler pulley retaining nut and lower the car to the ground.
18 Reconnect the battery, then run the engine for five minutes at a fast idle. Switch off, recheck the tension and repeat the adjustment procedure if necessary.

7   Alternator – removal and refitting

1   Remove the drivebelt as described in Section 6.
2   Undo the two nuts and remove the alternator rear cover.
3   Disconnect the electrical leads at the rear of the alternator (photo).
4   On cars with a rear-mounted power steering pump, remove the previously-slackened pivot bolt and adjustment arm bolt, then withdraw the alternator from the engine.
5   On cars with a front-mounted power steering pump, undo the alternator upper and lower mounting bolts, and remove the unit from the engine.
6   Refitting is the reverse sequence to removal, but adjust the drivebelt, as described in Section 6, before tightening the adjustment and mounting bolts.

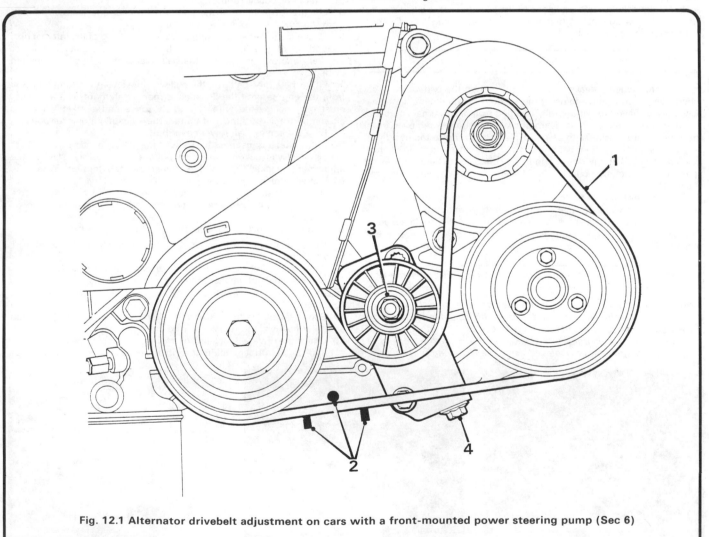

Fig. 12.1 Alternator drivebelt adjustment on cars with a front-mounted power steering pump (Sec 6)

1   Drivebelt   2   Checking gauge – Rover   3   Idler pulley retaining nut   4   Adjuster bolt
                        special tool

7.3 Disconnect the alternator electrical leads (arrowed)

8 Alternator – fault tracing and rectification

Due to the specialist knowledge and equipment required to test or repair an alternator, it is recommended that, if the performance is suspect, the car be taken to an automobile electrician who will have the facilities for such work. Because of this recommendation, information is limited to the inspection and renewal of the brushes and renewal of the voltage regulator. Should the alternator not charge, or the system be suspect, the following points should be checked before seeking further assistance:

(a) *Check the drivebelt condition and tension*
(b) *Ensure that the battery is fully charged*
(c) *Check the ignition warning light bulb, and renew it if blown*

9 Alternator brushes and regulator – removal, inspection and refitting

1 Remove the alternator as described in Section 7.
2 Undo the three small screws securing the regulator and brushbox assembly to the rear of the alternator (photo).
3 Tip the assembly upwards at the edge, and withdraw it from its location. Disconnect the wiring terminal and remove the regulator and brushbox from the alternator (photos).
4 Measure the brush length (photo) and renew the brushbox and

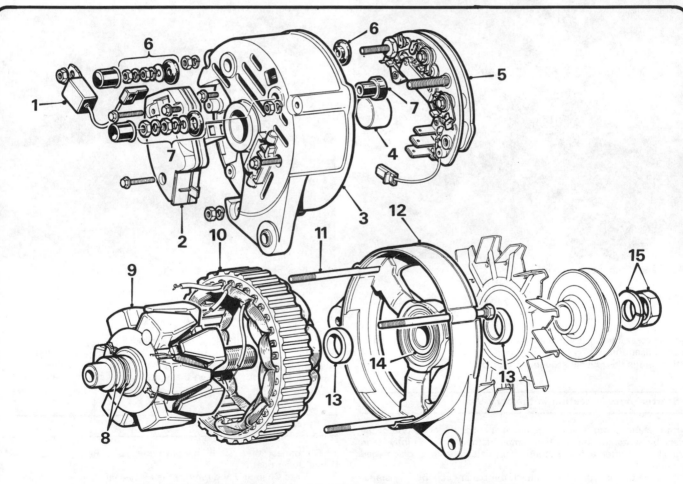

Fig. 12.2 Exploded view of the Lucas A127/65 alternator (Sec 9)

1	Suppression capacitor	6	Phase terminal attachments	9	Rotor assembly	13	Spacers
2	Regulator and brushbox		and insulating washers	10	Stator	14	Drive end bearing
3	Slip ring end bracket	7	Main terminal attachments	11	Through-bolts	15	Pulley retaining nut and
4	Slip ring end bearing		and insulating washers	12	Drive end bracket		washer
5	Rectifier pack	8	Slip rings				

9.2 Undo the regulator and brushbox retaining screws

9.3A Withdraw the regulator and brushbox ...

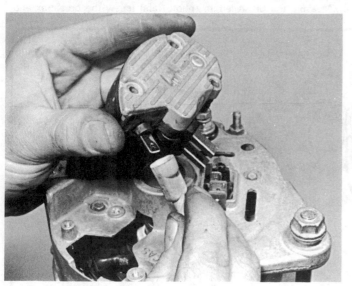

9.3B ... and disconnect the wiring

9.4 Checking alternator brush length

regulator assembly if the brushes are worn below the figure given in the Specifications.
5   Refitting is the reverse sequence to removal.

10 Starter motor – testing in the car

1   If the starter motor fails to operate, first check the condition of the battery by switching on the headlamps. If they glow brightly, then gradually dim after a few seconds, the battery is in a discharged condition.
2   If the battery is satisfactory, check the battery clamps, the starter motor main terminal and the engine earth cable for security. Check the terminal connections on the starter solenoid, located on top of the starter motor, for tightness.
3   If the starter still fails to turn, use a voltmeter, or 12 volt test lamp and leads, to ensure that there is battery voltage at the solenoid main terminal (containing the cable from the battery positive terminal).
4   With the ignition switched on and the ignition key in position III, check that voltage is reaching the solenoid terminal with the Lucar

connector, and also the starter main terminal.
5   If there is no voltage reaching the Lucar connector, there is a wiring, relay or ignition switch fault. If voltage is available, but the starter does not operate, then the starter or solenoid is likely to be at fault.

11 Starter motor – removal and refitting

1   Disconnect the battery negative terminal. (Refer to Section 1 before doing this).
2   Refer to Chapter 3 and remove the air cleaner air intake trunking as necessary to provide access to the starter motor.
3   Disconnect the main feed cable and the Lucar spade connector at the solenoid.
4   Support the weight of the engine/transmission with a jack, then unscrew and remove the starter motor retaining bolts. Withdraw the starter motor from the transmission (photo).
5   Refitting is the reverse sequence to removal, but tighten the retaining bolts to the specified torque.

11.4 Removing the starter motor

12 Starter motor – overhaul

1   Remove the starter motor from the car as described in Section 11.
2   Undo the two nuts and withdraw the commutator end bracket (photo).
3   At the rear of the solenoid, unscrew the nut and lift away the lead from the solenoid 'STA' terminal.
4   Release the rubber grommet from the side of the yoke (photo) and withdraw the brush holder assembly complete with brushes.
5   Withdraw the yoke from the drive end bracket and armature (photo).
6   Undo the two screws and remove the solenoid body from the drive end bracket (photo).
7   Disengage the solenoid plunger from the engaging lever and remove the plunger (photo).
8   Lift the armature out of the reduction gearbox, and remove it from the drive end bracket (photo). Recover the armature drivegear from the gearbox (photo).
9   Release the engaging lever pivot and grommet from the drive end bracket, then withdraw the reduction gearbox, engaging lever and drive assembly from the drive end bracket.
10 Using a suitable tubular drift, tap the thrust collar on the end of the pinion shaft towards the pinion, to expose the jump ring. Prise the

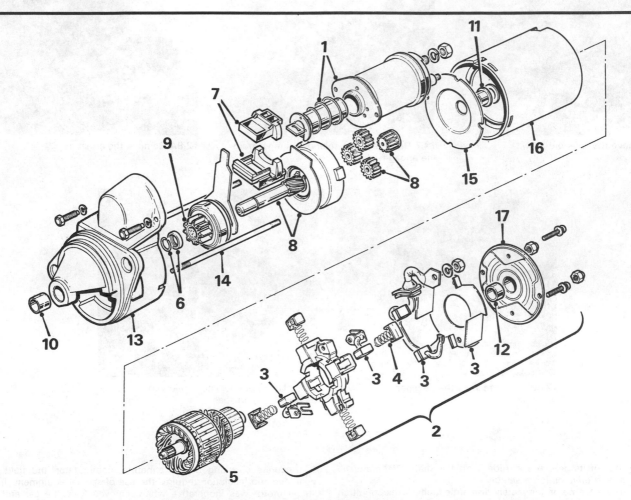

Fig. 12.3 Exploded view of the Lucas M78R starter motor (Sec 12)

1 Solenoid and plunger	6 Jump ring and thrust collar	9 Drive pinion assembly
2 Commutator end bracket and brush holder assembly	7 Engaging lever pivot and grommet	10 Drive end bracket bush
3 Brushes	8 Pinion shaft and reduction gears	11 Intermediate bracket bush
4 Brush springs		12 Commutator end bracket bush
5 Armature		

13 Drive end bracket	
14 Through-bolts	
15 Intermediate bracket	
16 Field coil yoke	
17 Commutator end bracket	

12.2 Withdraw the commutator end bracket

12.4 Release the rubber grommet (arrowed) and remove the brush holder

12.5 Withdraw the yoke

12.6 Remove the solenoid body

12.7 Disengage the solenoid plunger from the engaging lever

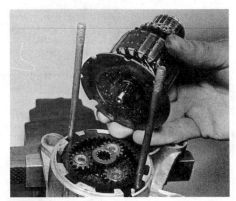

12.8A Remove the armature ...

12.8B ... and recover the drivegear

12.15 Using pointed-nose pliers to compress the brushes

jump ring out of its groove and slide it off the shaft. Withdraw the thrust collar and drive pinion assembly.

11 With the starter motor completely dismantled, check the condition of the brushes and the tension of the brush springs. If any appear excessively worn, or if the tension of any of the springs is suspect, renew the brush holder assembly.

12 Check the armature shaft for distortion, and examine the commutator for excessive wear or burns. If necessary, the commutator may be skimmed in a lathe and then polished with fine glass paper.

13 Check the drive pinion assembly, drive end housing, reduction gears, engaging lever and solenoid for wear or damage. Make sure that the drive pinion one-way clutch permits movement of the pinion in one direction only and renew the complete assembly, if necessary.

14 Accurate checking of the armature, commutator and field coil windings and insulation requires the use of special equipment. If the starter motor was inoperative when removed from the car and the previous checks have not highlighted the problem, then it can be assumed that there is a continuity or insulation fault, and the unit should be renewed.

15 If the starter is in a satisfactory condition, or if a fault has been traced and rectified, the unit can be reassembled using the reverse of the dismantling sequence. When refitting the brush holder assembly, carefully compress the brushes one at a time using pointed-nose pliers, tip the holder slightly and ease the brushes over the commutator (photo).

13 Fuses and relays – general

1   Two fuseboxes are used on Rover 820 models. One is located inside the car under the facia on the driver's side, and the other is located on the left-hand side of the engine compartment. The main vehicle system relays are located on a relay panel behind the interior fusebox, and also in the engine compartment fuse and relay box.

Interior fusebox

2   To gain access to the fuses, release the two turnbuckles at the base of the trim panel beneath the steering column, and lift away the panel (photo). The fuse locations, current rating and circuits protected are shown on a label attached to the inside of the panel (photo). Each fuse is also colour-coded, and has its rating stamped on it.

3   To remove a fuse from its location, withdraw the removal tool from the centre of the fusebox, push the tool over the fuse to be removed and pull out the fuse (photos). Refit the fuse by pressing it firmly into position. Spare fuses are located in a vertical row on the right-hand side of the fusebox.

4   Always renew the fuse with one of an identical rating. Never renew a fuse more than once without finding the source of the trouble.

5   To gain access to the relays behind the fusebox, undo the two fusebox retaining bolts, one at each end, and ease the unit away from its location. For greater access, mark the various wiring multi-plugs to avoid confusion when refitting, then disconnect them and remove the fusebox completely.

6   The fuse and relay locations, and circuits protected are shown in Figs. 12.4 and 12.5.

7   The relays can be removed by simply pulling them from their respective locations. If a system controlled by a relay becomes inoperative, and the relay is suspect, operate the system and if the relay is functioning it should be possible to hear it click as it is energised. If this is the case, the fault lies with the components of the system. If the relay is not being energised, then the relay is either not receiving a main supply voltage, a switching voltage, or the relay itself is faulty.

Engine compartment fuse and relay box

8   The engine compartment fuse and relay box contains additional fuses, some of the vehicle system relays, and the main wiring loom fusible links.

9   To gain access, press the upper edge of the retaining catch on the fuse and relay box cover, lift the cover at the front and disengage the rear tags (photo). A symbol identifying the function of each fuse is marked on the cover.

10   The fuses and relays can be renewed in the same way as for the interior fusebox described previously. The fuse removal tool, together with the spare fuses, is located at the front of the box. On certain models, additional fuses and relays are located on the outside edge of the box, with the fuses under a protective cover. Lift off the cover to renew each individual fuse (photo).

11   To gain access to the wiring loom fusible links, lift off the protective cover on the right-hand side of the fuse and relay box (photo). A blown fusible link indicates a serious wiring or system fault, which must be diagnosed before renewing it.

12   The fuse, relay, and fusible link locations and circuits protected are shown in Figs. 12.6 and 12.7.

14 Direction indicator and hazard flasher system – general

1   The combined direction indicator and hazard flasher unit is located adjacent to the interior fusebox. To remove the unit, release the turnbuckles and lift away the trim panel below the steering column. Pull the flasher unit from its mounting bracket and disconnect the wiring plug. Fit the new unit, then replace the trim cover.

2   Should the flashers become faulty in operation, check the bulbs for security, and make sure that the contact surfaces are not corroded. If one bulb blows, or is making a poor connection due to corrosion, the system will not flash on that side of the car.

3   If the flasher unit operates in one direction and not the other, the fault is likely to be in the bulbs or wiring to the bulbs. If the system will

13.2A Lift away the trim panel for access to the fusebox ...

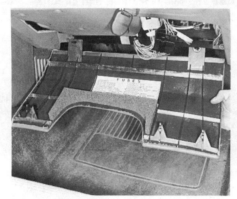

13.2B ... noting the fuse identification on the rear of the panel

13.3A Fuse removal tool location (arrowed)

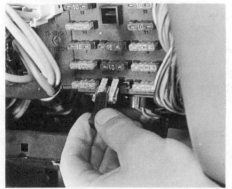

13.3B Using the tool to remove a fuse

13.9 Removing the engine compartment fuse and relay box cover

13.10 Additional fuse located under a cover on the outside of the fuse and relay box

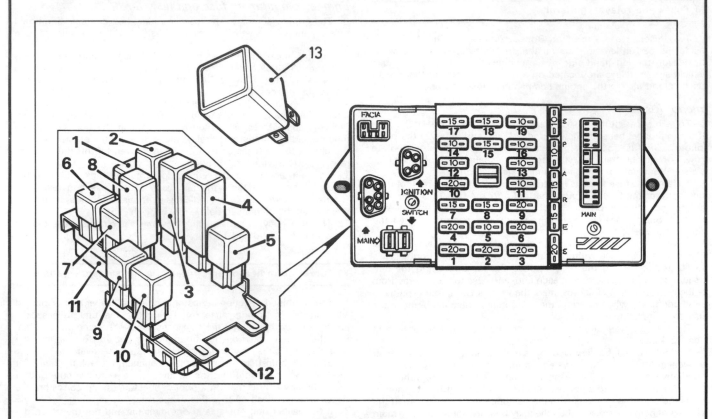

Fig. 12.4 Interior fusebox fuse and relay locations and circuits – pre-1988 models (Sec 13)

Note: *Some fuse and relay locations and circuits may vary from the following, according to model and equipment fitted*

Fuses

Fuse No	Circuit protected
1	Sun roof relays
2	Driver's front window relay
3	Passenger's front window relay
4	Cigar lighter, footwell lamp
5	Interior lamps, radio cassette player, headlamp delay unit, clock
6	Central door locking ECU
7	RH side/tail and number plate lamps, foglamp relay
8	LH side/tail and number plate lamps, panel illumination lamps
9	LH rear window relay
10	RH rear window relay
11	ABS voltage protection relay
12	Fuel ECU (multi-point injection models)
13	Inertia switch, fuel pump, oil pressure relay (single-point injection models)
14	Reversing lamps, direction indicators, instruments, digital clock, interior lamp delay unit
15	Ignition ECU (multi-point injection models), fuel/ignition ECU (single-point injection models)
16	Lighting, cooling fan, headlamp changeover, window lift and air conditioning compressor clutch relays
17	Washer pump, wiper relay
18	Heater relays, air conditioning relays, door mirrors
19	Radio memory, mirror memory

Relays

Relay No	Circuit
1	Wiper motor
2	Rear screen demister timer
3	Headlamp changeover unit
4	Headlamp delay timer
5	Rear window motors
6	Sidelamps
7	Rear foglamps
8	Interior lamps
9	Fuel pump
10	Front window motors
11	Wiper motor delay
12	Central door locking ECU
13	Flasher unit

Additional relays
Window lift control – located in driver's door
Sunroof – located in sunroof frame
ABS over-voltage protection – located in luggage compartment

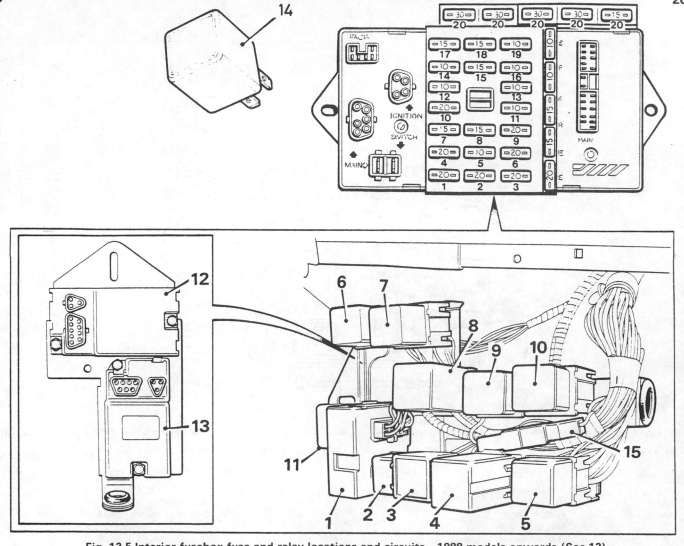

Fig. 12.5 Interior fusebox fuse and relay locations and circuits – 1988 models onwards (Sec 13)

Note: *Some fuse and relay locations and circuits may vary from the following according to model and equipment fitted*

Fuses

Fuse No	Circuit protected
1	Sunroof relays
2	Driver's front window relay
3	Passenger's front window relay
4	Cigar lighter, footwell lamp
5	Interior lamps, radio cassette player, headlamp delay unit, clock
6	Central door locking ECU
7	RH side/tail and number plate lamps, foglamp relay
8	LH side/tail and number plate lamps, panel illumination lamps
9	LH rear window relay
10	RH rear window relay
11	ABS voltage protection relay
12	Fuel ECU (multi-plug injection models)
13	Inertia switch, fuel pump, oil pressure relay (single-point injection models)
14	Reversing lamps, direction indicators, instruments, digital clock, interior lamp delay unit
15	Ignition ECU (multi-point injection models), fuel/ignition ECU (single-point injection models)
16	Lighting, cooling fan, headlamp changeover, window lift and air conditioning compressor clutch relays
17	Washer pump, wiper relay
18	Heater relays, air conditioning relays, door mirrors
19	Radio memory, mirror memory
20	Speaker power amplifier circuit

Relays

Relay No	Circuit
1	Rear wiper/washer timer (Fastback models)
2	Rear window motors
3	Headlamp changeover unit
4	Rear screen demister timer
5	Wiper motor
6	Front window motors
7	Cigar lighter
8	Interior lamp delay
9	Rear foglamps
10	Sidelamps
11	Front window motors
12	Windscreen wiper motor delay unit
13	Central door locking ECU
14	Flasher unit
15	Anti-run-on valve diode

Additional relays
Window lift control – located in driver's door
Sunroof – located in sunroof frame
ABS over-voltage protection – located in luggage compartment

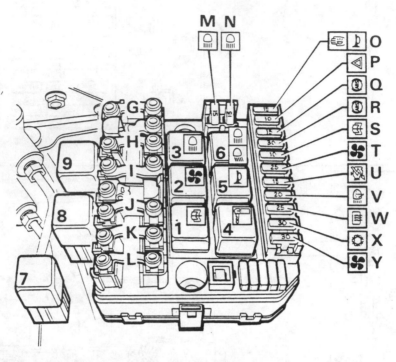

Fig. 12.6 Fuse and relay locations and circuits in the engine compartment fuse and relay box – pre-1988 models (Sec 13)

Note: Some fuse and relay locations and circuits may vary from the following according to model and equipment fitted

Fuses

Fuse	Circuit protected
M	RH headlamp
N	LH headlamp
O	Horn, stop-lamp relay
P	Hazard warning lamps
Q	ABS relay
R	ABS modulator
S	Fuel ECU (multi-point injection models)
T	Heater fan motor
U	Fuel/ignition ECU (single-point injection models)
V	Headlamp washer
W	Rear screen demister
X	Air conditioning fan/compressor clutch
Y	Radiator cooling fan

Fusible links	Circuit protected
G	Radio power amplifier
H	Ignition switch circuit
I	Alternator output
J	Window lift circuit
K	ABS braking system
L	Side and interior lamps, central locking

Relays

Relay No	Circuit
1	Cooling fan changeover, or inlet manifold heater (single-point injection models)
2	Radiator cooling fan
3	Lighting circuits
4	Starter solenoid
5	Horns
6	Headlamp main/dipped beams
7	Air conditioning changeover
8	Ignition/fuel ECU
9	Oil pressure transducer (single-point injection models)

Additional relays
Headlamp power wash timer – behind RH headlamp
Air conditioning compressor clutch – behind RH headlamp
ABS return pump – on top of ABS hydraulic modulator
ABS solenoid valve – on top of ABS hydraulic modulator

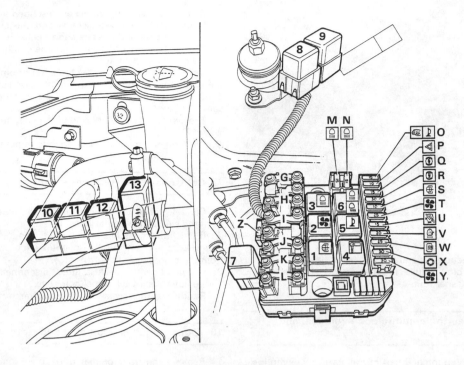

Fig. 12.7 Fuse and relay locations and circuits in the engine compartment fuse and relay box – 1988 models onwards (Sec 13)

Note: *Some fuse and relay locations and circuits may vary from the following according to model and equipment fitted*

Fuses

Fuse	Circuit protected
M	RH headlamp
N	LH headlamp
O	Horn, stop-lamp relay
P	Hazard warning lamps
Q	ABS relay
R	ABS modulator
S	Fuel ECU (multi-point injection models)
T	Heater fan motor
U	Fuel/ignition ECU (single-point injection models)
V	Headlamp washer
W	Rear screen demister
X	Air conditioning fan/compressor clutch
Y	Radiator cooling fan
Z	Headlamp dim/dip relay

Fusible links	Circuit protected
G	Radio power amplifier
H	Ignition switch circuit
I	Alternator output
J	Window lift circuit
K	ABS braking system
L	Side and interior lamps, central locking

Relays

Relay No	Circuit
1	Cooling fan changeover, or inlet manifold heater
2	Radiator cooling fan
3	Lighting circuits
4	Starter solenoid
5	Horns
6	Headlamp main/dipped beams
7	Air conditioning changeover
8	Inlet manifold heater (single-point injection models)
9	Ignition/fuel ECU

Additional relays

10 Fuel pump and oil pressure switch – RH headlamp
11 Not used on 820 models
12 Headlamp dim/dip – behind RH headlamp
13 Not used on 820 models

13.11 Lift off the protective cover for access to the fusible links

not flash in either direction, operate the hazard flashers. If these function, check for a blown fuse in position 14. If the fuse is satisfactory, renew the flasher unit.

15 Ignition switch/steering column lock – removal and refitting

The ignition switch is an integral part of the steering column lock, and removal and refitting procedures are given in Chapter 10.

16 Steering column switches – removal and refitting

1 Disconnect the battery negative terminal. (Refer to Section 1 before doing this).
2 Remove the steering wheel as described in Chapter 10.
3 Undo the three lower screws and the single upper screw, and remove the upper and lower steering column shrouds (photos).
4 Release the fibre optic lead from the bulbholder by carefully prising up the plastic tag (photo).
5 Depress the retainers at the top and bottom of the switch, then pull the switch out of the steering column boss (photos).
6 Disconnect the wiring multi-plug and remove the switch from the car.
7 The switch on the other side of the column is removed in the same way.
8 Refitting is the reverse sequence to removal.

17 Centre console switches – removal and refitting

1 Carefully prise up the coin holder or switch panel as applicable from the side of the centre console.
2 If individual switches are fitted, disconnect the wiring multi-plug, depress the lugs on the side of the switch and withdraw the switch from the coin holder panel (photo).
3 If a multi-switch pack is fitted, disconnect the wiring multi-plug and remove the switch panel complete.
4 Refitting is the reverse sequence to removal.

18 Door switches – removal and refitting

1 Remove the front or rear door inner trim panel as described in Chapter 11.

16.3A Undo the three lower screws ...

16.3B ... and single upper screw ...

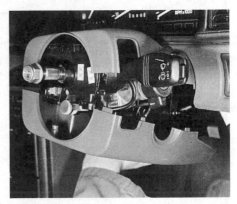

16.3C ... then lift off the steering column shrouds

16.4 Release the fibre optic lead from the bulbholder

16.5A Depress the top and bottom switch retainers ...

16.5B ... and remove the switch

2   Release the switch pack assemblies from the rear of the trim panel and carefully withdraw them. Note that the individual switches in the switch packs cannot be removed separately. If any are faulty, or if renewal of a switch is necessary for any reason, the complete switch pack must be obtained.
3   Refitting is the reverse sequence to removal.

19 Courtesy lamp door pillar switches – removal and refitting

1   Disconnect the battery negative terminal. (Refer to Section 1 before doing this).
2   Undo the retaining screw and withdraw the switch from the door pillar (photo).
3   Disconnect the wiring and remove the switch. Tie the wiring to the door striker plate while the switch is removed to prevent the wires dropping into the pillar.
4   Refitting is the reverse sequence to removal.

20 Instrument cowl and switch units – removal and refitting

1   Disconnect the battery negative terminal. (Refer to Section 1 before doing this).
2   Carefully prise out the cover plate at the extreme left-hand side of the cowl and undo the screw now exposed (photos).
3   Pull off the knobs on the heater and air conditioning controls as applicable (photo).
4   Undo the three screws securing the cowl to the facia above the instrument panel (photo).
5   Undo the two screws below the vent panel on the driver's side (photo) and the two screws below the heater control panel (photo).
6   Ease the cowl away from the facia slightly, and disconnect the switch panel and heater control wiring multi-plugs (photo).
7   Remove the cowl from the car.
8   If further dismantling is required, undo the four screws and remove the driver's vent panel.

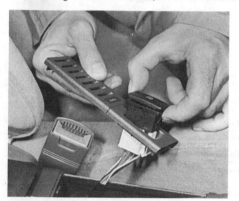
17.2 Centre console switch removal

19.2 Courtesy lamp door pillar switch location

20.2A Prise out the instrument cowl cover plate ...

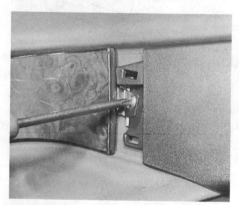
20.2B ... and undo the screw behind

20.3 Pull off the heater control knobs

20.4 Undo the three screws above the instrument panel (arrowed)

20.5A Undo the two screws below the driver's vent panel ...

20.5B ... and the two screws below the heater controls

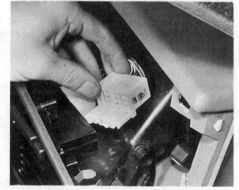
20.6 Withdraw the cowl and disconnect the multi-plugs

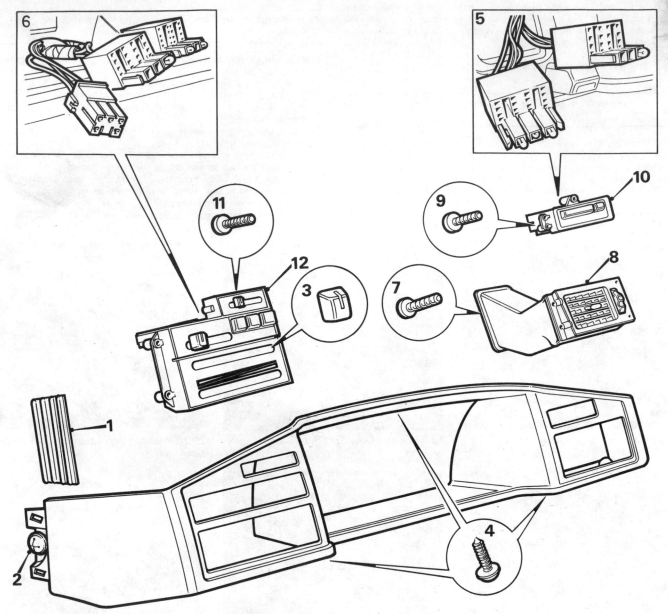

Fig. 12.8 Exploded view of the instrument cowl components (Sec 20)

1 Cover plate
2 Retaining screw
3 Air conditioning and heater
   control knobs
4 Retaining screw locations
5 Switch panel multi-plugs
   and bulbholders
6 Heater and air conditioning
   control multi-plugs and bulb
   holders
7 Vent panel retaining screws
8 Vent panel
9 Switch unit retaining screws
10 Switch unit
11 Heater and air conditioning
    control unit retaining screws
12 Heater and air conditioning
    control unit

9 Undo the three screws and remove the switch unit.
10 Undo the four screws and remove the heater and air conditioning control unit.
11 Refitting is the reverse sequence to removal.

21 Instrument panel – removal and refitting

1 Remove the upper and lower steering column shrouds as described in Section 16.
2 Remove the instrument cowl as described in Section 20.
3 Lower the steering column as far as it will go by means of the rake adjuster.
4 Undo the two screws at each end of the instrument panel (photo).
5 Ease the panel away from the facia, then disconnect the wiring multi-plugs and the earth lead Lucar connector (photos).

6 Remove the instrument panel from the car.
7 Refitting is the reverse sequence to removal.

22 Instrument panel and instruments – dismantling and reassembly

1 Remove the instrument panel from the car as described in Section 21.

Panel illumination and warning lamp bulbs

2 The bulbholders are secured to the rear of the instrument panel by a bayonet fitting, and are removed by turning the holders anti-clockwise (photo). Note that the illumination and warning lamp bulbs are renewed complete with their holders.
3 If a faulty bulb is not accessible, undo the five screws securing the

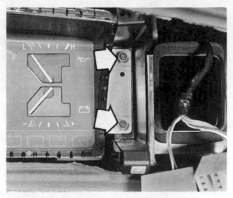

21.4 Instrument panel right-hand side retaining screws (arrowed)

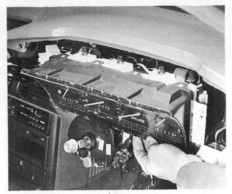

21.5A Withdraw the instrument panel ...

21.5B ... and disconnect the multi-plugs

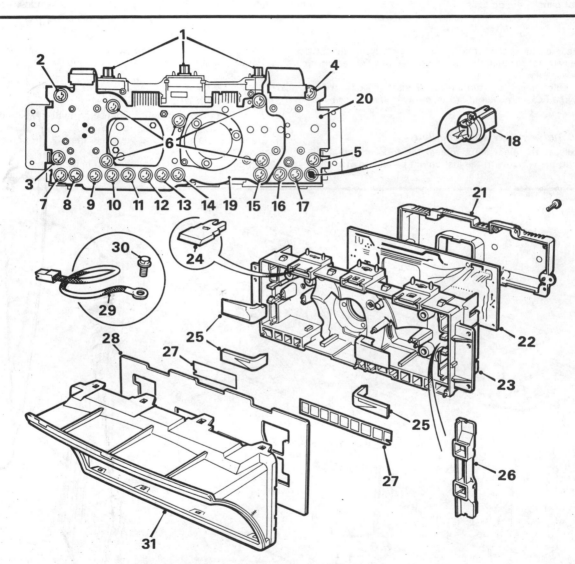

Fig. 12.9 Exploded view of the instrument panel (Sec 22)

1 Panel front illumination bulbs	7 RH direction indicator warning lamp bulb	15 Sidelamp warning lamp bulb
2 Low oil pressure warning lamp bulb	8 Spare bulb	16 Main beam warning lamp bulb
3 Ignition warning lamp bulb	9 Brake warning lamp bulb	17 Trailer direction indicators warning lamp bulb
4 High engine temperature warning lamp bulb	10 Spare bulb	18 LH direction indicator warning lamp bulb
5 Low fuel warning lamp bulb	11 ABS warning lamp bulb (where applicable)	19 Secondary printed circuit
6 Panel rear illumination bulb	12 Spare bulb	20 Main printed circuit
	13 Spare bulb	21 ECU cover
	14 Spare bulb	

22 ECU
23 Instrument panel body
24 Front illumination prism
25 Gauge illumination prisms
26 Side housing
27 Warning lamp colour strips
28 Faceplate
29 Earth strap
30 Screw
31 Cowl and faceplate

22.2 Instrument panel warning lamp bulb renewal

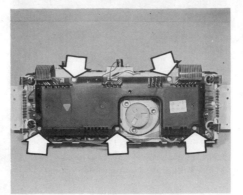

22.3 Instrument panel ECU retaining screws (arrowed)

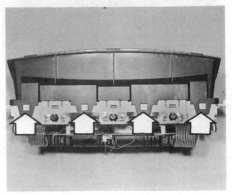

22.5 Instrument panel window upper retaining clips (arrowed)

ECU to the rear of the panel (photo), and carefully lift the ECU upwards. Take care not to strain the ribbon connectors. The remaining bulbs are now accessible.

4 Refit the bulbholders by turning clockwise to lock. Where applicable, lay the ECU in position and secure with the five screws.

Instrument panel window and faceplate

5 Carefully release the eight clips, four at the top and four at the bottom, securing the window to the instrument panel body (photo).

6 Withdraw the window and remove the faceplate.
7 Refitting is the reverse sequence to removal.

Electronic control unit (ECU)

8 Disconnect the two ribbon connector multi-plugs and the centre wiring multi-plug from the top of the ECU.
9 Undo the five screws and withdraw the ECU from the rear of the instrument panel.
10 Refitting is the reverse sequence to removal.

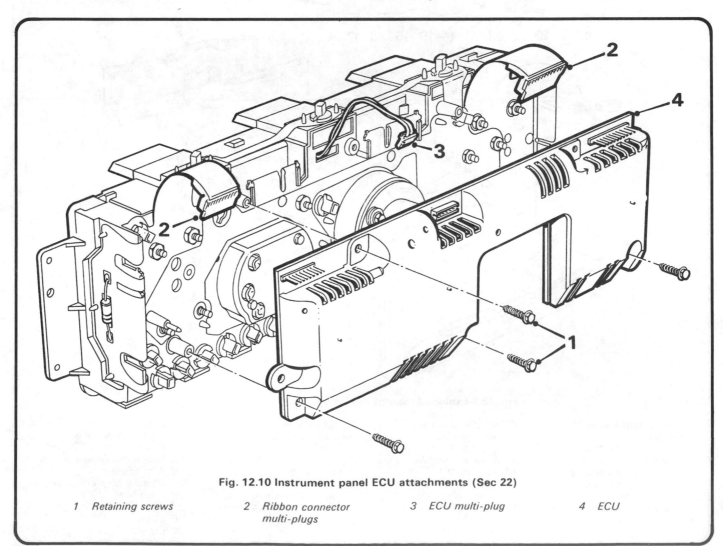

Fig. 12.10 Instrument panel ECU attachments (Sec 22)

1 Retaining screws
2 Ribbon connector multi-plugs
3 ECU multi-plug
4 ECU

Secondary printed circuit

11 Remove the ECU as described previously.
12 Undo the two voltmeter retaining nuts.
13 Remove the bulbholders as applicable.
14 Undo the five printed circuit retaining screws.
15 Release the five retaining studs.
16 Ease the printed circuit off the two locating pins, and remove it from the rear of the panel.
17 Refitting is the reverse sequence to removal.

Main printed circuit

18 Remove the instrument panel window and faceplate, the ECU and the secondary printed circuit as described previously.
19 Withdraw the warning lamp colour strips from the front of the panel.
20 Pull off the trip reset button.
21 Disconnect the ribbon connector from the tachometer by carefully levering off the metal retainer with a small screwdriver. Remove the metal retainer from the ribbon.
22 Remove the bulbholders.
23 Undo the nuts from the gauge studs.
24 Release the two printed circuit retaining studs.
25 Ease the printed circuit off the locating pins, and remove it from the rear of the panel.
26 Refitting is the reverse sequence to removal.

Speedometer

27 Remove the instrument panel window and faceplate, and the ECU as described previously.
28 Undo the three speedometer retaining screws, release the wiring harness and remove the speedometer from the instrument panel.
29 Refitting is the reverse sequence to removal.

Tachometer

30 Remove the instrument panel window and faceplate, and the ECU as described previously.

31 Undo the two tachometer retaining screws.
32 Disconnect the ribbon connector from the tachometer by carefully levering off the metal retainer with a small screwdriver. Remove the metal retainer from the ribbon.
33 Remove the tachometer from the instrument panel.
34 Refitting is the reverse sequence to removal.

Voltmeter, oil pressure, coolant temperature and fuel gauges

35 Remove the instrument panel window and faceplate, and the ECU as described previously.
36 Undo the two retaining nuts and remove the relevant gauge as applicable.
37 Refitting is the reverse sequence to removal.

23 Clock – removal and refitting

1 Disconnect the battery negative terminal. (Refer to Section 1 before doing this).
2 Undo the two screws at the base of the oddment tray opening.
3 Withdraw the oddment tray and disconnect the clock wiring multi-plug.
4 Remove the oddment tray. Undo the two clock retaining screws and remove the clock.
5 Refitting is the reverse sequence to removal.

24 Headlamp and sidelamp bulbs – renewal

Headlamp dipped beam bulb

1 From within the engine compartment, disconnect the wiring multi-plug at the rear of the headlamp bulb (photo), then pull off the rubber cover.

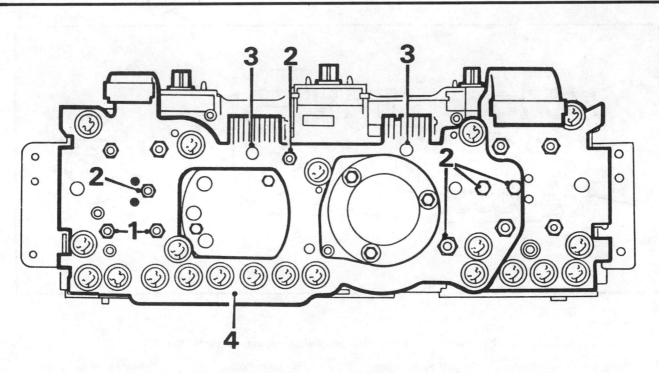

Fig. 12.11 Instrument panel secondary printed circuit attachments (Sec 22)

1 *Voltmeter retaining nuts*　　2 *Printed circuit retaining screws*　　3 *Printed circuit studs*　　4 *Printed circuit locating pins*

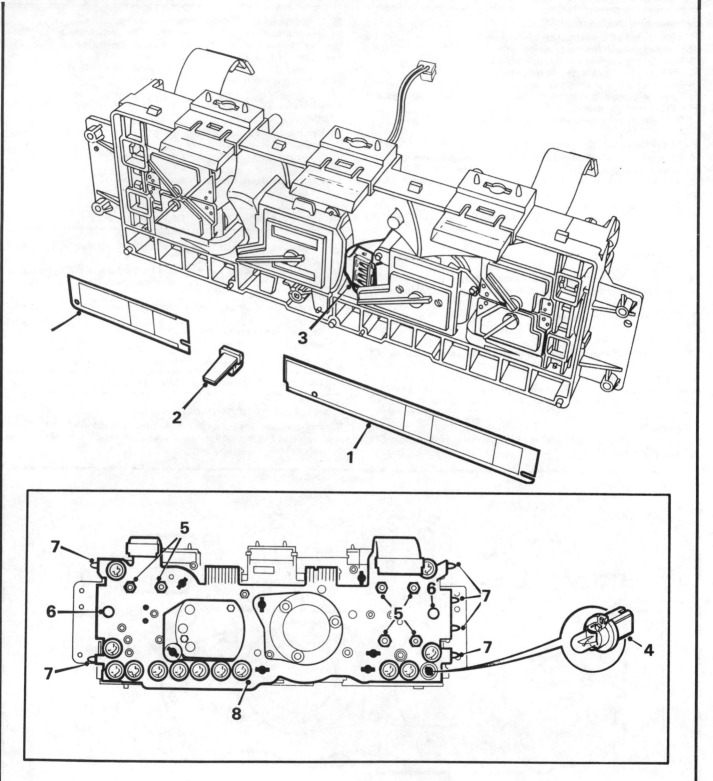

Fig. 12.12 Instrument panel main printed circuit attachments (Sec 22)

1 Warning lamp colour strips
2 Trip reset button
3 Tachometer ribbon
   connector
4 Bulbholders
5 Gauge retaining nuts
6 Printed circuit studs
7 Printed circuit locating pins
8 Printed circuit

2   Release the wiring retaining clip and withdraw the bulb from its location in the headlamp (photo). Take care not to touch the bulb glass with your fingers; if touched, clean the bulb with methylated spirit.
3   Fit the bulb, ensuring that the lugs in the bulb engage with the slots in the headlamp.
4   Refit the retaining clip, rubber cover and wiring plug. Ensure that the tab marked TOP on the cover is uppermost.

Sidelamp bulb

5   From within the engine compartment, disconnect the wiring multi-plug at the rear of the headlamp bulb, then pull off the rubber cover.
6   Withdraw the sidelamp bulbholder from the headlamp unit (photo) and remove the bulb from the holder.
7   Fit a new bulb to the holder and fit the holder to the headlamp.
8   Refit the rubber cover and headlamp wiring plug. Ensure that the tab marked TOP on the cover is uppermost.

Headlamp main beam bulb

9   Withdraw the plastic cover, release the wire clip and withdraw the bulb from the headlamp (photo). Take care not to touch the bulb glass with your fingers; if touched, clean the bulb with methylated spirit.
10 Disconnect the wiring connectors and remove the bulb.
11 Connect the wiring to the new bulb and place the bulb in the headlamp, ensuring that the flange cut-out locates in the housing ridge.
12 Refit the wire clip and the plastic cover.

25 Front direction indicator bulb – renewal

1   From within the engine compartment, unhook the retaining spring (photo) and withdraw the lens unit and seal from the front wing.
2   Press and turn the bulbholder anti-clockwise to remove it from the lens unit, then remove the bulb from the holder in the same way (photo).
3   Refit the bulb and holder, locate the lens unit in position and secure with the retaining spring.

26 Direction indicator side repeater bulb – renewal

1   Press the lamp unit to the right, free the left-hand retainer and withdraw the unit from the front wing.
2   Turn the bulbholder anti-clockwise to remove it from the lamp unit, then remove the push-fit bulb from the holder.
3   Fit a new bulb. Refit the bulbholder, and push the lamp unit into position in the wing.

27 Rear lamp cluster bulbs – renewal

1   From within the luggage compartment, press the retainer on the access panel and remove the panel (photo).
2   Lift the top retainer on the bulb panel, press the two bottom retainers and withdraw the panel (photo).
3   Remove the bulbs as required by depressing and turning anti-clockwise (photo).
4   Fit the new bulb(s), push the bulb panel into position and refit the access panel.

28 Number plate lamp bulb – renewal

Saloon models

1   Open the boot lid, turn the bulbholder anti-clockwise and withdraw the bulb and holder (photo).
2   Remove the push-fit bulb from the holder.
3   Refit the bulb and bulbholder.

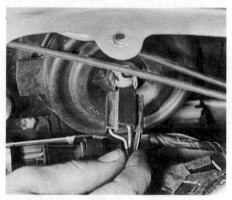
24.1 Disconnect the headlamp bulb multi-plug

24.2 Headlamp bulb withdrawn

24.6 Sidelamp bulbholder withdrawn

24.9 Headlamp main beam bulb withdrawn

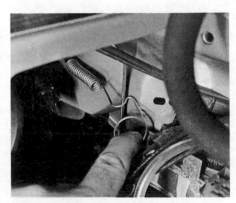
25.1 Unhook the direction indicator lens retaining spring

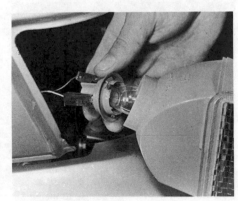
25.2 Withdraw the lens assembly and remove the bulbholder

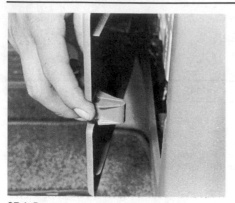

27.1 Press the retainer and remove the access panel

27.2 Remove the rear lamp cluster bulb panel

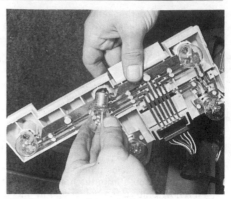

27.3 Rear lamp cluster bulb renewal

Fastback models

4 Open the tailgate, release the plastic retaining screws and remove the inner trim (photo).
5 Turn the bulbholder anti-clockwise (photo) and withdraw.
6 Remove the push-fit bulb from the holder.
7 Refit the bulb, bulbholder and trim.

---

29 Engine compartment lamp bulb – renewal

1 Open the bonnet, undo the two retaining screws and remove the lamp lens (photo).
2 Push and turn the bulb anti-clockwise to remove it from the holder.
3 Refit the bulb, lens and retaining screws.

---

30 Interior lamp bulbs – renewal

Interior courtesy lamp

1 Carefully prise the lens from the lamp body using a thin blade (photo).
2 Remove the festoon-type bulb from the contacts (photo).
3 Fit the new bulb and push the lens into place.

Map reading and courtesy lamp

4 Using a small screwdriver, carefully prise the map reading lamp from its housing, then turn the bulb anti-clockwise to remove.
5 Fit the new bulb and push the lens into place.
6 Renewal of the courtesy lamp bulb is the same as described in paragraphs 1 to 3.

28.1 Number plate lamp bulbholder on Saloon models

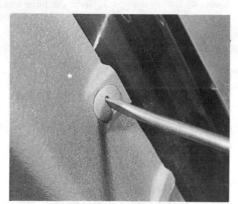

28.4 Release the screws and remove the trim panel

28.5 Number plate lamp bulbholder on Fastback models

29.1 Remove the lens for access to the engine compartment lamp bulb

30.1 Prise off the courtesy lamp lens

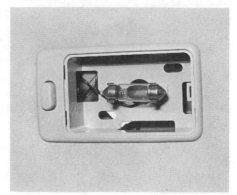

30.2 Remove the festoon bulb from the contacts

Footwell and glovebox lamps

7   From within the glovebox or under the footwell as applicable, carefully prise the lamp from its location using a small screwdriver.
8   Release the festoon-type bulb from its contacts (photo).
9   Fit the new bulb and push the lamp back into position.

Luggage compartment lamp

10   Using a small screwdriver, carefully prise the right-hand end of the lamp from its location under the rear parcel shelf on Saloon models, or on the rear side panels on Fastback models (photos).
11   Withdraw the lamp, turn the bulb anti-clockwise and remove it from the lamp (photo).
12   Fit the new bulb and push the lamp back into position.

31 Instrument panel illumination and warning lamp bulbs – renewal

Refer to Section 31.

32 Switch illumination bulbs – renewal

Facia switches and heater/air conditioner control switches

1   Remove the instrument cowl as described in Section 20.
2   With the wiring multi-plugs disconnected, remove the relevant bulb, which is a push-fit in the multi-plug holder.
3   Fit a new bulb, then refit the instrument cowl as described in Section 20.

Hazard warning switch

4   Lift off the switch lens on the steering column upper shroud, and remove the push-fit bulb.
5   Fit a new bulb, and press the lens into place.

Steering column switches

6   Undo the three lower screws and the single upper screw, and remove the upper and lower steering column shrouds.
7   Withdraw the bulbholder from the rear of the fibre optic diffuser unit (photo) then remove the bulb from the holder.
8   Fit a new bulb, push the bulbholder into place and refit the steering column shrouds.

33 Headlamp lens unit – removal and refitting

1   Remove the radiator grille as described in Chapter 11.
2   Remove the front direction indicator lamp assembly as described in Section 25.
3   Disconnect the wiring multi-plug at the rear of the headlamp dipped beam bulb, and separate the main beam wiring at the connector (photo).
4   Undo the two bolts securing the headlamp lens unit to the front body panel.
5   Release the unit from the two lower lugs (photo) and remove it from the car.
6   Refitting is the reverse sequence to removal.

34 Rear lamp cluster assembly – removal and refitting

1   From within the luggage compartment, press the retainer on the access panel and remove the panel.
2   Lift the top retainer on the bulb panel, press the two bottom retainers and withdraw the panel.
3   Undo the four nuts securing the lamp cluster to the rear wing, and withdraw the unit from the car (photos).
4   Refitting is the reverse sequence to removal.

30.8 Withdraw the glovebox lamp, and remove the bulb from the contacts

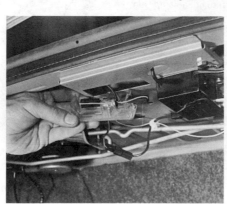
30.10A Renewing the luggage compartment lamp bulb on Saloon models

30.10B Withdraw the luggage compartment lamp lens from the rear side panel on Fastback models ...

30.11 ... for access to the bulb

32.7 Withdraw the bulbholder from the steering column switch fibre optic diffuser

33.3 Disconnect the headlamp lens unit wiring multi-plug

33.5 Release the lens unit from the lower lugs

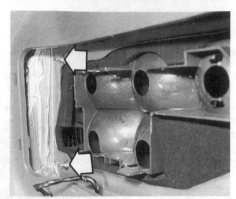

34.3A Rear lamp cluster side retaining nuts (arrowed)

34.3B Removing the rear lamp cluster assembly

35 Number plate lamp unit – removal and refitting

1   On Fastback models, remove the trim panel on the inside of the tailgate.
2   Undo the six retaining screws and remove the rear lens reflector and number plate assembly (photo).
3   Undo the two screws securing each number plate lamp unit and withdraw the unit(s) (photo).
4   Turn the bulbholder anti-clockwise to remove the bulb, then remove the lamp unit from the car.,
5   Refitting is the reverse sequence to removal.

36 Headlamp aim – adjustment

1   At regular intervals (see *Routine maintenance*) headlamp aim should be checked, and if necessary adjusted.
2   Due to the light pattern of the homofocal headlamp lenses fitted to Rover 820 models, optical beam setting equipment must be used to achieve satisfactory aim of the headlamps. It is recommended therefore that this work is entrusted to a dealer. If, however, you have access to beam setting equipment, the horizontal and vertical adjustment screws for each headlamp unit are shown in Fig. 12.13.

37 Wiper blades and arms – removal and refitting

Wiper blades

1   The blades should be renewed when they no longer clean the screen effectively.
2   Lift the wiper arm away from the screen.
3   Depress the spring retaining catch and separate the blade from the wiper arm (photos).
4   Insert the new blade into the arm, ensuring that the spring retaining catch engages fully. Note that the blade with the deflector is fitted to the driver's side.

Windscreen wiper arms

5   Open the bonnet, lift the wiper arm slightly and retain it in the raised position by inserting a pop-rivet, small drill bit or similar item through the hole in the side of the arm (photo).
6   Unscrew the arm-to-spindle retaining nut (photo) and withdraw the arm from the spindle.
7   If required, remove the blade from the arm as previously described, and pull out the rivet or drill bit. Relieve the spring tension of the arm as the rivet or bit is withdrawn.
8   Refitting is the reverse sequence to removal, but adjust the wiper arm park setting as described in Section 38 during the refitting sequence.

Tailgate wiper arm (Fastback models)

9   Lift off the cover over the wiper arm spindle.
10 Unscrew the wiper arm-to-spindle retaining nut and withdraw the arm from the blade.

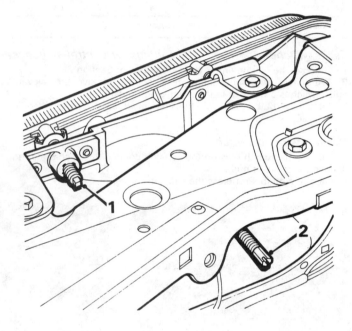

Fig. 12.13 Headlamp beam horizontal adjustment screw (1) and vertical adjustment screw (2) (Sec 36)

11 Refitting is the reverse sequence to removal, but position the arm along the bottom of the screen with the motor in the park position.

38 Windscreen wiper arm park setting – adjustment

1   Remove the wiper blades and wiper arms as described in Section 37.
2   Switch on the ignition and turn the wiper switch on and off, so that the motor operates then stops in the park position. Switch off the ignition.
3   Position the wiper arms so that they are resting on the top of the stop-pegs on the windscreen finisher. Engage the end of the arms with their respective spindles, and refit the retaining nut.
4   Refit the wiper blades, remove the rivet or drill bit, and position the arms in the normal park position against the side of the stop-pegs.
5   Operate the washers to wet the screen, then operate the wipers.
6   Switch the wipers off, and check that they park with the arms against the stop-pegs and the blades on the windscreen finisher.

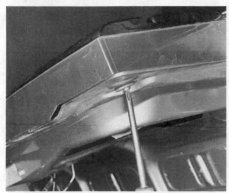

35.2 Remove the rear lens reflector and number plate assembly

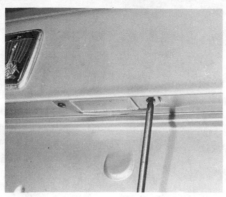

35.3 Removing the number plate lamp unit

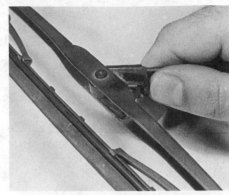

37.3A Depress the wiper blade spring retaining catch ...

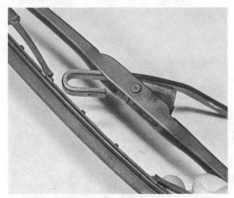

37.3B ... and release the blade from the arm

37.5 Insert a pop-rivet through the hole in the wiper arm

37.6 Wiper arm retaining nut

39 Windscreen wiper motor – removal and refitting

1 Disconnect the battery negative terminal. (Refer to Section 1 before doing this).
2 Remove the wiper arms as described in Section 37.
3 Carefully prise up the screw caps over the windscreen finisher retaining screws at the base of the windscreen (photo).
4 Undo the screws on the finisher front face and on the extreme edges, then remove the finisher from the car (photos).
5 Using pointed-nose pliers, release the rubber sealing strip retaining clips (photos). Be prepared for some of these clips to break during removal.

6 Lift off the centre grille and the left-hand plenum moulding (photos).
7 Working through the left-hand plenum chamber aperture, undo the retaining nut and remove the wiper linkage rotary link from the motor spindle (photo).
8 Disconnect the wiper motor wiring multi-plug (photo).
9 Undo the three bolts and remove the wiper motor and mounting bracket from the car (photo).
10 Withdraw the seal from the motor spindle, then remove the seal from the mounting plate.
11 Undo the three bolts and remove the motor from the mounting plate.
12 Refitting is the reverse sequence to removal.

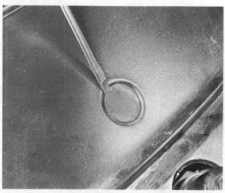

39.3 Prise up the windscreen finisher screw caps

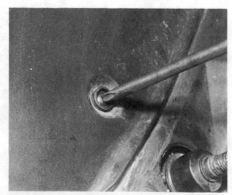

39.4A Undo the screws on the finisher front face ...

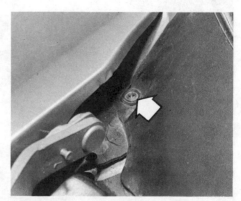

39.4B ... and at the extreme edges (arrowed)

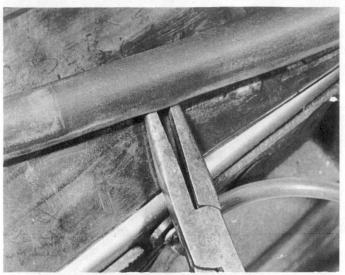

39.5A Release the rubber sealing strip retaining clips ...

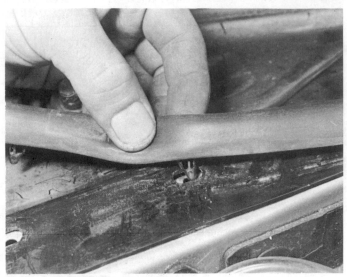

39.5B ... and withdraw the sealing strip

39.6A Lift off the centre grille ...

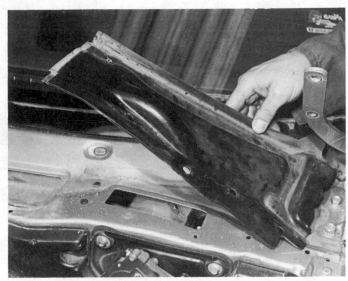

39.6B ... and the left-hand side plenum moulding

39.7 Undo the nut securing the linkage rotary link to the motor spindle

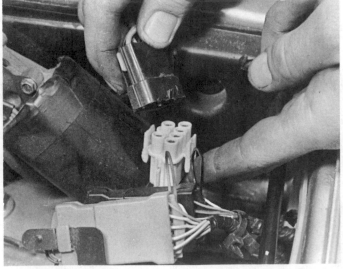

39.8 Disconnect the wiring multi-plug

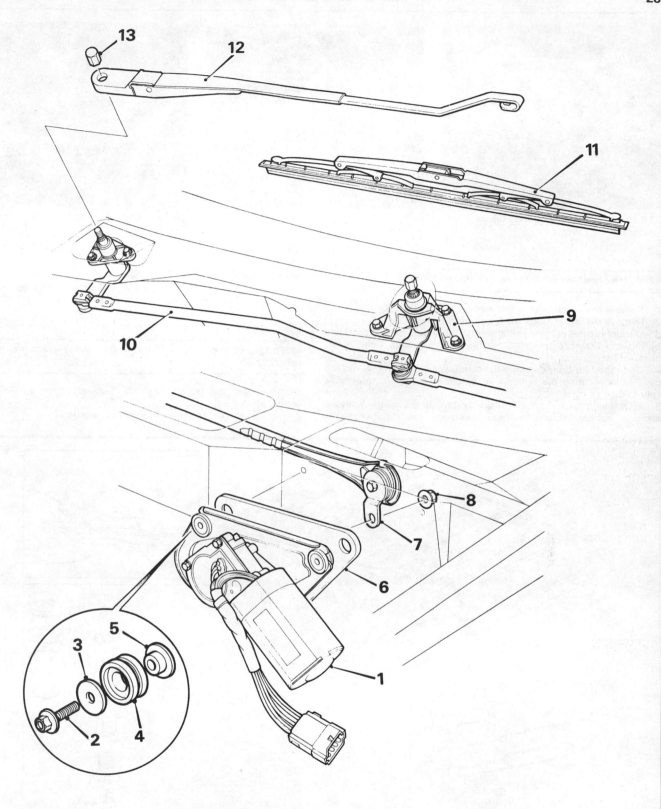

Fig. 12.14 Windscreen wiper motor and linkage components (Sec 39)

1	Wiper motor	4	Mounting bush	8	Rotary link retaining nut	11	Wiper blade
2	Mounting bracket retaining bolt	5	Sleeve	9	Linkage centre spindle	12	Wiper arm
3	Washer	6	Mounting bracket seal	10	Connecting link	13	Wiper arm retaining nut
		7	Rotary link				

39.9 Undo the motor mounting bracket retaining bolts (arrowed)

40.4A Wiper linkage centre spindle assembly ...

40.4B ... and right-hand spindle assembly

40 Windscreen wiper linkage – removal and refitting

1   Remove the windscreen wiper arms as described in Section 37.
2   Remove the wiper motor as described in Section 39.
3   Disconnect the primary link arm from the centre spindle assembly by pushing down to release the ball-and-socket joint. Remove the primary link.
4   Undo the four bolts securing the centre spindle assembly, and the three bolts securing the right-hand spindle assembly, to the scuttle (photos).
5   Feed the right-hand spindle assembly through the scuttle aperture, and draw out the linkage from the centre spindle opening. Remove the complete linkage assembly from the car.
6   Further dismantling is not possible, and if any of the parts are worn, a complete linkage assembly must be obtained.
7   Refitting is the reverse sequence to removal.

41 Tailgate wiper motor (Fastback models) – removal and refitting

1   Disconnect the battery negative terminal. (Refer to Section 1 before doing this).
2   Remove the wiper arm as described in Section 37.

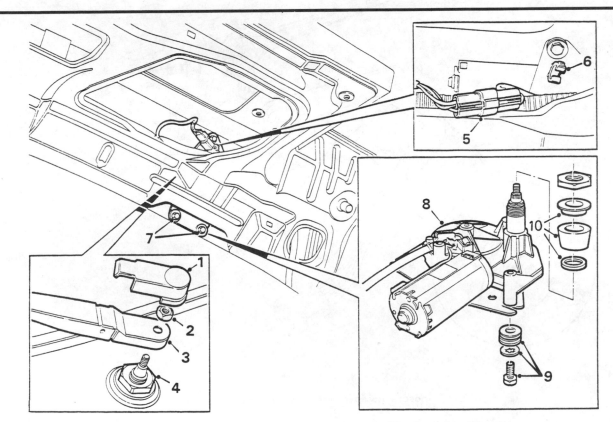
Fig. 12.15 Tailgate wiper motor attachments – Fastback models (Sec 41)

1 Wiper arm cover	retaining nut	bolts	washer
2 Wiper arm retaining nut	5 Wiring multi-plug	8 Motor assembly	10 Spindle seal, spacer and
3 Wiper arm	6 Wiring harness cable clip	9 Wiper motor-to-mounting	washer
4 Wiper motor spindle	7 Mounting plate retaining	plate bolt, spacer and	

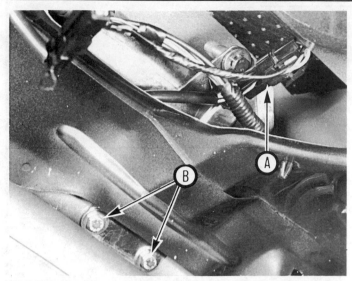

41.5 Tailgate wiper motor multi-plug (A) and mounting plate retaining bolts (B)

3 Release the plastic clip screws and remove the trim panel from inside the tailgate.
4 Undo the large retaining nut from the wiper motor spindle.
5 Disconnect the wiper motor multi-plug, and release the wiring from its cable clip (photo).
6 Undo the two bolts securing the motor mounting plate to the tailgate, then withdraw the motor and mounting plate.
7 Undo the three bolts and remove the motor from the mounting plate.
8 Withdraw the seal, spacer and washer components from the motor spindle.
9 Refitting is the reverse sequence to removal.

42 Washer reservoir and pumps – removal and refitting

1 Disconnect the battery negative terminal. (Refer to Section 1 before doing this).
2 Undo the screw securing the washer reservoir filler neck to the inner wing valance (photo).
3 Withdraw the filler neck from the reservoir, and disconnect the breather hose.
4 From under the wheel arch, undo the two screws and one bolt securing the access panel, and remove the panel.

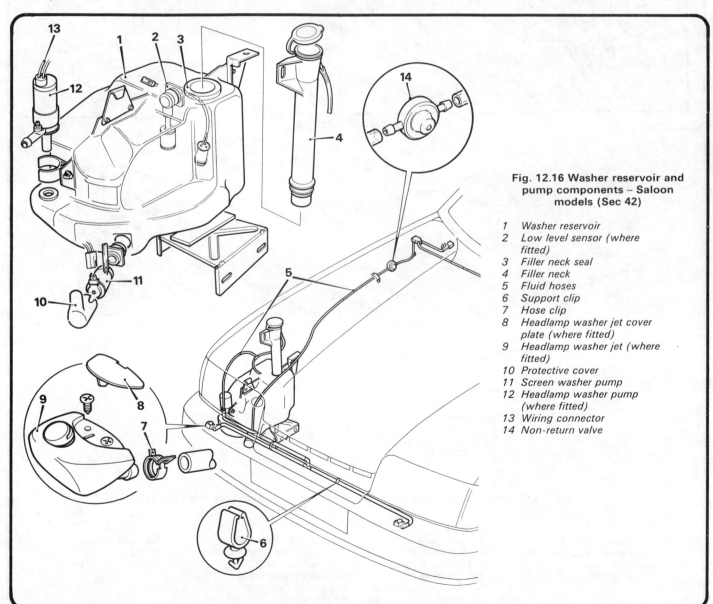

Fig. 12.16 Washer reservoir and pump components – Saloon models (Sec 42)

1   Washer reservoir
2   Low level sensor (where fitted)
3   Filler neck seal
4   Filler neck
5   Fluid hoses
6   Support clip
7   Hose clip
8   Headlamp washer jet cover plate (where fitted)
9   Headlamp washer jet (where fitted)
10 Protective cover
11 Screen washer pump
12 Headlamp washer pump (where fitted)
13 Wiring connector
14 Non-return valve

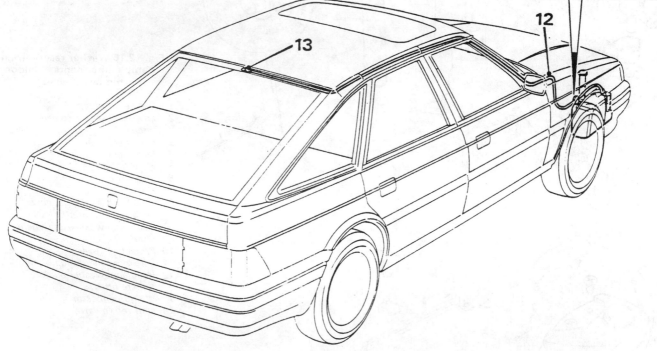

Fig. 12.17 Washer reservoir and pump components – Fastback models (Sec 42)

1   Washer reservoir
2   Low level sensor (where fitted)
3   Filler neck seal
4   Filler neck
5   Screen washer pump
6   Protective cover
7   Protective cover
8   Tailgate washer pump
9   Headlamp washer pump (where fitted)
10   Wiring connector
11   Non-return valve
12   Fluid hose
13   Tailgate washer jet

5 Undo the three reservoir retaining bolts and lower the unit slightly.
6 Disconnect the fluid hoses and wiring multi-plugs and remove the reservoir, complete with pumps, from under the wheel arch.
7 Remove the pumps as required from the reservoir by pulling them out of their locations.
8 Refitting is the reverse sequence to removal.

43 Headlamp washer jet – removal and refitting

1 Prise off the cover plate on the washer jet to expose the two retaining screws.
2 Undo the two screws and withdraw the jet from the front bumper.
3 Release the water hose clip, disconnect the hose and remove the jet.
4 Refitting is the reverse sequence to removal.

44 Horns – removal and refitting

1 Disconnect the battery negative terminal. (Refer to Section 1 before doing this).
2 From under the left-hand wheel arch, undo the two screws and one bolt securing the access panel and remove the panel.
3 Disconnect the electrical leads, undo the retaining nut and remove the horn(s) from the mounting bracket.
4 Refitting is the reverse sequence to removal.

45 Radio cassette player – removal and refitting

1 Disconnect the battery negative terminal. (Refer to Section 1 before doing this).
2 Insert a DIN standard radio removal tool into each pair of holes at the edge of the unit, and push the tools fully home to engage the radio retaining clips (photo). These tools are available from audio accessory shops or from Rover dealers.
3 Move the tools outward to depress the retaining clips, and withdraw the radio from the centre console sufficiently to gain access to the wiring at the rear (photo).
4 Note the location of the speaker wiring by recording the cable colours and their positions, then disconnect the speaker leads, aerial lead and wiring multi-plug (photo). Remove the unit from the car.
5 Disengage the removal tools from the retaining clips on the side of the radio, and remove the tools (photo).
6 Refitting is the reverse sequence to removal.

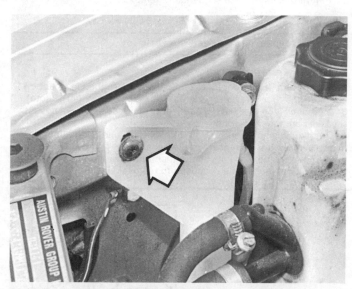

42.2 Washer reservoir filler neck retaining screw (arrowed)

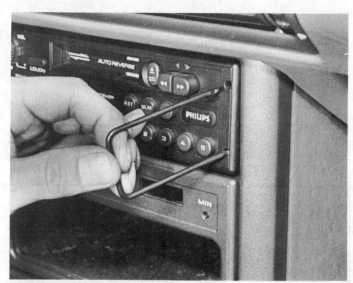

45.2 Insert the radio removal tools into the holes on the edge of the unit

45.3 Withdraw the radio, using the tools to release the retaining clips.

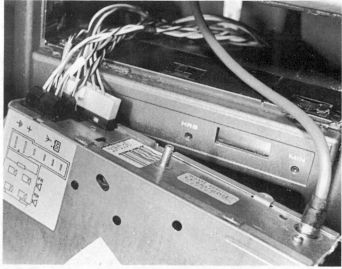

45.4 Disconnect the wiring at the rear of the radio

45.5 Release the removal tools from the retaining clips (arrowed)

5   Using a cotton wool pad moistened in a proprietary tape head cleaning fluid, clean the pinch wheel, capstan and tape head.
6   Return the arm to its original position and refit the unit cover.
7   Refit the radio cassette player as described in Section 45.

47 Rear speaker – removal and refitting

Saloon models

1   From inside the luggage compartment, disconnect the two leads and undo the four retaining nuts (photo).
2   Withdraw the speaker upwards into the car, and remove it from the rear parcel shelf (photo).
3   Refitting is the reverse sequence to removal.

Fastback models

4   Undo the three screws securing the trim panel to the parcel tray support (photo) and remove the trim panel.
5   Remove the speaker grille.
6   Undo the six speaker retaining screws (photo), lift the speaker from its location and disconnect the wiring connectors.
7   Remove the speaker from the car.
8   Refitting is the reverse sequence to removal.

46 Cassette unit tape head – cleaning

1   Remove the radio cassette player as described in Section 45.
2   Insert a screwdriver into the slot at the rear left-hand edge of the unit cover and lift the cover carefully upwards. Now insert the screwdriver into the slot on the other side, and lift carefully upwards until the retaining clips on the cover rear edge are released.
3   Pivot the cover upwards to disengage the retainer on the front edge and remove the cover.
4   Refer to Fig. 12.18 and press the arm on top of the unit rearwards to gain access to the playing mechanism.

48 Front speakers – removal and refitting

Main speaker and filter

1   Remove the front door inner trim panel as described in Chapter 11.
2   Undo the four screws securing the speaker to the door (photo).
3   Withdraw the speaker, disconnect the leads and remove the speaker from the door (photo).
4   To remove the filter, cut off the tape securing it to the wiring harness adjacent to the main speaker location.
5   Disconnect the leads at each end and remove the filter.
6   Refitting is the reverse sequence to removal.

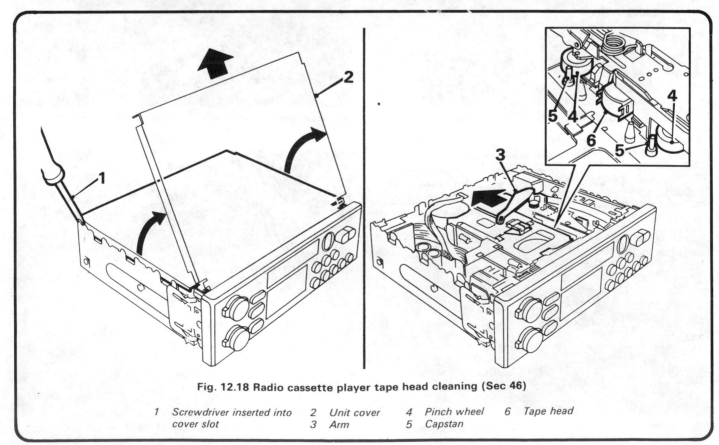

Fig. 12.18 Radio cassette player tape head cleaning (Sec 46)

1	Screwdriver inserted into cover slot	2	Unit cover	4	Pinch wheel	6	Tape head
		3	Arm	5	Capstan		

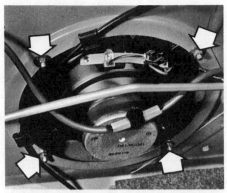

47.1 Rear speaker retaining nuts (arrowed) on Saloon models

47.2 Removing the rear speaker from the parcel shelf

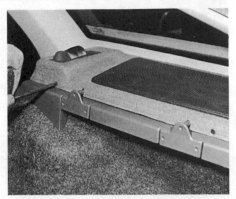

47.4 Remove the trim panel over the rear speaker on Fastback models

47.6 Undo the six screws and remove the speaker assembly

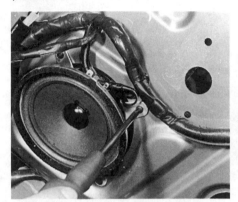

48.2 Undo the main door speaker retaining screws

48.3 Withdraw the speaker and disconnect the wiring

Tweeter

7   Refer to 'Front door inner trim panel – removal and refitting' in Chapter 11 and remove the escutcheon around the door inner release handle.
8   Rotate the tweeter clockwise to release it from the escutcheon, then disconnect the leads and remove the tweeter (photo).
9   Refitting is the reverse sequence to removal.

49 Aerial amplifier – removal and refitting

Saloon models

1   Disconnect the battery negative terminal. (Refer to Section 1 before doing this).
2   From inside the luggage compartment, disconnect the two leads at the amplifier unit located under the rear parcel shelf (photo).
3   Disconnect the two amplifer leads at the connections to the rear screen demisting element.

4   Disconnect the aerial co-axial lead at the amplifier.
5   Undo the two screws and remove the amplifier from under the parcel shelf.
6   Refitting is the reverse sequence to removal.

Fastback models

7   Disconnect the battery negative terminal. (Refer to Section 1 before doing this).
8   Remove the trim panel from inside the tailgate.
9   Disconnect the leads at the amplifier unit located behind the stiffener panel in the tailgate.
10   Disconnect the leads at the connector to the rear screen demisting element.
11   Disconnect the aerial co-axial lead at the amplifier.
12   Undo the two screws and remove the amplifier from the tailgate (photo). Note that one of the screws also secures the wiring earth cable.
13   Refitting is the reverse sequence to removal.

48.8 Disconnect the wiring and remove the tweeter

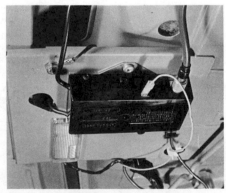

49.2 Aerial amplifier unit located under the rear parcel shelf on Saloon models

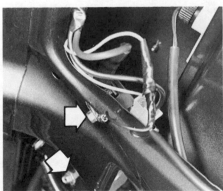

49.12 Aerial amplifier unit retaining bolts (arrowed) on Fastback models

50 Power amplifier – removal and refitting

Facia-mounted amplifier – early models

1 Disconnect the battery negative terminal. (Refer to Section 1 before doing this).
2 Release the turnbuckles and remove the trim panel over the fusebox, beneath the steering column.
3 Remove the radio cassette player as described in Section 45.
4 Disconnect the four multi-plugs connecting the speaker leads from the power amplifier to the wiring harness. Record the colour codes of each lead to ensure correct connection on reassembly.
5 Release the retaining stud and remove the small centre console trim panel from the footwell on the driver's side.
6 Working through the trim panel aperture, disconnect the power amplifier wiring multi-plug.
7 Undo the nut and two screws securing the power amplifier mounting bracket under the facia.
8 Withdraw the amplifier, release the wiring harness, and remove the unit from under the facia.
9 Refitting is the reverse sequence to removal.

Luggage compartment-mounted amplifier – later models

10 Disconnect the battery negative terminal. (Refer to Section 1 before doing this).
11 Remove the trim panel from the right-hand side of the luggage compartment.
12 Disconnect the rear speaker leads at the speakers or at the wiring connectors, and pass the disconnected leads through to the amplifier.
13 Disconnect the two multi-plugs and the DIN socket connector at the amplifier.
14 Undo the two amplifier mounting bracket screws, and remove the unit from the luggage compartment.

15 Refitting is the reverse sequence to removal.

51 Power amplifier filter – removal and refitting

1 Release the retaining stud and remove the small centre console trim panel from the footwell on the driver's side.
2 Working through the trim panel aperture, disconnect the multi-plugs at each end of the filter.
3 Release the cable tie and remove the filter from its location.
4 Refitting is the reverse sequence to removal.

52 Wiring diagrams – explanatory notes

1 The wiring diagrams included at the end of this Chapter are shown in continuous rail format. All the circuits which comprise the main wiring diagram for a particular model are positioned side by side in three rows, one above the other. The circuits are connected to each other by a common earth line, representing the vehicle chassis.
2 Grid references showing the location of the components on the diagram are included in the key. The component location on the diagram bears no relation, however, to the actual component location on the car.
3 Numbers shown within a triangle on the diagram represent interconnections from one circuit to another. An output is indicated by the lead being connected to the base of the triangle, and an input is indicated by the lead being connected to the triangle apex. A list of the connection point grid references is included in the key.
4 The numbers shown in boxes relate to the earth point locations, as shown on a supplementary diagram. A component without a number is earthed through its mountings, or through a cable earthed adjacent to the component.

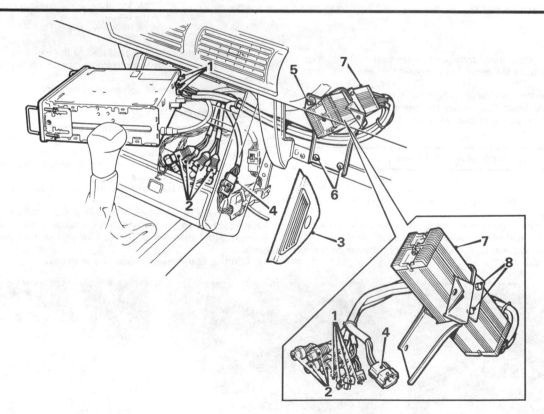

Fig. 12.19 Facia-mounted power amplifier attachments (Sec 50)

1 Speaker lead connections at radio
2 Speaker lead connections at amplifier
3 Console trim panel
4 Amplifier wiring multi-plug
5 Mounting bracket retaining nut
6 Mounting bracket retaining screws
7 Amplifier unit
8 Amplifier-to-mounting bracket retaining screws

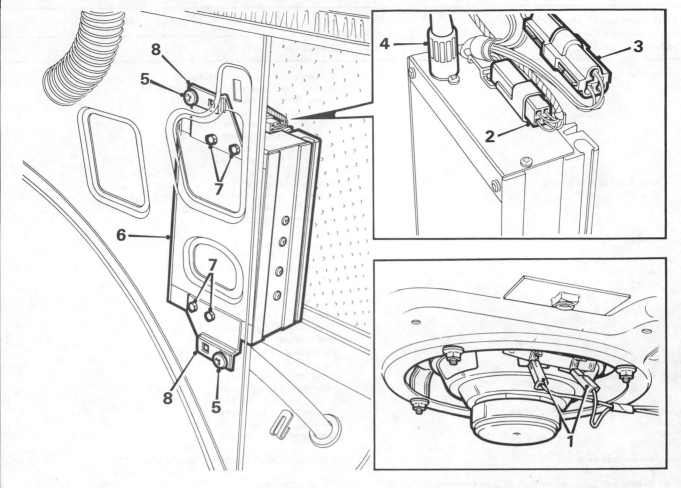

Fig. 12.20 Luggage compartment-mounted power amplifier attachments (Sec 50)

1 Left-hand speaker leads
2 Wiring multi-plug
3 Wiring multi-plug
4 DIN socket connector
5 Mounting bracket retaining
   screws
6 Luggage compartment
   stiffener panel
7 Amplifier-to-mounting
   bracket retaining screws
8 Amplifier mounting bracket

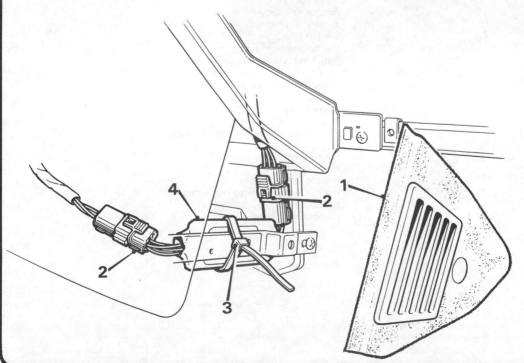

Fig. 12.21 Power amplifier
filter attachments (Sec 51)

1 Console trim panel
2 Multi-plugs
3 Cable tie
4 Filter

53 Fault diagnosis – electrical system

Symptom	Reason(s)
Starter fails to turn engine	Battery discharged or defective
	Battery terminal and/or earth leads loose
	Starter motor connections loose
	Starter solenoid faulty
	Starter brushes worn or sticking
	Starter commutator worn or dirty
	Starter field coils earthed
	Starter solenoid relay faulty
Starter turns engine very slowly	Battery discharged
	Starter motor or solenoid connections loose
	Starter brushes worn or sticking
	Poor earth connection
Starter noisy	Pinion or flywheel ring gear teeth broken or badly worn
	Mounting bolts loose
	Starter motor armature bushes worn
Battery will not retain charge	Battery defective internally
	Battery terminals loose
	Alternator drivebelt slipping
	Alternator regulator faulty
	Wiring fault
	Electrical system not switching off
Ignition warning lamp stays on	Alternator faulty
	Alternator drivebelt faulty
Ignition warning lamp fails to come on	Warning lamp bulb blown
	Warning lamp wiring open-circuit
	Alternator faulty
Instrument readings erratic	Faulty instrument electronic control unit
Fuel, temperature or oil pressure gauges give no reading	Wiring open-circuit
	Sender, thermistor or transducer faulty
	Faulty instrument electronic control unit
Lamps inoperative	Bulb blown
	Fuse blown
	Relay faulty
	Fusible link blown
	Battery discharged
	Switch faulty
	Wiring open-circuit
	Bad connections due to corrosion
Failure of component motor	Component motor faulty
	Fuse blown
	Relay faulty
	Fusible link blown
	Poor or broken wiring connections
Failure of an individual component	Fuse blown
	Relay faulty
	Fusible link blown
	Poor or broken wiring connections
	Switch faulty
	Component faulty

Wiring diagram symbols and colour code

Colour code

B	Black	P	Purple
G	Green	R	Red
K	Pink	S	Slate
LG	Light green	U	Blue
N	Brown	W	White
O	Orange	Y	Yellow

Symbols

1 Fusible links
2 Fuse
3 Sealed joint
4 Connection point input
5 Connection point output

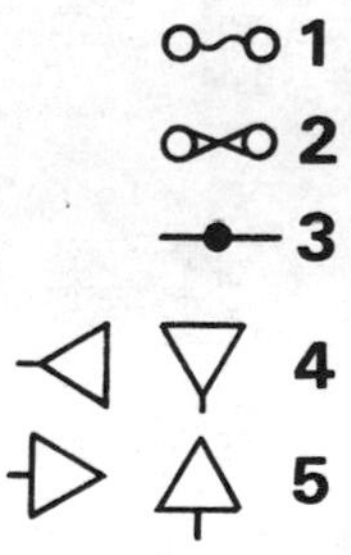

o—o **1**

o—o **2**

—•— **3**

◁ ▽ **4**

▷ △ **5**

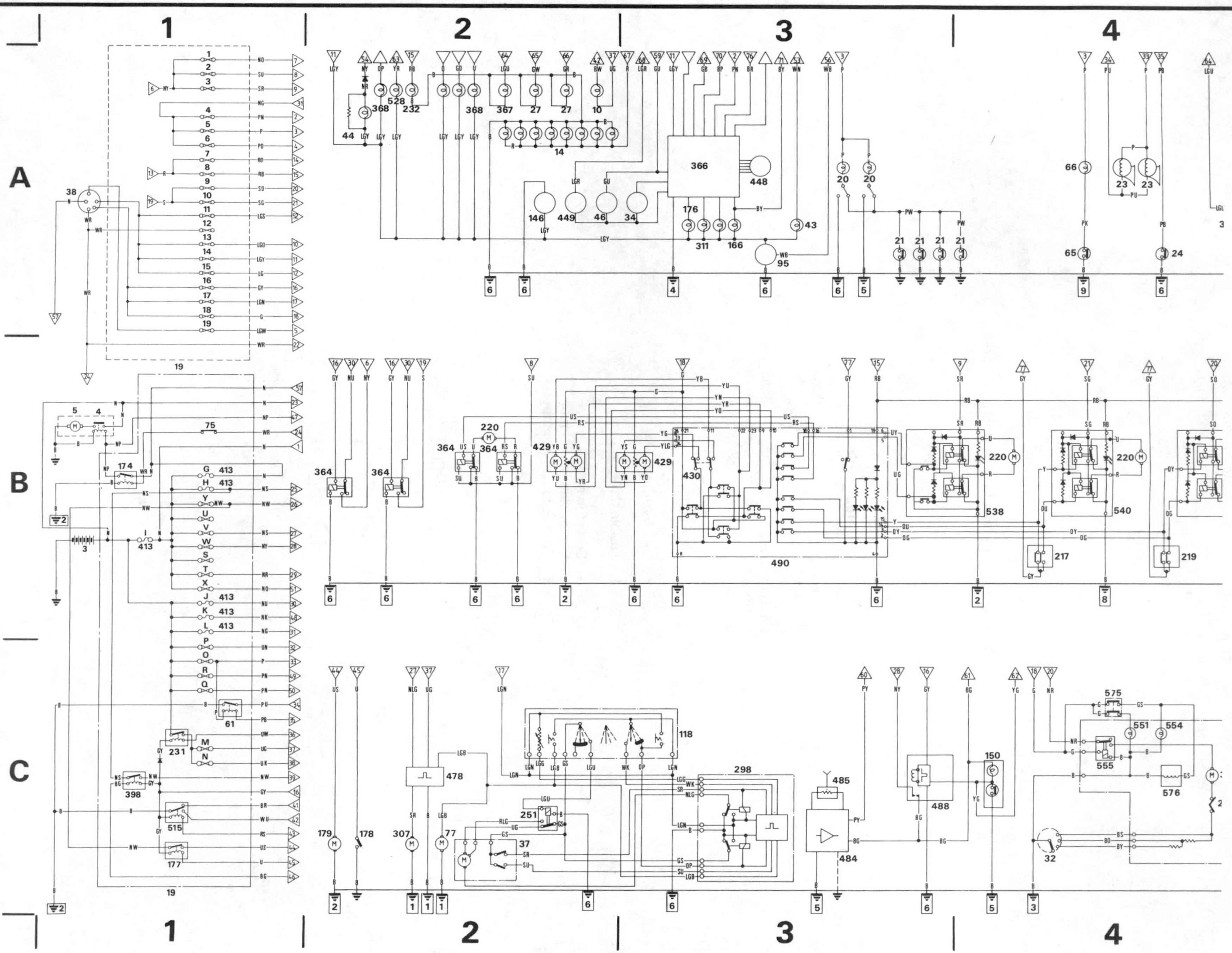

Fig. 12.22 Main wiring diagram – single-point fuel injection models

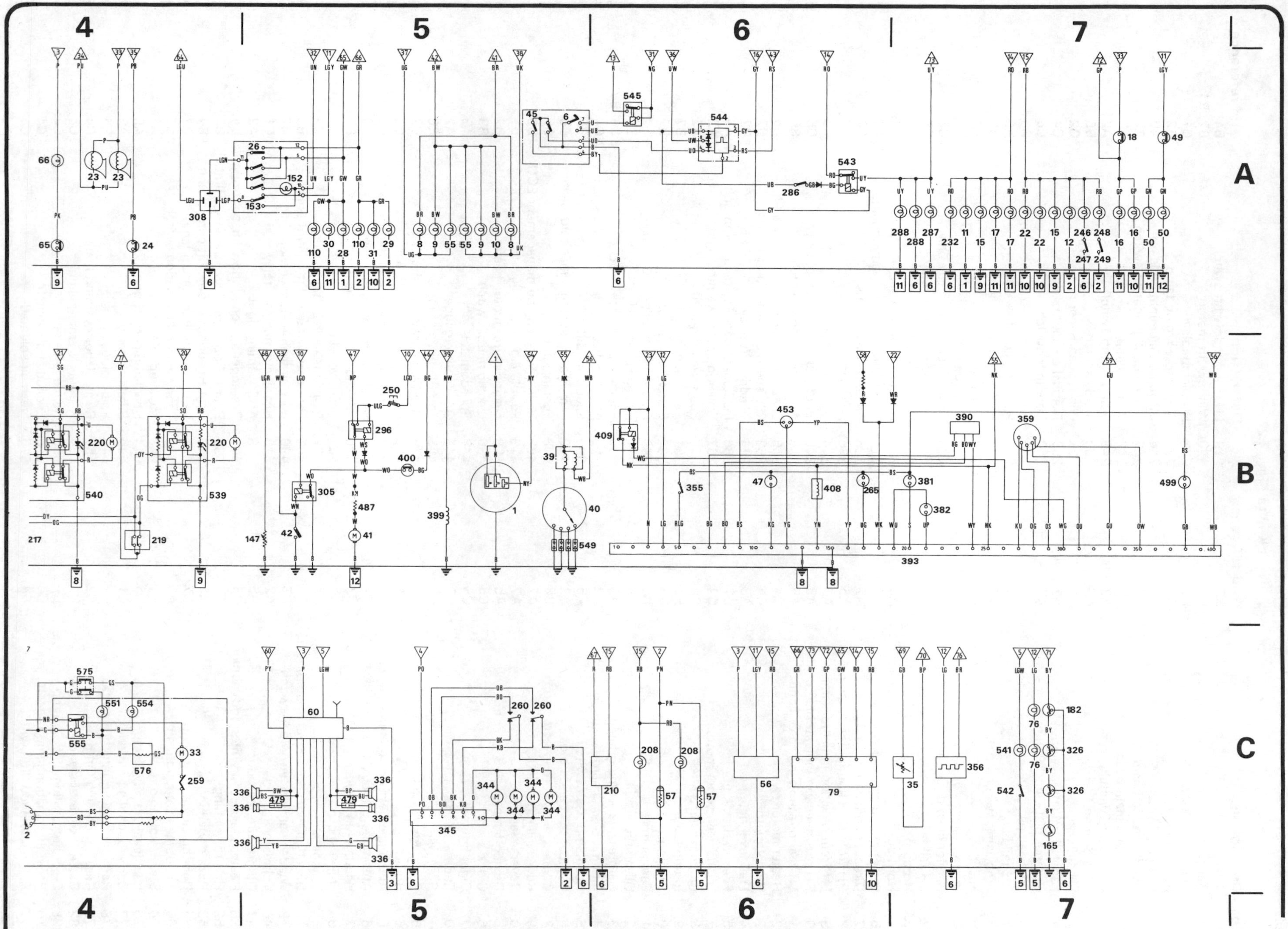

Fig. 12.22 Main wiring diagram – single-point fuel injection models (continued)

Key to Fig. 12.22

No	Description	Grid reference	No	Description	Grid reference
1	Alternator	B5	219	LH rear window lift switch	B4
3	Battery	B1	220	Window lift motor	B2, B4
4	Starter motor switch	B1	231	Headlamp relay	C1
5	Starter motor	B1	232	Sidelamp warning lamp	A2
6	Lighting switch	A5	246	Glove box illumination lamp	A6
8	Headlamp dip beam	A5	247	Glove box illumination switch	A7
9	Headlamp main beam	A5	248	Bonnet lamp	A7
10	Main beam warning lamp	A2, A5	249	Bonnet lamp switch	A2
11	RH sidelamp	A7	250	Inertia switch	B5
12	LH sidelamp	A7	251	Windscreen wiper relay	C2
14	Panel illumination lamps	A2	259	Thermal circuit breaker	C4
15	Number plate illumination lamps	A7	260	Door lock switch	C6
16	Stop-lamps	A7	265	Ambient air temperature sensor	B6
17	RH tail lamp	A7	286	Foglamp switch	A6
18	Stop-lamp switch	A7	287	Foglamp warning lamp	A7
19	Fusebox	A1,B1,C1	288	Foglamps	A7
20	Interior lamps	A3	296	Fuel pump relay	B5
21	Interior lamp door switch	A3	298	Windscreen wiper delay unit	C3
22	LH tail lamp	A7	305	Oil pressure switch relay	B5
23	Horns	A4	307	Headlamp wash motor	C2
24	Horn push	A4	308	Direction indicator/hazard flasher unit	A4
26	Direction indicator switch	A5	311	Coolant temperature warning lamp	A3
27	Direction indicator warning lamps	A2	326	Brake pad wear sensor	C7
28	RH front direction indicator lamp	A5	336	Speakers	C5
29	LH front direction indicator lamp	A5	344	Door lock motor	C5
30	RH rear direction indicator lamp	A5	345	Door lock motor control unit	C5
31	LH rear direction indicator lamp	A5	355	Accelerator pedal switch	B6
32	Heater motor switch	C4	356	Speed transducer	B6
33	Heater motor	C4	359	Idle speed stepper motor	B7
34	Fuel level gauge	A3	364	Window lift relay	B2
35	Fuel level tank unit	C7	366	Instrument pack multi-function unit	A3
37	Windscreen wiper motor	C2	367	Trailer indicator warning light	A2
38	Ignition/start switch	B5	368	Spare warning light	A2
39	Ignition coil	B5	381	Knock sensor	B7
40	Distributotr	B5	382	Crankshaft sensor	B7
41	Fuel pump	B5	390	Diagnostic junction – Engine management ECU	B7
42	Oil pressure switch	B5	393	Engine management ECU	B6, B7
43	Oil pressure warning lamp	A3	398	Manifold heater relay	C1
44	Ignition or no charge warning lamp	A2	399	Inlet manifold heater	B5
45	Headlamp flash switch	A5	400	Temperature switch – manifold heater	B5
46	Coolant temperature gauge	A2	408	Fuel injector	B6
47	Coolant temperature thermistor	B6	409	Main relay – Engine management ECU	B6
49	Reverse lamp switch	A7	413	Fusible link	B1
50	Reverse lamps	A7	429	Electric mirror motor/heater	B2
55	Driving lamps	A5	430	Electric mirror switch	B3
56	Clock	C6	448	Speedometer	A3
57	Cigar lighter	C6	449	Oil pressure gauge	A2
60	Radio cassette player	C5	453	Throttle potentiometer	B6
61	Horn relay	C1	478	Headlamp power wash timer unit	C2
65	Boot lamp switch	A4	479	Filter	C5
66	Boot lamp	A4	484	Aerial amplifier and isolator unit	C3
75	Automatic gearbox inhibitor switch	B1	485	Aerial and heated rear screen	C3
76	Automatic gearbox selector indicator lamp	C7	486	Resistor wire – harness	B5
77	Windscreen washer motor	C2	487	Resistive wire	B5
79	Trailer socket	C6	488	Heated rearscreen timer relay	C3
95	Tachometer	A3	490	Four door window lift control unit	B3
110	Direction indicator repeater lamps	A5	499	Inlet air temperature sensor	B7
118	Windscreen washer/wiper switch	C3	515	Headlamp main/dip relay	C1
146	Voltmeter	A2	528	ABS warning light	A2
147	Oil pressure transducer	B5	538	Passenger's door window lift control unit	B4
150	Heated rear screen switch and warning lamp	C4	539	Rear LH door window lift control unit	B4
152	Hazard warning lamp	A5	540	Rear RH door window lift control unit	B4
153	Hazard warning switch	A5	541	Vanity mirror illumination lamp	C7
165	Handbrake warning lamp switch	C7	542	Vanity mirror illumination switch	C7
166	Handbrake warning lamp	A3	543	Foglamp relay	A6
174	Starter solenoid relay	B1	544	Headlamp cut-off unit	A6
176	Fuel level warning lamp	A3	545	Sidelamp relay	A6
177	Radiator cooling fan relay	C1	549	Spark plugs	B5
178	Radiator cooling fan thermostat	C2	551	Recirculation warning lamp	C4
179	Radiator cooling fan motor	C2	554	Fresh air warning lamp	C4
182	Brake fluid level switch	C7	555	Heater relay	C4
208	Cigar lighter illumination lamp	C6	575	Recirculation switch	C4
210	Panel illumination lamp rheostat resistor	C6	576	Fresh air solenoid	C4
217	RH rear window lift switch	B4			

Key to Fig. 12.22 (continued)

Connection chart

No	Grid references	Supplementary circuit connections	No	Grid references	Supplementary circuit connections
1	B1, B5		37	A2, A5, C1	
2	A1, A3, C6	Courtesy lamp delay	38	A5, C1	
3	A1, A3, A4, C5, C6	Radio cassette player with power amplifier. Courtesy lamp delay	39	B5	
			40	A4, C1	
4	A1, C5	Central locking with remote control	41	A5, C1	
			42	A2, A5, C1	
5	A1, C5, C7	Radio cassette player with power amplifier	43	A5, C1	
			44	C1, C2	
6	A1, B2		45	C1, C2	
7	A1		46	A5, B5	
8	A1, B2		47	A5, B1, B5	
9	A1, B4	ABS brake system	48	B1, C1	ABS brake system
10	A1, B5		49	C1	ABS brake system
11	A1, A2, A3, A5, A7, C6	ABS brake system. Courtesy lamp delay	50	C1	ABS brake system
			51	B1	Cooling fans – models with air conditioning
12	A1, B6, C7				
13	A1, A6	ABS brake system	52	A2, B2	ABS brake system
14	A1, A6, A7, C6		53	A3, B5	
15	A1, A2, A7, B3, C6		54	A2, B5	ABS brake system
16	A1, A6, B2, C1, C3	Cooling fans – models with air conditioning	55	B5, B7	
			56	A3, B7	
17	A1, C2		57	A1, B1	
18	A1, B3, B6, C1, C4	Air conditioning	58	B6	Cooling fans – models with air conditioning
19	A1, B2				
20	A1, B4, C4		59	A3, B7	
21	A1, B4		60	C3, C5	Radio cassette player with power amplifier
22	A1, B7				
23	B1, B6		61	C4	Air conditioning
24	B1		62	C4	Air conditioning
25	B1	Radio cassette player with power amplifier	63	A2	ABS braking system
			64	A4, B2	
26	B1	Cooling fan – models with air conditioning	65	A5, B2, C6	
			66	A5, B2, C6	
27	B1, C2		67	A3, C6	Air conditioning
28	B1, C3		68	A3, B4	
29	B1, B6	Air conditioning	69	A3, C7	
30	B1, B2		70	A3, C7	
31	A1, A6, B1		71	A3, C7	
32	A5, C1		72	A7, C6	ABS brake system
33	A7, B1		73	A7, C6	
34	A4, B1, C1		74		Air conditioning
35	A4, B1, C1		76	A3, C7	
36	A6, B1, C1		77	B3, B4	

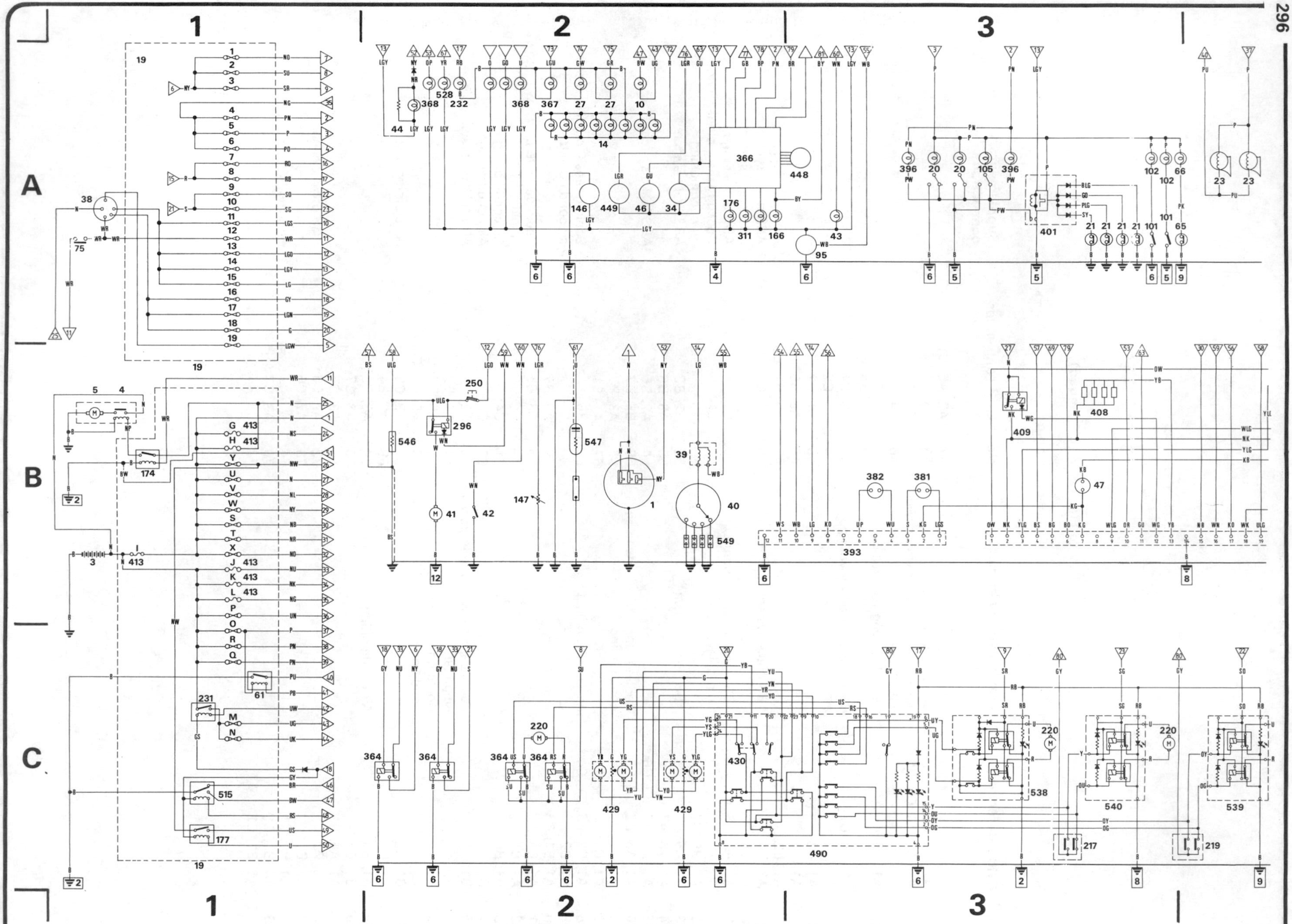

Fig. 12.23 Main wiring diagram – multi-point fuel injection models

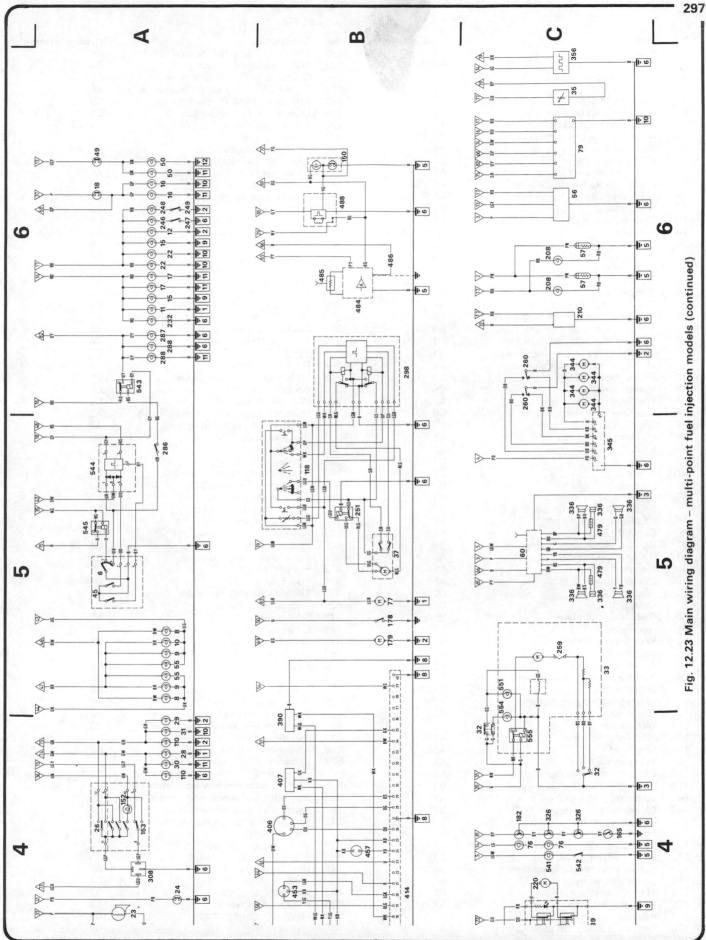

Fig. 12.23 Main wiring diagram – multi-point fuel injection models (continued)

Key to Fig. 12.23

No	Description	Grid reference	No	Description	Grid reference
1	Alternator	B2	179	Radiator cooling fan motor	B5
3	Battery	B1	182	Brake fluid level switch	C4
4	Starter motor switch	B1	208	Cigar lighter illumination lamp	C6
5	Starter motor	B1	210	Panel illumination lamp rheostat resistor	C6
6	Lighting switch	A5	217	RH rear window lift switch	C3
8	Headlamp dip beam	A5	219	LH rear window lift switch	C4
9	Headlamp main beam	A5	220	Window lift motor	C2, C3, C4
10	Main beam warning lamp	A2, A5	231	Headlamp relay	C1
11	RH sidelamp	A6	232	Sidelamp warning lamp	A2, A6
12	LH sidelamp	A6	246	Glove box illumination lamp	A6
14	Panel illumination lamps	A2	247	Glove box illumination switch	A6
15	Number plate illumination lamps	A6	248	Bonnet lamp	A6
16	Stop-lamps	A6	249	Bonnet lamp switch	A6
17	RH tail lamp	A6	250	Inertia switch	B2
18	Stop-lamp switch	A6	251	Windscreen wiper relay	B5
19	Fusebox	A1, B1, C1	259	Thermal circuit breaker	C5
20	Interior lamps	A3	260	Door lock switch	C6
21	Interior lamp door switch	A3	286	Foglamp switch	A5
22	LH tail lamp	A6	287	Foglamp warning lamp	A6
23	Horns	A4	288	Foglamps	A6
24	Horn push	A4	296	Fuel pump relay	B2
26	Direction indicator switch	A4	298	Windscreen wiper delay unit	B6
27	Direction indicator warning lamps	A2	308	Direction indicator/hazard flasher unit	A4
28	RH front direction indicator lamp	A4	311	Coolant temperature warning lamp	A2
29	LH front direction indicator lamp	A4	326	Brake pad wear sensor	C4
30	RH rear direction indicator lamp	A4	336	Speakers	C5
31	LH rear direction indicator lamp	A4	344	Door lock motor	C6
32	Heater motor switch	C4	345	Door lock motor control unit	C5
33	Heater motor	C5	356	Speed transducer	C6
34	Fuel level gauge	A2	364	Window lift relay	C2
35	Fuel level tank unit	C6	366	Instrument pack multi-function unit	A2
37	Windscreen wiper motor	B5	367	Trailer towing warning light	A2
38	Ignition/start switch	A1	368	Spare warning light	A2
39	Ignition coil	B2	381	Knock sensor	B3
40	Distributor	B2	382	Crankshaft sensor	B3
41	Fuel pump	B2	390	Diagnostic junction – Fuel ECU	B4
42	Oil pressure switch	B2	393	Programmed ignition ECU	B3
43	Oil pressure warning lamp	A3	396	Footwell illumination	A3
44	Ignition or no charge warning lamp	A2	401	Interior lamp delay unit	A3
45	Headlamp flash switch	A5	406	Air valve stepper motor	B4
46	Coolant temperature gauge	A2	407	Airflow meter electronic unit	B4
47	Coolant temperature thermistor	B3	408	Fuel injectors	B3
49	Reverse lamp switch	A6	409	Main relay – Fuel ECU	B3
50	Reverse lamps	A6	413	Fusible link	B1
55	Driving lamps	A5	414	Fuel ECU	B4
56	Clock	C6	429	Electric mirror motor/heater	C2
57	Cigar lighter	C6	430	Electric mirror switch	C2
60	Radio cassette player	C5	448	Speedometer	A3
61	Horn relay	C1	449	Oil pressure gauge	A2
65	Boot lamp switch	A3	453	Throttle potentiometer	B4
66	Boot lamp	A3	457	Fuel temperature sensor	B4
75	Automatic gearbox inhibitor switch	A1	479	Filter	C5
76	Automatic gearbox selector indicator lamp	C4	484	Aerial amplifier and isolator unit	B6
77	Windscreen washer motor	B5	485	Aerial and heated rear screen	B6
79	Trailer socket	C6	486	Aerial co-axial cable	B6
95	Tachometer	A3	488	Heated rearscreen timer relay	B6
101	Map light switch	A3	490	Four door window lift control unit	C3
102	Map light	A3	515	Headlamp main/dip relay	C1
105	Rear interior lamp	A3	528	ABS warning light	A2
110	Direction indicator repeater lamp	A4	538	Passenger's door window lift control unit	C3
118	Windscreen washer/wiper switch	B5	539	Rear LH door window lift control unit	C4
146	Voltmeter	A2	540	Rear RH door window lift control unit	C3
147	Oil pressure transducer	B2	541	Vanity mirror illumination lamp	C4
150	Heated rear screen switch and warning lamp	B6	542	Vanity mirror illumination switch	C4
152	Hazard warning lamp	A4	543	Foglamp relay	A6
153	Hazard warning switch	A4	544	Headlamp cut-off unit	A5
165	Handbrake warning lamp switch	C4	545	Sidelamp relay	A5
166	Handbrake warning lamp	A2	546	Lambda heater	B2
174	Starter solenoid relay	B1	547	Lambda sensor	B2
176	Fuel level warning lamp	A2	549	Spark plugs	B2
177	Radiator cooling fan relay	C1	551	Recirculation warning lamp	C5
178	Radiator cooling fan thermostat	B5	554	Fresh air warning lamp	C5
			555	Heater relay	C4

Key to Fig. 12.23 (continued)

Connection chart

No	Grid references	Supplementary circuit connections	No	Grid references	Supplementary circuit connections
1	B1, B2		39	C1	ABS brake system
2	A1, A2, A3, C6		40	A4, C1	
3	A1, A3, C3, C6	Radio cassette player with power amplifier	41	C1, A4	
			42	C1, A5	
4	A1, C5	Central locking with remote control	43	C1, A2, A5	
			44	C1, A5	
5	B1, C4, C5	Radio cassette player with power amplifier	46	A5, C1	
			47	A5, C1, A2	
6	A1, C2		48	C1, A5	
7	A1		49	C1, B5	
8	A1, C2		50	C1, B5	
9	A1, C3	ABS brake system	51	B4, B1	
10	A1		52	A2, B2	ABS brake system
11	A1, B1		53	A2, B3	
12	A1, B2		54	B2, B5	
13	A1, A2, A3, A4, A6, C6	ABS brake system	55	B2, A3, B3	
14	A1, B2, B3, C4, C6		56	B3, B4	
15	A1, A5		57	B2, B3	
16	A1, A6, C6		58	B2, B4	
17	A1, A2, A6, C3, C6	Air conditioning	59	B2, B4	
18	A1, A5, B6, C1, C2	Cooling fans – models with air conditioning	60	A3, B2	
			61	B4, B2	
19	A1, B5		63	B3, A2	
20	A1, C2, C4		64	B4	Cooling fans – models with air conditioning
21	A1, C2				
22	A1, C4		65	C5, B6	Radio cassette player with power amplifier
23	A1, C3				
24	B1	Radio cassette player with power amplifier	66	C5, B6	Radio cassette player with power amplifier
25	A1, B1		67	A2	ABS brake system
26	B1	Cooling fan – models with air conditioning	68	A6, C6	ABS brake system
			69	B6, B3	Air conditioning
27	B1, B3		70	B6	Air conditioning
28	B1	Headlamp power wash	72	C6, A2	Air conditioning
29	B1, B6		73	A4, A2	
30	B1, B4		74	A4, A2, C6	
31	B1, C4	Air conditioning	75	A4, A2, C6	
32	B1	Cooling fan – models with air conditioning	76	A2, B2	
			77	A2, C6	
33	B1, C2		78	C6, A2	
34	B1	ABS brake system	79	C6, A3, B3	
35	B1, A1, A5		80	C3	
36	B1, A4		81	A3, C4	
37	C1, A4, A6		82	A6, C6	
38	C1	ABS brake system	83	B5	Headlamp wash

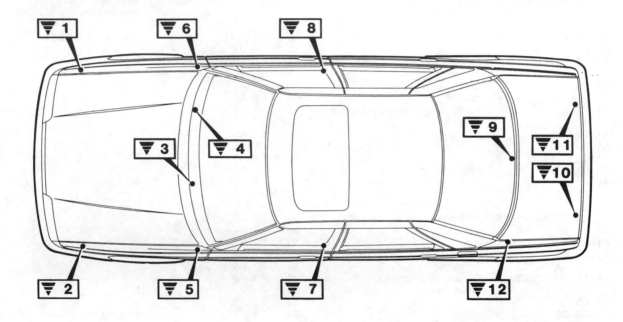

Fig. 12.24 Supplementary wiring diagram – earth point locations

1   Behind RH headlamp
2   Behind LH headlamp
3   Behind facia
4   Steering column bracket
5   Base of LH 'A' pillar
6   Base of RH 'A' pillar
7   Base of LH 'B' pillar
8   Base of RH 'B' pillar
9   Beneath rear parcel shelf
10 Beneath LH rear lamp
11 Beneath RH rear lamp
12 LH side panel in luggage
    compartment beneath carpet

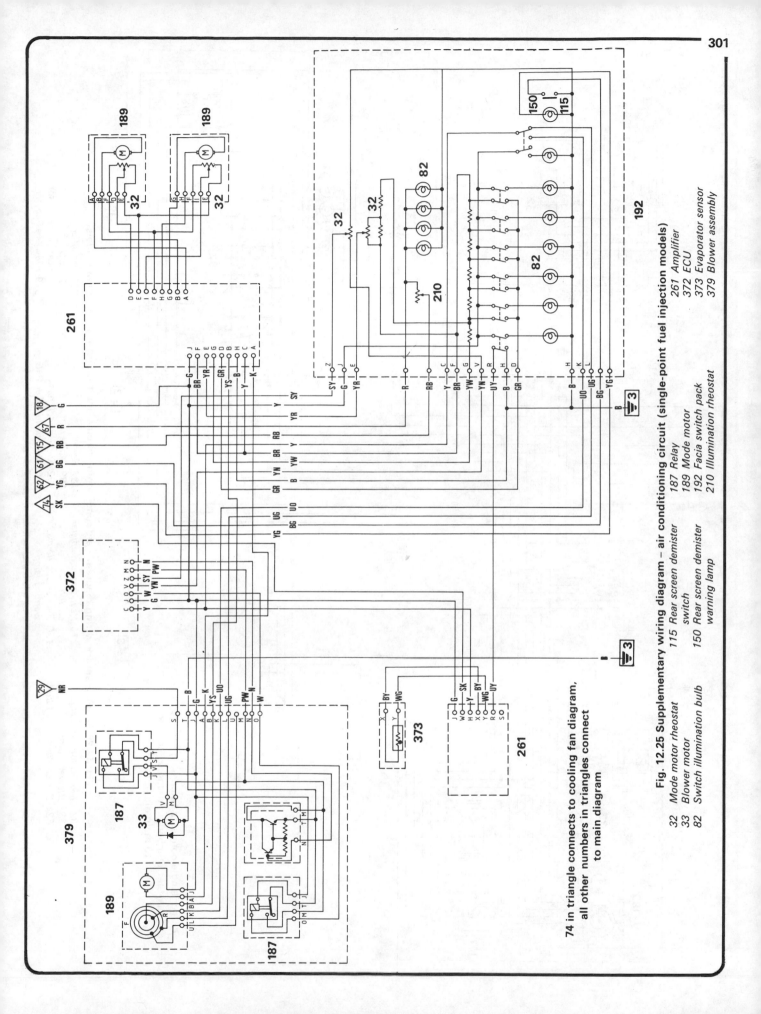

Fig. 12.25 Supplementary wiring diagram – air conditioning circuit (single-point fuel injection models)

32 Mode motor rheostat
33 Blower motor
82 Switch illumination bulb

115 Rear screen demister switch
150 Rear screen demister warning lamp

187 Relay
189 Mode motor
192 Facia switch pack
210 Illumination rheostat

261 Amplifier
372 ECU
373 Evaporator sensor
379 Blower assembly

74 in triangle connects to cooling fan diagram, all other numbers in triangles connect to main diagram

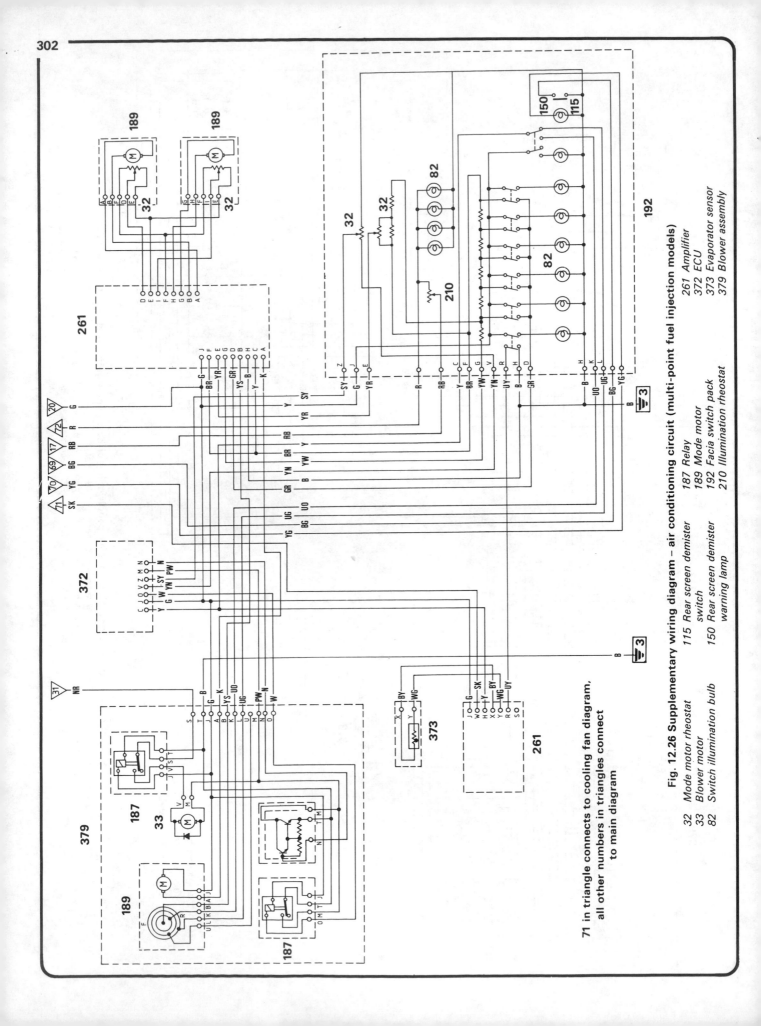

Fig. 12.26 Supplementary wiring diagram – air conditioning circuit (multi-point fuel injection models)

32 Mode motor rheostat	115 Rear screen demister	187 Relay	261 Amplifier
33 Blower motor	rheostat	189 Mode motor	372 ECU
82 Switch illumination bulb	150 Rear screen demister	192 Facia switch pack	373 Evaporator sensor
	warning lamp	210 Illumination rheostat	379 Blower assembly

71 in triangle connects to cooling fan diagram,
all other numbers in triangles connect
to main diagram

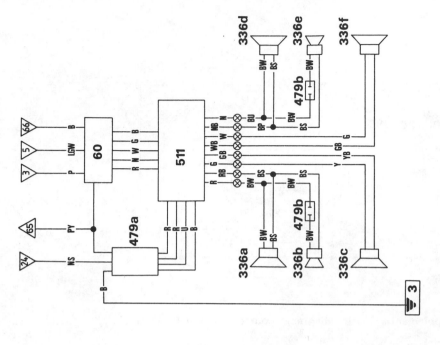

Fig. 12.28 Supplementary wiring diagram – radio cassette player with power amplifier circuit (multi-point fuel injection models)

60	Radio cassette player	336e	RH front tweeter
336a	LH front speaker	336f	RH rear speaker
336b	LH front tweeter	479a	Filter – power amplifier
336c	LH rear speaker	479b	Filter – speakers
336d	RH front speaker	511	Power amplifier

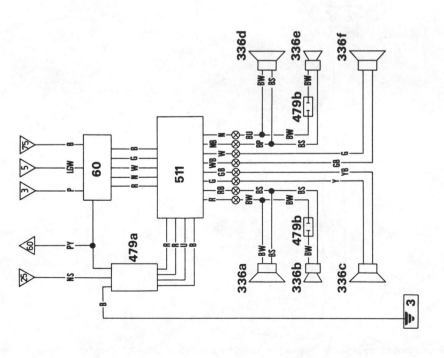

Fig. 12.27 Supplementary wiring diagram – radio cassette player with power amplifier circuit (single-point fuel injection models)

60	Radio cassette player	336e	RH front tweeter
336a	LH front speaker	336f	RH rear speaker
336b	LH front tweeter	479a	Filter – power amplifier
336c	LH rear speaker	479b	Filter – speakers
336d	RH front speaker	511	Power amplifier

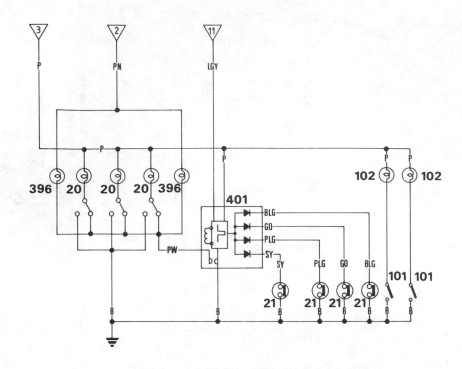

Fig. 12.29 Supplementary wiring diagram – courtesy lamp delay circuit

20 Interior lamps	21 Interior lamp door pillar switch	101 Map lamp switch	396 Footwell lamps
		102 Map reading lamps	401 Interior lamp delay unit

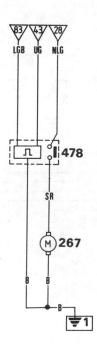

Fig. 12.30 Supplementary wiring diagram – headlamp washer circuit

267 Washer pump   478 Timer delay relay

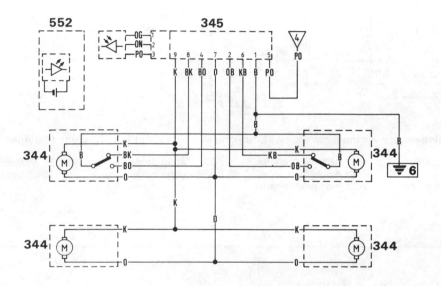

Fig. 12.31 Supplementary wiring diagram – central locking with remote control circuit

344 Door lock motor   *345 ECU*   *552 Remote control*

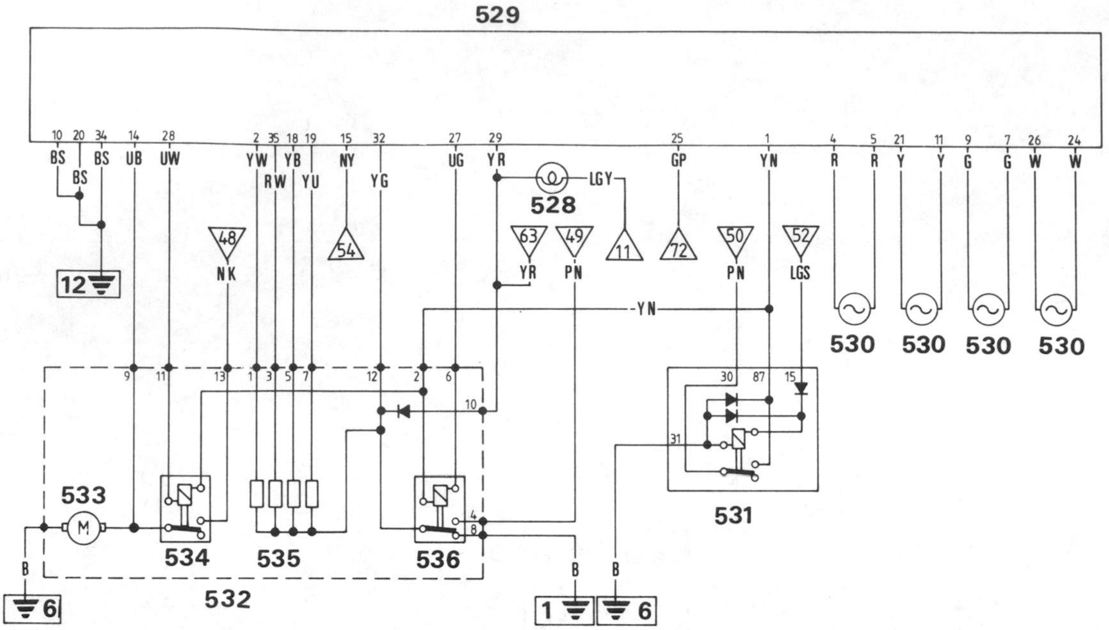

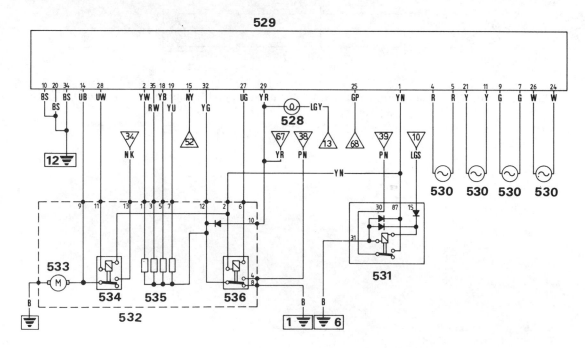

Fig. 12.32 Supplementary wiring diagram – ABS braking system circuit (single-point fuel injection models)

528 ABS warning lamp
529 ECU
530 Wheel speed sensor

531 ABS over-voltage
   protection relay
532 Hydraulic modulator

533 Return pump
534 Return pump relay

535 Solenoid valve
536 Solenoid valve relay

Fig. 12.33 Supplementary wiring diagram – ABS braking system circuit (multi-point fuel injection models)

528 ABS warning lamp
529 ECU
530 Wheel speed sensor

531 ABS over-voltage
   protection relay
532 Hydraulic modulator

533 Return pump
534 Return pump relay

535 Solenoid valve
536 Solenoid valve relay

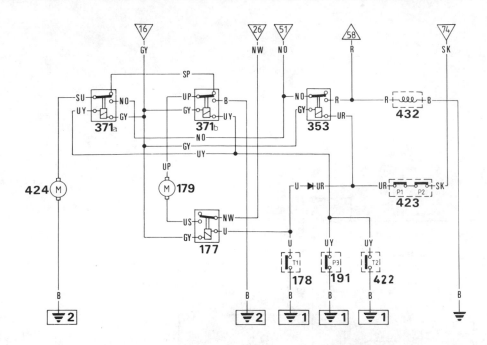

Fig. 12.34 Supplementary wiring diagram – cooling fan circuit (single-point fuel injection models with air conditioning)

177 Radiator cooling fan relay	191 Condenser cooling fan switch	371b Condenser fan changeover relay 2	423 Dual pressure switch
178 Radiator cooling fan switch	371a Condenser fan changeover relay 1	353 Magnetic clutch relay	424 Condenser cooling fan motor
179 Radiator cooling fan motor		422 Air conditioning thermostat switch	423 Compressor switch

74 in triangle connects to air conditioning diagram, all other numbers in triangles connect to main diagram

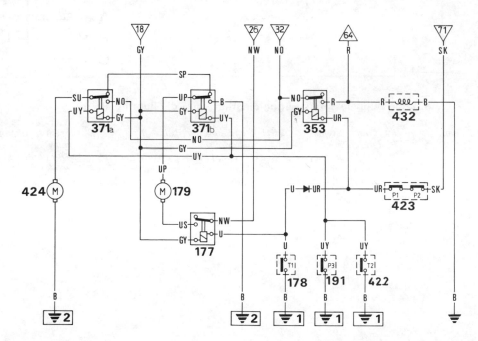

Fig. 12.35 Supplementary wiring diagram – cooling fan circuit (multi-point fuel injection models with air conditioning)

177 Radiator cooling fan relay	191 Condenser cooling fan switch	371b Condenser fan changeover ralay 2	423 Dual pressure switch
178 Radiator cooling fan switch	371a Condenser fan changeover relay 1	353 Magnetic clutch relay	424 Condenser cooling fan motor
179 Radiator cooling fan motor		422 Air conditioning thermostat switch	432 Compressor switch

71 in triangle connects to air conditioning diagram, all other numbers in triangles connect to main diagram

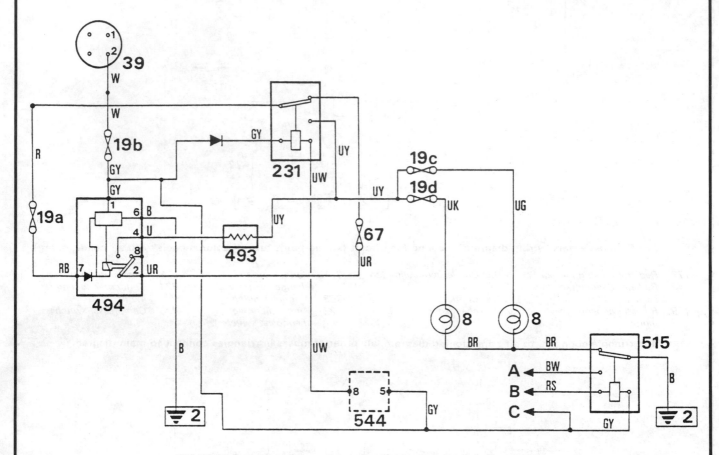

Fig. 12.36 Supplementary wiring diagram – dim-dip lighting circuit

8	Headlamp dipped beam	39	Ignition switch	515	Headlamp main/dipped	B	From headlamp changeover
19a	Fuse 7	67	Line fuse		beam relay		relay
19b	Fuse 16	231	Headlamp relay	544	Headlamp changeover relay	C	To radiator cooling fan
19c	Fuse M	493	Dim-dip resistor	A	From headlamp main		relay
19d	Fuse N	494	Dim-dip relay		beams		

Chapter 13 Supplement:
Revisions and information on later models

Contents

1 Introduction

This supplement contains information relating to models produced from 1988 onwards, and also material which is additional to, or a revision of, that contained in the preceding Chapters.

The Sections in this Chapter follow the same order as the Chapters to which they relate, and it is recommended that before any particular operation is undertaken, reference be made to the appropriate Section(s) of the Supplement. In this way, any changes to procedures or components can be noted before referring to the main Chapters.

2 Specifications

The following specifications are revisions of, or are supplementary to, those at the start of each of the preceding Chapters

Engine

Torque wrench settings

	Nm	lbf ft
Cylinder head bolts – from 1989:		
Stage 1	45	33
Stage 2	80	59
Stage 3	Angle-tighten a further 90°	Angle-tighten a further 90°
Timing belt upper idler pulley bolt – from 1989	50	36
Timing belt tensioner retaining bolt	45	33

Fuel and exhaust systems

Multi-point fuel injection engine – from 1988

Idle speed:	
ECU-controlled idle speed	850 to 950 rpm
Base idle speed	735 to 765 rpm
Exhaust CO content (non-adjustable)	0.25%

Multi-point fuel injection engine with catalytic converter – from 1991
Idle speed:
    ECU-controlled idle speed .... 825 to 925 rpm
    Base idle speed .... 735 to 765 rpm
Exhaust CO content (non-adjustable) .... 0.25% (maximum)

Torque wrench settings	Nm	lbf ft
Catalytic converter	30	22
Oxygen sensor	20	15

Ignition system
Ignition timing – from 1991
Multi-point fuel injection engine with catalytic converter:
    With vacuum connected .... 24° to 28° BTDC at 1500 rpm
    With vacuum disconnected .... 9° to 11° BTDC at 1500 rpm

Torque wrench settings	Nm	lbf ft
Spark plugs – from 1991	25	18
Distributor cap screws:		
Up to 1989	6	4
From 1989	3	2

Manual gearbox
Gear ratios – type V4DT – from 1988
1st 3.25:1
2nd 1.89:1
3rd 1.30:1
4th 0.93:1
5th 0.76:1
Reverse 3.00:1
Final drive 4.20:1

Suspension and steering
Rear wheel alignment – from 1991
Toe setting .... 0°11′ ± 0°6′ toe-in (each wheel)

Wheels and tyres – from 1988
Wheel size (optional) .... 6J x 16 (alloy)
Tyre sizes .... 195/70 VR 14, 195/65 VR 15 or 205/55 VR 16
Tyre pressures – cold, bar (lbf/in²):

	Front	Rear
195/70 VR 14 and 195/65 VR 15:		
Normal load	1.8 (26)	1.8 (26)
Full load	2.0 (29)	2.0 (29)
205/55 VR 16:		
All loads	2.2 (32)	2.2 (32)

For speeds above 100 mph (160 kph), increase pressures by 0.4 bar (6 lbf/in²) for 195/70 VR 14 and 195/65 VR 15 tyres, and by 0.6 bar (9 lbf/in²) for 205/55 VR 16 tyres

Torque wrench settings – from 1991	Nm	lbf ft
Front suspension		
Strut forked member clamp bolt	60	44
Tie-bar to lower suspension arm bolts	110	82
Roadwheel nuts	110	82

Electrical system
Alternator – from 1988
Alternative type .... Lucas A133-80
Maximum output .... 80 amps

General dimensions, weights and capacities
Weights (kerb) – from 1991
Saloon (with manual gearbox):*
    820i .... 1325 kg (2925 lb)
    820Si .... 1335 kg (2943 lb)
    820SLi .... 1345 kg (2965 lb)
Fastback (with manual gearbox):*
    820i .... 1355 kg (2987 lb)
    820Si .... 1365 kg (3009 lb)
    820SLi .... 1365 kg (3009 lb)

* Add 15 kg (33 lb) to the above weights for automatic transmission models

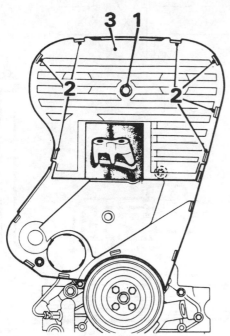

Fig. 13.1 Timing belt upper cover securing points on later models (Sec 4)

1	Bolt	3	Upper cover
2	Clips		

3 Routine maintenance – later models

1   The procedures and schedule given at the beginning of this manual apply equally to later models, with the following additions.
2   On models equipped with a catalytic converter, check the condition of the catalyst heat shield every 12 months or 12 000 miles (20 000 km).
3   Where applicable, check the condition of the evaporative emission control system components every 12 months or 12 000 miles (20 000 km).

4 Engine

Timing belt – removal, refitting and adjustment

1   The timing belt upper cover on later models is secured by a single bolt in the middle and seven clips around the periphery of the cover (Fig. 13.1).
2   To remove the later type cover, unscrew the retaining bolt and release the clips. Withdraw the cover.
3   With the exception of the upper timing cover and its fastenings, the timing components on later models are identical to those fitted on earlier models. The following special points, however, must be noted whenever the timing components are removed on any model:

(a)   *If the timing belt is removed with the cylinder head in position, it is most important that the crankshaft is not turned from the set position during belt removal. Such action will alter the valve timing and could cause the valves to touch the top face of the pistons*

(b)   *When refitting the timing belt upper idler pulley on models produced from 1989, it is important to ensure that the spacer washer is of sufficient thickness, otherwise the upper idler pulley and its retaining bolt will become loose in operation. When the idler pulley bolt is being tightened to its specified torque wrench setting, ensure that the pulley is tight against the spacer (not the back panel). The spacer is stepped and is fitted from behind the back panel*

(c)   *When turning the engine over to check the tension of the timing belt, do not turn the engine over using the camshaft sprockets or their retaining bolts*

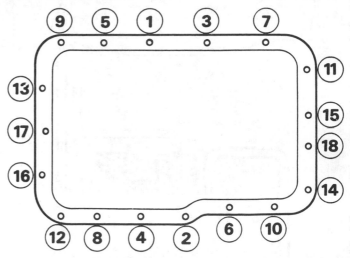

Fig. 13.2 Sump bolt tightening sequence from 1989 (Sec 4)

(d)   *When adjusting the timing belt tension, ensure that the tensioner retaining bolt is fully tightened prior to making the final tension check. Once the belt tension is correctly adjusted, the tensioner must not be disturbed further*

Sump bolt tightening sequence – revision

4   The sump bolt tightening sequence for models produced from 1989 on is as shown in Fig. 13.2. The sump removal/refitting procedures are otherwise the same as described in Chapter 1 for earlier models.

Cylinder head – removal and refitting

5   When refitting the cylinder head on later models (from 1989), refer to the specifications at the start of this Chapter for the torque wrench settings.

5 Fuel and exhaust systems (models with catalytic converter)

Multi-point fuel injection system – general

1   The component parts of this system and their method of operation are much the same as those fitted to the conventional system type described in Chapter 3. The mixture control adjustment is also affected by the readings supplied to the electronic control unit (ECU) by the oxygen sensor in the exhaust system.
2   In addition to the oxygen sensor and the catalytic converter, an evaporative emission control system is fitted.
3   The removal and adjustment procedures for the multi-point fuel injection system components are the same as described in Chapter 3 for the conventional system. Note that adjustment of the mixture control is not recommended because maladjustment of the mixture could have an adverse effect on the operation of the oxygen sensor and the catalytic converter. Any checks and adjustments to the mixture control must therefore be entrusted to a Rover dealer who has the specialised test equipment required.
4   The basic idle speed setting can be checked and adjusted as described for the conventional system in Sections 38 and 39 of Chapter 3, but ignore references to mixture adjustment.

Evaporative emission control system – description

5   The function of this system is to prevent fuel vapours escaping into the atmosphere. It achieves this by recirculating fuel vapours via a charcoal-filled canister, back into the engine inlet system where they are drawn into the combustion chambers and burnt in the normal combustion process.
6   The system layout is shown in Fig. 13.3. The system has two main controls – the fuel tank vapour control and the vapour purge control.
7   Fuel pressure in the fuel tank is controlled by a two-way breather valve. When the pressure rises above a given amount, the valve opens and the fuel vapour passes from the tank to the charcoal canister. When

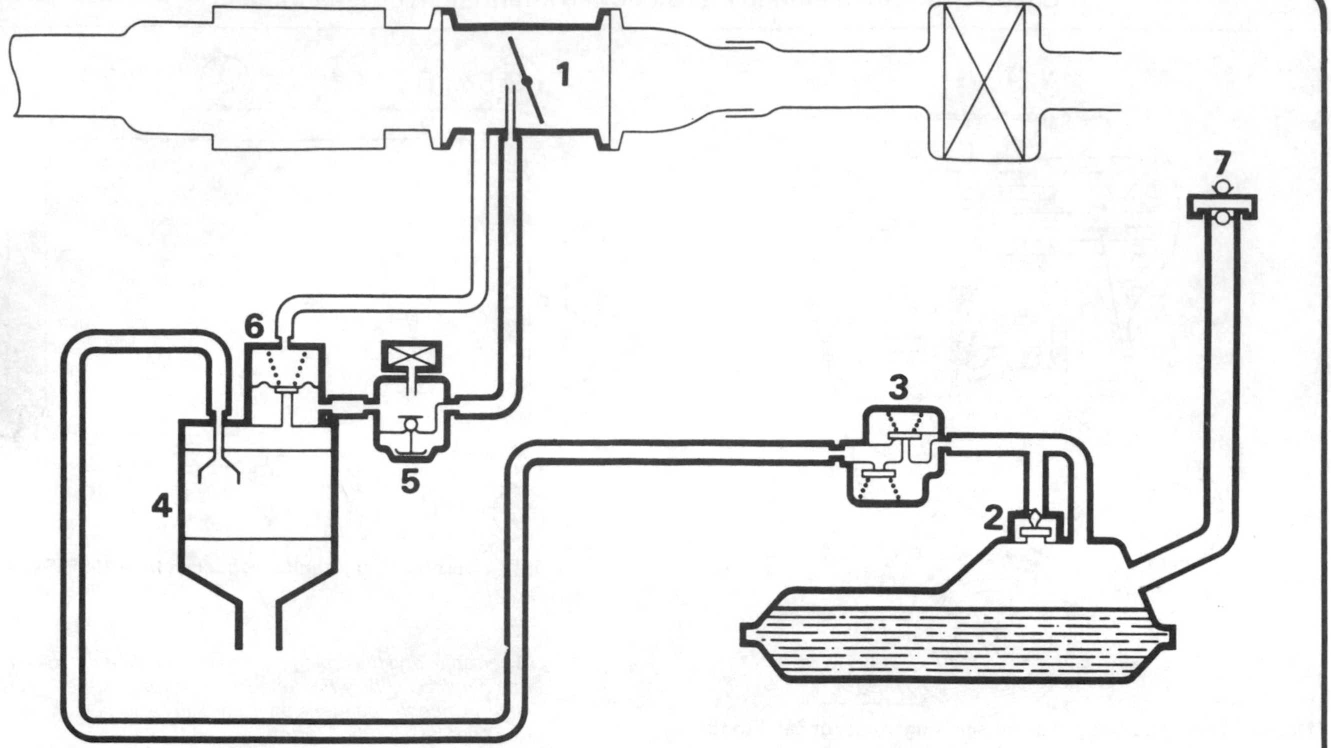

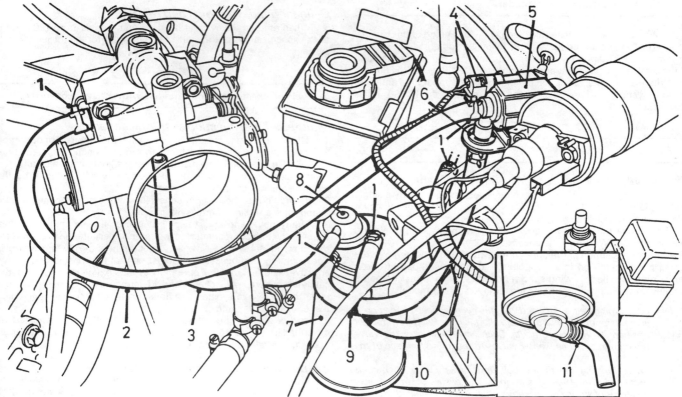

Fig. 13.3 Evaporative emission control system (Sec 5)

1 Throttle housing   3 Two-way breather valve   5 Purge control solenoid   7 Fuel filler cap
2 Tank cut-off valve   4 Charcoal canister   6 Diaphragm control valve

Fig. 13.4 Evaporative emission control system hose routing and component locations (Sec 5)

1 Retaining clips   5 Purge control solenoid   8 Diaphragm valve   Inset shows fresh air
2 Throttle hose   6 Circlip   9 Purge hose   hose (11) connection
3 Diaphragm valve hose   7 Charcoal canister   10 Top hose   on base of canister
4 Wiring multi-plug

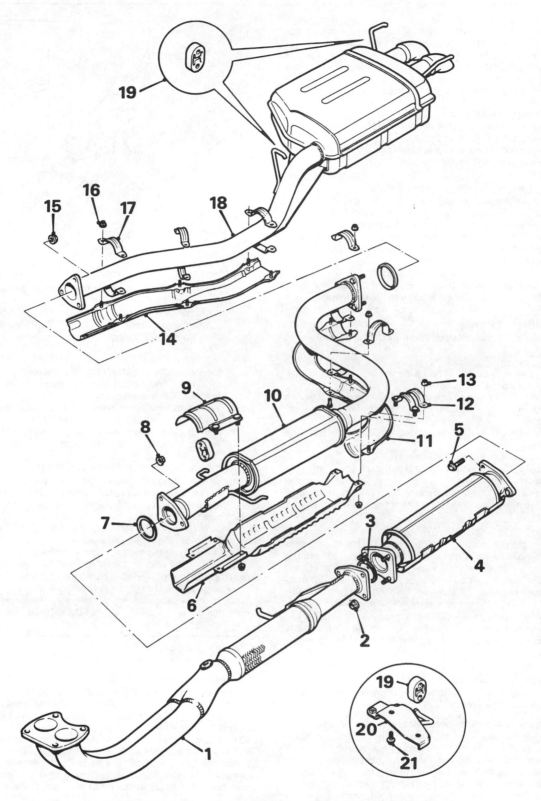

Fig. 13.5 Exhaust system components – with catalytic converter (Sec 5)

1 Front pipe	8 Nut	15 Nut
2 Nut	9 Intermediate pipe upper heat shield	16 Nut
3 Flange seal	10 Intermediate pipe	17 Heat shield bracket
4 Catalytic converter	11 Intermediate pipe rear heat shield	18 Tailpipe
5 Stud	12 Heat shield bracket	19 Mounting rubber
6 Intermediate pipe lower heat shield	13 Nut	20 Mounting bracket
7 Flange seal	14 Tailpipe heat shield	21 Bolt

the pressure drops below a given amount, the valve draws air through the charcoal canister, and this extracts fuel vapour from the granules of charcoal in the canister and returns the vapours to the fuel tank.

8   Liquid fuel is prevented from entering the vapour lines by means of a cut-off valve. In the event of the two-way valve failing, excess fuel vapour pressure in the tank will be released into the atmosphere through a valve in the fuel filler cap. The filler cap valve is otherwise normally closed.

9   The vapour purge control system comprises the canister purge solenoid and the charcoal canister. Fuel vapour flow from the canister to the engine is controlled by the fuel system ECU. This regulates the vapour flow rate in accordance with the engine coolant temperature, engine speed, road speed and throttle position.

Purge control solenoid – removal and refitting

10   Disconnect the wiring multi-plug from the solenoid unit.
11   Unclip and detach the throttle hose from the solenoid unit. Pull the hose straight from the solenoid, or the connecting pipe may break.
12   Prise free the circlip securing the purge hose to the support bracket and solenoid, then pull the hose from the solenoid connection. Collect the O-ring seal from the hose.
13   Slide free the solenoid from the support bracket.
14   Refit in the reverse order of removal. Ensure that all connections are securely made, and that the O-ring is fitted to the purge hose.

Charcoal canister – renewal

15   On ABS-equipped models, detach and remove the air intake duct for access.
16   Using a pair of suitable pliers, compress the tangs of the clip securing the top hose to the canister and slide the clip down the hose. Pull the hose from the canister connection.
17   Release the diaphragm valve hose securing clip, then pull the hose from its connection. Take care to pull the hose straight from its connection, or it may break.
18   Lift the canister bracket, then detach the fresh air hose from the base of the canister.
19   Remove the canister.
20   Transfer the plugs from the new canister to the old unit, then fit the new canister, reversing the removal procedures. Do not fit a new canister that has not had plugs fitted. Ensure that all hoses are in good condition and are securely reconnected with their retaining clips.

Exhaust system – description

21   A three-way catalytic converter is fitted to the exhaust system as an option on multi-point fuel injection engine models from 1988 on. The object of the catalytic converter is to further reduce the harmful CO and HC emissions from the exhaust by means of a high-temperature reaction in the exhaust process. To achieve this efficiently, the air/fuel mixture supplied to the engine must be finely regulated, and to assist in this, an oxygen sensor (lambda) is located in the exhaust downpipe. The sensor measures the contents of the exhaust gas and sends a signal to the fuel system ECU so that it can adjust the fuel mixture to the engine as required.

Precautionary notes – catalytic converter

22   Where a catalytic converter is fitted, the following special precautionary notes should be observed:

  (a) *Only unleaded fuel must be used, or the catalyst will be damaged*
  (b) *If the oxygen sensor malfunctions, it must be renewed at the first opportunity, or the converter could be damaged internally if the exhaust gas mixture is not measured and regulated*
  (c) *When working underneath the vehicle after it has been recently used, keep clear of the exhaust system (as normal), but particularly keep clear of the catalytic converter – it operates at a very high temperature and will take longer to cool off*

Exhaust system – removal and refitting

23   The procedures for checking, removing and refitting the exhaust system are the same as described in Chapter 3, but the following additional points should be noted:

  (a) *The catalytic converter heat shield is not removable*
  (b) *The catalytic converter operates at a higher temperature than the other parts of the exhaust system, and particular care must*

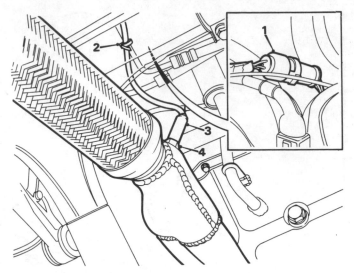

Fig. 13.6 Oxygen sensor location (Sec 5)

1	*Wiring multi-plug*	3	*Oxygen sensor*
2	*Wiring harness clip (to power steering pipe)*	4	*Seal washer*

be exercised to avoid scalding when working in close proximity to it. Where possible, allow the system to cool off completely before working underneath the vehicle
  (c) *When removing the exhaust system downpipe, it is also necessary to disconnect the oxygen sensor lead*
  (d) *Do not drop or knock the catalytic converter or the oxygen sensor, as they are easily damaged*

Oxygen sensor – removal and refitting

24   Raise and support the vehicle on axle stands.
25   Disconnect the oxygen sensor wiring multi-plug (noting the O-ring seal). Release the clip securing the wire harness to the power steering system pipe (see Fig. 13.6).
26   Unscrew the oxygen sensor unit and remove it from the exhaust downpipe. Collect the sealing washer.
27   Before refitting the sensor, clean its threads thoroughly.
28   Check that the washer is fitted, then screw the sensor into position, tightening it to the specified torque wrench setting.
29   Check that the O-ring seal is fitted to the wiring multi-plug, then reconnect the sensor lead and secure it to the power steering pipe. Ensure that the wire is routed clear of the exhaust pipe.

---

6   Manual gearbox

Manual gearbox type V4DT (from 1988) – general

1   From 1988 on, the V4DT type manual gearbox was fitted to Fastback models, and to some other models in the range. Apart from the gear ratios, the gearbox is identical to the G6DT type gearbox fitted to previous models, described in Chapter 6. Any work undertaken on the V4DT type gearbox is therefore the same as that described for the G6DT type, in the appropriate Section of Chapter 6.
2   When ordering replacement parts for the manual gearbox (or the associated components), it is important that the gearbox type and production number are specified to ensure that the correct items are obtained.

---

7   Braking system

Rear brake caliper – caution

1   If any work is undertaken on the rear brake caliper(s), it is important to note that the handbrake **must not** be applied until full reassembly is complete and the footbrake has been adjusted in the manner described in paragraph 18 of Section 7, Chapter 9. If the handbrake is applied

prematurely, the handbrake mechanism within the rear caliper(s) could move to an over-centre position, bringing the brake pads in permanent contact with the disc, even with the handbrake lever fully released. This will obviously cause a drop in performance and greatly reduce the life of the pads. In this event, the complete rear brake caliper unit(s) will require renewal.

Anti-lock braking system (ABS) – later models
2   The ABS modulator unit fitted to later models differs in appearance to that used on earlier models. It functions in much the same way as the earlier type, but to ensure the equal operation of the rear brakes when the system is in operation, the modulator incorporates a copy valve which operates in accordance with pressure changes in the modulator-controlled hydraulic circuit.

8   Suspension and steering

Steering arm/steering knuckle – inspection
1   When checking the front suspension arm/steering knuckle balljoint for wear, first raise the vehicle so that the front roadwheels are clear of the ground. Check for excessive wear by positioning a suitable bar between the ground and the tyre, then lever between the two and note the amount of free movement in the suspension arm/steering knuckle joint. Renew the joint if necessary.

Front tie-bar – removal and refitting
2   A second cup washer may be fitted to the bushed end of the tie-bar between the nut and the bush. Where this is the case, ensure that both washers are fitted during reassembly and locate them back-to-back as shown in Fig. 13.7.

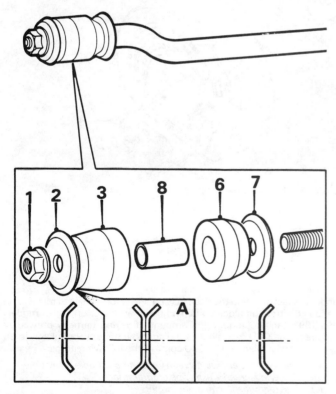

Fig. 13.7 Front suspension tie-bar end bushes and washers showing second cup washer orientation (inset A) – where applicable (Sec 8)

1	Nut	6	Bush
2	Washer	7	Washer
3	Bush	8	Spacer

9   Bodywork

Sunroof – later models
1   The sunroof fitted to later models is electrically operated. As with the mechanically-controlled roof panel, any problem encountered with the operation of the sunroof is best entrusted to a Rover dealer.
2   Should a malfunction occur, check the fuse and the electrical connections to and from the roof panel operating switch. If these prove to be in good order, have the roof panel motor and operating mechanism checked out by a Rover dealer.
3   If the panel suddenly malfunctions in the open position, it is possible to shut it manually using the key clipped to the topside of the access panel, to the rear of the interior mirror. Lift the access panel up at its rear edge and release it from the roof lining, then unclip the key from the access panel.
4   Insert the key into engagement with the sunroof motor and wind the roof panel shut by turning the key in a clockwise direction. When the panel is closed, turn the key slightly anti-clockwise to ensure that the drive mechanism re-engages.
5   Remove the key, attach it to the access panel clip, and refit the panel.

10   Electrical system

Battery and/or radio – removal and refitting
1   Whenever the battery and/or the radio are to be disconnected, it should be noted that the radio operating code will be cancelled. It will therefore be necessary to recode the unit when the battery is reconnected to enable the security switching circuit to be switched on, and to allow the radio to be operated. It is essential, therefore, to first check that you have a record of the personal identification number (PIN) before disconnecting the battery leads. Later models are fitted with a radio which has a code number specific to the vehicle, and the PIN is recorded during manufacture. This gives the advantage of the PIN being traced in the event of it being lost by the vehicle owner.
2   The special notes concerning battery disconnection in Section 2 of Chapter 12 are also to be adhered to.

Alternator type A133 – general
3   The Lucas type A133-80 alternator is fitted from 1988. Being similar in design to the Lucas A127 type used on earlier models, the removal and refitting procedures are the same as those described for the earlier type in Chapter 12. The drivebelt adjustment procedure is also the same.

Alternator brushes and regulator (type A133) – removal, inspection and refitting
4   Remove the alternator as described in Section 7 of Chapter 12.
5   Unbolt and remove the capacitor from the alternator rear cover.

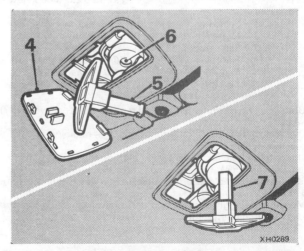

Fig. 13.8 Sunroof access panel (4) manual wind key (5) and key location (6 and 7) (Sec 9)

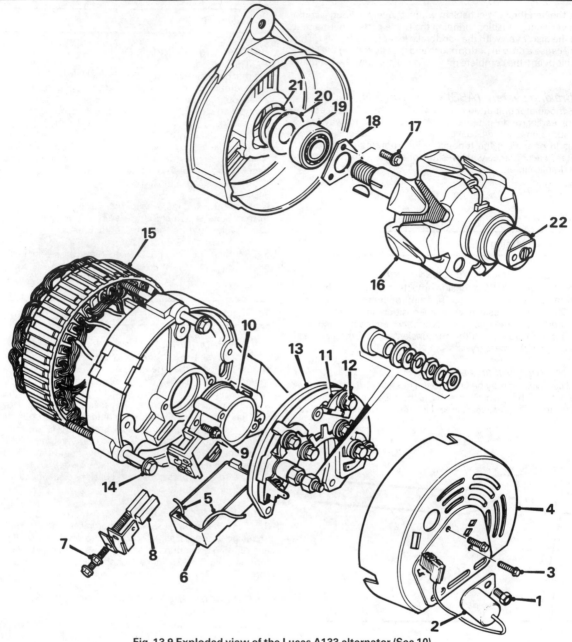

Fig. 13.9 Exploded view of the Lucas A133 alternator (Sec 10)

1 Setscrew	7 Setscrews	13 Rectifier unit	18 Clamp plate
2 Capacitor	8 Brushes	14 Through-bolts	19 Bearing
3 Setscrews	9 Setscrews	15 Stator	20 Felt washer retainer
4 End cover	10 Brush box/slip ring bracket	16 Rotor	21 Felt washer
5 Regulator leads	11 Rectifier wires	17 Setscrews	22 Bearing
6 Regulator	12 Setscrews		

6   Undo the two retaining screws and remove the rear cover from the alternator.

7   Disconnect the regulator leads, undo the retaining screws and remove the regulator.

8   Undo the retaining screws and extract the brushes from the holder/slip ring bracket. If required, undo the retaining screws and withdraw the brush holder/slip ring bracket from the rear face of the end bracket.

9   Measure the length of each brush and renew as a set if worn beyond the specified minimum length.

10   Refit in the reverse order of removal.

Central control unit (CCU) – later models

11   A central control unit (CCU) is fitted to later models, and is located under the facia, behind the dash fuse panel. Its function is to replace the various control units located behind the relay tower on earlier models (pre-1991), and to reduce the amount of wiring harness previously required. The CCU incorporates a diagnostic feature for linkage to an external test appliance. The CCU controls the following items:

(a)   *The intermittent windscreen wiper (and variable delay timer)*
(b)   *The windscreen wash/wipe programmer*
(c)   *The rear wash/wipe programmer*
(d)   *Rear intermittent wiper*
(e)   *Courtesy light delay*
(f)   *Lights-on warning buzzer*
(g)   *Heated rear window timer*
(h)   *Rear foglamps*
(i)   *Anti-theft alarm*

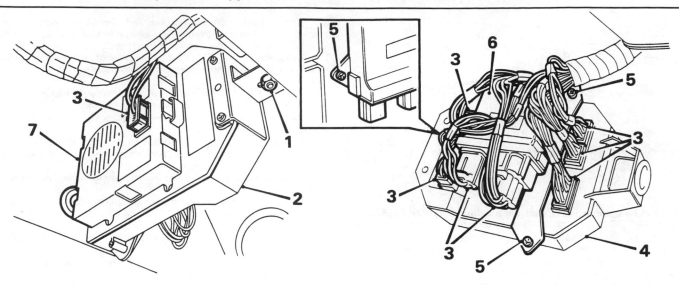

Fig. 13.10 Central control unit (CCU) (Sec 10)

1 Unit retaining nut	3 Wiring multi-plugs	5 Multi-function unit bracket screws	7 Audible signal unit
2 Central control unit (front face)	4 Central control unit (underside)	6 Multi-function unit	

(j) Headlamp changeover
(k) Headlamp courtesy off delay
(l) Headlamp dim-dip
(m) Headlamp power washer (where fitted)
(n) Electric windows (ignition off) and sunroof
(o) Seat adjustment (ignition off)
(p) Boot/tailgate release inhibitor
(q) Door locks (and mislock alarm)

Central control unit diagnostic features

12 The CCU incorporates two types of diagnostic features. The first (and more basic) type check enables each input to be monitored with visual and audible warnings, performing the functions in sequence. No external testing appliance is required to make these fault checks.

13 The second fault diagnosis method allows each input status to be checked using a serial port, and the outputs to be selectively driven, but this requires the use of a microcheck device, which is only available at a Rover dealer.

14 As mentioned above, the first diagnosis system incorporates an in-built test sequence, and this can be used to give an audible or visual indication of the operation of an input to the CCU. The outputs in the system can also be checked by switching them 'ON' and 'OFF' in a pre-set sequence. To actuate the in-built diagnostic system to check an input or output mode, first ensure that the ignition is switched fully off, then turn the ignition key to the auxiliary position. Move the headlamp flasher to the 'ON' position, then turn the ignition key to the ignition 'ON' position, and immediately release the headlamp flasher (within three seconds).

15 **Input checks:** Any particular input in the system can be checked. If checks on more than one circuit are to be made, they can be made in any order. To make a check on, for example the central door locking system (CDL), actuate the driver's (or front passenger's) door sill lock button. The input circuit to the CCU is in order if the CCU responds by giving an audible signal. This signal will be given by the CCU when any other circuit input check is made and is proved to be in satisfactory working order.

16 **Output checks:** The respective output circuits actuated by the CCU can be checked using the 'flick wipe' switch. Every time the 'flick wipe' switch is activated, the CCU checks the following circuit in the system in a set self-check sequence. The test sequence in the system is numerical, and each time the flick switch is actuated, the following circuit in the system is checked. The check sequence of the system is as follows:

Check number	Attrib*	Output circuit
1	SV	Lights-on warning buzzer
2	SI	Ignition switch (crank 'enable')
3	SV	Courtesy lights
4	OI	Infra-red receiver/decoder
5	SV	Central locking 'lock' relay
6	SV	Central locking 'unlock' relay
7	N	Not used
8	SV	Mislock alarm
9	SA	Boot/tailgate release
10	OV	Anti-theft alarm
11	OI	Not used
12	OV	Not used
13	SV	Wiper forward relay
14	SV	Wiper reverse relay
15	OV	Rear wiper relay
16	OV	Key alarm
17	SA	Electric windows
18	OA	Sunroof
19	SV	Heated rear window relay
20	OA	Seat adjustment
21	OV	Rear foglamp relay
22	SA	Main/dip relay
23	SI	Headlamp relay feed
24	OV	Lighting option relay
25	SV	Headlamp relay
26	OV	Headlamp power wash relay

* **Note:** *Attrib indicates attributes of output circuits relative to fitment as follows:*
S = Standard (on all models)
O = Optional (on some models only)
N = Not used
V = Visible (obvious visual or audible function, such as headlamps or horn)
A = Action required (a further control in the vehicle must be used in conjunction with the self-test system to obtain the 'positive' CCU signal)
I = Investigation required (further test using a voltmeter, and/or detach the circuit harness connectors)

17 As an example, to check say the output for the rear wiper relay, activate the flick wipe switch from the start fifteen times. When activating the switch from step fourteen to fifteen, the CCU will operate the key-in alarm, then when the switch is released, the circuit will be de-activated, and the alarm will stop. If the flick wipe switch is activated

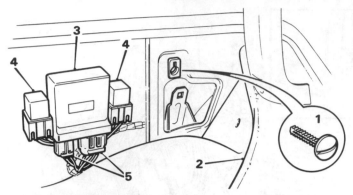

Fig. 13.11 Rear wiper and heated rear window relay module (Sec 10)

1	Trim turnbuckle	4	Relays
2	Side trim	5	Wiring multi-plugs
3	Multi-function trim		

again, it will move on to the next check (16). If it is wished to re-test a particular output circuit in the system, activate the intermittent wipe switch. When this is done, the key-in alarm should sound continuously until the intermittent wipe switch is released.

Central control unit – removal and refitting

18   Refer to the precautionary note at the start of this Section, then disconnect the battery earth lead.
19   Detach and remove the facia closing panel for access to the CCU unit.
20   Unscrew the nut securing the CCU, then withdraw the control unit from the mounting pin. Detach the five CCU wiring multi-plugs, the two multi-function unit plugs and the single audible signal unit multi-plug, then remove the control unit.

21   Undo the three retaining screws and remove the multi-function bracket, then separate the multi-function unit from the CCU.
22   Remove the audible signal unit from the CCU.
23   Reassemble and refit in the reverse order of removal. Ensure that all connections are correctly and securely made.

Rear wiper and heated rear window relay module (models from 1991) – removal and refitting

24   Refer to the precautionary note at the start of this Section, then detach the battery earth lead.
25   Remove the carpet in the luggage compartment, then turn the side trim turnbuckle a quarter of a turn, and release the trim for access to the multi-function unit and the relays.
26   Separate the appropriate unit from its wiring multi-plug and withdraw the unit.
27   Refit in the reverse order of removal, ensuring that the wiring connections are secure.

Rear (auxiliary) fusebox (models from 1991) – removal and refitting

28   Refer to the precautionary note at the start of this Section, then detach the battery earth lead.
29   Remove the luggage area carpet in the boot. Remove the left-hand rear light unit as described in Chapter 12.
30   Release the fuse block from its bracket.
31   Refit in the reverse order of removal.

Anti-theft alarm system – description

32   Later models are fitted with an anti-theft alarm system as an additional security measure. The system is armed automatically whenever the vehicle is locked (by key or infra-red handset); the system cannot be armed by pressing the internal door lock buttons.
33   In the event of the vehicle being broken into, the alarm will be activated. It will also sound if the ignition key is inserted into the ignition lock whilst the alarm is armed, and additionally, when the system is being armed and a door is not fully closed. Note that the bonnet must be fully closed to enable the system to be armed.

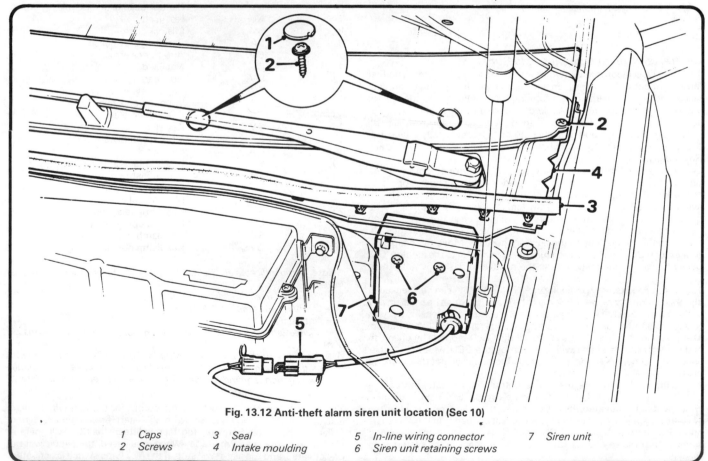

Fig. 13.12 Anti-theft alarm siren unit location (Sec 10)

1	Caps	3	Seal	5	In-line wiring connector	7	Siren unit
2	Screws	4	Intake moulding	6	Siren unit retaining screws		

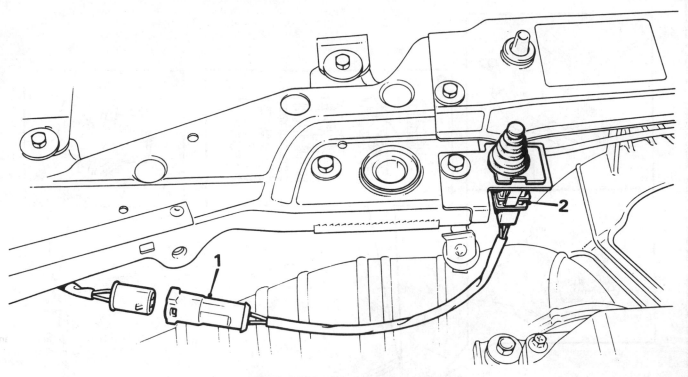

Fig. 13.13 Anti-theft alarm bonnet switch (Sec 10)

1   In-line wiring connector   *2   Bonnet switch*

34   The anti-theft alarm system is controlled by the ignition/starter circuit, the door courtesy light switches, the boot/tailgate light switches and the central control unit (CCU). If required, the alarm system can be checked for satisfactory operation in the following manner.

Anti-theft alarm system – checking
35   Open the door windows fully and ensure that all doors, the bonnet and the boot lid/tailgate are fully shut.
36   Lock the right-hand door with the key (from outside the car), then reach into the car (through the door window aperture) and release the bonnet catch. The alarm should sound. Unlock the right-hand front door using the key, and check that the alarm stops. Fully close the bonnet.
37   Repeat the procedure outlined in paragraph 36, but this time use the infra-red handset to lock/unlock the door, and release the boot lid/tailgate instead of the bonnet.
38   It should be noted that the alarm system will operate if the infra-red unit receives ten or more incorrect pulses.
39   Continue the checks by locking the left-hand door with the key, then lift one of the rocker panel buttons, open the door and check that the alarm is activated. The alarm system should remain operational when the door is closed. Unlock the door with the key to cancel the alarm.
40   Sitting in the driver's seat, shut the door and then lock the doors using the infra-red unit. Now insert the key into the ignition switch and turn it to operate the starter motor. The alarm should sound and the starter should fail to operate. Withdraw the ignition key, and unlock the doors using the infra-red unit to de-activate the alarm system.
41   If required, the alarm mode in the CCU can be checked as described earlier in this Section.

Anti-theft alarm siren – removal and refitting
42   Open and support the bonnet, then referring to Section 37 of Chapter 12, remove the right-hand windscreen wiper arm.
43   Carefully prise free the caps from the windscreen finisher retaining screws at the foot of the windscreen.
44   Undo the screws on the finisher front face and on the extreme edges, then remove the finisher from the car.
45   Using needle-nose pliers, release the rubber seal strip retaining clips from the top edge of the bulkhead. Note that some of the retaining clips may break, and will require renewal on refitting.

46   Remove the intake moulding from the plenum chamber.
47   Detach the in-line connector to the alarm siren unit, then undo the retaining screws and remove the siren.
48   Refitting is a reversal of the removal procedure. Set the wiper arm adjustment as described in Section 38 of Chapter 12.

Anti-theft alarm bonnet switch – removal and refitting
49   Open and support the bonnet. Detach the in-line wiring connector to the anti-theft switch.
50   Compress the retaining clips and withdraw the anti-theft switch from the mounting panel.
51   Refit in the reverse order of removal.

Infra-red central locking control – general
52   This system enables the doors to be automatically locked by the central locking system simply by aiming a hand-held infra-red transmit-

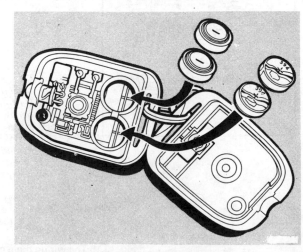

Fig. 13.14 Hand-held infra-red door lock transmitter battery renewal – note orientation of batteries (Sec 10)

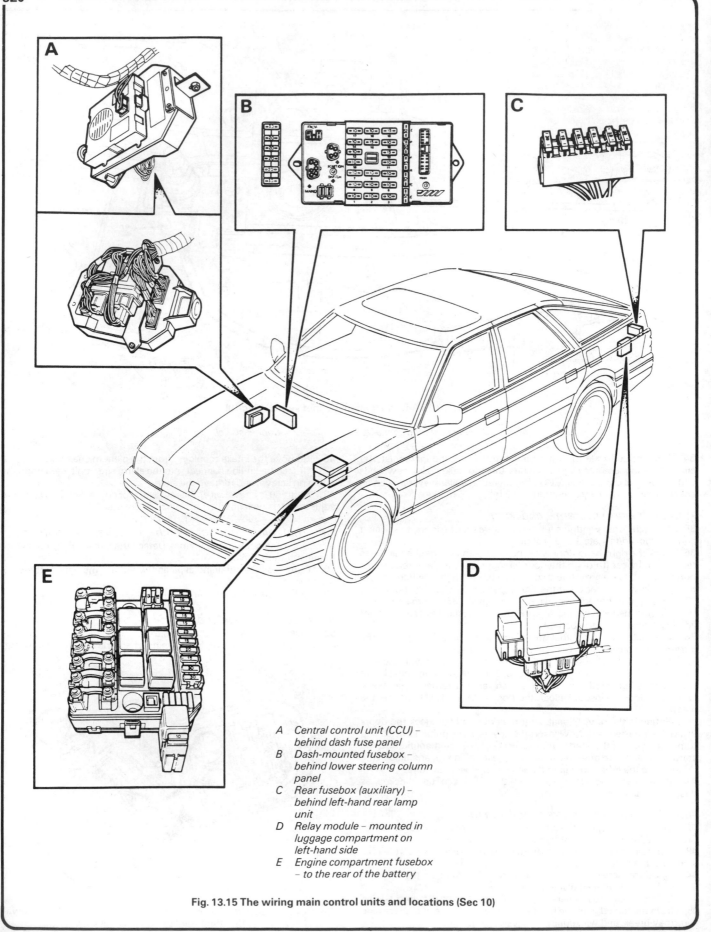

A Central control unit (CCU) –
   behind dash fuse panel
B Dash-mounted fusebox –
   behind lower steering column
   panel
C Rear fusebox (auxiliary) –
   behind left-hand rear lamp
   unit
D Relay module – mounted in
   luggage compartment on
   left-hand side
E Engine compartment fusebox
   – to the rear of the battery

Fig. 13.15 The wiring main control units and locations (Sec 10)

ter at a receiver unit within the vehicle. The receiver unit is located in the headlining, next to the interior rear view mirror. When the receiver unit is blipped by the hand-held (battery-powered) transmitter, the infra-red code transmitted matches the receiver code, and triggers the CCU to either lock or unlock the doors. Unless the correct code is received, the door lock circuit will not be actuated.

53   It is possible for the handset to fail in operating the locks even though the indicator is glowing. This is probably due to an unauthorised signal being picked up by the receiver unit. In this instance, operate the locks using the key; the infra-red locking system will then return to normal.

54   If the handset continuously fails to operate the infra-red receiver, this may well be due to the handset batteries having run down. Renew the batteries as a precaution before assuming that a more serious fault exists in the system.

55   To renew the handset batteries, carefully prise the two halves of the handset apart, then extract the old batteries, having taken note of their polarity. Check that the battery connections in the unit are clean to ensure a good contact, then insert the new batteries (type CLP 8951 or equivalent), making sure that they are correctly orientated as noted during removal. Reassemble the unit to complete.

Vehicle wiring and electrical control units – from VIN 276672

56   The main wiring control units and their locations on later models (manufactured from the above mentioned VIN) are shown in the accompanying illustrations (Figs. 13.15 to 13.18 inclusive).

57   Note that at the time of writing, it was not possible to include wiring diagrams for the 1991 model year vehicles, from VIN 276672 on.

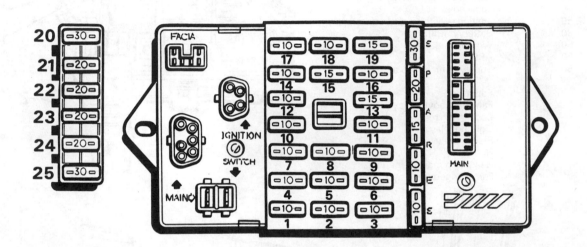

Fig. 13.16 Dash-mounted fusebox on later models, showing the fuse positions and details (Sec 10)

Fuse No	Rating (amps)	Circuit(s) protected	Fuse No	Rating (amps)	Circuit(s) protected
1	10	Switch and dash illumination	14	10	Instrument pack ignition supply, clock
2	10	Left-hand sidelamp	15	15	Ignition coil
3	10	Right-hand sidelamp	16	10	Cooling system, headlamps
4	10	CCU, ABS, and front courtesy lamps	17	10	Front wiper/washer
5	10	CCU, anti-theft alarm siren	18	10	Air conditioning system (where fitted)
6	10	CCU, CCU audible signal	19	10	Indicator lamps, reversing lamps, rear wiper
7	10	CCU auxiliary			
8	10	Cigar lighter, wipers, radio/cassette, vanity mirror lamp	20	30	Not used
			21	20	Right-hand front window regulator
9	10	CCU	22	20	Left-hand front window regulator
10	10	Not used	23	20	Right-hand rear window regulator
11	10	ABS	24	20	Left-hand rear window regulator
12	10	Starter relay	25	30	Not used
13	15	Fuel system circuits			

Fig. 13.17 Engine compartment fuse and relay identification on later models (Sec 10)

Note: *Some fuse and relay locations and circuits may vary from the following, according to model and equipment fitted*

Fuse No	Rating (amps)	Circuit(s) protected
M	15	Right-hand headlamp
N	15	Left-hand headlamp
O	15	Horns
P	10	Hazard warning
Q	15	Brake pedal switch
R	15	Relay module 1
S	15	Alternator, fuel injection control unit
T	30	Blower fan
U	15	Electronic fuel control unit
V	20	Headlamp power wash, dim-dip lighting
W	15	Radio/cassette unit connector, clock
X	30	Compressor clutch relay
Y	30	Cooling fan relay
Z	15	Bulb monitor

Fusible link No	Rating (amps)	Circuit function
G	50	Radio/cassette, power amplifier (if applicable)
H	50	Ignition switch supply, starter relay
I	80	Battery output
J	50	Window regulator
K	50	ABS
L	50	Supply to fuses 4, 5 and 6

Relay No	Function
1	Fan changeover relay 1
2	Cooling fan relay
3	Lighting relay
4	Starter relay
5	Horn relay
6	Headlamp main/dipped beam relay
7	Fan changeover relay 2

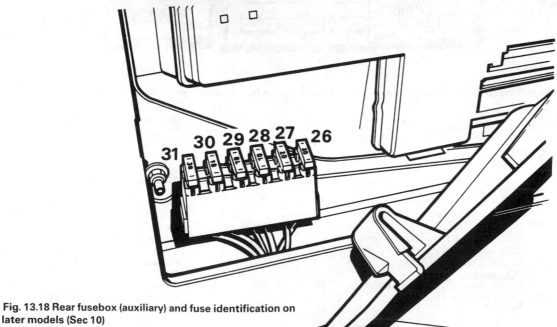

Fig. 13.18 Rear fusebox (auxiliary) and fuse identification on later models (Sec 10)

Fuse No	Rating (amps)	Circuit(s) protected		Fuse No	Rating (amps)	Circuit(s) protected
26	20	Sunroof and relay module		29	–	–
27	20	Central door locking and relay module 2		30	10	Luggage compartment lamps
28	20	Rear foglamp relay		31	30	Heated rear window relay

Index